EGYPT

目 次 CONTENTS

專論　Essays

附錄　Appendix

永生難忘的學習之旅

歡慶民國 100 年，許多珍貴的史料被重新發掘、整理，身處科技日新月異時代的我們，對過往不禁有懷古念舊，發思古幽情之感。

19 世紀的歐洲，科學開始展露鋒芒，同時也掀起一股「東方熱」，這股東方熱涵蓋對歐洲以外的所有古老異國文化的追捧，包括深深吸引著當時歐洲貴族的「埃及古文明」，許多人出資贊助發掘行動，甚或親赴埃及參與挖掘，將發現的各種文物當作紀念品帶回歐洲，放在家中做為擺飾，邀集朋友賞玩，蔚為風潮；當時多數發掘過程以現今的標準都無專業可言，但所收集的大量文物卻提供至今仍持續發展的考古科學充沛的研究資源。

隨著科技進步，世人不但能從文物了解古埃及人的日常生活，讚嘆當時工藝技巧的高度發展，甚至得以一窺木乃伊生前的面貌，但埃及文化的神祕面紗，卻仍待研究者們依循著謹慎的態度，一步步揭開。

英國伯頓博物館（Bolton Museum）從 20 至 30 年代英國駐埃及棉花商家族的私人蒐藏開始，藏有 10,000 件以上的古埃及文物，不同於大英博物館或羅浮宮的埃及館藏，有許多自大規模考古行動中發現的石雕等重量級文物，這些私人收藏的多是精巧華美的文物，當時的收藏者單純因喜好而珍藏在家中，特別引人入勝。

「木乃伊傳奇─埃及古文明特展」展出來自伯頓博物館精選之 250 多件精彩館藏、多具不同特色的木乃伊，以及完整複製的法老圖特摩斯三世墓室，提供台灣民眾絕無僅有、如同親至古埃及的現場，深切期待藉著「木乃伊傳奇─埃及古文明特展」在中正紀念堂展出，能帶領台灣民眾進入神秘的古埃及文化，進行一場永生難忘的學習之旅。

國立中正紀念堂管理處　處長

吳祖勝

An unforgettable journey of learning

In celebration of the R.O.C. Centennial, numerous valuable historical sources are being re-excavated and organized. Being in the era with advanced technologies, there is an irresistible sentiment of nostalgia for the past.

Science began to emerge in Europe during the 19th century, which also raised an Eastern Fever at the same time. This Eastern Fever covered the pursuance of all ancient foreign cultures other than Europe, including the Ancient Egyptian Civilization which deeply attracted European nobles of that time. Many people sponsored excavations, or even went to Egypt to participate in the digs. They brought the various discovered cultural relics as souvenirs back to Europe for decoration in their homes, and invited friends to visit. Many of the excavating procedures during then were not professional according to the current standard; however, a great amount of the collected cultural relics still act as abundant resources for the continuous development of archeological science.

With the advancement of technology, people may not only understand the daily life of ancient Egyptians through cultural relics, but further praise the high level of development for craftsmanship of that time, and even get the opportunity to get a glimpse at mummies. However, the mysterious veil of Egyptian culture still waits to be unveiled step by step with the researchers following a meticulous attitude.

The Bolton Museum in Britain has a collection of over 10,000 pieces of ancient Egyptian cultural relics from the private collections of British cotton businesses in Egypt during the '20s to the '30s. Differing from the Egyptian collections in the British Museum or the Louvre Museum, these collections include heavy cultural relics discovered from large scale archeological excavations such as stone sculptures etc. These private collections are mainly exquisite and extravagant cultural relics, which were collected in home purely due to collectors' interest, therefore they appear especially attractive.

Quest for Immortality exhibits over 250 selected pieces from the Bolton Museum, numerous mummies with different characteristics, and an exact replica of the Tomb of Tuthmosis III, offering Taiwanese people a unique exhibition of ancient Egypt. We deeply anticipate that through the exhibition of the Quest for Immortality at the CKS Memorial Hall, we may take the people of Taiwan into ancient Egyptian culture, and begin an unforgettable journey of learning.

Wu, Tsu-sheng
Director
National Chiang Kai-shek Memorial Hall

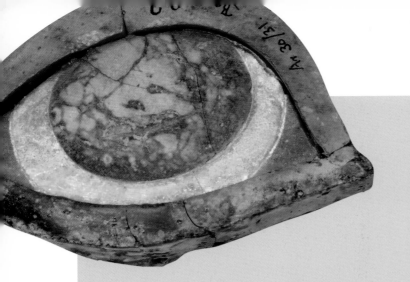

碰觸永生之謎，瞭解生死真諦！

自古以來，人們對於前世和來生就充滿無盡的好奇與想像。我們雖然活在今生，但是卻時時希望探索前世是否存在，以及如何轉世來生，這些想法創造出了各家各派的哲學思考，提供了人們多樣的人生觀，所衍生出來的各種因果緣分也增添了不少文學和宗教上的想像空間。

將生死之學推到極致的表現之一，就是古埃及的木乃伊，靈體雖遠，而肉身長存，讓後世可以直接瞻仰先人遺蛻，長留無盡去思。但是近年來的好萊塢電影風潮，賦予了木乃伊肉身重生大鬧乾坤的本事，這對於那些數千年來靜靜地躺在金字塔之下的木乃伊，也會帶來些許困擾吧！

2011 年的秋天，自然科學博物館和時藝多媒體合作，推出了「木乃伊傳奇－埃及古文明特展」，希望能碰觸古埃及人的「永生之謎」，也希望能讓國內的學生民眾，再一次近距離地接觸這些千年古物，更深刻地瞭解古埃及人是如何看待死生輪替的。

這次的展覽中，將會有四具來自波頓博物館的珍藏木乃伊，包含了男性、女性、大人，和小孩，除此之外，還有多種動物的木乃伊，和神廟建築、宮殿走道、生活用品，及文具器物等展品，內容豐富多樣，從生活的各個層面讓人體驗古埃及人從死亡到復活的整個過程，歡迎您撥冗眾蒞臨參觀！

古人有云：死生亦大矣！不同年代不同文化的人們，用不同的方法處理肉體的消逝；藏人實行天葬，將逝者身軀切割盡碎，和上糌粑，點起藏香，盤旋已久的老鷹就會下來大啖遺骸，吃得越乾淨表示逝者的德行越高，土葬則是針對德薄能鮮的惡人的儀式；但是對漢人而言，土葬卻是最為尊貴的方式；回族人則是挖了深坑，將遺骸裹了屍布，放入深坑，面向西方；各個文化都有不同的死生詮釋和對待之法，讓我們用寬宏的態度，來看待這個多元世界！

生死輪迴，是人們從古到今，總無法勘破的一關，希望在這次特展中，能藉著古埃及人的智慧，讓我們穿透世事的迷霧，接觸人生的真諦！

國立自然科學博物館 館長
台灣大學物理系及天文所 教授

孫維新

In touch with the mystery of eternity, understand the truth of life and death!

People have always been filled with infinite curiosity and imagination towards their previous life and next life since ancient times. Even though we live in the present, we are always hoping to explore the existence of our previous life, as well as how to transmigrate to the next life. These ideas created the philosophical concepts for various factions, and offered people with diversified perspectives of life, thus adding quite an imagination for literature and religion.

One of the demonstrations of pushing the theory of life and death to the extreme would be the ancient Egyptian mummies. Although the spirit is long gone, the body is preserved for the later generations to directly look at and pay respect to the ancestors' remains. However, the Hollywood movie trend during the recent years has endowed mummies with the power of coming back to life and disturbing the universe; this may have brought some hassles to the mummies lying quietly for several thousand years below the pyramids!

In fall of 2011, the National Museum of Natural Science collaborated with Media Sphere to launch the Quest for Immortality, hoping to get in touch with the mystery of eternity of the ancient Egyptians, as well as hoping to allow domestic people to be in touch with these thousand year old relics at a close distance, so as to understand comprehensively how the ancient Egyptians treated the alternation between life and death.

There will be four mummies from the Bolton Museum collection for this exhibition, including a male, female, adult and child. Moreover, there will also be several animal mummies, together with abundant exhibits such as from temples, palace aisles, articles for daily use and stationery etc. You are welcome to visit and experience the entire process of the ancient Egyptians from death to reanimation through the various aspects of living.

There is an old saying that: "Life and death are ultimate matters!" People from different eras with different cultures treat the fading of the flesh differently. Tibetans practice sky burial, where the body of the dead is cut into pieces and mixed with roasted barley flour together with lit Tibetan incense, and the hovering eagles would come down and feed on the corpse, the more being eaten represents the higher the moral conduct of the deceased, while interment is the ceremony for villains lacking virtue and ability. However, interment is rather the most respectful approach to the Hans. Where as for the people of the Hui nationality, they will dig a deep hole, wrap the body in textile, and then place it into the deep hole facing towards the west. Each culture has a different interpretation and treating approach regarding life and death, so let us look at this diversified world with a tolerant attitude!

The transmigration of life and death has always been the unsolved mystery for people since ancient times till now, thus it is hoped that through this special exhibition, we may see through the mystiques of life and get in touch with the truth of life via the ancient Egyptian wisdom!

Sun, Wei-Hsin

Professor
Department of Physics and Graduate Institute of Astrophysics, National Taiwan University
Director
National Museum of Natural Science

埃及古文明是神秘而美麗的

如同沙漠中蒙著面紗的女子，若隱若現的輪廓下，藏著讓人想一窺究竟的神秘；埃及古文明雖然已在電影、戲劇、文學當中被人們一再演繹與討論，但她主宰生命與追求永恆的神秘力量，以及跟宇宙間的微妙連繫，卻是人們尚未解開而充滿好奇的美麗傳說。

這一次，旺旺中時媒體集團特別與英國伯頓博物館（Bolton Museum）合作，引進200餘件珍貴的展品，帶著國人通過神秘的入口，一窺埃及古文明在面紗之後的傳說，並穿越時空進入古埃及的永恆世界。

在本次的展覽當中，除了國人耳熟能詳但難得一見的古埃及神祇、建築、文藝創作、飾品與生活器具；更重要的是讓國人投入古埃及的氛圍，來探討其對「永恆」追求的精神本質。而最令人期待的，莫過於圖特摩斯三世的等比例複製墓室，以及4具各具特色的木乃伊真品。

古埃及人相信，太陽從西方落下死亡之後，必須從地底向東返航，然後重新升起復活開始新的一天。「亡者之書」中記載，「亡者陪同太陽神一起乘船；共同度過地底的十二小時，共同突破12道關卡，以達到復活的明天。」而圖特摩斯三世墓室壁畫所描述的「來世之書」，即是全埃及最古老、最完整的紀錄。等比複製的墓室壁畫，完整呈現了亡靈隨同太陽進入黑夜之旅，直到獲得永生之前的12個小時之間，必須經過的種種險阻和考驗，讓觀眾更加了解埃及人的生死觀念，亦更增添看展的樂趣。另外，象徵古埃及永恆的代表—木乃伊，亦是本次展出的焦點，除了展出的數量堪稱歷年展覽之冠外，特別值得一題的是，展品中還包含了拉美西斯二世之子的「王子木乃伊」，當中隱含的種種神秘的故事，讓本展更添魅力。

最後，特別感謝國立中正紀念堂管理處、國立自然科學博物館及合作金庫銀行等單位的共襄盛舉，以實際行動展現對藝文活動的支持及回饋社會的一份心意。集眾力之心，「木乃伊傳奇—埃及古文明展」將為您打開古埃及的生命之眼，傳遞出永恆的幸福！

旺旺中時媒體集團 總裁

蔡紹中

Ancient Egyptian civilization is mystical yet beautiful

Resembling a female wearing a veil in the desert, the mystery concealed within the indistinctive silhouette makes one want to take a glimpse. Although ancient Egyptian civilization has been discussed in movies, dramas and literature, the mystical power of controlling life and pursuance for eternity, as well as its subtle connection with the universe are the beautiful legends still to be resolved.

This time, the Want Want China Times Inc. specially collaborated with the Bolton Museum from Britain to introduce over 200 pieces of valuable artifacts, to give the people of Taiwan a glimpse at the ancient Egyptian civilization's legend behind the veil of the mysterious entrance, and to cross over the era into the eternal world of ancient Egypt.

During this exhibition, other than Egyptian Gods, architectures, literature and art works, accessories and living utensils that are familiar to everyone but are rare to see, most important is that Taiwanese may delve into the atmosphere of ancient Egypt in order to explore its spiritual essence of pursuance for Immortality. What's most exciting is the exact replica of the Tomb of Tuthmosis III, and the 4 authentic mummies.

Ancient Egyptians believed that when the sun sets in the west, it must travel underground to return in the east for a new day. As recorded in the Book of Amduat, "The dead will accompany God of Sun on a boat to go through 12 hours underworld, and surmount 12 divisions in order to reach a new tomorrow." The wall paintings of the Book of Amduat depicted in the Tomb of Tuthmosis III are the most ancient and comprehensive documentation of Egypt. The exact duplication of the tomb wall paintings comprehensively demonstrate the journey in the night by the dead and God of Sun, where within the 12 hours before eternity is reached, they must go through various obstacles and ordeals, so that the audience may understand Egyptian's concepts of life and death even more, as well as enhancing the interest of the exhibition. Furthermore, mummies, the iconic symbolization of eternity for the ancient Egypt are also the highlight of this exhibition. The exhibited quantity of mummies exceed all exhibitions in the past, and includes the royal Mummy, son of Ramesses II, and the various mysteries concealed within, adding even more charisma to this exhibition.

Lastly, special thanks to the participation from the National Chiang Kai-shek Memorial Hall, National Museum of Natural Science and Taiwan Cooperative Bank etc., in which they demonstrated their support towards art and cultural events as well as contributing to society through concrete actions. With everybody's anticipation, the exhibition on the Quest for Immortality will open up the eyes of life to ancient Egypt, and convey the happiness of eternity!

Tsai, Eng-Meng
Chairman
Want-Want China Times Group

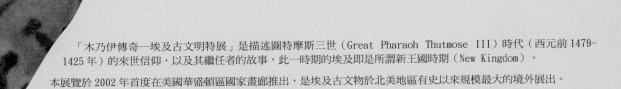

「木乃伊傳奇—埃及古文明特展」是描述圖特摩斯三世（Great Pharaoh Thutmose III）時代（西元前1479-1425年）的來世信仰，以及其繼任者的故事，此一時期的埃及即是所謂新王國時期（New Kingdom）。

本展覽於2002年首度在美國華盛頓區國家畫廊推出，是埃及古文物於北美地區有史以來規模最大的境外展出。

針對「木乃伊傳奇—埃及古文明特展」亞洲巡迴展，UEG策展公司與英國伯頓博物館（Bolton Museum）及伯頓議會（Bolton Council）達成協議，為本次展覽帶來超過200件源自埃及的文物，以闡述來生、「來世之書」（The Amduat）（在陰間的12小時）等極為重要的主題，以及日常生活、信仰等範圍更加廣泛的主題。

本次展覽核心為重建圖特摩斯三世陵墓裡的石棺室。最古老的陰間書「來世之書」的完整文本即首次出現在原墓室壁畫上。本次將整個陵墓包括壁畫皆絲毫不差地複製下來，要讓觀眾真假難分，有如身歷其境。

陵墓的壁畫也可讓觀眾探尋太陽神拉（Re）的夜行之旅，並且深入了解法老葬禮，以及亡者於黑夜12小時所經歷的旅程。本次展覽藉由來自伯頓博物館與埃及陵墓的收藏品及工藝品，提供觀眾絕佳的機會認識古埃及宗教與葬喪習俗。

「木乃伊傳奇—埃及古文明特展」亞洲巡迴展得以圓滿實現，主要歸功於伯頓議會的同意，允許珍貴的埃及古文物在亞洲地區巡迴展示數年，以台北為首站於2011年6月12日開展。

據我們所知，本次展覽是亞洲首次有如此長期巡迴的大規模埃及展，也是首度在全亞洲地區巡迴的大型埃及展。

因此我們很榮幸能與旺旺中時媒體集團的時藝多媒體傳播股份有限公司，以及參與本次浩大歷史工程的專業優良夥伴密切合作，在台灣為這場精彩展覽揭開序幕。

敬邀所有觀眾進入迷人的古埃及世界。

謹致誠摯的問候。

UEG 執行長

泰德・瑞索

The Exhibition "Quest for Immortality" follows and tells the story about the afterlife beliefs in the time of the Great Pharaoh Thutmose III (1479 – 1425 BC) and his successors in the period in Egypt we call the New Kingdom.

When the Exhibition was originally being presented at the National Gallery of Art in Washington DC in 2002 it presented the largest collection of Egyptian Antiquities ever to leave Egypt for a North American Exhibition.

At the core of the exhibition is a reconstruction of the sarcophagus chamber in the tomb of Thutmosis III. On the original walls of this chamber appeared for the first time the complete text of the Amduat, the oldest Book of the Netherworld. The whole and complete tombs including the walls are replicated so accurately that it is very difficult or nearly impossible for the visitor to determine if he or she is in the original tomb in Egypt or visiting the Exhibition.

For the Asian Tour of the "Quest for Immortality" Exhibition UEG ADM. has made an agreement with Bolton Museum / Bolton Council to deliver to the exhibition more than 200 original Egyptian objects illustrating very important themes such as the afterlife, The Amduat (the 12 hours in the netherworld) and also more broad themes such as daily life and beliefs.

The walls of the Tomb also allow the visitor to track the sun god Re on his nocturnal journey and to gain insight into the burial of pharaoh and the journey of the deceased through the twelve hours of the night. The Exhibition affords visitors a truly unique opportunity to learn about the religion and burial customs of the ancient Egyptians through the treasures and artifacts from Bolton Museum as well as from the tomb decorations.

The successful realization of the Quest for Immortality Exhibition in Asia is due to the very important agreement with Bolton Council which will allow the unique Egyptian Antiquities that is presented in the Exhibition to tour for several years in Asia, starting in Taipei the 12th of June 2011.

To the best of our knowledge this is the first major Egyptian Exhibition to travel through Asia for such a long period of time and also the first time a major Egyptian Exhibition will go on tour throughout Asia.

We are for all this reasons very pleased that the Premiere of this great Exhibition in Taiwan is realized in close cooperation with Media Sphere Ltd, China Times Want Want Group and equally professional and right partner for this great historical project.

We wish all visitors welcome to the fascinating universe of Ancient Egypt.

With kind regards,

CEO
UEG ADM. ApS

前言

起初眼前一片漆黑，從墓室裡逸散出的熱氣讓燭光搖曳得厲害，什麼也看不到。不一會兒，眼睛漸漸適應微弱的光源，房內的細節慢慢從霧裡浮現：有詭譎的動物、雕像，還有黃金！是的，就是黃金，燭光所及之處遍地黃澄澄…

Carter and Mace（1923），頁 95-96

埃及學剛開始發展的時候算不上是什麼顯學，頂多只能算是聖經研究中小小的旁門左道，為枯燥又生硬的學術研究增添娛樂。直到 1922 年 11 月 4 號，所有這些刻板印象因為一件事徹底扭轉——霍華德‧卡特（Howard Carter）和贊助他的加拿芬伯爵（Earl of Carnarvon）五世在帝王谷（Valley of the Kings）的考古工作，眼看就要有重大發現，可預見人們對埃及學的印象屆時將徹底改觀。

這是歷史時代以來考古學家首次發現未經入侵的陵墓，長眠於此的法老是年紀輕輕就逝世的圖坦卡門（Tutankhamun），學界對他尚且一無所知。陵墓的四個墓室裡滿是珍貴的寶物，有儀式用的器具也有俗世的用品，不僅建構出這位神祕法老生前的故事，也為埃及文明研究帶來一道曙光。

由於發現圖坦卡門的陵墓，使得埃及古文明變得不那麼遙不可及。就好像一位遠古時代的歷史人物突然和我們有了交集，處在同樣的時空，有同樣的品味和價值觀，甚至承擔一樣的苦痛、擁抱一樣的夢。圖坦卡門墓出土的文物不論在質、量上都很難得，最寶貴的是保存完整。透過這些古文物窺探歷史，3,500 年的時間距離似乎不存在了。

開啟時光膠囊，時間停滯——不只是一天、一個星期或一個月，而是幾千年的時間，完全隔絕任何時代的躁進變遷。圖坦卡門長眠在太久遠的從前，甚至連耶穌基督、佛陀或者穆罕默德這些為「存在」下註解的先哲都還未出生。當他和後繼們沉入亙古長眠的時候，我們熟悉的這些東西方的古老文明，例如：波斯、希臘、羅馬和古中國，曾歷經繁榮的文明也早已凋零。

對古埃及文明燃起興趣的人們很快發現，新發現的這些文物只不過是冰山的一角，圖坦卡門王也只是眾多古埃及法老中的其中一人，他們每一代法老王都曾統治著數百萬子民，跨越超過 3,000 個時空。

古埃及社會各階層的人們：王子、祭司、統治階級、士兵、藝匠、商人和農人等，他們一樣過著各自的生活，擁有信仰，並致力於修建廟宇，最後走向死亡。不論富人還是窮人，終其一生都在為自己一定會經過的階段——死亡做準備。他們相信死後的世界才是人們永恆的依歸，所以不僅張羅死後復生需要的器具，也準備許多私人用品，以保障在那個世界過得舒適。

圖坦卡門墓留給我們豐富的遺產，保存了這些倚仗尼羅河生活的人們的生與死，在我們已知的大略梗概上，加入最詳盡的細節。兩千多年以前古埃及人社會的權力與人性；宗教與俗世；物質生活與邏輯智慧；生與死，這些原本只存在於文字記錄上的一切，如今都透過真實物件重現在眼前。

本展透過 200 多件宗教或日常用途的工藝品，重現古埃及人對於他們生活的富饒大地所展現的熱情。當然，展品包括了與死亡有關的器具，古埃及人藉著這些器具試圖延續生命到永恆——儘管他們真正害怕的恐怕就是生命本身。

古埃及人絕不只是過份執著於死亡的民族，事實上，上至王族下至一般平民百姓，最關心的是「活著」這件事，尤其是尼羅河畔的生活。他們對永生的渴求建立在賴以生存的這條河上。環繞這份渴求的所有活動持續不斷地進行，創造高度生產力，相信所有的一切（包括最短暫的事物），都會快樂地持續下去直到永恆。

本展場很特別，我們希望完整複製、重現第十八王朝圖特摩斯三世（Thutmose III）的地下世界。它是埃及最了不起的建築成就之一，深埋在底比斯懸崖（Theban cliffs）之下，和神祕的圖坦卡門王陵墓同處於帝王谷。展場內可以看到包裹圖特摩斯三世的木乃伊使用的布料，是古埃及史上最好的亞麻布。本展也展出圖特摩斯三世紀念碑的遺跡，以及其忠臣奉獻的寶物。

在這個再現的墓室裡，您可以一探埃及學的興起與進程，解碼埃及古老而神祕的象形文字、參觀皇室成員的木乃伊，還有考古學家 Flinders Petrie 和其後的追隨者在那卡達（Naqada）、沙拉別艾卡錠（Serabit el-Khadim）等地區的重大發現，還有埃及探索學會（Egypt Exploration Society）在阿瑪爾那（El-Amarna）和薩卡拉（Saqqara）發現的神聖動物墓地（Sacred Animal Necropolis）。這些發現揭開了古埃及人從最早的起源，歷經古王國、中王國和新王國時期的盛事和中間期，一直到王國衰敗，先後受到波斯、希臘、羅馬入侵然後至今，其生活和死亡世界的各個面向。本展含括了 30 個朝代的生活與建樹。

從本展可以窺探古埃及生活的各個面向：工藝品、工具、化妝盤、陶器、化妝品研磨工具和剃刀等等，或者他們的服飾、不可思議地能展現他們容貌的鏡子，還有枕頭——可以想見他們躺在這上頭做著夢。您也可以看見他們的禱告儀式，包括在家裡、有祖先顯靈的祈禱；以及廟宇裡更複雜繁瑣的儀式：給掌管埃及人各生活面向的獸首神祇焚香，獻上食物、鮮花和藝術品等。您還可以透過殘缺的石雕、精工裝飾富有鮮明色彩的牆，和極具工藝價值的柱子，還原廟宇本來的樣貌。也可以一探阿肯那頓的理想城市「阿瑪納（El-Amarna）」的遺跡——一個完全獻給太陽神阿頓（或稱日輪）的城市。

本展邀您隨著文化傳播的腳步，看看埃及文化分別在其承平時期和動亂時代對其他地區的影響。不僅可以從戰爭武器上窺知一二，還有伊拉克尼姆羅德古城（Nimrud）的象牙板，在在顯示出國際性的「埃及化」現象。當然您絕不能錯過保存完好的木乃伊、面具、棺木、辟邪物，和為來世所做的準備。還有古埃及神秘的象徵符號「安卡」（ankh-strap）、傑得柱（the djed pillar）、聖甲蟲，和「假門」（false door）——埃及人相信死者可以透過假門和生者對話。

最後，本展也展出古埃及象形文字。象形文字最初是用來管理國家，隨著時間發展變得愈來愈成熟，成為宗教和文學的載具。高度發展的書面文字成為埃及官僚體系的推進力，使得法老統治下的埃及得以強盛、繁榮。超越死生、出現在廟堂與墓穴中的象形文字，不僅為個人和國家帶來榮景，也雋刻著一段埋藏數千年的歷史，在千年後的今日公諸世人眼前，也算是實現了古埃及人夢寐以求的永生。

考古學家
紐約大都會美術館埃及藝術區
希爾文科曼暨潘梅拉科曼紀念基金會研究員

尼可拉斯‧里夫

Introduction

At first I could see nothing, the hot air escaping from the chamber causing the candle to flicker, but presently, as my eyes grew accustomed to the light, details of the room within emerged slowly from the mist: strange animals, statues, and gold—everywhere the glint of gold ...

[Carter and Mace 1923: 95-96]

Egyptology has not always been the popular draw it is today: during its earliest decades the subject was seen as little more than a by-way of Biblical research, as a refuge for dry-as-dust academics and the downright peculiar. On November 4, 1922, however, all such preconceived notions were swept away: Howard Carter and his sponsor, the fifth Earl of Carnarvon, were on the brink of a discovery in Egypt's Valley of the Kings which would change the perception of the subject once and for all.

Oor the first time in recorded history, archaeologists had stumbled upon an undisturbed royal burial: that of a virtually unknown boy-king, Tutankhamun. The four chambers of this tomb were piled high with wonderful objects, ritualistic and mundane—a collection of unparalleled richness and splendour which cast not only this obscure king, but also the civilization of ancient Egypt as a whole in a new, unexpected and utterly compelling light.

Here was a culture more appealing, more accessible than had ever previously been imagined; an ancient people who, it seemed, shared recognizable tastes and values, similar fears and hopes. Through Tutankhamun's extraordinary treasures—gorgeous in their materials, pleasing in their proportions and perfectly preserved—the passage of three and a half thousand years seemed little more than the blink of an eye.

Egypt was revealed as the ultimate time-capsule—a place where time stands still, not for a day, a week, or even a month, but for a span of years wholly impossible for our hurried modern minds to take in. Tutankhamun had been laid to rest before the criteria which today govern how existence is gauged had even been conceived: before Christ, the Buddha, Mohammed had been born; a time so distant that, while pharaoh and countless thousands of lesser burials slumbered, every familiar civilization of east or west— Persia, Greece, Rome, ancient China itself—rose, flourished, and fell.

And, as the subject's new-found, popular audience soon discovered, Tutankhamun was but the tip of a veritable iceberg—one pharaoh among many; one of a hundred and more kings, who in total ruled multiple millions of subjects over a span of more than three millennia.

Princes, priests, administrators, soldiers, artisans, merchants and farmers— they too lived their lives, celebrated their gods, embellished their temples— all consumed by mortality; by the need to prepare in anticipation of their own inevitable passing similar burials, rich or modest, each and every one stocked not only with the equipment of resurrection upon which an individual's eternal survival depended, but with more personal items too—as much as could be afforded to guarantee a continuation into the beyond of this world's manifold pleasures.

Thanks to this cultural obsession, Egypt's physical legacy to our own world is a rich and diverse one, documenting every aspect of life and death on the River Nile—and not in the broad brush-strokes to which we are normally accustomed, but in the most exquisite, personal detail. Power and humanity; the religious and the secular; physicality and intellect; life and death—these are but some of the themes of two thousand years and more ago that are treated not only in the Egyptians' own words but in the actual objects which were made, used and enjoyed at the time.

This exhibition is an evocation of the ancients' boundless sense of enthusiasm for everything their bountiful land had to offer. It is a celebration here expressed through some 200 ancient works of art, objects of daily life and religion—and, of course, through the paraphernalia of death which had been intended to achieve for the ancients the continuation in perpetuity of what they truly held sacred: life itself.

For the Egyptians were as far from a people obsessed with death as can possibly be imagined. For king and commoner alike, the addiction was to living—and specifically life as experienced on the banks of the River Nile. Theirs was a quest for immortality, upon which all were determinedly embarked throughout their lives. The Egyptians' activities towards that ultimate end were unremitting, their productivity immense—and all in the context of an exceptional climate where even the most fugitive of materials happily survive, seemingly forever.

The setting of this show is unique: it is that of the Underworld itself, as conceived and represented in the tomb of Egypt's greatest warrior king, Thutmose III of the 18th Dynasty—a breathtakingly accurate replica of one of ancient Egypt's greatest architectural creations, dug and executed deep in the Theban cliffs, within the same mysterious Valley of the Kings as Tutankhamun himself. Its owner and occupant was that Thutmose III, a portion of whose mummy linen is here displayed—a textile among the finest ever produced by any Egyptian loom; a king whose fragmentary official monuments are also shown, alongside the offerings and possessions of pharaoh's loyal subjects.

Through the metaphorical contents of this recreated tomb we are able to trace Egyptology's extraordinary rise and progress, from the decipherment of Egypt's mysterious hieroglyphic script, through the discovery of the royal mummies, the ground-breaking archaeological discoveries of Flinders Petrie and his successors at Naqada, Serabit el-Khadim and elsewhere, down to the work of the Egypt Exploration Society at El-Amarna and Saqqara's famed Sacred Animal Necropolis. By finds from these and other sites all aspects of ancient Egyptian life and death are here highlighted—from Egypt's earliest beginnings, through the highs of the Old, Middle and New Kingdoms, the lows of the intervening Intermediate periods, through to the years of decline and occupation first by Persia, then by Greece and finally Rome and beyond. Thirty dynasties of tireless activity and wondrous achievement.

We observe the Egyptians at work and in a domestic setting—through their basketry and tools, their cosmetic palettes, pots and cosmetic grinders, their razors; through the clothes they wore, the mirrors which captured and magically held their image, the headrests upon which they wearily lay their heads to dream their dreams. We are witnesses to their worship, both at home in the magical presence of their revered ancestors and in the more rarefied atmosphere of their temples—making offerings of incense, food, flowers and art to the strange, animal-headed gods who regulated every aspect of their lives. We see the temples themselves, represented in fragmentary sculptures of hard and soft stones, exquisitely decorated walls with colours fresh and unsullied, and in their architectural columns. We see the exquisite, tentative fragments from Akhenaten's ideal city, El-Amarna, dedicated to the worship of the one god—the Aten, or solar disc.

We follow Egyptian influence abroad, during conflict and in peace; through the weapons of war and in the adoption of international, Egyptianizing modes of representation on exquisite ivory panels from the city of Nimrud in modern Iraq. And of course we see the Egyptians in death: their extraordinary preserved mummies, masks, coffins, amulets, models and provisions for the life to come; their mysterious symbols and emblems—the ankh-strap, the djed pillar, the scarab; the false doors through which the dead could commune with those they had left behind.

And above everything else we see their writing, the hieroglyphic script— that exquisite phenomenon whose appearance, initially for purposes of administering the early Egyptian State, would rapidly blossom into a sophisticated vehicle for the transmission of the deepest religious thought and an extraordinarily beautiful and varied literature. As the very motor of the bureaucratic machine, writing permitted pharaoh's Egypt to flourish and excel. Not only did it provide a means for advancement on a personal and national level, in life and in death, in temples and in tombs; through the medium of the hieroglyphic script would be conveyed and voiced the name itself—to generate, after a lapse of millennia, life itself—the immortality the deceased so earnestly desired.

Sylvan C Coleman and Pamela Coleman Memorial Fellow
Department of Egyptian Art
The Metropolitan Museum of Art
New York

伯頓博物館代表序

古埃及讓我們世世代代為之著迷。早在遠古時代，希臘人就視埃及為觀光勝地，對埃及的文明奇蹟感到驚艷不已，今日的我們也是如此。伯頓博物館裡的埃及藝廊是伯頓最受歡迎的景點之一。家庭觀眾前來藝廊探索古埃及文化遺產有數年之久，而且不斷重遊，就像是拜訪老朋友般。

我們很榮幸能藉由「木乃伊傳奇—埃及古文明特展」與更多觀眾分享伯頓博物館的古埃及珍藏。這個契機要歸功於 UEG 策展公司與時藝多媒體的協力。他們提供了極佳的舞台，讓觀眾得以欣賞古埃及文化中最精彩的文物。本次展覽重點為重建圖特摩斯三世的墓室。觀眾走進墓室就可橫跨三千年時空，一探古埃及宗教的祕密。這間墓室以及一旁展示的墓室文物，介紹的是古埃及人所期盼的來世生活。本展覽也安排觀眾與幾位古埃及人面對面，他們的身體為了永生，經木乃伊處理而保存下來。

古埃及人如此費盡心力為來世做準備，是為了要永續在埃及所過的生活。「木乃伊傳奇—埃及古文明特展」藉由展示古埃及人的日常生活文物，探索這種獨特的生活風格。觀眾可以看到非常私人的物品，例如項鍊、化妝品容器及鏡子，這些可能曾是距今4000 年前左右某位女性的早晨梳妝用品。觀眾也可以看到戰爭用武器，以及國王安撫諸神的形象，象徵埃及人對於社會免受外侮及自然災害的期盼。展品中最讓人動容的是古埃及人的肖像。我們可以看著這些人的面容，無論是君王或平民，想像許多年前他們所面對的生活。

伯頓博物館所收藏的埃及文物絕大部分是出自於安妮巴洛（Annie Barlow）的辛苦付出與慷慨捐獻。她的父親詹姆士巴洛（James Barlow）是伯頓富裕的紡織廠老闆，自埃及進口棉花。安妮擔任新成立的埃及探索學會的分會秘書，在伯頓當地募款資助埃及的考古挖掘。安妮獲得了一部分考古文物作為捐款回報。之後她又將這些文物交給伯頓當地的博物館。有感於安妮巴洛慷慨捐獻的精神，今日伯頓居民將這些寶物送至外地展出，讓其他人與我們共享欣賞的樂趣。

Foreword
Bolton Representative

Ancient Egypt has fascinated the world for generations. Already in ancient times, the Greeks went to Egypt as tourists and marvelled at the wonders of this great civilisation. Today we are no different. The Egyptian Gallery at Bolton Museum is one of the most popular attractions in Bolton. Families have been coming to the gallery for many years in order to explore the remains of ancient Egyptian culture and then return again and again, as if they were visiting old friends.

It is a great pleasure to be able to share some of Bolton Museum's treasures from ancient Egypt with a wider audience through the exhibition, *Quest for Immortality*. This opportunity could not have happened without the assistance of United Exhibits Group and Media Sphere. They have provided a stunning setting in which to view some of the finest products of ancient Egyptian culture. Central to this experience is the reconstructed tomb chamber of Thutmose III. Walking through this chamber allows us to cross the divide of over three millennia to encounter the mysteries of ancient Egyptian religion. The tomb chamber, and the objects found in tombs which are displayed nearby, illustrate what the ancient Egyptians expected their life after death to be like. It also prepares the visitor for coming face to face with some ancient Egyptians whose bodies were mummified to preserve them for eternity.

The ancient Egyptians went to such trouble to prepare for the afterlife because they wanted to extend forever the life they had in Egypt. The *Quest for Immortality* exhibition explores this unique style of life through objects that the ancient Egyptians used in their daily lives. Visitors can see very personal items such as necklaces, cosmetic containers, and mirrors that might have been part of a women's morning toilette around 4,000 years ago. They can also see the weapons of war and the representations of kings appeasing the gods, which symbolised Egypt's attempt to protect their society from foreign invaders and natural disasters. Among the most moving of all are the portraits of ancient Egyptians. Whether they are kings or commoners, we can look at their faces and imagine what life was like for them all those years ago.

Bolton Museum's collection of Egyptian objects arrived in Bolton largely through the hard work and generosity of Annie Barlow. She was the daughter of James Barlow, a wealthy mill owner in Bolton who imported cotton from Egypt. She acted as regional secretary to the newly formed Egypt Exploration Fund raising money locally to fund excavations in Egypt. In return for this funding, Annie Barlow was offered a division of the excavated material. In turn, Annie Barlow gave these materials to Bolton for its museum. It is in the spirit of Annie Barlow's generosity, that the people of Bolton now send these treasures out for others to enjoy as we have enjoyed them.

墓室假門

此石灰岩假門是獻給賽內珍（Sennedjsui），其擁有如唯一伴侶、皇家司庫以及管家等頭銜，而他的妻子埃烏提（Iuuti）據說是哈托爾神（Hathor）唯一的皇家裝飾員以及女祭司。賽內珍是梅若利（Mereri）的兒子，但奇怪的是，他並沒有繼承父親擔任祭司監督的最高職務或其他宗教頭銜。

賽內珍的假門來自於其座落於陵墓上方墓堂的墓室中，位於岩鑿軸底。其墓室佈置簡單，不像其父親的墓室較大型且更為複雜，但賽內珍的假門顯然在兩者中較大。

假門是墓堂的重點所在，其目的在於紀念死者，並作為一種生者與死者之間溝通的途徑，具有特定風格與象徵性，祭司與家庭成員會在此提供食物與飲料等供品。假門在古王國末期開始廢棄不用，並逐漸演變為石碑造型。

文字內容包括祭品配方、為死者援引之規定、特定祭品清單，其中包括七大聖油，給賽內珍的頭銜與讚揚。賽內珍和他的妻子埃烏提坐在低背獅腳椅上，前方有一張擺滿農產品的桌子，其中包括牛前腿、青蔥、排骨以及一排造型如羽毛般的麵包條。桌子底下是一組洗手用的器皿。埃烏提環抱著丈夫肩膀，而他將一罐香油拿往自己的鼻子。他們都穿戴著假髮與寬廣的衣領。賽內珍穿著一件突出的短裙，而埃烏提則穿著若隱若現的緊身裙。站在他們前方體型較小的是餐篷主管尼貝（Nebay）。假門的下半部份應該還有賽內珍的其他介紹，但目前已毀損。

其中人物以浮雕方式雕刻，文字部份則是以凹浮雕方式銘刻。假門上的設計包括在環面造型頂部及邊緣處的典型凹弧形屋簷（一種棕櫚葉的楣飾），此設計元素源自早期之泥磚與蘆葦編織的建築風格；當中構成的一仿製雙扇門、尺寸縮小，使文字和圖像面板能更加突出。獨特的星形排列並點綴著上緣。

賽內珍所在的丹德拉鎮是上埃及第六大省首都，同時是掌管愛與生育的女神「哈托爾神」的重要神廟所在地。在第九王朝時期，埃及並非集權控制，而是分裂為兩大相互衝突之王國，由位於北部的赫拉克雷奧波利斯（Herakleopolis）以及位於南部的底比斯（Thebes）所統治。賽內珍之家族成員曾在丹德拉擔任地方統治者以及哈托爾神的高級祭司，直到梅若利時期，其地方勢力才逐漸式微。其中原因可能是由於來自上埃及的督導阿比胡（Ab-ihu）的出現，其宣稱擁有丹德拉所在省份以及其他兩個省份的領導權。

此時期之權力分化造就各地地方藝術與書寫風格之發展，兩者皆顯著表現於賽內珍的墓室假門上。陳述內容避免重疊且支柱上的透視圖處理也相當特別，說明此時期之藝術自由風格有所增長。於賽內珍父親梅若利之時期，在丹德拉所發展出的鮮明書寫風格元素相當顯而易見，例如飛禽走獸站立的基準線，以及相當擁擠堆疊的象形文字。（作者：M.M.）

False door stela of Sennedjsui, son of Mereri

This limestone false door is dedicated to Sennedjsui, who held the titles sole companion, royal treasurer, and steward, while his wife 'Iuuti, was said to be a sole royal ornament and priestess of Hathor. Sennedjsui was the son of Mereri, but unusually, he did not inherit his father's highest office of overseer of priests or other religious titles.

Sennedjsui's false door comes from his mastaba, the building that housed the funerary chapel above the tomb itself, located at the bottom of a rock-cut shaft. The mastaba was simple in plan, unlike his father's, which was larger and more complex, but Sennedjsui's false door is significantly the larger of the two.

A false door was the focal point of a tomb chapel. It served to commemorate the deceased and functioned as a stylized, symbolic doorway of communication between the living and the dead, where priests and family members would give offerings of food and drink. False doors began to fall out of use at the end of the Old Kingdom, and began to evolve into stelae.

The texts contain an offering formula, invoking provisions for the deceased, lists of specific offerings, including seven sacred oils, as well as titles and praise for Sennedjsui. He and his wife 'Iuuti are shown seated on low-backed lion-footed chairs before a table of offerings laden with produce, including the foreleg of an ox, spring onions, ribs, and a row of bread loaves stylized as feathers. Underneath the table is a set of vessels for hand washing. 'Iuuti embraces her husband's shoulder, while he raises a jar of perfumed oil to his nose. They both wear wigs and broad collars. Sennedjsui wears a form of projecting kilt, while 'Iuuti wear an indistinctly indicated sheath dress. The smaller scale figure standing before them offering a cup is Nebay, Director of the Dining Tent. The lower half of the false door, which would have had further representations of Sennedjsui, is broken.

The figures are carved in raised relief, while the text is inscribed in sunk relief. The design includes the typical cavetto cornice (a decorative frieze of palm leafs) at the top and a border of 'torus' molding, both design elements originating from early mud-brick and reed matting architecture. They frame an imitation double-leafed door, reduced in size to allow for greater prominence of the text and image panel. An unusual row of stars adorns the upper border.

Sennedjsui's town of Dendera was the capital of the sixth province of Upper Egypt, and the site of an important temple to Hathor, goddess of love and fertility. During Dynasty 9, Egypt was not centrally controlled, but divided into two conflicting kingdoms, ruled from Herakleopolis in the north and Thebes in the south. Sennedjsui was part of a family who had served as local rulers in Dendera and high-ranking priests of Hathor until the time of Mereri, when their local power began to diminish. This was possibly due to the arrival of the Overseer of Upper Egypt Ab-ihu, who claimed leadership of the province of Dendera and two other provinces.

The decentralization of this period resulted in the development of localized provincial art and writing styles, both of which are evident in Sennedjsui's false door stela. The representations avoid overlapping and the treatment of the perspective on the legs is unusual, indicative of the increased artistic freedom characteristic of this period. Elements of the distinctive local writing style that developed at Dendera during the period of Sennedjsui's father Mereri are apparent, for example the baselines on which birds and quadrupeds stand and the rather crowded stacking of the hieroglyphs. (M.M.)

1. 墓室假門
來自丹德拉的古埃及墓室
第 9 王朝（西元前 2160-2025 年）
石灰岩
1170 x 1000 x 250 mm

False door stela of Sennedjsui,son of Mereri
From Dendera, mastaba of Sennedjsui
Dynasty 9 (2160-2025 BC)
Limestone

哈地亞墓室門楣

為了尋找處女地以追求其對太陽神（即阿頓神 Aten）的革命性崇拜，阿肯納頓（Akhenaten）國王將宮廷遷移至埃及中部一個荒涼之地，他將此地命名為阿肯大頓（Akhetaten，意為「阿頓神的地平線」）—即現在的阿瑪納（Amarna）。阿肯納頓的改革相當短暫，且其新城市在其統治結束後不久便遭遺棄。由於該城市已被遺棄，許多建築物似乎已被掠奪作為建築材料，因此值得注意的是，此門楣（原件收藏於開羅的埃及博物館）幾乎是毫髮無傷地保留下來。

此門楣源自該城市北部郊區一個較大且保存相當完好的房子中，研究人員發現，其墜落自該房北邊廊與中心房間的通道上。石材上原本漆著如圖所示之鮮豔顏色，由開鑿者約翰·潘德（John Pendlebury）的妻子海達（Hilda）所繪製的完整水彩畫，目前存放於埃及探險協會的檔案室中。此模製品是在該門楣被發現不久後製成，並且在 EES 探險隊帶回英國之物品展覽中展出。

在新王國時期官員的屋宅內，在位君王的橢圓形裝飾是通道週圍建築元素的常見主題。出於埃及人熱愛對稱的習慣，該屋的屋主哈提耶（Hatiay）出現了兩次。他非常喜愛阿肯納頓及其妻子娜芙蒂蒂（Nefertiti）的橢圓形裝飾，還有阿頓神之名，其字體更大上許多且同樣以橢圓形裝飾呈現。在埃及的許多遺跡當中，阿肯納頓的名字在其退位後便遭破壞 — 但皇后與阿頓神本身的名字卻毫髮無傷。門楣上的銘刻將哈提耶描述為該城市的「作品監督者」，他可能與阿肯納頓統治時代末期同名的「首席雕塑家」為同一人，據稱此人在修復傳統神祇的宗教雕像方面扮演著重要角色。（作者：C.P.）

Cast of Door Lintel of Hatiay

In search of virgin territory on which to pursue his revolutionary worship of the sun disc, the Aten, King Akhenaten moved the royal court to a desolate site in Middle Egypt that he named Akhetaten ('Horizon of the Aten') – modern Amarna. Akhenaten's reformation was short-lived, and his new city was abandoned soon after the end of his reign. Many buildings appear to have been stripped for building material as the city was deserted, so it is remarkable that this lintel – the original is in the Egyptian Museum in Cairo – survived almost unharmed.

The lintel came from a relatively large, exceptionally well-preserved house, numbered T.34.1, in the 'northern suburb' of the city. It was discovered, having fallen from above a doorway between the north loggia and central room of the house. The stone was originally brightly painted, as illustrated by a full-sized watercolour copy made by excavator John Pendlebury's wife Hilda, and now held in the archives of the Egypt Exploration Society. The cast was made shortly after its discovery and was displayed at an exhibition of finds brought back to Britain by the EES expedition.

In the houses of New Kingdom officials, the cartouches of the reigning king are a common motif on architectural elements around doorways. Respecting the Egyptian love of symmetry, the owner of house T.34.1, Hatiay, is shown twice. He adores the cartouches of Akhenaten and his wife Nefertiti, along with the much larger names of the god Aten – also in cartouches. As on many monuments throughout Egypt, Akhenaten's names have been destroyed after his demise – but those of the queen and the Aten himself are untouched. Hatiay is stated in the lintel's inscriptions to be the 'overseer of works' at the city. He is possibly to be identified with a 'chief sculptor' of the same name who claims to have played an important part in restoring the cult statues of the traditional gods after the end of Akhenaten's reign. (C.P.)

2. 哈地亞墓室門楣
來自阿瑪納
第 18 王朝，阿肯納頓統治時期（西元前 1352-1336 年）
石膏，顏料
2180 x 920 x 365 mm

Cast of Door Lintel of Hatiay
Original from Amarna.
1931, original New Kingdom,
Dynasty 18, reign of Akhenaten (1352-1336 BC)
Plaster and pigment

玻璃幻燈片

在電視和電影出現之前，公共及私人放映的幻燈片在娛樂和教育方面皆廣受歡迎。幻燈投影機以及在玻璃板之間以正片圖像製成的幻燈片，被用來在牆上或特殊螢幕上放映影像。隨著歐洲人更加頻繁的旅行異國他鄉，攝影師將其旅程拍攝下來，並對外銷售其照片以製作幻燈片。

這些幻燈片是歐洲人製作來表現「埃及」這個異國土地之幻燈片組中的一部份，包括古代以及照片拍攝時間左右的埃及。時至今日，這些影像可讓我們透過早期歐洲探險家的眼睛看見埃及。　（作者：C.R.）

Glass Lantern Slides

Before television and film, public and private showings of slides were popular both as entertainment and education. The Magic Lantern Projector was used, along with slides made of positive film images between glass plates, to project images on walls or a specially prepared screen. As Europeans travelled more frequently to foreign lands, photographers captured their journeys and sets of their pictures were sold to the public to produce slide shows.

These lantern slides are part of a set of slides produced to illustrate the exotic land of Egypt, both ancient and around the time the photographs were taken. Today these images let us see Egypt through the eyes of the early European explorers. (C.R.)

3. 玻璃幻燈片
埃及拍攝，曼徹斯特製造
維多利亞時代，約西元 1900 年
玻璃和底片
85 x 85 x 3 mm

Glass Lantern Slides
Taken in Egypt, produced in Manchester
Victorian, around AD 1900
Glass and film

1. 開羅 － Cairo from the Citadel
2. 尼羅河上的橋 － Bridge over river Nile at Cairo
3. 開羅堡壘 － The Citadel, Cairo
4. 開羅街道 － Cairo street scene
5. 吉薩金字塔和人面獅身像 － Giza sphinx and pyramid of Khafre
6. 班尼哈山墓室 － Tomb at Beni Hasan
7. 丹德拉的哈托爾神廟 － Hathor Temple at Dendara
8. 路克索神廟 － Luxor Temple at Luxor
9. 路克索神廟前尼羅河一景 － Boats on river Nile before Luxor Temple
10. 騎著驢子的埃及人 － Egyptian man riding a donkey
11. 路克索卡納克神廟的大多柱宮 － Great Hypostyle Hall in Karnak Temple at Luxor
12. 路克索卡納克神廟的方尖碑 － Obelisk in Karnak Temple at Luxor
13. 路克索孔蘇神廟大門 － Gate of the Khonsu Temple at Luxor
14. 底比斯西岸拉美西斯神廟 － The Ramesseum at the West Bank of Thebes
15. 底比斯西岸的阿蒙霍特三世大型坐姿雕像 － One of the Colossi of Memnon, a large seated statue of Amenhotep III at the West Bank of Thebes
16. 底比斯西岸的門農神像 － The other Colossi of Memnon, at the West Bank of Thebes
17. 底比斯西岸的哈布城神廟大門 － Gate of the Temple of Medinet Habu at the West Bank of Thebes
18. 艾德夫的荷魯斯神廟聖殿 － Shrine in the Horus Temple at Edfu
19. 大象島上的兩名埃及人 － Two Egyptians on Elephantine Island
20. 菲萊島 － The Island of Philae
21. 菲萊島上的伊西絲神廟 － Isis Temple at the Island of Philae
22. 菲萊島上被稱作「法老王座」的結構 － Formation called "Pharaoh's Throne" at Island of Philae
23. 菲萊島的圖拉真亭 － Trajan's Kiosk at Island of Philae
24. 菲萊島的古代遺跡 － Ancient monuments at Island of Philae
25. 尼羅河三角洲地區的農村景緻 － Rural scene in the Nile Delta region
26. 埃及村落景緻 － Egyptian village scene
27. 房屋旁的埃及村民 － Egyptian villagers near houses
28. 努比亞的古埃及遺跡 － Ancient Egyptian monuments in Nubia
29. 阿布辛貝的拉美西斯二世神廟 － Temple of Rameses II at Abu Simbel
30. 騎乘駱駝的埃及男子 － Egyptian man riding a camel

受擾陵墓的重建

當歐洲人來到埃及時，無論是考古學家或前來探險的遊客，經常遇到古埃及墓地。隨著老舊的墓地被新的墓地所推移，許多古埃及陵墓在數百年間已被使用多次。此外，有些陵墓也遭到劫掠，木乃伊往往被拆開並肢解以拿取由珍貴材料製成的珠寶及護身符。因此，早期的探險家所造訪的陵墓中，常發現許多雜亂的亞麻、陪葬品以及木乃伊的殘肢。探訪埃及經驗非常豐富的歐洲探險家—貝爾佐尼（Belzoni），描述於某次造訪位於底比斯古埃及陵墓的過程：

通過長達兩三百碼的通道之後，通常能找到一個更寬敞的地方，高度可能足以坐下。但這根本不是安息之處！週圍都是軀體，四面八方都是成堆的木乃伊；... 我完全沉沒在殘破的木乃伊與破碎的骨頭、破布以及木箱中。

此重建陵墓展示的物品來自英國維爾康研究所之收藏，並於英國伯頓博物館展出。原籍美國的亨利‧維爾康（Henry Wellcome，1853 年 -1936 年）移居至英國倫敦，並經營著一家成功的製藥公司。他對於醫學史相當感興趣，並開始收集材料以開設博物館。在他去世之前，便已收集到超過 100 萬件物品，且其醫學史收藏量被認為是全球最大宗者。這些收藏品包括數量相當龐大的古埃及文物，尤其是古埃及木乃伊以及製作木乃伊相關物品。英國維爾康及其所屬之收藏家，於 20 世紀初期在拍賣會中購買到其中大量文物。英國維爾康研究所收藏的古埃及文物多半於 1970 年至 1985 年間提供給擁有埃及文化收藏品的博物館，如伯頓博物館等。　（作者：C.R.）

A Recreation of a Disturbed Tomb

When Europeans came to Egypt, whether as archaeologists or adventurous tourists, they often encountered ancient Egyptian burials. Many ancient Egyptian tombs had been used multiple times during the centuries with old burials being pushed out of the way for new burials. Additionally, tombs had been robbed, often many times, and the mummies were unwrapped and dismembered to take the amulets and jewellery made from precious materials. Thus many of the tombs visited by these early explorers contained a jumble of mixed up linen, grave goods, and parts of mummies. Belzoni, one of the more colourful European explorers to visit Egypt, described one of his trips to an ancient Egyptian tomb in Thebes:

After getting through these passages, some of them two or three hundred yards long, you generally find a more commodious place, perhaps high enough to sit. But what a place of rest! Surrounded by bodies, by heaps of mummies in all directions;… I sunk altogether among the broken mummies with a crash of bones, rags and wooden cases.

The objects in this recreated tomb display came to Bolton Museum from the Wellcome Institute collection. Henry Wellcome (1853 -1936) was an American who moved to London England and ran a successful pharmaceutical company. He was interested in the history of medicine and began collecting material to open a museum. By his death, he had collected over 1 million objects and his medical history collection was considered the largest in the world. This collection included a very large number of ancient Egyptian objects, especially items related to ancient Egyptian mummies and mummification. Wellcome and his collectors purchased many of these items at auction in the first decades of the 20th Century. Most of the ancient Egyptian items in the Wellcome Institute Collection were disbursed to museums with Egyptological collection, such as Bolton Museum, between 1970 and 1985. (C.R.)

---

4. 受擾陵墓的重建

1. 木乃伊手部
來自埃及
新王國時期至後埃及時期
第 18 王朝（西元前 1550-332 年）
手部組織，亞麻纖維
225 x 80 x 30 mm

2. 木乃伊裹布
來自埃及
中王國時期
第 11 - 30 王朝（西元前 2055 年至 332 年）
亞麻布
1500 x 270 x 10 mm

3. 木乃伊裹布
來自埃及
中王國時期至後埃及時期
第 11 王朝（西元前 2055-332 年）
亞麻布
1200 x 600 x 10 mm

4. 木乃伊裹布
來自埃及
中王國時期至後埃及時期
第 11 王朝（西元前 2055-332 年）
亞麻布
1270 x 920 x 40 mm

5. 木乃伊包裹布
來自埃及
中王國時期
第 11 王朝（西元前 2055-332 年）
亞麻布
1240 x 450 x 10 mm

6. 木乃伊包裹布
來自埃及
中王國時期
第 11 王朝（西元前 2055-332 年）
亞麻布
830 x 500 x 10 mm

7. 薩布提人俑
來自亞比多斯
第三中間期
第 21 至 30 王朝（西元前 1069-332 年）
彩陶
90 x 35 x 25 mm

8. 奈夫圖神護身符
來自埃及
後埃及時期
第 26-30 王朝（西元前 664-332 年）
彩陶
50 x 30 x 20 mm

9. 人形棺耳部雕刻
來自底比斯西岸
新王國時期至後埃及時期
第 18-30 王朝（西元前 1550-332 年）
木，顏料
100 x 53 x 20 mm

10. 人型棺手部雕刻
來自底比斯西岸
新王國時期至後埃及時期
第 18-30 王朝（西元前 1550-332 年）
木，石膏，顏料
100 x 75 x 30 mm

11. 頭墊局部
來自埃及
新王國時期至第三中間期
第 18-25 王朝（西元前 1550 - 664 年）
木
185 x 85 x 80 mm

12. 木乃伊頭部
來自埃及
新王國時期至後埃及時期
第 18-30 王朝（西元前 1550-332 年）
人體組織
210 x 185 x 150 mm

13. 木乃伊頭部
來自埃及
新王國時期至後埃及時期
第 18-30 王朝（西元前 1550-332 年）
人體組織
250 x 185 x 150 mm

14. 木乃伊腳部
來自埃
後埃及時期
第 26 - 30 王朝（西元前 664-332 年）
人體組織，亞麻布，石膏，顏料
230 x 170 x 78 mm

A Recreation of a Disturbed Tomb

1. Mummified Human hand
From Egypt
New Kingdom to Late Period,
Dynasty 18 – 30 (1550–332 BC)
Human tissue, linen,
225 x 80 x 30 mm

2. Mummy wrapping cloth
From Egypt
Middle Kingdom to Late Period,
Dynasty 11 – 30 (2055-332 BC)
Linen,
1500 x 270 x 10 mm

3. Mummy wrapping cloth
From Egypt
Middle Kingdom to Late Period,
Dynasty 11 – 30 (2055-332 BC)
Linen,
1200 x 600 x 10 mm

4. Mummy wrapping cloth
From Egypt
Middle Kingdom to Late Period,
Dynasty 11 – 30 (2055-332 BC)
Linen,
1270 x 920 x 40 mm

5. Mummy wrapping cloth
From Egypt
Middle Kingdom to Late Period,
Dynasty 11 – 30 (2055-332 BC)
Linen,
1240 x 450 x 10 mm

6. Mummy wrapping cloth
From Egypt
Middle Kingdom to Late Period,
Dynasty 11 – 30 (2055-332 BC)
Linen,
830 x 500 x 10 mm

7. Shabti
From Abydos
Third Intermediate Period to Late Period,
Dynasty 21 – 30 (1069-332 BC)
Faience,
90 x 35 x 25 mm

8. Amulet of the god Nefertum
From Egypt
Late Period,
Dynasty 26-30 (664-332 BC)
Faience,
50 x 30 x 20 mm

9. Ear from a Coffin
From West Bank of Thebes
New Kingdom – Late Period,
Dynasty 18-30 (1550-332 BC)
Wood, pigment,
100 x 53 x 20 mm

10. Hand from a Coffin
From West Bank of Thebes
Third Intermediate Peraiod – Late Period,
Dynasty 21-30 (1069-332 BC)
Wood, plaster, pigment,
100 x 75 x 30 mm

11. Fragment from a Headrest
From Egypt
New Kingdom – Third Intermediate Period,
Dynasty 18-25 (1550 – 664 BC)
Wood,
185 x 85 x 80 mm

12. Mummified Human head
From Egypt
New Kingdom – Late Period,
Dynasty 18-30 (1550 – 332 BC)
Human tissue,
210 x 185 x 150 mm

13. Mummified Human head
From Egypt
New Kingdom – Late Period,
Dynasty 18-30 (1550 – 332 BC)
Human tissue,
250 x 185 x 150 mm

14. Mummified Human foot
From Egypt
Late Period,
Dynasty 26 – 30 (664-332 BC)
Human tissue, linen, plaster, pigment,
230 x 170 x 78 mm

蘆葦筆

由堅硬的蘆葦製成希臘風格的筆，底部帶有鋒利的對角線切割面，形成一個筆尖，取代了傳統的埃及抄寫配備鈍頭草筆。不僅是筆的樣式，此時期使用的墨水亦有所變化，埃及人的碳黑顏料被替換為鉛墨。希臘與拉丁文字比象形文字、僧侶體以及通俗體文字更需銳利且具稜角的筆尖來書寫，而新型式的筆能讓書記員以較小字體書寫所有語言。使用尖銳筆尖的蘆葦筆還需稍厚的紙莎草紙，以抵銷書寫時增加的壓力。

這些筆的筆尖仍保有些許墨水，而筆尖處也因使用而略有磨損。在法老時代，書記員往往被描繪成隨時帶著許多筆，有時甚至將筆塞在耳後 — 都屬於合理的寫照，因為書記員必須使用不同顏色的墨水，因而需要不同的筆以避免顏色受到污染。這些筆可能被用來書寫各種文件，我們目前所知的案例有表格及帳目、法律文件、人際之間的私人信件、咒語、讚美詩等，甚至有希臘羅馬時期的數學及天文學文本。　（作者：E.L.）

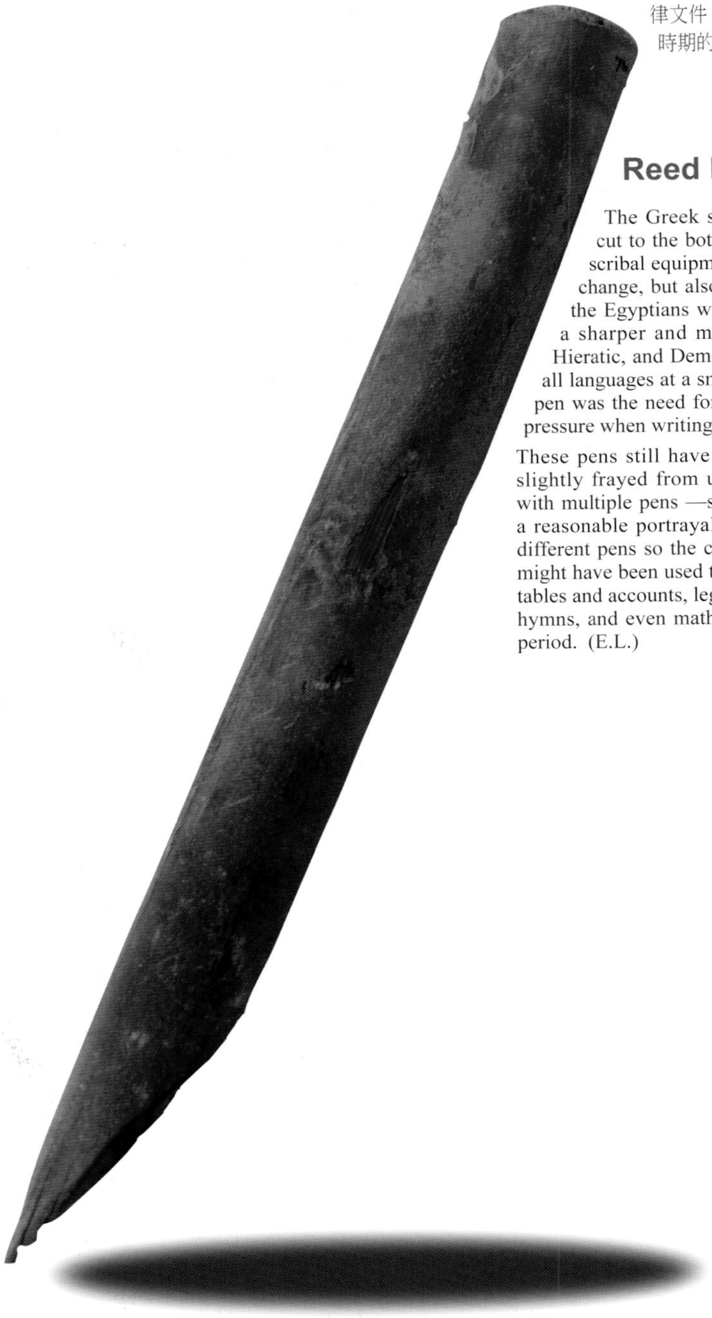

Reed Pens

The Greek style pen, made from a hard reed with a sharp diagonal cut to the bottom so as to form a nib, replaced the traditional Egyptian scribal equipment of the blunt ended rush pen. Not only did the pen type change, but also the ink used in this period; the carbon black pigment of the Egyptians was replaced by lead ink. Greek and Latin scripts required a sharper and more angular nibbed implement than the hieroglyphic, Hieratic, and Demotic scripts, but the new pen type allowed scribes to write all languages at a smaller scale. Another consequence of the sharp-tipped reed pen was the need for slightly thicker papyrus to compensate for the increased pressure when writing.

These pens still have the remains of ink preserved on the tip, which is also slightly frayed from use. In the pharaonic period scribes are often portrayed with multiple pens —sometimes even with the pens tucked behind their ears — a reasonable portrayal, since scribes used different coloured inks and needed different pens so the colours would remain uncontaminated. Pens such as these might have been used to write a wide variety of documents; we have examples of tables and accounts, legal documents, private letters between people, incantations, hymns, and even mathematical and astronomical texts from the Graeco-Roman period. (E.L.)

5. 莎草桿筆
來自奧克西林庫斯
希臘羅馬時期（西元前 332 年 - 西元 395 年）
莎草桿
90 x 10 x 7 mm

Reed Pens
From Oxyrhynchus
Graeco-Roman Period (332 BC-AD 395)
Papyrus reed

6. 莎草桿筆
來自法尤姆
希臘羅馬時期（西元前 332 年 - 西元 395 年）
莎草桿
166 x 9 x 8 mm

Reed Pens
From the Fayum
Graeco-Roman Period (332 BC- AD 395)
Papyrus reed

7. 書吏調色盤
來自阿比多斯，D9 號墓室
第 18 王朝，圖特摩斯三世統治時期（西元前
1479-1425 年）
黑檀木
356 x 60 x 13 mm

Scribal Palette of Inhertmes
From Abydos, tomb D9
Dynasty 18, reign of Thutmose III (1479-1425 BC)
Ebony

書吏調色盤

這項外型細長的長方形非洲黑木（黑檀木）製品是書記員的調色板。這是書記員的主要工具，象徵著書記的專業。這項由大衛・藍道麥克艾佛（David Randall-MacIver）及亞瑟・西・麥斯（Arthur C. Mace）在阿比多斯的墓園中的賽特胡（Sitepehu）陵墓所發現之物品，可追溯至圖特摩斯三世。這種狹長的形狀是新王國時代所使用的調色板特徵。原本其中包含著類似於現代畫筆的蘆葦筆（蘆筆管）以及紅色與黑色墨水，墨水存放在調色板一端的兩個小橢圓形凹槽內。黑色墨水是由碳（木炭）所製成，而紅色墨水則是由富含鐵的紅赭石製成。黑色是正常的書寫顏色，而紅色是用來指出文章的開頭或章節標題，並用於凸顯關鍵字或關鍵詞。此調色板表面的銘刻包含門黑貝雷（Menkheperre，意即圖特摩斯三世），其後題詞則是說明此調色板屬於提尼斯的糧倉監督者印何姆（Inhertmes）。

書記員的調色板是書記員工具組中的一個主要部分。然而，其他工具也同樣必要，包括用來研磨顏料的研缽及研杵、紙刀、讓紙莎草紙表面適於書寫的修光工具，以及書寫材料本身，通常是紙莎草紙，但也可能是木材、陶片（陶器碎片或石灰岩）和布料。這些物品被存放於木箱，且木箱通常以浮雕與彩繪的樣式出現在書記員旁。同樣地，在埃及雕塑中，經常把調色板雕刻在書記員坐姿雕像的某一邊肩膀上，而腿上則橫跨著一張紙莎草紙。

「調色板」與「畫筆」圖像則被當作象形文字符號，代表「書記員」這個名詞與動詞「寫」，以及其他有關書寫活動的詞彙。在整個古埃及歷史當中，書記員職業被賦予了崇高敬意，任何想要成為自身之主並過著良好生活的人，都會被鼓勵從事此行業。這部份記載於古埃及文學作品中，例如，在《The Satire on the Trades: The Instruction of Dua-Khety》一書裡，一名父親就對兒子講述書記員之外各行各業的慘況。由於僅有極少部分的古埃及人知道如何閱讀和寫字，因此書記員便成為一項專門職業。有效的行政管理是古埃及國家運作的重要面相。（作者：A.H.）

Scribal Palette of Inhertmes

This long, slim, rectangular object made of African blackwood (ebony) is a scribe's palette. It was the scribe's main tool and came to symbolize the scribal profession. This example was found in the Tomb of Sitepehu in Cemetery D at Abydos by David Randall-MacIver and Arthur C. Mace and dates to the reign of Thutmose III. The narrow shape is characteristic of palettes used throughout the New Kingdom. It would have originally contained reed pens (calami) similar to modern day paintbrushes and black and red ink, which would have been held in the two small oval wells located at one end of the palette. The black ink was made from carbon (charcoal), and the red ink was made from iron-rich red ochre. Black was the normal colour for writing, while red was used to indicate the start of a text or chapter headings and to highlight key words or phrases. The inscription carved on the surface of this palette contains a cartouche of Thutmose III (Menkheperre) at the top followed by an inscription, which indicates that the palette belonged to Inhertmes, Overseer of the Granary in Thinis.

The scribe's palette was an essential component of the scribe's tool kit. However, other instruments were also required, including a mortar and pestle to grind pigments, a paper knife and smoother to make the surface of the papyrus sheet suitable for writing on, and the writing material itself, which was usually papyrus, but could also be wood, ostraca (fragments of pottery or limestone), and fabric. These items would have been stored in wooden boxes, which are often presented next to scribes in reliefs and paintings. Similarly, in Egyptian statuary, palettes are often carved over one shoulder of statues of seated scribes with a papyrus across their lap.

The image of the scribal palette and brush case was used as the hieroglyphic sign for the word 'scribe' and the verb 'to write', as well as various other terms related to the act of writing. The scribe's profession was held in high esteem throughout ancient Egyptian history. Anyone who wanted to be his own master and make a good living was encouraged to take up this profession. This is indicated in the Instructions of ancient Egyptian literary texts, such as *The Satire on the Trades: The Instruction of Dua-Khety* where a father describes to his son the miserable conditions of professions other than the scribe's. The scribal profession was a specialized profession since only a small percent of the ancient Egyptian population knew how to read and write. An effective administration was an important aspect of ancient Egyptian state operation. (A.H.)

墨水槽

僅有極少數的古埃及人有書寫能力；其中部份能力原本就已存在，但僅介於那些只能夠辨認出一些符號以及那些能書寫新文體的人之間。象形文字大多用於古蹟，而較不正式的草書〔僧侶體〕則用於文件。識字者形成精英人士，而書記訓練則備受尊崇。在《The Satire on the Trades》一書中鼓勵年輕人接受培訓以成為書記員。一名男子對他的兒子說：

> 「我應當讓你愛書寫勝於愛你的母親，
> 我應當向你呈現書寫之美…」

他接著陳述從事其他工作者的艱苦生活，並以書記員的舒適生活作為對比。

這個小物件很可能是書記員工具組當中的一部份。僧侶體的文件中通常以黑色墨水書寫，某些部份則以紅色墨水書寫。因此，書記員的調色板除了包含用於攜帶的蘆葦筆，通常還包含兩個圓孔填裝乾燥顏料，一黑一紅。此橢圓形裝飾以皇室名稱的環形製成，這項小型物件帶有兩個圓柱孔以區隔開這些顏色，雖然現在已看不出任何痕跡。其他此類型物件皆刻有托特神（Thoth）之名，即書寫之神，可能是用來對該神祇還願的供品。 （作者：C.P.）

Ink Well

Only a very small percentage of the ancient Egyptian population would have been able to write. A range of ability would have existed, between those only able to recognise a few signs and those who could compose new texts. Hieroglyphs were mostly used for monuments, while the less formal, cursive script ('hieratic') was used for documents. The literate formed the elite, and scribal training was highly esteemed. One text, known as the Satire on the Trades, encourages young men to train to become scribes. A man addresses his son:

> 'I shall make you love writing more than your mother,
> I shall present its beauties to you…'

He goes on to describe the tough life of those doing other jobs, contrasting them with the easy life of a scribe.

This small object was likely part of the equipment of a scribe. Documents in hieratic were usually written in black ink, with some sections in red. Therefore scribal palettes – used to carry reed pens – usually also contained two circular cavities for dried pigments, one black and one red. Made in the shape of the royal name-ring, the cartouche, this compact example has two cylindrical holes to separate these colours, although no trace now remains of them. Other examples of this type of object are inscribed with the name of Thoth, the god of writing, and may represent votive offerings to that deity. (C.P.)

8. 墨水槽
來自壇尼斯
第三中間期至後埃及時期（西元前 1069-332 年）
彩陶
57 x 27 x 15 mm

Ink Well
From Tanis
Third Intermediate – Late Period (1069-332 BC).
Faience

印有銘文的陶罐碎片

在我們一般所說的埃及第一代法老等君王之前，曾有一連串統治者，其墳墓座落在阿比多斯的第一王朝皇家陵園附近，但其身為上下埃及國王的地位則較不明確。這些統治者的在位時間稱為埃及前王朝時期（Predynastic Period）或初期王朝。這短短幾年的時間必定目睹了埃及社會組織的急遽變化，在此期間，「兩塊土地」首次統一。掌管埃及近 3000 年的官僚體系迅速發展，包括象形文字系統以及皇室肖像，皆因此於早期即開始使用。

第一位名字書寫於埃及皇室（serekh）標誌的國王是卡（Ka）。其在位期間在納美爾（Narmer）之前。他也是第一位名字在上下埃及皆經過證實的統治者。[1] 我們透過在亞比多斯挖掘其帶有雙墓室的陵墓而得知這名「國王前身」（preking），並在圓柱罐上的銘文墨跡發現他的名字，也就是此殘留碎片的來源。圓柱罐在所謂波狀處理器皿製作上最後階段之特點為外形平直，邊框下有一條雕刻或繪畫線條環繞著容器上半部，此為波狀手把最後的裝飾遺跡。這些罐子似乎在模仿此時期之雪花石罐，也可能被視為經濟實惠的替代品。這些圓柱罐出現於埃及前王朝時期，並一直持續至第一王朝。考古學家利用其作為日期指標，以用於這個人們了解甚少的時期。如同此物件一般，其中某些部份由於已透過皇室銘文墨跡而確定年代，因而在排序時成為簡便的標記物。

雖然僅有片段，但保留下來的銘文墨跡顯示出朝上的臂部與手部，此為「卡」的名字在書寫時的特徵。宮殿外觀頂部已破損，但物件仍屬完整，一隻代表神聖王權的荷魯斯獵鷹位於頂上。在宮殿外觀旁的銘文墨跡意指上埃及國王國庫獲得的稅收，並說明即使在此早期階段，稅收制度在埃及北部與南部仍各自獨立。（作者：J.A.H.）

1. 書寫著其名字的圓柱罐在 Tarkhan 的墓園中尋得，此為下埃及首都孟菲斯在納美爾之前便已建立之有力佐證。

Cylinder Jar Fragment with Ink Inscription

Prior to the kings we commonly refer to as Egypt's first pharaohs, there was a succession of rulers whose graves are located near the First Dynasty royal cemetery at Umm el-Qa'ab, but whose status as kings of both Upper and Lower Egypt is less certain. These rulers occupy a period of time referred to as the Protodynastic Period or Dynasty 0. This brief span of years must have been witness to rapid change in the social organization of the country, a period during which the "Two Lands" were first united. The bureaucratic systems through which Egypt would be governed for almost 3000 years were quickly developing, including the hieroglyphic writing system and the royal iconography that would dominate its early use.

The first king whose name is written within the symbol of the Egyptian royal house (serekh) was Ka. He is the king whose reign immediately preceded Narmer. He is also the first ruler whose name is attested in both Upper and Lower Egypt.[1] We know of this "preking" through the excavation of his double chambered tomb (Tomb B7/9) at Abydos and from ink inscriptions of his name found on cylinder jars like the one from which this fragment survives. Cylinder jars, the very last stage of the so-called Wavy Handled Ware, were characterized by a straight profile and an incised or painted line around the upper body of the vessel below the rim, the last decorative vestiges of a wavy handle. The jars appear to imitate alabaster stone jars from this period and may have been considered economical substitutes. These cylinder jars appear at the very end of the Predynastic period and continue into Dynasty 1. Archaeologists use them as relative date indicators for this poorly understood period. Some of them, like this example, are convenient markers in the sequence because they have been dated with royal ink inscriptions.

Though fragmentary, the preserved ink inscription shows the upturned arm and hand that is characteristic of the writing of Ka's name. The top of the palace façade is broken away, but in complete examples, a Horus falcon, representing divine kingship, sits atop the serekh. The ink inscription beside the palace façade (ipw.t Sma.w) refers to revenues received in Upper Egypt by the king's treasury and indicates that tax collection even in this early period was organized separately for the northern and southern halves of the country. (J.A.H.)

1. A cylinder jar with his name written on it was found at the cemetery of Tarkhan, a strong indication that the Lower Egyptian capital of Memphis had been founded before Narmer.

9. 印有銘文的陶罐碎片
來自阿比多斯，B7 號墓室
早期王國，卡 (Ka) 統治時期（西元前 3200-3100 年）
陶瓷
177 x 67 x 35 mm

Cylinder Jar Fragment with Ink Inscription
From Abydos, Tomb B7
Naqada IIIb, reign of Ka (3200-3100 BC)
Ceramic

10. 家庭群像
來自埃及
第 18 王朝 (西元前 1550-1295 年)
砂岩
570 x 360 x 350 mm
杜漢大學東方博物館藏

Family Group Statue
From Egypt
Dynasty 18 (1550-1295 B.C.E.)
Sandstone
Durham University Oriental Museum

家庭群像

在埃及被發現的古王國到新王國時期夫妻雕像，外型往往像這樣，包括型體較小的孩童。在第十八王朝期間，這樣的家庭團體雕像經常被放置在陵墓所有人的墓室壁龕中。這些雕像提供了一個給予供品的焦點，以確保死者在死後收到寄託。這座雕像是獻給一名叫做阿美納斯（Amenmes）的男子以及一名可能是他的妻子的女性，儘管她的名字和頭銜不易辨識。有一名孩童站在這對夫婦之間。這在埃及藝術相當常見，這個女兒以較其父母為小的形體呈現，以強調其父母具有更高地位。有幾個兒子在座位兩旁以浮雕描繪出的人型當中。這座雕像原先是彩繪而成，目前仍保有些許彩繪痕跡。獨立雕刻出來插入雕像主體的女兒頭部已經遺失。　（作者：R.G.）

Family Group Statue

Husband and wife statues are found in Egypt from the Old Kingdom to the New Kingdom, often, as here, with smaller figures of children included. During Dynasty 18, family group statues like this were often placed in a niche within the owner's tomb chapel. These statues provided a focus for the giving of offerings, ensuring that the ka of the dead person received sustenance after death. This statue is dedicated to a man named Amenmes and a lady who is assumed to be his wife, though her name and titles are not legible. A child stands between the couple. As is common in Egyptian art, this daughter is shown at a smaller scale than her parents to emphasise their higher status. Several sons are among the figures depicted in the carved reliefs on either side of the seat. The statue would originally have been painted and some traces of paint remain. The head of the daughter, which appears to have been carved separately and inserted into a slot in the main statue, has been lost. (R.G.)

11. 記載供品列表的碎片
來自阿比多斯，奧塞里斯的大祭司溫奈尼法之墓
第 19 王朝，拉美西斯二世統治時期
（西元前 1279-1213 年）
石灰岩，顏料
235 x 200 x 200 mm

A text of endowment from Abydos
From Abydos, the tomb of the high priest of Osiris,
Wenennefer
Dynasty 19, reign of Rameses II (1279-1213 BC)
Limestone, pigment

記載供品列表的碎片

這是目前已知的長篇銘文四個片段之一，是英國考古學家佩托里（Petrie）於阿比多斯的開鑿期間，在被認定是奧塞里斯神（Osiris）的高級祭司衛南尼佛（Wenennefer）之陵墓中所發現。此座陵墓的位置不得而知，但其可能為佩托里發掘的墓園當中，位於阿比多斯的中央墓地。從該墓園之另一座建築構造出土的石灰岩磚上帶有衛南尼佛及其親屬米摩斯（Minmose），即歐努里斯（Onuris）的高級祭司之浮雕。此建築可能是奉獻給他們兩位的小教堂，倘若衛南尼佛的陵墓為獨立結構，應該就位於附近。

此碎片源自銘文上部，包含三組拉美西斯二世在位年份的連貫日期：「在位年份38，收穫季（shomu）第 1 個月第 3 天…在位年份 39，收穫季第 1 個月…」。最後已破損的一行記錄的日期似乎是播種季（peret）第 4 個月，在位年份可能是 40。這些象形文字被漆成黃色，而用來分隔的行列則帶有黑色顏料的痕跡。目前收藏於美國賓州大學考古學暨人類學博物館的其他兩塊碎片在個別日期之後包含著皇室人物雕像，據說其中之一為金屬材質。第四塊碎片目前在何處則無法確定，其記錄著土地面積以及酒與奶的單位。

從非王室陵墓出土的此種風格銘文，目前沒有其他相似的能夠比對，但其所列之日期、雕像以及糧食顯示出其記錄著衛南尼佛在阿比多斯各間寺廟之奉獻與皇室雕像捐贈。捐贈土地及一般糧食給廟宇雕像的行為在埃及新王國時期相當知名；在某種程度上，這屬於一種經濟策略，因為官方將可從該筆財產中獲得收入，或許還帶有稅收與其他義務之款項。這也是一種奉獻行為，能與神祇、廟宇以及國王之間，建立並永久保存著強烈的個人與體制關係。倘若衛南尼佛之銘文記載著此類奉獻，這也代表著相當大的資源投入。這四塊碎片的日期範圍為 21 年至 47 年，因此至少在此 28 年具備文件記錄的期間，雕像與捐獻內容均定期被建立與維護。透過在其墓室記錄這些奉獻內容，衛南尼佛便可確保一項永久，且或許具有法律約束力的財富展現及其虔誠奉獻。更廣泛而言，該年份列表可被解釋為一種制訂及列舉盡責服務之生活的方式。此舉可與銘刻於非王室陵墓傳統傳記文獻相比較，但後者用意在於講述個人正確行為的故事，以及對國王以及神祇的貢獻。（作者：L.F.）

A text of endowment from Abydos

This is one of four known fragments of a long inscription found by Petrie during his excavations at Abydos in a structure he identified as the tomb of Wenennefer, high priest of Osiris. The location of this tomb is not known, but it was probably in Petrie's 'cemetery G', part of the central necropolis area at Abydos. Limestone blocks from another structure excavated in cemetery G bear relief scenes of Wenennefer and his kinsman Minmose, high priest of Onuris. This building could have been a chapel dedicated to both of them ; Wenennefer's tomb, if it was a separate structure, may have been nearby.

This fragment is from the upper section of the inscription and gives three sets of dates in consecutive regnal years of Rameses II: "Regnal year 38, first month of shomu, day 3 … Regnal year 39, first month of shomu … ." The final, broken column seems to record a date in the fourth month of peret, probably in year 40. The hieroglyphs are painted yellow while the column dividers bear traces of black pigment. Two of the other fragments, now in the University of Pennsylvania Museum of Archaeology and Anthropology, Philadelphia (E. 9930), include figures of royal statues after each date, one of which is said to be metal. The fourth fragment, whose current location is unknown, records areas of land and measures of wine and milk.

There is no known parallel for this style of inscription from a non-royal tomb, but the listing of dates, statues, and provisions suggests that it records Wenennefer's dedication and endowment of royal statues in temples at Abydos. The practice of endowing temple statues with land and regular provision of goods is well-known in New Kingdom Egypt. It was, in part, an economic strategy as the official would receive an income from the property, perhaps with remittance of taxes and other obligations. It was also an act of devotion, creating and perpetuating strong personal, as well as institutional, ties to gods, temple, and king. If Wenennefer's inscription records such endowments, they represent a considerable investment of resources. The dates on the four fragments range from year 21 to year 47, thus at least 28 years during which statues and endowments were being regularly set up and maintained are documented. By recording these endowments in his tomb chapel, Wenennefer ensured a permanent and perhaps legally binding display of his wealth and his pious commitments. More broadly, the listing of years could be understood as a way of mapping out and enumerating a life of dutiful service. In this it may be compared with more traditional biographical texts that were inscribed in non-royal tombs to relate the individual's story of right action and service to king and gods. (L.F.)

記載有通俗體的陶器碎片

通俗（Demotic）這個詞用於代表埃及語言的文體與發展階段，其語言介於新埃及語和古埃及語之間－且共用兩者之語法與詞彙。和僧侶體（Hieratic）一樣，通俗體是埃及文手寫文體，但其個別符號遠較僧侶體簡略。

通俗體出現於薩美提克一世（Psammetichus I）統治時期（約公元前650年），為第二十六王朝初期，或稱為塞易特王朝（Saite）。在該王朝末期，通俗體已成為商業及日常事務的標準文體。整個托勒密時期直到羅馬時期皆使用此文體，所有類型的文本皆以通俗體書寫而成，包括如故事、說明、宗教、魔幻及醫學文獻等文學作品，以及非文學內容與行政文書，如信件、遺囑及合約。在紙莎草紙和陶片上曾發現以墨水書寫的通俗體題詞，此外亦雕刻於雕像、石碑，以及陵墓與寺廟等古蹟牆上。最近期的通俗體題詞時間為公元452年，地點在菲萊島（Philae）。

此陶片包含數行題詞，講述有關土地的內容。此內容中所使用的土地測量單位為「神聖腕尺」（divine cubit; mj-nor）。　（作者：J.H.W.）

Demotic Ostracon

Demotic is the name applied to both a script and a stage in the development of the Egyptian language, falling between Late Egyptian and Coptic -- and sharing grammar and vocabulary with both. Like Hieratic, Demotic is a cursive Egyptian script, but the individual signs are even more abbreviated than those found in hieratic.

Demotic appears during the reign of Psammetichus I (ca. 650 B.C.), early in the Twenty-sixth, or Saite, Dynasty. By the end of that dynasty, Demotic had become the standard script for business and everyday affairs. It was used throughout the Ptolemaic Period into the Roman Period and all genres of texts can be found written in Demotic including literary texts like tales and instructions, religious, magical and medical texts, as well as non-literary and administrative texts like letters, wills and contracts. Demotic inscriptions can be found written in ink on papyri and ostraca, as well as carved in stone on statuary, stelae, and the walls of monuments like tombs and temples. The latest dated Demotic inscription is from 452 AD and is located at Philae.

This ostracon contains an inscription of several columns dealing with a plot of land. The measurement used for the land in this text is the "divine cubit" (mj-nor). (J.H.W.)

12. 記載有通俗體的陶器碎片
來自哈拉耶
希臘羅馬時期（西元前332年 - 西元395年）
陶器，墨水
165 x 112 x 25 mm

Demotic Ostracon
From Harageh
Graeco-Roman Period (332 BC-AD 395)
Pottery and ink

化妝品調色板

以沙泥岩等軟石雕刻成各種尼羅河流域動物形狀的調色板，通常就是內加達 I-IIb 時期（西元前 4000-3600 年）的代表文物。類似此一魚狀調色板的獸形外觀器皿，於史前時代晚期數量減少，取而代之的是在一端裝飾有兩隻動物頭部相對的簡單長方形或長菱形器皿。這種調色板為個人物品，用來將鉛礦中的方鉛礦或銅礦中的綠色礦物（孔雀石）研磨成眼線顏料，並調和油或脂肪做為黏著劑。眼部化妝除了是一種美容儀式，同時在健康考量上也有其益處，因為這些礦物不僅有助於減低埃及艷陽的刺眼強光，亦能防止蒼蠅或其他昆蟲飛入眼睛造成感染。

此調色板雕刻為魚狀，雖屬風格化且略為抽象，但應是以羅非魚（Tilapia nilotica）為描摹對象，此圖案延續至埃及歷史時期仍為化妝品容器和個人護身符的熱門裝飾主題。此化妝品調色板原有一枚鑲嵌的眼睛，很可能是以獸骨或象牙雕製成，但現已佚失。調色板頂部鑽設的洞孔可供穿線，以便於未使用時可提線攜帶。此調色板出土自一處先前未發掘的前王朝時期晚期墓地中，此墓地在 1925 年至 1926 年阿比多斯挖掘季時由亨利‧法蘭克福（Henri Frankfort）首次發掘。此調色板發現時旁邊另有一件小型晚期陶器，其位置鄰近蘆葦靈柩中的死者臉部。（作者：J.A.H.）

Cosmetic Palette

Palettes carved from soft stone such as siltstone in the shapes of various Nilotic animals are usually the hallmark of the Naqada I-IIb period (4000-3600 BC). Zoomorphic types such as this palette in the shape of a fish decline in number in later prehistoric periods to be replaced by simple rectangular or rhomboidal shapes decorated at one end by the opposing heads of two animals. Such palettes were personal articles used to grind eye paint made from either the lead ore mineral galena or malachite, a green mineral found in copper ore, mixed with oil or fat as a binding agent. The application of eye makeup was both a beautification ritual and healthy practice as these minerals not only lessened the glare of the Egyptian sun, but discouraged flies and other pests from flying into the eyes and causing infection.

This palette carved in the shape of a fish, though stylized and slightly abstract is likely meant to represent the bolti fish (Tilapia nilotica), which continues to be a popular decorative motif for cosmetic containers and personal amulets in Egypt's historic period. This cosmetic palette at one time had an inlaid eye, likely made of bone or ivory, which is now missing. The hole drilled in the top of the palette allowed it to be strung and carried when it was not in use. The palette was discovered in an undisturbed late Predynastic burial excavated by Henri Frankfort in a 1925-1926 excavation season at Abydos. The palette was found in association with a small Late Ware vessel and placed close to the face of the deceased who rested inside a reed coffin. (J.A.H.)

13. 魚形化妝盤
來自阿比多斯，1629 號墓室
前王國時期，內加達文化 (西元前 3350-3150 年)
沙泥岩
155 x 100 x 5 mm

Cosmetic Palette
From Abydos, Tomb 1629
Predynastic, Naqada IId-Naqada IIIa (3350-3150 BC)
Siltstone

達干石碗

這枚精緻的石碗說明了前王國及早王國時期石器工匠的技術水準。佩托里（Petrie）發掘這件器皿的地點為達干（Tarkhan），此地是一處專供第一王朝時期孟斐斯新都精英人士下葬的墓地。此展品的材質為較軟的沙泥岩或硬砂岩[1]；埃及人自古以來已使用這種採自埃及東方沙漠中哈馬特乾谷的材質來加工為器皿。沙泥岩這種石材很適合雕刻前王國時期用於研磨眼線顏料的調色板；此材質亦用於製作石質紀念調色板，如著名的那爾邁調色板上最具歷史價值的持久圖案，就為我們見證了埃及的早期王權。在此石碗所屬的早王朝時期，石器皿是為了皇室陪葬所造，因此通常銘刻有已逝亡者的名字，或刻有為其先人葬禮製作此石器的王位繼承人名字。

在埃及史前時期結束之際，平民墓穴中陪葬陶器的數量及種類皆有大幅減少的現象，但社會精英份子的墓葬中卻開始出現大量由石材所仿製出的高品質陶器。當時雖然有多種石材都被取來鑽孔、研磨和拋光製成容器，但以柔軟細緻的沙泥岩進行操作時，工匠們更能利用這種石材如黏土般柔軟可塑的特性，創造出極為精緻的器皿。諷刺的是，當石器皿大受重視，甚至成為陪葬品主流之後，卻換成陶匠開始裝飾陶作來模仿石器了。（作者：J.A.H.）

1. 或有人將此材質誤認為石板。然而，石板為沉積而成的石材，質地極為脆硬，無法充分展現出如本件作品或紀念調色板之類的精緻雕工。

Tarkhan Bowl

This graceful bowl is a fine example of the skill attained by stone artisans during the Protodynastic and Early Dynastic periods. W. M. F. Petrie excavated the vessel from Tarkhan, one cemetery serving the elites of the new Memphite capital during Dynasty 1. It is carved from the relatively soft medium of siltstone or greywacke[1]. Egyptians had a long history of working with this material which is quarried in the Wadi Hammamat in Egypt's Eastern Desert. Siltstone was the preferred stone from which to carve the palettes used for grinding eye paint throughout the Predynastic. It was also the medium used to create the monumental stone palettes such as the Narmer Palette, which provide us the most memorable and enduring images of early Egyptian kingship. In the Early Dynastic Period to which this bowl dates, stone vessels meant for royal burials were inscribed with the deceased king's name or the name of the king's successor who donated stone vessels to his predecessor's burial equipment.

As Egypt's prehistoric period drew to a close there was a marked decline in the quality and variety of ceramics being produced for burial offerings in the graves of commoners, but a marked increase in the number of high quality ceramic vessel forms being imitated in stone and placed in the burials of elite members of society. While a wide variety of stones were drilled, ground and polished to make these containers, artisans working with the relatively soft, fine grained siltstone were able to create vessels of surprising delicacy, making it appear as though stone were as pliant and plastic a medium as clay. The irony is that the stone vessels became so highly prized as burial goods that potters began to decorate their ceramics to imitate their stone imitators. (J.A.H.)

1. The material is sometimes erroneously labeled slate. However, slate is a much more brittle and flaking sedimentary stone which would not respond well to the type of detailed carving exhibited in this piece or the monumental palettes.

14. 達干石碗
來自達干
早期王國時期，第 1 王朝（西元前 3000-2890 年）
沙泥岩
212 x 210 x 45 mm

Tarkhan Bowl
From Tarkhan
Early Dynastic, Dynasty 1 (3000-2890 BC)
Siltstone

薩卡拉石碗

此件修復石碗可能為埋葬於薩卡拉的墓穴中，第一王朝皇后的葬禮筵席中所使用的眾多餐具之一。發掘此墓室的考古學家艾默利（W.B. Emery）考證墓穴中的女性為赫爾奈特（Herneith），亦即哲爾王（Djer）之妻。赫爾奈特的墓穴年代應屬哲爾繼承人丹（Den）的統治時期所建造。如同丹在阿比多斯的墓穴，此墓穴亦包含許多當時的新興特徵，包括採用建築石材。墓穴入口上方的石灰石門楣上雕有臥獅，此門楣所支撐的石板跨越內室木製屋頂橫樑。墓穴南側佈置有陶器及石器。而艾默利在墓室北側發現木棺遺跡及部分人類遺骸。靈柩周圍壁面設置的小型磚砌壁龕中擺放有石製及陶製小碟，其中盛裝有食物並殘存有牛骨。在此時期流行在淺碗中裝滿食物，以備亡者隨時之需，其他食物則放置於墓穴內他處的儲存罐中。到了晚期，祭品形態轉為亡者墓穴壁面或墓穴前方石碑的豐富食物祭品畫像。艾默利在這裡也發現了以彩陶、天青石、紅玉髓及黃金製成的珠寶首飾，以及原本由象牙和石材打造的破碎手鐲。墓穴中的封印內包含有丹及赫爾奈特的名字。

墓室兩側的平台上放置超過 300 頭古代野牛（現已絕種）的頭骨做為裝飾。赫爾奈特的墓穴也是最早於內部設有階狀土墩結構的墓穴之一，艾默利主張此結構即是金字塔形式的濫觴。不同於此時期的其他皇室墓址，赫爾奈特的墓穴中並沒有用來容納陪葬朝臣屍體的墓室。唯一陪她走入幽冥世界的只有一隻薩路基獵犬，他的遺骨被發現時是橫陳於赫爾奈特墓穴的門檻上。（作者：J.A.H.）

Saqqara Bowl

This reconstructed stone bowl was perhaps part of a dinner service for the funerary banquet laid out for a queen of Dynasty 1 buried in Tomb 3507 at Saqqara. W.B. Emery, the archaeologist who excavated the mastaba tomb identified this woman as Herneith, the wife of King Djer. Herneith's tomb dates to the reign of Djer's successor, Den. Like Den's tomb at Abydos, hers contained many new features, including the use of architectural stone. A limestone lintel carved with images of recumbent lions was set over the doorway to the tomb. The lintel supports stone slabs laid across the wooden roof beams of the inner chamber. The southern part of the burial chamber contained pottery and stone vessels. In the northern part of the burial chamber Emery found the remains of a wooden coffin along with some human remains. Set into small brick niches in the walls around the coffin were small dishes of stone and ceramic containing food, the surviving remnants of the banquet included ox bones. In this period it was the practice to lay out a full meal in shallow bowls for the immediate needs of the deceased, while additional provisions were placed in storage jars elsewhere in the tomb. In later periods this provisioning was performed magically by representing a cornucopia of food offerings on the deceased's tomb walls or on slab stelae placed before the tomb. Emery also discovered jewelry made of faience, lapis lazuli, carnelian and gold, as well as broken bracelets of ivory and stone. Seal impressions in the tomb contained the name of Den as well as that of Herneith.

The skulls of more than 300 auroch (an ancient breed of cattle) mounted on platforms decorated either side of her mastaba. Her tomb was also one of the earliest to contain the stepped mound structure in its interior, which Emery theorized led to the pyramid form. Unlike other royal monuments from this period, Herneith's mastaba contained no burial chambers to receive the bodies of court retainers. Her sole companion to the netherworld was a saluki hound whose body was found lying across the threshold to her tomb. (J.A.H.)

15. 薩卡拉石碗
來自薩卡拉，3507 號墓室
早期王國時期，第 1 王朝丹 (Den) 統治時期（西元前 3000-2890 年）
沙泥岩
190 x 187 x 45 mm

Saqqara Bowl
From Saqqara. Tomb 3507
Early Dynastic, Dynasty 1, Reign of Den (3000-2920 BC)
Siltstone

皇室戳印的泥土封罐

埃及早期王國時期的國王將其墓穴建造於初期王國的國王所埋葬的墓地以西，此地點即今日我們所知的烏姆卡伯（Umm el-Qa'ab，阿拉伯文，亦為陶罐之鄉），由於此地一度被認為是埃及首位神王奧塞里斯（Osiris）的葬身之所，因此此處皆散佈著世代代埃及朝聖者所帶來供奉的小型許願祭品器皿。第一王朝的前半時期，繼位的國王們建立了更大的墓室和側殿，也增加了宮庭成員用的小型周邊墓穴。[1]考古學證據顯示，國王的僕役在國王下葬之時也遭到殺害陪葬，所有墓穴一次封死。國王墓葬中提供有統治者來生所可能需要的一切事物，包括細亞麻布疋、皇室禮服、傢俱、以黃金薄片封口的石罐、以黑檀或象牙雕製的物品、香料油、食物和酒等等。

此件在丹國王的墓穴中發現的黏土罐為泥土封口，其上載有這位國王的名字。丹的墓穴是烏姆卡伯最為精美的墓穴之一。主墓室鋪有紅黑花崗岩板，周圍設有136間附屬墓室。這是第一處包含樓梯及入口的皇家墓穴，入口處並以石閘防盜。墓穴南側為三個長形儲藏室，此一裝酒或裝油的大陶罐可能即是來自這三個儲藏室之一。銘刻於泥土封罐上的符號是以大型筒狀印章製作，此印章可能以木、石或象牙為材質，以陰刻鐫有國王的名字，附上皇室徽章（serekh）。皇室徽章頂部的獵鷹是另一個代表神性王權的標誌，象徵荷魯斯神。負責籌備皇室葬禮祭品的官員，會以國王的印信標示統治者對特定物品的所有權。有時皇家封印上也會刻有負責官員的名字以明確標示陪葬物品的管理責任。封印可以保護物品免於遭竊，因為除非手上握有印信，否則難以竊取封印罐內的物品而不被察覺。以往有人主張埃及直到第一王朝時期才開始使用筒狀印章，但德國在烏姆卡伯墓地的挖掘結果顯示埃及於前王朝時期後期即已將印信用為管理工具。　（作者：J.A.H.）

1. 值此習俗全盛時期，哲爾王墓室周圍環繞多達325名陪葬朝臣。

Jar Sealing with Royal Seal Impression

Egypt's Early Dynastic kings constructed their tombs to the west of Cemetery B where the kings of Dynasty 0 were interred. This site is today known as Umm el-Qa'ab (Mother of Pots in Arabic) because the site is littered with small votive offering vessels brought by generations of Egyptian pilgrims to this sacred site, once believed to be the burial place of Egypt's first divine king, the god Osiris. For the first half of Dynasty 1, succeeding kings built larger burial chambers and annexes and increased the number of small satellite tombs for members of the royal court[1]. Archaeological evidence suggests that the king's servants were killed and buried at the time of his interment and that all the tombs were sealed in once. Kings' burials were provisioned with everything the ruler might need in the next world including, bolts of fine linen, royal regalia, furniture, stone jars sealed with gold leaf, objects carved from ebony and ivory, scented oils, food and wine.

This preserved mud sealing, bears the name of King Den in whose tomb it was discovered. Den's tomb is one of the most elaborate at Umm el-Qa'ab. The burial chamber was paved with slabs of red and black granite and surrounded by 136 subsidiary burial chambers. It is the first royal tomb to include a staircase and an entrance, which was blocked by a portcullis stone to discourage robbers. On the south side of the tomb were three long storage chambers. This sealing probably closed a large ceramic jar containing wine or oil from one of these chambers. The signs impressed into the mud sealing were made by a large cylinder seal, a piece of stone, wood or ivory carved with intaglio relief of the king's name enclosed within a symbol representing the royal house called a serekh. On top of the serekh is another symbol of divine kingship, the falcon, representing the god Horus. Officials charged with provisioning the royal burial would use the king's seal to mark particular goods as belonging to that ruler. Sometimes a second seal with the name of the official carved into it is used to counter stamp the royal seal so that the administrative chain of responsibility for the goods is clearly known. Seals protected goods from plundering because unless one owned a seal, he could not steal sealed goods without being detected. It was once thought that cylinder seals were not used in Egypt until Dynasty 1, but German excavations in Cemetery U at Umm el-Qa'ab have revealed that seals were used as administrative tools in the late Predynastic period. (J.A.H.)

1. At the height of this practice, the tomb of king Djer was surrounded by the tombs of 325 courtiers.

16. 皇室戳印的泥土封罐
來自阿比多斯，墓室 T
早期王國時期，第 1 王朝丹 (Den) 統治時期
(西元前 3000-2890 年)
未燒過的尼羅河黏土
215 x 195 x 195 mm

Jar Sealing with Royal Seal Impression
From Abydos, Tomb T
Early Dynastic, Dynasty 1, Reign of Den (3000-2920 BC)
Unfired Nile Clay

17. 波浪刀鋒石刀
來自阿比多斯，墓室 E
前王國時期，內加達文化 (西元前 3500-3200 年)
褐色打火石
288 x 63 x 5 mm

Ripple-flaked Knife
From Abydos, Cemetery E
Predynastic, Naqada II (3500-3200 BC)
Brown Flint

波浪刀鋒石刀

這件以上埃及火石敲擊出的展品，展現了史前時代晚期的高超工藝水準。瑞士埃及學家艾德華・那維爾（Édouard Naville）在阿比多斯前王朝時期的墓地地面上發現這把刀，因此很遺憾無法確知其於考古學上的由來。不過，其形式為內加達 II（Naqada II）時期典型的專用刀，在此時期中，製作精美的石刀常是供做陳列裝飾之用，而非實用工具。保存最佳的範例如：現存放於羅浮宮的貝爾阿拉克刀及存放於開羅埃及博物館的貝爾塔里夫刀，都裝有河馬牙刀柄。有些更精心雕刻了來自貿易對象美索不達米亞文化的設計圖案或與歷史時期埃及王權有關的圖像。刀具本身不僅為個人物品，也展現了上埃及與貿易對象交易異國商品的連結。早期貴族以購買賜贈這種物品贏取權力及名望。

這種刀具的製作首要選擇尺寸符合目標刀具大小的高品質火石，而後研磨製成薄片，再經拋光，形成頂緣平直且底緣具有緩和弧線的半成品形。重點是火石必須保留平滑未處理的一面，如此才能供以骨或角製成的尖頭工具在此平面上施加集中壓力，藉以達到另一面去除碎屑的效果。當時工匠採用這種手法從剝落面的頂部及底部刻下大小長度相同的碎片，創造波紋效果，並形成縱貫刀具全長的中央刀脊。

此刀具的特殊之處在於製作工匠直接於刀片下敲鑿出與刀片連成一體的柄狀握把。此柄狀握把當初應是插設於一枚骨製或牙製把手中，可惜外部把手現已佚失。「刀刃」邊緣也可見細微的整補薄片。製作此種刀具的技巧使部分埃及學家主張史前時代晚期已經設有專用刀具工坊，顯示當時統治階級會招募藝匠，專為他們製作奢華藝品。　（作者：J.A.H.）

Ripple-flaked Knife

This fine example of the late Predynastic flint knapping tradition in Upper Egypt is a member of the class of so-called "ripple flaked knives" which demonstrate the superior workmanship of this late prehistoric period. Swiss Egyptologist Édouard Naville discovered this blade on the surface of the ground in the Predynastic E Cemetery at Abydos so it is unfortunately without good archaeological context. However, its style is typical of specialized blades dating to the Naqada II period during which stone knives of exceptional beauty were made as ornaments of display rather than as utilitarian tools. The best preserved examples, such as the Gebel el-Arak knife in the Louvre and Gebel el-Tarif knife in the Egyptian Museum in Cairo, were hafted with handles made of hippopotamus ivory. Some were elaborately carved with designs and images derived from interregional trade with the cultures of Mesopotamia or images of power associated with Egyptian kingship in historic periods. As such the knives represented not only sumptuary objects in themselves, but a connection to foreign lands with which the Upper Egyptians traded for exotic goods. Early elites derived some of their power and prestige from the consumption and redistribution of these goods.

The blades were created first by selecting a cobble of high quality flint large enough to create the size blade desired, then through a process of grinding, flaking and polishing a pre-form with a straight top edge and a gently curved bottom edge. It was important that one face of the flint be left smooth and unworked, because from this platform it was possible to remove small flakes from the opposite face by applying concentrated pressure using a pointed tool made of bone or horn. Such was the skill of the craftsmen of this period that they executed collateral flakes of the same size and length from the top and bottom of the flaked face, creating a ripple effect and forming the central ridge which runs the length of the blade.

The Cemetery E example is unusual in that the artisan knapped a handle-like haft as part of the blade. This haft at one time was undoubtedly inserted into a handle made of bone or ivory but which is unfortunately lost. It also shows some fine retouch flaking on the "cutting" edge of the blade. The skill exhibited in the creation of these blades has led some Egyptologists to suggest that specialized lithic workshops were already in place during the late prehistoric period, an indication of a ruling class who supported skilled craftsmen for the sole purpose of creating luxury items for their patrons. (J.A.H.)

彩繪陶罐

此小型漆罐係放置於上埃及瑪哈薩前王國時期某墓地中埋葬的成年男性面前。在同時出土的四件陪葬器皿中，此件是唯一一鄰近遺體放置的物品；遺體及漆罐皆以蘆蓆包裹。此小罐可能曾有麻線或皮帶穿過其水平管狀握把，以便攜帶，罐身以紅褐色塗料裝飾，並繪有尼羅河船隻與植物圖像。罐身圖案分為大小相同且構圖相似的兩區。一側所繪為 25 槳船隻，船上設有兩處構造物，一般稱為船艙或神壇。右側船艙設有向上延伸的桿體，其上繪有向內彎曲的獸角。船隻下方為三株樹狀植物，並有一組 S 形符號，有些學者將之解讀為鳥群。罐身另一側是一艘 26 槳船隻，甲板上同樣設有兩處構造物，且右側船艙亦設有向上延伸的桿體，支撐著像是閃電般的符號。船艙上方飄浮著樹狀符號。船隻下方一樣繪有三株樹狀植物或樹狀符號，但有更多行 S 形符號。器皿基部繪有螺旋圖紋。學者針對船艙上方符號研究後認為這些符號可能代表上埃及地理區域，應可對應歷史時期的行政區或省份，但也有學者認為這是表達對於不同神祇的崇拜。陶藝研究則指出此類器皿是由專業工坊製作，僅供少數人擁有。

佩托里（Petrie）首先將此類陶器稱為裝飾器皿，其上的人物動物圖案意義則尚有待研究闡明。有些人主張這些場景是如實刻劃送葬隊伍護送亡者，從尼羅河東岸搭乘船隻到西岸的最後旅程，尼羅河西岸即是公認的死亡之地。哈森（Hassan）認為此畫面代表遠征貿易隊沿尼羅河光榮返航的場景；維金森（Wilkinson）則主張這些圖案是描繪人類、自然與超自然領域之間的關係，這些關係也可見於正在發展的皇室肖像研究之中。近年來則有葛盧夫（Graff）主張這些圖像為符號字彙，可依其呈現的視覺元素和相對順序加以「閱讀」。　（作者：J.A.H.）

Painted Jar

This small jar was placed before the face of an adult male buried in the Predynastic Cemetery H at Mahâsna in Upper Egypt. Of the four offering vessels left in the grave, this jar was the only one placed close to the body; both were wrapped in a reed mat. This small jar might once have been carried by twine or leather thongs strung through its horizontal tubular handles. The vessel is decorated in reddish brown paint with figural scenes of Nile river boats and plant life. The vessel is divided into two scenes of equal size and similar composition. On one side there is a boat with 25 oars and two structures, often referred to as cabins or shrines. The cabin on the right has a pole extending up from it and on top it carries the emblem of inward curving animal horns. Below the boat are three plants that look like trees and sets of s-shaped symbols that some scholars have interpreted as birds. On the opposite side of the vessel is another boat with 26 oars, two cabins on its deck and a pole extending up from the right cabin, supporting a symbol that resembles a lightning bolt. Above this cabin floats a tree symbol. Beneath the boat again are three more plant or tree symbols and more lines of s-shaped symbols. The base of the vessel is decorated with a spiral pattern. Studies of the emblems above the cabins have suggested that the symbols may represent geographic areas of Upper Egypt which correspond to districts or nomes in historic periods. Others propose that they are cult fetishes for different gods and goddesses. Ceramic studies suggest that the vessels were created in specialist workshops and were available to relatively few people.

The meaning of the figural representations on this type of pottery, called Decorated Ware by W. M. F. Petrie who first classified it, is open to interpretation. Some have argued that the scenes are literal representations of funeral processions depicting the deceased's final journey by boat from the east bank to the west bank of the Nile, the eponymous land of the dead. Hassan has suggested that the scenes represent the return of successful trading expeditions up the Nile. Wilkinson argues that the scenes depict relationships between the human, natural, and supernatural spheres, some of which are adopted in the developing royal iconography. More recently Graff has suggested that the representations employ a semiotic vocabulary that can be "read" depending on the visual elements present and their relative order. (J.A.H.)

18. 彩繪陶罐
來自瑪哈薩，H133 號墓地
前王國時期，內加達文化（西元前 3500-3200 年）
陶器，顏料
130 x 93 x 85 mm

Painted Jar
From Mahâsna, Grave H133
Predynastic, Naqada IId (3500-3200 BC)
Ceramic and pigment

前王國時期墓群

這組物件為前王國時期早期中埃及的巴達里男性墓穴中的墓葬品，此墓穴先前已經人盜挖，並於 1923-24 年由蓋・布朗登（Guy Brunton）及埃及學早期女性先鋒之一的葛楚‧卡登-湯普森（Gertrude Caton-Thompson）正式發掘。由於此墓葬先前已經人盜挖，我們無從得知當初究竟哪些陪葬品伴隨墓主前往來世，但剩餘的證據顯示他在世時應是名偉大的獵人。他的遺體以蘆蓆包覆，墓室中並有若干具有魔法或宗教性質的物件相伴，其中包括兩枚大型河馬牙。如此大型的牙齒僅可能來自成年河馬，牠們是棲息於尼羅河谷中最為危險的動物。墓中河馬牙外表面雕有三組三條線的紋飾，其中填有黑色顏料，且牙心挖空。此種獸牙有時可作為容器，用來盛裝樹脂、作為眼線顏料的孔雀石粉，或皮革碎片。但此墓穴中的河馬牙並未盛裝物品。另外，此墓穴中另有一件河馬狀的陶器，以紅漆繪有三名獵人以繩索搬運河馬。可能是為了紀念墓穴主人曾經參與的成功河馬狩獵活動，也可能是為了預言超越精神世界中渾沌力量的象徵性勝利。

墓中共發現三枚同樣以河馬牙製成的精美護身符。此類護身符常見於前王國時期上埃及墓葬中，但確實目的則不得而知。有人認為護身符底部的弧形為兩隻鳥，但護身符上嵌入的「眼睛」說明其應是代表具有彎角的公牛。護身符頂部穿孔，可以細皮繩懸掛於人類頸部。亡者佩帶的其他個人飾品包括象牙手環或手鐲，及經過研磨並混予油脂用來繪製眼線的方鉛礦 。[1] 墓葬器皿中有一件品質極佳的黑漆紅土瓶，瓶身塗有紅色漆帶，不但賦予誘人光澤，也提升其盛裝液態祭品的能力。（作者：J.A.H.）

1. 近年來有人主張亡者遺體是一種連結，透過此連結，亡者與親密之人和社群整體的關係能夠在葬禮儀式中獲得調解與讚美。飾品、珠寶、身體彩繪及墓葬中的彩繪陶器並不應被視為個人物品，而是亡者親友選擇用以紀念亡者的禮物。

Predynastic Tomb Group

This group of objects represents some of the burial equipment found in a disturbed tomb of a man who lived in the early to mid-Predynastic period at the site of Badari in Middle Egypt. His tomb was excavated in 1923-24 by Guy Brunton and one of Egyptology's early female pioneers, Gertrude Caton-Thompson. Because the burial was disturbed we will never know everything that was meant to accompany this man into the afterlife, but the remaining evidence suggests that he was a great hunter.

His body was wrapped in reed matting and several different objects of magical or religious purpose were placed in the tomb with him, including two large hippopotamus tusks. Tusks of this size can only come from a fully grown hippo, one of the most dangerous animals to inhabit the Nile Valley. This tusk has been carved on the exterior with three bands of three lines each that were filled with black pigment. The tusk is also hollowed out. Some tusks like this were used as containers and have been found to hold resin, powered malachite for eye paint, or fragments of leather. This one however is empty. Another object found in this tomb, a ceramic vessel in the shape of a hippopotamus, is decorated with red painted images of three hunters carrying harpoons with coils of rope. It could commemorate a successful hippopotamus hunt in which the tomb owner participated or it could represent the forerunner of a more symbolic triumph over the forces of chaos in the spiritual world.

A finely worked amulet made of the same kind of ivory was found with two others of its kind in this burial. The purpose of these amulets is not known though they appear in many Predynastic burials in Upper Egypt. The curved shapes at the bottom of the amulet have been described as double birds, though the inlaid "eyes" on the body of this amulet suggest that it might have been meant to represent a bull with elaborately curved horns. The top of the amulet is pierced and would have been worn around the neck strung from a thin strip of leather. Other personal adornments worn by the deceased included ivory bangles or bracelets and the mineral ore galena which was ground and mixed with fat to create eye paint. [1] Among the vessels included in the burial was a Black-topped Red Ware vase of high quality, being coated in a red slip which gives the vessel its attractive sheen and makes it better able to hold liquid offerings. (J.A.H.)

1. More recently it has been argued that the deceased's body was the nexus thorough which his relationships with his intimates and the community as a whole was mediated and celebrated in funerary ritual. Ornaments, jewelry, body paint and painted pottery included in burials could be considered not as personal effects but as gifts through which people who knew the deceased chose to remember him.

19. 黑口瓶
來自巴達里，3759 號墓室
前王國時期，內加達文化（西元前 3500-3200 年）
陶器
252 x 98 x 98 mm

Black-topped Red Ware Vase
From Badari, Tomb 3759
Predynastic, Naqada IIb-c (3500-3200 BC)
Ceramic

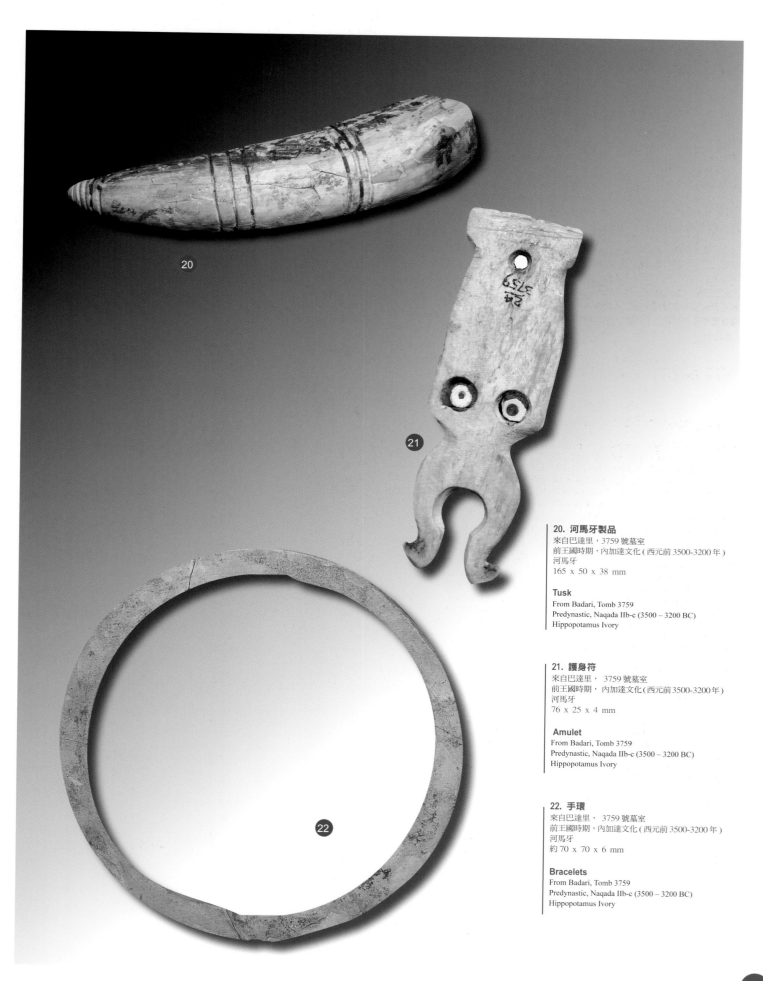

20. 河馬牙製品
來自巴達里，3759 號墓室
前王國時期，內加達文化 (西元前 3500-3200 年)
河馬牙
165 x 50 x 38 mm

Tusk
From Badari, Tomb 3759
Predynastic, Naqada IIb-c (3500 – 3200 BC)
Hippopotamus Ivory

21. 護身符
來自巴達里， 3759 號墓室
前王國時期，內加達文化 (西元前 3500-3200 年)
河馬牙
76 x 25 x 4 mm

Amulet
From Badari, Tomb 3759
Predynastic, Naqada IIb-c (3500 – 3200 BC)
Hippopotamus Ivory

22. 手環
來自巴達里， 3759 號墓室
前王國時期，內加達文化 (西元前 3500-3200 年)
河馬牙
約 70 x 70 x 6 mm

Bracelets
From Badari, Tomb 3759
Predynastic, Naqada IIb-c (3500 – 3200 BC)
Hippopotamus Ivory

23. 黑口罐
來自內加達或巴拉斯
前王國時期，內加達文化（西元前 4000-3350 年）
陶器
268 x 185 x 185 mm

Jar
From Naqada or Ballas
Predynastic, Naqada I-IId (4000-3350 BC)
Ceramic

黑漆紅土陶

黑漆紅土是埃及前王國時期（約西元前 4000-3150 年）最早也最具特色的陶器。雖然在高超製造工藝、優雅形式，以及美觀外型上或有不及巴達里時期條紋器皿之處，但此種特別加工的陶器是前王國時期早期（內加達 I-IIb）上埃及墓葬最為時興的風格。到了前王國時代後期，對於此種器皿的風潮已有衰減，不過此種器皿加工處理手法仍延續到早王國時期。這批出土器皿是在專攻埃及史前文物的英國考古學家佩托里（Petrie）指揮下，從內加達／巴拉斯和胡（或希烏）這兩處最大的上埃及墓地中挖出。

一般而言，這類器皿是利用多種技法手製而成，包括在模子上塑形底部，以盤繞的黏土條建構主體，而後在墊子或可移動表面上轉動器皿以修整邊緣。陶藝工匠也會將黏土板黏合至模塑基座的方式來製作這種風格的器皿。接著將器皿外部以卵石磨平和磨光，以消除盤繞痕跡。若使用黏土板，則是在「砧」上形成器皿，砧是一種以黏土或石頭為材質，利用槳型工具製成的物件。此種技法可製作出極薄的壁面，如此類物件中最精美範例所呈現。

學者們爭論埃及人如何製作器皿邊緣周圍和上方部分的獨特黑色區域。多數人認為必須在燒製過程之中或燒製之後立即使器皿上方部分脫氧。一種可能的方法是將器皿自火中取出，趁溫度仍高時，將頂部埋在如木屑等有機材質中，以於器皿冷卻過程中阻斷氧氣，使邊緣周圍表面呈現黑色，與本體表面氧化的紅色產生對比。這種器皿有時也塗佈有黏土和紅赭石的混合物，因此賦予陶器獨特的光澤外觀。這種塗佈及表面處理也使得器皿較不易滲水，由於早期墓葬祭品多為食物及液體，因此這種器皿更利於盛裝食物及液體等祭品。

埃及學家也懷疑黑漆紅土的鮮明對比顏色對於古代埃及人是否有特殊涵義。阿凱爾（Arkell）認為器皿邊緣黑化是來自新石器時代薩哈啦文化傳統影響，當時薩哈啦人會將以火烤瓠瓜製成的杯碗邊緣來提高邊緣強度。也有些人主張顏色對於埃及人而言有其特定文化涵義，表示他們從環境中察知的二元性：在歷史時期，埃及人將生存之地的尼羅河谷稱為「黑地」(kemet)，並將死亡之地的沙漠稱為「紅地」(desheret)。（作者：J.A.H.）

Black-Topped Red Ware Ceramics

Black-Topped Red Ware is some of the earliest and most distinctive pottery from Egypt's Predynastic period (ca. 4000-3150 BC). Second only to Badarian period combed ware in its superior manufacture technique, graceful forms, and aesthetically pleasing appearance, this specially treated pottery was the dominant style placed in Upper Egyptian burials of the early Predynastic period (Naqada I-IIb). Although it becomes less prominent in the later phases of the Predynastic, examples of this treatment of vessels persist into the Early Dynastic. The vessels in this collection were excavated in two of the largest early cemeteries of Upper Egypt – Naqada/Ballas and Hu (or Hiw) under the direction of W.M.F. Petrie, the British archaeologist credited with discovering Egypt's prehistoric cultural sequence.

In general, these vessels are built by hand using a variety of techniques including shaping the base on a mould, building the body using coiled ropes of clay and finishing the rim by turning the vessel on a mat or movable surface. Potters created other vessels in this style by joining slabs of clay to a moulded base. Signs of coiling were eliminated by smoothing and burnishing the interior and exterior of the vessel with a pebble. Slab built vessels were formed over an "anvil" – a specially shaped clay object or a stone – using a paddle. This technique created the thin walls found in the finest examples of this type.

Scholars debate how Egyptians created the distinctive black field around the rim and upper part of the vessel. Most agree that depriving the upper part of the vessel of oxygen either during or immediately after firing was necessary. One possible method was to remove the vessel from the fire and, while it was still very hot, bury the top in an organic medium, such as sawdust, which would cut off oxygen as the vessel cooled, blackening the surface around the rim while the body surface oxidized red. Some of these vessels were also coated with a mixture of clay and red ochre, giving this pottery its distinctive shiny appearance. This coating and surface treatment also made the vessels less permeable and therefore better containers for the food and liquids that played a major role in early funerary offerings.

Egyptologists have questioned whether the starkly contrasting colours of Black-Topped Red Ware carried some significance to the ancient Egyptians. Arkell proposed that the blackening of the rim of the vessels was a cultural carryover from a Neolithic Saharan tradition of burning the rims of cups and bowls made from gourds to toughen their edges. Others have suggested that the colours held cultural meaning for the Egyptians, signifying a duality they perceived in their environment. In historic periods, Egyptians refer to the Nile Valley – the land of the living – as the "Black Land" (kemet) and the desert – the land of the dead – as the "Red Land" (desheret). (J.A.H.)

24. 黑口罐
來自胡 (Hu)
前王國時期，內加達文化 (西元前 4000-3350 年)
陶器
145 x 88 x 85 mm

Jar
From Hu
Predynastic, Naqada I-II (4000 – 3350 BC)
Ceramic

25. 黑口杯
來自胡 (Hu)
前王國時期，內加達文化 (西元前 4000-3600 年)
陶器
125 x 95 x 95 mm

Beaker
From Hu
Predynastic, Naqada Ia-b (4000-3600 BC)
Ceramic

26. 陶碗
來自胡 (Hu)
前王國時期，內加達文化 (西元前 4000-3350 年)
陶器
313 x 300 x 140 mm

Bowl
From Hu
Predynastic, Naqada I-IId (4000-3350 BC)
Ceramic

27. 黑口瓶
來自胡 (Hu)
前王國時期，內加達文化 (西元前 4000-3600 年)
陶器
305 x 110 x 110 mm

Vase
From Hu
Predynastic, Naqada Ia-b (4000-3600 BC)
Ceramic

28. 黑口杯
來自胡 (Hu)
前王國時期，內加達文化 (西元前 4000-3500 年)
陶器
230 x 180 x 175 mm

Beaker
From Hu
Predynastic, Naqada I-IIa-b (4000-3500 BC)
Ceramic

木乃伊面具

保存一種有生命般的外觀是製作木乃伊的目標之一，而且保護木乃伊的頭部和臉部相當重要。為了確保這點，面具被放置於包裹住的木乃伊頭上。面具亦可提供死者一個理想化的形象。如果沒有銘文伴隨其中，往往難以從面具確定死者的性別。

這件木乃伊面具裝飾簡單。死者配戴著厚重的假髮，並穿著藍色與米色條紋相間的寬闊衣領，頂上其餘部份則是網狀圖案。面具的眼睛和眉毛以黑色顏料凸顯出來。死者的皮膚被漆成淺黃色。此面具的簡單性可能是由於面具擁有者之財力或是在製造面具時被當地流行風格影響所致。
（作者：J.H.W.）

Cartonnage Mummy Mask

The preservation of a life-like appearance was one of the goals of mummification and the protection of the head and face of the mummy was essential. In order to ensure this, masks were placed over the head of the wrapped mummy. The mask also presented an idealized image of the deceased. It is often difficult to identify the gender of the deceased from a mask if there is no accompanying inscription.

This cartonnage mask is simply decorated. The deceased is shown wearing a heavy blue wig and a simple broad collar of alternating rows of blue and cream stripes which rests atop a net pattern. The mask's eyes and eyebrows are highlighted with black pigment. The skin of the deceased is painted a buff colour. The simplicity of this mask may be due to the relative wealth of its owner, or is perhaps due to local styles popular at the time of its manufacture. (J.H.W.)

29. 木乃伊面具
來自塞德蒙
托勒密時期 (西元前 332-30 年)
木乃伊盒，顏料
310 x 280 x 280 mm

Cartonnage Mummy Mask
From Sedment
Ptolemaic Period (332-30 BC)
Cartonnage, pigment

木製木乃伊面具

在新王國時期和第三中間時期，古埃及人創造出包裹木乃伊形狀的棺木，且頭部風格自然。這些棺木頭部的髮型精巧，並以理想化的方式呈現死者的臉部與頸部。這些棺木的臉部往往與棺木分開雕塑，然後再用木梢加以接合。臉部上可看到一些為木梢預留的孔洞。一般情況下，完整的棺木上無法看出這些獨立的面具，因為接合部份已透過石膏或亞麻，以及顏料等隱藏起來。

這些棺木面具背面平整，且帶有用於接合棺木的木梢。較大型的面具在下巴底下還留有木梢痕跡。此木梢來自於一件假鬍子，相當類似於本書編號32的展品。此類鬍鬚能讓死者與掌管來世的奧塞里斯神產生共鳴。這些面具代表著死者希望在來世呈現的樣子－年輕且寧靜。

古埃及人希望當他們在來世時，他們的棺材外觀能如同死者的樣子，以便使墳墓及埋葬能正常運作。在古埃及的信仰中，靈魂的一部分稱為「巴（Ba）」，其必須來往於墳墓與來世之間。巴能夠藉由辨識棺木上的臉來認出自己的墳墓以及棺木中的遺體。（作者：C.R.）

Wooden Coffin Faces

In the New Kingdom and Third Intermediate Period the ancient Egyptians created coffins in the shape of wrapped mummies with naturalistic heads. These heads had elaborate hair styles and idealised representations of the faces and necks of the deceased. The faces of these coffins were often carved separately from the coffin and then attached using pegs. Some of the holes for the pegs are visible on these faces. In general, the separate faces cannot be detected on complete wooden coffins as the joins are hidden by plaster or linen and the pigment.

These wooden faces are flat on the back and have pegs to attach them to coffins. The larger face has the remains of a peg under the chin. This peg was from a false beard, much like catalogue #32. Such beards identified the deceased with the god Osiris who was the ruler of the afterlife. The faces represent the deceased as they hoped to be in the afterlife; young and serene.

The ancient Egyptians wanted their coffins to look like the deceased as they would be in the afterlife so that the tomb and burial could function properly. In ancient Egyptian belief, the part of the soul called the Ba needed to travel between the tomb and the afterlife. The Ba would recognise its tomb and the body in the coffin partially by recognising the face on the coffin. (C.R.)

31. 木製木乃伊面具
來自底比斯西岸
新王國時期至第三中間期，第 20-25 王朝
（西元前 1186-664 年）
木，灰泥，顏料
143 x 140 x 75mm

Wooden Coffin Face
From Thebes, West Bank
New Kingdom-Third Intermediate Period,
Dynasty 20-25 (1186-664 BC)
Wood, linen, pigment

30. 木製木乃伊面具
來自底比斯西岸
新王國時期至第三中間期，第 20-25 王朝
（西元前 1186-664 年）
木，灰泥，顏料
243 x 180 x 124mm

Wooden Coffin Face
From Thebes, West Bank
New Kingdom-Third Intermediate Period,
Dynasty 20-25 (1186-664 BC)
Wood, plaster, pigment

假鬍子

此件製作精良的假鬍子是由考古學家大衛（David Randall-MacIver）及亞瑟（Arthur C. Mace）在阿比多斯的墓園挖掘賽特胡（Sitepehu）陵墓的期間尋獲。此件假鬍子年代可追溯至第十八王朝，由整塊木材雕刻而成，其頂部帶有一個榫，作為與棺木接合之用。鬍子的正面曲線約略朝外，並以模仿編結的雕刻線條加以裝飾。

古埃及法老們的王室特徵之一就是狹長的鬍子。至少從前王國時期開始，貴族男性刮除所有鬍鬚便成為一種時尚，因為鬍子與不潔淨的狀態以及低等級的生活有關。然而，某些鬍子類型在宗教概念中與神祇之神性相關。有些神祇的鬍鬚及頭髮在宗教經文中被形容為如青金石般（一種罕見的半寶石），因而使鬍子被認為是一種神聖的屬性。出於此原因，法老王在特定慶典或公開露面的場合中會配戴一種人造鬍子，透過細繩連接到耳朵上，以強調其如神一般的特質，並展現其權威地位。即使是女王哈謝普蘇（Hatshepsut）亦在一些雕像和浮雕中被描繪成配戴假鬍子，以作為其統治埃及的力量與神聖權力之象徵，正如其前輩所做的一般。

在死亡的世界裡，法老與奧塞里斯神有所關聯，且經常被描繪成配戴著神聖奧塞里斯形式的鬍鬚，其外觀狹長而帶有編結，且邊端凸出，可在圖坦卡門（Tutankhamun）的黃金面罩上看到。自中王國時期開始，有些非王室男性在死後則被描繪成鬍鬚造型較短的模樣，這似乎與此處崇高的賽特胡描繪的鬍子是相同的形式，賽特胡是提尼省的祭司監督者。事實上，這種類型的鬍子最後也出現在許多一般埃及人的棺木上，表示非王室人民具有更多機會獲得永生。（作者：A.H.）

False Beard

David Randall-MacIver and Arthur C. Mace recovered this fine false beard during their excavations of the Tomb of Sitepehu in Cemetery D at Abydos. Dating to the Eighteenth Dynasty, this false beard was carved out of one piece of wood and has a tenon at the top for attachment to a coffin. The front of the beard curves slightly outwards and is decorated with incised lines imitating plaiting.

One of the royal characteristics of ancient Egyptian Pharaohs was a long, narrow beard. Since at least the Early Dynastic Period, it had become fashionable for noble men to shave off all facial hair as it eventually became associated with an unclean state and a low rank in life. However, certain types of beards were associated with the divinity of the gods in religious concepts. Some gods' beards and hair were described as being like lapis lazuli (a rare semi-precious stone) in religious texts, so that wearing a beard was considered to be a divine attribute. For this reason, the Pharaoh would wear an artificial beard that was attached to the ears by a string during certain ceremonial celebrations or public appearances in order to emphasize his god-like qualities and demonstrate his position of authority. Even the Queen Hatshepsut was depicted wearing a false beard in some of her statues and reliefs as a symbol of her power and divine authority to rule Egypt just as her predecessors had done.

In death, the Pharaoh was associated with the god Osiris and was often depicted wearing the divine Osiris form of the beard, which was a long, narrow plaited beard with end jutting forward, as can be seen on the gold mask of Tutankhamun. From the Middle Kingdom onwards, some non-royal men were depicted with a shorter form of this beard after death, which appears to be the same form as the beard depicted here for the noble Sitepehu, who was Overseer of Priests in the Thinite nome. The fact that this type of beard eventually appeared on the coffins of many ordinary Egyptians, indicates that non-royal people had greater access to immortality. (A.H.)

32. 假鬍子
來自阿比多斯，D9 號墓室
第 18 王朝，哈謝普蘇統治時期（西元前 1473-1458 年）
第 25 王朝時重複使用（西元前 747-656 年）
Wood
178 x 50 x 20 mm

False Beard
From Abydos, tomb D9
Dynasty 18, reign of Hatshepsut (1473-1458 B.C.E.);
reused Dynasty 25 (747-656 B.C.E.)
Wood

33. 黃金面具
來自法尤姆
羅馬時期 (西元前 30 年 - 西元 100 年)
亞麻，木
495 x 310 x 270 mm

Gilded Mummy Mask
From the Fayum
Roman Period (30 BC-AD 100)
Linen, cartonnage

黃金面具

此件木乃伊面具經過精心裝飾，並且已確定為一名女性所有。面具的皮膚經過鍍金，以模仿神祇不朽的金色皮膚。死者的眼睛從背面進行鑲嵌，眉毛為藍色。死者配戴著一條帶有橢圓形垂飾的串珠項鍊，其用意或許是代表一個心形的護身符。

死者的長假髮被漆成藍色，並以宗教圖像覆蓋於兩側，這可能是表達出死者希望能成功進入來世的希望。眉頭上方是一個帶有日輪的頭帶，另一個帶翼日輪置於其上：兩個相對的陪葬神奧塞里斯圖像坐在寶座上，出現在垂飾兩側。垂飾底部是一排頭上有日輪的神蛇鏡像裝飾。在其兩側下方的是四名安坐的神祇。棋盤圖案裝飾著垂飾兩側，其上有位於神龕上的阿努比斯圖像。面具兩側也以站立的神祇景像進行高度裝飾，由長方形邊界所包圍，上方則是一排豎起的神蛇。面具背面之特色為垂飾的打結兩端，末端是垂下的神蛇。在打結處下方是一個馬特女神的大型站姿圖像，帶有伸展的翅膀。她雙手各握住一根羽毛，還有一根羽毛在她的頭上。在馬特兩側，有一個人頭狀的巴形體以站姿出現在神龕上。面具頂部是一隻兩側帶有烏加眼 (udjat) 的禿鷹。 （作者：J.H.W.）

Gilded Mummy Mask

Elaborately decorated, this cartonnage mask has been identified as belonging to a woman. The skin of the mask is gilded to imitate the imperishable golden skin of the gods. The eyes of the deceased are rimmed in back with blue eyebrows. The deceased wears a beaded necklace with an oval pendant perhaps meant to represent a heart-shaped amulet.

The deceased's long wig is painted blue and is overlaid on all sides with religious imagery, which may address the deceased's hope for a successful entry into the afterlife. Above the brow is a fillet with a sun disk. A winged sundisk hovers above it. Two facing images of the funerary deity Osiris, seated on a throne, appear on each lappet. At the bottom of each lappet is a mirror-image decoration of a row of uraei with sun disks on their heads. Below this on either side are four seated deities. A checkerboard pattern decorates the sides of each lappet with an image of Anubis on a shrine on either side. The sides of the mask are also highly decorated with scenes of standing deities enclosed within a rectangular border topped by a row of rearing uraei. The back of the mask features the tied ends of the fillet, which end in pendant uraei. Below the ties is a large standing image of the goddess Maat with extended wings. She holds a feather in each hand and also has a feather on her head. On either side of Maat, a human headed ba figure appears standing atop a shrine. On the top of the mask, is a vulture flanked by udjat eyes. (J.H.W.)

黃金面具

此類面具可保護木乃伊的頭部，這些物件並非死者的真實肖像，而是其主人的風格化代表。如同此一時期相似的面具，其面部鍍金或許是為了模仿神祇的皮膚。大眼睛以黑漆鑲邊，眉毛亦同。死者戴著帶有風格化辮子的厚重假髮，以黃金隔珠裝飾，並配戴一條浮雕裝飾的項鍊。在其頭部上有一條帶有鍍金烏加眼（udjat）垂飾的頭帶。這類主題在此時期的面具中相當常見，而烏加眼是一種廣受歡迎的護身符，代表荷魯斯的真實之眼，其在遭受塞特所傷後獲得痊癒。這是一種廣為流行的符號，代表再生和保護。在假髮的兩個垂飾之間是一種包含數列浮雕裝飾的衣領。面具表面可看到亞麻製的木乃伊包裹布所造成的壓痕。（作者：J.H.W.）

Gilded Mummy Mask

Masks such as this one protected the head of the mummy. These objects were not true portraits of the deceased but instead were stylized representations of their owners. As with similar masks of this period, the face is gilded perhaps to mimic the gold skin of the gods. The large eyes are rimmed in black paint, as are the eyebrows. The deceased is shown wearing a heavy wig with stylized braids decorated with gold spacer beads and wears a necklace executed in raised decoration. On its head is a fillet with a pendant of a gilded udjat eye. This motif is commonly seen on masks of this period and the udjat was a popular amulet representing the sound eye of Horus, which was made whole after its damage by Seth. It was a popular symbol of regeneration and protection. Between the two lappets of the wig is a collar consisting of several rows of raised decoration. Traces of impressions from the linen mummy wrappings can be seen in places on the surface of the mask. (J.H.W.)

34. 黃金面具
來自哈瓦拉或古若卜
希臘羅馬時期（西元前 100-1 年）
金色彩繪的木乃伊盒
440 x 296 x 150 mm

Gilded Mummy Mask
From Hawara or Gurob
Graeco-Roman Period (100-1BC)
Gilded, painted cartonnage

刻有三個男子的浮雕（局部）

三個面向左側的光頭男子以凹浮雕的方式雕刻於此砂岩片段。此雕刻使用白色石膏塗底以添加生氣，隨後被漆為紅褐色，此為埃及藝術中男性皮膚的典型顏色。

這些男性的皮膚顏色，以及一排人被以重疊輪廓的方式描繪，是埃及藝術長期固有的傳統。阿肯納頓（Akhenaten）統治期間有新意，此為一個宗教變革與藝術創新的時期，其中包括男性的特點，長形的禿頭蓋骨、傾眼、厚唇、渾圓、下巴略下垂、以及長脖子。其身體較不明顯：細手臂、纖弱的手與手指、胸前皮包骨、大肚子、肥臀以及細長的小腿。阿瑪納（Amarna）時期的人物代表與該在位君王（這裡指阿肯納頓）與其他時期並無差異，因為他已設定描繪其臣民的模板。一些沒有說服力且有多處矛盾的醫學理論解釋阿肯納頓、其妻娜芙蒂蒂（Nefertiti）以及他們的女兒們擁有不尋常的外表，但他們忽略了一個事實，就是埃及體系從未真正的忠實複製身體特徵。而阿肯納頓所提出的新宗教將需要一種新的藝術風格來連續地突破。

此片段構成部份以浮雕裝飾的牆面，其座落於阿瑪納的阿頓神（Aten）大神廟中，周圍面積達 800 x 300 公尺，位於阿瑪納中部北端。整個神廟包含上千個祭壇，祭品在此供奉，還有一個屠宰場專門供應鮮肉，此區域內的東方後側座落著神殿，約為 50 x 30 公尺的複合建築，朝東，陽光通透，包含約 150 張祭桌。

如此小碎片是源自一個遠比其大的場景，可能顯示出該寺廟的運作。因此這些頭髮剃光的男子可能是祭司或神廟官員，永遠在描繪中盡責服侍著阿頓神。（作者：T.H.）

Relief of Three Men in Procession

Three bald-headed men, facing left, are carved in sunk relief on this fragment of sandstone. The carving was further elaborated and enlivened with the addition of a white plaster coating which was in turn painted a reddish brown, the typical colour of male skin in Egyptian art.

The men's skin colour, and the way in which a row of people is depicted by overlapping the outlines of the figures, were long-established conventions of Egyptian art. What was new to the reign of Akhenaten, a period of religious change and artistic innovation, are the men's features, with their elongated bald skulls, slanted eyes, thick lips, rounded, slightly drooping chins, and long necks. Their bodies would have been no less distinctive: thin arms with attenuated hands and fingers, scrawny chests, pot bellies, fat hips and spindly calves would have completed the picture. Human representations of the Amarna Period were no different from those of other periods in that the reigning king – here Akhenaten – set the template for the way in which his subjects were depicted. A number of medical theories, none convincing and many contradictory, have been advanced to explain the unusual appearance of Akhenaten, his wife Nefertiti, and their daughters; they ignore the fact that Egyptian systems of representation were never primarily concerned with faithful copying of physical traits. A new religion such as Akhenaten proposed would require a new artistic style to help mark the break with continuity.

The fragment formed part of the relief-decorated walls of the sanctuary of the Great Temple to the Aten at Amarna, a gigantic enclosure measuring 800 by 300 metres at the northern end of the centre of Amarna. The whole temple enclosure contained over a thousand altars on which offerings were made, and a butcher's yard which supplied them with fresh meat; at the eastern rear end of the enclosure stood the "Sanctuary", a complex of buildings about 50 by 30 metres in dimension, oriented east, open to the sun throughout, and containing about 150 offering tables.

So small a fragment would have come from a far larger scene, probably showing the temple in operation. The shaven-headed men could therefore be priests or temple officials, depicted eternally carrying out their duties serving the Aten. (T.H.)

35. 刻有三個男子的浮雕（局部）
來自阿瑪納
新王國時期，第 18 王朝，阿肯納頓統治時期
（西元前 1352-1336 年）
砂岩，灰泥，顏料
113 x 105 x 97 mm

Relief of Three Men in Procession
From Amarna, sanctuary of the Great Temple, T.A. 26-27-S.11
New Kingdom, Dynasty 18, Reign of Akhenaten
(1352-1336 BC)
Sandstone, plaster, pigment

搬東西的男子浮雕（局部）

頭戴普通假髮的兩名男子被描繪成面向左側，各扛著一個圓形的布袋或包裹。左手邊人物胸部上的線條顯示他們因為負重而彎下腰。儘管此展品是從藝術市場中取得，但從材料、主題，及其凹浮雕之風格可追溯年份及原始尋獲點：其來源為底比斯的阿蒙霍特（Amenhotep）四世（即阿肯納頓）之神廟「塔拉塔石」的一部份，底比斯為第十八王朝的舊都。

阿蒙霍特（即「滿意的阿蒙神」）直到其即位的第五年才將自己的名字改為阿肯納頓（即「有益於阿頓神」），且約在同時間將首都從底比斯遷往阿瑪納（Tell el-Amarna）。然而，即使在這之前，他一直積極推動信奉阿頓神，即神聖的日輪。在其統治期間初期，曾在眾神之王阿蒙神（Amun）之宗教核心東卡納克（East Karnak）建造眾多神龕並奉獻給阿頓神。不同於鄰近的阿蒙神廟那封閉、黑暗的神殿，阿頓神的神龕圍繞著大型的柱廊牆，能向太陽的光芒開放。為了便於快速施工，這些廟宇以小型的沙岩塊建成（目前稱其阿拉伯名，塔拉塔），約為1埃及腕尺乘0.5腕尺乘 0.5 腕尺（約 50 厘米 x 25 厘米 x 25 厘米）。

位於卡納克的阿蒙霍特四世廟宇裝飾和其建築一樣創新。阿蒙霍特並未使用眾神前的國王之景像，而是採用自己與家人一起到神廟旅行並祭祀阿頓神的場景，其以日輪呈現，伴隨著光芒結束於手中。該場景亦呈現出神廟本身、人們以及祭司、音樂家、舞蹈家，以及僕人，如同描繪於此的兩名男子。

阿蒙霍特的寺廟在其治理期間結束後便遭到毀壞，其中的塔拉塔石塊則用作卡納克寺廟的地基與新塔門填充物。這種破壞行為反而將其以良好狀態保留至今。過去 50 年來，塔拉塔石塊已取自塔門內部，並加以記錄和研究。（作者：T.H.）

Relief Fragment: men with burdens

Two men with plain wigs are depicted facing left, each carrying a rounded-edged sack or package. The line of the left hand figure's chest shows that they were orignally shown bent over under the weight of their loads. Although acquired on the art market, the material, subject, and style of this sunk-relief carving allow it to be assigned a date and original findspot with some certainty: it is part of a 'talatat' block from the temples of Amenhotep IV / Akhenaten at Thebes, the old capital of Dynasty 18.

Amenhotep ("Amun is satisfied") did not change his name to Akhenaten ("Beneficial for the Aten") until his fifth regnal year, around the same time as he moved the capital from Thebes to Tell el-Amarna. Even before this, however, he had been actively promoting the cult of the Aten, the divine sun-disc. The earliest years of his reign saw the construction of a number of shrines dedicated to the Aten at East Karnak, the heart of the cult of Amun, the king of the gods. The Aten shrines were unlike the enclosed, dark sancuaries of the neighbouring temple of Amun, and consisting of several large enclosures with colonnaded walls, open to the rays of the sun. To aid quick construction, these temples were built of small sandstone blocks (now called by their Arabic name, talatat), around one Egyptian cubit by half a cubit by half a cubit (c. 50cm x 25cm x 25cm) in dimension.

The decoration of Amenhotep IV's temples at Karnak was as innovative as their construction. Instead of scenes of the king before the gods, Amenhotep showed himself and his family travelling to the temple and making offerings to the Aten, shown as a sun-disc with rays ending in hands. Scenes like this would also show the temple itself, peopled with priests, musicians, dancers, and servants like the two depicted here.

Amenhotep's temples were torn down after the end of his reign, and the talatat were used as the foundation and filling for new pylons in the temple of Karnak. This act of destruction paradoxically preserved them in excellent condition until the present day. Over the past 50 years the talatat have been retrieved from the interior of the pylons, documented, and studied. (T.H.)

西奈的書記官潘尼法石碑

至少從中王國時期早期開始，在西奈西南方山區內高聳的塞拉比爾卡丁高原（Serabit el-Khadim），向來主要是奉獻給「綠松石的主人」哈托爾神，以及其他與綠松石、銅，和當地其他礦產有關的神祇之神廟所在地。此石碑在其後約 800 年左右設立，時間約在新王國時代末期，神廟生命進入最後階段左右。此件是由書記員潘尼法（Panefer）所奉獻，其站立於左側，在阿蒙雷神（Amun-Re）的面前手臂高舉，表現出高度崇拜之意。該神祇則站立於右側，面對著潘尼法。祂伸出手部，手持權杖，此為一種統治的象徵，而且幾乎快要碰觸到潘尼法，其後方的手拿著 T 形十字章安卡（ankh），並配戴著其特有的雙羽冠。阿蒙雷神在該石碑上出現並不尋常，塞拉比爾卡丁高原的主要神祇是哈托爾，而索度（Sopdu）則是次要神祇。眾多在神廟中的石碑都是奉獻給這兩位神祇。阿蒙雷神可能是潘尼法所在地的神祇，在該地讓其形象與兩位當代的主要神祇產生關聯可能是一種展現聲望的方法，其他額外解釋之後的內容提出。這些形象的位置也別具特色，通常在石碑上，會將神祇描繪於左側，面向右方。在此場景內之方向相反可能與神廟內原本的位置有關，潘尼法可能是朝向一座神龕或宗教雕像。

潘尼法頭部上方的題詞分為三個欄位，敘述該石碑是「獻給書記員與軍隊副代表 潘尼法之靈魂」。「副」這個字延伸到銘文框線下方，表示此石碑在這一點上的設計失算。神祇的題詞寫在其面前的單一欄位內：「兩片土地與寶座之主阿蒙雷神的發言內容」，神祇的實際發言內容則未寫出，可能對於這種非王室場景太過神祕且威力強大。然而，這種公式化的內容，常見於寺廟牆壁上的王室場景，這顯示潘尼法是值得獲得此類言論的人。

潘尼法代表國王參與建設工作的記錄下方有五行文字：「第五年，shomu 季第二個月（四月／五月）：其命令在哈托爾的領域內，女主人的綠松石，建造一座拉美西斯四世之百萬年神廟，透過軍隊之派遣書記員潘尼法，派瑞（Pairy）之子」。潘尼法的石碑是若干設立於神廟以紀念遠征西奈的第五年，但目前僅存唯一的一座石碑可記錄該座「百萬年神廟」。被埃及學家稱為祭廟的「百萬年神廟」之建築，用意在於維護並創新新王室地位，包括在君王的此生及來生期間。最負盛名的神廟位於底比斯西岸，包括為拉美西斯二世所建造的拉美西斯之屋（Ramesseum），其將王室宗教與阿蒙神以及其他當地神祇相互連結。這些機構同時設在屬於其他神祇的神廟內，可能和此處的例子一樣。拉美西斯四世並未在塞拉比爾卡丁高原委任製作獨立建築，反而是對現有的哈托爾神廟之主要房間進行擴充與改善。或許拉美西斯四世的「百萬年神廟」便是在這些區域中構成，因此將其宗教與哈托爾神靈緊密結合。潘尼法則負責監督這項工作。儘管其石碑上並未記載該原始位置，其可能設立於國王的「神廟」中以強調自己在創造與參與宗教永恆性方面的角色。在潘尼法的石碑上出現的阿蒙雷神描繪可能與此「神廟」有所關聯，顯示拉美西斯四世可自神祇接受獲得永恆王權，而此神祇可能是阿蒙神。因此，潘尼法對阿蒙雷神的崇敬或許和其石碑上的場景內容一致，並使其對其君王產生認同。（作者：L.F.）

Stela of the Scribe Panefer from Sinai

From at least the early Middle Kingdom, the plateau of Serabit el-Khadim, high in the mountains of south-west Sinai, had been the site of a temple dedicated primarily to Hathor, 'mistress of turquoise', as well as other deities associated with the mining of turquoise, copper, and other minerals in the area. This stela was set up in the temple some 800 years later, during what seems to have been the final phase of the temple's life at the end of the New Kingdom. It was dedicated by the scribe Panefer who is shown standing on the left with his arms raised in adoration before the god Amun-Re. The god stands on the right, facing Panefer. He holds a was-sceptre in his outstretched hand, a symbol of dominion which Panefer almost touches, an ankh in his rear hand, and wears his characteristic double-plumed crown. Amun-Re's presence on the stela is unusual; the primary deity of Serabit el-Khadim was Hathor, with Sopdu as an important secondary god. Many stelae in the temple were dedicated to these two deities. Amun-Re may have been Panefer's local god, or his inclusion in the scene could have been a way to display Panefer's prestige by associating him with the most important state deity of the time; an additional interpretation is suggested below. The positioning of the figures is also distinctive. Normally on stelae gods are depicted on the left, facing right. It is possible that the reverse orientation of Panefer's scene relates to its original position in the temple, with Panefer perhaps facing towards a shrine or cult statue.

The caption above Panefer's head, in three columns, states that the stela is "for the ka (soul) of the scribe and deputy of the army Panefer." The word for "deputy" extends below the framing line of the inscription, indicating a miscalculation in the stela's design at this point. The god's caption is written in a single column in front of him: "Words spoken by Amun-Re, lord of the thrones of the Two Lands." The actual words of the god's speech are not given and may have been too secret and potent for this non-royal context. However, this formulaic statement, common in royal scenes on temple walls, shows that Panefer was the worthy recipient of such a speech.

Five lines of text beneath the scene record Panefer's involvement in building works on the king's behalf: "Year 5, second month of shomu (April/May): Command of His Person (to) build a temple of millions of years of Rameses Heqamaat Meryamun (Rameses IV) in the domain of Hathor, mistress of turquoise, by the dispatch scribe of the army, Panefer, son of Pairy, true of voice." Panefer's stela is one of a number that were set up in the temple to commemorate an expedition to the Sinai mines in the fifth year of Rameses IV, but is the only surviving stela to record the construction of a "temple of millions of years." Also referred to by Egyptologists as a mortuary temple, a "temple of millions of years" was a building or institution focused around the maintenance and renewal of the royal status of an individual king during his life and after his death. The most famous are those on the Theban West Bank, including the Ramesseum built for Rameses II, which linked the royal cult with that of Amun and other important state and local gods. These institutions could also be located inside temple structures belonging to another deity, as is probably the case here. Rameses IV did not commission a separate building at Serabit el-Khadim, instead central rooms in the existing Hathor temple were extended and elaborated. It is these areas which probably comprise Rameses IV's "temple of millions of years," thus closely binding his cult to the cult of Hathor. Panefer would have overseen this work. Although the original position of his stela was not recorded, it may have been set up within his king's 'temple' to emphasize his role in its creation and to participate for eternity in its cult. The depiction of Amun-Re on Panefer's stela may relate to a scene in this 'temple' which shows Rameses IV receiving eternal kingship from a god that is probably Amun. Thus Panefer's worship of Amun-Re may align his stela with such scenes and identify him with his king. (L.F.)

37. 西奈的書記官潘尼法石碑
來自塞拉比爾卡丁高地，西奈半島南方
新王國時期，第 20 王朝，拉美西斯四世統治時期
（西元前 1153-1147 年）
砂岩
645 x 310 x 90 mm

Stela of the Scribe Panefer from Sinai
From Serabit el-Khadim, South Sinai (probably from the Hathor temple)
New Kingdom, Dynasty 20, reign of Rameses IV
(ca. 1153-1147 BC)
Sandstone

凱基之子，土地登記官易（Iy）石碑

以凹浮雕刻成的圓頂石碑仍顯示出紅漆及黃漆的痕跡。此石碑高度 51 公分，幾乎正好是古埃及一腕尺高，在泥磚祭堂的壁龕原址中發現，高度為 153 公分，或接近三腕尺平方。

第一個位於頂部的記錄顯示出兩個面對面的陪葬之神 - 胡狼神偉布華偉特（Wepwawet），其名字意味著「開路者」。這種表現方式有助於確認此物件的年份約在中王國時期，更精確的時間為第十三王朝。在月形記錄下的前兩行文字提供了傳統的祭祀配方，其中寫著：「國王所奉獻的祭品，（獻給？）偉布華偉特，聖地之主，他可給予祈求祭品（包括）麵包、啤酒、牛肉和家禽給土地（文件）負載者 Iy 之靈魂，房子女主人 Keki 的真實心聲。」

在這底下是一個廣泛的記錄，包含數字及識別文字。左邊是石碑主人坐在一張椅子上，前方桌子堆滿供品，有各種麵包、蔬菜，以及一隻鴨子。他的皮膚被漆成紅褐色，是男性的傳統膚色，他穿著短裙和寬闊的衣領，他的假髮未遮住耳朵，長度到他的肩膀。他左手持蓮花或藍荷花，朝往他的鼻子，而他的右手正好伸向在他面前的成堆祭品。有四個人像面向著他，皆以相同姿勢：坐在地上，右膝蓋朝上，右手持花朝向自己的鼻子，左手則放在膝上。在他正前方的是一名坐在地上的女性，認定是他的妻子 Atu。她穿著附有肩帶的緊身裙與寬闊的衣領，她的長假髮顯示黑漆的痕跡。在她身後有三個人形成一列。第一個標示為「他的兒子 Ibi」，第二個是一名女子，標示為「他的女兒 Keki」，第三名認定為「他的兒子 Snefru」。請注意前兩名因為他們的爺爺奶奶而分別獲得了相同的名字。

在其下方式是兩個類似的記錄：兩對人像面對著彼此，而第五位則自己坐在最右邊。從左邊開始，是「他的父親 Ibi」、「他的母親 Keki」、「祭司 Id」、「祭司 Neh」，以及「房屋女主人 Titi」。最下層的記錄是五名婦女。這五人皆命名為房屋女主人和他們的名字，由左到右，分別是 Horemheb、Renseneb、Mery、Satjedut，以及 Sahi。推測這些人是 Iy 的兄弟姐妹。

該石碑是嵌在泥磚教堂牆上的四件物品當中的一部分。不同石碑之間的關聯為 Iy 和他的父親 Ibi，而教堂可能是為了一名叫做 Nemty-em-weskhet 的高級官員而豎立，他可能和 Iy 及其家人來自同一地區。（作者：R.L.）

Stela of the Carrier of Land (Documents) Iy, son of Keki

Round-topped stela carved with sunk relief, which still shows traces of red and yellow paint. Measuring 51 cm, the stela is almost exactly one ancient Egyptian cubit high; it was found in situ in a niche in a mud-brick offering chapel that was 153 cm, or close to three cubits, square.

The first register at the top shows two facing standards of the jackal-god Wepwawet, a funerary god whose name means 'The Opener of the Roads'. This representation helps date the piece to late in the Middle Kingdom period, and more precisely to the Thirteenth Dynasty. The first two lines of text below the moon-shaped register offer the traditional Offering Formula, which reads: "An offering that the king gives, (to?) Wepwawet, Lord of the Sacred Land, that he may give invocation-offerings (consisting of) of bread, beer, beef, and fowl to the ka-spirit of the carrier of land (documents) Iy, true-of-voice, whom the house mistress Keki bore."

Below this is a wide register that contains figures and captions that identify them. At the left is the stela owner seated on a chair before a table of offerings piled high with various loaves of bread, a vegetable, and a duck. His skin is painted reddish brown, the traditional colour for men, he wears a short kilt and a broad collar, and his wig, which leaves his ears uncovered, reaches his shoulders. His left hand holds a lotus flower -- or blue water lily -- up to his nose while his right extends toward the pile of offerings before him. Four figures face him, all shown in the same posture: they sit on the ground with their right knee up, their right hand holds a flower to their nose, while their left rests on their knee. Immediately before him is a woman who sits on the ground, identified as 'his wife Atu'. She wears a tight-fitting dress held up by straps at the shoulders, a broad collar, and her long wig shows traces of black paint. Behind her is a row of three figures. The first is labelled 'his son Ibi'; the second is a woman labelled 'his daughter Keki', and the third figure is identified as 'his son Snefru'. Note how the first two were given the same names as their paternal grandparents.

Below this are two similar registers: two pairs of figures face one another while a fifth sits on her own on the far right. From the left, they are 'his father Ibi, 'his mother Keki', 'the wab-priest Id', 'the wab-priest Neh', and 'the house mistress Titi'. In the lowest register are five women. All are designated as a 'house mistress' and their names, from left to right, are given as Horemheb, Renseneb, Mery, Satjedut, and Sahi. These were presumably Iy's brothers and sisters.

The stela is part of a group of four such objects embedded in the walls of the mud-brick chapel. The links between the various stelae are Iy and his father Ibi, and the chapel was probably erected for a high official named Nemty-em-weskhet, who may have come from the same geographical area of the country as Iy and his family. (R.L.)

38. 凱基之子，土地登記官易（Iy）石碑
來自阿比多斯，易墓室
中王國時期，第 13 王朝（西元前 1773-1650 年）
石灰岩，顏料
515 x 340 x 50 mm

**Stela of the Carrier of Land (Documents) Iy,
son of Keki**
From Abydos, tomb of Iy
Middle Kingdom, Dynasty 13 (1773-1650 BC)
Limestone, pigment

德迪與其子朝臣瑞森涅卜石碑

此凹浮雕圓形平頂石碑是在阿比多斯現場的地面上發現。頂部有兩個神聖之眼，石碑主人可透過它們以神奇的方式觀看，在其下方是兩個水的標誌，象徵著一個未來的路人代表他執行奠酒祭神。

下一段記載包含了傳統的葬禮祈禱，記載著：「國王（獻給？）奧塞里斯，布塞里斯（Busiris）之主，偉大的神，阿比多斯之主的祭品，他可以奠酒祭神、（焚）香，並（奉獻）神油給皇室朝臣瑞森涅卜（Renseneb）的靈魂，真實心聲，以及他父親（同樣為了靈魂），保鏢德迪（Dedi），真實心聲。」「為了靈魂」這些用詞寫在第三個紀錄的中間，意思是要讀兩次，由右至左，反之亦然。

其下是瑞森涅卜和他的妻子，左側標記為「Nub-en-ib 侍女」，而右側則是德迪和他的妻子，「總管的僕人 Mut-pu-senbet」。在他們當中的是一張祭品桌。

最下方的記錄顯示一系列簡單的清單，僅列出姓名和頭銜。左側較大的欄位則寫著「Nekhen Neb-su-menu 的官員及管理員」的名字。右側 14 個較短的欄位應由右方讀至左方，其中有些人特別稱為「他的哥哥」或「他的姐姐」，而有些人僅給予頭銜和名字，可能是瑞森涅卜和德迪的同事。此處值得一提的是頭銜的多樣化。其中六人是「上埃及十大偉人」，這可能與大臣職務相關的頭銜，以及兩名普通的祭司。在女性當中，出現兩次「房屋女主人」，意思是掌管家務的已婚婦女，以及前面提到的「侍女」和「總管的僕人」；前者表示與宮廷有遠親關係的女性，而後者則是指嫁給基層官員的女性，雖然她們也有可能與宮廷有間接關係。因此，臆測這些男性可能在宮廷中身為基層官員，而這些女性亦與跟王室宮廷有著某種關聯。（作者：R.L.）

Stela of the True King's Acquaintance Renseneb and his father, the Bodyguard Dedi

Round-topped stela engraved with sunk relief found on the ground surface at the site of Abydos. At the top are two sacred eyes, through which the stela owner could magically see, below which are two signs of water, signifying a libation performed on his behalf by future passers-by.

The next register contains a traditional funerary prayer which reads: "An offering that the king gives (to?) Osiris, lord of Busiris, great god, and lord of Abydos, that he may give a libation, (burn) incense, and (offer) sacred oil for the ka-spirit of the true king's acquaintance Renseneb, true-of-voice, and (also for the ka-spirit of) his father, the bodyguard Dedi, true-of-voice". The words 'for the ka-spirit of' are written in the middle of the third register and are meant to be read twice, from right to left and vice-versa.

Below is a scene of Renseneb and his wife, labelled as 'the lady-in-waiting Nub-en-ib' on the left, and of Dedi and his wife, 'the servant of the ruler Mut-pu-senbet' on the right. Between them is a table of offerings.

The lower register shows a series of columns which simply list names and titles. The larger column on the left names 'the functionary and keeper of Nekhen Neb-su-menu'. The fourteen short columns to the right of this are meant to be read from right to left. Some of the people are specifically called 'his brother' or 'his sister', while others are simply given a title and a name and may have been co-workers of Rensenb and Dedi. What is noteworthy here is the diversity of titles met. Among the men are six 'great one of the tens of Upper Egypt', a function that may have been attached to the vizier's office, and two ordinary wab-priests. Among the women, there are two occurrences of 'mistress of the house', which simply meant a married woman in charge of a household, as well as the previously mentioned 'lady-in-waiting' and 'servant of the ruler'. The former indicated a woman with remote family ties to the royal court while the latter was given to women who were married to minor officials, although it is possible that they too had indirect ties to the palace.

Thus, it seems possible that the men worked together as minor officials of the palace while the women named also had some connection to the royal court. (R.L.)

39. 德迪與其子朝臣瑞森涅卜石碑
來自阿比多斯
中王國時期，第 13 王朝（西元前 1773-1650 年）
石灰岩
432 x 290 x 75 mm

Stela of the True King's Acquaintance Renseneb and his father, the Bodyguard Dedi
From Abydos
Middle Kingdom, Dynasty 13 (1773-1650 BC)
Limestone

著羅馬服飾的男子石碑

從埃及歷史初期,陪葬石碑就被用以紀念死者。這種做法一直持續到希臘羅馬時期。這些石碑往往設立於陵墓附近,但其亦可能在遠離個人墓地的紀念堂中豎立起來,因此其功能並不完全等同於現代的墓碑。

1906 年至 1907 年間,位於阿比多斯的開鑿地點發現了一座大型的希臘羅馬時期墓園,數百座可追溯至此時期的石碑被發現。此陪葬石碑結合埃及和古希臘羅馬風格,反映出建造時的多元文化背景。石碑的圓形頂部刻有帶蛇的雙翼日輪。此石碑中間刻有死者之形象,兩側伴隨著胡狼神的圖像,但並未保留其擁有者的名字。死者面部朝前方,並穿戴著束腰外衣與披風,此造型代表他並非典型的埃及人。木乃伊形式的胡狼頭人像可能代表阿努比斯神,這些神像各持有一個鉤子與連枷,象徵著王權的傳統。此外,他們每位都戴著王冠 — 左側人形上可看到阿提夫冠,右側人形則戴著雙皇冠。(作者:J.H.W.)

Stela of a Man in Roman-style Clothing

From the beginning of Egyptian history, funerary stelae were used to commemorate the deceased. This practice continued into the Graeco-Roman period. These stelae were often set up in or near a tomb, but they could also be erected in memorial chapels far from an individual's burial site, so their function is not exactly equivalent to modern day tomb stones.

Excavations at Abydos in 1906-07 revealed a large Graeco-Roman cemetery and hundreds of stelae dating to this time period were found. The motifs on this Abydene funerary stele combine both Egyptian and Classical motifs reflecting the multicultural time in which it was created. A traditional winged sun disk with pendant uraei appears on the top of this round-topped stele. Decorated with a central image of the deceased flanked by images of jackal-headed gods, this stele does not preserve the name of its owner. The deceased is shown facing forward and wears a tunic and a mantle. His appearance is not typically Egyptian. The mummiform jackal-headed figures likely represent the god Anubis, although Anubis was not the only canide god in the Egyptian pantheon. The divine figures each hold a crook and a flail, the traditional emblems of kingship. In addition, each wears a royal crown -- the atef-crown can be seen on the figure on the left, the double crown is worn by the figure on the right. (J.H.W.)

男性形象浮雕（局部）

此件浮雕描繪一個男人穿著簡單的短裙，留著短髮且頭上未配戴物品。其來自中王國時期的創建者 - 尼布赫帕特拉・蒙圖荷泰普二世（Nebhepetre Mentuhotep II）的神廟，位於底比斯西岸的巴哈里（Deir el-Bahri）。

蒙圖荷泰普二世是來自底比斯的當地統治者，他在赫拉克雷奧波利斯（Herakleopolis）成功擊敗敵對統治者並重新統一埃及。其神廟是一座特殊的皇家陵墓，其創新建築之靈感取自於當地底比斯先人的岩石切割柱廊陵墓，以及古王國時代的金字塔。如同其具有的古王國風格，該複合式建築包含河谷神廟與堤道。神廟本身帶有平台且前方面向廊柱大廳。該廊柱大廳和庭院是奉獻給蒙圖 - 雷神（Montu-Ra）；而直接在懸崖上進行雕刻的內院和多柱大廳內，則被獻給已經神化的國王。奉獻給阿蒙神的小型聖殿是後來才添加至後側的多柱大廳。在聖殿的遠端處陳列著祭桌以及一座置於神龕內的國王雕像，此外則是深入懸崖 150 公尺的皇家陵墓。

寺廟中的大部分，浮雕的藝術風格不再遵循當地的底比斯傳統，而受到第五至六王朝孟斐斯城模型的影響。然而，一些神廟外區則包含著非王室及宗教的場景，例如描繪放牧的男性或士兵部隊，其風格較接近於第一中間期。

此件作品的人物表現仍保有統一以前的底比斯風格之元素，包括四肢幾乎不帶有肌肉的渾圓造型，大眼睛以及一個顯著且向下轉折的內眼角、寬鼻，且鼻孔到嘴巴之間有一道重刻線。手臂部份特別細，且雕刻有些漫不經心，浮雕深度相對較淺，不像神廟內為國王及神靈所保存的極高品質浮雕。彩色油漆仍保存在物件上：黑色的頭髮及紅褐色的皮膚，儘管臉部已有些褪色。（作者：M.M.）

Relief Fragment of a Male Figure

This relief block depicts a man wearing a simple kilt, bareheaded with closely cropped hair. It comes from the mortuary temple of King Nebhepetre Mentuhotep II, founder of the Middle Kingdom, at Deir el-Bahri, on the west bank of Thebes.

Mentuhotep II was a local ruler from Thebes, who succeeded in defeating rival rulers in Herakleopolis and re-unified Egypt. His mortuary temple is an unusual royal tomb, with innovative architecture drawing inspiration from the rock-cut, colonnaded tombs of his local Theban predecessors, and Old Kingdom pyramid temples. Like its Old Kingdom inspiration, the complex had a valley temple and a causeway. The temple itself was terraced and fronted by pillared halls. The large front pillared hall and courtyard were dedicated to the god Montu-Ra, while the inner court and hypostyle hall, which were carved directly into the cliffside, were dedicated to the cult of the deified king. A small sanctuary dedicated to the god Amun was subsequently added to the rear of the hypostyle hall. At the far end of the sanctuary stood offering tables and an enshrined statue of the king, beyond which was the royal tomb, 150 metres into the cliff.

In much of the temple, the artistic style of the reliefs no longer followed local Theban tradition, but were instead influenced by Dynasty 5-6 Memphite models. However, some of the outer areas of the temple included non-royal, non-religious scenes, such as depictions of men herding animals or troops of soldiers, some of which are executed in a style more typical of the First Intermediate Period.

The figural representation on this block still retains elements of pre-unification Theban style, including rounded modelling of the limbs with little musculature, a large eye with a pronounced, downward turn of the inner corner, and a broad nose with a heavily incised line from the nostril to the mouth. The arms are especially thin and somewhat carelessly carved, as well as executed in relatively shallow raised relief, unlike the temple's highest quality reliefs, which were reserved for the king and deities. Coloured paint is still preserved on the block: black for the hair and red-brown for the skin, although it is somewhat faded on the face. (M.M.)

41. 男性形象浮雕（局部）
來自巴哈里，蒙圖荷泰普二世神廟
中王國時期，第 11 王朝，蒙圖荷泰普二世統治時期
（西元前 2055-1985 年）
石灰岩
530 x 280 x 90 mm

Relief Fragment of a Male Figure
From Deir el-Bahri, temple of Mentuhotep II
Middle Kingdom, Dynasty 11, reign of Mentuhotep II
(2055-1985 BC)
Limestone

42. 奧塞里斯的大祭司溫納尼法雕像頭部
來自阿比多斯，奧塞里斯神廟
新王國時期，第19王朝，拉美西斯二世統治時期（西元前 1279-1213 年）
紅花崗岩
330 x 310 x 300 mm

Head from a Monumental Statue of the High Priest of Osiris, Wenennefer
From Abydos, the temple of Osiris
New Kingdom, Dynasty 19, reign of Rameses II (1279-1213 BC)
Red granite

奧塞里斯的大祭司溫納尼法雕像頭部

佩托里（Petrie）在阿比多斯的奧塞里斯神廟挖掘期間拍攝的照片顯示，此受損頭部片段曾經一度是超越真人大小的溫納尼法（Wenennefer）雕像的一部分，其在拉美西斯二世時期曾擔任奧塞里斯神的大祭司。佩托里的報告指出，該雕像受到鹽份嚴重侵蝕，因而僅剩頭部能夠挽救。此塊狀雕塑的原始外觀應為其主人之坐姿，膝蓋移至胸前並以長斗篷包覆；此類雕像由寺廟中的官員們奉獻，以彰顯其在神靈宗教中的地位。包覆住的斗篷亦提供一個長篇文字撰寫的表面。然而，這些溫納尼法雕像的照片僅記錄到來自已遺失柱子上的四欄銘文的某些部份。這些部份記錄著他的名字與頭銜，以及他的妻子與母親之名字與頭銜，她們兩人都是侍奉奧塞里斯神的女吟唱者。他們的頭銜強調著其家族與奧塞里斯神廟的密切關係—溫納尼法的父親亦曾擔任大祭司，而其後代也繼續在阿比多斯保有大祭司等頭銜。

溫納尼法在此處配戴著一頂普通假髮，長度直達肩膀，且耳朵外露。他寬闊、扁平的臉部沒有明顯顴骨，而豐滿的嘴唇是拉美西斯時代的典型風格。眉毛與眼睛週圍的眼線精雕細琢，包括另一條在眼線上方用以指出眼瞼的線條。在造型與風格方面，此雕塑比溫納尼法在阿比多斯的其他雕像更具傳統性，或許能顯示出其對不同工作坊的贊助，或是一間工作坊內多元化與實驗方面的可能性。他的慷慨贊助蹤跡遍及整個阿比多斯。溫納尼法從新王國時代晚期便在當地奉獻了，而且比其他非王室人物更多，目前尚存有部分私人文物。其中包括一座墓堂（請參見本書11號展品）以及眾多還願物品、雕像和石碑，這些都在整個區域中極重要的聖地內被發現。四尊他的雕像，包括這件雕像局部，在奧塞里斯神廟的轄區內被發現。奧塞里斯神廟中的古物相當難以重建，但這尊雕像似乎是在座落於第十八王朝較早期的皇室聖堂前之建築中所發現。儘管此建築之作用並不明確，但溫納尼法的文物連同一件屬於塞提一世（Sety I）且重複使用的塊狀物件出現在其中，此部份顯示該建築是在拉美西斯二世時期所建。溫納尼法可能負責監督該項建設作業。（作者：L.F.）

Head from a Monumental Statue of the High Priest of Osiris, Wenennefer

Photographs taken during Petrie's excavations in the temple of Osiris at Abydos show that this damaged fragment of a head was once part of an over-life-size block statue of Wenennefer, high priest of Osiris under Rameses II. Petrie reported that the statue was so badly eroded by salt that only the head could be salvaged. Block statues, which show their owners seated with their knees drawn to their chests and wrapped in a long cloak, were often dedicated by officials in temples to assert their presence and participation in the divine cult. The enveloping cloak also provided a surface for long texts. However, the photographs of Wenennefer's statue record only parts of four columns of inscription from the lost back pillar. These give his name and titles as well as those of his wife and mother who were both songstresses of Osiris. Their titles stress the family's close institutional ties with the temple of Osiris – Wenennefer's father had also been high priest and his descendants went on to hold high priestly titles at Abydos.

Wenennefer is shown here wearing a plain wig that was worn to shoulder-length, leaving his ears exposed. His broad, flat face, without any modelling of cheekbones, and full lips are typically Ramesside in style. The eyebrows and the cosmetic lines around the eyes have been delicately carved, including a second line above the upper cosmetic line to indicate the eye-lid. In form and style, this statue is more traditional than some others Wenennefer dedicated at Abydos, perhaps showing his patronage of different workshops or the possibility for variety and experimentation within one workshop. Traces of his generous patronage can be seen across Abydos. Wenennefer dedicated more surviving personal monuments at the site than any other non-royal individual from the late New Kingdom. These include a tomb-chapel (see catalogue #11) and numerous votive objects, statues, and stelae found at significant sacred locations throughout the landscape. Four statues of his, including this fragment, were recovered from the precinct of the temple of Osiris. The archaeology of the Osiris temple is very difficult to reconstruct, but it seems that this statue was found inside a structure located in front of an earlier, Dynasty 18, royal chapel. Although the function of this structure is unknown, Wenennefer's presence inside it, along with a reused block belonging to Sety I, suggest that it was built under Rameses II. Wenennefer probably oversaw this building work. (L.F.)

鏡子手柄

在第十八王朝陵墓的一個井狀通道中，佩托里（Petrie）發現此處存放著骨頭與長牙，連同六個瓶罐、兩個石瓶、眼線瓶以及貝斯神像。此陵墓曾遭掠奪，且物品混合在一起，因此無法確認哪些屬於原來的墓葬，哪些是之後存放其中。此地與位於高（Qau）墓園的存放地點相當鄰近，使蓋‧布朗登（Guy Brunton）推測其可能為同時期物品，年代可追溯至第十九王朝。

以風格而言，此件鏡子手柄之年代可追溯至第十九王朝，並顯示其為後期存放之物。類似的形象也在拉美西斯時代陵墓的長牙中發現，儘管其風格，即厚重的浮雕假髮、平台冠以及左手肘彎曲等，可追溯至第十八王朝。該名女性臉部渾圓，雙眼狀如杏仁，虹膜處由帶有黑色顏料的鑽孔所組成。其髮際與王冠之間的頭髮週圍有一條帶子，手上可能捧著小貓。此人形雕塑由整塊河馬牙雕刻而成：河馬門牙適用於製作柱狀的鏡子手柄以及眼線盒。此件物品曾遭受相當大的破壞，特別是在右側，且雙腳已遺失。王冠頂部有一個洞，用於固定鏡子的柄腳。（作者：N.H.）

Mirror Handle

In the shaft of a Dynasty 18 tomb, Petrie found a deposit of bone and ivory, along with six pots, two stone vases, kohl tubes and a figure of Bes. The tomb had been robbed and the objects mixed together, so it was not clear which items belonged with the original burial and which had been deposited there subsequently. The proximity of this deposit to that of Cemetery 500 at Qau prompted Guy Brunton to suggest that they may have been contemporary, both dating to the Dynasty 19. Stylistically, this mirror handled can be dated to Dynasty 19, indicating that it was part of the later deposit. Similar figures were found among the Ramesside Tomb 562 ivories, though the style, with a heavy embossed wig, platform crown and the left arm bent at the elbow, can be traced back to Dynasty 18. The woman has a rounded face and almond-shaped eyes with irises consisting of drilled holes containing black pigment. She has a band around her hair between her hairline and crown, and may have held a kitten in her cupped hand. The figure was carved from a single piece of ivory: hippopotamus incisors are ideal for making cylindrical mirror handles and kohl tubes. It has suffered considerable damage, particularly on the right side and the feet are missing. There is a hole in the top of the crown for the tang of the mirror. (N.H.)

43. 鏡子手柄
來自高艾爾喀勃，7260 號墓室
新王國時期，第 19 王朝，拉美西斯二世統治時期
（西元前 1279-1213 年）
河馬牙
167 x 40 x 33 mm

Mirror Handle
From Qau el-Kebir, Cemetery 7000, Tomb 7260
New Kingdom, Dynasty 19, Ramesses II (1279-1213 BC)
Hippopotamus ivory

鏡子手柄

鏡子在古埃及具有實用性和象徵性的意義。其被用於化妝並且在婦女產後隔離期間使用。其亦包括在陪葬品以及奉獻給神祇的物件中。埃及詞彙中的鏡子（安卡，ankh）也同時意指生命以及花束，顯示出鏡子與新生命之間在字詞上的關聯性。帶有圓形反射面的鏡子讓人聯想到太陽，手柄部份的設計也加強了這種連接性。另外紙莎草繖狀花序、裸體的年輕女性，以及手柄上哈托爾女神面具等結合皆暗示著青春、活力與生育力。

此件鏡子手柄的風格相當獨特：該女性的臉龐是倒置的淚滴形狀，由一頂沉重的假髮勾勒出線條，其上的垂飾剛好低於頸部下側。乳房雕刻不均勻，而放在右側乳房下方的手部末端為點狀：手指無法各別呈現。其左手臂懸放在其側邊。兩腳之間有一個洞，可能曾用於固定木梢，以將人偶與底座接合。腿部有一部分經過重製，假髮頂部有一個洞，用於固定鏡子的柄腳。（作者：N.H.）

Mirror Handle

Mirrors had practical and symbolic properties in ancient Egypt. They were used for the application of makeup and presented to women during their post-partum seclusion. They were also included among burial equipment and objects offered to deities. The Egyptian term for mirror (ankh) is also that for life and bouquets of flowers, indicating a word association between mirrors and new life. The mirror with its circular reflective surface is reminiscent of the sun, and the design of some handles reinforces this connection. Youth, vitality and fertility are alluded to by the incorporation of papyrus umbels, young nude women, and Hathor masks on the handles.

The style of this mirror handle is unusual: the woman's face is an inverted teardrop shape, framed by a heavy wig with lappets that almost meet just below the neck. The breasts are unevenly carved and the hand that rests beneath the right breast ends in a point: the fingers are not individually rendered. Her left arm hangs by her side. A hole between her feet may have held a pin attaching the figure to a base. The legs have been partially reconstructed, and there is a hole in the top of the wig to hold the tang of the mirror. (N.H.)

44. 鏡子手柄
來自高艾爾喀勃，562 號墓室
新王國時期，第 19 王朝，拉美西斯二世統治時期
（西元前 1279-1213 年）
象牙
101 x 25 x 15 mm

Mirror Handle
From Qau el-Kebir, Cemetery 500, Tomb 562
New Kingdom, Dynasty 19, Ramesses II (1279-1213 BC)
Elephant ivory

杯子

在拉美西斯二世統治期間，位於高（Qau）墓園中的一座第二王朝陵墓主要被用來存放大量的河馬骨與河馬牙，重量約在2至3噸左右。混合在廢棄骨頭當中的是一些由象牙、石頭、貝殼、玻璃、金屬以及一些人骨雕成的物品。開鑿者認為，此存放地點跟佩托里（Petrie）在附近發現的類似存放地點可說明這些河馬殘骸受到恭敬的擺放，第十九王朝掘墓者在該遺址意外發現這些河馬殘骸。

在古埃及時代，河馬出現在整個尼羅河流域。他們對農作物造成損害，且具有危險性，特別是在保護小河馬免於遭受潛在威脅時。他們經人格化後形成塞特神（Seth）的一股混沌勢力，以及孕婦、分娩與生育女神塔沃里特（Taweret）的保護力量，其擁有河馬的臉和身體、鱷魚尾巴、獅爪、假髮，以及女人的乳房。

河馬牙杯雕刻自河馬的下側犬齒及門齒，並以刻劃之線條裝飾。這種牙杯並不常見，但有五個牙杯連同許多裝飾性物品在該墓園中發現，例如眼線瓶、雕刻精緻的勺子、鏡子手柄及珠子。事實上，這只牙杯與上述物品一同被發現，表示其被用來作為化妝品或芳香物質之容器。（作者：N.H.）

TUSK CUP

During the reign of Ramesses II, a Dynasty 2 tomb in Cemetery 500 at Qau was used to deposit a vast quantity of mainly hippopotamus bone and ivory, weighing between two and three tons. Mixed in with the discarded bone were objects carved from ivory, stone, wood, shell, glass and metal, and some human bones. The excavator believed that this deposit and a similar one found by Petrie nearby were evidence for the reverential disposal of the remains of hippopotami, accidentally uncovered at the site by grave diggers in Dynasty 19.

Hippopotami were present throughout the Nile Valley in ancient Egypt. They caused damage to crops and could be dangerous, particularly in protecting their young from perceived threats. They became personified as a force for chaos in the god Seth, and of protection in Taweret, the goddess of pregnant women, childbirth and fertility, who has the face and body of a hippo but the tail of a crocodile, paws of a lion, and the wig and breasts of a woman.

Tusk cups were carved from the lower canines and incisors of hippopotami and decorated with incised lines. They are not common, but five were found in the Cemetery 500 deposit, along with many decorative items, such as kohl tubes, intricately carved spoons, mirror handles and beads. The fact that this cup was found with these objects suggests that it was used as a container for cosmetics or perfumed substances. (N.H.)

45. 杯子
來自高艾爾喀勃，7260 號墓室
新王國時期，第 19 王朝，拉美西斯二世統治時期（西元前 1279-1213 年）
河馬牙
116 x 55 x 45mm

TUSK CUP
From Qau el-Kebir, Cemetery 500, Tomb 562
New Kingdom, Dynasty 19, Ramesses II (1279-1213 BC)
Hippopotamus ivory

雙化妝墨管

眼影或眼線（埃及文稱為 mesdemet）是作為一種化妝品，以強化外貌特徵，並用以降低太陽眩光。在新王國時期曾製造出多種眼線瓶，其中可能包含各種準備工作，以應付眼部在不同的季節發生的問題。自中王國時期（公元前 2040 年至 1648 年）便開始生產眼線棒以應用於眼線的使用，而眼線容器則經過改良用以保存眼線棒。此樣本在兩個眼線瓶中間有個空心處可用於置放眼線棒，該眼線棒現今已遺失，有可能是在存放於陵墓的過程中自容器脫離，雖然也有許多物品是在處置前便早已損壞。兩個眼線瓶側頂部鑽有孔洞，用於附著瓶塞（現已遺失），以防止眼線乾涸。這些瓶子模仿連結成一體的空心蘆葦叢，並帶有黑 / 灰色粉末痕跡。新王國時期最流行的顏色是黑色，但眼線瓶內亦曾證實存在綠色眼影並曾被描繪於陵墓中。（作者：N.H.）

Double Kohl Tube

Eye paint or kohl (Egyptian mesdemet) was used as a cosmetic to enhance physical appearance and as a prophylactic to reduce the glare of the sun. In the New Kingdom, multiple kohl tubes were produced, possibly containing separate preparations to combat eye problems that occurred during different seasons. From the Middle Kingdom (2040-1648 BC) onward, sticks were produced for the application of kohl, and eye paint containers were modified to hold them. This example has a hollow between the tubes for a kohl stick that is missing, possibly separated from the container during the process of deposition in Tomb 562, though many objects were damaged prior to disposal. Holes were drilled into the side of the two tubes near the top for the attachment of stoppers (now lost) to prevent the kohl from drying out. The tubes imitate clusters of hollow reeds bound together, and contain traces of black/grey powder. The most popular colour for kohl in the New Kingdom was black, but green eye paint is also attested in kohl tubes and depictions in tombs. (N.H.)

46. 雙化妝墨管
來自高艾爾喀勃，562 號墓室
新王國時期，第 19 王朝，拉美西斯二世統治時期
（西元前 1279－1213 年）
象牙
125 x 48 x 17 mm

Double Kohl Tube
From Qau el-Kebir, Cemetery 500, Tomb 562
New Kingdom, Dynasty 19, Ramesses II (1279-1213 BC)
Elephant ivory

化妝墨管

這種八角形眼線瓶是用整塊骨頭或象牙雕刻成紙莎草芽柱的形狀。瓶身中空且不完整，但其中能保存著一塊眼線墨。眼線瓶在全新的時候能站立在圓形底座上，之後底座會固定在一塊長方形象牙上，並保存著另一只眼線瓶和眼線棒容器。這些眼線瓶中有十三只在「骨坑」中被發現，而在蓋•布朗登（Guy Brunton）發表的七只中（例如「荷花柱」眼線瓶），沒有一個帶有底座，這表示它們在存放於陵墓之前便已受到破壞。在側面和頂部的小孔是用於一個旋鈕，細繩能綁在其上以固定住蓋子（有一個對應的旋鈕），這些小孔也用於能讓蓋子旋轉開啟與關閉的象牙栓子。在柱桿與柱頭之間有兩條刻線，這是大多數紙莎草形眼線瓶及其所仿製的完整尺寸柱子之常見特點。（作者：N.H.）

KOHL TUBE

This octagonal kohl tube is carved from a single piece of bone or ivory in the shape of a papyrus bud column. The tube is hollow and incomplete, but a lump of kohl is preserved inside. When new it would have stood on a rounded base which in turn may have been fixed to a rectangular piece of ivory holding another tube and a container for the kohl stick. Thirteen of these tubes were found in the 'bone pit', and of the seven published by Guy Brunton (as 'lotus-pillar' kohl tubes), none have bases, suggesting that they were all damaged before being deposited in Tomb 562. Holes in the side and top were for a knob to which string could be tied to secure the lid (which would have had a corresponding knob), and for an ivory pin that allowed the lid to swivel open and closed. There are two incised lines between the shaft of the column and the capital, a feature common to most papyriform kohl tubes and to the full-sized columns that they imitate. (N.H.)

47. 化妝墨管
來自高艾爾喀勃， 562 號墓室
新王國時期，第 19 王朝，拉美西斯二世統治時期（西元前 1279-1213 年）
動物骨或象牙
110 x 25 x 25 mm

KOHL TUBE
From Qau el-Kebir, Cemetery 500, Tomb 562
New Kingdom, Dynasty 19, Ramesses II (1279-1213 BC)
Bone or ivory

48. 兒童罩衫
來自梅特瑪,第 100 號墓地,1012 號墓室
科普特時期 (西元 700-800 年)
羊毛與亞麻
910 x 570 x 25 mm

Child's Tunic
From Matmar, Cemetery 100, Tomb 1012
Coptic Period (AD 700-800)
Wool and linen

兒童罩衫

這是一件相當罕見的完整兒童服裝,是在梅特瑪(Matmar)兒童墓地中發現的數樣物品之一,當中還包括骨製與玳瑁殼製的手鍊及皮革鞋子。這件服裝的長度約超過兒童的膝蓋部位,呈現 T 字形並有窄短的衣袖,此一件式的連身服裝兩邊袖口上方直接連接,縫線則各自從手臂下開始接合至衣角,連接前後兩片衣料,頸部的開口則是沿著服裝上方的折疊處剪開。這是從羅馬時期至中世紀早期的典型男子、女子與兒童服裝樣式,但通常會也有其他變化,如雕像上的服裝會出現長袖、無袖款式,以及搭配腰帶或拿掉腰帶等裝扮。

其主要的布料為平織的紅色羊毛料,搭配嫩黃緯紗(即穿過基本花紋的橫向線),再縫上五彩繽紛的織錦飾片,係屬 clavi 樣式,亦即領口兩邊有平行短帶、底部與袖口有垂直的帶子以及獎章。部分飾片已脫落,特別是肩膀部位與衣角的獎章,織錦的部分則是使用黃、橘、綠與海軍藍等有色羊毛製成,飾片邊緣與 clavi 內部的連鎖扣製成黃色與橘色的花朵與動物圖形,其中多數皆已無法辨識,但已被重新製作。(作者:J.A.C.)

Child's Tunic

This is a rare example of a complete child's tunic. It was one of several items found within a child's burial at Matmar, which also includes bone and tortoiseshell bracelets and leather shoes. It is long, reaching beyond the child's knee, and T-shaped with short, narrow sleeves. The garment was manufactured in one piece, from sleeve edge, to sleeve edge, with its seams under the arms and down each side, joining the front and back pieces. The neck opening was cut along the top fold. This is the standard form of tunic worn throughout the Roman world and the early Middle Ages for men, women, and children, although variations are common. For example, in statuary, tunics are represented with long sleeves, be sleeveless, and be worn either belted or unbelted.

The base material is plain woven red wool, with a yellow-cream weft (i.e. the transverse thread running through the base weave). Polychrome tapestry panels were appliquéd to the tunic to provide decoration. These are in the form of clavi, i.e. short vertical bands on either side of the neck and horizontal bands along the base and the cuff, and medallions. Some of these panels have been pulled off, especially the medallions at the shoulders and along the bottom edge. The tapestries are produced using yellow, orange, green, and navy blue wool. Yellow and orange are used for the panels' borders and also for the interlocking chains within the clavi, within which images of floral and fauna - many of which are difficult to identify - are reproduced. (J.A.C.)

皮製涼鞋

對古埃及的上流階層而言，涼鞋為整體裝扮中不可或缺的一部分，最早在納美爾石板（3100 BC）中便曾描述過涼鞋的用途。在法老王時期，涼鞋是以紙莎草製成，但在西元 30 年之後，皮革成為最普遍的材質，由於大部分的埃及人皆打赤腳，因此涼鞋便使成為上流階級居高位的象徵，但可能只會在特殊場合穿戴，也包括作為上流社會的重要陪葬品。

本次展出的涼鞋，主要的特色為尖頭外形以及經過穿孔與雕刻的鞋底，並綴有裝飾鞋帶。一般而言，涼鞋是以兩片皮革縫合而成，皮革間還加了一層紙莎草或棕櫚葉，而沿著鞋底邊緣縫製的收邊用縫線亦是裝飾圖案的一部分；縫至涼鞋中軸的第二部分縫線，則具有穩固的作用。左邊這雙涼鞋的鞋跟背面，同樣有鏽蝕的銅合金支撐固定兩片皮革，兩隻涼鞋上的多數鞋帶皆保存完整，包括鞋後跟鞋帶與鞋底連結的部分，以及連接鞋子前方大姆指與食指間的鞋帶。雖然左邊的涼鞋有較清楚的裝飾，但兩雙涼鞋其實是類似的同款鞋，沿著縫線皆有一個壓入皮革的雙重圓圈裝飾。鞋跟的底座上有一個以雙重線條刻於皮革上的 X 圖樣，此種刻在方格中的 X 圖樣，也同樣出現在鞋子的蹠骨區域，這些花樣通常能令人想起以紙莎草編織涼鞋之時代製作的鞋型，而兩個 X 刻紋之間則是以連續的波浪線段連接。儘管這些涼鞋的寬度較窄，但確實是標準尺寸的成人涼鞋。（作者：E.L.）

Pair of Sandals

Sandals were an integral component of costume for the ancient Egyptian elite, with representations of the footwear used as early as the Narmer palette (3100 BC). In the pharaonic period, sandals were predominantly made from papyrus, but post-30 BC, leather became the most popular material. Egyptians went barefoot, thus sandals signified a high rank in the elite classes and were presumably used only for special occasions, including for the elite as essential tomb goods.

Sandals such as these are grouped in a typology which includes the pointed toe and the punched and incised designs on the sole that are further enhanced by decorative accents on the thong. In general, sandals are manufactured by stitching two pieces of leather together with a layer of papyrus or palm leaf in between them. These sandals use the stitching along the perimeter of the sole as an integral component of the decoration by providing a perimeter for the punched decoration. The second section of stitching down the middle axis of the sandal is for stability's sake. The left sandal also has the remains of corroded copper alloy at the back of the heel, simply an extra anchoring tack between the two pieces of leather. On both sandals much of the twisted thong is intact, and one can see how the thong connected to the underside of the shoe behind the heel as well as where it would have connected at the front of the shoe between the first and second toe. Although the decoration on the left sandal is clearer, both sandals are a matched pair consisting of a double circle decoration that is punched into the leather at regular intervals along the stitching. At the heel base an X figure formed by double lines incised into the leather, while an X figure inscribed in a box also composed of double lines is present at the ball of the foot. These patterns are reminiscent of the shapes made when sandal were made from woven papyrus. Connecting these two incised X shapes are a series of incised wavy lines. Despite the narrow width of the sandal, it is the standard size for adult shoes. (E.L.)

織錦片段

此碎片保留了兩種裝飾性掛毯的元素，亦即在淺色底布上有大型的橢圓獎章與長方形飾片，且從尺寸上亦可看出原本的織品應為掛飾或壁毯，而非服裝（其尺寸與縫飾的製造技術皆與本書編號 48 的兒童服裝不同）。兩種底部編織皆為紫色羊毛材質，搭配未染色的亞麻線設計，長方形飾片上則保留了三面花邊，顯示此碎片為完整織品的尾端，邊緣還有一連串的幾何圖形。橢圓編織上有兩個同心橢圓花樣，兩者之間則排列了十四個小圓圈，中央還搭配了其他設計，且除右方的額外 E 形符號外，橢圓編織中還有一條由上至下的對稱中線。（作者：J.A.C.）

Tapestry Panel

This fragment preserves two decorative tapestry elements, a large oval medallion and a section of a rectangular panel, on a light-coloured ground weave. The size of these features indicates that the original textile was a cover or wall hanging, rather than a tunic (they are very different in size and production technique to the appliquéd tapestries on the child's tunic, # 48). The background weave of both tapestries is purple wool, with designs in undyed flax thread. On the rectangular panel, three edges of the decorative border are preserved, suggesting that the surviving fragment is from the end of the original piece. Within this border are a series of geometric shapes. The oval is patterned with two concentric ovals, between which are 14 small circles, with another design in the central space. With the exception of some of the E-form symbols on its right side, the oval has one line of symmetry, running from top to bottom. (J.A.C.)

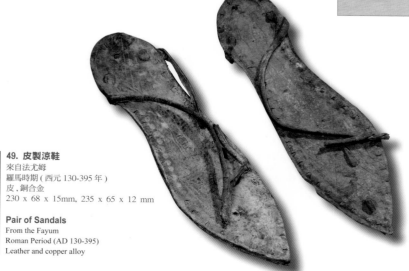

織錦飾帶

此碎片為較大織品飾片的一部分，可能是服裝的 clavus 部分（請參見本書編號 48 的織錦設計，以瞭解此飾片的可能位置），底布為深棕色羊毛料，飾片上的精緻裝飾則以染色羊毛與未染色亞麻線製成，但僅上半部邊緣完整存留。布料上的連續波浪完美映襯出徜徉於水生植物間，以綠色背景襯托的裸體人物與海豚，這些人物是以神話經典中的海上仙子，即海神尼爾尤斯（Nereus）之女內芮蒂絲（Nereïdes）為靈感，身邊則陪伴著許多無法辨識種類的生物。在殘留的片段中央有一隻小鴨，但其他有腳、尾巴與耳朵的生物則非普通的水生動物，而是整個神話主題圖樣的一部分。（作者：J.A.C.）

Tapestry Band

This fragment is part of the decorative panel of a larger textile, probably the clavus of a tunic (see the layout of the tapestries on the child's tunic, # 48, for possible locations for the panel). The ground fabric is a dark brown wool and the fine decoration of the panel is provided by coloured wools and undyed flax thread. Only the top border survives in its entirety. This shows a series of waves, which are an appropriate frame for the main theme of naked figures and dolphins swimming on a green background among water plants. These figures, inspired by classical mythology's Nereïdes (sea nymphs, daughters of the sea spirit Nereus), are accompanied by a number of animals, the exact nature of which is not always easy to identify. In the centre of the surviving fragment is a small duck, but the other creatures, with legs, a tail, and ears are certainly not aquatic, but serve to contribute to the overall mythological motif. (J.A.C.)

流蘇衣飾

這塊亞麻織品碎片保留了清楚邊緣，而邊緣八條流蘇中的剩餘部分是由布料的經紗製成。在此碎片中有許多額外的緯紗塞在單一處，形成一條獨特的線條，此特色可能是裝飾、補強，或用以提醒編織工人開始製作經紗流蘇的記號。這一片織品不是使用最高級的布料製成，但上面的垂綴流蘇則為高極的裝飾效果，在新王國時期，服裝通常都會加上流蘇飾邊，且質料大多較本次展出的碎片高級與輕巧，因此，此碎片應為飾帶或床單的一部分。在新王國時期，布製品皆屬家庭工業。（作者：T.H.）

Fringed Textile Fragment

This fragment of linen preserves a plain selvedge and the remains of eight tassels from a fringe made from the cloth's warp threads. Halfway along the fragment a number of extra weft threads are inserted in a single pick, forming a distinctive line; this may have been intended as decoration, strengthening, or as a note to the weaver to begin the warp fringe. The texture of the cloth is not of the finest quality, but the fringing is quite decorative. While New Kingdom garments often had fringed edges, they often are finer and lighter than this example. It has been suggested that this fragment may have come from a sash or decorative bed cover. Production of cloth was a household industry throughout the New Kingdom. (T.H.)

51. 織錦飾帶
來自奧克西林庫斯
科普特時期（西元 300-800 年）
羊毛與亞麻
252 x 82 x 1 mm

Tapestry Band
From Oxyrhynchus
Coptic Period (AD 300-800)
Wool and linen

52. 流蘇衣飾
來自阿瑪納，11， 21/324 號房屋
新王國時期，第 18 王朝，阿肯納頓統治時期
（西元前 1352-1336 年）
亞麻
210 x 100 x 1 mm

Fringed Textile Fragment
From Amarna, Workmen's Village, Gate Street House 11, 21/324
New Kingdom, Dynasty18 , reign of Akhenaten (1352-1336 BC)
Linen

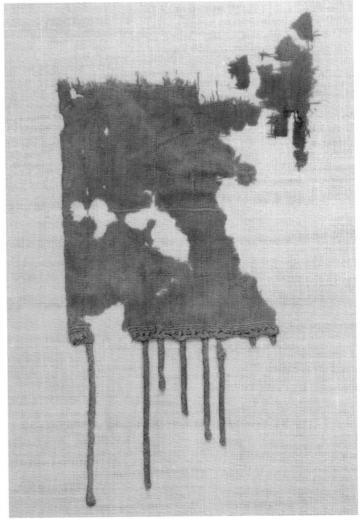

亞麻布料

在古埃及，不論男女皆穿著以長亞麻布製成的圍裹式服裝。亞麻布的品質與細緻度會隨穿衣者的地位與氣候變化而改變，穿戴方式是先以亞麻布圍裹住全身，再以腰帶固定。亞麻服裝的長度依穿著對象決定，因此會因作為女用的洋裝、裙子，或作為男性的短裙、披風等不同用途而改變。

這一塊棉袍可能原本是屬於此圍裹式服裝，但也可能是當作壽衣使用。這一塊棉袍的大小與磨損狀況皆符合圍裹式服裝的特徵，是非常細緻的布料，長的一邊還採用了綴邊與修飾技術，因此很難辨別此棉袍的真正功能，但在棉袍的其中一邊卻可看到明顯的整齊針腳，皆符合其他已鑑定為圍裹式服裝先捲起布料再一針一針縫邊的技術。流蘇是一種修飾技術，流蘇的縫線擁有獨立的起始線頭，且會將部分縫線縫入棉袍中，具有補強功能。在棉袍中還發現了一個打結處，由於近代曾多次從這塊布料剪下樣本，因此可能還有另一個長邊的飾邊。（作者：C.R.）

Linen Sheet

Both men and women in ancient Egypt wore wrap-around garments made of long sheets of linen. The quality or fineness of the linen related to both the status of the owner and climatic needs. The linen was wrapped around the body and then held in places with sashes. The length of linen required depended on whether the garment was a dress or skirt for a woman or a kilt or cloak for a man.

This sheet was probably such a wrap-around garment, but may have been reused for burial cloths. The size and wear patterns on this sheet are very similar to examples identified as wrap-around dresses. The fabric is relatively fine and the fringing is applied to the long edge, which has a finishing technique, the exact nature of which is difficult to determine, however neat stitches visible on one side. In other examples of sheets identified as wrap-around dresses, this technique is a rolled and whipped hem. The fringe has been attached to this finishing technique. The separate thread used to form the fringe has its starting end interwoven a few threads into the sheet itself - as a means of securing it. One knot was also found. There have been a number of samples cut from this fabric in modern times, including what was probably the other fringed, long edge. (C.R.)

53. 亞麻布料
來自埃及
新王國時期後期，第 18-30 王朝 (西元前 1550-332 年)
亞麻
2250 x 1240 x 1 mm

Linen Sheet
From Egypt
New Kingdom – Late Period, Dynasty 18-30 (1550-332 BC)
Linen

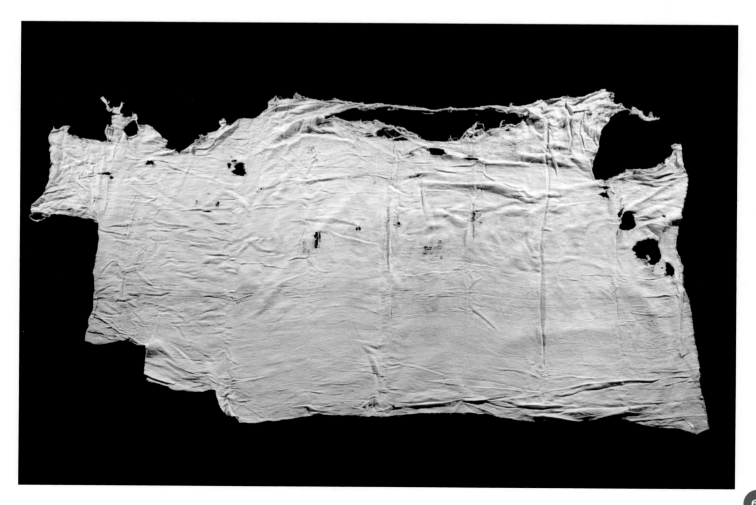

織布機重錘與紡錘軸

在法老王統治時期的埃及人，大多是使用以亞麻植物（Linum usitatissimum）莖部的長纖維製成的亞麻布，製作方法是先從植物的莖部取出纖維，經過浸泡、曬乾與敲打等步驟後，再製作成織線。這兩個木製紡錘軸是用於將鬆散捲起的纖維紡成較緊密的紗線，也就是可使用的織線：先將最初的一圈粗紗纏繞在木軸的長端上，並繞過盤形的紡輪，再繞至木軸較短一邊的頂端切口（可由本頁下方圖清楚檢視）。紡錘軸為活動式設計，通常會快速捲到紡織工人的腳後再落下，而紡輪具有飛輪的功能，可讓紡錘軸轉動得更持久、更穩定，以使笨重的紡錘軸將粗紗拉出並扭轉，之後再緊緊鎖成織線。完成織線，紡織工人就會停止紡錘軸，並從木軸頂端拿下全新的織線纏繞於紡錘軸底部，再重新開始整個程序。在本頁下方圖中可看見纏繞的古老織線。

完成織線後，接著就是使用織布機將織線製成布匹。織布機會交錯編織固定於機器上的（垂直移動）經紗與水平緯紗，若改變經紗與緯紗的比例，或變化緯紗與經紗交織形成的網孔，就能製造出不同強度、重量與質感的布匹。在新王國之前，埃及人都是使用織布區域與地面平行的臥式織布機（ground loom），但至新王國後，由於垂直式織布機（vertical loom）能更有效率地利用空間，並能執行更複雜的織法，而受到廣泛使用。經辨識後發現，此處展示的兩顆石頭是織布機的砝碼，因為垂直式織布機需要利用砝碼的重量拉緊經紗線，石頭上的凹槽即是為了能方便地固定石頭。由於過去曾於博物館中展示，因此砝碼與紡錘軸上皆已換成現代的織線。

阿瑪納（Amarna）的挖掘者，為埃及紡紗與布匹技術提供了重要證據，其證明織品製作是屬於家庭工業，且為家庭工作中極為重要的一部分。在阿瑪納有許多小房子都是將織布機設備設置於主要的房間內，若為大型複合式莊園則是設置於庫房中。此處展示的砝碼與紡錘軸的作工都較為粗糙，且皆是使用棕櫚木、鵝卵石等當時容易取得的材料製成，由此亦可顯示紡紗與織布對埃及家庭經濟的重要性。（作者：T.H.）

Loom Weights and Spindles

The majority of cloth made and used in Pharaonic Egypt was linen, made from the long fibres of the stem of the flax plant (Linum usitatissimum). The fibres are removed from the stem and prepared by soaking, drying, and beating, before they can be turned into thread. These two wooden spindles were used to spin loosely pre-rolled fibres ('rovings') into tighter spun, useful threads: a starting loop of rovings was wrapped around the longer end of the shaft and passed over the disc-shaped spindle whorl before being guided through the notch at the tip of the shorter end of the shaft (visible most clearly on 1922.15.7.b). The spindle was set in motion, usually by being rolled quickly up the spinner's leg, and then dropped free. The whorl acted as a fly-wheel to keep the spindle rotating longer and more evenly, so the heavy, spinning spindle would pull out and twist the rovings, locking them together into a piece of thread. Once a length of thread had been produced, the spinner would stop the spindle, un-hook the new thread from the top of the shaft, and wind it round the bottom of the spindle before beginning the process again. Ancient thread is still wound on 1922.15.7.b.

The thread would then be made into cloth on a loom, where fixed warp threads (running vertically) were interwoven with horizontal warp threads. Varying the ratios of warp and weft threads, and the way in which the weft threads meshed with the warps, would produce cloths of different strengths, weight, and texture. Until the New Kingdom the Egyptians used ground looms, with a working area parallel to the ground; from the New Kingdom onwards the vertical loom was more popular, as it allowed for more efficient use of space, and for more complicated weaving techniques to be used. Warp threads were kept taut on vertical looms by weights such as the two stones shown here, identified by their excavators as loom weights, and grooved for easy attachment. Both weights and spindles were supplied with modern thread for an early museum display.

Excavations at Amarna provided important evidence for the production of yarn and cloth in Egypt. Textile manufacture was carried out within the home, and would have formed a significant part of the household's work; fixtures for looms have been found in the main rooms of many smaller houses, or in the outhouses of the larger villa compounds at Amarna. Both the spindles and loom weights shown here are relatively crudely made from materials that would have been readily available at the time – palm wood and pebbles. They emphasise the vital nature of spinning and weaving in the Egyptian domestic economy. (T.H.)

54. – 55. 紡錘軸
來自阿瑪納工人村
新王國時期，第 18 王朝，阿肯納頓統治時期（西元前 1352-1336 年）
木，亞麻
210 x 44 x 42 mm, 215 x 53 x 53mm

Spindles
From Amarna, Workmen's Village
New Kingdom, Dynasty 18, reign of Akhenaten (1352-1336 BC)
Wood, linen

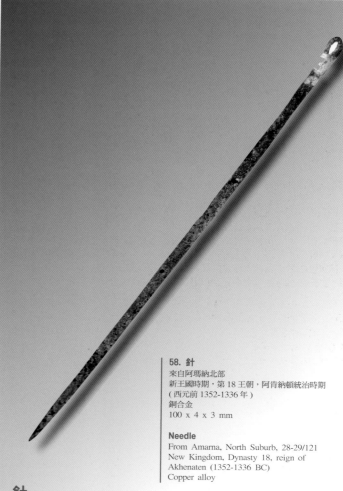

56. – 57. 織布機重錘
來自阿瑪納，11，21/324 號房屋
新王國時期，第 18 王朝，阿肯納頓統治時期
（西元前 1352-1336 年）
石灰岩
82 x 53 x 48mm, 92 x 58 x 54mm

Loom weights
From Amarna, Main City
New Kingdom, Dynasty 18, reign of Akhenaten
(1352-1336 BC)
Limestone

58. 針
來自阿瑪納北部
新王國時期，第 18 王朝，阿肯納頓統治時期
（西元前 1352-1336 年）
銅合金
100 x 4 x 3 mm

Needle
From Amarna, North Suburb, 28-29/121
New Kingdom, Dynasty 18, reign of
Akhenaten (1352-1336 BC)
Copper alloy

針

在埃及最早的歷史中即已發現針的蹤跡。儘管埃及的衣物沒有繁複的剪裁，卻仍有許多證據顯示埃及人會使用針縫紉，包括簡單的縫合、縫飾、繡花與織補痕跡，當時最普遍的縫邊技術就是將布料捲起互相堆疊，再一針一針地將捲起部分固定。針的材質有很多類型，包括骨頭、木頭、銅合金與銀，因此針縫的品質也各不相同，但依然出現了許多精緻與合宜的縫紉作品。埃及人當時已會使用各種粗細不一，甚至顏色多變的亞麻線，且從古埃及的許多衣物上都會發現有縫補的痕跡，或許這也代表衣物是屬於昂貴的物品，所以修補比替換新衣物更符合經濟效益。繡花在古埃及時期較為稀少，但在圖坦卡門（Tutankhamun）的墓中也曾發現繡有精緻繡花的服裝。本次展出的這支針相當大，一端鋒利，另一端則是穿線用的針眼，是於室內區域中發現。（作者：C.R.）

Needle

Needles have been discovered from the earliest periods in Egyptian history. While Egyptian garments were not heavily tailored, evidence for the techniques of sewing with a needle include simple seams, appliqué, embroidery, and darning. One of the most common hemming techniques was to roll the fabric over on itself and then whip stitch the roll in place. Needles were made from a variety of materials including bone, wood, copper alloy, and silver. The quality of stitching varied but there are many examples of very fine and regular work. Egyptians used flax thread in a variety of thicknesses, sometimes coloured. Darning has been found on many examples of cloth from ancient Egypt, perhaps suggesting cloth was expensive and it was more economical to repair than replace. Embroidery was rare in ancient Egypt, but very fine embroidery was found on garments from the tomb of Tutankhamun. This needle is moderately large and is sharp at one end with a hole for the thread at the other. It was found in a domestic area. (C.R.)

59. 項鍊組
來自巴達里，5544 號墓室
古王國時期，第 6 王朝（西元前 2345-2181 年）
動物骨，動物牙，貝殼，銅，彩陶，紅玉髓，塊滑石
500 x 52 x 8 mm

Set of Necklaces
From Badari, Tomb 5544
Old Kingdom, Dynasty 6 (2345-2181 BC)
Bone, ivory, shell, copper, faience, carnelian, and steatite

項鍊組

自古王國時期開始，就會讓男性、女性與兒童佩戴串珠與護身符下葬，且此習俗一直延續至第一中間王國時期。這一串項鍊是在一位成年女性的身上發現，是墓中唯一的陪葬品，且此墳墓無任何曾遭人侵入的跡象。墓中共挖掘出五串串珠與護身符，這些串珠在歷經四千年的時間後依然串連在一起未斷落，這些珠子的材質大多為象牙、石頭、貝類、彩陶與半寶石，皆屬簡樸的飾物。這一串項鍊雖不同於其他該時期的護身符般以珍貴黃金打造，但因當時是將彩陶稱為 tjehenet，意指「埃及之光」，類似新王國時期用於描述太陽神的辭彙，因此很難判斷其價值。即使在古王國時期，有時候也會以彩陶代替半寶石裝飾在頭冠等重要物品上，證明彩陶於該時期是一種良好的替代材質。

點綴於樸素珠子之間的護身符能為亡者提供魔力與保護。由於埃及人於在世時及逝去後皆會配戴護身符，因此我們無法判斷這些護身符是專為葬禮製作，或是亡者生前喜愛的物品。這一串項鍊上的護身符神像，包括了象徵愛與美神哈托爾（Hathor）的牛頭，以及代表生育之神塔瓦里特（Taweret）的懷孕河馬，還能賦予佩戴者視覺、聽覺與言語能力的抽象人頭像、能讓佩戴者擁有圖像動物般迅速腳程與勇猛，極抽象的獅子／狗護身符（由於圖像過於模糊，無法辨識出護身符上的確切圖樣）。此墓中還發現了其他鱷魚和聖甲蟲護身符。（作者：L.A.W.）

Set of Necklaces

Beginning in the Old Kingdom, men, women, and children were commonly buried wearing beads and amulets. The trend further increased in the First Intermediate Period. The necklaces shown here were found on the body of an adult woman. They were the only grave goods found in her grave, despite the burial being intact. A total of five strings of beads and amulets were excavated, having survived for almost four thousand years still strung. The beads are composed largely of ivory, bone, shell, faience, and semi-precious stones, forming simple adornment. The value of the necklace is difficult to determine. While it is not made of precious materials such as gold, like other amulets from the period, material like faience was called tjehenet, 'gleaming' in Egyptian, similar to words which would be used to describe the sun god in the New Kingdom. Even in the Old Kingdom, faience was commonly used in lieu of semi-precious stones, sometimes in important objects like diadems, suggesting that it was an acceptable alternative.

The amulets interspersed between the simple beads provide the deceased with magical capabilities and protections. Amulets would have been worn by Egyptians both during life as well as in death, and it is impossible to know if these amulets were purpose made for the burial or favourite objects worn during the woman's lifetime. The amulets on this necklace include images of deities such as the cow-head representing Hathor, goddess of love and beauty, and the pregnant hippopotamus representing Taweret, goddess of childbirth. Stylized human heads also appear which endowed the wearer with use of her sense of sight, hearing, and speech. The highly stylized lion/dog amulets – it is impossible to tell which of the two the amulets represent, as they are very crude – lend the wearer the fleetness of foot or ferocity of these animals. Additional amulets from this burial include crocodiles and scarabs. (L.A.W.)

60. 紫水晶項鍊
來自阿比多斯，E204 號墓室
中王國時期，第 12 王朝（西元前 1985-1773 年）
紫水晶
225 x 45 x 15 mm

Amethyst Necklace
From Abydos, tomb E204
Middle Kingdom, Dynasty 12 (1985-1773 B.C.E.)
Amethyst

紫水晶項鍊

這一串項鍊是以顏色飽和且尺寸逐漸分級的二十五顆紫水晶珠串成。紫水晶為半透明的石英，顏色範圍可自深紫色變化至透明中帶有少許淡紫色調，是中王國時期的代表特色，當時通常是將紫水晶製作成珠寶飾品，主要是開採自埃及最南邊之象島（Elephantine）東南方的瓦迪護堤（Wadi el-Hudi）採石場。在中王國時期的富人墓中便曾發現過極類似的項鍊，其特色為每一顆紫水晶珠的兩邊都加了黃金飾片。

這些珠子經過鑽孔、以沙子或金鋼砂研磨後，再使用串線穿孔，最後進行拋光。在古王國時期，鑽孔器是以銅製成的手持敲打器具，但到新王國時期，已改為具青銅尖端、製作精巧的弓鑽。

發現這一串項鍊的阿多比斯（Abydos），是埃及在中王國時期很重要且與奧塞里斯神（Osiris）有關的葬禮祭祀中心。這一串項鍊是在位於阿比斯北方的墓地中尋獲，由約翰·加斯唐（John Garstang）進行開挖，墓地的東北區域最珍貴，也最靠近城鄉與奧塞里斯神廟。在該墓地中還包含強行設於更南方位置的第十二王朝與第十三王朝墳墓。（作者：M.M.）

Amethyst Necklace

The necklace consists of a string of 25 amethyst barrel beads, rich purple in colour and graduated in size. Amethyst is a translucent crystalline form of quartz, which ranges in colour from deep purple to a transparency with a faint violet-tinge. Amethyst is characteristic of the Middle Kingdom, the period when it was most popularly used in jewellery. It was sourced chiefly from the quarry at Wadi el-Hudi, southeast of Elephantine, in southernmost Egypt. Similar necklaces to this, from very wealthy Middle Kingdom burials, feature gold caps on either ends of each individual amethyst bead.

The beads would have been made through a process of drilling, aided by sand or emery abrasive, to provide a stringing perforation, followed by polishing. In the Old Kingdom, drills were apparently copper-made, hand-held, and percussive, but by the New Kingdom, bronze-tipped, sophisticated bow-drills were being used.

During the Middle Kingdom, Abydos, the site where the necklace was found, was a funerary cult centre of national importance, associated with the god Osiris. The tomb was located in the Abydos North Cemetery, specifically Cemetery E, which was excavated by John Garstang. The north-eastern area of the cemetery was the most desirable, closest to the town and Osiris temple. Cemetery E included both Twelfth Dynasty and later Thirteenth Dynasty tombs, which forced to locate further to the south. (M.M.)

心型護身符和串珠項鍊

這些物品都是在同一個墳墓中發現，但使用的串線為現代產品，且排列方式可能與原始設計不同。貝殼、石頭與陶珠為埃及最早的飾品原料，且在前王國時期的墓中即曾發現，是法老王統治時期相當普遍的素材，因此在各社會階層的墓中都曾發現過，而玻璃則是新王國後才出現的物品，其製造技術是由西亞傳至埃及。在法老王時期，石珠必須各別進行鑽孔，但到了新王國，製造商便能如索貝克侯特普（Sebekhotep）墳墓中描繪的方法，使用弓鑽一次啟動數根鑽桿為數顆（通常為三至四顆）石頭鑽孔，進而開始量產。埃及的彩陶包括以粉碎的石英／石英沙與小部分石灰及泡鹼／植物灰製成的陶瓷主體，再加上一層以小蘇打、石灰與矽石製成的釉，若再加入銅就能製造出藍、綠色彩，如展出的珠子。僅管自新王國時期後便能製造出新的色彩，但是在法老王統治的期間，藍、綠仍最受歡迎的顏色，有時也會使用彩陶代替綠松石和青金石等較普遍但常用於珠寶上的石頭，本次展出的項鍊中，就有一兩顆以此類材料製成的珠子；事實上，古埃及的彩陶名稱即等同於綠松石（tjehenet，意指「閃閃發亮、隱約含光、燦爛明亮」）與青金石（hesebedj）。早期的珠子皆是以手工塑模，珠孔也是個別穿洞，但到了古王國時期，已能利用銅線塑造珠子的主體部分，且已開始量產。在出土文物中有無數與此處展出之珠子相似的物品，是目前最常見的古埃及飾品。

這個水晶護身符的外形雖然簡約，但製作精美，表面經過拋光後顯現出如玻璃般的反光亮度，主要象徵心臟。自新王朝時期起，此類護身符即成為陪葬品之一，更出現在《亡者之書》（Book of the Dead）第 26-29 首的咒語中。第 29 首咒語中指出，此類護身符應以瑪瑙製成（紅色象徵鮮血），但也經常出現如本次展出，使用其他材質製作心型護身符墜飾的情形。當時視心臟為人體的中心，不僅具有生理上的重要功能，同時也是智慧所在，在描繪亡者審判的繪畫中，便曾出現心臟由代表世界正義秩序之馬特女神 (Maat) 進行秤重的畫面，因此留在亡者身上的心臟必須進行秤心程序。上述提及的第 29 首咒語此心型護身符直接有關，它能確保亡者的心臟不會在地府中被奪走。此心型護身符與聖甲蟲護身符的作用不同，但兩者之間有密切的相關性，且能互相搭配。心型護身符通常不會如本次展出般穿成項鍊，而是置於木乃伊的繃帶內、外，或直接置於亡者的胸口上。（作者：C.W.）

Beads and Heart Amulet

These objects were found together in the same tomb, but their current stringing is modern and their original combination was probably different. Shell, stone and faience beads are among the earliest jewellery items produced in Egypt and are already found in tombs of the early Predynastic period. They remained popular throughout the pharaonic period and are found in tombs of all social strata. Glass was produced in Egypt only since the New Kingdom, the technology having been imported from western Asia. In the Predynastic period, stone beads were drilled individually, but by the time of the New Kingdom manufacturers were able to drill several beads (usually three or four) at a time employing a bow drill driving several drilling rods, as depicted for example in the tomb of Sebekhotep, allowing for mass production. Egyptian faience consists of a ceramic body composed of crushed quartz/ quartz sand and small amounts of lime and natron/ plant ash, and a glaze of soda, lime and silica. Copper is added to produce a green to blue colour, as seen in the beads here. This remained the most popular colour throughout the pharaonic period, although from the Middle Kingdom onwards other colours are produced. Faience was used as an imitation of stones such as turquoise and lapis lazuli, both equally popular for jewellery, though less ubiquitous. One or two beads in the necklace here are made of these materials. In fact, the names used for faience in ancient Egyptian are identical to turquoise (tjehenet; meaning 'shining, gleaming, dazzling') and lapis lazuli (hesebedj). The earliest beads were hand-modelled and the holes drilled individually, but this technique was replaced in the Old Kingdom by moulding the body material around a copper wire, allowing for mass manufacture. Indeed, beads such as those exhibited here are found in countless number, being the most popular item of adornment by far.

The crystal amulet is simple in shape, but superbly finished, the surface polished to a glass-like gleam. It most likely represents a heart. This type of amulet is introduced into the funerary equipment in the New Kingdom and is mentioned in spells 26 to 29 of the Book of the Dead. Spell 29b states that such amulets should be made of carnelian (the red colour resembling blood), but other materials such as the one shown here are not uncommon. The heart was considered to be the centre of the human existence, not only important for the bodily functions, but also as the seat of the intellect. As such, it is seen in illustrations of the so-called judgement of the deceased being weighed against the symbol of Maat, the goddess and principle of rightful world order. It was therefore important that the heart remained with the deceased for this weighing procedure. The spells mentioned above, of which spell 29 is directly linked to the heart amulet through the heading 29b, should make certain the heart was not taken away from the deceased in the netherworld. Therefore the heart amulets have a different function than the heart scarabs (see other exhibits), but both are closely linked and complementary to each other. Heart amulets were usually not worn on necklaces - as shown in this exhibit – but placed either outside of or within the mummy bandages, or directly onto the chest of the deceased. (C.W.)

61. 心型護身符和串珠項鍊
來自阿比多斯，T3 號墓室
新王國時期，第 18 王朝，圖特摩斯一世統治時期
（西元前 1504-1492 年）
水晶，彩陶，貝殼，寶石，玻璃
260 x 25 x 20 mm

Beads and Heart Amulet
From Abydos, Tomb T3
New Kingdom, Dynasty 18, reign of Thutmose I
(1504-1492 BC)
Rock crystal, faience, shell, stone, glass

62. 紅玉髓項鍊
來自阿比多斯，D161 號墓室
中王國時期，第 12 王朝（西元前 1985-1773 年）
紅玉髓
720 x 15 x 15 mm

Necklace of graduated carnelian beads
From Abydos, tomb D161
Middle Kingdom, Dynasty 12 (1985-1773 BC)
Carnelian

紅玉髓項鍊

這一串瑪瑙串珠項鍊的作工相當精巧，八十四顆珠子的尺寸都經過非常精細的分級，瑪瑙則呈現出半透明狀的玉髓，顏色為紅棕色或橘色到透明帶著些許紅色，在阿拉伯沙漠 (Eastern Desert) 與努比亞 (Nubia) 有極豐富的蘊藏，但在歷代埃及中仍屬高價寶石。埃及人將瑪瑙稱為 herset，瑪瑙珠子必須經過鑽孔、以沙子或金鋼砂研磨後才能以串線穿孔，最後再進行拋光。

發現這一串項鍊的阿比多斯，是埃及在中王國時期很重要，且與奧塞里斯神有關的葬禮祭祀中心；奧塞里斯神是被視為已故的國王，且是獲得來生的重要關鍵。在此時期，許多造訪阿比多斯的朝聖者皆會留下紀念石碑作為標記，並期望能因參加神的祭祀慶典而獲得永生。

這一串項鍊的發現地，是一個有兩個南向開口墓室的豎井墓，較低的墓室在發現當時，外面還封著一道磚牆，是過去從未發現過的墓室。墓室中的女性亡者，脖子上即佩戴著這一串項鍊，身邊則散置著幾顆赤鐵珠子和一面銀盤，身體下還有小顆的藍色陶珠與護身符、未刻字的綠色聖甲蟲飾品，以及一串較大的灰斑石串珠。該墳墓的尺寸與貴重陪藏品，皆顯示此墓應屬上流階級的墳墓。（作者：M.M.）

Necklace of graduated carnelian beads

This necklace of carnelian spheroids is finely made, each of the 84 beads being carefully graduated in size. Carnelian is a translucent form of chalcedony, ranging in colour from red-brown or orange to a red-tinged transparency. It was relatively plentiful in both the Eastern Desert and Nubia, but was still highly valued throughout Egyptian history. The Egyptian name for carnelian was herset. The beads would have been made through a process of drilling, aided by an abrasive, in order to provide a stringing perforation, followed by polishing.

Abydos, the site where the necklace was found, was a funerary cult centre of national importance, especially during the Middle Kingdom. The site was connected to the god Osiris, who was associated with the deceased king and was considered to be the key god of the afterlife. Many pilgrims visited the site during the period, often leaving commemorative stelae marking their visit, hoping to be able to participate in the god's cultic celebrations for eternity.

The necklace was found in a shaft tomb with two chambers opening to the south, the lower one being still intact and bricked up when discovered. The chamber contained the burial of a woman, with the necklace placed around her neck, along with a few haematite beads and a silver disc. Lower on the body were found small blue faience beads and amulets, an uninscribed green scarab, and a string of larger beads of grey speckled stone. The size of the tomb and comparative wealth of the burial suggests that it was relatively elite grave. (M.M.)

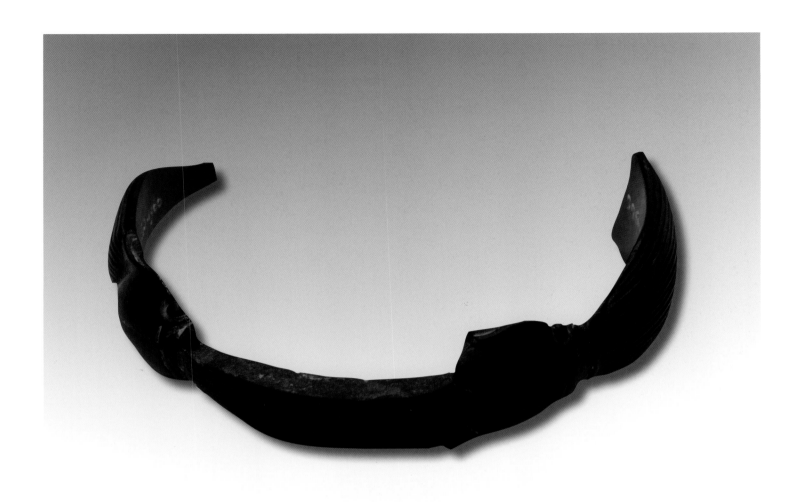

63. 叩頭蟲手環
來自阿比多斯
第 1 王朝（西元前 3150-2920 年）
沙泥岩
70 x 57 x 20 mm
＊埃及發現學會捐贈

Click Beetle Bracelet
From Abydos
Early Dynastic Period, Dynasty 1 (3150-2920 BC)
Siltstone
Donated by the Egypt Exploration Society

叩頭蟲手環

此手環雖然僅殘留一部分，但在細密沉積砂岩上的雕刻，卻能證明埃及早期石匠即已具備處理此類創作材料的驚人能力與技術。手環上的裝飾圖樣為叩頭蟲（Agrypnus notodonta），此蟲為古埃及極普遍的昆蟲，主要棲息於尼羅河的沼澤河岸，名稱源自於牠們跳過空中時發出的喀嚓聲響。這種甲蟲與主宰埃及早期王朝時期的奈特（Neith）女神有關，許多貴族女性會將奈特女神之名融入自己的姓名中[1]，而奈特也與尼羅河三角洲的伊斯有關，在早期王朝時期是狩獵與戰爭的代表。

目前收藏於布魯塞爾皇家歷史博物館（Musèes Royaux d'Art et d'Histoire）的奈特石板（Neith Palette）碎片上，便有兩隻嗑頭蟲與一面盾牌及弓箭緊鄰著奈特神像。根據紀錄，這塊石板是發現於阿多比斯，且有磨損的痕跡，顯示該石板原本是用於研磨眼部彩妝粉。雖然這些物品的相關考古學資料極為貧乏，但從關聯性進行判斷，顯示其中一項或兩項物品可能是屬於第一王朝的貴族家庭。（作者：J.A.H.）

1.King Djer 之妻 Herneith 與 King Den 之母 / 攝政王 Merneith，都是在名字中結合奈特女神之名的貴族女性。

Click Beetle Bracelet

Although fragmented this bracelet, carved from the fine grained sedimentary rock siltstone, is a stunning example of the skill with which stone artisans were able to manipulate the medium during this early period of Egyptian history. The design uses click beetles (Agrypnus notodonta) as a decorative motif. Click beetles were common insects in ancient Egypt inhabiting the marshy banks of the Nile river. They are called click beetles because of the clicking sound they make as they jumped through the air. The beetle is associated with the goddess Neith, a deity whose iconography dominates Egypt's Early Dynastic period. Many royal women incorporated this goddesses name in their own names.[1] Neith is associated with the site of Saïs in the Delta and during this early period she was identified with hunting and warfare.

Two click beetles appear next to the Neith fetish, a shield and crossed arrows, on the so-called Neith Palette fragment now at the Musèes Royaux d'Art et d'Histoire, Brussels. The palette is recorded as being recovered at Abydos and shows sign of wear, indicating that it was used to grind eye makeup. Archaeological context for both these objects is poor, but given their associations it is possible that one or both of the items belonged to women of the First Dynasty royal family. (J.A.H.)

1.The wife of King Djer, Herneith, and the mother/regent of King Den, Merneith are examples of royal ladies associated with this goddess.

鏡子

由於鏡子的外形以及具備照耀明亮的特質，人們經常會將鏡子與太陽進行聯想，因此鏡子不僅實用，還具有宗教與葬禮方面的作用。這些盤形鏡子是以銅合金材質製成，並附有一個連接握把的柄舌，最初這兩面鏡子皆因氧化而出現斑點，其中一面更黏附著一塊布，但經過清理與拋光後，已恢復類似原本於遠古時代的明亮狀態。

這兩面鏡子都是以銅合金材質製成，銅合金在中王國時期之前極為普遍，之後則逐漸由青銅取代成為鏡子的主要製作材料。銅大多是開採自西奈半島（Sinai）的亭納（Timna）礦區或阿拉伯沙漠（Eastern Desert），鏡子的製作程序包括鑄造、錘煉、鍛冶與打磨。

每一面鏡子皆有能連接握把的柄舌。在中王國時期，握把大多以木頭或象牙等易腐蝕或不易保留的材質製成，至新王國時期，則開始出現不同材質的握把，其中以金屬握把最普遍。象徵富饒與重生的圖像是握把的基本樣式，最常見的就是象徵植物生長與重生的紙莎草稈，或是象徵富饒與性慾的哈托爾（Hathor）女神或裸女塑像，此外，握把上也可能會裝飾與鏡子有關的哈托爾女神頭像。在部分古王國時期的墳墓中，亦可見看哈托爾女神在舞蹈表演中使用鏡子的圖繪。

在陪葬品中，由於鏡子與美麗、富饒及生產有關，而具有重生的意義，因此多數鏡子皆是屬於女性的陪葬品。墳墓內與亡者個人（多半為女性）有關的繪畫中，亦會將鏡子放置在座椅下方、亡者的面前或由一旁的隨從獻上，事實上，有許多從墓穴中挖出的鏡子，皆是細心地置於亡者的臉上。

這些鏡子是挖掘自一個重複使用的墳墓，為眾多集合陪葬品之一。此墳墓原為第一中間期的墳墓，因之後遭到入侵破壞，而約在第十二王朝時期又重複用於埋葬了「許多名彼此明顯無關係的亡者」，在北方與南方墓室即各自埋葬了兩位男性與一位女性。除了鏡子外，還同時發現了陶製器皿、六個白色雪花石膏花瓶、許多瑪瑙與金屬串珠，以及有微量木頭棺木的跡象。

此墳墓係位於第一與第二王朝等早期國王的大型泥磚圍場中央，尤其是哲爾王（King Djer）的圍場，且周遭圍繞著哲爾王的朝臣之墓。雖然至今尚不瞭解這些大型圍場的作用，但一般認為它們是「陪葬宮殿」或「神之堡壘」。（作者：M.M.）

Mirrors

Mirrors were associated with the sun disc because of their shape and radiant shine. They were functional but also had religious and funerary uses. These disc-shaped mirrors are made of a copper alloy with a tang to attach to a handle. Originally both mirrors were tarnished by oxidization, with cloth adhering to one of them, but this mirror has been cleaned and polished to bring it back to an approximation of the shine it would have possessed in ancient times.

Both are made of a copper alloy, which was common up until in the Middle Kingdom, when bronze slowly began to replace copper as the material chiefly used for mirrors. The copper most likely came from the Egyptian mines in the Sinai at Timna, or the Eastern Desert. Mirrors were generally made through a process of casting, hammering, annealing, and polishing.

Each mirror has a tang for its attachment to a handle. In the Middle Kingdom, handles would generally have been made of wood or ivory, perishable materials that have survived less often, while in the New Kingdom materials for handles diversified and metal handles became popular. Typical forms for handles were motifs associated with fertility and rebirth, the most common being a papyrus stalk, symbolic of green growth and regeneration, or a figure of the goddess Hathor or a nude female figure, both of which signified fertility and sexuality. A handle could also be surmounted by the head of Hathor, who was particularly associated mirrors. In several Old Kingdom tombs, mirrors were depicted being used in performing dances associated with Hathor.

Within a tomb context, mirrors were symbols of rebirth because of their association with beauty, fertility, and procreation. The majority come from female burials. In funerary depictions of deceased individuals, often women, mirrors could be represented underneath their chairs, placed before their face, or presented to them by attendants. Indeed, many of the mirrors found in tombs were carefully placed by their owner's face.

These mirrors were part of a burial assemblage in a reused tomb that was originally dated to the First Intermediate Period, but was broken into and reused for 'several apparently independent burials of later date', probably during the Twelfth Dynasty. The north and south chambers each contained a group of two males and one female. Along with the mirrors, there were found small pottery vessels, six alabaster vases, many carnelian and metal beads, and the traces of wooden coffins.

The tomb was located in the midst of the once massive mud-brick enclosures of the earliest kings of Egypt from the First and Second Dynasties, specifically in the enclosure of King Djer, surrounded by the graves of his courtiers. The function of these huge enclosures is still uncertain, though it has been variously suggested that they were 'funerary palaces' or 'fortresses of the gods'. (M.M.)

64. & 65. 鏡子
來自阿比多斯，797 號墓室
中王國時期，第 12 王朝（西元前 1985-1773 年）
銅合金
170 x 160 x 2mm, 185 x 185 x 2 mm

Mirrors
From Abydos, tomb 797
Middle Kingdom, Dynasty 11-12 (2055-1773 BC)
Copper alloy

化妝品容器組

這一組化妝品罐皆來自同一個墳墓。從尺寸與附設鏡子等特點判斷,這些罐子極可能是用於裝盛化妝油或油膏的罐子,尤其是罐子 A 更進一步確立此說法,因為其外型與「開口」儀式('Opening of the Mouth' ceremony)中使用的小罐子十分相似。在製作雕像與木乃伊時,皆會實行「開口」儀式以使其復活,並讓接受儀式的對象能展現身體的完整生理功能,在進行儀式時需要七種油脂(現代稱為七聖油,但在古埃及僅稱其為「油脂」),這些油脂是各別出現於第一王朝時期,其名稱會分別寫在象牙、骨頭與木頭製成的標籤上,至古王國時期,這些油脂變成了一個組合,並可見於祭獻程序中。我們同樣在葬禮物品中發現寫有名稱的石板,放置於盛了少量油脂的凹洞旁,但僅有四個名稱能完成轉譯,且譯文無法直接與原本代表的物質對應,而是用以代表儀式中的特定情況與步驟,如「讚揚之油(oil of praising)」。我們對其他油脂與油膏的了解是來自於更廣泛的祭獻清單,古埃及人認為這類物品對死後的存在極為重要。油脂與動物脂肪亦可在加入花瓣浸泡到完全吸收花香後,取出花瓣,以製成香氛,或再加入沒藥等樹脂。香味能有效掩蓋身體的腐敗氣味,樹脂與樹膠則能進一步將香氣牢牢鎮在油膏中,羅馬詩人普林尼(Pliny)即曾在西元 1 世紀時,將埃及描寫為當代能製作出最完美油膏的國家,並指出許多油膏的製作成分非常複雜,不僅融合了油脂、花朵與樹脂,還添加了辛香料與酒,但是,我們無法確知古王國時期是否同樣是使用此種製作方式。

這四個罐子都是第五、第六王朝的典型樣式,其中的 D 罐子的外型更延用至第一中王國時期(First Intermediate Period),所有的罐子都是以石灰華材質製成,或稱為埃及雪花華石膏(Egyptian alabaster)。由於雪花石膏較柔軟且具有透光特性,在埃及石器製造業中最被普遍使用,且最適合製成油燈的石材。在古王國時期,開羅南方靠近赫勒萬(Helwan)的瓦地吉布拉威(Wadi Gebrawi)與中埃及阿瑪納(Amarna)北方的赫努布(Hatnub),皆設有雪花石膏的採石場,後者還能開採更多其他類的礦石,且至法老王統治時期仍在持續運作。

現代已能全面瞭解古埃及石器皿的製作程序。許多墳墓中皆有古王國到新王國時期之器皿工廠的圖繪,而且在眾多開挖場中都曾發現如工具、廢棄與失敗的手工藝品,甚至曾發現過兩個工廠,包括位於尼羅河三角洲西北方布圖(Buto)的第一王朝時期工廠,以及位於象島上,面對靠近現代蘇丹邊界之亞斯文鎮的古王國時期工廠。後人曾依據這些資訊,重新打造出一組工具,並實際體驗石器皿的製作過程,結果非常成功:一個小型(約 10 公分高)石灰器皿,從最初的塑造外型到最後的打磨程序,需花費 10 小時才能完成,由於雪花石膏的硬度與石灰相當,因此製作 C 罐也同樣需要花費約 10 小時。因為石製器皿的製作時間較陶器長,更顯出石製器皿的重要性,由此可見,現在展出的化妝品罐組,包括內容物與器皿本身,都極為珍貴。(作者:C.W.)

Four Cosmetic Vessels

This set of vessels was found together in the same tomb. Their size and their association with a mirror make it very likely that these were used for cosmetic oils or ointments. This is further underlined by Vessel A, the shape of which has close parallels in small vessels associated with the 'Opening of the Mouth' ceremony. This ritual was performed on statues and mummies to bring them to life and to enable them to take on the full physical functions of the body. Seven different oils were required for this ritual – today known as the seven sacred oils, but in ancient Egypt only called the oils. Individually these oils were known from Dynasty 1, where their names appear on ivory, bone and wooden labels. In the Old Kingdom, they form a group, as can be seen in their mentioning within the offering formula. As funerary equipment we also find stone palettes with their names next to depressions for holding small quantities of these oils. Only four of the names can be translated, although not straightforwardly as the substance they represent, but more as belonging to a specific occasion or step within the ritual, e.g. the 'oil of praising'. Further oils and ointments are known from the even more extensive offering lists, an inventory of those items considered vital for the existence beyond death. Oils and animal fats could be perfumed by adding flower petals and leaving them to soak until their scent was absorbed, after which they would be removed again, or by adding resins such as myrrh. The scent would help to mask the tendency of rancidness of such materials. Resins and gums could further be employed in aid of fixing the fragrance within the unguent. The Roman writer Pliny, writing in the first century AD, describes Egypt as the country best suited for the production of unguents, and also mentions that many of these products were very complex compositions, not only consisting of oils, flowers and resins, but also spices and wine. We do not know, however, if this was already the case in the Old Kingdom.

The forms of the all four vessels are typical for the Dynasty 5-6, although the vessel shape of D continues into the First Intermediate Period. The material used for the four vessels is travertine, also frequently called Egyptian alabaster, which is the most popular stone used in Egyptian stone vessel manufacture, possibly due to its relative softness and its translucent quality, which makes it also suitable for oil lamps. Quarries for this stone can be found in the Old Kingdom at Wadi Gebrawi near Helwan, south of Cairo, and Hatnub in Middle Egypt, north of Amarna. The latter is the more extensively exploited quarry and continues to be in use throughout the pharaonic period.

The process of making stone vessel is well understood today thanks to numerous tomb depictions showing vessel workshops from the Old to the New Kingdom – the technology remains basically unchanged throughout the periods - and artefacts such as tools, waste products and mishaps found at various sites, including two actual workshops, an Early Dynastic example in Buto in the north-western Nile Delta and an early Old Kingdom one on the island of Elephantine in the First Nile Cataract opposite of the town of Aswan near the modern border to the Sudan. On the basis of these sources a set of tools was recreated in experiments to produce stone vessels. These experiments were successful: it turned out that it would take more than 10 hours to produce a small limestone vessel (circa 100 mm in height) from the initial outer shaping to the final polish. As travertine is of similar hardness, the manufacture of Vessel C, for example, would have taken equally long. This underlines the great value of stone vessels, the production of which is vastly more time-consuming than that of pottery. Therefore a set of vessels such as the one displayed here is valuable not only for its contents, but is also an asset in itself. (C.W.)

(A)

66. – 69. 化妝品容器組(A-D)
來自高艾爾喀勒,590 號墓室
古王國時期,第 5-6 王朝(西元前 2494-2181 年)
埃及雪花石膏
58 x 29 x 28 mm,80 x 48 x 48 mm
105 x 33 x 33 mm,56 x 44 x44 mm

Four Cosmetic Vessels
From Qau el-Kebir, Tomb 590,
Old Kingdom, Dynasty 5-6 (2494-2181 BC)
Egyptian Alabaster

有裝飾的梳子

這一把窄長型的梳子與右頁的梳子同樣擁有兩組不同的梳齒，並由一個裝飾精美的飾板區隔為兩邊。精緻雕刻的圖像亦分為兩種風格，上方為三個人物，從服裝即可辨識出為三位女孩，底部的圖像則是一頭豬。埃及殘存了許多此類梳子，最常見的裝飾圖樣則為四足動物與鳥類。精美的雕刻與梳子整體的精細度，皆顯示這一把梳子擁有與右頁的梳子不同的功能：這一把梳子不是日常生活中使用的梳子，比較可能是從未使用過的結婚禮物。（作者：J.A.C.）

Decorated Comb

This long and narrow comb has two different sets of teeth, like #71, which are separated by a decorative panel. The delicately carved images are divided onto two registers. The top one shows three figures, by their clothing three girls, and the bottom a single pig. Numerous examples of such combs survive from Egypt, in which images of quadrupeds and birds are particularly common. The fineness of the carving and the overall fragility of the comb suggest that this was not used daily by its owners, as would certainly be the case for #71, but may have been a marriage gift that was never used. (J.A.C.)

70. 有裝飾的梳子
來自埃及
科普特時期（西元 300- 800 年）
木
240 x 70 x 10 mm

Decorated Comb
From Egypt
Coptic Period (AD 300-800)
Wood

梳子

梳子為男女打扮時的器具之一,可用於日常生活與宗教活動中。本次展出的這一把梳子,為羅馬時期至伊斯蘭早期的埃及與地中海地區最常見的樣式,共有兩組梳齒,其中一組的梳齒較厚實且間距較大,另一組則纖細並排列緊密。這些梳子的功能與現代梳子無異:第一組梳齒能梳開揪結的髮絲,第二組則是用於梳製造型。這一把梳子的飾板狹窄且無多餘的裝飾, 與左頁的梳子完全不同:僅管較為樸實,卻是以含芬芳香味的木頭製成,且至今仍留有明顯的香氣。(作者:J.A.C.)

Comb

Combs were part of the toilette of both women and men, and were used both in daily and religious life. This example is of the type commonly found throughout Egypt and the Mediterranean world from the Roman to early Islamic periods. There are two sets of teeth, those of one set are thicker and well spaced, while those of the other are fine and close together. The function of these combs is no different to that of today: the first set was used to untangle hair, while the second for other hairdressing needs. The central panel on this example is narrow and undecorated, unlike # 71. While plain, the comb is made from an aromatic wood that still has a strong scent. (J.A.C.)

71. 梳子
來自埃及
科普特時期 (西元 300- 800 年)
木
125 x 89 x 15 mm

Comb
From Egypt
Coptic Period (AD 300-800)
Wood

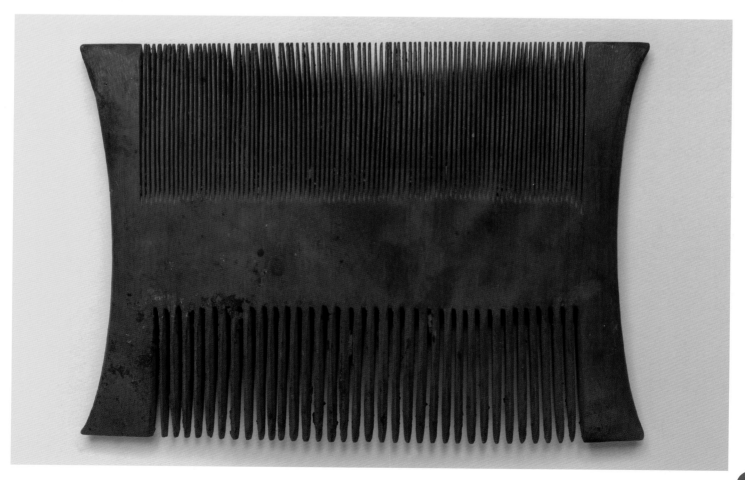

剃刀

在埃及,剃刀是上流階級男女的重要工具,不僅由於當時的潮流與儀式上要求剃除臉部與身體的毛髮,也是因為新王國時期的精緻捲曲編髮大多是戴在光頭上的假髮。

這一把剃刀為五邊形的青銅刀片,切口已鏽蝕,刀片上更以兩個金屬卵釘接合了一把彎曲的把手與圓形旋鈕,為新王國最常見的款式。刀片可使用楔形磨刀石磨利,不使用時則可收藏於木頭或皮革材質的盒子中。在阿瑪納(Amarna)的同一間屋子中共發現了三組剃刀,本次展出的剃刀即是其中之一。(作者:T.H.)

72. 剃刀
來自阿瑪納北部
新王國時期,第18王朝,阿肯納頓統治時期
(西元前1352-1336年)
銅合金
157 x 135 x 15 mm

Razor
From Amarna, North Suburb, House U.35.26, 29/254
New Kingdom, Dynasty 18, reign of Akhenaten
(1352-1336 BC)
Copper alloy

Razor

Razors were an essential tool for élite men and women in Egypt. Not only did fashion and ritual purity dictate that facial and body hair should be removed, but the elaborate curled and echeloned hairstyles of the New Kingdom were often wigs worn over a shaven head.

This razor is made from a pentagonal bronze blade, the cutting edge now corroded, and a cast curved handle with a round knob, attached to the blade by two metal rivets. This is a common form in the New Kingdom. The blade would have been sharpened on a wedge-shaped whetstone, and perhaps kept sharp by being placed in a wooden or leather case when not in use. The razor was one of a group of three discovered in the same house at Amarna. (T.H.)

73. 蘆葦籃
來自薩卡拉
後埃及時期（西元前 664-332 年）
蘆葦桿
420 x 410 x 130 mm

Basket
From Saqqara.
Late Period (664-332 BC)
Reeds

蘆葦籃

籃子是在日常生活中使用的一種常見物品。不同於木材，這些用於製作籃筐的材料很容易取得：蘆葦、棕櫚樹葉及草類等最為常見。在古埃及，人們運用一系列不同的技術來製作籃筐。這類方法被用來製造各類物件，包括涼鞋與傢俱。此件樣品展示出盤繞技術，是最常獲得證實，也是樣式最為多變者。關於形成籃框的盤繞構造，是將數捆纖維以螺旋狀緊緊包裹，以製作成一個圓形或橢圓形的底部。個別的盤繞構造再透過縫合來相互連接，且時至今日，埃及仍採用這種技術。

籃子的主要目的很可能用於儲存，因其提供了一個堅實且輕量的容器以保存或運輸其他物件。有眾多籃框樣本在墓葬中存留下來，說明其在來世的持續效用。此件樣品來自薩卡拉（Saqqara），很可能屬於當地繁忙的聖獸墓地部落。（作者：C.P.）

Basket

Baskets were a common class of object used in daily life. Unlike wood, the materials that were used to create basketry were easily obtainable: reeds, palm leaves and grasses are the most common. A series of different techniques were employed to create basketry in ancient Egypt. These methods were used to create items including sandals and furniture. This example exhibits the coiling technique, which is the most frequently attested and also the most versatile. Coiled construction involves forming a basket by coiling tightly wrapped bundles of fibres in a spiral to create a circular or oval base. The individual coils of this foundation are then bound by stitching, and this technique remains in use in Egypt today.

The chief purpose of baskets is likely to have been for storage, as they provided a sturdy but lightweight container in which to hold or transport other objects. Many examples survive from tombs illustrating their continued utility in the afterlife. This example comes from Saqqara and likely belonged to the community that served the busy sacred animal necropolis at the site. (C.P.)

74. 美杜姆陶碗
來自高艾爾喀勃，656 號墓室
古王國時期，第 5 王朝（西元前 2494-2345 年）
陶器
260 x 258 x 103 mm

Meidum Bowl
From Qau el-Kebir, Tomb 656
Old Kingdom, Dynasty 5 (2494-2345 BC)
Ceramic

美杜姆陶碗

這只碗來自於一名男子的墓地，其地位較低，居住在埃及中部，距離首都都甚遠。這是兩件物品當中的一件，與其未經木乃伊化的遺體一同埋葬。兩件物品皆為盆狀物：一個是碗，另一個則是罐子。不像石頭或金屬，陶器相對而言較廉價，因此陶製容器在各個社會階層皆方便取得。此處展出的碗稱為「美杜姆碗」。這種類型的碗很容易辨識，其帶有彎邊以及拋光的櫻桃紅滑面。美杜姆碗在古王國時期是最精緻的陶瓷器皿之一。此類型是古王國特有造型，之後時期便不再製作，其邊緣的特有形狀可用來確定各個碗製造的具體時代。美杜姆碗在生者與死者之間都受到使用，並同時在住宅區和陵墓中發現。有人推測早期的美杜姆碗是用於牛奶發酵，同時亦有人推測其為裝飾用品，用來盛裝漂浮的蓮花。這些類型的碗可能有許多用途。此類容器是當地所製造，並且不太可能被廣泛交易。（作者：L.A.W.）

Meidum Bowl

This bowl comes from the burial of a lower-class man who lived in Middle Egypt, far from the capital. It was one of only two objects to be buried with his un-mummified body. Both objects were pots: one a bowl, the other a jar. Pottery was relatively inexpensive, unlike stone or metal, and therefore pottery vessels were accessible to all strata of society. The bowl shown here is called a 'Meidum Bowl'. This type of bowl is easily distinguishable by its recurved rim and polished, cherry-red slip. Meidum Bowls were one of the finest ceramic wares in the Old Kingdom. The type was exclusive to the Old Kingdom and was not made in later periods; the specific shape of the rim can be used to determine a specific dynasty for each bowl's manufacture. Meidum Bowls were used by both the living and the dead, being found both in settlements and in tombs. It has been suggested that early Meidum Bowls were used in milk fermentation; it has also been suggested they were ornamental, used to hold floating lotuses. It is probable that these types of bowls actually served many purposes. These vessels were manufactured locally and it is unlikely that they were widely traded. (L.A.W.)

美杜姆陶碗、陶罐、陶盆

這三件盆狀物品來自同一名男子的墓地，其規模小而完整。該墓地僅包含骨骼本身、一只木製棺材，以及五件盆狀物品。這些容器代表著古王國時期常見的陪葬陶器。此處展示的美杜姆碗，是古王國時期特有的類式，經常用作推測年代的標準（請參見本書編號74）。陶瓷水盆有手工完成的平底、略帶閃爍的表面，以及平直的邊緣。水壺則有些精雕細琢、平底、肩部高，以及模造邊緣。陶藝師傅藉由拉動邊緣製作一個小壺口，很可能是當粘土呈半乾狀時便在其中一側形成端點。水壺與水盆很可能是用於沐浴，並曾當做一個個體來使用。水壺與水盆有時是用銅製成，並可在貴族陵墓中發現，包括與實際尺寸相同的容器及模型。陶瓷可做為銅的替代品，使該類型在平民階層中更易取得。儘管成本較低，這些陶製容器亦製作精良，是古王國時期精緻器皿的良好範例。這些陶器表面製作精細，每一件都塗有一層厚實的櫻桃紅滑面，然後加以磨光。這些陶器被發現置於棺木頂部，美杜姆碗在其軀幹上方，而水壺和水盆則在其骨盆上方。（作者：L.A.W.）

Tomb group including a Meidum Bowl, Ewer, and Basin

These three pots are from the same small, intact burial of a man. The tomb included only the skeleton itself, a wooden coffin, and five pots. These vessels represent common burial pottery from the Old Kingdom. The bowl shown here is called a Meidum Bowl and is a distinctive Old Kingdom form frequently used as a dating criterion (see #74). The ceramic basin has a hand-finished flat base, slightly flaring walls, and direct rim. The ewer is a bit more elaborate, with flat base, high shoulder, and modelled rim. The potter made a small spout by pulling on the rim, likely when the clay was leather hard, to form a point to one side. The ewer and basin were probably intended for ablutions and would have been used as a unit. Ewers and basins were sometimes made of copper and have been found in elite tombs both as full-sized vessels and as models. Ceramic was an affordable alternative to copper, making the forms more accessible to the non-elite classes. Despite being less costly, these pottery vessels are very well made and are good examples of Old Kingdom fine wares. They are also finely finished, each being coated with a thick, cherry-red slip and then burnished. These pots were found placed on top of the coffin, the Meidum Bowl over his torso and the ewer and basin over his pelvis.
(L.A.W.)

75. 美杜姆陶碗
來自高艾爾喀勃，1108 號墓室
古王國時期，第 5 王朝（西元前 2494-2345 年）
陶器
275 x 275 x 82mm

Meidum Bowl
From Qau el-Kebir, Tomb 1108
Old Kingdom, Dynasty 5 (2494-2345 BC)
Ceramic

76. 陶盆
來自高艾爾喀勃，1108 號墓室
古王國時期，第 5 王朝（西元前 2494-2345 年）
陶器
210 x 158 x 150mm

Basin
From Qau el-Kebir, Tomb 1108
Old Kingdom, Dynasty 5 (2494-2345 BC)
Ceramic

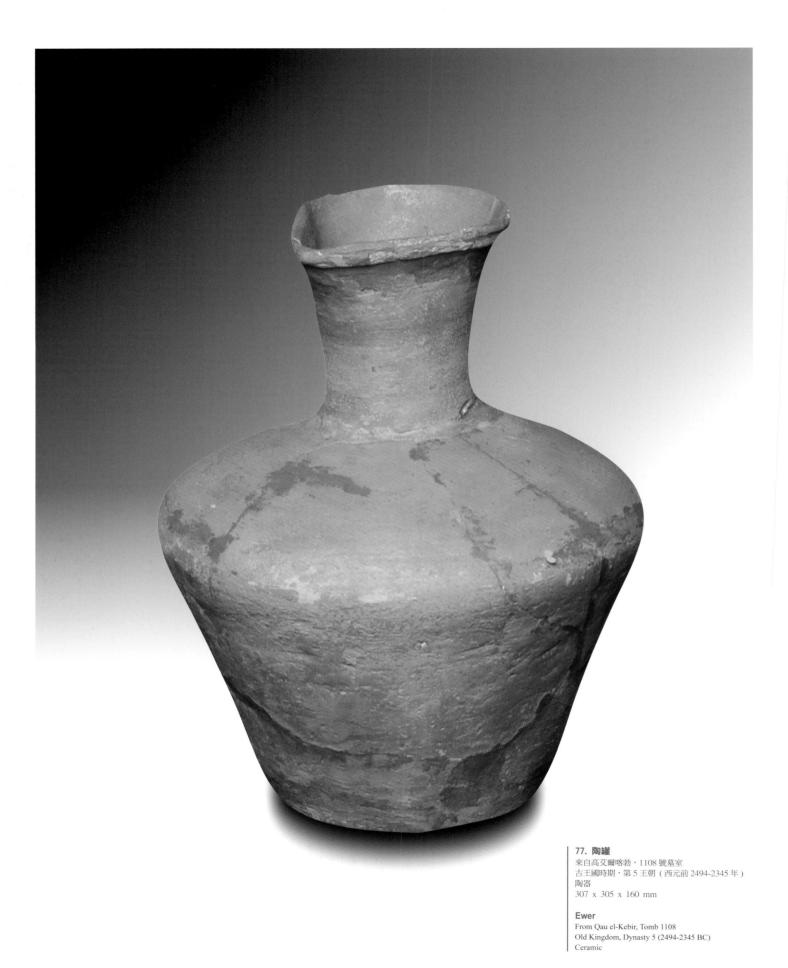

77. 陶罐
來自高艾爾喀勃，1108 號墓室
古王國時期，第 5 王朝（西元前 2494-2345 年）
陶器
307 x 305 x 160 mm

Ewer
From Qau el-Kebir, Tomb 1108
Old Kingdom, Dynasty 5 (2494-2345 BC)
Ceramic

78. 荷花飲杯
來自阿比多斯，E153 號墓室
新王國時期， 第 19 王朝（西元前 1295-1186 年）
彩陶
140 x 84 x 84 mm

Blue Water Lily Chalice
From Abydos, Tomb E153
New Kingdom, Dynasty 19 (1295-1186 BC)
Faience

荷花飲杯

儘管在墓地以及容器上經常被描繪的花卉通常被認定為蓮花，但此處呈現的植物卻是荷花：蓮花（Nelumbo 與 Nymphaea 截然不同）於新王國時期並未在埃及出現。古埃及人熟知兩個品種的荷花：即 Nymphaea cerulean Savigny （藍色）與 Nymphaea lotus Linnaeus Willdenow （白色）。開花週期為期三天的藍荷花象徵著重生以及太陽之通道，在古王國時期因奈夫圖神（Nefertum）而受到認識，文中提及「在拉神（Re）鼻子旁的荷花…」。埃及貴族們希望能在死亡中轉化為這種花卉，在圖坦卡門〔Tutankhamun〕陵墓出土的一塊著名的石膏木雕上，描寫到「這朵純淨的（荷花）…在拉神（Re）鼻子旁」。

有人推測，這些白荷花造型的杯子是做為酒器，而那些仿藍荷花者則在儀式中使用，特別是關於死亡的儀式，這或許能解釋為何此聖杯會在墓地中發現。除了宜人的香味之外，荷花花朵與根部含有麻醉物質，在與葡萄酒或啤酒混合後，能有助於打破生者與死者之間的壁壘。在一些新王國時期的石碑上曾描述到在死者面前倒入液體類祭品到荷花形狀的容器內；此處的容器可能同時象徵著死者重生，以及生者與死者能在儀式活動中進行互動的能力。

荷花聖杯之設計首次在第十八王朝獲得證實，並在新王國時期獲得發展：此樣品是第十九王朝的典型作品，以其長形杯體及鐘形邊緣為特色。花瓣和葉子是以凹浮雕模造，雕刻線條佈滿每一片葉子，邊緣有一圈線條。杯腳已經過重製，但其原本是經過模造而成並各別連接到杯子。（作者：N.H.）

Blue Water Lily Chalice

Although the flowers frequently depicted in tomb scenes and on vessels are commonly identified as lotuses, the plants represented were lilies: the lotus (Nelumbo as opposed to Nymphaea) was not present in Egypt in the New Kingdom. Two species of water lily were known to the ancient Egyptians: Nymphaea cerulean Savigny (blue) and Nymphaea lotus Linnaeus Willdenow (white). The three-day flowering cycle of the blue lily came to symbolise rebirth and the passage of the sun, and was identified by the Old Kingdom with the god Nefertum, the "water lily at the nose of Re". In death elite Egyptians hoped to be transformed into this flower, and it is as "this pure (water lily) that ... is at Re's nose" that Tutankhamun is depicted in a famous plastered wooden sculpture from his tomb.

It has been suggested that cups in the form of the white lily were used as drinking vessels and those imitating blue lilies for ritualistic purposes, particularly in relation to the cult of the dead, which may explain why this chalice was found in a tomb. Aside from a pleasant scent, lily blossoms and roots contain narcotic substances that when mixed with wine or beer could help to break down the barrier between the living and the dead. The act of pouring liquid offerings into lily-shaped vessels before the deceased is depicted on several New Kingdom stelae: the vessel in this context may be symbolic of both the renewal of the recipient and the ability of the living and the dead to interact during ritual activity.

The design of lily chalices, which are first attested in Dynasty 18, developed during the course of the New Kingdom: this example is typical of Dynasty 19 with its long body and flared rim. The petals and leaves are moulded in low relief, with incised lines running up each leaf, and a single line around the rim. The foot has been reconstructed but would originally have been moulded and attached separately. (N.H.)

鐘形碗

約在公元前 50 年左右，在敘利亞海岸發現吹製玻璃。以小型容器和珠子呈現的製造用玻璃在整個美索不達米亞和埃及獲得佐證，自由吹製讓容器造型琳瑯滿目並帶有裝飾新意，且玻璃生產已不再是一種昂貴和勞力密集的程序。吹製玻璃的過程開始於在一根長吹管末端收集熔融玻璃，工匠在此處將空氣吹入其中以膨脹成泡，並操縱吹管塑形，以便創造一個形狀。通常容器上仍留有痕跡，無論是出於當其仍在吹管尾端時各種用於塑形的工具，或是幾乎位於底部，在工匠斷開吹管以完成容器頂部作業時，用來固定容器的鐵棒（固體金屬桿）所造成。沿海商城亞歷山大港是奢華玻璃製造的中心，尤其是浮雕技術，但其亦有可能是玻璃工業之樞紐，將奢華製品分銷至東西兩方。到了晚古時期，玻璃工藝被公認具有極高工藝地位，而若干優惠措施，例如豁免強制公共服務，亦由康士坦丁皇帝在狄奧多西法典（Theodosian Code）中頒布，此舉可證實工匠所具有之價值。

此具有深度的鐘形碗可看到製造過程中所產生的氣泡，由於此類型之碗在埃及法尤姆的卡拉尼斯（Karanis）被大量發現，因此通常稱為卡拉尼斯深碗。此容器有一實用襯墊，且邊緣形狀外捲，這可能是因為該容器原本有個蓋子。此類型容器很少在埃及以外的地方發現。（作者：E.L.）

Bell-shaped Bowl

By around 50 BC, most likely on the Syrian coast, glass blowing was discovered. Manufacturing glass was well attested in small vessels and beads from throughout Mesopotamia and Egypt, but it was free blowing that allowed for an endless variety of vessel forms and decorative innovations as well as glass production was no longer a costly and labour intensive process. The process of glass blowing started with collection of molten glass at the end of a long blowpipe, where the craftsman would blow air into the mass so as to inflate a bubble while the pipe was manipulated so as to create a shape. Often there remain marks on vessels, either from the variety of tools used to refine the shape of the piece while it was still on the end of the blow pipe, or almost always on the base, when the pontil (a solid metal rod) was applied to hold the vessel while the craftsman cracked off the blow pipe to allow further work to finish the top of the vessel. Alexandria, the coastal emporium, was the centre of luxury glass manufacturing, in particular the cameo technique, but it was likely also the hub of the glass industry for distribution of luxury products to the East and West. By the Late Antique period, glassmaking was recognised as a high status craft and concessions, such as exemption from compulsory public service, were granted by Emperor Constantine in the Theodosian Code, attesting to the value placed on craftsmen.

This deep bell-shaped bowl with visible air bubbles from the manufacturing process is often referred to as the Karanis deep bowl, since a large group of this type was found at Karanis in the Fayum, Egypt. The vessel has an applied pad base and outward rolled rim shape, which was likely because the vessel originally had a lid. This type of vessel is rarely found outside of Egypt. (E.L.)

錐形的燈或杯子

簡單的圓錐形容器造型向來被認定為各種燈具或燒杯，且似乎這種簡單並以工業規模進行生產的造型相當適合任一形式。到公元 300 年，玻璃油燈越來越受到歡迎，不僅在家庭及工作坊內，並且在地位較高的地方亦是如此，例如教堂。支架及保留下來的玻璃吊燈顯示，眾多玻璃容器能聚集在一起以強化光線。儘管此物件有一個相應的盤繞底座，使其能夠直立於平面上，卻不一定是一只杯子，因為其框邊附近的玻璃線條能讓該容器更容易扣住支架邊緣。（作者：E.L.）

Conical Lamp or Beaker

Simple conical vessel forms have been variously identified as lamps or beakers and it seems this form, uncomplicated to manufacture on an industrial scale, was suited to either form. By AD 300, glass oil lamps were gaining in popularity, not only in homes and in workshops, but also in high status places like churches. Brackets and surviving chandeliers show that multiple glass vessels could be grouped together so as to intensify the light. Although this object has an applied base coil which allows it to stand upright on a flat surface, it is not necessarily a cup since the single line of trailed glass near the rim would allow the vessel to catch the edge of a stand more easily. (E.L.)

80. 錐形的燈或杯子
來自高艾爾喀勃，7780 號墓室
科普特時期 (西元 300-400 年)
褐色玻璃
156 x 80 x 78 mm

Conical Lamp or Beaker
From Qau el Kebir (Antaeopolis) tomb 7780
Coptic Period (AD 300-400)
Blown glass

有四個把手的玻璃罐

此作品由球根狀壺體延伸為鐘形邊緣的高壺頸，但真正令此作品別具一格的是位於邊緣底下，壺頸部藍色玻璃上的明顯線條，以及四只同樣由藍色玻璃製成的手柄。至少有一只手柄與明顯線條相融合。這種以無色玻璃搭配對比之綠色或藍色手柄的玻璃罐，手柄數目由二至九皆有，其添加目的是做為裝飾。此類型容器被發現於埃及，但有人推測該造型起源於地中海東部（可能是敘利亞）。（作者：E.L.）

Jug with Four Handles

The bulbous body of the jug transitions into a high neck with flared rim, but what makes the piece exceptional are the accent threads of blue glass at the collar of the piece and just below the rim and the four added handles which are also in blue glass. At least one handle is joined to the accent threads. The specimen type of colourless glass with contrasting green or blue handles has anywhere from two to nine handles that have been added for decoration. The vessel type is found in Egypt but it is suggested that the form originated in the Eastern Mediterranean (possibly Syria). (E.L.)

81. 有四個把手的玻璃罐
來自埃及
科普特時期 (西元 350-450 年)
褐色玻璃
70 x 47 x 45 mm

Jug with Four Handles
From Egypt
Coptic Period (AD 350-450)
Blown glass

82. 打磨工具
來自巴達里, 3400 號現場
前王國時期（西元前 4000-3200 年）
玄武岩
135 x 125 x 31, 172 x 170 x 70 mm

Pounding Stone and Platform
From Badari, Locality 3400
Predynastic Period (4000-3200 BC)
Basalt or Dolorite

打磨工具

錘石或搗具在古埃及各個時期中被廣泛應用於採石場、粗糙石頭，以及敲擊片狀打火石工具上。這些錘石是從採石場及國內環境取得。一般都是由堅硬的石頭製成，例如玄武岩、石英岩或粗玄岩。從巴達里（Badari）出土的搗石及平台初期可能是設計用於研磨穀物等簡單任務。然而，奇怪的是這種手磨器具是呈圓形而且非常小。此工具組的另一個不尋常方面為磨石及平台之搭配平面。手磨平台一般呈長方形，並帶有凹槽或孔洞，可讓穀物存放其中等待研磨，而磨石則相對渾圓，以便能恰好嵌入凹槽。

根據館長筆記顯示，此平台與磨床可能是用來錘打銅箔。很少有人知道早期埃及的金屬工人如何執行工藝。首篇冶金介紹直到古王國晚期才在墓室浮雕與彩繪中出現。位於上埃及阿代瑪（Adaïma）勘測現場，可追溯至埃及前王國晚期內加達（Naqada）第二階段的金屬文物顯示，銅斧或銅錛已可公開鑄模並經由捶打而製成。極少數金屬物件在此時期保存下來，因此說明難以重現埃及人所採用的冶煉、鑄造，以及精加工技術。銅以及其他貴重金屬在埃及是寶貴與稀有的資源，導致人們經常僅為了獲取其中的金屬而盜墓。（作者：J.A.H.）

Pounding Stone and Platform

Hammer stones or pounders were commonly used during all periods of ancient Egyptian history to quarry and rough dress stone and percussion flake flint tools. These hammer stones have been recovered from quarries and domestic contexts. They are generally made of hard stone such as basalt, quartzite or dolorite. It may at first appear that this grinding stone and platform recovered from the site of Badari were designed for the simple task of grinding grain. However, it is unusual for such hand mills to be circular and so small. Another unusual aspect of this tool kit is the matching plane surfaces of the grinder and the platform. Hand mill platforms generally are rectangular and have a groove or cavity in which grain can rest to be ground and mill stones are relatively rounded so that they can fit into this groove.

Curatorial notes suggest that this platform and grinder may have been used to hammer copper foil. Little is known about how early Egyptian metal workers practised their craft. The first representations of metallurgy do not appear until late Old Kingdom mastaba tomb reliefs and paintings. Metal artefacts dating to the late Predynastic Naqada II phase at the site of Adaïma in Upper Egypt indicate that copper axe heads or adzes had been cast in open moulds and finished by hammering. Few metal objects survive from this period, so it has proven difficult to reconstruct the smelting, casting, and finishing techniques the Egyptians employed. Copper, as well as other precious metals, was so valuable and scarce a resource in Egypt that people frequently robbed graves simply to retrieve the metal that lay within. (J.A.H.)

83. 刀
來自阿瑪納北部，U.36.46, 29/141 號房屋
新王國時期，第 18 王朝，阿肯納頓統治時期
(西元前 1352-1336 年)
銅合金，纖維
117 x 15 x 10 mm

Knife
From Amarna, North Suburb, House U.36.46, 29/141
New Kingdom, Dynasty 18, reign of Akhenaten
(1352-1336 BC)
Copper-alloy and fibre

刀

這把小刀是由一種粗略鑄造的金屬所製成，其後再進行錘打和加工完成最後的形狀與鋒利度。手柄部份源自未經加工的金屬厚片，其在重疊後以纖維線段包裹起來，讓使用者能舒適且安全地握住刀柄。像這樣的小刀必定是用在細膩、嚴謹的工作上。也許這把刀亦屬於書記員配備之一，可用於畫筆和紙莎草紙的修邊。（作者：T.H.）

Knife

This small knife would have been made from a roughly-cast blank of metal which was then hammered and worked into its final shape and sharpness. The handle was formed from the unworked end of the metal blank, which was doubled over and wrapped around with fibre thread to provide a comfortable and secure grip for the user.

A small knife like this must have been intended for delicate, precise work. Perhaps it formed part of a scribe's equipment, used for trimming brushes and sheets of papyrus. (T.H.)

84. 扁斧
來自阿瑪納北部，U.35.24，29/255 號房屋
新王國時期，第 18 王朝，阿肯納頓統治時期
（西元前 1352-1336 年）
銅合金
195 x 51 x 50 mm

Adze blade
From Amarna, North Suburb, House U.35.24, 29/255
New Kingdom, Dynasty 18, reign of Akhenaten
(1352-1336 BC)
Copper-alloy

扁斧

這件厚重的青銅工具應該是由厚片金屬鑄造製作而成，在其中一端鍛打為尖銳的刀刃，另一端則成為配件接口。最後刀刃會以大約 60 度的角度固定於木柄，並以生牛皮繩捆紮牢固。這種類型的鑿是用來切割和雕塑木材以及石灰岩等軟質石頭。這個尺寸是用於較繁重、粗糙的工作，而更精細的塑形會經由較小的車床和鑿子進行加工。

金屬工具實在太過珍貴而無法輕易丟棄，無論是金屬本身的價值或投入其中的工藝。破損或破舊的工具會交還給鐵匠進行熔化重製。阿瑪納（Amarna）遺址在阿肯納頓（Akhenaten）死後逐漸被廢棄，且其貴重物品亦遭受離開該地的居民大量掠奪，因此像這樣較大的金屬工具很少能在該遺址尋獲。這把鑄連同其他兩把是在一座房屋附屬建築中所發現。（作者：T.H.）

Adze blade

This hefty bronze tool would have been worked up from a cast blank of metal, hammered into a cutting edge at one end and the other turned into a socket for attachment. The resulting blade would have been fixed into a wooden handle at an angle of approximately 60 degrees, and lashed securely into place with rawhide thongs. Adzes of this form were used to cut and shape wood and softer stones like limestone. One this size would have been intended for heavier, rougher work, and more precise shaping would have been carried out with smaller lathes and chisels.

Metal tools were too precious, both in terms of the value of the metal and the craftsmanship put into them, to be discarded lightly. Broken or worn-out tools were returned to the smith who would melt them down and re-make them. The site of Amarna was abandoned gradually after the death of Akhenaten, and was largely stripped of its valuables by the departing inhabitants, so large metal tools like this are rare finds at the site. This adze was discovered with two other ones in a complex of outhouses. (T.H.)

刀

此薄型刀是由大衛・藍道麥克艾佛（David Randall-MacIver）及亞瑟・西・麥斯（Arthur C. Mace）在阿比多斯的賽特胡〔Sitepehu〕陵墓的北側所發現。其頂部為一單片彎刃，且帶有狹長手柄，其底部寬度略增。底部向外彎曲，形成第二把刀刃。頂部刀刃稍微向後彎曲，在其下端形成一個彎鉤，頂部則有些上翻。

開鑿者將此物件稱為切割刀，或許可用來切割亞麻布。然而，在與其他新王國陵墓所發現之同類型的刀比較後顯示，這種刀其實是一種如手術刀般的多功能剃刀。這類型物件是新王國時期特有的裝飾用品，且似乎是從中王國時期帶有各種凹口的剃刀發展而成。在同一剃鬚設備中，這個剃刀常常和另一種帶有手柄的剃刀同時出現。這種如手術刀般的剃刀名稱是 dega，且儘管使用該剃刀的方式並不是非常清楚，但其卻可能提供更精細的剃鬚過程。其形狀與其他被發現的第十八王朝時期之剃刀相同，而第十九王朝時的剃刀則較花俏，頂部帶有明顯彎鉤，底部則向外開展。

該剃刀連同其他各種物件在陵墓中被發現，包括書記員的木製調色板、木製假鬍鬚、雪花石卡諾皮克罐、包含在本書中的青銅矛尖，以及金製的紅碧玉戒指、一塊帶有圖特摩斯三世之橢圓裝飾的彩釉飾板，以及一對青銅鑷子。（作者：A.H.）

Knife

This slim knife was found at Abydos in the tomb of Sitepehu in the north section of cemetery D by David Randall-MacIver and Arthur C. Mace. It consists of a single curved blade at the top with a long narrow shaft that widens slightly at the bottom. The bottom is curved outwards and forms a second blade. The top cutting edge curves back slightly to form a hook at its lower end and the top is turned over a little.

The excavators termed this object a cutting-out knife, which could have perhaps been used for cutting linen cloth. However, a comparison of knives of similar type found in other New Kingdom tombs indicates that this knife was actually a multifunctional scalpel-like razor. Objects of this type were characteristic toilette implements of the New Kingdom and appear to have developed from the notched variety of razor found during the Middle Kingdom. In the same shaving equipment, this razor often appears alongside the hafted mechak razor. The name of this scalpel-like razor was dega, and, although it is not entirely clear how this razor was used, it may have provided more precision in shaving. Its shape is typical of similar razors found during Dynasty 18, which become fancier in Dynasty19 with noticeably curved hooks at the top and widely flared bottoms.

It was found in tomb D9 with a variety of other objects, including the wooden palette of the scribe Inhertmes, the wooden false beard, the alabaster canopic jar of Neb, and the bronze spearhead included in this catalogue, as well as gold and red jasper rings, a glazed plaque with the cartouche of Thutmose III, and a pair of bronze tweezers. (A.H.)

85. 刀
來自阿比多斯，D9 號墓室
新王國時期，第 18 王朝，圖特摩斯三世統治時期 (西元前 1479-1425 年)
銅合金
167 x 20 x 2 mm

Knife
From Abydos, Tomb D9
New Kingdom, Dynasty 18, reign of Thutmose III
(1479-1425 BC)
Copper alloy

魚鉤

尼羅河的魚是古埃及人的主要食物來源，這一點也不奇怪；由於太陽的熱度，魚在捕獲後不久就必須食用，或是加工乾燥並儲存於陶罐中。用鉤子和線垂釣或使用魚叉似乎曾是新王國時期廣為流行的消遣，且偶爾會描繪在社會精英的陵墓中。最嚴肅的捕魚是由男性帶著織網乘船或於河岸旁進行拖網作業來完成，織網會利用小型鉛塊或石灰岩加重，並在水中拖曳。

這種單鉤金屬魚鉤在末端有一個附有線圈的垂直軸，用來連接以亞麻或亞麻纖維製成的線。這種鉤子可能被列入陪葬品中，讓死者能在來世繼續享受這項釣魚運動，或為自己提供食物。某些魚類，例如羅非魚（Tilapia），與重生有關，而釣魚活動與死後重生之間的象徵性連接，可能是在陵墓內存放釣魚設備的另一個原因。（作者：N.H.）

Fish Hook

Perhaps unsurprisingly, fish from the Nile river was a major food source for the ancient Egyptians. Due to the heat of the sun, fish had to be eaten shortly after it was caught, or prepared and dried then stored in pottery jars. Angling with a hook and line or harpoon seems to have been a popular New Kingdom pastime, and is occasionally depicted in elite tombs. Most serious fishing was done with woven nets by men in boats or by trawling from the river banks. The nets were weighted with small lead or limestone sinkers and dragged through the water.

This single-barbed metal fish hook has a straight shaft with a coil at the end for attachment to a line that would have been made from linen or flax. The hook may have been included among grave goods to enable the deceased to continue enjoying the sport of fishing in the afterlife, or to provide himself with food. Certain fish, such as the Tilapia were associated with rebirth, and the symbolic connection between the act of fishing and being reborn after death may be another reason for the deposition of fishing equipment in tombs. (N.H.)

86. 魚鉤
來自阿比多斯，T3 號墓室
新王國時期，第 18 王朝（西元前 1540-1295 年）
銅合金
48 x 21 x 3 mm

Fish Hook
From Abydos, Tomb T3
New Kingdom, Dynasty 18 (1540-1295 BC)
Copper alloy

研缽和杵

這裡展示的研缽與兩個杵是由湯瑪斯‧艾瑞克‧皮特（Thomas Eric Peet）在阿比多斯開鑿墓園期間尋獲。皮特在某陵墓的井狀通道下方發現這些物件。該墓園座落於大窪地南部，通往將阿比多斯一分為二的大峽谷。在此處存在著不同時期的墓園建築。命名為字母 T 的陵墓座落於耕地區邊緣陡峭斜坡的南面。

T 陵墓中包含一個通往北部及南部的房間。研缽與杵，連同一組物件，便是在該井狀通道內發現，包括九個敘利亞式暗黃色粘土花瓶、兩個藍釉聖甲蟲（其中一個帶有圖特摩斯一世的名字）、三件粉紅珊瑚、一個青銅鉤和鑷子、一個帶有蓋子的小型雪花石化妝墨罐等。在陵墓的南側房間內，皮特發現了一些曾受擾亂的墓葬遺跡，其中包括一名孩童的墓葬。

研缽和杵是第十八王朝許多大型墓園中經常發現的常見配備。其往往是由埃及雪花石膏（方解石）所製成，因為該材質極具柔軟性，且加工廉價又簡便。自埃及前王國時期至古王國早期，雪花石主要是用來製作容器，而新王國時期的出土次數則有限。地點位於西奈半島及東部沙漠，顏色為白色或黃白色，其紋理往往如大理石般。

研缽和杵的作用主要是搗碎並研磨固體顏料。兩者在整個古代世界均與美食和醫藥相關。此研缽之造型為凸邊與方形手把，是新王國時期的特色。在第三中間時期期間，研缽形狀則改為直邊；而在希臘羅馬時期，手把部份則變得更加傾斜。研缽內部似乎有磨損及使用跡象。（作者：A.H.）

Mortar and Pestles

The mortar and two pestles displayed here were recovered by Thomas Eric Peet during his excavations of the cemeteries of Abydos. Peet found these objects in the lower part of the shaft of tomb T3 located in Cemetery S (the South Cemetery). This cemetery is located south of the great depression which leads to the Great Valley at Abydos and which divides Abydos in two halves. Here, there exists a complex of cemeteries of various periods. The tombs designated with the letter 'T' lay in the southerly portion of a steep slope on the edge of the cultivation.

Tomb T3 contained a chamber to the north and south. The mortar and pestles were discovered with a group of objects found in the shaft, including nine vases of buff clay of Syrian type, two blue glaze scarabs (one bearing the name of Thutmose I), three pieces of pink organ coral, a bronze hook and tweezers, and a small alabaster kohl pot with lid, among other finds. In the south chamber of the tomb, Peet discovered the remains of several disturbed burials, including one of a child.

Mortar and pestles were common equipment found in many large cemeteries of the Dynasty18. They were often made of Egyptian alabaster (calcite) because of its extreme softness and its ability to be worked cheaply and easily. Alabaster was predominantly used to make stone vessels from the Predynastic to the early Old Kingdom with limited occurrence in the New Kingdom. It occurs in the Sinai and the Eastern desert and is a white or yellowish white colour, often striped like marble.

The function of mortar and pestles was primarily to pound and grind solid pigments. They were associated with cuisine and medicine throughout the ancient world. The form of this mortar, with convex sides and square bottom handles, is typical of the New Kingdom. During the Third Intermediate Period, the mortar shape changed to straight sides, and in the Graeco-Roman Period, the handles became more sloped. The interior of this mortar seems to show signs of wear and use. (A.H.)

87. – 89. 研缽和杵
來自阿比多斯，T3 號墓室
新王國時期，第 18 王朝 (西元前 1540-1295 年)
埃及雪花石膏
80 x 60 x 60, 79 x 25 x 25, 69 x 18 x 18 mm

Mortar and Pestles
From Abydos, tomb T3
New Kingdom, Dynasty 18 (1550-1295 BC)
Egyptian alabaster

木槌

木槌屬於各種工藝活動的標準工具組，如石砌工程、雕刻、木工以及造船等，並結合金屬鑿子或石鑿來使用。已有眾多物件出自所有法老時期中，並且自古王國到新王國時期經常在陵墓中被描繪出來，以展示上述活動，例如，位於薩卡拉（Saqqara）的第六王朝尼安克克努姆（Niankhkhum）和克努姆霍特普（Khnumhotep）陵墓以及位於貝尼哈珊（Beni Hassan）的第十二王朝巴凱特（Baket）三世陵墓中的雕塑工作坊，還有位於西底比斯的謝赫阿卜杜勒古爾奈（Sheikh Abd el-Qurna），第十八王朝萊克米爾（Rekhmire）陵墓之石砌建築。其中描繪往往與此展品之木槌類型略有不同。前者槌頭較為細長，而後者則是鐘形槌頭且中間部份帶有寬槽。兩種類型皆雕刻自單件木材，且帶有渾圓把手。鐘形槌較常見，特別是在古王國之後各個時期。凹槽部份應是刻意雕刻出來用於置放金屬帶以避免木槌分裂，或者是因鑿子不斷衝擊而造成。此件展品之手把處展現出高度的光面處理，以及因頻繁且密集使用而形成的光澤。（作者：C.W.）

Mallet

Mallets belong to the set of the standard tools in various crafts activities such as stone masonry, sculpture, carpentry and ship building, where they are used in combination with metal or stone chisels. Numerous examples are known from all pharaonic periods and they are often depicted in tomb scenes from the Old to New Kingdom showing the aforementioned activities, e.g. sculpture workshops in the Dynasty 6 tomb of Niankhkhum and Khnumhotep at Saqqara and in the Dynasty 12 tomb of Baket III in Beni Hassan, and stone masonry in the Dynasty 18 tomb of Rekhmire (TT 100) in Sheikh Abd el-Qurna, Western Thebes. The depictions often show a slightly different type of mallet than this example. The former have a more slender, elongated head, while the latter displays a bell-shaped head with a broad groove around the middle. Both types are carved out of a single piece of wood and have rounded handles. The bell-shaped type is more common, especially in the periods after the Old Kingdom. The groove could have either been intentionally carved for accommodating a metal band in order to prevent the mallet from splitting or be the result of the repeated impact of the chisel. This piece shows a strongly polished handle, with the polish being the result of frequent, intensive use. (C.W.)

90. 木槌
來自底比斯， 蒙圖荷泰普二世神廟
新王國時期，第 18 王朝 (西元前 1540-1295 年)
木
260 x 145 x 140 mm

Mallet
From Thebes, Deir el-Bahri, Temple of Mentuhotep II
New Kingdom, Dynasty 18 (1550-1295 BC)
Wood

鋤頭柄

此手柄由劣質的當地木材雕刻出，並將木製的鎬狀或鏟形刀片安放於插槽中，用布料固定（有些許痕跡遺留下來）。此手柄與刀刃會以麻繩或牛皮帶綑綁起來，手把上會切割一道凹痕，使帶子固定其中。

鎬與鋤頭是農業和建築業的基本工具，用於打散並移動土壤，而其實用意義使其能描繪於正式場景中。為死者的來世生活所準備的薩布提人俑用於替代工人角色，經常被描繪成手持鋤頭；而寺廟之基本儲存物也包含鋤頭與鎬的模型，並在該地的破土儀式中使用。（作者：T.H.）

Handle

Carved roughly out of poor-quality local wood, this handle would have held a wooden pick-like or spatulate blade in the socket, secured with cloth (of which some traces remain). The handle and blade would have been braced into position with a twisted linen or rawhide cord, half-way up the handle where a notch was cut to keep the cord in place.

Picks and hoes were essential tools in agriculture and construction for breaking up and shifting soil, and their practical significance ensured their depiction in formal contexts. Ushabti figures, which substituted as workers for the dead person in the afterlife, were usually depicted holding hoes, and temple foundation deposits contained models of the hoes and picks used in the ritual groundbreaking of the site. (T.H.)

91. 鋤頭柄
來自阿瑪納，TA79 號工人村
新王國時期，第 18 王朝，阿肯納頓統治時期
（西元前 1352-1336 年）
木，亞麻布
485 x 65 x 52 mm

Handle
From Amarna, Workmen's Village, TA79
New Kingdom, Dynasty 18, reign of Akhenaten
(1352-1336 BC)
Wood and linen

（92）

麻繩

儘管紙莎草、蘆葦以及草繩也會被使用，但埃及繩索最常使用粗糙且耐用的棗椰樹纖維製成。其尺寸與使用範圍包括家庭日常使用的細繩，到用於重型施工、相當於人類手腕粗細的繩索。

學者將此繩索外型歸類為 Z,3S：其整體為順時針 Z 形旋轉的繩索，由三條逆時針 S 形旋轉的細繩所形成。其中一端已被捆綁成一個滑結，使其能根據需要收緊或放鬆。已腐爛的另一端之排列方式則較不確定。（作者：T.H.）

Fragment of rope

Rope in Egypt was most commonly made from the coarse, durable fibres of the date palm tree, although papyrus, reed, and grass ropes were also used. It could range in size and use from thin cord for everyday use around the house to ropes the thickness of a human wrist used for heavy construction work.

This piece of rope is of a form scholars would classify as Z, 3s: it is overall a clockwise ("Z")-spun rope, formed from three anticlockwise ("s")-spun cords. One end has been tied into a slip-knot, allowing it to be tightened or loosened as needed. The arrangement of the more decayed other end is less certain. (T.H.)

92. 麻繩
來自阿瑪納
新王國時期，第 18 王朝，阿肯納頓統治時期
（西元前 1352-1336 年）
植物纖維
175 x 52 x 30 mm

Fragment of rope
From Amarna, possibly from the Workmen's Village
New Kingdom, Dynasty 18, reign of Akhenaten
(1352-1336 BC)
Plant fibre

木匙

這件被粗略削成的木材，其長柄末端為一個淺勺，作用無法理解。此勺太淺而難以做為湯匙使用，或許是一件多用途器具，可用於撥動、刮，以及攪拌。其在阿瑪納（Amarna）工人村落一間房屋廚房內樓梯底下的櫥櫃中被發現。

工人村落（由其首批開鑿者稱為東方村落，並同時進行街道命名與房屋編號）是一處獨立的居住地，大致位於阿瑪納主城市東方 1 公里處。其四面有外牆圍繞，面積約 70 平方公尺，區分為六條街道、十二間連棟房屋。其地點相對孤立，且其所在位置靠近阿瑪納皇家私人墓園，因而推測該遺址之作用為工人構建陵墓的根據地。

雖然工人村落的房屋幾乎以完全相同的平面設計建成，但其很快便加入個人元素。主要街道中某房屋的屋主便在其主臥室內安裝了一組石浴盆。（作者：T.H.）

Spoon

This crudely whittled piece of wood, with a shallow scoop at the end of a long handle, is enigmatic. Too shallow to be much use as a spoon, it may perhaps have been a multi-purpose implement for poking, scraping, and stirring. It was found in the under-stairs cupboard in the kitchen of a house in the Workmen's Village at Amarna.

The Workmen's Village (called the 'Eastern Village' by its first excavators, who also named the streets and numbered the houses) is a separate settlement which lies approximately 1km east of the main city of Amarna. It is a walled enclosure some 70 meters square, divided within into six streets of twelve terraced houses. The relative isolation of the site, and its location near the royal and private necropoleis of Amarna, suggest that it served as the base for the workmen building the tombs.

Although the houses in the Workmen's Village were originally built to nearly identical plans, they were soon personalised. The owner of 8 Main Street had installed a stone bath in the central room of his house. (T.H.)

93. 木匙
來自阿瑪納，8, 22/123 號房屋
新王國時期，第 18 王朝，阿肯納頓統治時期
（西元前 1352-1336 年）
木
362 x 40 x 32 mm

Spoon
From Amarna, Workmen's Village,
Main Street House 8, 22/123
New Kingdom, Dynasty 18, reign of Akhenaten
(1352-1336 BC)
Wood

（93）

釀造場模型組

農業、糧食生產以及工匠的木製模型場景在中王國早期是廣受歡迎的陪葬品。此模式的神奇用意在於提供食物、衣物和其他產品，以維持墓主來世的靈魂卡（ka）。這組物件與雕像是在中王國創建者蒙圖荷泰普（Nebhepetra Mentuhotep）二世之祭廟及墓塚內發現，最有可能是其中一名宮廷婦女的隨葬品

該模型容器有可能來自於啤酒廠模型。此類模式可能還包括麵包店，因為麵包和啤酒這兩種古埃及人飲食之主要原料，是產自相同設備與基本成份 — 小麥、大麥、酵母和水。該淺型大桶可能是代表用於發酵麵包混合物，即醪液容器。高大的圓柱型大桶將被用來過濾醪液，將啤酒液體轉移至高大的凸肩瓶。

男性雕像是否出自同一模型尚不確定。此蹲姿男性雕像為各類模型的通用類型，包括在釀酒廠、糧倉以及船隻中。其皮膚被塗成紅色，是埃及藝術中男性的典型代表。兩個站姿雕像較可能是用來代表書記員或其他官員。他們的皮膚呈黃色，而非常見的紅棕色，表示其職業使他們能夠在室內工作，而其前方帶有圍裙的偏長正式短裙，是地位較高的紳士之典型特徵。（作者：D.D.）

Figures From a Model Brewery

Wooden model scenes of agriculture, food production and craftspeople were popular funerary offerings during the early Middle Kingdom. Such models were intended magically to provide food, clothing and other products to sustain the ka of the tomb owner in the afterlife. This group of objects and figures was discovered in the mortuary temple and tomb complex of Nebhepetra Mentuhotep II, the founder of the Middle Kingdom, where they were most likely burial goods for one of the women of the royal court.

The model vessels probably come from a model or models of a brewery. It is likely such a model also included a bakery, since bread and beer, both staples of the ancient Egyptian diet, were produced in the same facilities and from the same basic ingredients -- emmer wheat, barley, yeast and water. The shallow vat probably represents the container for the fermenting bread mixture known as mash. The tall cylindrical vat would have been used to strain the mash, leaving the liquid beer to be transferred into the tall, shouldered jars.

Whether the male figures derive from the same model is uncertain. The squatting male figure is a versatile type that was used in a variety of models, including breweries, granaries and boats. His skin is painted red, as is typical for representations of men in Egyptian art. The two standing figures are more likely to portray scribes or other officials. Their yellow, rather than the more common reddish brown, skin suggests that their professions allowed them to work indoors, while their long, formal kilts with aprons at the front are typical of relatively high status gentlemen. (D.D.)

94. 釀造場模型
來自底比斯，公主墓室
中王國時期，第 11 王朝，蒙圖荷泰普二世統治時期
（西元前 2055-2004 年）
木，顏料
109 x 50 x 40mm

Figures From a Model Brewery
From Thebes, Deir el-Bahri, Tomb of the Princesses
Middle Kingdom, Dynasty 11, reign of Mentuhotep II
(2055-2004 BC)
Wood, pigment

95. 釀造場模型
來自底比斯，公主墓室
中王國時期，第 11 王朝，蒙圖荷泰普二世統治時期
（西元前 2055-2004 年）
木，顏料
240 x 62 x 50mm

Figures From a Model Brewery
From Thebes, Deir el-Bahri, Tomb of the Princesses
Middle Kingdom, Dynasty 11, reign of Mentuhotep II
(2055-2004 BC)
Wood, pigment

96. 釀造場模型
來自底比斯，公主墓室
中王國時期，第 11 王朝，蒙圖荷泰普二世統治時期
（西元前 2055-2004 年）
木，顏料
192 x 45 x 35mm

Figures From a Model Brewery
From Thebes, Deir el-Bahri, Tomb of the Princesses
Middle Kingdom, Dynasty 11, reign of Mentuhotep II
(2055-2004 BC)
Wood, pigment

97. 釀造場模型
來自底比斯，公主墓室
中王國時期，第 11 王朝，蒙圖荷泰普二世統治時期
（西元前 2055-2004 年）
木，顏料
57 x 57 x 35 mm

Figures From a Model Brewery
From Thebes, Deir el-Bahri, Tomb of the Princesses
Middle Kingdom, Dynasty 11, reign of Mentuhotep II
(2055-2004 BC)
Wood, pigment

98. 釀造場模型
來自底比斯，公主墓室
中王國時期，第 11 王朝，蒙圖荷泰普二世統治時期
（西元前 2055-2004 年）
木，顏料
57 x 57 x 35 mm

Figures From a Model Brewery
From Thebes, Deir el-Bahri, Tomb of the Princesses
Middle Kingdom, Dynasty 11, reign of Mentuhotep II
(2055-2004 BC)
Wood, pigment

99. 釀造場模型
來自底比斯，公主墓室
中王國時期，第 11 王朝，蒙圖荷泰普二世統治時期
（西元前 2055-2004 年）
木，顏料
100 x 30 x 25 mm

Figures From a Model Brewery
From Thebes, Deir el-Bahri, Tomb of the Princesses
Middle Kingdom, Dynasty 11, reign of Mentuhotep II
(2055-2004 BC)
Wood, pigment

100. 釀造場模型
來自底比斯，公主墓室
中王國時期，第 11 王朝，蒙圖荷泰普二世統治時期
（西元前 2055-2004 年）
木，顏料
81 x 44 x 43 mm

Figures From a Model Brewery
From Thebes, Deir el-Bahri, Tomb of the Princesses
Middle Kingdom, Dynasty 11, reign of Mentuhotep II
(2055-2004 BC)
Wood, pigment

酒罐

此圓柱狀雙耳酒瓶帶有模糊的僧侶體銘文，內容敘述一名叫做阿蒙霍特普（Amenhotep）的男子之農產品產業。此酒罈製作於一個輪子上方，有一個圓形底座，並已用泥塞密封，其上印有內容物與出處等資訊。除了銘文之外，該容器並未經過修飾：呈現白色之褪色作用是由於黏土內的鹽份在罈身乾燥後移動到表面所致。

葡萄酒製作過程以簡略形式被描繪於社會精英的陵墓中，例如位於底比斯的納赫特（Nakht）。葡萄在採摘後在大桶內以腳踩碎。由此產生的汁液經採集、裝瓶並在密封保存至酒罈之前先加以發酵。（作者：N.H.）

Wine Jar

This cylindrical wine amphora bears a faint hieratic inscription identifying the contents as the produce of the estate of a man named Amenhotep. The jar was made on a wheel, has a rounded base, and would have been sealed with a mud stopper stamped with information about its contents and origin. Aside from the inscription the vessel is undecorated: the white discolouration is a result of salt in the clay moving to the surface as the pot dried. The wine-making process was depicted in abbreviated form in the tombs of the elite, such as Nakht at Thebes. The grapes were picked and crushed underfoot in a vat. The resulting juice was collected, bottled and allowed to ferment before the jars were sealed and stored. (N.H.)

101. 酒罐
來自阿比多斯
新王國時期，第 18 王朝 (西元前 1540-1295 年)
陶器
675 x 245 x 245 mm

Wine Jar
From Abydos
New Kingdom, Dynasty 18 (1540-1295 BC)
Ceramic

藍色彩繪陶罐

多數埃及陶器皆未經過修飾，但在第十八王朝末期，埃及人發展出一種傳統的藍彩陶，現今有時稱為馬卡達（Malkata）器皿。這個名字源自底比斯的馬卡達宮殿，大量的此類陶器在這裡被發現。這種陶器主要出現在皇室宮殿座落的城市，且似乎是由少數專業工匠所製成。

此瓶瓶身格外大型，且為藍彩陶之優良範例。陶器的基本部份覆蓋著經過打磨的紅色滑面。藍色裝飾是模仿藍色蓮花花瓣之花環，埃及人在節慶時配戴藍色蓮花花瓣，並將其置於所使用的陶器上。如此大型的瓶身需耗費非常高超的技術技能。陶藝家必須各別製作頂部與底部，再由瓶頸處底部連接兩個部份。

像這樣的大型瓶罐可能是於佳節時混合各種酒用。這些陶器的底部通常會保持裸露，以讓瓶罐結成水珠，從而冷卻內容物。根據陵墓現場情形顯示，此瓶罐會放置在一個瓶架上，以促進其結成水珠並展現此容器之美。（作者：C.R.）

Blue-painted Biconical Jar

Most Egyptian pottery was undecorated, but during the last part of Dynasty 18 the Egyptians developed a tradition of blue painted pottery, today sometimes called Malkata ware. The name comes from the palace of Malkata at Thebes where relatively large quantities of this pottery was found. Such pottery has been found primarily in cities where royal palaces were located and seems to have been made by a small number of specialist craftsmen.

This pot is an exceptionally large and fine example of blue-painted pottery. The base pottery is covered in a red slip that has been burnished. The blue decoration imitates garlands of blue lotus petals that the Egyptians wore and placed on pottery used at festivals. Very high technical skill would have been needed to make such a large pot. Potters would have constructed the top separately from the bottom and then joined the two parts at the base of the neck.

Large jars such as this one were probably used for the mixing of wine for festive occasions. The bottom of these pots were normally left bare to allow the pot to 'sweat' thereby cooling the contents. Based on tomb scenes, the jar would have been placed on a pot stand that facilitated the sweating and displayed the beauty of the vessel. (C.R.)

102. 藍色彩繪陶罐
來自阿瑪納
新王國時期，第 18 王朝，阿肯納頓統治時期
（西元前 1352-1336 年）
陶器
720 x 460 x 460 mm

Blue-painted Biconical Jar
From Amarna, 24/163
New Kingdom, Dynasty 18, reign of Akhenaten
(1352-1336 BC)
Ceramic

貝斯神頭像

由於貝斯神（Bes）的角色是一種裝飾性的保護神，其圖像在家居用品中廣為流行，例如床、頭枕以及美容用品。雖然形象怪異，他的本質卻是仁慈的。他的奇特外表具有避邪作用，並可抵禦邪惡勢力。他經常被召喚來協助分娩的婦女。僅需對貝斯神的粘土雕像複誦一段神奇的咒語四次，便能抵抗分娩時的危險。他與生育和性聯繫在一起。因此其圖像裝飾著 mammisi（誕生房），圖像中的他若不是參與著生育過程，就是在一名新生兒身旁。我們在薩卡拉（Saqqara）發現古埃及晚期的保溫室，其牆面排列著貝斯神的石膏雕像。尋求神祇援助的朝聖者會在此處過夜，希望能獲得具有療癒效果的夢。[1] 目前已發現眾多貝斯神的陪葬人俑，這可能是由尋求神祇調解的朝聖者所奉獻。（作者：J.H.W.）

1. Kaiser注意到，在附近房間內關於性愛的奉獻人俑顯示，有夫婦可能在部份房間內嘗試懷孕。

Head of Bes

Due to his role as a decorative protective deity, images of Bes were popular on household items such as beds, headrests and cosmetic items. While his image was grotesque, his nature was benevolent. His strange appearance served an apotropaic function and warded off evil forces. He was often called upon to assist women in labor. A magical spell exists which was supposed to recited over a clay image of Bes four times to ward off the dangers of childbirth. He was linked with fertility and sexuality. Consequently, his image decorates mammisi (birth houses) where he is shown either attending a birth or nearby a newborn baby. During the Late Period at Saqqara we find incubation chambers with walls lined with plaster figures of Bes. Pilgrims seeking the god's assistance would spend the night there hoping to have healing dreams. [1] Numerous examples of terracotta figurines of Bes have been found, which may have been dedicated by pilgrims who sought the gods' intercession. (J.H.W.)

1. Kaiser notes that the discovery of erotic votive figurines in some of the nearby rooms suggests that couples may have tried to conceive in some of the rooms.

103. 貝斯神頭像
來自薩卡拉，1422 號區
托勒密時期（西元前 332-30 年）
陶器，顏料
140 x 93 x 35 mm

Head of Bes
From Saqqara, area 1422
Ptolemaic Period (332-30 BC)
Ceramic, pigment

貝斯神花瓶

作為一件人形瓶的樣本，所謂的貝斯神花瓶是一種在埃及已流行上千年的類型。這些以矮神的形象裝飾的容器，通常被認為是貝斯神。第一批樣本出現於阿蒙霍特（Amenhotep）三世統治期間，直到希臘羅馬時期仍繼續順利進行製造。此類型容器分佈範圍廣泛，已在整個埃及各點，以及近東地區和努比亞等埃及以外的地區發現。

本希臘羅馬時期樣本是一只大型的模製雙耳瓶，其瓶身裝飾著風格怪誕的貝斯神立體圖像。其極具風格的面部特徵以及細長的手臂被應用於容器表面。此瓶罐的裝飾僅包括貝斯神圖像上方的五條褐色橫帶，及圖像下方的彩繪。

學者繼續推測此類容器的功能，及其原本之內容物可能為何。水、啤酒、葡萄酒、牛奶、香水、藥膏、軟膏和油都曾被提出為可能內容，並且有人推測，這些內容物是用於宗教儀式等場合。針對貝斯神花瓶的二十三種內容物，近期的科學研究已在這些經過檢測之容器中的一小部分取得牛奶蛋白的痕跡。（作者：J.H.W.）

Bes Vase

As an example of a figure vase, the so-called 'Bes Jar' is of a type popular in Egypt for over a thousand years. These vessels are decorated with an image of the dwarf god commonly referred to as Bes. The first examples appear during the reign of Amenhotep III and continue to be manufactured well into the Graeco-Roman period. Vessels of this type have a wide geographic range and are found at sites throughout Egypt as well as in areas outside of Egypt in the Near East and Nubia.

This Graeco-Roman example is a large, wheel made amphora whose body is decorated with a three-dimensional image of Bes executed in a grotesque style. His stylized facial features and spindly arms are applied to the surface of the vessel. The jar's decoration is limited to five brown horizontal bands above and below the Bes image, which has some painted highlights.

Scholars continue to speculate on the function of vessels of this kind and on what their original contents may have been. Water, beer, wine, milk, perfume, ointments, unguents, and oils have all been put forth as possibilities and its been suggested that these contents were used in circumstances relating to rituals or offerings. Recent scientific study of the contents of twenty-three of these Bes jars has yielded traces of milk proteins in a small percentage of the vessels tested. (J.H.W.)

104. 貝斯神花瓶
來自埃及
希臘羅馬時期（西元前 332 年 - 西元 332 年）
陶器，顏料
470 x 255 x 245 mm

Bes Vase
From Egypt
Graeco-Roman Period (332BC -AD 332)
Ceramic, pigment

貝斯神小銅像

在埃及的萬神殿中,有一些矮人般的神,其中一位就是貝斯神。貝斯神很有可能是若干早期神祇的混合體,例如像能在中王國時期的魔杖上看到的哈(Aha,戰士)。直到托勒密時期,才出現我們在此處看到的人形肖像,且銘文內容亦與貝斯神的名字產生關聯。

貝斯神(以及其他早期類似的矮神)具有不同於其他埃及神祇的外觀。他通常會以正面的外表出現,而非側面,並且有一個怪誕的外表,推測具有避邪作用。他通常戴著羽毛頭飾並且雙腿向外彎曲。

貝斯神因其對家庭之保護而聞名,特別是孩童以及分娩中的母親。貝斯神護身符廣受歡迎,且其圖像亦裝飾於所有個人物品上,例如傢俱和頭枕。黏土及青銅製成的貝斯神人俑可能使用在巫術方面,或用於還願。

儘管貝斯神的面貌頗具有威嚇性,且其可能以攜帶寶劍或揮舞蛇的形象出現,但他仍與娛樂、歡笑,以及幸福等相關,且同樣能以演奏鼓或鈴鼓等樂器的形象露面。然而,演奏這些敲擊樂器有可能是為了避開邪靈。(作者:J.H.W.)

Figure of Bes

In the Egyptian pantheon, there are a number of dwarf-like gods, one of whom is Bes. It is possible that Bes came to be an amalgamation of several earlier deities, including, for example Aha (the Fighter) who can be seen on Middle Kingdom magical wands. It is not until the Ptolemaic period that the iconography of the figure we see here and inscriptional material is linked to a god by the name of Bes.

Bes (and other similar earlier dwarf gods) has an appearance that is not typical of Egyptian divinities. He is usually shown frontally, rather than in profile and he has a grotesque appearance, which presumably served an apotropaic function. He typically wears a feathered headdress and is shown bandy-legged.

Bes was known for his protection of the household, especially children and mothers in childbirth. Amulets of Bes were popular and his image decorated all manner of personal objects such as furniture and headrests. Figurines of Bes in both clay and bronze may have been used during magical practices, or perhaps dedicated as votives.

Although Bes' mien is somewhat menacing and he could be shown carrying a sword or wielding snakes, he was also associated with entertainment, laughter, and happiness and could likewise be shown playing musical instruments like drums or tambourines. However, it is possible that these percussive musical instruments may also have been played to ward off evil spirits. (J.H.W.)

105. 貝斯神小銅像
來自奧克西林庫斯
托勒密時期(西元前 250-150 年)
銅合金
95 x 46 x 19 mm

Figure of Bes
From Oxyrhynchus
Ptolemaic Period (250-150 BC)
Copper alloy

106. 人形胸像
來自阿比多斯，D9 號墓室
新王國時期， 第 18 王朝（西元前 1540-1295 年）
石灰岩，顏料
100 x 67 x 22 mm

Anthropoid Bust
From Abydos, Tomb D105
New Kingdom, Dynasty 18 (1540-1295 BC)
Limestone, pigment

人形胸像

類人猿或「始祖」半身像以立體形式製成，自第十八王朝開始遍及整個新王國。有關半身像的最早已知描繪是在第十一王朝時，一名來自巴哈里（Deir el-Bahri）的女性之石棺上的裝飾圖案。其伴隨的文字，即棺材文咒語，係用於節慶香水與頭枕：「你的頭為了你而被支撐著，以便讓你活下去…而你可能成為神」。在其他物件的帶狀裝飾中，兩個半身像上標註著：「把他的頭給他，以便他能活下去」。這表示半身像被認為是死者頭部的代替品，而半身像基座能提供支撐，或許能使死者成為神。在新王國時期，該咒語已發展為死亡之書中的咒語，即用於「秘密」或「神秘」頭顱的咒語，有時會伴隨著一個半身像的描繪。死者的靈魂，或稱為 akh，可居住在半身像內以獲得供品，以作為在生者發生困境期間提供協助的交換。

在 189 件已知的半身像裡，其中 83 件是在德瑞爾美狄亞（Deir el-Medina）的工匠村落發現，其他則來自埃及各地，包括阿瑪納（Amarna）、古洛（Guro）、米特拉希納（Mit Rahina）以及卡納克（Karnak）的神廟，有多件起源不明。這些半身像具有區域性差異，但基本上包含一個在無臂軀幹人頭，沒有頭髮／配戴緊身帽或三部分組成的（三重的）長假髮，軀幹往底座方向漸寬。有些半身像會以寬闊的衣領及垂下的荷花裝飾：此類半身像有可能會在節慶或祭典中以花環裝飾。類人猿半身像的尺寸範圍包括 2 公分的護身符到 70 公分高左右，並且由各種材料製成，包括石灰岩、砂岩、花崗岩、黏土、彩陶以及木材。

伯頓博物館收藏的半身像輪廓平整，且帶有漆成黑色的三重假髮，其上有兩個垂飾構成三角形面部。類人猿半身像的性別具有爭議性，但非條紋假髮表示其代表的是一名女性，因為男性半身像通常有短髮和鬍鬚。眼睛部份是透過石灰岩上的水平切割來呈現，而髮際則是由未均勻雕刻的眉毛描繪出輪廓。雕像的其餘部份被漆成黃色：表面已有擦傷，而基座週圍和側面的漆已磨損。此半身像是在一座陵墓中發現，連同黑色石灰岩化妝墨罐、彩陶垂飾和珠子，以及釉面滑石聖甲蟲。雖然半身像通常與家庭場景有所關聯，有若干半身像仍在陵墓和寺廟中發現。此件樣本可能曾被存放於墳墓內以抵抗邪惡力量，具有相同避邪作用的半身像護身符有時會和死者一同埋葬，以保護他們在此世與來世免受傷害。（作者：N.H.）

Anthropoid Bust

Anthropoid or 'ancestor' busts were produced in three-dimensions throughout the New Kingdom from Dynasty 18 onwards. The earliest known depiction of the busts is a vignette on the Dynasty 11 stone sarcophagus of a woman named 'Ashyt from Deir el-Bahri. The accompanying text, Coffin Texts Spell 934, is a request for festival perfume and a headrest: "your head is supported for you so that you may live ... and you may be a god". In another frieze of objects, two busts are captioned: "giving his head to him so that he may live". This suggests that the busts are to be understood as substitute heads for the deceased, and the plinth provides support so that the dead may become divine. By the New Kingdom Spell 934 had developed into Book of the Dead Spell 151, the spell for the 'secret' or 'mysterious' head, which is sometimes accompanied by a depiction of a bust. The spirit or akh of the deceased could inhabit the bust in order to receive offerings in exchange for assisting the living during times of need.

Of 189 known busts, 83 were found at the artisans' village of Deir el-Medina; others derive from sites throughout Egypt, including Amarna, Gurob, Mit Rahina, and Karnak temple, and many are unprovenanced. The busts show regional variations, but consist essentially of a human head, without hair/wearing a tight-fitting cap or a long three-part (tripartite) wig, on an armless torso that usually widens towards the base. Some of the busts were decorated with broad collars and pendant water-lily blossoms: it is possible that they could have been adorned with garlands of this type during festivals or as part of offering ceremonies. Anthropoid busts range in size from 2cm amulets to 70cm, and were made in a variety of materials including limestone, sandstone, granite, clay, faience and wood.

The Bolton bust is flattened in profile and has a black-painted tripartite wig, with two lappets framing the triangular face. The gender of anthropoid busts is disputed, but the non-striped wig suggests that a woman may be represented here, since male busts usually have close-cropped hair and a beard. The eyes are represented by horizontal cuts in the limestone, and the hairline is delineated by unevenly carved eyebrows. The rest of the sculpture is painted yellow: the surface is abraded and some of the paint has worn away around the base and sides. The bust was discovered in a tomb along with a blackened limestone kohl pot, a faience pendant and beads, and a glazed steatite scarab. While busts are generally associated with domestic contexts, several have been found in tombs and temples. This example may have been deposited in a grave to repel malevolent forces, with the same apotropaic purpose as the bust amulets that were sometimes buried with the deceased to protect them from harm in this world and the next. (N.H.)

銅鉗

這些由經過雕鏤的彎曲銅鉗太過精雕細琢，應不曾在工作坊或廚房中被使用，其可能是用來將香球放入火盆中做為馨香祭品。在此宗教情境中，銅鉗的末端形狀是一雙優雅且戴著手鐲的手，看來格外相稱。其令人聯想起古埃及太陽神阿頓（Aten）的光芒，並呈現在人類雙手愛撫，以及向阿瑪納（Amarna）王室奉獻 T 形安卡（ankh）標誌上。

陵墓及廟宇之浮雕不斷展示出阿肯納頓（Akhenaten）及王室在祭祀阿頓神的景象，但這個小範圍以外的人並未直接祭拜阿頓神。他們專注於其奉獻，而非擔任人與神之中間人的王室。因此，阿瑪納地區在宗教方面的核心裝飾品 — 重點可能在於使用鉗子 — 是一座石碑，描繪著在阿頓神光芒下的王室。此銅鉗在阿瑪納北郊一間規模中等的房屋內被發現，然而，其中還包含兩只小型鱷魚物件，其中一個帶有小孔，可做為頭飾配件。這是否表示，儘管阿肯納頓明令禁止崇拜其他神祇，卻仍有居民在阿瑪納供奉祂們呢？（作者：T.H.）

Bronze tongs

These tongs, made from a chased and bent strip of bronze, are too elaborate to have been used in a workshop or kitchen, and were probably used to drop pellets of incense in a brazier as a fragrant offering. In this cultic context the shape of the tongs, ending in a graceful pair of hands wearing bracelets, is especially fitting. They recall the rays of the Aten, which are shown with human hands caressing and offering ankh-signs to the Amarna royal family.

Tomb and temple reliefs ceaselessly show Akhenaten and the royal family making offerings to the Aten, but people outside this small circle did not worship the Aten directly. They focused their devotion instead on the royal family, who served as intermediaries between the human and the divine. As a result, the centerpiece of domestic cults at Amarna – and the likely focus of use for the tongs – would be a stela depicting the royal family under the rays of the Aten. The mid-sized house in the North Suburb at Amarna where the tongs were discovered, however, was found to contain two small figures of crocodiles, one of which had a hole for the attachment of a headrest. Do these show that in spite of the official proscription of the cults of the other gods by Akhenaten, some inhabitants at Amarna were still making offerings to them? (T.H.)

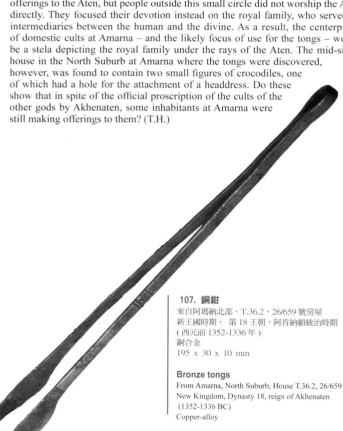

107. 銅鉗
來自阿瑪納北部，T.36.2，26/659 號房屋
新王國時期， 第 18 王朝，阿肯納頓統治時期
（西元前 1352-1336 年）
銅合金
195 x 30 x 10 mm

Bronze tongs
From Amarna, North Suburb, House T.36.2, 26/659
New Kingdom, Dynasty 18, reign of Akhenaten
(1352-1336 BC)
Copper-alloy

108. 頭墊
來自底比斯
新王國時期， 第 18 王朝（西元前 1540-1295 年）
木
212 x 193 x 63 mm

Headrest
From Thebes
New Kingdom, Dynasty 18 (1540-1295 BC)
Wood

頭墊

在古埃及時代，雕刻自石材或木材的頭墊是傢俱中常見的物品。頭墊上貝斯神（Bes）與塔沃里特（Taweret）的形象，是用來保護睡眠者或已故者免於遭受蛇類、蠍子，以及如邪惡亡靈等魔鬼所傷。類人猿半身像（本書編號 106）以及頭枕之間的關聯顯示在夢境中可與祖先們聯繫，這些物件目前仍在非洲某些區域。頭枕的曲線造型類似於地平線上的山丘，而太陽則從其中升起。頭部、頭墊，以及太陽之間的聯結在一個從圖坦卡門（Tutankhamun）陵墓出土的頭枕中明顯呈現，空氣之神出現在其中支撐著頭墊（以及國王的頭部），兩側是地平線上的兩隻獅子，象徵著昨日與明日。他的肩膀上扛著保護標誌，表示即使是國王，也需要保衛自己以抵抗夜晚和來世之險境。

這個簡單、未經雕琢的頭墊外型高雅，長形的頸部由橢圓形底座向外開展而逐漸狹窄。頭墊部份是由兩塊木板製成，其餘則是分別雕刻後，透過位於中央部份的定位梢固定於底座。植物纖維製成的枕頭可能是用來緩衝頭墊，但僅有極少部分能通過時間考驗。此頭墊的確切出處並不明確，儘管其可能是來自底比斯地區的一座墓地。（作者：N.H.）

Headrest

Headrests carved from stone or wood were common items of furniture in ancient Egypt. Many headrests bear figures of Bes and Taweret to protect the sleeper or the deceased against snakes, scorpions, and demons including malevolent spirits of the dead. The association between anthropoid busts (catalogue #106) and headrests suggests that the ancestors could be contacted in dreams, as they still are in some parts of Africa. The curved shape of headrests is similar to the hills of the horizon between which the sun rose. This connection between the head, the headrest and the sun is made explicit on one of the headrests from the tomb of Tutankhamun, where Shu, the god of air, is shown supporting the headrest (and thereby the king's head) flanked by the two lions of the horizon, symbolising yesterday and tomorrow. Over his shoulders, Shu bears the sign for protection, suggesting that even the king needed defending against the dangers of the night and the afterlife.

This simple, undecorated headrest is elegant in form, with a long tapering neck that splays out to an oval base. The headrest is made from two pieces of wood; the rest itself was carved separately and fixed to the base by a dowel through the centre. Pillows made from woven plant fibres were probably used to cushion headrests, but few have survived the test of time. The exact provenance of this headrest is unknown, though it probably derived from a tomb in the Theban area. (N.H.)

109. 模型屋
來自英國
當代，西元 1990 年
紙，木，顏料
900 x 540 x 300 mm

House Model
From United Kingdom
Modern, 1990
Card, wood, pigment

模型屋

此模型表現出新王國時期的埃及標準住宅（公元前 1550 年至 1069 年）。此模型是以工人住房為基礎，主要位於阿瑪納（Amarna），但並非任何特定住房。

此房之特點在其庭院入口，並於此處從事家務。庭院後方是主接待室的入口。通常接待室的特徵是帶有一座壁爐以及一塊高起的區域，讓房子的主人能坐在其中接待客人。接待室後面是一些用於儲物和烹飪的小房間。上方樓層的出現是來自出土房屋牆壁厚度之推斷。在此模型中，上方樓層被想像成一個睡眠區域。許多埃及房屋內都設有供奉當地神祇的神龕。此模型的神龕內有女神塔沃里特（Taweret）的圖像。塔沃里特是由不同動物結合而成，具有河馬、鱷魚、人類以及獅子的特徵。她是家庭以及分娩婦女的保護神。此類神龕亦包括如貝斯神（Bes，本書編號 103-105）、祖先（本書編號 106）等神祇，有時也包括王室人物。（作者：C.R.）

House Model

This model represents a standard Egyptian house from the period of the New Kingdom (1550-1069 BC). It is based on workers houses, primarily at Amarna, but is not any particular house.

The house features a courtyard entry where domestic work took place. Behind the courtyard was the entry to the main reception room. The reception room often featured a hearth and a raised area where the master of the house might sit to receive guests. Behind the reception room were small rooms for storage and cooking. The presence of an upper story is inferred from the thickness of the walls in the excavated houses. In this reconstruction, the upperstory is imagined as an area for sleeping. Many Egyptian houses had shrines to domestic gods. In this reconstruction, the shrine contains an image of the goddess Taweret. Taweret was a composite animal, part hippopotamus, crocodile, human, and lion. She was a protector of the home and women in childbirth. Such shrines also contained gods like Bes (Catalogue #103-105), ancestors (catalogue #106) and sometimes royalty. (C.R.)

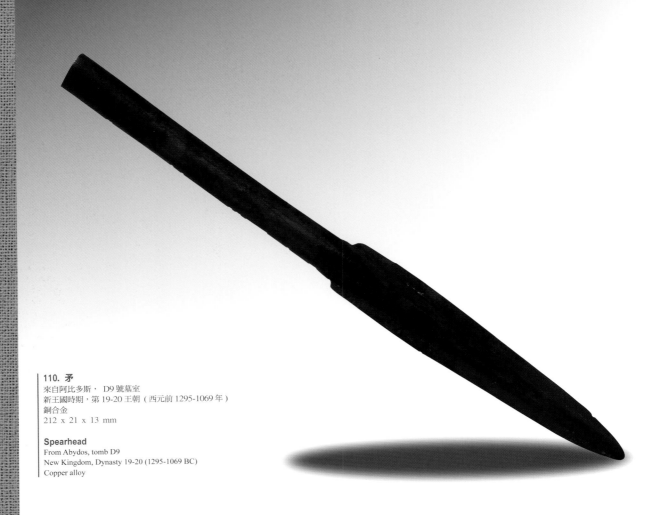

110. 矛
來自阿比多斯，D9 號墓室
新王國時期，第 19-20 王朝（西元前 1295-1069 年）
銅合金
212 x 21 x 13 mm

Spearhead
From Abydos, tomb D9
New Kingdom, Dynasty 19-20 (1295-1069 BC)
Copper alloy

矛

此處展出的矛尖擁有葉形刀鋒與突起中脈，而中脈逐漸加寬形成一個環形的錘打與重疊凹槽。考古學家大衛（David Randall-MacIver）與亞瑟（Arthur C. Mace）在阿比多斯的賽特胡〔Sitepehu〕之墓發現這支矛，極可能為之後另一個葬禮的陪葬品。這支矛的握柄應為木製，並藉由凹槽與刀鋒連接。有凹槽的青銅矛是新王國時期相當普遍常見的類型，取代古王國與中王國時期利用刀鋒延伸部分和握柄相連的銅製和打火石製刀鋒。

矛的使用方式多為推刺與拋擲，主要與埃及的軍事方面相關；但矛也能用於狩獵大型動物。在與埃及士兵相關的浮雕作品與模型中經常會出現矛的蹤影；曾發現的文物包括一對第十一王朝的彩繪木製埃及士兵模型，以及來自梅斯諦（Mesehti）之墓的努比亞弓箭手，40 位埃及持矛士兵皆手持一面盾牌與一支類似此處展示的葉形刀鋒長矛。

青銅的出現是銅製工具與武器製造上的一大進步，青銅工具與武器較易投擲，並會在鍛鍊後變得更堅硬、耐用。青銅為銅合金，多數成分為銅和錫。錫礦自然而然地就出現於埃及，但卻未有證據顯示古埃及曾開採過錫礦，所以應是自國外進口。因此，埃及早期的青銅器或許是將銅與其他自然界金屬，如銅意外混合後才製成，直到中王國時期，埃及才有製造青銅，可能是由敘利亞進口。除了武器與工具外，青銅也用於鑄造雕像、器皿與其他如戒子和護身符等小物品。（作者：A.H.）

Spearhead

This spearhead has a leaf-shaped blade with raised midrib. The midrib widens and continues to form a circular hammered and lapped socket. It was discovered by David Randall-MacIver and Arthur C. Mace in the Tomb of Sitepehu in Cemetery D at Abydos, probably from a later burial. The shaft of this spear was likely made of wood and would have been attached to the blade by means of the socket. This type of bronze spearhead with socket was common during the New Kingdom and replaced the copper and flint blades of the Old and Middle Kingdoms, which were attached to the shaft by a tang.

Spears were commonly used as thrusting and throwing weapons, being primarily associated with military contexts in Egypt. But, they could also be used for hunting larger animals. Spears are frequently depicted in relief scenes and models involving Egyptian soldiers. For example, from the Eleventh Dynasty, a pair of painted wooden models of Egyptian soldiers and Nubian archers from the tomb of Mesehti, show forty Egyptian spearmen each carrying a shield and a spear with a long leaf-shaped blade similar to the one depicted here.

The introduction of bronze was a great improvement on copper in tool and weapon manufacture. It was easier to cast and could become harder and tougher through annealing. Bronze is an alloy of copper, consisting largely of copper and tin. Tin ore occurs naturally in Egypt, but there is no evidence that it was ever mined in antiquity, so it would have had to have been imported. Thus, early bronze artefacts in Egypt were probably the result of the accidental mixing of copper and other metals, such as arsenic, in nature. It was not until the Middle Kingdom that man-made bronze appeared in Egypt, probably being imported from Syria. Apart from weapons and tools, bronze was also used to cast statuettes, vessels, and other smaller objects, such as rings and amulets. (A.H.)

戰斧

這把戰斧有著對稱的外寬式斧面與細長手柄，為銅合金材質，其中的多數成分為銅與砷，且已有部分遭腐蝕。原本應搭配一根利用皮帶綁住的木製握把，只是兩者皆已腐朽分解。在墓穴中，這把斧頭原本由其擁有者緊握於手上，其發現地是一個位於中埃及高（Qau）的深坑墓穴之中，旁邊還有一個木頭棺木與一個埃及雪花石膏製成的眼影罐。高是最大的非皇室墓地，其年代可追溯至中王國時期。

在第一和第二中間王朝時期內戰頻繁，斧頭開始出現了最重要的發展，包括在外形上有了重大改變。經常出現士兵或領主隨從握持斧頭的描繪，而中王國棺木上也常繪有斧頭，斧頭更逐漸成為常見的陪葬物品。直至第十八王朝，斧頭都是最主要的雙手武器，之後便逐漸由圓月彎刀（curved Khepesh-sword）所取代。

此處展示的斧頭有著細長手柄、內彎的側邊與一個較窄小的腰身，並搭配比切面更寬的底部。其手柄部分有稜角，切面邊緣則呈圓形。根據佩托里（Petrie）與布蘭登（Brunton）的紀錄，此墓穴的年代可追溯至中王國與第二中間王朝時期，但從斧頭的型式進行判斷，墓穴的年代較可能為中王國晚期或第二中間王朝時期；而根據戴維斯（W.V. Davies）所稱，有著細長手柄的斧頭便是在這個時期「首度現身」。斧頭的型式也在這時出現了重大改變，由外寬式斧頭取代了過去普遍呈圓形當作工具與武器使用的斧頭。不同於過去的圓式斧頭需穿孔以連結刀鋒和握把，外寬式斧頭可利用兩邊的突出手柄連接握把。雖然出現此種轉變的原因並不明確，但一般認為其型式較適合執行貫穿的功用，是為了對付更具防護效力的盔甲而發展出的設計。最早的外寬式斧頭其手柄部分較短，而刀鋒最窄的部分則相當接近握把；在同時期中有著較長手柄與中間部位窄小的斧頭，如本次所展出的斧頭，都屬於戰斧。

木匠使用的斧頭工具多為銅合金材質，而戰斧則多為由銅與大量砷的合金或青銅材質。檢驗古埃及銅製工具的結果顯示，斧頭皆於開放式模具中鑄造，而已發現的數個模具皆為燒製黏土與石製模具。在鑄造之後，斧頭上方的扁平側邊尚需經過多項程序方能完成，特別是切面需經過冷卻加工，可以增加其硬度。（作者：M.M.）

111. 戰斧
來自高 (Qau)，7489 號墓室
中王國時期至第二中間期（西元前 2055-1550 年）
銅合金
100 x 58 x 4 mm

Axe head
From Qau, tomb 7489
Middle Kingdom-Second Intermediate Period (2055-1550 BC)
Copper alloy

Axe head

This symmetrical splayed axe-head with elongated lugs would have served as a battle-axe. It is composed of a copper alloy, most likely copper-arsenic, which has suffered some corrosion. It would originally have had a handle made of wood attached using leather thongs, both of which decomposed in ancient times. The axe-head was found placed by the hand of its owner, who was buried in a pit grave in the Middle Egyptian site of Qau along with a wooden coffin and an Egyptian alabaster kohl pot. Qau is the site of the largest non-royal tombs dating to the Middle Kingdom.

It was during the increased internal warfare during the First and Second Intermediate Periods that the most significant developments in axes occurred, including a major evolution in form. Axes are frequently depicted in the hands of soldiers and local rulers' attendants, as well as in the depictions of objects on Middle Kingdom coffins, and they also became more common among burial goods. The axe was the primary hand-weapon of soldiers up until Dynasty 18, after which it was gradually replaced by the curved Khepesh-sword.

The axe has elongated lugs, incurved sides, and a relatively narrow waist, with the base wider than the cutting edge. The lugs are angular and the corners of the cutting edge are rounded. Petrie and Brunton recorded its tomb as dating to both the Middle Kingdom and Second Intermediate Period, but considering the form of the axe, a late Middle Kingdom or Second Intermediate Period date may be most likely. According to W.V. Davies, this is the period when axes with elongated lugs 'make their first definite appearance'. A major change in axe forms occurred at this time, with the previously prevalent rounded form of axe being replaced as both a tool and weapon by the splayed type. Unlike the earlier rounded axe, which was perforated in order to fasten the blade to the handle, the splayed type had protruding lugs on either side to allow for attachment. The reason for the change in form is uncertain, but it has been suggested that its shape is more suited for penetration and was developed in reaction to more effective body armour. The earliest splayed axe had relatively short lugs, with the narrowest point of the blade close to the handle. A contemporary form with longer lugs and a narrow mid-point, such as the axe shown here, served specifically as a battle-axe.

Axes that served as carpenter's tools were almost always made of unalloyed copper, while battle-axes were usually composed of either copper alloyed with a high level of arsenic, or bronze. Examination of ancient Egyptian copper tools show that they were cast in open moulds. Several axe moulds have been found, made of baked clay and stone. After casting, the upper flat side of the axe would require further work to shape it into its final form, mostly through cold-working, especially at the cutting edge to increase its hardness. (M.M.)

象牙浮雕

在古代的近東地區，象牙雕刻製品主要用來裝飾容器或木製傢俱與箱子的鑲嵌飾板。象牙浮雕製品主要出現於黎凡特地區，而黎凡特地區自西元前 4000 年便建立起主要的工藝傳統。

古代的象牙浮雕原料主要來自大象的長牙與犀牛的犬齒。從這兩種動物身上取得的象牙原料都是從埃及出口至地中海東部與古代近東地區。然而，在黎凡特的地中海沿岸與奧倫特（Orontes）河谷曾出現過大象與犀牛的蹤影，只是在西元前 1000 年便完全滅絕。因此，若未進行化學或同位素分析，將難以判斷製造特定古代工藝品的象牙來源。

從第二中間期開始，在黎凡特的象牙浮雕便深受埃及藝術圖樣與圖像的影響。廣泛地來說，這是由於黎凡特地區深受埃及經濟與政治影響力所產生的副作用。大約從西元前 1550-1150 年，從現在的以色列、巴勒斯坦、約旦西部、黎巴嫩與敘利亞南部，全都含括在新王國時期的埃及法老王的統治範圍內。埃及人並未全面地介入受其統治之黎凡特地區的日常生活之中，但埃及藝術深具影響力的圖樣與圖像卻深深吸引著象牙工匠與其贊助者，且至今仍受到現代人的喜愛。

深受埃及藝術吸引的情形還產生了另一個副作用：約在西元前 1000 年，黎凡特的工匠全面地將埃及圖像與圖樣同化，其內化之徹底讓人無法再將其視為是借用了埃及的藝術精隨；其中尤以腓尼基藝術最為明顯，即與黎巴嫩的地中海沿岸如 Tyre、Sidon 和 Byblos 等腓尼基城邦有關的藝術。

本次所展出的三件象牙浮雕皆為西元前 850-700 年間的腓尼基象牙作品。三件作品皆採用了埃及圖樣，但都不是來自腓尼基或埃及，而來自尼姆魯德的「Fort Shalmanseser」軍事宮殿中，即現在的伊拉克北部。在西元前 800-700 年間，尼姆魯德是亞述帝國的首都，而至今仍殘存的多數腓尼基象牙作品便都是發現於亞述國王的宮殿中。在亞述征服多數古代的近東地區後，亞述王便接受象牙浮雕容器與鑲嵌傢俱作為貢品與戰利品；顯然亞述王也相當讚賞結合了埃及圖像與黎凡特工藝的象牙浮雕所展現出的美學特質。（作者：B.R.）

Carved Ivories

In the ancient Near East, ivory was primarily carved to make decorative containers and panels for inlaying on wooden furniture and boxes. Ivory carving was particularly identified with the Levant, where it had been established as a major craft tradition since the 4000 BC.

Ancient craftsmen carved ivory from both the tusks of elephants and the canine teeth of hippopotami. Ivory from both of these animals was exported from Egypt to sites around the Eastern Mediterranean and ancient Near East. However, elephants and hippopotami were also found along the Mediterranean coast of the Levant and in the Orontes river valley, only becoming extinct after the 1000 BC. This makes it difficult to identify the origin of ivory used in specific ancient artefacts without conducting chemical or isotopic analysis.

From the Second Millennium onwards, ivory carving in the Levant was heavily influenced by the motifs and images of Egyptian art. To a large extent, this was a by-product of Egypt's economic and political importance in the Levant. From about 1550 BC until 1150 BC, what is now Israel, Palestine, western Jordan, Lebanon and southern Syria were incorporated into an empire ruled by the New Kingdom pharaohs of Egypt. Egyptians did not intervene extensively in the day-to-day life of the areas they ruled in the Levant. However, the powerful motifs and images of Egyptian art were very attractive to both ivory carvers and their patrons, much as they are to us today.

One by-product of this strong attraction to Egyptian art is that, by around 1000 BC, Levantine craftsmen had assimilated Egyptian images and motifs so extensively that we can no longer describe them as being borrowed. This is most notable in Phoenician art; the art associated with Phoenician city-states of the Mediterranean coast of Lebanon such as Tyre, Sidon and Byblos.

The three carved ivory panels in this exhibit are examples of Phoenician ivories from between 850 and 700 BC. All three make use of Egyptian motifs; however, these pieces were not discovered in Phoenicia or Egypt. All three originate from 'Fort Shalmanseser', a military palace located in the city of Nimrud, in what is now Northern Iraq. Between 800 and 700 BC. Nimrud was the capital of the Assyrian Empire. The majority of the Phoenician ivories that survive today were found in palaces belonging to kings of Assyria. Assyrian kings received carved ivory containers and inlaid furniture as tribute or booty after Assyria had conquered much of the ancient Near East. Clearly, Assyrian kings also appreciated the aesthetic qualities of Egyptian images married with Levantine craftsmanship. (B.R.)

象牙飾板—二個男子和聖樹

這個飾板上有兩個分站在棕櫚樹兩旁的男性人物。右手邊的人物於遠古時期便已受損，但從其他尼姆魯德（Nimrud）文物，可判斷右邊的人物除了左手臂的姿態，其餘部分應與左邊人物相同。兩個人物皆穿戴著雙重頭冠與埃及法老王的典型短裙，而右手也都持有一根飾有山羊彎角的權杖（太陽神阿蒙的象徵）。左邊人物的左手拿著一個細頸壺，而右邊的人物則拿著古埃及十字架，但兩項物品皆已磨損。整件作品原本鑲於一個埃及皇室涼亭上，其簷部正面飾有雙翼日輪，而沿著屋頂則飾有一排共八隻古埃及聖蛇烏瑞（uraei）。

儘管這塊飾板上的多項元素都直接取自埃及皇室象徵，但飾板本身是腓尼基作品。經考證後，發現拿著山羊頭權杖與倒出祭酒的人物圖樣自西元前十三世紀便已出現於黎凡特地區，並用於腓尼基印章與其他尼姆魯德象牙製品上。在最早發現的文物中，獻祭的對象多為就座的神祇或逝去的國王；而在尼姆魯德象牙製品上，則以繪製的棕櫚樹取代就座的人物。就某種程度上，這是為了藝術上的美觀，因為棕櫚樹能區隔不同風格，並在視覺上提供飾板間的一致性。然而，在鐵器時代的黎凡特地區與塞普勒斯，棕櫚樹多與皇家的藝術、建築有關，顯示棕櫚樹如同此飾板所使用的許多埃及圖樣一樣，皆能象徵王者的身分。（作者：B.R.）

Ivory Plaque – 2 Men and a Sacred Tree

This plaque depicts two male figures on either side of a stylized palm tree. The right-hand figure was damaged in antiquity, but other examples from Nimrud suggest that it duplicated the left-hand figure in all ways except for the position of his left arm. Both figures wear the double crown and kilt typical of Egyptian pharaohs. Both figures also hold a sceptre in their right hand decorated with the head of a ram with curved horns (a symbol of Amun-Re). The figure on the left holds a narrow necked jug in his left hand, while the figure on the right holds an ankh, although both items are partially worn away. The entire scene is framed within an Egyptian royal kiosk, decorated with a winged sun-disk on the face of the entablature and a row of eight uraei along the roof.

While many of the individual elements in this scene are taken directly from Egyptian representations of royalty, the scene itself is distinctly Phoenician. Figures pouring out libation offerings while holding up a ram's-headed sceptre are attested in the Levant already by the Thirteenth Century BC and appear on Phoenician seals as well as on other ivories from Nimrud. In the earliest examples, offerings are being made to a seated figure who is either a deity or a deceased king. In the Nimrud ivories, the seated figure has been replaced by the stylized palm tree. In part this is for artistic reasons, as stylized trees are used to divide registers and provide visual unity between plaques. However, stylized palm trees are frequently associated with royal art and architecture in the Iron Age Levant and Cyprus, suggesting that it was a symbol of kingship like many of the Egyptian motifs used in this scene. (B.R.)

112. 象牙飾板 - 二個男子和聖樹
來自伊拉克尼姆羅德，ND 11003(2) 號平原
新亞述時期 (西元前 850-700 年)
象牙
148 x 60 x 13 mm

Ivory Plaque – 2 Men and a Sacred Tree
From Nimrud (Kahlu), Iraq, Fort Shalmaneser,
Field No. ND 11003(2)
NeoAssyrian (850-700 BC)
Ivory (elephant)

113. 象牙飾板 – 雙翼獅鷲
來自伊拉克尼姆羅德，ND 10483 號平原
新亞述時期 (西元前 850-700 年)
象牙
63 x 45 x 8 mm

Ivory Plaque – Winged Griffin
From Nimrud (Kahlu), Iraq, Fort Shalmaneser, Field
No. ND 10483
NeoAssyrian (850-700 BC)
Ivory (elephant)

象牙飾板—雙翼獅鷲

此浮雕飾板的主題為神話動物—雙翼獅鷲，為長了一對翅膀的獅身鷹首動物。和許多繪製於尼姆魯德（Nimrud）象牙上的獅鷲一樣，牠們頭上都有著類似迦南巴爾神（Ba'al）髮型的長捲羽毛；其側邊同樣裝飾著棕櫚葉。獅鷲圖像於西元前 4000 年便出現在現在的伊朗蘇薩（Susa）與埃及地區；在埃及，沒有翅膀的鷹首獅鷲即為帝王的象徵。西元前 2000 年地中海東部開始出現獅鷲圖像，而直至現代在歐洲的建築物與紋章中仍能看見獅鷲的蹤影。這類的梯形飾板共有六塊，這是其中的一塊；六塊組合後會形成一個斜截錐，可能具有杯架的用途。（作者：B.R.）

Ivory Plaque – Winged Griffin

The subject of this plaque is a winged griffin, a mythical creature formed by the body of a lion and the wings and head of an eagle. Like many griffins depicted on the Nimrud ivories, the tuft of feathers on its head are depicted in form of long curls, similar to those shown in the hair of the Canaanite god Ba'al. Also like other examples at Nimrud, this griffin would have flanked a stylized palm tree. Images of griffins appear already in both Susa, Iran and Egypt in the Fourth Millennium BC. In Egypt, a falcon-headed griffin without wings serves as a symbol of kingship. Images of griffins begin to appear in the Eastern Mediterranean in the Second Millennium BC and can still be seen today in European architecture and heraldry.

This trapezoidal plaque was one of six such plaques that would have fitted together to form a truncated cone, which may have been used as a cup holder. (B.R.)

114. 象牙嵌板—母牛與小牛
來自伊拉克尼姆羅德，ND 11080(201) 號平原
新亞述時期 (西元前 850-700 年)
象牙
61 x 30x 11 mm

Ivory Panel—Cow and Calf
From Nimrud (Kahlu), Iraq, Fort Shalmaneser, Field
No. ND 11080(201)
NeoAssyrian (850-700 BC)
Ivory (elephant)

象牙嵌板—母牛與小牛

這個雕刻描繪了一隻母牛轉頭舐拭躺在其身下的小牛。「母牛與小牛」為古代近東地區最早與最普及的藝術圖樣，而早在埃及古王國時期（第五王朝）與捷姆納薩期（Jemdet Nasr Period，西元前 3000 年早期）便出現過這些圖樣。在尼姆魯德（Nimrud）與敘利亞北部阿爾斯蘭塔什（Arslan Tash）同時代的象牙上，均看得到這些圖樣。一般而言，此圖樣象徵著大自然的豐沛資源與豐饒多產。

這個浮雕飾板外圍有個長方形邊框，為戶外飾板，但其外圍邊框現已遺失。母牛與小牛的眼睛皆經過挖空以鑲上埃及藍釉料，意謂著此象牙飾板原本並非只有單一色彩，而是綴以有色石頭或釉料與黃金葉子。（作者：B.R.）

Ivory Panel—Cow and Calf

This panel depicts a cow turning her head to lick her calf as it nurses at her udder. The 'cow and her calf' motif is one of the earliest and most widespread in the art of the ancient Near East. Examples occur already in Old Kingdom Egypt (Dynasty 5) and the Jemdet Nasr Period in Mesopotamia (early 3rd Millennium BC). Numerous examples occur amongst the ivories from Nimrud, as well as amongst contemporary ivories from the site of Arslan Tash in northern Syria. This motif is generally associated with scenes of natural fecundity and abundance.

The panel is carved as open-work within a rectangular frame that is now missing. The eyes of both the cow and the calf were excised in order be inlaid with Egyptian Blue frit. This fact reminds us that the ivories were originally not monochrome, having once been highlighted with coloured stone or frit and gold leaf. (B.R.)

西克索王朝聖甲蟲戒指

於燒製前先將聖甲蟲縱向貫穿，以銜接青銅環。背面有一道解剖聖甲蟲的刻痕。基座上刻畫了一個大步跨走的隼首神祇，並置於簡單的橢圓框架內。隼首神祇面向右方，為埃及藝術中的主位，並出現於代表「君主」neb 之象形文字之上。這位神祇穿著尖角短裙，左手持著一朵蓮花。短裙上的交叉線條與作品的挖空部分均為迦南當地的聖甲蟲特色，而圖像與神話圖樣則完全為埃及風格。在青銅器時代中期與西克索物品的文化中，融合埃及與地中海黎凡特（Levant）區域的傳統肖像是相當普遍的作法。可配戴聖甲蟲作為護身符，以祈求冥神奧塞里斯（Osiris）之子，天神（sky-god）荷魯斯（Horus）的幫助，而隼即為荷魯斯的象徵。在埃及神話中，蓮花象徵著重生與創造；蓮花經常出現於陪葬品之列，因此代表亡者對生命的渴求與在冥界中的繁榮。（作者：D.N.）

Hyksos Scarab on Ring

The scarab was pierced through lengthwise, before firing, to help attach the bronze ring. The back shows an incised tracing of the anatomy of the scarab beetle. The base depicts a striding falcon-headed deity placed inside a simple oval frame. The figure is facing to the right, which is the dominant position in Egyptian art, and is represented on top of the hieroglyph for 'lord', neb. The deity wears a pointed kilt and holds a lotus flower in its left hand. The cross-hatched pattern on the kilt and the hollowed out execution of the scene are characteristic of the local Canaanite scarabs, while the imagery and mythological motifs are completely Egyptian. Such a mixture of Egyptian and Levantine iconographic traditions is quite common for the Middle Bronze period and Hyksos material culture. The scarab might have been worn as a protective amulet invoking the help of the sky-god Horus (in his aspect as the son of Osiris, the god of the underworld), who is usually represented as a falcon. The lotus plant symbolises rebirth and creation in Egyptian mythology - as this object was a part of a grave goods assemblage it refers to the aspirations of the deceased for life and prosperity in the underworld. (D.N.)

116. 聖甲蟲戒指
來自巴勒斯坦
第二中間期，第 15 王朝（西元前 1650-1550 年）
彩陶，銅合金
31 x 20 x 8 mm

Scarab on Remains of Ring
From the Palestinian Territories, Gaza Tell el-Ajjul
Second Intermediate Period, Dynasty 15 (1650-1550 BC)
Faience, copper-alloy

聖甲蟲戒指

這個彩陶聖甲蟲背部僅展現聖甲蟲的基本線條，附有一個青銅環（僅戒子兩端殘存），應為繫上鍊子後戴在脖子上的護身符。底部的裝飾融合了青銅器時代埃及與地中海黎凡特（Levant）區域常見的花朵圖樣。邊框材質為象徵著「年輕」與「創造」的兩種紙莎草植物，並圍繞著一對自中心位置扭曲延伸而形成的對稱樹枝。在迦南當地的圖像學中，樹枝與女性身體和裸體女神具有相關性，因而更具意義。在整個西亞，這些圖像皆象徵在埃及諸神中居最重要位置的哈托爾（Hathor）女神，並代表愛情、美麗與母性等意義。女性會配戴這類聖甲蟲飾品守護自己度過艱困的生產過程，而聖甲蟲飾品也能作為贈送新生兒或年幼兒童的禮物，讓他們獲得這位美善女神的守護。（作者：D.N.）

Scarab on Remains of Ring

The back of this faience scarab shows only the basic outline of a scarab beetle. It was attached to a bronze ring (of which only the two ends remain) to be worn as a protective amulet, possiby on a string along the neck. The decoration on the base consists of a mixture of floral motifs common to both Egypt and the Levant during the Middle Bronze age. The frame is made of two papyrus plants symbolysing youth and creation. These enclose a pair of symmetrical branches coming out of the centrally positioned twisted cable. Branches are particularly significant in the local Canaanite iconography through their association with female figurines and nude goddesses, such as Anat and Astarte. Throughout Western Asia these were closely identified with Hathor, one of the most important goddesses of the Egyptian pantheon, and represent ideas of love, beauty, and motherhood. A woman could have worn this object to guard her through the rigours of childbirth, or it could have been a gift to a newborn or a young child, ensuring the protection of a benign deity. (D.N.)

聖甲蟲

縱向穿孔顯示這個聖甲蟲飾品原本應是穿在繩子上，
或為金屬戒子的戒臺，只是戒子現已遺失。甲蟲與底
座上的圖片設計均相當簡略，而花朵的圖樣則是古埃
及最普遍的「皇家」象徵之一即：sema tawy，象徵上下埃
及的統一。此圖像由蓮花與紙莎草植物彼此纏繞於代表統
一的象形文字 sema 外圍。蓮花是南埃及（亦即上埃及）的
紋章符號，而紙莎草植物則代表著北埃及（亦即下埃及）。
就古埃及人的世界觀而言，分裂與混亂是他們相當厭惡之事，
因此法老王的主要職責之一即為維持國家的穩定狀況，讓北
方與南方結合、沙漠地區與尼羅河流域統一、讓神的精神世界
與人類的物質世界結合。彼此纏繞的繩索成為聖甲蟲底座上的框
架，並強調 sema tawy 圖樣的結合面向。在青銅器時期中期，或
更明確地說，在第二中間時期，迦南當地曾模仿這個純埃及設計，並
再增添一些風格上的變化，如植物環形中的交叉線條。這類圖樣常用於
器皿或珠寶裝飾上、神廟或墳墓的牆面上，並作為傢俱的裝飾鑲嵌。（作者：
D.N.）

Scarab

The longitudinal piercing on this scarab indicates that it was supposed to be
worn on a string or as the bezel of a metal ring which is now lost. The designs of
both the beetle and the image on the base are quite schematic. The floral motif
represents one of the most common 'royal' symbols from ancient Egypt - sema
tawy, the union of the two lands. The image consists of the lotus and papyrus
plants knotted together around the hieroglyph for union, sema. The lotus is the
heraldic sign for the southern part of the country, Upper Egypt, while the papyrus
stands for the north, Lower Egypt. Division and chaos were abhorrent to the
ancient Egyptian worldview and it was one of the main duties of the pharaoh to
preserve the stability of his country, the north united with the south, the desert
regions with the Nile valley, the spiritual world of the gods with the physical
world of the mortals. The binding aspect of the sema tawy motif is visually
strengthened by the string of twisted rope acting as a border frame at the scarab
base. Local Canaanite imitations of this purely Egyptian design are known from
all periods of the Middle Bronze age but some stylistic variations, such as the
cross lines inside the loops of the plants, might point at a more specific date in the
Second Intermediate Period. It is commonly seen on decorated vessels, jewellery,
on the walls of temples and tombs, and as decorative inlays for furniture. (D.N.)

117. 聖甲蟲
來自巴勒斯坦
第二中間期，第 15 王朝（西元前 1650-1550 年）
塊滑石
23 x 16 x 8 mm

Scarab
From the Palestinian Territories, Gaza Tell el-Ajjul
Second Intermediate Period, Dynasty 15 (1650-1550 BC)
Steatite

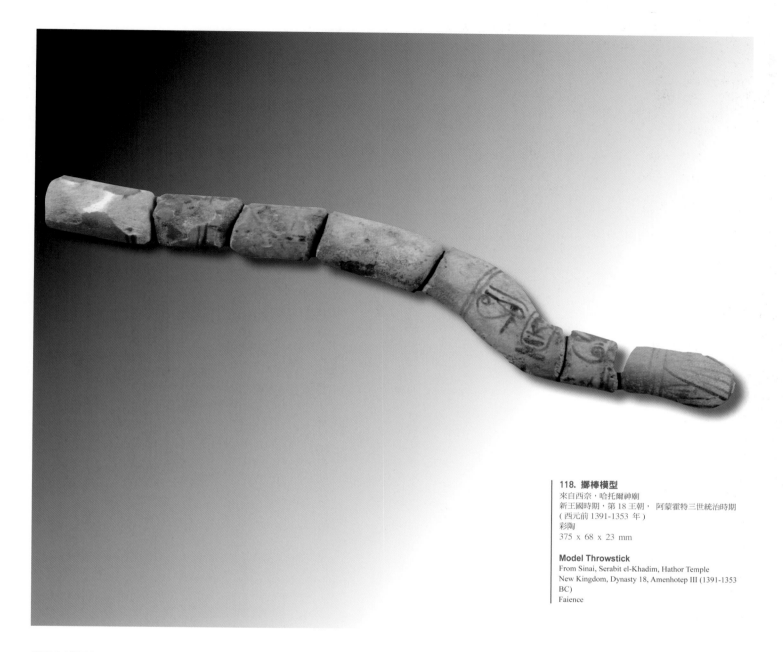

118. 擲棒模型
來自西奈，哈托爾神廟
新王國時期，第 18 王朝， 阿蒙霍特三世統治時期
（西元前 1391-1353 年）
彩陶
375 x 68 x 23 mm

Model Throwstick
From Sinai, Serabit el-Khadim, Hathor Temple
New Kingdom, Dynasty 18, Amenhotep III (1391-1353 BC)
Faience

擲棒模型

在西奈的沙拉別艾卡錠（Serabit el-Khadim）的哈托爾女神廟中，佩托里（Petrie）在獻給哈托爾女神的還願祭品中，找到約 60 個彩陶投擲器（棍）。神廟的聖殿與柱廊上有著厚厚一層可追溯至新王國時期的彩陶，包括花瓶、碗、杯子、飾板、莫那特平衡鎚（menat-counterpoises）與手環。在第十八王朝時期的底比斯墓中普遍有著描繪在尼羅河畔沼澤使用木製投擲器獵鳥的情景，而投擲器的一端多半會刻著蛇首。在墓中擺放投擲器是為了讓亡者在來世仍能繼續打獵，更重要地，讓亡者戰勝由飛行鳥類所代表的混亂。在獵鳥場景中所描繪的女神是沼澤之神絲梅特（Sekhet）；而以牡牛形象出現的哈托爾同樣也與沼澤地有關，因此投擲器也是獻給哈托爾的合宜祭品。此外，投擲器的埃及文為 gema，近似於「創造」、「產生」，因此投擲器也象徵著豐饒肥沃。

這個藍色彩陶投擲器已碎裂為七個部分，綴有白色的睡蓮花瓣與一對荷魯斯之眼（烏加眼，udjat-eyes），旁邊是阿蒙霍特三世（Amenhotep III）王名圖，外圍有著雙重飾帶。這根投擲器已褪色並磨損，而終端部分也遺失部分碎片。由於彩陶重擊堅硬表面時會碎裂，因此這根投擲器極可能不具有實際的使用目的；主要價值在於其象徵意義而非實用性。（作者：N.H.）

Throwstick

William Flinders Petrie found fragments of around 60 faience throwsticks ('wands') among the votive offerings dedicated to the goddess Hathor at her temple at Serabit el-Khadim in the Sinai. The sanctuary and portico of this temple contained a thick layer of broken faience dating to the New Kingdom, including vases, bowls, cups, plaques, menat-counterpoises, and bracelets. Wooden throwsticks were used for hunting birds in the marshes on the banks of the Nile, as commonly depicted in Dynasty 18 Theban tombs, and often have the head of a snake carved at one end. They may have been deposited in tombs to enable the deceased to continue to hunt in the afterlife, and perhaps more importantly, to overcome the chaos represented by the birds in flight. The goddess mentioned in fowling scenes is Sekhet, the deity of the marshes; in her bovine form Hathor was also associated with marshland, and throwsticks were therefore an appropriate offering for her. In addition, the throwstick may have had symbolic connections to fertility, since its Egyptian name (gema) is similar for the word for 'to create' or 'beget'.

This blue faience throwstick is broken into seven sections and is decorated with white water lily petals and a pair of udjat-eyes flanking the cartouche of Amenhotep III enclosed within a double band. It is faded and abraded, and flakes are missing from the terminal segment. It is likely that this throwstick was never intended for use, since the faience would shatter on impact with a hard surface: its value was symbolic rather than practical. (N.H.)

莫那特護身符

莫那特平衡鎚（Menat counterpoises）能平衡依附上方角落兩個鑽孔上的多條串珠重量。附有莫那特的項鍊與哈托爾女神有關，尤其是以牡牛形象現身的哈托爾女神，通常會搭配由女祭司搖動叉鈴（sistra，儀式用搖鈴），撫慰眾神。當在墓地進行此動作呈獻給亡者時，即象徵著授予哈托爾的恩典：生命、健康、豐饒與重生。這片不完整莫那特寫著：「阿蒙霍特三世（Amenhotep III）（Nebmaatre），蒙綠松石女神（Mistress of Turquoise）哈托爾之恩典」。

綠松石（mefkat）與其替代品，彩陶（tjehnet），皆為代表哈托爾女神的聖物。彩陶本身即帶有亮度，是非黏土的陶瓷原料，以石英砂（粉碎的石英礫石）、石灰與鹼（泡鹼或植物灰）再和入水製成；混合銅礦、孔雀石或藍銅礦後，能創造彩陶的獨特色彩；而依據添加物質的多寡，會出現綠色到深藍等不同色彩。陶土是在拉坯輪上的模具中以手工進行塑形，在燒製前先塗上錳或氧化鐵顏料，並以800-1000°C的溫度於窯中燒製，就能完成此莫那特與本書中數項物品上的黑色裝飾。最常見的上釉方法為風化或自身上釉（self-glazing）。隨著水分蒸發，塗在陶土表面的鹽會形成表層，並於溶化與溶合後創造出光澤感。（作者：N.H.）

Menat

Menat counterpoises were designed to balance the weight of numerous strings of beads, which were attached by two holes drilled into the top corners. Necklaces with menats were associated with Hathor, particularly in bovine form, and were often paired with sistra (ceremonial rattles) and shaken by priestesses to pacify the gods. They are shown being presented to the deceased in tomb scenes, an act that may have been symbolic of conferring Hathor's favours: life, health, fertility and rebirth. The inscription on this fragmentary menat reads "Amenhotep III (Nebmaat[re]), beloved of Hathor, Mistress of Turquoise".

Both turquoise (mefkat), and its substitute, faience (tjehnet), were sacred to the goddess Hathor. Faience itself is a glazed, non-clay ceramic material, made from quartz sand (crushed quartz pebbles), lime, and alkalis (natron or plant ash) combined with water. Copper ore, malachite or azurite were mixed in to create its characteristic colours, from light green to deep blue depending on the quantity added. The paste was shaped by hand, in moulds on a pottery wheel. The black decoration on this menat and several other objects in this catalogue was achieved by the application of manganese or iron oxide paint prior to firing in the kiln at 800-1000°C. The most common glazing method is efflorescence, or self-glazing. Salt, drawn to the surface of the paste as the water evaporates, forms a layer which melts and fuses to create a varnished effect. (N.H.)

119. 莫那特護身符
來自西奈，哈托爾神廟
新王國時期，第18王朝，阿蒙霍特三世統治時期
（西元前1391-1353年）
彩陶
108 x 56 x 10 mm

Menat
From Sinai, Serabit el-Khadim, Hathor Temple
New Kingdom, Dynasty 18, reign of Amenhotep III
(1391-1353 BC)
Faience

120. 彩陶環形支撐座
來自西奈，哈托爾神廟
新王國時期，第 19 王朝， 塞堤二世統治時期 (西元前 1391-1353 年)
彩陶
110 x 110 x 37 mm

Ring Stand
From Sinai, Serabit el-Khadim, Hathor Temple
New Kingdom, Dynasty 19, reign of Sety II (1214-1204 BC)
Faience

彩陶環形支撐座

多數埃及器皿皆為圓底，因此直立時需緊靠牆面並置於凹陷平面上，或立在環形支撐底座上。要區分自沙拉別艾卡錠（Serabit el-Khadim）出土的環形底座與擁有類似外型的彩陶手環時，可從兩者的不同寬度與外壁厚度來進行辨識。此展品包含了上半表面的一圈黑線、戴著「polos」或厚底皇冠的哈托爾頭像、一隻貓底座已碎裂為七塊碎片，原本為明亮藍色，但如今其表面已變色且磨損。黑色裝飾與一段文字：「上下埃及共主塞堤二世（Userkheperure Setepenre），蒙哈托爾（綠松石女神）之恩典」。貓的身體部分只以側面輪廓表現，但頭部則以正面展現；由於哈托爾的頭像或面具也展現正面，因此或許是藉此將貓與哈托爾進行連結。貓或許是哈托爾較為少見的象徵形象，但在西奈神廟中卻相當普遍。（作者：N.H.）

Ring Stand

Many Egyptian vessels were round-bottomed, which meant that in order to stand vertically they were leant against a wall, placed in a hollow in the ground, or stood on a ring-shaped support. Ring stands from Serabit el-Khadim can be distinguished from similar-looking faience bracelets by their width and the thickness of their walls. The Bolton stand is broken into seven pieces, and was originally bright blue: the surface is now discoloured and abraded. The black decoration consisted of a single line running around the upper surface, a Hathor head with 'polos' or platform crown, a cat, and an inscription: "The lord of the two lands, Sety II (Userkheperure Setepenre), beloved of Hathor [Mistress of Turq]uoise". The cat's body is shown in profile, though its head is depicted frontally, perhaps to link it iconographically with Hathor whose head or mask is depicted in the same manner. The cat is probably a representation of the goddess in her less common feline form, which seems to have been popular at the Sinai temple. (N.H.)

121. 陶瓶碎片
來自西奈，哈托爾神廟
新王國時期，第 19 王朝，拉美西斯二世統治時期（西元前 1279-1213 年）
彩陶
55 x 50 x 17 mm

Vessel Fragment
From Sinai, Serabit el-Khadim, Hathor Temple
New Kingdom, Dynasty 19, reign of Ramesses II
(1279-1213 BC)
Faience

陶瓶碎片

彩陶上的明亮藍色與藍綠色能使人聯想到蔬菜、水，與反射陽光的瀲灩水面。或許由於彩陶能在燒窯中從暗淡、無色的泥團幻化為鮮艷、令人眼花撩亂的釉面陶瓷，因此被稱為 tjehnet，意指「明亮」或「閃閃發光」，象徵著生命與新生。哈托爾女神被稱為彩陶之神（Mistress of Faience）與綠松石女神（Mistress of Turquoise），而在綠松石礦場沙拉別艾卡錠（Serabit el-Khadim）將彩陶貢品呈獻予哈托爾，更具雙重意義。

此器皿上有著拉美西斯二世（Ramesses II）的王名圈（cartouche），因此極可能為由官員或國王本人於巡視礦區時作為獻給哈托爾女神的貢品。「（完美之神），上下埃及（共主），拉美西斯（Usermaatre）；Re 之子，美（之女神），拉美西斯蒙受阿蒙之愛，（如）Re 賦與生命」。拉美西斯二世之名的寫法相當少見，但已經過驗證。右方的碑文大多已消失，但依然可看出「蒙哈托爾，天界之神，綠松石女神之恩典」。從彩陶碎片的外壁厚度判斷，顯示原本應為存放液體（酒、水、牛奶）的器皿，於獻祭或受洗儀式中使用。（作者：N.H.）

Vessel Fragment

The bright blue or blue-green of faience is reminiscent of vegetation and water, with a shiny surface that reflects the sun. It was known as tjehnet, meaning that which is 'brilliant' or 'gleaming', and was symbolic of life and renewal, probably partly due to the transformation in the kiln from a dull, virtually colourless paste to a vivid and dazzling glazed ceramic. The goddess Hathor was both Mistress of Faience and Mistress of Turquoise, which renders the faience offerings to her at Serabit el-Khadim, the site of a turquoise mine, doubly appropriate.

This vessel bears the cartouches of Ramesses II and may have been dedicated to the goddess by an official or the king himself during a mining expedition. "[The perfect god, lord of the] two lands, Usermaatre; the son of Re, [lord of] appearances, Ramesses-beloved-of-Amun, given life [like] Re". The writing of Ramesses' prenomen is unusual but not unattested. The inscription to the right is largely missing, but may have read "Beloved of Hathor, Mistress of the Sky, Mistress of Turquoise". The thickness of the walls suggests that it might have held liquid – wine, milk, or water – for offering or washing rituals. (N.H.)

陶瓶碎片

許多自沙拉別艾卡錠（Serabit el-Khadim）挖掘出土的彩陶器皿都擁有相當不尋常或獨特的造型，就像這個中型花瓶。在佩托里（Petrie）從沙拉別艾卡錠運至英國的六個碎片中，其中的三片在不常見的水滴狀帶飾下方繪有阿蒙霍特三世（Amenhotep III）的王名圖（cartouche）；有一個抽象的植物圖與類似現代花瓶上的一朵盛開睡蓮與花苞，但這些花樣或王名圖與其他元素之間的相關性卻難以判定。其中一塊碎片上描繪了一個葡萄棚架，似乎下方應該還有一根直立叉棍與橫桿，但剩下的花瓶部分顯示其餘支撐部分皆已破裂。這些裝飾可能與花瓶的內容物有相關性：意謂著睡蓮被浸泡於飲酒中，以增添風味。

部份學者表示，將睡蓮垂墜於酒瓶四周代表睡蓮會與瓶中的內容物有所混合。若是如此，那麼在宴會時傳遞給墓室主人及其妻子的金色器皿便極具重要性，因為這些器皿的邊緣同樣繪有抽象的花朵，顯示睡蓮會浸泡於獻祭的液體中（可能為祭酒）。在少數殘存的幾個同類器皿中，其中一兩個飾有牡牛形象的哈托爾女神，並且底部突起，讓花柄得以從中穿過。睡蓮所釋放出來的麻醉化學作用能夠加強酒精效果，實為獻給西奈神廟中的酩酊女神（Mistress of Drunkenness）哈托爾的最佳祭品。（作者：N.H.）

Vessel Fragments

Many of the faience vessels from Serabit el-Khadim are of unusual or unique types. This medium-sized vase seems to be one of these. Of the six fragments transported to England from the site by Petrie, three have cartouches of Amenhotep III (Nebmaatre) beneath an unusual teardrop-shaped band. A stylised plant motif and a water lily blossom and bud have parallels on contemporary vessels, though it is difficult to see a pattern or how the cartouches relate to the other elements. One fragment appears to depict a grape arbour, insofar as there is one vertical forked stick with a horizontal pole suspended from it, the section of the vase showing the other support having broken away. It is possible that the decoration was related to the contents of the vessel: wine which had been fortified by steeping lily flowers in it.

Some scholars have suggested that the water lilies draped over and around wine jars indicate that the contents had been mixed with them. If this is the case, then the golden vessels passed to the tomb owner and his wife during banquets may be significant as they also have stylised blossoms around the rim, suggesting that lilies were steeping in the liquid offering, probably wine. Of the few surviving examples of this bowl type, a couple contain a figure of the goddess Hathor in bovine form, with a projection in the base through which flower stalks may have been threaded. The narcotic chemicals released by the lilies would have enhanced the effects of alcohol: such gifts would be appropriate for Hathor at her Sinai temple in her aspect as Mistress of Drunkenness. (N.H.)

122. 陶瓶碎片
來自西奈，哈托爾神廟
新王國時期，第 18 王朝，阿蒙霍特三世統治時期
（西元前 1391-1353 年）
彩陶
75 x 65 x 28 mm

Vessel Fragment
From Sinai, Serabit el-Khadim, Hathor Temple
New Kingdom, Dynasty 18, reign of Amenhotep III
(1391-1353 BC)
Faience

123. 陶瓶碎片
來自西奈，哈托爾神廟
新王國時期，第 18 王朝，阿蒙霍特三世統治時期（西元前 1391-1353 年）
彩陶
94 x 69 x 29 mm

Vessel Fragment
From Sinai, Serabit el-Khadim, Hathor Temple
New Kingdom, Dynasty 18, reign of Amenhotep III
(1391-1353 BC)
Faience

124

125

哈托爾模型

哈托爾是埃及少數幾位呈現正面形象（en face）而非側面輪廓的神祇，部分是因為太陽神偶爾會出現正面的形象，而哈托爾正為太陽神拉（Re）之女。哈托爾有著一對母牛耳朵，讓人聯想起哈托爾象徵富饒滋養的母牛女神的身份；頭上戴著 polos 或厚底皇冠與綁著三條髮帶的直紋假髮。由於臉部相當平面不具立體感，因而呈現如面具般的外表。保留了原有明亮藍色的那一面，顯示該面並非如另一面般因穿戴者的使用而遭受磨損。如此處所展示的哈托爾頭像，上方通常會再加上一個儀式用搖鈴（圓圈或神殿叉鈴），但此哈托爾頭像上方的皇冠並沒有過去曾連接其他物品的跡象；相反地，此頭像應為迷你紀念柱的一部分，是仿製大型紀念碑或作為節慶中使用的可攜式紀念柱。以相同方式受到崇拜的神祇包括了底比斯的阿蒙雷神（Amun-Re）與阿努奇斯（Anukis）。在沙拉別艾卡錠（Serabit el-Khadim）的神廟中找到的彩陶碎片顯示為設於紀念柱上的哈托爾面具；而佩托里（Petrie）更表示它們即為豎立於節慶場合中的柱子。（作者：N.H.）

Bifrontal Hathor Mask

Hathor is one of the few Egyptian deities to be shown frontally (en face) rather than in profile. This may be due in part to her status as the daughter of Re, since the sun-god is also sometimes depicted in this way. Hathor's ears are those of a bovine, evocative of her role as the nurturing cow goddess. She wears the polos or platform crown and a striated wig tied with three bands. The face seems flattened, giving it a mask-like appearance. One face has retained its original bright blue, indicating that it was protected from exposure to both the weather and abrasion that has damaged the other one. Often Hathor heads like this are surmounted by a ceremonial rattle (loop or naos/shrine sistrum), but the top of the crown shows no sign of breakage as would be expected if another element had been attached. Instead, this head is part of a miniature column, imitating a large-scale fixed monument or a portable version that could be carried in festival processions. Deities honoured in a similar manner include Amun-Re and Anukis at Thebes. Faience plaques from the temple at Serabit el-Khadim show Hathor masks on columns; Petrie suggested that they depict poles set up on festive occasions. (N.H.)

柱狀握柄

這個淡藍綠色彩陶手柄自底部些微展開，上面連接著哈托爾神像面具（參見本書編號 124）。上面寫著兩列呼應兩個面具的文字，其譯文分別為「由國王獻給綠松石女神哈托爾」以及「上下埃及共主，Usermaatre-Meryamun；美之女神，Ramesses-Hekaiunu」。顯示這項物品是依據進貢的程序，由不知名官員（可能為代表團領袖）獻給女神；也可能是皇室以還願目的獻給哈托爾女神的貢品。設置迷你手柄的習俗似乎始於阿蒙霍特一世（Amenhotep I）的統治時期（西元前 1525-1504 年），並沿續了整個新王國時期。（作者：N.H.）

Miniature Column

This pale blue-green faience column flares slightly towards the base and was once surmounted by a bifrontal Hathor mask (see Catalogue #124). It has two vertical lines of text corresponding with the two masks that may be translated as: "An offering which the king gives to Hathor, Lady of Turquoise", and "Lord of the Two Lands, Usermaatre-Meryamun, Lord of Appearances, Ramesses-Hekaiunu." It has been suggested, based on the presence of the offering formula, that this object was dedicated to the goddess by an unnamed official, perhaps an expedition leader. It is equally possible that the column was part of royal votive offerings to Hathor: the deposition of miniature columns seems to have begun in the reign of Amenhotep I (1525-1504 BC) and continued throughout the New Kingdom. (N.H.)

124. 哈托爾模型
來自西奈，哈托爾神廟
新王國時期，第 20 王朝，拉美西斯三世統治
時期（西元前 1184-1153 年）
彩陶
82 x 67 x 36 mm

Bifrontal Hathor Mask
From Sinai, Serabit el-Khadim, Hathor Temple
New Kingdom, Dynasty 20, reign of Ramesses III
(1184-1153 BC)
Faience

125. 柱狀握柄
來自西奈，哈托爾神廟
新王國時期，第 20 王朝，拉美西斯三世統治
時期（西元前 1184-1153 年）
彩陶
115 x 33 x 31 mm

Miniature Column
From Sinai, Serabit el-Khadim, Hathor Temple
New Kingdom, Dynasty 20, reign of Ramesses III
(1184-1153 BC)
Faience

126. 哈托爾浮雕
來自西德塔特拉納
托勒密時期，托勒密一世統治時期（西元前
305-285 年）
石灰岩
855 x 830 x 250 mm

Relief of Hathor
From Terraneh, Western Delta
Ptolemaic Period, reign of Ptolemy I (305-285 BC)
Limestone

哈托爾浮雕

特瑞納（Terraneh，古稱 Terenouthis）的哈托爾（Hathor）神廟，位於西三角洲（Western Delta）邊陲地帶，靠近恐阿布必羅（Kom Abu Billo）墓地出土了三座緊鄰的石碑。非常幸運地，這些浮雕因葛瑞菲斯（F. Ll. Griffith）於 1887 至 1888 年間，代表埃及探索學會（Egypt Exploration Fund）勘查該地而得以保存至今，未如其他許多石灰岩石碑般，遭到後人重複利用或在石灰窯中燒毀。

托勒密王朝之開朝君主托勒密一世（西元前 305-285 年）建造的所有建物中，僅有特瑞納的哈托爾神廟成為少數存留至今的範例。這些同時收藏在英國牛津、格拉斯哥和美國的精美淺浮雕，最能代表托勒密王朝早期的藝術，由淺薄的石碑厚度，即可推斷建物本身的規格亦極為樸實。這些浮雕原本可能是內牆的一部分，雕工十分精緻，與托勒密二世時期以沉雕雕鑿，應屬外部結構之一的石碑大相逕庭。

該雕刻係描繪古埃及人向神廟主神哈托爾獻祭的儀式。畫面中有一個人手持一種通常由女祭司持有，在儀式中使用，稱為又鈴（sistrum）的搖鈴，走向女神神像。又鈴的古埃及原文為 sesheshet，讀音可能是模仿該樂器發出的聲響，此字亦以古埃及象形字，出現在又鈴圖案的上方，由此可見，古埃及藝術經常以圖案作為隨後之文字的限定詞或類詞。女神像前面的其他象形文字，則是強調古埃及人對該儀式之人神互惠的理解：祂說祂會「施予」某樣東西，也許是生命，或是健康，做為獻祭的回報。

通常，哈托爾女神係被描繪成頭上長牛角的女人，有時也會以頭長牛耳的正面出現，而當地版本的哈托爾女神（稱 Mistress of Mefket），是以牛頭女的形象出現，戴著長長的假髮，並有兩條烏瑞（uraei）眼鏡蛇作為傳統頭飾的一部分，手握紙莎草權仗，為女神的典型特徵。（作者：C.P.）

Relief of Hathor

These three adjoining blocks come from a temple to the goddess Hathor at Terraneh, ancient Terenouthis, located near the cemetery site of Kom Abu Billo on the edge of the Western Delta. Fortunately, unlike many other limestone monuments which were reused or destroyed totally in lime-kilns, these reliefs were saved by F. Ll. Griffith, who investigated the site on behalf of the Egypt Exploration Fund between 1887-1888.

The temple at Terraneh is one of the few surviving structures built by Ptolemy I Soter (305-285 BC), founder of the Ptolemaic dynasty. These fine, low relief carvings – others are in Oxford, Glasgow and the United States – are among the best examples of the art of the early Ptolemies. The shallow depth of the blocks suggests a building of modest dimensions. These reliefs likely belonged to interior walls; their delicacy of execution can be contrasted with those of other blocks, carved in sunk relief by Ptolemy II, that seem to have belonged to the outside of the structure.

This scene depicts an offering ritual for the chief deity of the temple, Hathor. A figure approaching the goddess holds a sistrum, or ritual rattle, often held by priestesses. The Egyptian word for 'sistrum' is sesheshet and was likely supposed to imitate the sound the instrument made. This word appears in hieroglyphs above the image of the sistrum. Thus, as is typical in Egyptian art, an image acts as a determinative, or classifier, of the word it comes after. The remaining hieroglyphs directly in front of the goddess highlight the reciprocal understanding of such rituals: she says that she will 'give' something – perhaps life, or health – in return.

Usually, Hathor is shown as a woman with cow's horns on top of her head, or sometimes full-face with a cow's ears. Here, the local form of Hathor 'Mistress of Mefket' is shown as a cow-headed woman, with a long wig and two cobras – called uraei – added to her traditional headdress. The papyrus sceptre she holds is a typical attribute of female deities. (C.P.)

刻有女神舒（Shu）的神殿壁畫

蘇（Shu）是初始創造之神阿圖姆（Atum）的兒子，也是一位生命與創造之神，在圖中，是以正常人的形體出現，面朝左站立，似乎在接受一位國王或王子（浮雕部分已不可考）的獻祭。頭上的羽毛是王冠象徵，上面則以象形文字書寫著祂的名字，蛇型頭冠（王冠）的束帶以淺浮雕的方式刻在頭部後方，另外還穿戴了其他神聖飾物，如三角假髮、長假鬍以及摺裙，軀幹部分則保持裸露。這塊石碑是艾朵納威爾（Edouard Naville）在位於東三角洲（Eastern Delta）特貝斯塔（Tell Basta，或以希臘文 Bubastis 著稱）的獅身（貓身）神貝斯特（Bastet）神廟中挖掘而出。蘇被納入貝斯特神廟中，可能與祂本身也是施予生命之神有關，也可能與祂對應之女神特夫娜（Tefnut）的獅身型體和貝斯特極為相似有關，但這些只是祂被納入神廟的諸多可能原因的其中兩個。古埃及金字塔創造、納入並展現了各種不同的神聖星座和宇宙論，而蘇在貝斯特神廟出現，也代表了相同的複合性及多元性。

西元前五世紀之古希臘歷史學家希羅多德（Herodotus），描述貝斯特神廟為：「最值得注目的建物。其他神廟可能更大，花費更多，但沒有一座比此神廟更引人注目。」這塊石碑原是屬於希羅多德最敬仰之建物的一部分，且在他造訪該建物 前幾百年即已雕刻並安置完成。貝斯特神廟與其他古埃及神廟一樣，都曾經歷多次拆遷、重建及擴建，這塊石碑也見證了神廟波折不斷的過去。與蘇圖像垂直的石面上，雕有清晰可見之擬人形體的腿部和腳部，可能是木乃伊形體的神（Mummiform deity），祂和蘇圖像方位顛倒，且沒有正對著蘇圖像。蘇圖像的浮雕可能較早雕刻完成，時間可能為第十九王朝或第三中間期。納威爾還記錄了該遺址的一塊石碑，上面刻有拉美西斯二世（Rameses II）的兒子梅尼普塔王子（Merenptah），圖中梅尼普塔正面的形體與石碑上之蘇的神像近似，正在焚香祭拜。該浮雕也可能是第三中間期神廟擴建的一部分，擴建時間為奧索爾孔一世（Osorkon I）與二世（Osorkon II）任內，且這兩位君王都曾在貝斯特神廟追溯自己的源頭。經過一段時間過後，石碑被翻面，另外雕上木乃伊形體的浮雕圖案，由於此圖案周圍有重新修繕的痕跡，即顯示石碑曾在過去的其他時期中遭到重複使用，且推測刻有蘇神像的一面可能緊靠其他石碑，才會變得模糊不清。第二個浮雕人物的完工時間，以及與其有關的神廟改建與變革部分的時間，皆已難以判定。（作者：L.F.）

127. 刻有女神舒 (Shu) 的神殿壁畫
來自貝斯塔神廟
新王國時期至第三中間期，第 19 至 25 王朝（西元前 1295-664 年）
紅花崗岩
1000 x 410 x 350 mm

Temple Block with an Image of the God Shu
From Tell Basta (Bubastis), the temple of Bastet
New Kingdom – Third Intermediate Period, Dynasty 19 – 25
(1295-664 BC)
Red granite

Temple Block with an Image of the God Shu

Shu, as child of the primeval creator god Atum, was also a god of life and creation. He is shown here in his normal human form, standing and facing left, probably in order to receive offerings from a now lost figure of a king or prince. The feather on his head is his emblematic crown and the hieroglyph that writes his name. The tie for a filet or diadem is carved in low relief behind his head. He wears other, typical divine accoutrements such as the tripartite wig, long false beard, and pleated kilt which leaves his torso bare. This block fragment was found by the excavator Edouard Naville in the temple of the lion- or cat-headed goddess Bastet, in the city of Tell Basta (also known by its Greek name of Bubastis) in the eastern Delta. Shu was included in scenes in Bastet's temple perhaps in his capacity as life-giver, or through his relationship with his female divine counterpart Tefnut whose leonine form linked her closely to Bastet. These are two of many possible reasons for his representation. Egyptian temples created, enclosed, and displayed a myriad of divine constellations and cosmologies; Shu's presence in Bastet's temple is expressive of this plurality and diversity.

The temple of Bastet was described by the Greek historian Herodotus in the fifth century BC as "a building most worthy of note. Other temples are greater and more costly, but none pleasanter to the eye than this." This fragment would have been part of the structure that Herodotus admired, having been carved and set in place a few hundred years before his visit. Like all major Egyptian cult temples, Bastet's went through many phases of dismantling, rebuilding, and expansion; this fragment bears witness to some of this complex history. On the face perpendicular to that bearing the image of Shu, the foot and leg of another male anthropomorphic figure is visible, possibly a mummiform deity. This figure is upside-down in relation to Shu and oriented away from him. The scene with Shu was probably carved first, perhaps in Dynasty 19 or early Third Intermediate Period. Naville recorded a block from the site which shows prince Merenptah, son and heir of Rameses II, censing before a figure of Shu which is similar to the one on this fragment. However the scene may also date to the Third Intermediate Period, as part of extensive building works undertaken in the temple by Osorkon I and Osorkon II, kings who traced their origins to Tell Basta. Some time later, the block was turned around and carved with a scene that included the mummiform figure. There are traces of reworking around this image indicating additional stages of reuse. The surface bearing Shu was probably pushed against other blocks, thus made invisible. It is difficult to date the carving of the second figure and the associated reshaping and transformation of part of Bastet's temple that it implies. (L.F.)

供品台

宏偉的古埃及神廟和神殿所有的室內陳設，皆早已撤出，因此當我們面對這些偉大建物時，實在難以想像，過去在這些建物內主持過的無數儀式中，究竟使用了多少陳列物品、器皿以及器具。此供品台常見於神廟牆壁上的裝飾浮雕中，在浮雕中，供品台通常擺滿了各樣的供品、酒、燈或香爐。

此供品台是以青銅敲打製成，並附有一個小圓盤，由一支細桿支撐，尾端則是華麗的喇叭狀，但供品台上擺設的供品已無從得知了。發現地點係位於薩卡拉（Saqqara）之神聖動物墓地的主神殿區。此供品台是在開挖當時，由成堆的神殿器物中挖掘而出，當時供品台已被拆解，並以亞麻布包裹，小心翼翼地與瓶裝木乃伊老鷹埋在同一個地方。此器物與其他同時出土的器物一樣，都有使用過的痕跡，底部還寫有四行供奉文字，雖然文字只剩片段，但部分仍可辨識：「在奧塞里斯-阿匹斯（Osiris-Apis）偉大神尊前…帕…，索德坦（Thotertain）之子，母親為鞈…公羊，孟德斯（Mendes）之主，偉大神…」。（作者：J.H.W.）

Offering Stand

When faced with the monumental temples and shrines of ancient Egypt -- which now stand largely emptied of their furnishings -- it is hard to imagine the vast amount of furniture, vessels and equipment used for the countless rituals these buildings hosted. This offering stand is of a type often seen in reliefs decorating the walls of temples, where the stands support various kinds of offerings, libation vessels, lamps or incense burners.

Made of hammered bronze, this stand has a small circular pan supported by a narrow stem that ends in a flaring trumpet-shaped base. It is uncertain what the stand may have supported. It was discovered in the main temple area of the sacred animal necropolis at Saqqara. Excavators found this stand in a large deposit of other temple materials, which had been dismantled, wrapped in linen and carefully buried in an area that also contained jars containing mummified falcons. Like many of the other objects with which it was found, the object shows sign of use and also bears a dedicatory inscription in four lines around its base. The inscription is fragmentary, but can be read in part: "Before Osiris-Apis, the great god […] Pa-[…], son of Thotertain whose mother is Ta […] the ram, Lord of Mendes, the great god […]". (J.H.W.)

128. 供品台
來自薩卡拉
希臘羅馬時期（西元前 332 年 - 西元 100 年）
銅合金
1410 x 465 x 465 mm

Offering Stand
From Saqqara
Graeco-Roman Period (332 BC-AD 100)
Copper-alloy

長柄勾杓

這種杓子是在室內及儀式中盛酒的重要器具。在宗教典禮上，此杓子通常是用於倒貢酒，或品嚐之後將酒灑在祭物頭上，在希臘羅馬時期，這種杓子會出現在各種媒介物品中，最著名的就是刻在羅馬硬幣背面，代表祭祀的器具。杓子也曾出現在古埃及的器物歷史中，出土於坦尼斯（Tanis）之第二十一王朝的銀杓，便是早期歷史的印證，而且無論在托勒密時期早期或希臘羅馬時期，杓子都是祭祀伊西斯（Isis）以及賽拉皮斯（Serapis）的重要儀式用具。

本件器具雖僅有握柄及勾勾兩個部分，但是杓子上的蝕刻、壓印、鑄造裝飾，卻非常值得注意。頂部彎曲的部分是一個勾子的形狀，而形成上下雙勾的造型，並有鑲綴飾帶的鑄造裝飾，雕刻技巧近似高品質青銅器小雕像的鬍鬚雕刻方法。此勾子可將杓子掛在牆上、架子邊緣或更大容器的把手上，長長的手柄亦刻有奪目的裝飾樣式，最後則是以一個圓圈加上一個方形裝飾，該方形是以徒手蝕刻而成，搭配了一個X形，並在劃分出的三角形中間打了一個圓洞。下面則是一個圓圈，還有作為標記的蝕刻盒，盒子是由兩條平行線構成，中間有對角線，盒中有一個十字形，分支尾端也以徒手蝕刻完成。長手柄的邊緣是以單一線條作為裝飾，搭配一系列不規則的圓洞。根據館藏資料顯示，該物件是以紅色黏土裝飾，很可能是黏附在這些圓圈上，但如今已無跡可循，可能是清理過後的結果。（作者：E.L.）

Decorated simpulum handle

The simpulum, or hadle, was an essential piece of equipment for the serving of wine in domestic and ritual situations. In religious ceremonies, the simpulum was used to pour libations and to taste wine poured over the heads of sacrificial victims. The simpulum appears in various media from the Graeco-Roman world, most prominently on the reverse of Roman coins as a representation of priestly equipment. The ladle also occurs in the Egyptian material record, as attested by an early example in silver from Dynasty 21 also from Tanis. In the Ptolemaic and Roman periods, the simpulum was an essential piece of ritual equipment for the worship of Isis and Serapis.

This example consists of only the long handle and hook but is notable for its etched, stamped and cast decoration. The top curved section forms a hook that doubles back on itself and the cast braided decoration is reminiscent of the technique used on high quality bronze figurines for beards. This hook allowed the simpulum to be hung from a wall or stand or from the handle of a larger vessel. The long handle is notable for its decorative form that terminates with a circle surmounted by a square. The square is etched freehand with an X shape, the triangular shapes made as a result have punched circles in the centre of them. Below is a circle, demarked by an etched box that consists of two parallel lines, with diagonal lines in-between. Inside the box is a cross-shape with branches at the ends also etched free hand. The long handle is edged with a single line, and a series of unevenly punched circles. The museum entry records that this piece was decorated with a red paste, most likely in these circles, but no traces remain, likely the result of cleaning. (E.L.)

129. 長柄勾杓
來自壇尼斯桑哈傑爾
希臘羅馬時期（西元前 332 年 - 西元 395 年）
銅合金
142 x 25 x 18 mm

Decorated simpulum handle
From Tanis San el-Hagar
Graeco-Roman Period (332 BC-AD 395)
Copper-alloy

聖瓶

Situla 為拉丁文，是指一種附有手柄，可盛裝液體的小型桶狀器皿，主要是用於古埃及神廟的儀式中，通常為青銅或彩陶製，有一行行的圖片水平並列，環繞於整個瓶身，作為此儀式用器皿的裝飾，祭祀者也會將此類器物當成請願物，在神廟擺滿這些供物時，依儀式燒毀。這一件青銅器皿是出土於薩卡拉當地的動物大墓地，在挖掘當時亦發現大量的其他器物，包括一件裝飾更精美的器物。

此器皿的主要裝飾有三層，上層的圖案為太陽神坐在神聖的小船上，身邊有兩隻狒狒做出祭祀的姿勢，同時還刻有烏加眼（udjat，荷魯斯之眼）。中間層最寬，圖像中有一位崇拜者奉獻金字塔形狀的蛋糕給刻有陽具的阿蒙神（Amun），神像面前則是以古埃及象形文字寫著「Opet 的阿蒙」。阿蒙的身旁站著分成兩組的六位神明，第一組有三位女神，分別是伊西斯（Isis）、幕特（Mut）與奈芙蒂斯（Nephthys），另一組則是孟菲斯眾神，包括普塔（Ptah，置於神殿中）以及祂的配偶瑟魅特（Sekhmet）和小孩那夫坦（Nefertem），小孩頭戴著一朵大蓮花。最底層刻有帶翼日輪，亦即稱為「安卡」的象形字母（意指「生命」）以及另一隻烏加眼。此器皿的底部為乳頭狀，上有蓮花圖案，容器的邊緣下方有部分雕刻了象形文字，上面寫著：「願伊西斯將生命賦予…」。（作者：J.H.W.）

Situla

Situla is a Latin term for a small bucket-shaped vessel with a handle that was used for holding liquid. Situlae were used in Egyptian temple rituals and were usually made of bronze or faience. Rows of scenes running horizontally around the object decorate these ceremonial vessels. This type of object was also dedicated as a votive object by worshippers. When a temple became too crowded with these offerings, they were ceremonially buried. The bronze example here was excavated at Saqqara in the area of the sacred animal necropolis. It was found in a horde together with another more elaborately decorated example.

The main decoration on this vessel is in three registers. At the top is a scene of the sun god in a sacred boat together with two baboons shown in a worshipping pose. An udjat eye (the sound eye of Horus) also appears. The central register is the tallest and contains a scene of a worshipper making offerings of pyramid shaped caked to an ithyphallic Amun, identified by a hieroglyphic inscription before the god reading 'Amun in Opet'. Amun is flanked by series of six deities. First are three goddesses, Isis, Mut and Nephthys. The next group is the triad of Memphis, which consists of Ptah (shown in a shrine), his consort Sekhmet and the child god Nefertem who wears a large lotus flow on his head. The bottom register is decorated with winged sun disks, ankh hieroglyphs (meaning 'life' and another udjat eye. The bottom of the situla is nipple-shaped and has a lotus motif. Below the rim of the vessel is a fragmentary incised hieroglyphic inscription reading "May Isis give life (to)…" (J.H.W.)

130. 聖瓶
來自薩卡拉，動物大墓地
後埃及時期，第 26 王朝（西元前 664-525 年）
銅合金
174 x 69 x 69 mm

Situla
From Saqqara, Sacred Animal Necropolis
Late Period, Dynasty 26 (664-525 BC)
Copper alloy

伊西斯抱荷魯斯坐像

這一座小雕像不僅表現出母親保護子女的特質，也述說了古埃及最重要的神話之一，因為此神話賦予了埃及君主持有王權及統治的正當性。荷魯斯的母親伊西斯，藉由魔法懷有死去的丈夫及哥哥奧塞里斯（Osiris）的小孩，之後即生下荷魯斯，他是一位象徵與君王有密切連結的神，而伊西斯既是他的母親，也是他的守護者，當然與古埃及王座有關聯。事實上，古埃及王座的圖樣就是伊西斯名字的象形字母，且伊西斯經常被描繪成將王座的象形文字圖樣戴在頭上作為王冠。此處的伊西斯是佩戴著一頂三角假髮，上有一頂小王冠，王冠的形式是由一隻眼鏡蛇構成的圓環支撐著一對牛角，中間則包圍著一個日輪。此頭飾通常較容易讓人聯想到哈托爾，因為哈托爾能以母牛的形體顯現，且在新王國時期（西元前1550-1069年）與伊西斯有密切的關聯。若仍對該神像的身分感到懷疑，神像底部則有象形文字，表示該座小雕像是為了紀念伊西斯而雕製。

伊西斯原本是安置在另一個王座上，但該王座圖樣未保存下來。另外在伊西斯大腿上的小孩就是他的兒子荷魯斯，母親則以左手扶持著小孩。此處的荷魯斯是一位赤身露體的小孩，頭戴在古埃及作為幼年象徵的單摺邊鎖，荷魯斯和他的母親一樣，都是受眼鏡蛇的力量保護，且眼鏡蛇於前額上方豎起亦是代表他的君王身分。在神話中，伊西斯是在尼羅河三角洲的沼澤中扶養年幼的荷魯斯，有又高又密的草堆保護祂們不受塞特（Seth）的威脅；塞特是荷魯斯的叔叔，殺害了他的父親，而從正統繼承人手中奪取王位。（作者：A.C.）

Figure of Isis and Horus

This statuette captures the protective qualities of motherhood and one of the most important myths that validated divine kingship and legitimate rule. Isis was the mother of Horus, god child she had conceived through magic with her dead husband and brother Osiris. Horus was a god symbolically identified with the king and since Isis was his mother and protector she was associated with kingship. Indeed, the royal throne formed the hieroglyph for her name and she is often depicted wearing the hieroglyph of a throne on her head as a crown. In this example she wears a tripartite wig with a small crown consisting of a ring of rearing cobra heads that supports a pair of cow horns enclosing a solar disc. This headdress is more commonly associated with the goddess Hathor who could manifest herself in the form of a cow who was closely linked with Isis from the New Kingdom (1550-1069 BC). If the identity of the goddess were in doubt the hieroglyphic inscription on the base indicates that the statuette was dedicated in honour of Isis.

Isis would originally have been seated on a separate throne but this has not survived. Separately cast and attached to Isis's lap is her young son Horus, who she supports with her left hand. He is shown as a naked child wearing a large single plaited side-lock, a common symbol of youth. Like his mother he is protected by the powers of a uraeus cobra that rears above his forehead, and symbolizes his identity as a king. In mythology Isis nursed the young Horus in the marshlands of the Delta where the tall dense vegetation offered protection from Seth, the uncle who murdered Horus's father and stole the throne from the rightful heir. (A.C.)

131. 伊西斯抱荷魯斯坐像
來自薩卡拉，動物大墓地
後埃及時期，第26王朝（西元前664-525年）
銅合金
247 x 74 x 63 mm

Figure of Isis and Horus
From Saqqara, Sacred Animal Necropolis
Late Period, Dynasty 26 (664-525 BC)
Copper-alloy

奧塞里斯三人群像

從第三中間期（西元前1069-664年）開始，埃及人越來越重視將三位神明看成一家，通常包含父母親及一位兒子。這一件小雕塑中，位於中間的奧塞里斯，是由妻子伊西斯和兒子荷魯斯支撐著，奧塞里斯家族是豐饒和重生的強力象徵，由於重生在古埃及宗教中是一項很重要的概念，因此，奧塞里斯家族也成為最受廣泛敬拜的神明。

雕塑底部周圍以及神像背面圍繞著許多圓圈，代表奧塞里斯家族是由一條繩索或連接至神廟的條狀物提供保護，此圖像可能會用在神殿中，也可能會作為神聖器物的裝飾品，例如載負神明的小船，或是用於葬禮中。此雕塑是於1964至1976年間，從薩卡拉動物大墓地出土的八座奧塞里斯神像中的一座，在這段期間出土的1800件青銅器文物中，約有百分之七十五都是埋在底部的坑洞中，位置在今日稱為動物大墓地的墳場。這些小神像在神殿中上呈後，就成為祝禱過的器物，這些獻給眾神明的禮物會不斷堆積，最終只能定期送進神廟內外的儲藏間燒毀。

這些青銅器大部分都是就地製作，地點可能是神廟旁的工作室。西元前一千年之後，這些祭品的產量遽增，於是人們開始販售給外來朝聖者，大規模生產的器物，包括小神像或獻祭用的木乃伊，不僅可販售給更多的人供其與神溝通，也為祭司帶來大量的收入。（作者：A.C.）

Triad of Osiris

From the beginning of the Third Intermediate Period (1069-664 BC), there was a greater emphasis on imagining gods as family groups of three, usually composed of father, mother and son. This small sculpture consists of Osiris at the centre, being supported by his wife Isis and their son Horus. This Osirian triad was a powerful symbol of fertility and rebirth. Regeneration was an important concept in Egyptian religion, which made the Osirian triad the most widely worshipped family group of deities.

The loop on the side of the base and on the back of the figure of Isis suggest this triad of Osiris was secured with rope or a rod to a temple wall, perhaps in a shrine, or as decoration to sacred equipment such as a bark used to carry statues of gods in festival or funerary processions. This is one of eight Osirian triads excavated at the sacred animal necropolis at Saqqara between 1964 and 1976. About 75 percent of the 1800 bronzes discovered at this time were found buried in low level pits around the part of the cemetery now called the Sacred Animal Necropolis. Following presentation to the divine statue of a god in a shrine, statuettes would have been considered as blessed objects. As the number of these gifts to the gods built up they were periodically buried in caches within and around the temple precinct.

Most of these bronze objects are likely to have been made locally, probably in workshops attached to the temples. After 1000 BC there was a huge rise in the production of votive objects to be sold to pilgrims visiting cult centres. The manufacture and sale of mass produced objects such as statuettes and votive mummies allowed a greater scale of people to commune with the gods and created large revenues for the priesthood. (A.C.)

132. 奧塞里斯三人群像
來自薩卡拉，動物大墓地
後埃及時期，第26王朝（西元前664-525年）
銅合金
90 x 74 x 28 mm

Triad of Osiris
From Saqqara, Sacred Animal Necropolis
Late Period, Dynasty 26 (664-525 BC)
Copper-alloy

133. 阿蒙雷像
來自埃及
後埃及時期，第 26 王朝（西元前 664-525 年）
銅合金
121 x 35 x 25 mm

Figure of Amun-Ra
From Egypt
Late Period, Dynasty 26 (664 -525 BC)
Copper-alloy

阿蒙雷像

這一座實心鑄造的青銅器小神像，頭戴圓頂帽，上面有一個日輪和兩根長羽毛。加上日輪的意思，係表示這一位神明是底比斯神阿蒙（Amun）和主太陽神拉（Ra）的合體，祂穿戴著摺襴裙，屬站立的姿態，左腿向前跨，雙手則緊握靠在身體兩側。阿蒙通常是描繪成此形貌，看似國王、半人半神的神明，但是有時也會以公羊，甚至鵝的形象顯現，他的名字意思為「隱藏」，即代表可使用繁多的形體呈現，幾乎沒有人清楚知道祂能表現出多少種樣貌。

阿蒙神原本是南方城市底比斯（Thebes）的地方神明，最後卻一躍成為埃及諸神殿的至高神明。在新王國時期（西元前 1550-1069 年），人們通常稱祂為「阿蒙 - 雷，眾神明的君王」，並且是全埃及的神廟中受人膜拜的神明，他不僅是至高神，也是埃及諸君王神聖的父親。神廟內的圖畫顯示，「隱藏」的神 - 阿蒙，事實上已變身為未來君王母親的丈夫，以藉此讓她們懷胎。（作者：A.C.）

Figure of Amun-Ra

This solid cast bronze statuette wears a headdress of a domed cap surmounted by a solar disc and two tall plumes. The incorporation of the solar disc identifies the deity as a combination of the Theban god Amun and the principal solar god, Ra. He wears a pleated wrap-around kilt and stands in a traditional pose with his left leg striding forward and with clenched hands held against his side. Amun is most commonly portrayed in this way, as an anthropomorphic deity looking rather like the king, but he could also be shown in the form of a ram and even a goose. His name means 'hidden' which suggests no one was ever sure of what form he could assume.

Amun rose from being the local god of the southern city, Thebes, to being the preeminent god of the Egyptian pantheon. In the New Kingdom (1550-1069 BC) he was commonly referred to as 'Amun-Ra, King of the Gods' and was worshipped in temples throughout Egypt. At this time not only was he the supreme god, but also he was believed to be the divine father of all kings. Images within temples reveal that Amun, the 'hidden' one, actually impregnated the mothers of future kings by assuming the form of their husband. (A.C.)

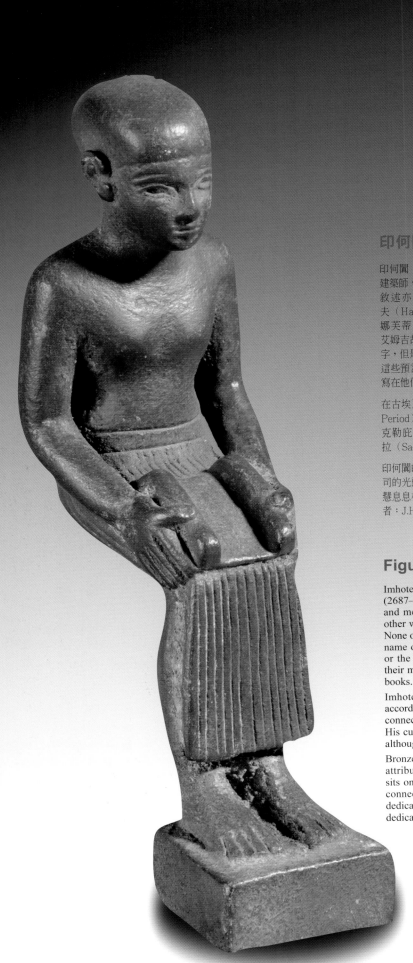

印何闐像

印何闐（Imhotep）是第三王朝期間，為約瑟王（King Djoser）建造階梯金字塔的建築師，至中王國時期（Middle Kingdom），印何闐則被奉為智者，因此他的相關敘述亦與其他智者的名字一起出現在智慧文獻中。「這裡有人能像哈底德夫（Hardedef）一樣嗎？有人能勝過印何闐嗎？在我們宗族之中，無人能與娜芙蒂（Neferti）或克緹（Khety）相比，他們是智者中的翹楚。我能告訴你撻 - 艾姆吉胡帝〔Ptah-emdjehuty〕以及卡克佩睿 - 索尼（Khakepperre-soneb）等名字，但是有其他人能與普塔霍特普（Ptahhotep）或凱勒斯（Kaires）並駕齊驅嗎？這些預言未來的智者，只要說出來的事必然會發生，事情也會如他們昭告的一般，寫在他們的書中。」

在古埃及歷史中，印何闐是少數被埃及人賦予神性的真人，至後埃及時期（Late Period），埃及人甚至將印何闐當成醫治之神膜拜，之後還被比擬為希臘神明阿斯克勒庇俄斯（Asclepius）。印何闐的神廟係位於孟菲斯，可能是安葬在薩卡拉（Saqqara），但墓地位置至今仍不明。

印何闐的神像通常是做成青銅器小雕像，與神像的特徵一致。印何闐有著古埃及祭司的光頭外型，坐在椅子上，大腿上放著一卷展開的紙莎草紙，代表他與寫作及智慧息息相關。此類小雕像可能是朝聖者的供物，用以祈求醫治疾病或獲得智慧。（作者：J.H.W.）

Figure of Imhotep

Imhotep was the architect of the Step Pyramid built in Dynasty 3 for King Djoser (2687–2668 BC). During the Middle Kingdom, Imhotep was revered as a sage and mention of him can be found in wisdom texts together with the names of other wise men: "Is there one here like Hardedef? Is there another like Imhotep? None of our kin is like Neferti, or Khety, the foremost among them. I give you the name of Ptah-emdjehuty, of Khakepperre-soneb. Is there another like Ptahhotep, or the equal of Kaires? Those sages who foretold the future, what came from their mouth occurred; It is found <as> their pronouncement, It is written in their books..."

Imhotep is a rare example of a living person to whom the ancient Egyptians accorded divinity. By the Late Period, the Egyptians worshipped Imhotep as a god connected to healing and later he was identified with the Greek god Asclepius. His cult center was at Memphis and he likely was buried in the area of Saqqara, although his tomb has never been located.

Bronze statuettes of this god are common and he is always shown with the same attributes. Imhotep is shown with the shaved head of an Egyptian priest. He sits on a chair and holds an open roll of papyrus on his lap indicating his close connection to writing and wisdom. Statuettes such as this one may have been dedicated by pilgrims for help with a medical problem or perhaps to endow their dedicators with wisdom. (J.H.W.)

134. 印何闐像
來自埃及
後埃及時期，第 26 王朝（西元前 664-525 年）
銅合金
143 x 57 x 40 mm

Figure of Imhotep
From Egypt
Late Period, Dynasty 26-30 (664-332 BC)
Copper-alloy

奧塞里斯像

奧塞里斯為亡者之神,可透過重生為古埃及人死後的生命帶來希望。古埃及的神話很多,其中一則述說荷魯斯(Horus)與塞特(Seth)爭奪奧塞里斯王位之爭戰的神話,已成為古埃及信仰的基礎。在此神話中,奧塞里斯是一位廣受愛戴的埃及君王,但是心懷妒忌的壞心哥哥塞特,為了要從弟弟手中奪取王國的統治權,而殺害了奧塞里斯,並將他的屍體肢解,散落於各地。同為奧塞里斯妻子與妹妹的伊西斯(Isis)將他的屍塊收集起來,在木乃伊之神阿努比斯(Anubis)的協助下,以棉布包裹屍體,透過魔法,讓伊西斯懷有成為木乃伊之奧塞里斯的小孩,並生下兒子荷魯斯,將他扶養長大成為了王國的正統繼承者。奧塞里斯到異世界後繼續統治著亡者的世界,而年幼的荷魯斯則被帶到尼羅河三角洲的沼澤,以脫離弒父之叔塞特的威脅。伊西斯將荷魯斯扶養長大,且苗壯至足以對抗塞特後,奪回王位,並將塞特放逐到沙漠,這就是正義戰勝邪惡的故事,也是賦予埃及王族統治正當權的神話。

阿比多斯是上埃及的沙漠區,據傳奧塞里斯就是安葬於此,來到亡者聖城朝聖的人,一般都會參與膜拜奧塞里斯的相關慶典,有些人還會奉獻供具、搭建紀念碑,或於死後埋葬於此,期盼能與這位已逝的君王連結,使自己在紀念奧塞里斯的儀式中成為永恆。他們希望能透過與奧塞里斯的連結,於死後復活,在他的王國中永生。在安葬文獻中,死者皆被稱為奧塞里斯,且在西元前兩千年之後,棺材也都是做成奧塞里斯木乃伊的形狀,以這些木乃伊形狀的棺材將死者與奧塞里斯連結-成為一位最完美的木乃伊。

實心鑄造的青銅器小雕像是朝聖者會在阿比多斯及埃及其他聖地奉獻的供具。這一件奧塞里斯像與其他六百件青銅器供具一樣,都是埋在阿比多斯的一個木箱內,而該等木箱則與其他埃及埋藏於地底之木製文物的遭遇一樣,大部分都已遭白蟻蛀蝕,只剩下木屑。箱內的青銅器為供具,推測應該是從一間堆滿器物的神廟內清理出來的物品,由於經過獻神而具有神聖性,因此將這些供具埋藏於此。圖中的奧塞里斯以亞麻布緊緊包紮,僅露出雙手,握住象徵王室的鉤與樺枷。他戴著假的捲鬍鬚,頂著阿特夫(atef)羽冠,上面飾有向前豎起的烏瑞(uraeus)眼鏡蛇,兩旁則突出一對公羊角。(作者:A.C.)

Figure of Osiris

Osiris was the god of the dead that offered the hope of life after death to the people of Egypt through regeneration. There are many Egyptian myths but one that makes up the basis of religious belief is the conflict between Horus and Seth for the inheritance of Osiris. In mythology Osiris was once a popular king of Egypt but his wicked brother Seth became jealous and decided to steal the kingdom away from him. Seth murdered Osiris, dismembered his body and scattered parts throughout the land. Isis, the widow and sister of Osiris, collected his body parts and with the help of Anubis, the god of mummification, she wrapped the corpse in bandages. Using magic Isis was impregnated by the mummified Osiris and conceived the son Horus who she would raise as the rightful heir to the throne. Osiris went to the Otherworld to rule as the king of the dead and the young Horus was taken to the marshlands of the Delta away from his murderous uncle. Isis nursed Horus until he was strong enough to fight Seth, seize the throne and banish Seth to the deserts. This is a triumphant tale of good over evil and a myth that legitimises divine kingship.

Abydos is a desert site in Upper Egypt where it was believed Osiris was buried. Those that could made pilgrimages to this sacred city of the dead and participate in the festivals associated with the cult of Osiris. Some dedicated votive objects, built cenotaphs, or were buried here so that they could connect themselves with the king of the dead and perpetuate their involvement in the ceremonies that celebrated the power of Osiris. Through connection with Osiris people hoped to be resurrected after death and to live forever in his kingdom. In funerary texts the dead were referred to as being an Osiris and from about 2000 BC coffins were made in the shape of a mummified Osiris. These mummiform coffins identified the dead as Osiris, the most perfect mummy ever.

Solid cast bronze statuettes are the type of votive offering pilgrims would have donated to shrines at Abydos and at other sacred places throughout Egypt. This Osiris figure was buried in what remained of a wooden box with another 600 bronze votives at Abydos. As with many wooden artefacts buried in the Egyptian sands, termites had eaten away at the box reducing most of it to powder. The bronze contents were votives, presumably cleared from a cluttered temple and buried because they had acquired sacredness after being dedicated to a deity. Osiris is shown in the tight wrap of his linen bandages with his hands exposed to hold the royal insignia of crook and flail. He wears an artificial curled beard and the plumed atef crown with a uraeus cobra rising from the front and ram horns protrude from the sides. (A.C.)

135. 奧塞里斯像
來自阿比多斯
後埃及時期,第26王朝(西元前664-525年)
銅合金
182 x 52 x 28 mm

Figure of Osiris
From Abydos
Late Period, Dynasty 26 (664- 525 BC)
Coppery-alloy

神帶領法老蒙圖荷泰普二世浮雕（局部）

本件浮雕局部描繪著中王國時期創建者蒙圖荷泰普二世，由一名身份不明的男性神祇所帶領。此件作品來自位於底比斯西岸巴哈里（Deir el-Bahri）之祭廟內殿。

右側人像是一名神祇，牽著手帶領著位於左側的國王：這是王室與神聖古蹟中常見的場景。兩個人像皆朝向內殿，有可能是要走向阿蒙神（Amun），亦即此祭廟所奉獻之神。兩個人像都穿著樣式簡單的短裙。該神祇之短裙為白黃色相間，國王則穿著串珠裝飾圍裙。該神祇手持權杖（只能看到右側有一條垂直線），表示其神權，其穿戴公牛尾巴並懸於短裙後側，亦是古埃及權力象徵之一，此國王人像同樣配戴著一條公牛尾巴。國王的腿部肌肉組織輪廓清晰，繪製精細。此浮雕品質極高，有鑑於此浮雕主題及所在位置之重要性，其可能是由王室裡最優秀的藝術家所完成。浮雕顏色仍然生動地保存下來，祭廟的內殿坍塌正好保護許多石塊免於遭受風化，不像有些來自外部柱廊之作品，大部分皆已褪色。

這些神殿浮雕被發現時已呈零碎狀態，艾德華 · 那維爾（Edouard Naville）在首次廣泛挖掘現場期間收集到此塊浮雕。近 60 年後，迪特 · 阿諾（Dieter Arnold）發現此塊浮雕之連接處，當中描繪了該神祇腳部其餘部份以及其他象形文字，因此能重建更多的場景。此塊浮雕來自神殿南側內牆西端，僅有右側之象形文字符號邊緣可見，但在另一塊浮雕局部中，能看到「大量」這個詞彙，以及常見的王室稱號「如拉（Ra）一般被賜予永生」。

此浮雕場景與神殿中另一塊浮雕類似，其描繪了國王荷魯斯（Horus）及塞特（Seth）所共同帶領，代表著蒙圖荷泰普二世之關鍵成就，即上、下埃及之統一。在第十八王朝期間，女法老哈謝普蘇（Hatshepsut）透過在巴哈里以蒙圖荷泰普二世之原架構來建造自己的祭廟，藉以強化其王權正統性。（作者：M.M.）

Relief of King Mentuhotep II Being Led by a God

This fragmentary relief block depicts the King Nebhepetre Mentuhotep II, founder of the Middle Kingdom, being led by an unidentified male deity. The block comes from the king's mortuary temple at Deir el-Bahri, on the west bank of Thebes, and comes from the inner sanctuary of the temple.

The right hand figure is a god, leading the king, on the left, by the hand: a common scene in both royal and divine monuments. The figures face towards the inner sanctuary and were likely approaching the god Amun, to whom the sanctuary was dedicated. Both figures wear short, simple kilts. The god's kilt is white and yellow, and the king wears a decorative beaded apron. The god carries a was-sceptre (of which only a vertical line to the right is visible) signifying his divine dominion, and he wears a bull's tail hanging from the back of his kilt, one of the oldest ancient Egyptian symbols of power. The figure of the king would have also worn one. The musculature in the king's legs is well defined, but subtly modelled. The quality of the raised relief carving is very high and was likely carried out by the best artists in the king's service, considering the importance of the subject matter and location of the reliefs. The colour is still vividly preserved, as the collapse of the inner portion of the temple largely protected many of the blocks from weathering, unlike some of the scenes from the outer colonnade, which are mostly faded.

The sanctuary reliefs were discovered in a fragmentary state when this block was collected by Edouard Naville, during the first extensive excavation of the site. Almost sixty years later, Dieter Arnold found the adjoining relief section to this block, depicting the rest of the god's foot and further hieroglyphs, and was able to reconstruct more of the scene. The blocks come from the west end of the southern interior wall of the sanctuary. Only the edges of the hieroglyph symbols are visible on the right hand side of the original block, but with the other fragment, it is possible to read the phrase 'a great many' and the common royal epithet 'given life like Ra forever'.

The scene is similar to another in the sanctuary, depicting the king being led by the Horus and Seth, who together represent the union of Upper and Lower Egypt, Mentuhotep II's defining achievement. In Dynasty 18, the female pharaoh Hatshepsut sought to strengthen her legitimacy by building her own mortuary temple at Deir el-Bahri in a style inspired by the architecture of Mentuhotep II. (M.M.)

136. 神帶領法老蒙圖荷泰普二世浮雕（局部）
來自底比斯，蒙圖荷泰普二世神廟
中王國時期，第 11 王朝，蒙圖荷泰普二世統治時期
（西元前 2055-2004 年）
石灰岩，顏料
715 x 510 x 120 mm

Relief of King Mentuhotep II Being Led by a God
From Thebes, Deir el-Bahri, temple of Mentuhotep II
Middle Kingdom, Dynasty 11, reign of Mentuhotep II
(2055-2004 BC)
Limestone, pigment

阿蒙霍特三世神廟浮雕

這五件相連之浮雕片段是由佩托里 (Petrie) 所發現，其在阿比多斯之奧塞里斯神廟圍牆的阿摩斯 (Ahmose) 教堂南側中被重新用於鋪面，並形成某場景的一部份。其右側是面向右方的奧塞里斯頭部上部。奧塞里斯身著上埃及之白色王冠並手持權杖，但此部分幾乎完全斷裂。權杖是權力之象徵，並且從早期開始便是由神祇以手持的方式呈現。奧塞里斯頭部右側是構成其頭銜的部份象形文字。

此塊浮雕左側是蒙圖荷泰普三世的頭部上部，其頭戴頭籬與阿泰夫 (Atef) 王冠。阿泰夫王冠之特色為兩側有兩道羽毛裝飾，王冠中央之設計類似於白色王冠，但頂端有一個小型日輪。這種王冠主要由奧塞里斯配戴，並成為冥界之象徵。王冠下方能看到兩側水平的波狀羊角，可藉此確定其為身份為克努姆 (Khnum) 神。國王額上還配戴著一個蛇形裝飾 (uraeus)，為其職務標記。這種阿泰夫王冠、公羊角，以及蛇形裝飾之組合是一種常見的頭飾，由國王在其即位週年慶典時所配戴，在新王國時期許多神廟浮雕中均有此類國王描繪。

蒙圖荷泰普三世頭部右側有一段銘文片段，意指其三十年慶典 (Heb-Sed)，而左側的上部則是 sekhem 權杖以及橢圓形裝飾之殘餘部份，其中載有國王之出生名稱。在浮雕作品中，國王會手持 sekhem 權杖，以作為一種權力與威望的象徵。這是冥界神祇奧塞里斯及阿努比斯 (Anubis) 之常見特徵，且似乎會在有關奉獻祭品之神廟及祭典儀式中，由國王手持。在 sekhem 權杖上方可看到國王 Ra (拉) 之稱號「like Re」。

蒙圖荷泰普三世神廟建造於阿比多斯之圖特摩斯三世神廟前方，僅管原開鑿者除了存放於其中的物件之外，無法確定該建築為何。埃及神廟的牆壁重現了國王與神祇之間的永恆交流，這是為了維護宇宙秩序和真理正義之神馬特 (Maat) 的關係。

此件作品以精細之浮雕刻製而成。五塊浮雕的外側邊緣已磨損，而表面的部份損傷可能是開鑿者使用丁字斧移開石板而導致。儘管其在古代原本裝飾精美，但目前彩繪痕跡已不復存在。（作者：A.H.）

Temple Relief of Amenhotep III

These five adjoining fragments were discovered by Sir William Matthew Flinders Petrie reused in a late paving south of Ahmose's chapel in the Osiris Temple Enclosure at Abydos, and form part of a scene. On the right side is the upper part of the head of Osiris facing right. He wears the White Crown of Upper Egypt and holds a was-sceptre, which is almost entirely broken off. The was-sceptre was a symbol of power and was shown carried by deities since early times. To the right of Osiris's head are hieroglyphs which form part of his titles.

On the left side of the block is the upper part of the head of Amenhotep III shown wearing a seshed circlet and Atef crown. The Atef crown features two feather plumes on either side of a central crown similar in design to the White Crown, but with a small solar disc on the tip. It was predominately worn by Osiris and became an emblem of this god of the underworld. Below the crown, one can see two horizontal undulating horns of the Ovis longipes species of sheep, which was identified with the god Khnum. The king is also wearing a uraeus on his brow, the insignia of his office. The combination of Atef crown, ram horns, and uraeus was a common headdress worn by the king at the celebration of his jubilee and was depicted in representations of the king in many temple relief scenes of the New Kingdom.

There is a fragment of an inscription to the right of Amenhotep III's head, which refers to his Heb-Sed festival, while to the left is the upper part of a sekhem-sceptre and the remains of a cartouche, which contained the birth-name of the king. In reliefs, the king would hold the sekhem-sceptre as a sign of power and prestige. It was a common emblem of the underworld deities, Osiris and Anubis, and appears to have been used by the king in temple and mortuary rituals involving the presentation of offerings. Above the sekhem-sceptre, one can see the epithet mi Ra "like Re."

The temple of Amenhotep III was built in front of the temple of Thutmose III at Abydos, although the building could not be defined by the original excavators, except for foundation deposits. The walls of Egyptian temples reproduced the permanent exchange between the king and the gods. It was a relationship upon which cosmic order and the maintenance of maat depended.

This block was carved in fine raised relief. The outer edges of the five pieces are worn and some of the damage to the face may have been caused by the excavators' use of pick-axes to remove the slabs. No traces of paint remain, although it would have been beautifully decorated in antiquity. (A.H.)

慶典浮雕

此塊浮雕來自東部三角洲布巴斯提斯（Bubastis）遺址，即第二十二王朝諸位國王的居住地。該城市的守護神是貓首女神貝斯塔（Bastet），而此塊浮雕源自於其寬闊的神廟遺址，是神廟中央大廳與歐索肯（Osorkon）二世節慶廳之間通道的一部分，其表面描繪內容與國王即位週年慶典儀式（sed）有關。

該慶典通常會在一名國王即位三十年時舉行。根據記錄顯示歐索肯當時僅即位24年（公元前874年至850年），這表示該國王提早慶祝自己的即位週年慶典。通道上的其他場景描繪著儀式程序：眾神歡迎國王，國王向眾神獻祭並由眾神加冕。位於埃及各地之神廟神像將於即位週年慶典時特別聚集於一地，以確認國王之正統性，並重申其統治權。

大量人物亦出現於該場景中，參與遊行和儀式。此浮雕顯示出其中部份人物。浮雕頂部區塊為四名手持法杖、頭戴假髮、身著短裙的男性，其被標記為顧問。其下為三名女性，配戴著植物製成的高大頭飾，並手持羚羊頭權杖。她們被稱為吟唱者，並攜帶著T形十字架，即生命的象徵。銘文週圍描述著作為即位週年慶典部份儀式的歌唱喜悅。較低區塊的殘餘部份描繪著俯臥的內侍與大臣高官，其確切角色如同以上所列人物一樣尚不清楚。（作者：C.P.）

Relief of a Jubilee Ritual

This block comes from the site of Bubastis in the eastern Delta, the residence of the kings of Dynasty22. The patron deity of the city was the cat-headed goddess Bastet, and the block comes from her extensive temple at the site. It formed part of a gateway between the temple's Central Hall and Festival Hall of Osorkon II, the surfaces of which depicted rituals associated with the king's jubilee ('sed') festival.

Usually, the festival was held after thirty years of a king's rule. Records show Osorkon to have had only a 24 year reign (874-850 BC), implying that the king celebrated his sed-festival earlier than was customary. Other scenes on the gateway depict the ritual proceedings: gods welcoming the king, the king offering to and being crowned by a series of them. Gods, in the form of their statues from temples around Egypt, were assembled especially for the jubilee to confirm the king's legitimacy and to renew his right to rule.

Large numbers of human participants are also shown taking part in processions and rituals. This scene shows some of them. On the top register four male figures holding staves, wearing bag wigs and long kilts, are labelled as councillors. Below, three female figures wear tall headdresses made of plants, and hold gazelle-headed sceptres. They are labelled chantresses, and also carry ankhs, the sign for life. Surrounding inscriptions describe the vocal rejoicing that would have been part of the jubilee rites. Remains of a lower register show prostrate chamberlains and dignitaries, although – like those above – their precise role remains unclear. (C.P.)

138. 慶典浮雕
第三中間期，第 22 王朝，奧索爾孔二世統治時期
（西元前 874-850 年）
紅花崗岩
1090 x 640 x 360 mm

Relief of a Jubilee Ritual
Third Intermediate Period. Dynasty 22, reign of Osorkon II (874-850 BC).
Red granite

拉美西斯二世神殿巨柱

此兩塊大型花崗岩局部在連接後可共同形成石柱的上段與中段，其曾經座落於埃及中部伊納西亞艾爾梅迪納（Ihnasya el-Medina）的赫莉雪芙（Herishef）神廟中，鄰近法尤姆河口。兩塊片段刻劃著拉美西斯二世向奧塞里斯獻祭之場景，其中較大片段位於次大片段的下方，而次大片段上則刻劃著該國王之橢圓形裝飾。該場景之上部可在上方片段之最底下看到，包括原本位於拉美西斯頭上兩側帶有蛇形裝飾的日輪。完整石柱之原始高度約為 5 公尺，此石柱之棕櫚葉柱形部份目前已遺失。此石柱與其他七根相稱的石柱共同構成神廟柱廊的其中一列，此為開闊的宮廷轉變為神廟之多柱式大廳的標記性結構。其他石柱及石柱局部目前收藏於澳大利亞（阿德萊德）、美國（波士頓、費城）及英國（曼徹斯特、倫敦）等地之博物館中。

這些石柱有可能取自於一個更古老的建築，並且由拉美西斯的建造者將其融入柱廊中，作為重新改造神廟主體的一種方式。它們可能來自第五王朝之金字塔複合建築，阿布什（Abusir）或 薩卡拉（Saqqara）向北約 50 公里處，此處曾証實存在類似的棕梠葉頂紅色花崗岩石柱，表面刻劃著拉美西斯之橢圓形裝飾與場景。部份石柱後來則刻有拉美西斯之子及其繼承人梅潤塔（Merenptah）的名字，以作為他與赫莉雪芙神廟以及其父親功業之聯繫。這些文字內容可在石柱下部看到，位於這些場景下方，與其父親的部份相間。這些文字僅輕微刻劃，並未完整雕刻。這裡只有橢圓形裝飾記錄著梅潤塔的寶座名稱，即 Baenra Merynetjeru（以一種公羊象形文字書寫），並獲得完整保存。

羊頭的赫莉雪芙與奧塞里斯有著密切關聯，並經常被比作奧塞里斯。一個位於伊納西亞艾爾梅迪納，叫做納瑞福（Naref）的神秘地點，被認為是奧塞里斯的其中一個墓地，因此造成他在該地區之重要性。下方石柱局部的兩個場景顯示出拉美西斯站在奧塞里斯前，向其進獻牛奶，以換取其在阿圖姆（Atum）之王權，牛奶壺位於拉美西斯伸出的雙手上。奧塞里斯在此並未以其一貫的木乃伊式造型出現，反而在其中主動大步行走，身穿短褶裙，頸部環繞著胸飾。奧塞里斯在此處之姿勢與外型與其他石柱上描繪的赫莉雪芙及荷魯斯（Horus）相似，形成石柱裝飾的視覺對稱，並強調神祇之間的密切關係。在托勒密王朝時期，赫莉雪芙之地位等同於希臘英雄赫拉克力士（Herakles），因此該城市之古典名稱為赫拉克雷奧波斯（Herakleopolis Magna）。（作者：L.F.）

Temple column fragments of Rameses II

These two massive granite fragments join together to create the middle and upper sections of a column that once stood in the temple of Herishef at Ihnasya el-Medina in Middle Egypt, near the mouth of the Fayum. The larger of the two fragments, which bears scenes of Rameses II offering to Osiris, would have been positioned beneath the second, which is inscribed with cartouches of this king. Remains of the upper sections of the scenes can be seen in the lowest part of this top fragment, including the sun discs flanked by uraei which would have been above Rameses' head. The complete column, with its now lost palm capital, was originally about 5 metres high. It formed a row with seven other matching columns in the temple's portico, a structure that marked the transition from the open court into the enclosed space of the temple's hypostyle hall. Other columns, or their fragments, are now in museums in Australia (Adelaide), America (Boston, Philadelphia), and England (Manchester, London).

The columns were probably taken from a much older structure and incorporated by Rameses' builders into the portico as a way of dramatically reshaping the main temple axis. They may have come from the Dynasty 5 pyramid complexes of Abusir or Saqqara some 50 km further north, where similar palm-topped, red granite columns are attested. Rameses' cartouches and scenes were then deeply carved into the surface. Some of the columns were later inscribed with the names of Rameses' son and heir, Merenptah, as a way of associating him with Herishef's temple and his father's work there. These texts are visible on the lower block, beneath the scenes, alternating with his father's. They are only lightly incised and were never fully carved. Here only the cartouche enclosing Merenptah's throne name, Baenra Merynetjeru (written with a ram hieroglyph), is fully preserved.

The ram-headed Herishef was closely associated with, and assmiliated to, Osiris. A mythical place in Ihnasya el-Medina, called Naref, was thought to be one of the burial places of Osiris, hence his importance in the area. The two scenes on the lower column fragment show Rameses standing before Osiris of Naref, offering him milk in return for the 'kingship of Atum'; milk-jugs are shown in Rameses' outstretched hands. Osiris is not represented here in his usual mummiform pose. Instead he is shown actively striding, wearing a short pleated kilt and a pectoral around his neck. In this, his pose and appearance are similar to those of Herishef and Horus who are depicted on some of the other columns, contributing to the visual symmetry of the column decoration and emphasizing the affinities between the deities. In the Ptolemaic period Herishef, called Harsaphes in Greek, was identified with the Greek hero Herakles, hence the city's Classical name Herakleopolis Magna. (L.F.)

139. & 140. 拉美西斯二世神殿巨柱
來自印納西亞艾密地納
新王國時期，第 19 王朝，拉美西斯二世統治時期
（西元前 1279-1213 年）
紅花崗岩
1500 x 750 x 750 mm, 1495 x 700 x 700 mm

Temple column fragments of Rameses II
From Ihnasya el-Medina (Herakleopolis Magna), the
temple of Herishef
New Kingdom, Dynasty 19, reign of Rameses II
(1279-1213 BC)
Red granite

飛舞的鴨子－宮殿走道（局部）

位於阿瑪納（Amarna）最南端的主要古蹟 Maru-Aten（意為「阿頓神的瞭望處」）包含一些奉獻給 阿肯納頓（Akhenaten）之長女梅莉塔譚（Meritaten）的建築。此龐大建築的中央部份面積約 250 平方公尺，是一座大型湖泊或沼澤區，使其首位開鑿者里歐納・伍立（Leonard Woolley）於 1921 年期間將其視為王室遊樂渡假勝地，國王及其家人在此處舉辦歡樂的野餐派對。較近期之研究則強調阿瑪納之城市規劃且其原本安排做為阿頓神（Aten）與王室之宗教中心，而馬魯譚（Maruaten）目前則解釋為阿肯納頓及其第二任妻子奇亞（Kiya）之「遮陽」神廟（後來又改為其長女梅莉塔譚），其帶有陰涼清爽的花園與湖泊，使太陽賦予生命的特質能在此被欣賞和享受。

位於馬魯譚圍牆東北方角落的「水上宮廷」，是一個設有連鎖 T 形水池的柱廊區，週邊有許多描繪著沼澤植物群和動物群的裝飾石膏地板。

儘管只是復原品，英國伯頓博物館精確地闡釋出該水上宮廷之裝飾內容。兩隻針尾鴨從一叢翠綠的紙莎草上迅速飛入空中（在完整的樣品內會搭配第二個灌木叢，通常是藍色）。然而，該景像不僅僅是一種裝飾或是大自然的簡單描繪：近來一項由蓋・羅賓（Gay Robins）所提出的研究內容顯示，針尾鴨在這些場景中特別被選作為一種象形文字的雙關語。一隻飛行的針尾鴨代表 pa 之聲音，其延伸意義為 pawty 這個字，意即「原始時期」。沼澤中的鴨子形象因而喚起原始肥沃濕地的景象，即生命的起源處，因此在國王跨過這些彩繪地板同時，亦重新建立起原始造物時刻。

除了圖像本身，這些地板的彩繪技術亦值得評論。埃及陵墓及宮廷壁畫被藝術史學家稱為乾壁繪畫（secco）技術：漆料被應用於乾燥的石膏表面，使線條及色彩得以精確控制，但其表面脆弱，容易受磨損所傷，顯然不適合用於地板。位於阿瑪納之馬魯譚和其他地方的地板在埃及繪畫中皆屬於早期且罕見，部份是由濕壁畫（fresco）技巧所繪製，漆料被應用於潮濕的石灰石膏表面，而隨著石膏逐漸乾燥，顏料便會緊附在其上，創造出光滑的表面。這種技術的缺點在於，畫家必須根據其在數小時內可繪畫之面積來準備石膏表面，使石膏部份能保持濕潤以附著漆料。伯頓博物館所收藏之物件中，有部份區域保有像是布料印記的痕跡，或許是來自放在潮濕石膏上以避免其乾燥的布料。然而，該件馬魯譚鋪面並非真正的濕式壁畫：此藍色及綠色顏料由粗糙研磨的人造釉料製成，在濕壁畫中會失去其色彩，因此必須在乾燥地板上以乾壁繪畫方式使用。

此件伯頓博物館收藏之當前狀態有些誤導意味：因其並非單一完整之面板，而是來自整個遺址之局部片段的復原品，由挖掘團隊於 1920 年代將其彙整並復原，於 1990 年代進行保存處理，並為 2008 年之展覽進行修復，形成此塊地板目前之外觀。（作者：T.H.）

Ducks in flight: fragment of a painted pavement

The southernmost major monument of Amarna, the Maru-Aten ('Viewing place of the Aten') was the location of a number of buildings dedicated to Meritaten, the oldest daughter of Akhenaten. The central part of this vast complex, nearly 250 metres square, was a large lake or marshy area, which led Leonard Woolley, its first proper excavator in 1921, to regard it as a 'royal pleasure resort' in which the king and his family would hold 'gay picnic parties'. More recent studies emphasise the way in which Amarna was planned and laid out as a centre for the cult of the Aten and the royal family, and the Maruaten is now interpreted as a 'Sunshade' temple of Akhenaten and his secondary wife Kiya, later replaced by his eldest daughter Meritaten; in the refreshing setting of a shaded garden and lake, the life-giving qualities of the sun would be better appreciated and enjoyed.

At the north eastern corner of the Maruaten enclosure was the 'Water-court', a colonnaded area with interlocking T-shaped pools surrounded by a plaster floor decorated with numerous panels depicting marsh flora and fauna.

Although a composite, the Bolton panel accurately exemplifies the decoration of the water-court. Two pintail ducks rocket into the air above a thicket of green papyrus (in complete examples this would be paired with a second thicket, usually in blue). The scene is more than just decoration or a simple depiction of nature, however: a recent study by Gay Robins has suggested that the pintail ducks were specifically chosen as a hieroglyphic pun in these scenes. The sign of a flying pintail duck represents the sound pa, and by extension the word pawty – 'primeval time'. The image of ducks in the marsh would thus evoke the original fertile marshland out of which life emerged in the beginning, so the king's crossing the painted floors would also re-enact the moment of creation.

Iconography aside, the technique with which the panel was painted is also worth comment. Wall paintings in Egyptian tombs or palaces were executed in what art historians call the secco technique: paint was applied to the surface of a dry, plastered surface. This allowed for precise control of line and colour but produced a fragile surface easily damaged by wear and tear, obviously unsuitable for a floor. The floors in the Maruaten and elsewhere at Amarna are early and rare Egyptian examples of painting in partial fresco technique, where paint is applied to a wet lime plaster surface. Chemical reactions as the plaster dries and sets bind the pigment firmly into the plaster, providing a durable surface. A disadvantage of this technique is that the surface has to be prepared according to the amount the painter can cover during the few hours the plaster remains wet enough to take the paint. A few areas of the Bolton fragment preserve what appear to be textile imprints, perhaps from cloths placed on the wet plaster to keep it from drying out. The Maruaten pavements are not, however, true frescoes: the blue and green pigments, made from coarsely ground man-made frits, would lose their colours in fresco so had to be applied afterwards in secco to the dry floor.

The Bolton object is somewhat misleading in its present state: it is not a single intact panel, but is instead a composite of fragments from all over the site, brought together and restored in the 1920s by the excavation team. Conservation treatment in the 1990s, and restoration for an exhibition in 2008, have resulted in the panel's present appearance. (T.H.)

141. 飛舞的鴨子－宮殿走道（局部）
來自阿瑪納
新王國時期，第 18 王朝，阿肯納頓統治時期（西元前
1352-1336 年）
灰泥，顏料
1750 x 750 x 150 mm

Ducks in flight: fragment of a painted pavement
From Amarna, Maruaten, Water-court
New Kingdom, Dynasty 18, reign of Akhenaten (1352-1336 BC)
Plaste, pigment

142. 柱頂雕刻（局部）
來自印納西亞艾密地納
新王國時期，第19王朝，拉美西斯二世統治
時期（西元前1279-1213年）
紅花崗岩
350 x 260 x 130 mm

Fragment of Column Capital
From Ihnasya el-Medina (Herakleopolis Magna)
New Kingdom, Dynasty 19, reign of Rameses II
(1279-1213 BC)
Red granite

柱頂雕刻（局部）

此塊紅色花崗岩局部源於一根大型石柱頂部，其可能類似於本展覽中的拉美西斯二世石柱（本書編號139&140），由佩托里（Petrie）於數年後在相同遺址挖掘出土。赫莉雪芙（Herishef）神廟石柱的主要部份為棕櫚樹狀裝飾，頂部如同棕櫚樹頂端，有大型葉子在頂部朝外拱出。此件石柱局部保留了棕櫚葉中央骨幹處以及從此處拱出的枝葉。八根帶有棕櫚葉裝飾的石柱構成了赫莉雪芙神廟前側入口的柱廊。這一列石柱可在赫莉雪芙神廟前營造出一列棕櫚樹的印象。

棕櫚狀石柱在古埃及已有悠久歷史，年代可追溯至第五王朝。有人推測，這些源於第五王朝的石柱在中王國時期被帶到伊納西亞（Ihnasya），並且於第十九王朝時被拉美西斯二世再次使用。這些石柱得以長期流行，或許能反映出紅色花崗岩之價值，並與埃及思想中的太陽及神廟之意式型態相連結，其中植物形態亦與地球孕育及生命起源相關。（作者：C.R.）

Fragment of Column Capital

This red granite fragment is a small part of the top of a large column, possibly similar to the columns of Ramses II in this exhibition (Catalogue #139 &140). It was excavated from the same site several years later by Flinders Petrie. The capitals of the columns of the temple of Herishef were in the shape of palm trees, with the top looking like the bound top of the tree with the large fronds arching outwards at the top. This fragment preserves the centre rib of the palm frond and the branching leaves arch in gentle and regular curves from this rib. There were 8 columns topped with the palm capitals that formed a portico on the front entry to the temple of Herishef. This row of columns would have created the impression of a row of palm trees fronting the temple of Herishef.

Palm columns have a long history in ancient Egypt dating as early as Dynasty 5. It has been suggested that these columns originally date to Dynasty 5 and were brought to Ihnasya during the Middle Kingdom and then reused again by Ramses II in Dynasty 19. The long popularity of the columns probably reflects the value of red granite, linked to the sun in Egyptian thought and the ideology of the temple where plant forms were connected to the fertility of the earth and the origins of life. (C.R.)

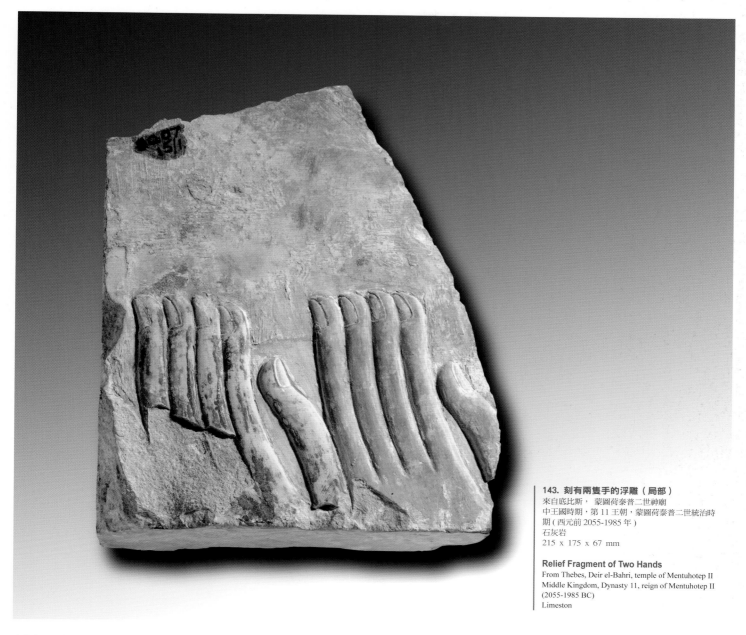

143. 刻有兩隻手的浮雕（局部）
來自底比斯，蒙圖荷泰普二世神廟
中王國時期，第 11 王朝，蒙圖荷泰普二世統治時
期（西元前 2055-1985 年）
石灰岩
215 x 175 x 67 mm

Relief Fragment of Two Hands
From Thebes, Deir el-Bahri, temple of Mentuhotep II
Middle Kingdom, Dynasty 11, reign of Mentuhotep II
(2055-1985 BC)
Limeston

刻有兩隻手的浮雕（局部）

此件描繪著兩隻手的浮雕局部來自於中王國時期創建者蒙圖荷泰普二世之祭廟，座落於底比斯西岸的巴哈里（Deir el-Bahri）。蒙圖荷泰普二世是底比斯當地統治者，由於戰勝其赫拉克雷奧波利頓（Herakleopolitan）之對手而受後人所尊崇，此舉亦終結第一中間期之國家分裂狀態，並重新統一埃及。其祭廟建築表現出建築發展之創新，其靈感來自當地石雕、柱廊式底比斯陵墓，以及早期王室金字塔之複合建築。

在古埃及，可藉膚色表現區分性別，男性膚色一般被描繪成紅棕色，而女性則以黃色皮膚表現。這表示左邊的手屬於男性，右邊的手則屬於女性。然而，此處所使用的男性膚色並非標準的紅棕色，而是用於區別人物重複線條的棕色，可進而推測有一些人物位於這兩隻手附近。手指曲線經過精密著色，而指甲部份則精雕細鑿。此件作品以浮雕方式呈現，為用於室內之典型裝飾。在古埃及，舉起的雙手意味著尊崇與崇拜，因此這些人物有可能是站立於神祇之前。另一種可能性是，這雙手屬於有著深色皮膚與淺色皮膚的外地人士，其中深膚色者代表埃及之南部人，淺膚色者則代表埃及之北部及西部人，因為戰爭及戰俘獻祭的場景亦發現於此座神廟中。（作者：M.M.）

Relief Fragment of Two Hands

This fragmentary relief block depicting two hands comes from the mortuary temple of King Nebhepetre Mentuhotep II, founder of the Middle Kingdom, at Deir el-Bahri, on the west bank of Thebes. Mentuhotep II, a local ruler from Thebes, was revered by later generations for his victory over his Herakleopolitan rivals, which ended the state fragmentation of the First Intermediate Period and re-unified Egypt. His mortuary temple represented an innovative architectural development, drawing inspiration from both the local rock-cut, colonnaded Theban tombs and earlier royal pyramid complexes.

The representation of skin colour was gendered in ancient Egypt, with men generally depicted with red-brown skin and women with yellow skin. This indicates that the hand on the left belonged to a man, and the hand on the right belonged to a woman. However, the male colouring used here is not the standard red-brown shade, but rather a brown that is typically used when differentiating a repetitive line of figures. A group of figures is further suggested by the close placement of the hands. The curve of the fingers is sinuously rendered and the detail of the fingernails delicately carved.

It is executed in raised relief, which was typically used indoors. In ancient Egypt, upraised hands signified worship and adoration, so the figures in question might be standing before a deity. The other possibility is that these hands belonged to foreigners with the dark and light colours referring to the darker colouring of peoples to the south of Egypt and the lighter to peoples north and west of Egypt. Scenes of warfare and the sacrifice of war captives were located in this temple. (M.M.)

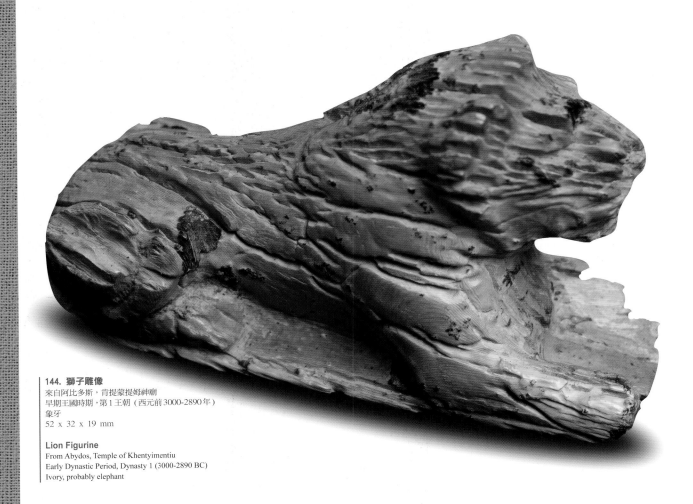

144. 獅子雕像
來自阿比多斯，肯提蒙提姆神廟
早期王國時期，第1王朝（西元前 3000-2890 年）
象牙
52 x 32 x 19 mm

Lion Figurine
From Abydos, Temple of Khentyimentiu
Early Dynastic Period, Dynasty 1 (3000-2890 BC)
Ivory, probably elephant

獅子雕像

這件小型獅子雕像是神廟還願祭品之一，出土自古王國時代晚期位於阿比多斯之喪葬神（Khentyimentiu）神廟。其存放位置在一道牆下的坑，開鑿者佩托里（Petrie）認為其出自更早期之神廟建築中，應可回溯至王朝早期（第一至二王朝），其後上方又加蓋古王國時期建築。在埃及，祭司埋葬舊的還願物和雕像，以騰出空間給新廟的設備與祭品，此為常見之做法。如果沒有銘文方面的佐證，要追溯這類物品的年份相當困難，但在這存放位置中發現的物品，其風格類似於其他在大象島供奉女神莎特（Satet）的早期王朝神廟中所發現的還願祭品。這隻獅子是一組由彩陶、石灰石和象牙所製成的雕像之一，這組雕像描繪著人類、動物、瓶罐模型、船隻以及糧食祭品等。

這隻精雕細鑿的獅子以經典的伏臥姿勢坐著，該坐姿在後期被應用於獅身人面像。其眼睛和腳掌位置朝向前方，捲起的尾巴靠近其右側，後軀捲曲，似乎準備跳起。其四肢並未清晰呈現，而是靠在雕刻自同一塊象牙的長方形平台上。其頭部環繞鬃毛，且不具備母獅雕像常配戴項圈的特徵，顯示其為公獅。

學者們曾將其他小獅俑描述為博弈物件，因為它們是在王朝早期之墓葬傢具中被發現。位於薩卡拉（Saqqara）的海斯雷（Hesy-Re）陵墓（第三王朝）中出現的遊戲是在一塊板上進行，板子形狀像盤繞的蛇。整套博弈物件包括三隻公獅、三隻母獅以及六顆彩色彈珠。然而，此雕像之背景與其他神廟還願祭品，說明其可能是宗教用途而非為娛樂所用。（作者：J.A.H.）

Lion Figurine

This small figure of a make lion was a member of a cache of temple votive objects excavated from beneath a wall of a late Old Kingdom Temple to the mortuary god Khentyimentiu at Abydos (Deposit M69). The cache's location in a pit beneath a wall led the excavator, W.M.F. Petrie, to conclude that it was a deposit from an earlier temple building phase dating back to the early Dynastic Period (Dynasties 1-2) that was built over by an Old Kingdom construction phase. It was common practice in Egypt for priests to bury old votive objects and statuary to make room for new temple furniture and offerings. Without inscriptional evidence dating such finds is difficult, but the style of the objects found in Deposit M69 is similar to other votive objects found in an Early Dynastic temple dedicated to the goddess Satet in Elephantine. This lion was among a group of figurines made of faience, limestone and ivory depicting humans, animals, and models of pots, boats and food offerings.

This delicately carved lion is seated in the classic recumbent pose adopted by sphinx figures in later periods. His eyes and paws are positioned forward, tail curled close to his right flank and hindquarters coiled as though ready to spring. Rather than articulated his limbs rest on a thin rectangular platform carved from the same piece of ivory. That he is male is indicated by the raised mane encircling his head and by the fact that he does not have a collar, a common feature on lioness figurines.

Scholars have described other small lion figurines as gaming pieces because they have been discovered among the burial furniture in Early Dynastic tombs. The game, as shown in the tomb of Hesy-Re at Saqqara (Dynasty 3), was played on a board shaped like a coiled serpent. The full set of gaming pieces included three lions, three lionesses and six colored marbles. However, the context of this figurine with other temple votive object indicates that it likely served a religious rather than recreational purpose. (J.A.H.)

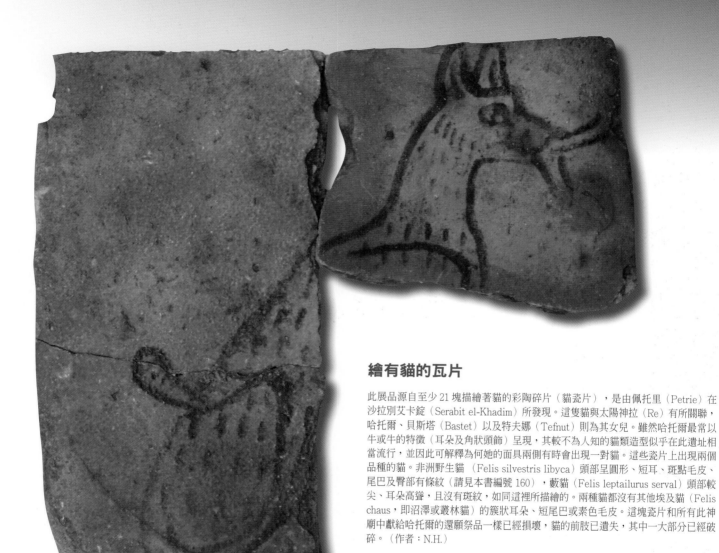

繪有貓的瓦片

此展品源自至少21塊描繪著貓的彩陶碎片（貓瓷片），是由佩托里（Petrie）在沙拉別艾卡錠（Serabit el-Khadim）所發現。這隻貓與太陽神拉（Re）有所關聯，哈托爾、貝斯塔（Bastet）以及特夫娜（Tefnut）則為其女兒。雖然哈托爾最常以牛或牛的特徵（耳朵及角狀頭飾）呈現，其較不為人知的貓類造型似乎在此遺址相當流行，並因此可解釋為何她的面具兩側有時會出現一對貓。這些瓷片上出現兩個品種的貓。非洲野生貓（Felis silvestris libyca）頭部呈圓形、短耳、斑點毛皮、尾巴及臀部有條紋（請見本書編號160），藪貓（Felis leptailurus serval）頭部較尖、耳朵高聳，且沒有斑紋，如同這裡所描繪的。兩種貓都沒有其他埃及貓（Felis chaus，即沼澤或叢林貓）的簇狀耳朵、短尾巴或素色毛皮。這塊瓷片和所有此神廟中獻給哈托爾的還願祭品一樣已經損壞，貓的前肢已遺失，其中一大部分已經破碎。（作者：N.H.）

TILE WITH A SKETCH OF A CAT

Fragments from at least 21 faience tiles with depictions of cats ('cat plaques') were discovered by Petrie at Serabit el-Khadim. The cat was associated with the sun-god Re and with Hathor, Bastet and Tefnut as his daughters. Although Hathor is most commonly represented as a cow or with bovine features (ears and horned headdress), her lesser-known feline form seems to have been popular at this site, and would explain why her mask is sometimes flanked by a pair of cats. Two species of cat are shown on the plaques. African wild cats (Felis silvestris libyca) have rounded heads, short ears, spotted coats, and stripes on their tails and haunches (see Catalogue #160); servals (Felis leptailurus serval) have pointed heads, tall ears and no stripes, as depicted here. Neither species has the tufted ears, short tail or plain coat of the other Egyptian feline – Felis chaus, the swamp or jungle cat. In common with all votive offerings dedicated to Hathor at this temple, this plaque is damaged, and the cat's forelegs are missing where a large section has broken away. (N.H.)

145. 繪有貓的瓦片
來自西奈，沙拉別艾卡錠，哈托爾神廟
新王國時期，第18王朝，圖特摩斯三世統治時期（西元前1479-1425年）
彩陶
88 x 85 x 6 mm

Tile with a scatch of a Cat
From Sinai, Serabit el-Khadim, Hathor Temple
New Kingdom, Dynasty 18, Thutmose III (1479-1425 BC)
Faience

貝斯塔神雕像

這隻坐著的貓耳朵高聳，且尾巴靈巧地捲曲在其右臀，具有吸引力的形象被公認為古埃及物質文化之特色。然而，出乎人們意料的是，貓本身在古埃及並未被崇拜，而名為貝斯塔（Bastet）的女神，以貓的外形呈現，在古埃及後期及托勒密王朝時期（公元前 664 年至 30 年）是廣受歡迎的神祇。作為奉獻給貝斯塔神之象徵，像這樣的小雕像是由朝聖者購買來作為貓之女神神廟中之還願祭品。其中一些中空的青銅雕像是用來包裹貓木乃伊，或裝飾為青銅或木製棺材頂部。朝聖者藉由給予貓一個體面的墓葬，以虔誠的尋求貝斯塔神之恩寵。

我們目前知道在埃及有二十座與其宗教相關的貓墓園，這就是貝斯塔神廣受歡迎的程度。若干來自這些大規模墓葬的貓類奉獻品目前已成為博物館收藏，但大部分已在公元 1800 年至 1900 年之間被摧毀，在埃及或國外作為肥料使用。1890 年 2 月 10 日，約有 180,000 具重達 19.5 噸的貓木乃伊，在英國利物浦的拍賣會上售出。幾乎所有貓木乃伊皆被粉碎，並且如糞肥般灑在農田上，但有少數被保存下來並收藏於利物浦國家博物館。這些貓木乃伊於前一年在埃及中部的貝尼哈森（Beni Hasan）墓園尋獲，當時有一名農民掉入一個充滿貓木乃伊的地下墓穴中。

此件小雕像是獻給位於薩卡拉（Saqqara）供奉著貝斯塔的神廟。這裡有數以百萬計不同種類的動物木乃伊存放在一個巨大的地道網絡中，甚至是翻造的陵墓中，在許多世紀以前由石灰岩基岩雕刻而成。地上有神廟建築與裝飾著神祇圖像的神殿，形成其宗教焦點。該神廟建築不僅是神祇的棲身之所，同時也飼養、捕捉即將被殺死並製成木乃伊的還願用動物與鳥類，其規模如同一項產業。在超過 2500 年以前，薩卡拉必定曾在慶典期間擠滿成千上萬來自埃及和地中海東部的男性與女性，並且在即將成為祭品的貓、狗、狒狒和鳥類的噪音中參觀著神廟。朝聖者對於來自神廟工作坊之還願祭品的需求，為埃及各地神廟提供了一個重要的收入來源，對此時期的國家經濟來源也是一個顯著特色。（作者：A.C.）

Figure of Bastet

With its ears erect and tail neatly curled around its right haunch this seated cat is an attractive image widely recognised as a feature of ancient Egyptian material culture. However, contrary to popular belief the cat itself was not worshipped in ancient Egypt; it was a goddess called Bastet, who could take on the appearance of a cat that was a popular deity of the Late and Ptolemaic Periods (664-30 BC). As a sign of devotion to Bastet, statuettes like this one were purchased by pilgrims and dedicated as votives in temples where a cult of the cat goddess existed. Some of these hollow bronze statuettes were used to contain the mummified remains of a cat, or to decorate the top of a bronze or wooden coffin. By providing a cat with a decent burial pilgrims were seeking the favour of Bastet through piety.

Such was Bastet's popularity that we now know of over twenty cat cemeteries for her cult in Egypt. Some cat donations from these mass burials are now in museum collections, but most were destroyed in the between AD 1800 and 1900 for use as fertilizer in Egypt and abroad. On 10th February 1890 an estimated 180,000 mummified cats, weighing 19.5 tons, were sold at auction in Liverpool, England. Almost all were crushed and spread on fields like manure, but a few were saved and remain in National Museums Liverpool. They were discovered the previous year, near the cemetery of Beni Hasan in Middle Egypt, when a farmer fell through a hole into a catacomb completely filled with cat mummies.

This statuette was dedicated in a temple at Saqqara where an important cult of Bastet existed. Here millions of mummified animals of different types were deposited in a vast underground network of galleries and even in reclaimed tombs, carved into the limestone bedrock many centuries earlier. Above ground were temple complexes with shrines that housed divine images of a god that formed the focus of the cult. The temple complex was not just a dwelling place for the gods but a facility to breed, capture and contain votive animals and birds to be killed and mummified on an industrial scale. Over 2500 years ago Saqqara must have been a congested place on festival days with thousands of men and women from Egypt and the Eastern Mediterranean visiting the temples amid the noise of cats, dogs, baboons and birds awaiting their sacrifice. Pilgrims' demand for votive offerings from the temple workshops provided an important source of income for temples throughout Egypt and was a significant feature of the national economy at this time. (A.C.)

146. 貝斯塔神雕像
來自薩卡拉， 動物大墓地，第 4 區
後埃及時期， 第 26 王朝（西元前 664-525 年）
青銅
195 x 123 x 75 mm

Figure of Bastet
From Saqqara, Sacred Animal Necropolis, sector 4
Late Period, Dynasty 26 (664-525 BC)
Bronze

貓木乃伊

在所有被製成木乃伊的動物中，埃及人可能與貓的關係最為密切。這件展品的出處不明，但可能源於一座貓類墓園。在東部三角洲的布巴斯提斯（Bubastis）是貓女神貝斯塔（Bastet）的宗教中心，而據希羅多德（Herodotus）表示，所有死去的貓都會被帶到這裡埋葬。事實上，在史塔普安塔（Stabl Anta，接近埃及中部的貝尼哈森）及薩卡拉（Saqqara）亦有大型貓類墓園座落其中，較小的墓地則分佈於其他眾多地點。

貓木乃伊之主要目的是作為奉獻給神的還願祭品。從古埃及晚期開始，供應朝聖者對於聖獸木乃伊需求的產業便逐漸蓬勃，且在薩卡拉等地相當活躍。因此，大量的貓被飼養來屠宰，透過勒斃或重擊頭部致死，並經常有早逝情況。此需求似乎導致製造「假」木乃伊的必要，利用一隻貓或數隻貓的部份軀體製成一具木乃伊。的確，位於薩卡拉的新王國時期再生陵墓中，有一組貓木乃伊的分析顯示，約有近三分之一的「木乃伊」中僅包含泥漿、黏土或鵝卵石。

雖然有些貓木乃伊的四肢經過個別包裹，但大多數都如同這件展品般，腿部及尾巴皆包裹於圓柱狀裹布內。最引人注意的部份是頭部，以亞麻、石膏及油墨來模擬生命之細節。交錯縱橫的裹布圖案是羅馬時期之典型。（作者：C.P.）

Cat mummy

Of all the animals that they mummified, the Egyptians are perhaps most closely associated with the cat. This example is unprovenanced, but may have originated from a number of cat cemeteries. Bubastis, in the eastern Delta, was the cult centre of the cat goddess Bastet, and Herodotus states (II, 67) that all dead cats were to be brought here for burial. In fact, large cemeteries for felines were also located at Stabl Antar (near Beni Hasan in Middle Egypt) and at Saqqara, with smaller burials at many other sites.

Cat mummies were in principal intended as a votive gift to the gods. Beginning in the Late Period, a booming industry catering to the demand from pilgrims for sacred animal mummies was active at sites like Saqqara. Thus large numbers of cats were reared for slaughter, and commonly appear to have died young, through either strangulation or a blow to the head. Demand seems to have necessitated the creation of 'fake' mummies, with only a part of a cat – or parts from several – in one packet. Indeed, analysis of a group of cat mummies from reused New Kingdom tombs at Saqqara showed that almost a third of 'mummies' contained only mud, clay or pebbles.

While some cat mummies have individually-wrapped limbs, most have their legs and tail bound up within a cylindrical package such as this. Most attention was paid to the head, with linen, plaster and ink used to model details in imitation of life. Criss-crossed patterned wrappings are typical of the Roman period. (C.P.)

147. 貓木乃伊
來自埃及
後埃及時期 - 羅馬時期（西元前 664 年 - 西元 100 年）
動物組織，亞麻
280 x 88 x 87 mm

Cat mummy
From Egypt
Late Period – Roman (664 BC-AD 100)
Animal tissue and linen

148. & 149. 鑲嵌於牛木乃伊的眼睛
來自巴卡利亞，阿曼特
後埃及時期 – 托勒密時期（西元前 360-30 年）
玻璃
88 x 56 x 29 mm， 91 x 59 x 13 mm

Inlaid eyes from a cow mummy
From the Baqaria, Armant
Late Period – Ptolemaic Period (360-30 BC)
Glass

鑲嵌於牛木乃伊的眼睛

在法老時期的埃及，有些公牛的宗教相當活躍。其中最著名位於曼菲斯（Memphis）的阿匹斯（Apis）聖牛，已證實早在埃及歷史剛開始時便已存在。公牛因其力量象徵與性能力而受到尊崇。不像其他多數被飼養來屠宰、製成木乃伊，並銷售給朝聖者的聖獸，僅有公牛在任何時期皆被視為某位神祇。在曼菲斯，阿匹斯聖牛與該城市之守護神普塔（Ptah）有所關聯，並且在薩卡拉（Saqqara）附近塞拉皮雍（Serapeum）的地下墓穴中給予厚葬。

這對牛眼的起源顯示其曾經屬於一隻生下布奇斯（Buchis）聖牛的母牛木乃伊，而布奇斯聖牛是蒙圖（Montu）神之神獸。蒙圖神是亞曼達（Armant）當地神祇，被稱為「上埃及的赫雷奧波利斯（Heliopolis）」。

太陽神的宗教中心在北方，其中之關聯可能是布奇斯聖牛在生活中被稱為太陽神拉的「傳令官」的原因。該聖牛會周遊於城鎮中，而有機會看到此動物的人民可能會闡釋聖牛之動作，以作為詢問其問題之回覆。聖牛的選擇方式是根據其身體記號：據古早資料記錄顯示，布奇斯聖牛必須為白色，而頭部是黑色。

布奇斯之地下墓穴布闊安（Bucheum）目前位於亞曼達現代城鎮北方。聖牛之墓葬證實最早於內克坦布（Nekhtanebo）二世即位後第 14 年（公元前 366 年）便已開始。產下布奇斯的母牛同樣會被認為是神聖的，且能在附近擁有一座獨立的墳墓建築，稱為巴卡利亞（Baqaria）。這對眼睛來自巴卡利亞第 32 墳墓。儘管此特殊墳墓似乎受到的影響最小，但來自地下水的損害導致布闊安和巴卡利亞兩地有機物質之保存情形極差，因而僅有此類配件得以被發現。大部分的公牛木乃伊都戴有面具或玻璃和石頭製成的眼罩以獲取視覺能力。眼角（canthi）部份使用帶有自然風格的紅色玻璃也使其形成一個格外逼真的外觀。（作者：C.P.）

Inlaid eyes from a bull mummy

A number of bull cults were active in pharaonic Egypt. The most famous, that of the Apis bull at Memphis, is attested from the very beginning of Egyptian history. The bull was revered as an embodiment of strength and sexual potency. Unlike the majority of other 'sacred' animals, which were raised for slaughter, mummification and sale to pilgrims, only one bull was considered the incarnation of a certain deity at any one time. At Memphis the Apis bull was associated with Ptah, the patron deity of the city, and was given an elaborate burial in the catacombs of the Serapeum at nearby Saqqara.

The provenance of this pair of eyes indicates that they once belonged to a mummified cow that had borne a Buchis bull, an animal sacred to the god Montu. He was the local god of Armant, known as 'Upper Egyptian Heliopolis'. This association with the sun god's cult centre in the north may be one reason why in life the Buchis bull was known as a 'herald' of the sun god Re. The bull would travel around towns, and people who had the opportunity to see the animal might interpret its movements in response to questions asked of it. Selection of the bull was based on its markings: ancient sources record that the Buchis was to be white, with a black head.

The Buchis catacomb – the Bucheum – lies to the north of the modern town of Armant. A bull burial is first attested here in year 14 of Nekhtanebo II (366 BC). The cows who gave birth to the Buchis bulls were also considered sacred, and had a separate tomb complex nearby, known as the Baqaria. This pair of eyes comes from tomb 32 at the Baqaria. Although this particular tomb appeared the least affected, damage from ground water resulted in the poor preservation of organic material in both the Bucheum and the Baqaria, so often only fittings such as this have been recovered. The majority of bull mummies would have had masks or coverings with eyes made of glass and stone in order to enable the power of sight. The naturalistic use of red glass for the canthi gave an especially lifelike appearance. (C.P.)

阿匹斯牛雕像

動物宗教在古埃及晚期愈發流行。其中最重要的是公牛崇拜，早在第一王朝時便已出現。在所有聖牛崇拜中，阿匹斯（Apis）聖牛或許是其中最著名，且神聖性最高者。阿匹斯聖牛起初被認為是卜塔（Ptah）神的化身。之後阿匹斯聖牛則與奧塞里斯神有關。在一段時間內僅有一隻公牛可被視為阿匹斯聖牛，在該隻聖牛死亡時，將尋求一隻替代的公牛。阿匹斯聖牛可透過特定記號來確認。其為黑色且前額帶有白色鑽石圖形，背上有鷹形圖像，尾巴毛髮為雙倍數量，且舌下有聖甲蟲印記。在阿匹斯聖牛死亡時，其屍體會經防腐處理，並安葬於塞拉皮雍（Serapeum）一座巨型石棺中。（作者：J.H.W.）

Figure of the Apis Bull

Animal cults became increasingly popular during the Late Period. Among the most important were the bull cults, which appeared as early as Dynasty 1. The Apis bull cult is probably the best known of the divine bull cults, and it was the most sacred. The Apis bull was originally believed to be the incarnation of the god Ptah. Later the Apis became associated with the god Osiris. Only one bull was considered to be the sacred Apis at a time; a replacement would be sought upon the death of the bull. The Apis bull could be identified by certain distinct markings. The animal was black with a white diamond on its forehead, an image of an eagle on its back, double the number of hairs on its tail, and a scarab mark under its tongue. When an Apis bull died, the body was embalmed and buried in the Serapeum in a massive stone sarcophagus. (J.H.W.)

150. 阿匹斯牛雕像
來自薩卡拉
後埃及時期，第 26-30 王朝（西元前 664-332 年）
銅合金
78 x 71 x 20 mm

Figure of the Apis Bull
From Saqqara
Late Period, Dynasty 26-30 (664-332 BC)
Copper-alloy

鱷魚木乃伊

鱷魚是棲息於尼羅河岸邊最危險的動物之一。其為索貝克（Sobek）神之聖獸，索貝克神若不是被描繪成一隻鱷魚，就是被描繪成一個有著鱷魚頭的人，這種極強大的生物在尼羅河流域的陵墓場景中，常以捕食者之形象出現。鱷魚在文學作品中亦以作為命運之代理人為特色。在古王國時期之墓葬詛咒中，死者會威脅將以鱷魚之形體返回攻擊那些損害其陵墓的人。

目前已知的大型鱷魚墓園位於柯蒙波（Kom Ombo）、伊斯納（Esna），以及馬貝德（Maabad）的沙目（Samun）洞穴。部份聚集在法尤姆地區，索貝克神在此地區被尊崇為「湖地之主」。這些爬行動物的木乃伊通常都年紀都非常小，有些才剛從卵中孵化，且經常埋葬於這些木乃伊身旁。同樣地，這些樣本在年紀還小的時候就被擊斃，即使是較大的木乃伊亦同，或許這是為了防止牠們因尺寸變大而變得難以操控且危險。（作者：C.P.）

151. 鱷魚木乃伊
來自埃及
後埃及時期，第 26-30 王朝（西元前 664-332 年）
動物組織、亞麻
1150 x 80 x 70 mm

Crocodile mummy
From Egypt
Late Period, Dynasty 26-30 (664-332 BC)
Animal tissue and linen

Crocodile mummies

Crocodiles were among the most dangerous animals that lived along the banks of the Nile. Sacred to the god Sobek, who id depicted as either a crocodile or as a man with a crocodile's head, this extremely powerful creature was shown as a predator in Nilotic scenes in tombs. Crocodiles also feature in literary texts as the agents of fate. In Old Kingdom tomb curses the deceased threatens to return in the form of a crocodile to attack those who would damage his tomb.

Large crocodile cemeteries are known at Kom Ombo, Esna, and in the Samun caves at Maabad. Several are clustered around the Fayum region, where Sobek was worshipped as 'Lord of the Land of the Lake'. The mummified reptiles were often very young; some found had only just hatched from their eggs, which are often buried alongside the mummies. Likewise, these examples were killed when still young, even the larger mummy – perhaps to prevent them from becoming unmanageable, and thus dangerous, in size. (C.P.)

152. 鱷魚木乃伊
來自哈瓦拉
後埃及時期，第 26-30 王朝（西元前 664-332 年）
動物組織、亞麻
288 x 125 x 70 mm

Crocodile mummy
From Hawara
Late Period, Dynasty 26-30 (664-332 BC)
Animal tissue, sand, linen

153. 蛇木乃伊和棺木
來自埃及
後埃及時期 – 托勒密時期（西元前 664-30 年）
木，亞麻，動物組織
172 x 50 x 48 mm

Coffin for a Snake
From Egypt
Late Period-Ptolemaic Period (664-30 BC)
Wood, linen, animal tissue

蛇木乃伊和棺木

蛇與一般小型動物，例如蠕蟲、老鼠、蜥蜴以及鼩鼱等，亦被製成木乃伊。這具小型棺木安放著蛇的遺體，作為獻給神的禮物。在這種更為精細的物件上，其象形文字表明此類禮物是為了獲取神祇恩寵而製作。這種還願祭品可能也用於控制並重新引導蛇的危險力量。

有個神話故事敘述了女神伊西斯（Isis）用來發現太陽神拉（Re）之實名的魔法。該神祇已衰老且容易流口水，所以伊西斯收集其唾液並與泥土混合以形成一條毒蛇。由於拉自己並未創造出該生物，因此不具有避免該毒蛇咬牠的力量。伊西斯要求知道神的秘密名字以作為治療傷口的回報，並因此獲得其部份神力。出現於古埃及晚期之「治療雕像」上的銘文特別強調治療蛇咬傷的部份，或許奉獻這件小型作品之目的是為了對這種治療表示感謝，或對這種治療表示期待之意。（作者：C.P.）

Coffin for a Snake

Snakes were among the small animals such as worms, rats, lizards and shrews that were also mummified. This small coffin contains the remains of snake, given as a gift to the gods. Hieroglyphic texts on more elaborate versions of this type of object make clear that such gifts were made in expectation of divine favour. Such a votive offering may also have been intended to harness and redirect the dangerous powers of serpents.

One myth narrates the magic used by the goddess Isis to discover the true name of the sun-god Re. The aging god was prone to drooling, so Isis collected his saliva and mixed it with earth to form a venomous serpent. Because Re had not created the creature himself, he did not have power over it and was unable to prevent it from biting him. In return for curing the bite, Isis demanded to know the god's secret name – and was thus able to acquire some of his magical power. Inscriptions on so-called 'healing statues' from the Late Period place particular emphasis on curing snake bites; perhaps this small object was offered in gratitude for – or anticipation of – such a cure. (C.P.)

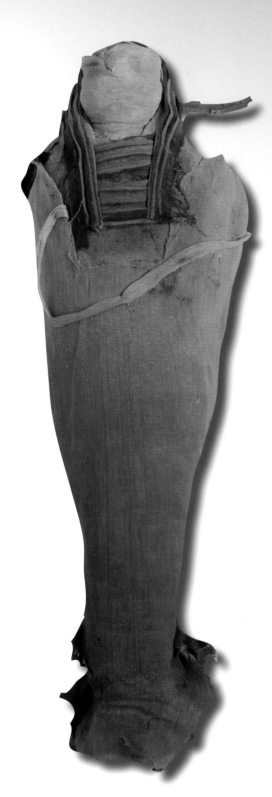

154. 鷹木乃伊
來自埃及
後埃及時期 - 托勒密時期（西元前664-30 年）
動物組織
270 x 70 x 45 mm

Hawk Mummy
From Egypt
Late Period-Ptolemaic Period (664-30 BC)
Animal tissue

鷹木乃伊

鷹（或獵鷹）最常與荷魯斯神有所關聯，荷魯斯神是被謀殺的冥神奧塞里斯之子，亦為其父親之復仇者。荷魯斯因而成為合法王權之典範，而每一位國王皆被認為是其活生生的化身。活鷹便成為奧塞里斯之子荷魯斯之聖獸，而一般則認為奧塞里斯是以阿匹斯（Apis）聖牛的形體出現，阿匹斯聖牛因而成為薩卡拉（Saqqara）神獸墓地之動物崇拜焦點。

首批至埃及旅行的歐洲遊客曾描述到薩卡拉的「鳥坑」之事，而近來已遺失。在1965 至 1976 年間，由埃及探索學會在現場挖掘到的物品中發現無數具動物木乃伊，通常放置在陶罐裡並堆積於地下陵墓的長隧道中，其中包括五十萬隻鷹。這座「木乃伊動物園」反映出古埃及後期眾多朝聖者對於神獸墓地之虔誠。一般人希望藉由奉獻神獸標本以獲得神的青睞。在放置著鷹的地道中即取得與動物崇拜相關的儀式配備：盤子、香爐，甚至還有剃刀，其用來剃去祭司頭髮，使他們在動物崇拜儀式中能保持純潔。（作者：C.P.）

Hawk Mummies

The hawk – or falcon – was most frequently associated with the god Horus, son and avenger of his murdered father Osiris, god of the dead. Horus was thus the model for legitimate kingship, and each king was considered his living incarnation. Living hawks were sacred to Horus, the son of Osiris – who was believed to take the form of the Apis bull, the focus of the animal cult at the Saqqara sacred animal necropolis.

The first European travellers to Egypt describe 'bird pits' at Saqqara, which latterly became lost. Excavations at the site by the Egypt Exploration Society between 1965 and 1976 revealed countless numbers of animal mummies – usually placed in pottery jars and stacked up in long, tunnelling catacombs – including half a million hawks. This 'mummified zoo' reflects the piety of the many pilgrims to the sacred animal necropolis in the Late Period. It seems that by offering a specimen of their sacred species to a deity, ordinary people hoped to gain divine favour. The hawk galleries in particular have yielded examples of ritual equipment associated with the animal cult: dishes, incense burners, even razors to shave the heads of priests in order to make them ritually pure for service in the temples associated with the animal cults. (C.P.)

155. 鷹木乃伊
來自薩卡拉
後埃及時期，第 26-30 王朝（西元前664-332 年）
動物組織，亞麻
465 x 105 x 90 mm

Hawk Mummy
From Saqqara
Late Period, Dynasty 26-30 (664-332 BC)
Animal tissue, linen

156. 荷魯斯雕像
來自薩卡拉，動物大墓地，第 3 區
後埃及時期，第 26 王朝（西元前 664-525 年）
銅合金
109 x 73 x 28 mm

Figure of Horus the Falcon
Excavated at Saqqara, Sacred Animal Necropolis, sector 3
Late Period, Dynasty 26 (664-525 BC)
Copper-alloy

荷魯斯雕像

有大量的神祇與獵鷹有所關聯。由於其獨特的雙王冠（稱為 peschent），這座站立的小雕像可確認其身份為荷魯斯。這是一頂上埃及王冠與下埃及王冠的組合，象徵著這兩片由該國王統治的土地之統一（分別為北方與南方）。王冠前側擴張的帽圍以及豎起的眼鏡蛇可給予配戴者保護，並代表國王之權力，而荷魯斯與國王之關係最密切。確實如此，其關聯性可追溯至埃及前王國時期（公元前 5300 年至 3000 年），早期的統治者在當時被稱為「荷魯斯追隨者」。

其雕刻裝飾包括頸上環繞的珠子，以及鏨雕的羽毛細部，已不如其製成初期般清晰。此外，還可能有一件包含獵鷹遺體的青銅或木製棺材，並形成此件雕像之底座，以滿足其作為荷魯斯獻祭品之作用。此類青銅包裝的木乃伊遺體以更為精細的型態呈現在神廟還願物品中，當中亦可能包含經完整防腐處理或火化的動物遺體，或是跟一些較大型、亞麻布包裹的動物木乃伊一樣，由各種動物肢體，甚至是樹枝混合而成。（作者：A.C.）

Figure of Horus the Falcon

There are a large number of deities associated with the falcon. This statuette of a standing falcon can be indentified as Horus because of the distinctive double crown called the peschent. This is a combination of the crowns of Lower Egypt and Upper Egypt and represents the unity of these 'two lands' ruled over by the king (north and south respectively). The rearing cobra with dilated hood at the front of the crown offers protection to the wearer and represents the power of the king, with whom Horus is most closely connected. Indeed, the association goes back to the Predynastic Period (c. 5300-3000 BC) when the early rulers were referred to as the 'followers of Horus'.

The incised decoration comprising a broad collar of beads and chased feather details are now not as clear as when the statuette was first made. Also, there may have been a bronze or wooden casket containing the remains of a falcon which formed the base of this statuette and satisfied its role as a votive offering for Horus. Bronze packaged mummified remains of this type were a more elaborate form of presenting a votive in a temple. They may have contained the complete embalmed or cremated remains of the animal. Or, like some of the larger linen wrapped mummified animals, a mix of body parts from various animals and even twigs. (A.C.)

荷魯斯雕像

鷹在古埃及受到崇拜並視為神獸。伊西斯（Isis）與奧塞里斯之子荷魯斯經常被描繪成一隻鷹，且其象徵著神聖王權之概念。荷魯斯是國王的守護神，一般認定其與國王為同一人，國王所擁有的五個王銜中以「黃金荷魯斯」之名最具特色。

此尊雕像之造型為站立於長方形底座的一隻鷹，其身份為荷魯斯，雕刻自同一塊軟質白色石灰岩。殘餘的漆料痕跡顯示，此雕像原先經過彩繪。不幸的是，由於其石材柔軟，大部分的臉部細節已經遺失。

自古埃及晚期開始，面積廣闊的地下陵墓便建造於薩卡拉（Saqqara），以安置大量的神獸，其中包括荷魯斯神之神獸，即鷹木乃伊。這些還願用的木乃伊是由來訪者奉獻給神祇，並零星埋葬於地下陵墓中。鷹神荷魯斯之雕像，例如此件樣本，同樣是由來訪者獻給神祇之祭品，作為人與神之間的媒介，並同時祈禱神祇的幫助或恩寵。（作者：作者：A.G.）

Statue of Horus

The hawk was worshipped in ancient Egypt as a sacred animal. The god Horus, the son of Isis and Osiris, was usually depicted as a hawk, and he embodied the concept of divine kingship. Horus was the guardian deity of the king and was identified with the living king, whose five-fold titulary featured the 'Golden Horus' name.

This statue takes the form of a standing hawk upon a rectangular base, identified with Horus, carved in one piece from a single block of soft white limestone. Remaining traces of paint suggest that the figure would originally have been painted. Unfortunately, due to the softness of the stone, much of the detail of the face has since been lost.

From the Late Period vast catacombs were built at Saqqara to house huge quantities of sacred animals, including mummified hawks which were sacred to the god Horus. These votive mummies were donated by visitors to the deity, and buried sporadically in the catacombs. Votive statues of the hawk-god Horus, such as this example, would also have been left by visitors to the site as offerings to the deity with prayers for the god's help or favour, acting as intermediaries between the human and the god. (A.G.)

157. 荷魯斯雕像
來自薩卡拉，動物大墓地
後埃及時期，第 26-30 王朝（西元前 664-332 年）
石灰岩，顏料，鍍金
405 x 328 x 193

Statue of Horus
From Saqqara, Sacred Animal Necropolis
Late Period, Dynasty 26-30 (664-332 BC)
Limestone, pigment, gilt

朱鷺木乃伊

在埃及探索學會的挖掘過程中，曾在薩卡拉（Saqqara）地區某處發現四百萬件朱鷺木乃伊。位於此處的神獸墓地大部分可追溯至古埃及晚期，但包含動物木乃伊的地下墓穴有時與更為早期的深豎井有關，如古王國時期陵墓。此件木乃伊即來自於這些早期墓葬豎井之一。

像這件一樣包裹細緻的標本往往會隱藏一些（在某些情況下，如果有的話）預期的神獸遺體。雖然這可能不會影響其實質效益，試圖規範此行業之內容以明確指示出現，以確保「一個容器裝載一個神」。一位名叫赫（Hor）的書記員約在公元前 100 年左右活躍於薩卡拉地區，根據其文件所述，大規模之朱鷺墓葬每年舉辦一次，這些木乃伊之前則集中在一個稱為「客棧」的地方。考古證據亦指出，這些地下墓穴一旦完全填滿後，將依區塊進行封鎖。

此件亞麻繃帶上的貼花作品描繪著一位女神，其以一名配戴著頭飾的女性呈現，該頭飾上的牛角之間帶有日輪。她坐在寶座上，手持紙莎草權杖。此類肖像通常是哈托爾女神之典型，但在薩卡拉她更可能是伊西斯，因為其角色為「阿匹斯（Apis）之母」，而阿匹斯則是埋葬於此地的聖牛。朱鷺是托特（Thoth）神的神獸，在當地的神祇家譜中，被認為是阿匹斯之母伊西斯的父親，因而為聖牛的祖父。朱鷺似乎也是印何闐（Imhotep，在階梯金字塔附近被奉為神明的建築師）的神獸，其墳墓被認為位於附近的墓穴中。（作者：C.P.）

Ibis mummy

Somewhere in the region of four million mummified ibis birds were discovered at Saqqara during the course of excavations by the Egypt Exploration Society. The sacred animal necropolis at the site largely dates to the Late Period, but the underground catacombs containing mummified animals sometimes connect with the deep shafts of much earlier, Old Kingdom tombs. This mummy comes from one of these early burial shafts, numbered 3508.

Finely wrapped specimens such as this often conceal few – in some cases, if any – remains of the expected sacred species. While this may not have affected their perceived effectiveness, an attempt to regulate the industry appears in the explicit instruction to ensure 'one god in one vessel'. According to documents belonging to a scribe named Hor, who was active at Saqqara around 100 BC, mass burials of ibises took place once a year, the mummies having previously been collected together in a so-called 'rest house'. Archaeological evidence also indicates that the catacombs, once sufficiently full, were blocked up in sections.

Appliqué work on the linen bandages of this mummy depicts a goddess, shown as a woman with a headdress consisting of a solar disk between cow's horns. She is seated on a throne and holds a papyrus sceptre. This iconography typically represents the goddess Hathor, but at Saqqara she is more likely to be Isis, in her role as the 'Mother of the Apis' – the sacred bull buried at the site. Ibis birds were sacred to the god Thoth, who in the local divine genealogy was thought to be the father of Isis, Mother of Apis, and thus the sacred bull's grandfather. Ibises also appear to have been sacred to Imhotep, the deified architect of the nearby Step Pyramid, whose own tomb was believed to lie nearby the catacombs. (C.P.)

158. 朱鷺木乃伊
來自薩卡拉，古王國墓地，朱鷺坑道
後埃及時期 - 托勒密時期（西元前 664-30 年）
動物組織，亞麻
510 x 190 x 130 mm

Ibis mummy
From Saqqara, Old Kingdom Cemetery, Ibis Galleries
Late Period – Ptolemaic Period (664-30 BC)
Animal tissue and linen

159. 串珠項鍊和朱鷺護身符
來自梅特瑪，539 號墓室
第一中間期，第 9-10 王朝（西元前 2160-2055 年）
彩陶，金
75 x 75 x 4 mm

Beaded Necklace with Ibis Amulet
From Matmar, tomb 539
First Intermediate Period, Dynasty 9-10 (2160-2055 BC)
Faience, gold

串珠項鍊和朱鷺護身符

這條項鍊由一串藍綠色彩陶珠子環繞而成，並附有朱鷺護身符。該護身符是由黃金製成，並帶有一個環作為扣件。其位於護身符基線之下垂尾部顯示，朱鷺原本棲息在一根對角橫木上，目前已遺失。朱鷺造型的護身符最早出現於第一中間期，通常棲息在一根支柱上，目的在強調其代表托特（Thoth）神。其可與其他件樣品相比較，例如來自於第一中間期摩斯他卡達（Mostagedda）附近，一隻站立於支柱上的琥珀金朱鷺。這種造型的護身符幾乎都是由金、琥珀金，或銅所製成。

朱鷺是托特神的象徵，與寫作和知識有所關聯。然而，「以朱鷺造型呈現的托特神護身符可能具有特別的陪葬意涵。」至少第三中間期時，這種類型的護身符便是以一隻朱鷺面向著馬特（Maat）女神或是象徵著她的鴕鳥羽毛為其特色，強調著托特神在審判死者時，記錄著心在秤重後之結果的角色。

該護身符本身之成份主要是黃金，並結合少量的銅。黃金常常與銅或銀形成合金以達到完美與實用之目的。此外，銅的添加可降低黃金的熔點。在此護身符製作當時，埃及的黃金主要來源是在東部沙漠的採礦場，主要透過卡普多斯（Koptos）當地控制。

組成此項鍊其餘部份的珠子是由彩陶製成，這種彩陶是由人造石英砂與透明鹼性釉結合而成。埃及人將這種釉製合成物稱為 tjehnet，意思是「閃爍之物」。彩陶最常見的顏色分別是綠色和藍色，以模仿半寶石，尤其是綠松石，其為古埃及最珍貴的材料之一。這條項鍊的顏色在陪葬場景中相當重要，因為綠色是植物的顏色，表示生育和復活。Wadj 這個字代表綠色，同時意味著「蓬勃發展」與「身體健康」。

位於埃及中部梅特瑪（Matmar）墓園，發現此件作品的墓葬中已經過相當程度的侵擾，且並未有任何其他發現物品之紀錄。這條項鍊曾被重新串起，因此無法確定這是否為其原始配置。（作者：M.M.）

Beaded Necklace with Ibis Amulet

This necklace consists of a string of blue-green faience ring beads with an ibis amulet. The amulet is made of gold and has a loop at the back for attachment. The tail hanging down at the end of the baseline of the amulet suggests that the ibis originally perched on a standard, with the diagonal crosspiece from the corner now missing. Ibis-form amulets are first found in the First Intermediate Period and are usually depicted perching on a standard, which emphasises that a representation of the god Thoth is intended. It is comparable to other examples, such as an electrum ibis on a standard from nearby Mostagedda during the First Intermediate Period. This form of amulet is almost always made of gold, electrum, or copper.

The ibis was a symbol of the god Thoth, who was associated with writing and knowledge. However, "amulets of Thoth in ibis form may have had particularly funerary connotations." By at least the Third Intermediate Period, this type of amulet features the ibis facing a figure of the goddess Maat, or an ostrich feather symbolizing her, emphasizing the role of Thoth in recording the outcome of the weighing of the heart in the judgement of the dead.

The composition of the amulet itself is mainly gold, alloyed with a small amount of copper. Gold often had copper or silver alloyed with it for both aesthetic and practical purposes. The addition of copper lowered the melting point of gold. At the time when the amulet was made, the main source of gold in Egypt was the quarries in the Eastern Desert, controlled mainly through the site of Koptos.

The beads that make up the rest of the necklace are made of faience, a man-made composition of sand and quartz with a vitreous alkaline glaze. The Egyptians called this glazed composition tjehnet 'that which gleams'. The most commons colours for faience were green and blue, in imitation of semi-precious stones, especially turquoise, which was one of the most highly prized materials in ancient Egypt. The necklace's colour is significant for a funerary context, since green was the colour of vegetation, fertility, and resurrection. The word for green, wadj, also meant 'to flourish' and 'be healthy'.

The burial in which it was found, at the cemetery of Matmar in Middle Egypt, was quite disturbed and nothing else was recorded as being found there. The necklace has been restrung and it cannot be certain that this was its original configuration. (M.M.)

160. 刻有圖特摩斯三世名字的陶片
來自西奈，沙拉別艾卡錠，哈托爾神廟
新王國時期，第 18 王朝，圖特摩斯三世統治時期（西
元前 1479-1425 年）
彩陶
70 x 40 x 15 mm

Fragment of Tile with Cartouche of Thutmose III
From Sinai, Serabit el-Khadim, Hathor Temple
New Kingdom, Dynasty 18, Thutmose III (1479-1425 BC)
Faience

刻有圖特摩斯三世名字的陶片

透過與佩托里（Petrie）在沙拉別艾卡錠（Serabit el-Khadim）之哈托爾神廟發現的其他物件相比較，或許能重建此件小碎片之景像。兩件由佩托里所發表的貓的圖像瓷片目前收藏於倫敦與布魯塞爾，兩者在風格上極為相似，包括其中的象形文字以及貓鬚的描繪方式。這三塊瓷片幾乎能確定出自同一人手中，且皆有部分遺失。在伯頓博物館所收藏之碎片上，其尾巴頂端帶有橫條紋，意味著其屬於非洲野生貓（Felis silvestris libyca），與其他兩件樣品一起。其獻詞亦與收藏於倫敦之瓷片一模一樣：「完美的神、兩地之主，圖特摩斯三世（Menkheperre）」，收藏於布魯塞爾之瓷片銘文則有部份已遺失，但在風格與內容上似乎相同。所有貓圖像瓷片之年代可追溯至第十八王朝，在沙拉別艾卡錠一地相當獨特，並可能被視為綠松石之主哈托爾以貓之形態的方式呈現。沙漠在古埃及時代被視為一種蠻荒、危險且混亂的地方，探險考察隊因而將哈托爾之具有警覺且兇猛的貓類外形視為一種保護作用。（作者：N.H.）

Fragment of Tile with Cartouche of Thutmose III

It is possible to reconstruct the scene on this small fragment by comparison with the other objects found by Petrie at the Hathor temple of Serabit el-Khadim. Two cat plaques published by Petrie and now in London (BM EA 41842) and Brussels (E 1982 B) are very similar in style, from the hieroglyphs to the manner in which the cats' whiskers are drawn. All three plaques were almost certainly produced by the same person, and all have pieces missing. The tip of the tail on the Bolton fragment bears a horizontal stripe indicating that it belonged to an African wild cat (Felis silvestris libyca), in keeping with the other two examples. The dedication is also identical to the London plaque: "the perfect god, lord of the two lands, Thutmose III (Menkheperre)"; the Brussels inscription is partly lost but seems to match in style and content. All cat plaques date to Dynasty 18, seem to be unique to Serabit el Khadim, and may be understood as representing statues of Hathor, Mistress of Turquoise, in cat form. The desert was seen as an untamed, dangerous and chaotic place in ancient Egypt, and expedition parties therefore evoked Hathor in her watchful and fierce feline form for protection. (N.H.)

包裹圖特摩斯三世的亞麻布

此塊亞麻碎片是由大英博物館贈予伯頓博物館，以提供館長湯瑪斯麥格雷（Thomas Midgley）做研究，其為古埃及紡織品知名專家。據大英博物館所述，此碎片是由埃米爾布魯格施（Emile Brugsch）於圖特摩斯三世之木乃伊被移至巴哈里（Deir el-Bahri）附近發現的王室木乃伊存放區後取出。

此塊亞麻布以古埃及文字描述為「王室亞麻」，且為生產品質最佳的亞麻。該亞麻之精細程度已超出現代商業紡織人員之能力。此件特殊樣品由庫克（Cooke）及艾爾蓋蒙（el-Gamal）連同幾件極精細亞麻樣本進行檢驗，其中有些來自圖坦卡門的陵墓。此件樣本是所有受檢測亞麻中最為精細者，需要非常高超的技巧，以及編織程序生產自亞麻纖維。來自新王國時期的埃及景像透過精細亞麻描繪出王權實力，並可藉此看到身體輪廓。此件作品之亞麻布便具備此般品質，且適合作為如此偉大的法老之墓葬包裹布。（作者：C.R.）

Fragment of Royal Linen

This fragment of linen was given to Bolton Museum by the British Museum for the curator, Thomas Midgley to study as he was a known expert on ancient Egyptian textiles. According to the British Museum, the fragment was taken by Emile Brugsch from the mummified body of Thutmose III after he was removed from the cache of royal mummies found near Deir el-Bahri.

The linen is of a quality described as 'royal linen' in ancient Egyptian texts and was the finest quality produced. Linen of this fineness is beyond the capability of modern commercial weavers. This particular sample was examined by Cooke and el-Gamal along with several samples of very fine linen, including several from the tomb of Tutankhamun. This sample was the finest of those tested and would have required very great skill to produce from the production of the flax thread through the weaving process. Egyptian scenes from the New Kingdom picture royalty in very fine linen under which it is possible to see the outlines of the body. This piece of linen would have had this quality and would have been suitable as funerary wrapping for such a great pharaoh. (C.R.)

161. 包裹圖特摩斯三世的亞麻布
來自西奈，沙拉別艾卡錠，哈托爾神廟
新王國時期，第 18 王朝，圖特摩斯三世統治時期（西元前 1479-1425 年）
亞麻
150 x 105 mm

Fragment of Royal Linen
From Thebes, Theban tomb 320
New Kingdom, Dynasty 18, reign of Thutmose III (1479-1425 BC)
Linen

162. 巴哈里圖特摩斯三世浮雕
來自底比斯，巴哈里圖特摩斯三世神廟
新王國時期，第 18 王朝，圖特摩斯三世統治時期 (西元前
1479-1425 年)
砂岩，灰泥，顏料
1115 x 650 x 180 mm

Relief of Thutmose III from Deir el-Bahri
From Thebes, Deir el-Bahri, Thutmose III temple
New Kingdom, Dynasty 18, reign of Thutmose III (1479-1425 BC)
Sandstone, plaster, pigment

巴哈里圖特摩斯三世浮雕

此件大型不規則砂岩區塊是以浮雕方式進行雕刻，並加以粉刷與彩繪。此區塊包含牆體下部，且僅有人物之下半身被保留下來。位於左側的是諸神之王阿蒙雷（Amun-Ra）的坐姿圖像，前方是堆滿物品的供桌。位於右側的是一名跪著獻酒給神的國王，銘文上刻著「獻酒」。葡萄酒被放置在兩個一模一樣的小型 nu 瓶中（各在國王的每隻手裡），代表著上、下埃及。伸出的手臂與手拿碗祭碗在埃及象形文字中以 derep 之符號呈現。在新王國時期，此類國王與神祇互動的典型場景常見於神廟之室內裝飾中，這也是埃及藝術中最受喜愛的主題，表現出國王的謙卑以及對神祇之虔誠。

此景象在重建後將可看到阿蒙雷神的上半身配戴其特有之雙羽狀頭飾，一隻手拿著象徵生命的安卡（ankh），另一隻手則拿著權杖（was-sceptre）。國王則配戴傳統的條紋頭飾（nemes）。相對於坐著的阿蒙雷神，位在低處的國王及其臣服性的跪姿表現出神祇的優越地位。阿蒙雷神的雙羽頭飾高度會超越圖特摩斯三世之頭部。然而，其中人物亦以一種相互尊重的平衡狀態面向彼此，國王獻祭給阿蒙雷神，而阿蒙雷神同時賜福給國王。阿蒙雷神之圖像被擦除，並於後來重新雕刻、粉刷，且於雕刻表面彩繪。此浮雕裝飾風格正式且古典，保存完好的彩繪亦顯示出神廟浮雕的色彩是多麼美麗與燦爛。

此座圖特摩斯三世之小型神廟於 1962 年被賈德維加李平加（Jadwiga Lipińska）所指揮的波蘭與埃及代表團發現，其佇立於巴哈里（Deir el-Bahri）之哈謝普蘇（Hatshepsut）與蒙圖荷泰普的古蹟之間，主要由爵貝西西勒（Gebel Silsila）之砂岩所建成，並搭建於蒙圖荷泰普神廟上方的人工平台上。此神廟被命名為卓瑟阿克特（Djeser Akhet，意即「神聖的地平線」），進獻給阿蒙神，且與山谷的美麗盛宴儀式相關。此神廟之建造日期可追溯至該國王之統治末期，圖特摩斯三世於此時開始除去哈謝普蘇之名字與圖象。有數以千計的浮雕碎片與雕塑在此遺址出土。(作者：A.H.)

Relief of Thutmose III from Deir el-Bahri

This large, irregular-shaped block of sandstone was carved in raised relief and is plastered and painted. The block comprised the lower part of a wall scene and only the lower parts of the figures are preserved. On the left is a seated figure of Amun-Ra, King of the Gods, before a heaped offering table. On the right is a kneeling figure of the king offering wine to the god with the inscription 'giving wine.' The wine would have been placed in two small identical nu jars (one in each of the king's hand) representing Upper and Lower Egypt. This image of an outstretched arm with the hand holding an offering bowl appears as the sign derep in Egyptian hieroglyphs. In the New Kingdom, this type of scene is typical of interior temple decoration where the king is shown interacting with deities, and was a favourite motif in Egyptian art. It illustrated the king's humility and piety toward the gods.

A reconstruction of the scene would show the upper half of Amun-Ra wearing his signature double feathered (plumed) headdress holding an ankh, the sign for life, in one hand and a was-sceptre in the other. The king would be wearing the nemes headdress. The lower height of the king in comparison to the seated Amun-Ra and the king's subservient kneeling position demonstrates the superior status of the god. Amun-Ra's two double feathers would tower over the head of Thutmose III. However, the figures also face each other in a balanced composition of mutual respect; the king shows his devotion to Amun-Ra while he gives his blessing to the king. The figure of Amun-Ra was re-erased and later re-carved, plastered, and painted on the cut down surface. The relief decoration is in the formal, classical style and the well preserved paint shows how beautiful and brilliant the colour would have been on temple reliefs.

The small temple of Thutmose III was discovered in 1962 by a Polish-Egyptian mission directed by Jadwiga Lipińska erected between the monuments of Hatshepsut and Mentuhotep at Deir el-Bahri. It was predominately built of Gebel Silsila sandstone and was constructed on an artificial platform above the temple of Mentuhotep. The temple was named Djeser Akhet ('Sacred Horizon'), was dedicated to the god Amun, and was connected to the ritual of the Beautiful Feast of the Valley. The date of the construction of the temple was towards the end of the king's reign during the period when Thutmose III began to erase the name and images of Hatshepsut. The site uncovered thousands of fragments of reliefs and sculptures. (A.H.)

阿比多斯圖特摩斯三世浮雕

著名的英籍埃及古物學家佩托里（Petrie）修復了這件位於阿比多斯奧塞里斯神廟圍牆內，第十八王朝神廟遺跡之方形結構中的石灰岩塊。該岩塊以浮雕方式雕刻，且經過彩繪。有部份殘餘漆料被保存下來，尤其是浮雕右側，其中包含著黑色及紅色邊界。在邊界上方，還保留著站立的人物雙腳。浮雕左側是以詳細的象形文字浮雕刻著即位週年慶典稱號，其中包括兩行垂直書寫的荷魯斯（Horus）稱號「拉（Re）摯愛的強大公牛」以及圖特摩斯三世之王銜「（所有土地）的崇敬偉大之王」。這種類型的銘文常見於與圖特摩斯三世之即位週年慶典相關的古蹟上，並開始出現於其即位後第 21 年，即其統治期間之後半部時期。即位週年慶典是在統治者即位後三十週年，用以慶祝法老持續不斷的統治與成就而舉行，其後每三年一次。圖特摩斯三世之荷魯斯稱號中的公牛與配備武器之形象（權力或勝利之象徵）喚起了強大國王之象徵，其獲勝之實力同時踐踏著敵人。

帶有圖特摩斯三世之名的石塊於埃及各地被發現，最遠至南方努比亞（Nubia）的博爾戈爾山（Gebel Barkal），此舉也證明這名法老廣泛的建設活動及其深具野心的特質。有大量帶有圖特摩斯三世之名的石塊在阿比多斯的奧塞里斯神廟圍牆中發現。從極早期開始，此地點一直是墓地之神肯提伊門提烏（Khentiamentiu）之宗教中心，其後來與奧塞里斯神同化。在中王國時期，奧塞里斯神廟已成為冥界統治者最重要的宗教建築，並且是許多國王之多項建築活動重點。許多來自較早期結構的石塊被發現使用於後期國王的建築中。從現場發現的文物看來，活動之時間範圍從早期王國時期一直延伸至希臘羅馬時期。時至今日，這座一度宏偉壯觀的神廟建築已幾乎所剩無幾。這主要是由於神廟本身幾乎完全是由泥磚所建造，且其中有些部份不斷被拆除與重組所造成。（作者：A.H.）

163. 阿比多斯圖特摩斯三世浮雕
來自阿比多斯，奧塞里斯神廟
新王國時期，第 18 王朝，圖特摩斯三世統治時期（西元前 1479-1425 年）
石灰岩，顏料
895 x 446 x 115 mm

Relief of Thutmose III from Abydos
From Abydos, Osiris Temple Enclosure
New Kingdom, Dynasty 18, reign of Thutmose III (1479-1425 BC)
Limestone, pigment

Relief of Thutmose III from Abydos

The noted English Egyptologist, Sir William Matthew Flinders Petrie recovered this limestone block from the square mass of Dynasty 18 temple ruins situated within the Osiris Temple Enclosure at Abydos. The block was carved in raised relief and was painted. Some remnants of the paint have been preserved, most notably on the right side of the relief, which contains a border in black and red. Above this border, only the feet remain of the figure that once stood there. On the left side of the block there is part of a jubilee titulary inscribed in detailed raised hieroglyphs, which comprises the Horus name 'Mighty Bull, beloved of Re' and Nebty name 'Great of Reverence in (all lands)' of Thutmose III in two vertical columns. This type of inscription is commonly found on monuments associated with the Heb-Sed festivals of Thutmose III and appeared during the second half of his reign beginning in year 21 of his reign. The Heb-Sed festival celebrated the continued rule and success of the pharaoh after the ruler had held the throne for thirty years and then every three years after that. The image of the bull and arm with weapon (the sign for power or victory) in Thutmose III's Horus name invokes the symbolism of a powerful king whose victorious strength tramples his enemies.

Blocks with the name of Thutmose III have been found throughout Egypt and reached as far south as Gebel Barkal in Nubia, which attests to the extensive building campaign and ambitious nature of this pharaoh. At Abydos, a large quantity of blocks with the name of Thutmose III was discovered within the Osiris Temple Enclosure. From very early times, this site was a cult centre of the necropolis god Khentiamentiu, who later became assimilated with the god Osiris. By the Middle Kingdom, the Osiris Temple had become the most important religious structure of the ruler of the dead and was the focal point of multiple building activities of numerous kings. Many blocks from earlier structures can be found reused in the buildings of later kings. Artefacts found at the site show that activity ranged from the Early Dynastic Period to the Graeco-Roman Period. Today, very little survives of this once magnificent temple complex. This is largely due to the fact that the temple itself was built almost entirely of mud-brick and that parts of it were constantly being dismantled and reassembled. (A.H.)

奧塞里斯雕像

奧塞里斯（Osiris）代表了死亡、重生與豐饒，為古埃及最重要的神祇之一。這個精緻雕琢的塑像展現奧塞里斯特有的木乃伊形象，而精美的雕工顯示此雕像原本應出自皇室工匠之手。奧塞里斯從繃帶中伸出雙手，緊握著代表皇室的曲柄杖與槤枷，清楚展現其身為逝去國王與亡者之王的雙重身分。頭上戴著高聳的阿特夫冠（atef-crown），兩側飾有獨具特色的羽毛。王冠的正面為眼鏡蛇的頭部，而雕像的雙腳與底座部分皆已遺失。雕像所緊靠著的回柱並未刻上銘文。（作者：R.G.）

Statue of Osiris

Connected with death, resurrection and fertility, Osiris was one of the most important deities in ancient Egypt. This finely carved statue depicts the god in his characteristic form as a mummy and is of a quality that suggests it originated in a royal workshop. The god's hands project through the mummy wrappings to hold the royal insignia of crook and flail. In this way it is made clear that he is both a dead king and King of the Dead. On his head is the tall atef-crown with its distinctive plumes on either side. The head of the cobra on the front of the crown and the legs and feet of the statue have been lost. The statue stands against an uninscribed back pillar. (R.G.)

164. 奧塞里斯雕像
來自埃及
後埃及時期，第 26 王朝（西元前 664-525 年）
玄武岩
580 x 220 x 150 mm

Statue of Osiris
From Egypt
Late Period, Dynasty 26 (664-525 BC)
Basalt

康亞契斯外棺

此外棺是連同本書編號 166 之展品一起取得，這個人形棺明顯曾裝納了一個內棺，但此外棺上的名字卻不同於編號 166 展品上的名稱，因此引發兩者是否屬於同一位女性的質疑。可能的情況包括了：康亞契斯（Tjenkhaykhetes）與塔克漢姆斯（Takhenmes）為同一人交替使用的兩個名字，而當塔克漢姆斯取得以康亞契斯之名完成的外棺後，卻未改變名字；或者兩個棺木實際上並不屬於同一組，只是同時一起交給伯頓博物館罷了。

另外，同樣讓人感到困惑之處在於，根據挖掘報告，康亞契斯的墓穴裡包含了一個人形棺（外棺）與一個內棺，且兩者皆漆上了「神話主題」。雖然內棺（166 號展品）上有精美的裝飾，但目前展示的外棺卻相當樸素，顯示若不是在撰寫報告時有失誤，便是還有一個最外層的棺木遺失了－或許是由於狀況過於不佳而無法帶回英國。

除了頭部與衣領，外在裝飾僅限於一列寫了制式進獻程序的文字，延伸至棺蓋的正面底部。而內棺在額頭部分繪有一圈鮮花頭冠，並非聖甲蟲，頭部頂端裝飾以橫向的象形文字，與從中升起的太陽。兩側飾以代表東方與西方的圖式。棺木槽底部繪有擁有全臉部與等身高的天神努特（Nut）圖像，兩側則繪有「孕育眾神（who bore the gods）」的象形文字。（作者：A.M.D.）

Outer Coffin of Tjenkhaykhetes

Acquired with Catalogue #166, this coffin is certainly of the type that would have enclosed such a mummy-case, but the writing of the owner's name is sufficiently different from that written on that object to lead to doubts as to whether they indeed belonged to the same woman. Options include that Tjenkhaykhetes and Takhenmes were alternate names for the same person; that Takhenmes had acquired an outer coffin made for another, but had failed to have the name changed; or that the coffins were not actually found as a set and were only brought together when given to Bolton.

The confusion is increased by the fact that the burial of Tjenkhaykhetes is described in the excavation report as comprising a coffin and a mummy-case, both painted with 'mythological scenes'. While the mummy-case is richly decorated, the present coffin is extremely plain, suggesting either that a mistake was made in compiling the report, or that there may have been a further (outermost) coffin which is now lost - perhaps ultimately in too poor a condition to be brought back to the United Kingdom.

The exterior decoration, apart from the head and collar, is restricted to a single column of text, containing a standard offering formula, down the front of the lid. As with the mummy-case, a floral chaplet is depicted around brow but, rather than the scarab, the top of the head is here adorned with the hieroglyph of the horizon, with the sun rising from it. This is flanked by the signs for the east and the west. The floor of the coffin trough is adorned with a full-face, full-length, image of the sky-goddess Nut. Her head is flanked by the hieroglyphic signs reading 'who bore the gods'. (A.M.D.)

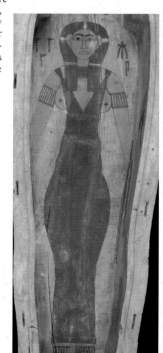

165. 康亞契斯外棺
來自底比斯，哈謝普蘇神廟
第三中間期，第 25 王朝早期（西元前 747-656 年）
木，灰泥，顏料
1850 x 640 x 630 mm

Outer Coffin of Tjenkhaykhetes
From Thebes, Deir el-Bahari, temple of Hatshepsut
Third Intermediate Period, Early Dynasty 25 (747-656 BC)
Wood, plaster, paint

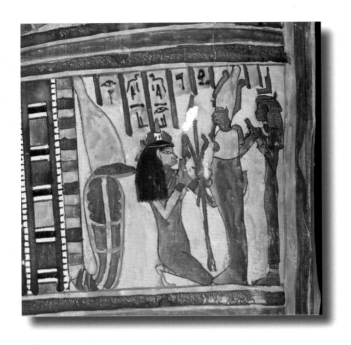

塔克漢姆斯人形棺

這個木乃伊盒的內棺混合了亞麻布與灰泥，與本書上的編號 165 外棺一起取得，原本被埋藏於哈謝普蘇（Hatshepsut）神廟中間列柱北部的殘骸之中，自該神廟建造後已埋藏了 800 年之久。這類木乃伊盒屬於基本款式，最初出現於示薩一世（Shoshenq I）的統治期間（西元前 945-924），取代早期以面具覆蓋木乃伊頭部，或為整個木乃伊蓋上一片等身長的面具木乃伊蓋板的習慣作法。在新的製作方法中，木乃伊被密封於事先製作的合身堅固束衣中，繫緊背後的束帶後，就能緊緊包著木乃伊，接著裹以灰泥並上色，最後再於雙腳下方釘上木板。因此，若不先將內棺切開，便無法移走木乃伊；而此處所展示的內棺便在木乃伊出土時被切開過，而當中的木乃伊顯然被遺留在埃及。如腳下的基座所顯示一這是一種新型木乃伊內棺的特色，約在西元前 600 年取代了早期的木乃伊盒。

在木乃伊的頭頂部繪有一個聖甲蟲，周圍環繞著一個花冠，底下則伸出鳥的身體、雙腳與軀幹，而鳥更在臉部兩側保護性地展開雙翅。一個製作精美的衣領覆蓋著肩膀與軀幹上半部，底部的空白部分則繪有一隻有著公羊首的猛禽圖像，代表著太陽的化身。其下區域則描繪了塔克漢姆斯（Takhenmes）跪在奧塞里斯與伊西斯面前的場景。

底下有一隻張開雙翅且頭上頂著日輪的猛禽，在鳥的尾巴下方，繪有奧塞里斯的祭祀，一直延伸至腳踝處，因此將剩下的區域切割為兩部分，上半部的一端繪有坐著的阿努比斯（Anubis）；下一個區域內有著一對奧塞里斯、伊西斯和奈芙蒂斯（Nephthys）站在平台上的圖像，搭配繪於木乃伊右邊的托特（Thoth），與左邊的荷魯斯（Horus）。底部飾有一對猛禽，皆張開雙翅，頭上頂著日輪。在腳部兩側則飾有阿努比斯的橫臥圖像，兩腳之間的空間則寫上來自《亡者之書》（Book of the Dead）的韻文，此並出現於內棺的其餘部分。

塔克漢姆斯擁有 Lady of the House 的稱號，因此表明了她的已婚身分，此外再沒有其他關於其身分的敘述；但由於在第二十五王朝期間，許多埋葬於卡納克北方哈謝普蘇神廟者皆為蒙圖（Mentu）神的祭司團成員，因此塔克漢姆斯可能是該祭師團成員的妻子或女兒。（作者：A.M.D.）

Mummy-case of Takhenmes

This mummy-case of cartonnage - a mixture of linen and plaster, not dissimilar to papier mâché - was acquired with the outer coffin Catalogue #165, found in the debris that had accumulated in the northern part of the Middle Colonnade of the temple of Hatshepsut in the eight centuries since the building of that structure. The case is of a basic type first found during the reign of Shoshenq I (945-924 BC), replacing earlier customs of covering the mummy's head with a mask, or laying a full-length board in the shape of masked mummy atop the whole mummy. In the new approach the mummy was sealed in a solid envelope, made on a former and fitted round the wrapped mummy before being laced up at the rear, receiving a final coat of plaster and being painted. A wooden board pegged under the feet completed the process. As a result, the mummy could only be removed by cutting the case open: this has been done with the present piece when the mummy was unwrapped at the time of its excavation; the mummy was apparently left in Egypt. This mummy-case is one of the very latest of the genre, as is shown by the pedestal below its feet - a feature of a new kind of inner coffin that had replaced such cartonnage cases by around 600 BC.

A scarab beetle is painted on the crown of the head, surrounded by a floral chaplet, below which protrude the body, legs and wings of a bird, the latter spread protectively either side of the face. An elaborate collar swathes the shoulders and upper torso, its lower margin covered by the image of a ram-headed raptor, a personification of the sun. Under this is a register including two scenes of Takhenmes kneeling before Osiris and Isis.

Below is a raptor with outstretched wings and a sun-disc on its head; beneath the bird's tail, an Osiris-fetish extends to the ankles. This divides the remaining three registers into two, the upper one having a seated figure of Anubis at either extremity. The next register has a pair of images of Osiris, Isis and Nephthys on a podium, accompanied on the right side of the case by Thoth and Horus on the left. The lower register is decorated with a pair of raptors, wings outstretched with sun-discs on their heads. Each side of the foot is decorated with a recumbent image of Anubis, the area in between by verses from the Book of the Dead, which also features elsewhere on the case.

Takhenmes bore the title of Lady of the House, implying that she was a married woman. Nothing else is known for certain about her, but as many of the burials made in Hatshepsut's temple during Dynasty 25 were members of the priesthood of the god Mentu at Karnak-North, it is likely that Takhenmes was the wife or daughter of a member of that priesthood. (A.M.D.)

166. 塔克漢姆斯人形棺
來自底比斯，哈謝普蘇神廟
第三中間期，第 25 王朝早期（西元前 747-656 年）
亞麻，灰泥，顏料
1700 x 500 x 330 mm

Mummy-case of Takhenmes
From Thebes, Deir el-Bahari, temple of Hatshepsut
Third Intermediate Period, Early Dynasty 25 (747-656 BC)
Linen, plaster, pain

普塔 – 蘇卡 – 奧塞里斯雕像

這座普塔 – 蘇卡 – 奧塞里斯（Ptah-Sokar-Osiris）雕像有著黑色身體與鍍金的臉部，與後期王朝時期和托勒密王朝時期的彩色雕像皆屬同時期作品，且與新王國時期塗上了黑色亮光漆的皇室木雕已無相似之處，反映了關於奧塞里斯、土堆上的普塔（Ta-tenen）與墓地之主蘇卡等喪葬觀點。藉由讓自己與陰間的神祇產生連結，獲取創造與繁盛的力量，亡者因而能確保自己的復生，並被接納成為奧塞里斯神所統治之來世世界中備受崇敬的一員 akh。依照慣例，這些雕像必須展現纖長渾圓的外形，並戴著以兩根鴕鳥羽毛與放在山羊角的日輪所製成的 shuty 頭冠。這類雕像也大多會戴著藍色假髮與神明的鬍鬚。許多雕像上會銘刻著獻給小型神祇雕像的讚美詩，但此處所展示的雕像卻未刻有讚美詩。有趣地是，這類雕像多數都缺少usekh-en-bik 衣領，反映了當代的石棺裝飾特色。

這座普塔 – 蘇卡 – 奧塞里斯神雕像顯示這位神祇包裹以黑色裹屍布。黑色所代表的意義相當不明確，不僅能暗示埃及的肥沃土地 kemet，同時也象徵了死亡（即陰間）與來世。頭上分為三部分的假髮為紅色，不同於常見的藍色假髮，可能是特定地方工作坊的獨特印記。雕像頭上原本應戴著 shuty 頭冠，但現已遺失。其臉部與頸部皆鍍上金色，以表現有著金黃膚色神像的神性，並強調亡者勝利精神的耀眼外表。雕像的手臂與雙手皆隱藏在繃帶下。這座雕像的回柱設計與其擁有繽紛色彩的同類作品相似，並依稀可見雕像正面的銘文。雕像的身體部分共分為兩半，並以六根釘子接合，因而可以在雕像的空心部分放入紙莎草紙或木乃伊等物體，而「埋藏」在創造之神聖體中的任一物品都能確保亡者通往來世的旅程。這個雕像的腳部並未直接站立於底座上，而是立於一個紅色基座上，象徵讓亡者從中復生再出現的土堆與沙地。

雕塑的長方形底座鋪了灰泥，並以多種色彩塗上宮殿外牆圖樣（或 serekh），暗示著亡者即將加入的陰間王者奧塞里斯所擁有的不朽皇室建築中。雖然許多底座皆有著鷹隼或棺木外形的小盒，但這個底座卻是實心設計，且並未放有紙莎草紙或木乃伊物體。（作者：A.J.M.）

Ptah-Sokar-Osiris Figure

The statuettes of Ptah-Sokar-Osiris with black body and gilded face were contemporary to their Late Period and Ptolemaic Period polychrome parallels. Their resemblance to the New Kingdom black-varnished royal wooden statues is minimal as they are the reflection of mortuary ideas concerning not only Osiris but also Ptah in his form of primordial mound (Ta-tenen) and the lord of the necropolis Sokar. By associating himself with a deity of the netherworld gifted with powers of creation and fertility, the deceased ensured his resurrection and acceptance as a venerated spirit (akh) in the community of Osiris in the afterlife. As a rule these statuettes present slender but rounded shapes, wearing a shuty-crown consisting of two ostrich feathers and a sun disc on ram's horns. Most of the exemplars also wear a blue wig and divine beard. Many specimens were inscribed with a hymn to the god represented by the figurine, although that is not the case here. Interestingly, several statuettes of this type lack the usekh-en-bik collar, mirroring the decoration of the contemporary stone sarcophagi.

This figure of Ptah-Sokar-Osiris shows the deity covered in a black shroud, a colour with ambiguous meaning since it simultaneously alludes to the black fertile land of Egypt (kemet) while also symbolizing death (i.e. the netherworld) and afterlife. His tripartite wig is red, which seems a deviation from the common blue wig, perhaps the mark of a distinctive provincial workshop. Originally the head would have been topped with a shuty-crown, now lost. Its face and neck are gilded so as to portray the god's statuette with a golden skin, as a divine being, and enhance the gleaming aspect (hedjet) of the deceased's triumphant spirit. Arms and hands are hidden beneath the wrappings. The statuette has a back pillar in the same fashion as its polychrome counterparts, and traces of a frontal inscription are observable. The body of the statuette was manufactured in two halves that were joined by means of six spikes, allowing for the placement of a papyrus, corn-mummy or mummified fragment in the hollow core of the statuette. Any of these objects, 'buried' within the sacred body of the creator god, guaranteed the deceased's voyage to the afterlife. The figure's feet do not stand immediately on the base but on a red plinth, which conveys the idea of the primeval mound or sands from which the deceased symbolically re-emerges into life.

The oblong base of the statuette is plastered and painted in several colours with the palace-façade motif (or serekh), alluding to the monumental royal architecture of the king of the netherworld, Osiris, to whose community the deceased is to join. Although many bases have caskets with falcon or coffin-shaped lids, this base is solid and did not contain any papyrus or mummified fragment. (A.J.M.)

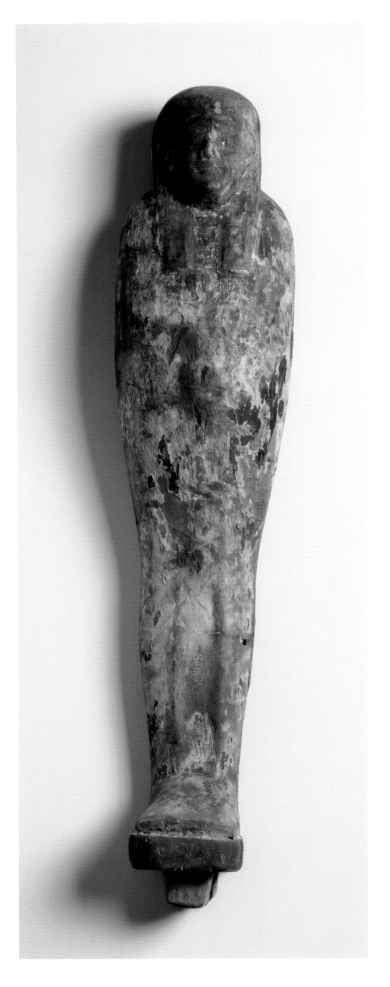

167. & 168. 普塔－蘇卡－奧塞里斯雕像
來自埃及
托勒密時期 (西元前 332-30 年)
木，灰泥，顏料，鑲金
370 x 125 x 80 mm, 565 x 125 x 90 mm

Ptah-Sokar-Osiris Figure
From Egypt
Ptolemaic Period (332-30 BC)
Wood, plaster, pigment, gilding

169. 普塔－蘇卡－奧塞里斯雕像
來自阿克敏
托勒密時期早期（西元前 332-150 年）
木，顏料
550 x 105 x 75 mm

Ptah-Sokar-Osiris Figure
From Akhmin, Panopolis
Early Ptolemaic Period (332-150 BC)
Wood, pigment

普塔－蘇卡－奧塞里斯雕像

有著紅色與黑色身體以及華麗服飾，這種融合普塔 - 蘇卡 - 奧塞里斯三神的雕像常見於托勒密王朝時期的墓穴之中。在第二十六王朝出現了所謂的埃及文藝復興時期（Egyptian Renaissance），改以精緻陪葬物品取代空心的奧塞里斯神像與較樸實無華的普塔 - 蘇卡 - 奧塞里斯神雕像（如本書編號 168）。每一個墓穴皆埋入一個人俑，並放置於石棺附近，這些陰界神衹的雕像不僅能藉由巫術確保亡者的復生─即讓亡者與三神（普塔、蘇卡與奧塞里斯）合為一體；更能將奧塞里斯的木乃伊遺體或具防護能力的紙莎草紙《亡者之書》[1] 獻給亡者，這些雕像原本被稱為紙莎草紙束衣（papyrus-sheaths）或空心雕像（hollow statues）。

這件文物展現早期托勒密王朝雕像的基本特色，同時又帶著地方工作坊的特色。雕像上有著深藍色的三方假髮、黃色皮膚（可能經過鍍金程序），而眼睛則塗上黑白色，強調奧塞里斯戰勝死亡的臉部表情。頭上有一個能夠擺置 shuty 頭冠的洞；shuty 頭冠以兩根鴕鳥羽毛與山羊角上的日輪製成。雕像纖細的身體包裹著紅色裹屍布與一個五彩繽紛的胸飾，並飾以華麗的 usekh-en-bik 衣領，上面有著兩個鷹隼首（象徵蘇卡），與數列同心花朵圖樣與水滴形設計。在衣領下方，努特（Nut）女神在亡者身上伸展雙翼，象徵著保護與復原。頭上的日輪則象徵女神讓太陽神拉（Re）復活的能力，而亡者亦能從中獲益。雕像背面有一個顯示地方工作坊創意的特色：只要移開回柱上半部的移動式木板，即能看見一個可放入紙莎草紙的小凹洞。獻給亡者的短文刻印在前柱與回柱上有著綠色鑲邊的黃色區域，並詳細描述作品的出處：（前柱）奧塞里斯背頌辭：西方的先鋒，親愛的神明呀，Ta-wer 之主 [2]，蘇卡 - 奧塞里斯」；（回柱）「在 Ipu（即 Akhmin）心中，偉大的母親伊西斯，您存在於 Ipu 心中，（與）阿努比斯，聖地之主，您為奧塞里斯提供保護……公平正義者。」此外，這個雕像站立於黑色基座上，暗示著復活（kemet）的黑土；雕像上有著一個能插入底座的榫舌，而底座現已遺失。（作者：A.J.M.）

---

1. 雕像上的小凹洞是設備以放入紙莎草紙捲，而底座上的盒子則是用以收藏衣物、假木乃伊、骨頭或屍體的一部分，如內臟或陰莖。
2. 意指鄰近的 Ta-wer 地區，以阿比多斯為中心，在這個奧塞里斯的稱謂中並非公認用來指涉奧塞里斯的來世之神身分，與其受歡迎的祭祀中心。

Ptah-Sokar-Osiris Figure

Statuettes of the syncretistic god Ptah-Sokar-Osiris, with red or black bodies and sumptuous apparels, became familiar objects in the tombs of the Ptolemaic Period. These elaborate specimens replaced the hollow Osirian figurines and the less opulent Ptah-Sokar-Osiris types (e.g.Catalogue #168) in the funeral equipment since the times of the so-called Egyptian Renaissance (Dynasty 26). With one specimen per burial and placed in proximity to the sarcophagus, these statuettes of the netherworld deity not only ensured the resurrection of the deceased by means of sympathetic magic: by identifying the deceased with the triad of divine mortuary aspects (Ptah, Sokar and Osiris), but also providing the deceased with the mummified remains of Osiris or a protective papyrus (Book of the Dead),[1] hence the former name of these statuettes as papyrus-sheaths or hollow statues.

This example shows the basic principles of the early Ptolemaic statuettes, but also some particularities of a provincial workshop. It has a dark blue tripartite wig, yellow face (possibly once gilded), and the eyes are painted black and white for enhancing the facial expression of Osirian triumph over death. On the head there is a hole to place a shuty-crown consisting of two ostrich feathers and the sun disc over a pair of ram's horns. The slender figure of the body is protected by a red shroud as well as a multicolor pectoral, and it is decorated with an opulent usekh-en-bik collar with two falcon heads (symbols of Sokar) and several concentric rows with floral motifs and drop-shaped elements. Below the collar, the sky goddess Nut stretches her double-wings over the deceased as a sign of protection and reconstitution. Her head bears the sun disc as a symbol of the resurrecting capacities of the goddess for the solar god Re, from which the deceased also benefits. The back of the statuette presents an exceptional feature, the result of a provincial workshop innovation: a small cavity for a piece of papyrus that can be revealed by removing the top half of the back pillar manufactured as a loose panel. The inscriptions on the fore and back pillar of the statuette are written on a yellow ground with blue bands and give details of the provenance of the piece: (front) "Words recited by Osiris, Foremost of the West, Good God, Lord of Ta-wer,[2] Sokar-Osiris"; (back) "who is at the core of Ipu (i.e. Akhmin), Isis the Great Mother, who is (also) at the center of Ipu, (and) Anubis, Lord of the Sacred Lands, who offer protection for Osiris […] justified". In addition, the statuette stands on a black plinth, which alludes to the black land of resurrection (kemet), and shows a tenon for fitting the body to its base, now lost. (A.J.M.)

1.The small cavities on the statuettes were made to contain rolls of papyrus while the large cavities on the bases or the trunk caskets were used for keeping pieces of cloth, corn-mummies, bones, or parts of the corpse, such as the entrails or even the penis.
2.The allusion to the neighbouring province of Ta-wer, whose main centre was Abydos, in this epithet for Osiris is not usually attested for referring to the role of Osiris as god of the afterlife and the awareness of its popular cult centre.

普塔－蘇卡－奧塞里斯雕像

在晚期托勒密王朝時期的墓穴中多置有以木乃伊形象出現的神祇木雕，這些木乃伊神祇融合了象徵復活的普塔 - 蘇卡 - 奧塞里斯三神。亡者與神的關係是為了確保亡者的轉世與復活。如此一來，亡者的外表，即其包裹在壽衣內的身體、與神明相仿的鬍鬚與受到崇拜的地位（即外表軀殼「sah」形體），以及胸前的文字皆讓亡者與奧塞里斯神產生聯結，因而奧塞里斯神便能夠確保來生的存在。其他雕像上還包含了獻給神的讚美詩。而另外兩位神祇，蘇卡和普塔則代表著死亡的神秘與墓地。此外，這些雕像皆飾有以兩根鴕鳥羽毛與山羊角的日輪所製成的 shuty 頭冠。雕像多立於底座之上，而底座多半擁有一個有蓋空間，並裝飾為鷹隼或棺木，但此處所展的文物則缺少了底座。在其他的文物中，顯示底座內可能還會放置一個假木乃伊（與奧塞里斯神話相關的復活象徵）或木乃伊物體。

此雕像為艾瑞 - 艾瑞魯（Iret-Ireru）的陪葬人俑，並以神化的形象表現亡者。特別強調眼部與鬍鬚部分，以讓人偶顯現奧塞里斯的外貌；略帶綠色的臉部則指涉了植物的繁盛與倖存的能力。亡者有著藍色假髮與雙色的同心帶衣領，能夠保護他的胸口。壽衣為紅色，為歡慶蘇卡節日的顏色。獻給亡者的短文則刻印在前柱與回柱上有著綠色飾邊的黃色區域。碑文包括了亡者的姓名與家譜：（前柱）背頌辭：哦，奧塞里斯，西方的先鋒，阿比多斯之主，親愛的神明呀，…」；（回柱）「背頌辭：哦，奧塞里斯，「Mut」-ir-rud 之子，公平正義者，與 Pa-di-asha-ikhet，公平正義者，女主人，Iret-Ireru」[1]。此外，這座雕像在腳部還有一個榫舌，剛好能放入底座的榫眼內。根據分類學上的形式特徵來看，這座雕像應製作於塞特（Saite）時期。（作者：A.J.M.）

....
1. 多數證據顯示 Iret-Ireru 為晚期時期的女性姓名。

Ptah-Sokar-Osiris Figure of Iret-Ireru

Wooden statuettes of a mummiform deity who is identified as Ptah-Sokar-Osiris, a syncretistic god of resurrection, were often placed in tombs of the Late and Ptolemaic periods. The relationship of the deceased with the god was thought to ensure his transfiguration and resurrection. In this instance, the deceased's external appearance, namely his body enveloped in a shroud, his divine beard, and his privileged deified status (a sah-figure), as well as the details of the inscription on his front, associate him with the god Osiris, a guarantor of an existence in the afterlife. Other statuettes include a hymn to the god. The other two forms of the deity, Sokar and Ptah, allude to the mysteries of death and the territories of the necropolis. In addition, the statuettes were decorated with a shuty-crown consisting of two ostrich feathers and a sun-disc over ram's horns. Besides, they usually stand on a base in which there was often a cavity with a lid decorated with a falcon or a coffin, although this specimen lacks its base. Other exemplars show that a miniature corn-mummy (symbol of resurrection connected with the mysteries of Osiris) or a mummified fragment might have been placed inside the base.

The present statuette was provided for the burial of Iret-Ireru and represents the deceased in the form of a deified being. The eyes and beard are outlined to make him look like Osiris; the greenish face also refers to the faculties of vegetation to flourish and emerge. The deceased has a blue tripartite wig and a bicolour collar of concentric bands that protects his chest. His shroud is red, the colour used in the celebration at the Sokar festival. Short texts for the deceased are inscribed on a yellow ground with green bands on the fore and the back pillar. The inscription includes the name and filiation of the deceased: (front) "Words to be recited: O Osiris, Foremost of the West, Lord of Abydos, Good God, […]"; (back) "Words to be recited: O Osiris, [son of Mut]-ir-rud, justified, and Pa-di-asha-ikhet, justified, Lady of the House, Iret-Ireru". Additionally, the statuette shows a tenon below the feet that would fit into a mortise on the base. Based on the typological formal features, the statuette must have been produced in the Saite Period. (A.J.M.)

....
1.Most of the attestations of the name Iret-Ireru corresponds to female individuals of the Late Period.

170. 普塔－蘇卡－奧塞里斯雕像
來自埃及
第 26 王朝（西元前 664-525 年）
木，顏料
340 x 85 x 60 mm

Ptah-Sokar-Osiris Figure of Iret-Ireru
From Egypt
Dynasty 26 (664-525 BC)
Wood, pigment

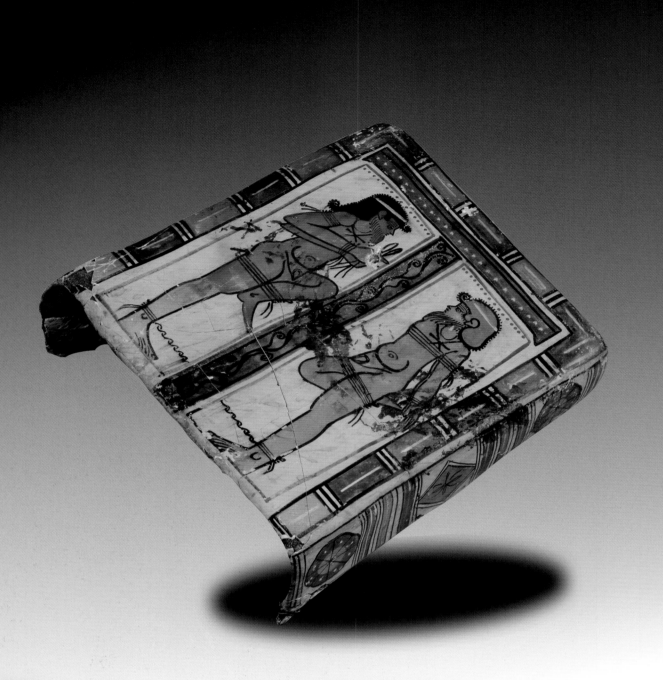

裝飾用腳蓋板

羅馬時期的木乃伊通常會有腳蓋板，可以覆在亡者的木乃伊腳部。鍍金後的腳部裝飾在腳蓋板上。前方中央裝飾以蓮花，而聖蛇之眼則裝飾於其中一側；玫瑰花形飾物則裝飾著兩側。

更有趣的部分在於會遮蔽雙腳底部的蓋板底部裝飾。最常見的圖樣即為遭捆綁的犯人，而在早期的埃及藝術中便曾出現關於俘虜的描述，且有平面與立體的表現方式。這些人物通常都是努比亞人與亞細亞人等埃及的古老敵人，且人物圖像多繪於可以遭到粉碎、勒緊或踐踏的位置，最知名的物件即為在圖坦卡門墓中所尋得的一雙涼鞋。當國王穿著涼鞋時，他就能以每一個步伐以具法力、象徵性地摧殘埃及的敵人。在托勒密與羅馬時期，這些圖樣開始被用於非皇室的葬禮物品中，如此處所展示的腳蓋板。如同早期的皇室文物，這些裝飾的目的皆在於能夠確保永遠戰勝敵人，包括外敵與危險猛獸。（作者：J.H.W.）

Decorated Footcase

Mummies of the Roman period often have cartonnage foot cases that were fitted over the mummified feet of the deceased. Natural-looking feet that have been gilded decorate the top of this foot case. The front is decorated with a central lotus flower and udjat eyes on either side. Floral rosette elements decorate the sides.

Even more interesting is the decoration found on the underside of the case, which would have covered the soles of the feet. Images of bound prisoners are a popular motif and representations of bound captives appear quite early in Egyptian art and can be found in both two and three dimensions. The figures, usually representing generalized Nubian and Asiatic captives (the traditional enemies of Egypt), are often found in places where these images could be crushed, throttled, or trod upon. A particularly well-known example can be seen on a pair of sandals found in the tomb of Tutankhamun. When the king wore these sandals, he would magically and symbolically trample the enemies of Egypt with each footstep. In the Ptolemaic and Roman periods, the motif came to be used on non-royal funerary trappings such as this cartonnage foot case. As with the earlier royal examples, the impetus for such decoration was to ensure eternal victory over enemies, be they foreigners or dangerous creatures. (J.H.W.)

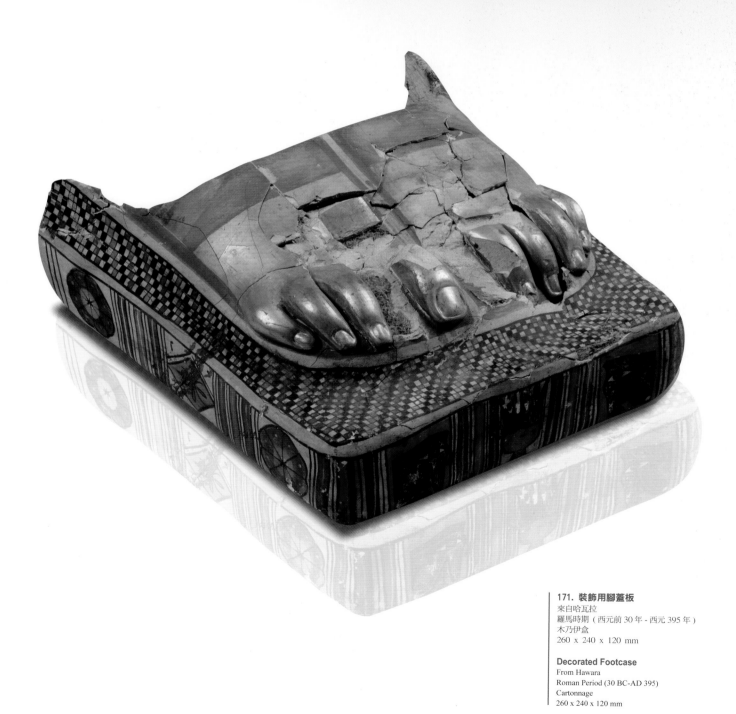

171. 裝飾用腳蓋板
來自哈瓦拉
羅馬時期（西元前 30 年 - 西元 395 年）
木乃伊盒
260 x 240 x 120 mm

Decorated Footcase
From Hawara
Roman Period (30 BC-AD 395)
Cartonnage
260 x 240 x 120 mm

172. 聖甲蟲護身符
來自丹德拉
後埃及時期－托勒密時期（西元前664-30 年）
彩陶
90 x 46 x 10 mm

Winged scarab amulet
From Dendera
Late Period – Ptolemaic Period (664-30 BC)
Faience

聖甲蟲護身符

聖甲蟲是古埃及人眾多護身符樣式中最普遍可見的樣式。埃及聖甲蟲，或稱為糞金龜（Scarabaeus sacer）會將卵產在動物埋在地底下的糞便中，再從中孵化其後代，且經常可以看見聖甲蟲將糞便滾成球狀作為食物。

顯然埃及人將自無移動力的物品中出現的新生命，與甲蟲持之以恆的滾動糞球行為變成一種象徵，並對照為賜予眾人生命的太陽的移動過程。因此，在葬禮的文本，如新王國的《通道之書》（Book of Gates）中，便明確描述聖甲蟲會伴隨著太陽的升起。有時聖甲蟲會展現出翅膀，如此處所示；翅膀代表的不僅是聖甲蟲的真實飛翔能力，也代表天神的移動能力。

代表聖甲蟲的象形文字寫出了動詞 kheper「復活」，而在黎明時分的太陽神則展現了有著聖甲蟲頭部的凱布利（Khepri）神形象。因此，聖甲蟲結合了數個重生與新生的譬喻，也成為伴隨亡者進入來世的最適切象徵。從第二十五王朝（約西元前747-656 年）開始，如此處展出的雙翼聖甲蟲護身符便經常以光亮材質製作而成，上面通常有小洞，以縫在串珠樣式的壽衣上或直接縫在木乃伊繃帶上。（作者：C.P.）

173. 聖甲蟲護身符
來自阿比多斯
後埃及時期－托勒密時期（西元前664-30 年）
彩陶
155 x 60 x 10 mm

Winged scarab amulet
From Abydos
Late Period – Ptolemaic Period (664-30 BC)
Faience

Winged scarab amulets

The scarab is the most ubiquitous of the ancient Egyptians' many amuletic forms. An Egyptian scarab, or dung beetle (Scarabaeus sacer), lays its eggs in animal dung underground, from which baby beetles hatch. The beetles can also commonly be seen rolling balls of dung for consumption as foodstuff.

The Egyptians seem to have combined the symbolism of new life emerging from an inert mass and the beetle's persistence in moving balls of dung, comparing them with journey of the life-giving sun across the sky. Thus, in funerary texts such as the New Kingdom Book of Gates, the rising of the sun is explicitly said to be accomplished by a scarab. Sometimes the beetle is shown with wings, as here. This reflects not only the real scarab's ability to fly but also the potential movement of a celestial being.

The hieroglyphic symbol of a scarab writes the verb kheper 'to come into being' and the sun god takes the form of the scarab-headed deity Khepri at dawn. Thus, the scarab combines several metaphors of regeneration and rebirth, and so was an apt symbol to accompany the deceased into the afterlife. From Dynasty 25 (c. 747-656 BC), winged scarab amulets such as these were commonly made of glazed composition. They often include small holes, as here, in order to be attached to a bead-work shroud or to the mummy wrappings directly. (C.P.)

174. 聖甲蟲護身符
來自阿比多斯
後埃及時期－托勒密時期（西元前664-30 年）
彩陶
145 x 65 x 10 mm

Winged scarab amulet
From Abydos
Late Period – Ptolemaic Period (664-30 BC)
Faience

175. 聖甲蟲護身符
來自阿比多斯
後埃及時期（西元前 664-332 年）
玄武岩
50 x 35 x 15 mm

Heart Scarab Amulet
From Abydos
Late Period (664-332 BC)
Basalt

聖甲蟲護身符

對於古埃及與來世的一個重要關鍵為奧塞里斯神面前的亡者審判。為了能夠進入極樂的蘆葦之野（Field of Reeds），亡者必須先將心臟與真理的象徵（馬特神的羽毛）進行秤重。心臟不僅為情感的中心，更是智慧之所在，因此在製做木乃伊的過程中，會將屍體的內臟器官都移除，只留下心臟。每一位埃及人皆期望自己的心臟能和馬特神的羽毛達成平衡，因此便能獲得「真理之聲」的宣判，並獲允進入來世。然而，心臟若因罪惡而過重，便會遭到名為阿穆特（Ammut）的「吞噬者」（混合了鱷魚、獅子與河馬的混種怪獸）所吞噬。

審判中最重要的部分為「反面懺悔」（negative confession），記述於收藏葬禮咒語之《亡者之書》（Book of the Dead）的第 125 章。在懺悔中，亡者會否認曾犯過惡行；然而，亡者的心臟卻有可能反駁其主人的言論。為了避免發生這類情形，便會將心臟聖甲蟲護身符放在木乃伊身上，這是聖甲蟲的多種護身符圖樣最重要的意義。許多存留的聖甲蟲文物上都有著出自《亡者之書》中的特別刻文。這項咒語直接針對心臟，祈求心臟能夠忠於其主人：

「哦，由母親賜予我的心臟呀！……

請勿挺身而出，提出不利於我的證詞！..

切勿在神的面前編造不利於我的謊言！」

在其他的文本中，心臟聖甲蟲是以 Nemehef 石製成，安置於黃金之上，並放在心臟上方，而 Nemehef 可能即為綠碧玉。雖然部分皇室文物皆嚴密地遵循這些規範，但一般私人所擁有的心臟聖甲蟲卻是由各種深色堅硬石頭打造而成。伯頓博物館所收藏的心臟聖甲蟲在橢圓底座上繪製了一個自然寫實的聖甲蟲，兩側刻有昆蟲前部（額板），在翅鞘上則刻有精緻的條紋。雖然這件物品並未刻有文字，但其尺寸、材質與缺少吊掛用的穿孔，皆顯示這是一件心臟聖甲蟲，包裹於木乃伊的繃帶內。代表只要有護身符，即使缺少銘文，也足以幫助亡者度過審判過程。（作者：C.P.）

Heart Scarab Amulet

A central expectation of the ancient Egyptian afterlife was the judgement of the dead before the god Osiris. In order to gain entry into the blissful Field of Reeds, the deceased had to have his heart weighed against the symbol for truth – the feather of maat. The heart was not only the centre of the emotions, but the seat of intelligence. Thus, when the corpse had its internal organs removed during mummification, only the heart was left in place. It was every Egyptian's hope that the heart and the maat feather would balance and that the deceased would be declared 'true of voice', and therefore entitled to enter the afterlife. However, if a heart was heavy with sin, it would be swallowed by a hybrid monster named Ammut, 'the devourer' – part crocodile, part lion, part hippopotamus.

A key part of the judgement was the so-called 'negative confession,' known from Chapter 125 of a collection of funerary spells known as the Book of the Dead. In the confession, the deceased denied having committed a series of wrong-doings. Potentially, however, a dead man's heart might contradict the statements of its owner. In order to prevent this, an amulet known as a heart scarab was placed on the mummy. This was the most significant of the many amuletic images of the scarab beetle. Many examples carry a special inscription, Chapter 30B from the Book of the Dead. This spell addresses the heart directly, and pleads with it to stay loyal to its owner:

'O my heart which I had from my mother!…

Do not stand up as a witness against me!..

Do not tell lies about me in the presence of the god!'

An additional text instructs that the heart scarab be made of nemehef stone, set in gold and placed over the heart. Nemehef probably indicates green jasper. While some royal examples follow these recommendations closely, heart scarabs belonging to private individuals are made from a range of dark, hard stones. The Bolton example depicts a naturalistically modelled scarab on an oval base, with flared front parts (clypeus) and finely detailed striations on its wing cases (elytra). Although this example does not carry an inscription, its size, material and lack of any pierced holes for suspension indicate that it functioned as a heart scarab, bound up within a mummy's wrappings. It may have been considered that the mere presence of the amulet, even without an inscription, was sufficient to assist the deceased at the Judgement. (C.P.)

鍍金眼鏡蛇飾物

聖蛇有時又被稱為「偉大魔女」，展現的形象包括了直立起的眼鏡蛇或人首蛇身。眼鏡蛇為帝王身分的重要象徵，包括在皇室標誌上出現代表下埃及的瓦潔特（Wadjet）女神，以及代表上埃及的禿鷹女神奈荷貝特（Nekhbet）。這兩位女神被稱為「兩位女士」（Two Ladies），象徵著埃及的二元性。代表瓦潔特與奈荷貝特的聖蛇與禿鷹像會從王冠的前額部分突出，利用法術向敵人吐出火燄與毒液，達到保護帝王的目的。最重要地，眼睛蛇為具保護性的神祇，被視為太陽神拉（Ra）的雙眼。

這件物品是以單塊木頭打造而成，先全部抹上石膏再鍍金。其上依然殘留著刻入木頭內的刻度細節。眼鏡蛇展現其特有的攻擊姿態，背部呈弧形，頭上則覆蓋著日輪。根據下方可以插入底座內的延伸部位判斷，這個眼鏡蛇可能屬於神殿上方聖蛇簷壁的一部分，也或許是葬禮設備的一部分。在日輪後的一個縱向穿孔則顯示聖蛇原本應連結著簷壁上其他並列的眼鏡蛇。（作者：A.G.）

Gilded Uraeus

The uraeus was sometimes described as 'the great enchantress', and was depicted either as a rearing cobra or as a cobra with a human head. The cobra was an important symbol of kingship, included in the royal insignia as a representation of the goddess Wadjet who represented Lower Egypt alongside the vulture goddess of Upper Egypt, Nekhbet. Together the goddesses were known as the 'Two Ladies' and symbolized the duality of Egypt. Figures of a uraeus and a vulture representing Wadjet and Nekhbet protruded from the forehead of the royal crown to protect the king by magically spitting fire and venom at his enemies. Most importantly the cobra was a protective deity, identified as the eye of the god Ra.

This example was made from a single piece of wood, which was plastered over with gesso and then gilded. The details of the scales still survive, which were incised into the wood. The cobra is depicted in the characteristic striking position with a curved back, the head being surmounted with the sun disk. This cobra may have formed part of a frieze of uraei from the top of a shrine, perhaps as part of funerary equipment, based on the survival of the tang below for insertion into a base. A longitudinally pierced hole behind the sun disk shows that the uraeus would have been attached to the adjoining cobras in the frieze. (A.G.)

176. 鍍金眼鏡蛇飾物
來自薩卡拉
後埃及時期 (西元前 664-332 年)
木，鑲金
172 x 45 x 40 mm

Gilded Uraeus
From Saqqara, Sacred Animal Necropolis
Late Period (664-332 BC)
Wood, gilding

177. 托特神雕像
來自薩卡拉
後埃及時期，第26-30王朝（西元前664-332年）
銅合金
100 x 45 x 27 mm

Figure of Thoth
From Saqqara
Late Period, Dynasty 26-30 (664-332 BC)
Copper-alloy

托特神雕像

托特神（Thoth）發明了語言，為智慧與療癒之神。托特神同時也是月神，戴著以滿月和新月組成的頭冠。托特神的形象多為人身鷺首，有時也會以完整的朱鷺或狒狒形象現身。托特神備受愛戴，從各王朝時期到羅馬時代皆廣受埃及人的崇拜。托特神為抄寫員之守護神，其標誌為石版與筆，但在這座小型青銅像上，托特神手上卻抱著焚香用的香爐。

托特的主要祭祀中心為中埃及的赫爾莫普利斯（Hermopolis），但在埃及全國皆有膜拜儀式，在發現這座青銅像的薩卡拉（Saqqara）更是將動物獻祭給托特神的大型祭祀場，埋葬了超過五十萬個朱鷺與狒狒的木乃伊。（作者：J.H.W.）

Figure of Thoth

The god Thoth was the inventor of language and a god of wisdom and healing. He also was a lunar deity and could wear a headdress consisting of the full and crescent moons. Often shown as a man with the head of an ibis, Thoth could also appear fully in ibis form, or as a baboon. A popular deity, Thoth was worshipped from the early Dynastic Period well into Roman times. As a patron of scribes, the gods's usual attributes are a palette and brush. However, in this small bronze statuette, Thoth appears to hold a censer used for burning incense.

His main cult center was the site of Hermopolis in Middle Egypt, but he was worshipped throughout Egypt and the site of Saqqara (where this statue was found) was the location of a massive animal cemetery dedicated to Thoth wherein more than five hundred thousand mummified ibises and baboons were buried. (J.H.W.)

178. 賽克麥特神雕像
來自薩卡拉
後埃及時期，第26-30王朝（西元前664-332年）
銅合金
220 x 45 x 35 mm

Figure of Sekhmet
From Saqqara
Late Period, Dynasty 26-30 (664-332 BC)
Copper –alloy

賽克麥特神雕像

古埃及人將貓、獅子等貓科動物與神祇產生聯結[1]，他們視貝斯特（Bastet）為守護與和平女神，與較具威脅性的賽克麥特（Sekhmet）獅子女神形成抗衡。貝斯特會協助人類解決難題，因此備受愛戴；而儘管賽克麥特具有毀滅性神力，但同樣被視為守護女神而受到崇拜。

賽克麥特的日輪強調了祂與太陽的關聯性。在某些神話故事中，賽克麥特被描繪成太陽神拉（Re）之女，並出現於人類之毀滅（Destruction of Mankind）的神話中。在神話中，年邁的太陽神相信人類正密謀策畫要反抗自己，因而派出祂的「眼線」（即太陽神之女）到人間毀滅人類。賽克麥特的名字意為「有能力者」，而她正是執行毀滅人類任務的女神。賽克麥特以擔任殘暴的屠殺者為傲，而當太陽神改變心意後，便需要有人出面以詭計阻止賽克麥特的行動。

獅首的賽克麥特被視為令人害怕的戰神，但同時也擁有驅邪的能力，例如，賽克麥特的箭便具有驅趕疾病的效果。賽克麥特再加上普塔（Ptah）與奈夫圖（Nefertem），即為曼菲斯（Memphis）的三神，而賽克麥特更是曼菲斯守護神普塔的伴侶。（作者：J.H.W.）

---

1. 其他可能以獅子形象出現的女神包括了 Tefnut，Mafdet 與 Pakhet。

Figure of Sekhmet

The ancient Egyptians associated felines – both cats and lions -- with many deities[1]. The ancient Egyptians saw the goddess Bastet as a protective and peaceful counterpart to the more threatening lion goddess, Sekhmet. Bastet was popular for help with human problems and, although Sekhmet was perceived as a destructive force, she was also worshipped as a protective goddess.

Sekhmet's sun disk highlights her solar associations. In some myths, she is thought of as a daughter of the sun god, Re and she appears as a participant in the myth of the Destruction of Mankind. In this story, the aging sun god sends his "eye" (his daughter) to earth to destroy mankind, whom he believes is plotting against him. Sekhmet, whose name means "the Powerful One" is the goddess who undertakes this task. She glories in the bloody slaughter and must be stopped (by means of deception) when the sun god has a change of heart.

The lioness-headed Sekhmet could be seen as a fearsome warlike deity, but she also serves an apotropaic function; for example with her arrows, she could ward off diseases. Together with Ptah and Nefertem, she was part of the triad at Memphis. Sekhmet is the consort of Ptah, the patron deity of Memphis. (J.H.W.)

1.Other goddess who could appear in leonine form include Tefnut, Mafdet, and Pakhet.

179. 普塔神小雕像
來自薩卡拉
後埃及時期，第 26 王朝（西元前 664-525 年）
銅合金
160 x 45 x 30 mm

Statuette of Ptah
From Saqqara, Sacred Animal Necropolis, sector 3
Late Period, Dynasty 26 (664-525 BC)
Copper-alloy

普塔神小雕像

由於普塔的外型很像木乃伊，以緊身的亞麻長袍包裹住全身，僅露出雙手與頭部，因此乍看之下非常類似奧塞里斯神。然而，不同於奧塞里斯，普塔頭上並非戴著頭冠，而是戴著一頂無邊小帽，如同創造神與工匠守護者的打扮。在普塔筆直的鬍子上僅刻有些許垂直線條，較類似法老王的鬍鬚特色，而不同於奧塞里斯神的捲曲鬍子。普塔脖子周圍配戴的寬邊串珠同樣有著精緻的雕刻細節。普塔的雙手緊握著一根以動物頭部為裝飾且尾端呈分叉狀的權杖，是一根名為瓦司（was）的權杖，為普塔或國王所持有的特別手杖。在象形文字中，其代表意義為「統治」，象徵著普塔的力量，且如同其王者鬍鬚，也意謂著他與國王的關聯性。

薩卡拉（Saqqara）為孟菲斯墓地的一部分，為埃及北部的一個古老墓地，座落於孟菲斯西邊的沙漠峭壁上。孟菲斯為埃及的首都，並以普塔為守護神。身為創造神與工匠守護者，孟菲斯墓地的神廟與墳墓皆被視為其建造石匠與工匠的創作，展現普塔的想法與作為。

這個普塔青銅鑄造雕像為 1964-1976 年間埃及探索學會（Egypt Exploration Society）在薩卡拉挖掘出 1800 多件青銅藝品之一。這些工藝品包括了朝聖者獻給眾神的禮物與祭師的祭祀工具。這件雕像發現於神廟石板下方的坑洞中。考古學家發現了以亞麻布仔細包裹的大量雕像與三座裝滿青銅雕像的木造聖壇。發現的團隊在神廟內與四周皆發現許多這類的隱藏物品，並提出三項將物品埋藏起來的解釋理論，包括了因神廟遭受危難、為了拓展神廟，或是因為祭品皆為聖物而無法投入工匠的熔爐回收再利用，而單純地收藏起舊祭品。（作者：A.C.）

Statuette of Ptah

At first sight this figurine looks very similar to the god Osiris, since Ptah appears like a mummy, wrapped in a tight-fitting linen gown with only his hands and head left exposed. However, unlike Osiris he wears a simple skullcap rather than a crown, just like those worn by some of the craftsmen who worshipped him as their patron god. He wears a straight beard decorated with incised vertical lines, more characteristic of a pharaoh, rather than the curled beard usually worn by gods such as Osiris. Just as carefully detailed as his beard is the broad collar of beads he wears around his neck. With both hands he grips an ornamented animal-headed staff with a forked end, called a was sceptre, a distinctive staff carried by Ptah or the king. As a hieroglyphic symbol it means 'dominion' and signifies Ptah's power and, like his royal beard, associates him with the king.

Saqqara was part of the Memphite necropolis, an ancient burial ground in the north of Egypt, located upon the desert escarpment to the west of Memphis, Egypt's capital city where Ptah was the patron deity. As a creator god and patron of craftsmen, the temples and tombs of the Memphite necropolis were considered as much the creation of the stonemasons and artists who built them, as they were the will and action of Ptah.

This solid cast bronze statuette of the Ptah is one of over 1800 bronze artefacts found at Saqqara by the Egypt Exploration Society between 1964 and 1976. These artefacts represent the gifts given to the gods by pilgrims and cult equipment used by the priests. This statuette was found in a pit below the stone paving of a temple floor. Archaeologists discovered an array of sculpture and three wooden shrines neatly packed with bronze statuettes carefully wrapped in linen cloth. The team found many of these caches within and around the temple complex and proposed three theories for why they had been buried: hidden in times of trouble when the temple was in danger; buried to consecrate new extensions of the temple complex; or as storage of old offerings considered too sacred to be recycled in the metal craftsmen's melting pot. (A.C.)

180. 馬特神小雕像
來自埃及
後埃及時期,第 26 王朝(西元前 664-525 年)
銅合金
80 x 25 x 22 mm

Figure of Maat
From Egypt
Late Period, Dynasty 26 (664 - 525 BC)
Copper-alloy

馬特神小雕像

從神像所配戴的獨特羽毛便能讓人輕易區別此女神像與其他神祇的不同。這位女神的名字是馬特,意指「真理」、「正義」或「秩序」。馬特神的象形文字是一根鴕鳥羽毛,如這個小雕像頭上的羽毛。馬特是世上導向真理與正義的力量,為埃及人相當重視的概念,特別是面對死亡時。

埃及人相信有個稱為杜瓦(Duat)的地方;而我們可視其為一個稱為「來世」精神世界。那個地方和埃及極為相似,但也充滿神秘與危險,如有著滿地的火燄與四處的魔鬼;那裡也是奧塞里斯的王國,一旦復活的亡者被宣判清白無罪,便可居住於奧塞里斯的王國內。為了達成此目標,埃及人必須找出危險的障礙,以成功找到審判廳(Hall of Judgement),讓奧塞里斯與進行審判的諸神利用天秤決定自己的命運。亡者的心臟必須與羽毛相秤,有時則是與此雕像的馬特神相秤。為了通過測試,心臟的重量必須完美地相當於馬特神的重量,否則心臟就會被「吞噬怪獸(swallowing monster)」吞噬,無法獲得奧塞里斯的永生。(作者:A.C.)

Figure of Maat

The goddess represented by this figure, is easily distinguished from other deities by the distinctive plume that she wears. Her name is Maat, a word that meant 'truth', 'justice' or 'order'. It was a word that was written with the hieroglyph of a single ostrich feather just the same as the feather on this little statuette's head. Maat was a guiding force of truth and justice in the world, a concept that was very important to the Egyptians, especially in death.

The Egyptians believed in a place called Duat that we may think of as a spiritual realm called the 'Otherworld'. It was a land similar to Egypt, but it was also mysterious and full of danger, such as fields of fire and demons. It was also where the kingdom of Osiris existed, a place the resurrected dead could only live once they had been declared innocent of any wrongdoing. To achieve this they had to navigate dangerous obstacles to successfully search out the Hall of Judgement were Osiris and a jury of gods decided on their fate using a balance. The deceased's heart was weighed against a feather, or sometimes an image of Maat just like this statuette. To pass the test the heart needed to be in perfect balance with Maat, otherwise the heart was fed to a 'swallowing monster', denying eternal life with Osiris. (A.C.)

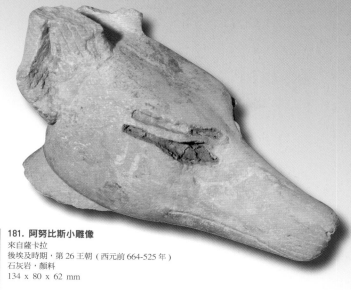

181. 阿努比斯小雕像
來自薩卡拉
後埃及時期，第 26 王朝（西元前 664-525 年）
石灰岩，顏料
134 x 80 x 62 mm

Statue of Anubis
From Saqqara, Sacred Animal Necropolis
Late Period, Dynasty 26-30 (664-332 BC)
Limestone, pigment

阿努比斯小雕像

阿努比斯（Anubis）為死亡之神，擁有狗或胡狼的外形，與成為木乃伊的過程有著密切的關係，根據神話，將奧塞里斯神製作包裹成木乃伊的正是阿努比斯。古埃及人相信使用胡狼的樣子表現死亡之神，經防腐處理的屍體將能獲得保護，不會遭胡狼吞食。

阿努比斯同時也是墓地的守護者，他最常見的兩個稱號為：「站在山頂者（he who is upon his mountain）」與「西行者的先峰（foremost of the westerners）」，兩者皆指稱阿努比斯監督著在觀念上與西方有密切關聯的墓地。

這個雕像發現於阿努比安（Anubieion），是有著地下墓穴的阿努比斯神廟，於晚期與托勒密王朝時期建於薩卡拉。這些地下墓穴中埋著數以千計的狗木乃伊，是由朝聖者作為獻給阿努比斯的祭品，並祈望逝去的動物能成為自己與阿努比斯神中間的媒介。

這座雕像僅殘存了頭部，但原本可能是呈現仰躺姿勢。臉部的雕刻相當精美，耳朵（現以破損）部分以模型塑造，展現了耳朵精緻的摺痕，眼部深切地以石灰雕刻而成。相對而言，鼻口部份的製作則使用了較細緻的線條，加上少許鬍鬚與鼻孔的細節。眼睛與眼皮為凹陷設計，以進行嵌入程序，並殘留了一些藍色顏料；沿著嘴巴的線條裡同樣殘留了些許紅色顏料痕跡。（作者：A.G.）

181. Statue of Anubis

Anubis was the god of the dead, taking the form of a dog or jackal. He was closely associated with the process of mummification, and according to myth it was Anubis who wrapped the mummy of the god Osiris. It is thought that by using the image of a jackal for the god of the dead, the embalmed corpse would be magically protected from being consumed by jackals.

Anubis was also the guardian of the necropolis: two of his most common epithets were 'he who is upon his mountain' and 'foremost of the westerners', both illustrative of Anubis watching over the necropolis which was conceptually associated with the west.

This statue was found at the site of the 'Anubieion', a temple of Anubis with associated catacombs constructed at Saqqara during the Late and Ptolemaic Periods. These catacombs were filled with thousands of mummified dogs which were offered to the cult of Anubis by pilgrims at the site, hoping that the deceased animal would act as an intermediary for them with the god.

Only the head of the figure survives, but it was probably originally depicted in the recumbent position. The carving of the face was highly detailed; the ears (now broken) were modelled to show the intricate folds of the ear, and the eyes were deeply carved into the limestone. In contrast, the nose and mouth were produced with a much finer line, together with the subtle detail of the whiskers and nostrils. The eyes and eyebrows were recessed to be inlaid and some blue pigment remain. There also are traces of red pigment surviving along the line of the mouth. (A.G.)

奧塞里斯雕像

古埃及殘存了大量的奧塞里斯青銅像。身為來世之王，在充滿危險的來世之途上，埃及人極需要奧塞里斯的協助以成功獲得來世。同時埃及人也相信，要成功獲得來世，就必須將自己與奧塞里斯神視為一體。此信念的思考邏輯在於，若奧塞里斯能成功通過所有危險與難關，而自己成為奧塞里斯後，便能同樣成功度過。

各處都曾挖掘出奧塞里斯像，包括從神廟與墓地之中；可能都是人們為了祈求來世，或家族成員為了亡者而獻上的祭品。根據自古埃及所找到的信件，我們瞭解埃及人相信已進入來世者能從活著的人的行為中獲益；同樣地，他們也深信，若亡者對生者心懷憤怒，則亡者將會有害於使其感到不滿之對象的生命。

這個青銅像上有許多損壞痕跡，且過去或許一直被收藏在神器儲藏室中，儘管仍為聖物，但已不再適宜使用。青銅像的雙眼似乎曾被加上紅色的玻璃眼珠，可能是由維多利亞時代的收藏家所加上來的。（作者：C.R.）

Figure of Osiris

Large number of bronze figures of Osiris survive from ancient Egypt. As king of the afterlife, the Egyptians needed the help of this god to successfully reach the afterlife after many dangers on the road. There also was a belief that one way to be successful was to identify yourself with Osiris. The thinking behind this idea may have been that if Osiris could make it past all the dangers and guardians, than if you were Osiris, you could too.

The figures of Osiris come from a variety of contexts, including temples and cemeteries. It is possible that the figures were offered in anticipation of the journey to the afterlife or by family members on behalf of the deceased. From letters to the dead found in ancient Egypt, it is clear that the Egyptians believed their actions on earth could benefit those who had gone to the afterlife. Similarly, they believed that if the deceased were angry with the living, they could adversely influence the lives of those at whom they were upset.

This figure shows many signs of damage and may have been buried in a cache of temple objects that were still sacred, but not suitable for use. The eyes seem to have been enhanced with red glass eyes, probably by Victorian collectors. (C.R.)

182. 奧塞里斯雕像
來自薩卡拉
後埃及時期，第 26-30 王朝（西元前 664-332 年）
銅合金，鑲金，玻璃
305 x 65 x 60 mm

Figure of Osiris
From Saqqara
Late Period, Dynasty 26-30 BC
Copper-alloy, gilding, glass

183. 模型船
來自班尼哈山
第 11-12 王朝（西元前 2055-1773 年）
木，顏料，亞麻
490 x 400 x 150 mm

Model Boat
From Beni Hasan
Dynasty 11-12 (2055-1773 BC)
Wood, pigment, linen

模型船

尼羅河在古埃及的各種生活層面中皆扮演了重要角色，不僅能夠藉由每年的洪水淤積讓耕地變得肥沃，也是埃及進行運輸、聯絡與貿易的主要方法。自相當早期，埃及人便將船隻納入陪葬物品與墳墓的裝飾之中。在法老王統治時期，埃及人相信太陽神於白日乘船於空中，到了晚上則是進入地下世界。同樣地，通往來世的旅程也有一部分必須依賴船隻。從中王國開始，目的在於促進通往來世的木製船隻模型便成為標準的陪葬物品。陪葬用的複製船隻有許多不同類型，包括帆船與划船、陪葬三桅帆船、運輸船、廚房艇、遊行船與打獵或釣魚小船。此處展出的模型係利用在中埃及貝尼哈山（Beni Hasan）出土的古代船隻模型於現代打造而成，為一艘運輸船，上面載有行動小屋，能讓墓穴主人舒適地通往來世。小屋的拱型屋頂繪上顏色代表縫製在骨架上的皮革，並支撐以六根木樁。在兩側各懸掛著以黑白斑點牛皮製成的護罩。一名瞭望員站在船頭觀望著沙洲與其他危險，而其身後則站著一群士兵操控現已消失的風帆。漆成黃色的墓穴主人坐在罩篷下方，後面則站著一位侍從。捆綁在船尾木柱上的大型舵槳則是船隻的方向舵，原本應有一名坐著的舵手進行操控。（作者：D.D.）

Model Boat

The Nile River played a critical role in almost all aspects of ancient Egyptian life, fertilizing the farmland with silt from the annual flood and providing Egypt's principal means of transportation, communication and commerce. From a very early date the Egyptians included representations of boats on grave goods and in tomb decoration. In pharaonic times they believed that the sun god sailed across the sky by day and through the underworld by night. Likewise, the journey to the afterlife took place partly by boat. Beginning in the early Middle Kingdom, wooden models of boats, intended to facilitate the journey, became standard burial offerings.

The repertoire of funerary boats could include several types of vessels, including sailing and rowing boats, funerary barques, transport boats, kitchen boats, procession boats, and skiffs for hunting and fishing. This model, constructed in modern times from components of ancient boat models excavated at Beni Hasan in central Egypt, represents a transport boat with a portable cabin in which the tomb owner could travel in comfortable shade. The arched roof of the cabin is painted to represent leather sewn onto a frame and supported by six posts. On each side hangs a shield made of black and white spotted cowhide. A lookout stands on the prow watching for sandbars and other hazards, while a group of sailors behind him manipulates a now-missing sail. The tomb owner, painted yellow, sits beneath the canopy, while an attendant stands behind it. The large steering oar lashed to a pole at the stern would serve as a rudder. A seated helmsman would originally have been shown operating it. (D.D.)

納卜卡諾皮克臟器罐

至少自第四王朝開始，在製作木乃伊的過程中將亡者的內臟取出放入墓穴中的容器內便成為古埃及人的慣例。這些容器被稱為卡諾皮克臟器罐，為來世保存器官，且通常置於胸口或石棺、棺木旁的盒子內[1]。卡諾皮克臟器罐多以石灰岩、木頭、彩陶與陶土雕刻製成，因此具備各種材質。此卡諾皮克罐是獻給尼布（Neb），奧努里斯的牧牛人，以方解石製成，又稱為埃及雪花石膏。

最早的卡諾皮克臟器容器是將器官捆束起來然後放置於墓穴牆上的凹洞中。在中王國時期，以人首形狀蓋子取代平面或圓頂蓋子，這個習慣一直沿續至第十八王朝才取代為荷魯斯的四位兒子的頭形蓋：伊姆塞特（Imsety）、多姆泰夫（Duamutef）、凱布山納夫（Qebehsenuef）和哈比（Hapy）等四位神祇。每位神祇負責保護一種器官，並受到特定守護女神的保護，且各與指南針上的四個方位有關。伊姆塞特守護肝臟，代表南方，有著人首，他的守護女神為伊西斯。多姆泰夫擁有胡狼的頭，與奈特（Neith）女神有關並代表著東方，負責守護胃。凱布山納夫擁有鷹隼的頭，保護腸子，而其守護女神為塞勒凱特（Selket），並代表西方。最後是有著狒狒頭部的哈比，負責保護肺，並與奈芙蒂斯（Nephthys）女神與北方有關。

這一個卡諾皮克臟器罐原本有著狒狒的頭部，因此應保存著經木乃伊程序處理的肺，正如罐子上的題辭談到了哈比。刻在罐身上的題辭共有四列，閱讀順序為自右往左，由上至下：「奈芙蒂斯詳述：我將深藏內心之物擁入懷中。我在心中守護著哈比。奧塞里斯，祭師；奧努里斯的牧牛人，尼布，公平正義者。」這個卡諾皮克臟器罐由大衛・藍道 - 麥克艾佛（David Randall-MacIver）與亞瑟・西・麥斯（Arthur C. Mace）發現於阿比多斯的賽特胡（Sitepehu）之墓中，且內部中空，顯示使用過的痕跡。（作者：A.H.）

---

1. 最早存放著木乃伊內臟的卡諾皮克臟器罐是發現於吉薩的王后海特菲瑞斯之墓室。

Canopic Jar of Neb

Since at least Dynasty 4, it was common practice for ancient Egyptians to remove the viscera of the deceased during the mummification process and place them in containers set within the tomb. These containers, termed canopic jars, preserved the organs for the afterlife and were typically placed in chests or boxes set beside the sarcophagus or coffin.[1] Canopic jars were commonly carved from limestone, wood, faience, and pottery, and were thus produced from a variety of materials. This canopic jar inscribed for Neb, the Overseer of the Cattle of Onuris, was made from calcite, also known as Egyptian alabaster.

The earliest canopic containers were in the form of wrapped organ bundles placed in a built cavity in the tomb wall. In the Middle Kingdom, human-headed lids replaced flat or domed lids and became the norm until they were later replaced, during Dynasty 18, by heads associated with the four sons of Horus: the deities Imsety, Duamutef, Qebehsenuef, and Hapy. Each of these gods was responsible for protecting a specific organ, was under the protection of a specific companion goddess, and was associated with one of the four cardinal points of the compass. Imsety, who guarded the liver, represented the south and was human-headed. He was protected by the goddess Isis. Duamutef was jackal-headed, was associated with the goddess Neith and the east, and protected the stomach. Qebehsenuef, who was hawk-headed, protected the intestines and was guarded by the goddess Selket. He was associated with the west. Finally, Hapy, who was depicted with the head of a baboon, protected the lungs and was associated with the goddess Nephthys and the north.

The canopic jar depicted here was originally baboon-headed and would have contained the mummified lungs, as indicated by the reference to Hapy in its inscription. The inscription, incised on the exterior of the body, appears in four vertical columns and reads from right to left, top to bottom as follows: "Recitation by Nephthys: I embrace in my arms that which is within me. I protect Hapy who is within me. The honoured by Hapy. The Osiris, priest, Overseer of the cattle of Onuris, Neb, the justified." This canopic jar was found in the Tomb of Sitepehu in Cemetery D at Abydos by David Randall-MacIver and Arthur C. Mace and has a hollowed-out interior, which shows signs of use. (A.H.)

1.The earliest canopic chest with mummified viscera was discovered in the burial chamber of Queen Hetepheres at Giza .

184. 納卜卡諾皮克臟器罐
來自阿比多斯，D9 號墓室
新王國時期，第 18 王朝，哈謝普蘇統治時期（西元前 1473-1458 年）
埃及雪花石膏
203 x 180 x 180 mm

Canopic Jar of Neb
From Abydos, tomb D9
New Kingdom, Dynasty 18, reign of Hatshepsut (1473-1458 BC)
Egyptian Alabaster

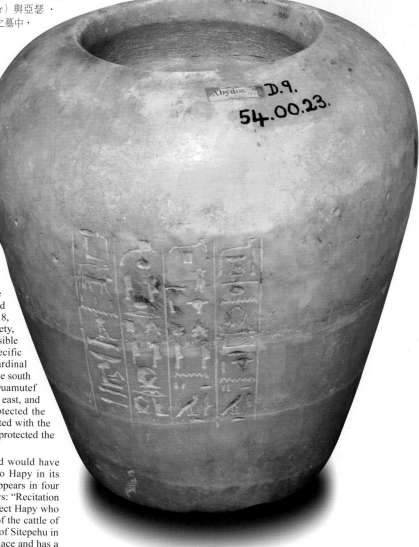

185. 傑得柱
來自薩卡拉， 動物大墓地
後埃及時期，第26-30王朝（西元前664-332年）
木，顏料
268 x 98 x 30 mm

Djed Pillar
From Saqqara, Sacred Animal Necropolis
Late Period, Dynasty 26-30 (664-332 BC)
Wood, pigment

傑得柱

艾梅里（Emery）於 1966-1967 年發現傑得柱（Djed-pillar），當時他正在挖掘薩卡拉（Saqqara）北部一個賽斯與波斯期間圍場西北角落的神廟圖像與傢俱。出土文物的年代可追溯至新王國到賽斯時期：傑得柱可追溯至晚期時期（西元前 600-400 年）。傑得柱以木頭打造而成，並鋪平與漆上不同色彩。主幹部分以細黑線條分隔，將平行條紋染上藍、綠、紅與白等色彩。傑得柱的頂端擁有四個以凸起浮雕表現的帶飾。柱子頂端的凸榫與底下的榫眼顯示這個傑得柱原本應連結了神廟或葬禮傢俱上的精緻簷壁。

傑得柱代表著修剪掉樹枝的樹幹，或倚靠著一捆一捆作物的柱子。從古王國（約西元前 2687-2190 年）該圖案便與創造之神普塔（Ptah）有關，到了新王國（約西元前 1569-1076 年）便與來生之主奧塞里斯神產生聯結。傑得柱代表了奧塞里斯的脊椎骨，因此象徵卓越的耐力與穩定性，並被視為護身符，或繪於棺木底部以保護亡者的脊椎，守衛亡者的復活。因此，傑得柱多半為藍色或綠色等與重生有關的色彩。神廟中所進行的「豎立傑得柱」儀式同樣也是皇室的祭祀，象徵奧塞里斯戰勝其敵人，具有穩固王者身分的寓意。（作者：C.G.）

Djed Pillar

The Djed-pillar was discovered by Emery in 1966-7, while he was excavating a deposit of temple images and furniture in the north-west corner of an enclosure of the Saite-Persian Period in Saqqara North. The deposit comprised finds dating from the New Kingdom to the Saite Period; the Djed pillar dates to the Late Period (600-400 BCE). The object is made out of wood and was plastered and painted with different colours. The stem is divided by thin black lines that separate the horizontal bands coloured in blue, green, red, and white. The top part of the item exhibits four bands in raised relief. The presence of a tenon on top of the pillar and a mortise below it makes it probable that the Djed-pillar was originally attached to an openwork frieze from an object belonging to temple or funerary furniture.

The Djed-pillar possibly represents a tree trunk with lopped-off branches or a pole with attached grain sheaves. The emblem was connected with the creator god Ptah since the Old Kingdom (c.2687-2190 BCE) as well as with the god Osiris, the lord of the afterlife, since the New Kingdom (c.1569-1076 BCE). As a representation of Osiris' backbone, the Djed-pillar was the symbol for endurance and stability par excellence, and was used as an amulet or drawn on the bottom of coffins to protect the deceased's backbone, guaranteeing his resurrection. Accordingly, the Djed-pillar is often represented blue or green, colours connected with regeneration. The ritual action of the "erection of the Djed-pillar" is known from the temple as well as the royal cult where it symbolizes the triumph of Osiris over his enemies, an allegory for the stability of kingship. (C.G.)

186. 模型棺
來自阿比多斯
後埃及時期，第 26 王朝（西元前 664-525 年）
木，顏料，鑲金
230 x 180 x 90 mm

Model Coffin
From Abydos
Late Period, Dynasty 26 (664-525 BC)
Wood, pigment, gilding

模型棺

這個四方形盒子上有個拱形上蓋，是一個模型棺。這個物品可能擁有一個中空的空間，可以容納一張陪葬的紙莎草紙、一個動物木乃伊，或是一個奧塞里斯神像，但蟲蛀造成的損壞讓人難以做出正確判定。這件物品漆上白色，並在長邊有著兩條橫線，方形柱上則有兩條較粗的直線。拱形蓋上有著四名坐著的神祇；兩位穿著紅色衣物，兩位穿著綠色，四位皆拿著一支鞭子。在另一邊則是一個有著狒狒頭部的身影，其次是一位有著隼頭的神祇，以及兩位擁有人首的神。另一邊則繪有一名有著人首的神祇，其次為一名有著胡狼頭部與兩位有著人首的神祇。這些神祇皆代表陰間。在窄的一邊繪有一根象徵復活與耐力的綠色傑得柱；另一邊已受到嚴重損壞，但依舊可看見相同的棺木尾端輪廓。兩個刻有文字的圓柱描繪在輪廓的左右兩側，而在輪廓內繪有一個人物舉起一隻手。在其中一個方形柱頂端站著一隻隼，而另一根方形柱頂端則蹲踞著另一隻形似鳶的鳥類。在另外的方形柱上皆設有暗榫，因此這些方形柱上可能還有其他塑像。在棺蓋上有一個墓穴之神阿努比斯的塑像，但幾乎已遭蟲完全蛀蝕破壞。

在阿比多斯的墓室中共發現了四個模型棺，其年代可追溯至第二十六王朝，而此模型棺即為其中之一。他們被放置在靠近四個棺木的位置，並搭配一個奧塞里斯的雕像。和雕像放在一起顯示這些模型棺與普塔 - 蘇卡 - 奧塞里斯神的雕像有關。這些雕像或其底座多半為中空狀態，可以放入一張陪葬紙莎草紙、動物部位，或一個假木乃伊。底座通常會再蓋上一隻鷹隼或象徵奧塞里斯之墓的石棺。（作者：C.G.）

Model Coffin

The rectangular box with a vaulted top and four square pillars at each side represents a model coffin. The object may have had a cavity that could have included a funerary papyrus, an animal mummy, or a corn Osiris, but the insect damage makes this difficult to determine. The piece is painted in a white colour with two horizontal lines on the long sides as well as two thicker vertical lines on the square pillars. The vaulted lid shows on the four seated deities; two are featured in red and two in green. All four carry a flagellum. On one side is a baboon-headed figure, followed by a deity with a falcon head and two with human heads. The other side depicts a deity with a human head, followed by one with a jackal head and two with human heads. The gods may represent underworld deities. A green Djed-pillar, the symbol of resurrection and endurance, is illustrated on one narrow side. The other side is badly damaged, but the same outline of the coffin end is still visible. This time two columns with inscriptions are depicted to the left and right of the outline. A human figure with raised hands seems to be illustrated inside the outline. A figure of a standing falcon is attached to the top of one of the square end pillars, while a squatting bird, reminiscent of a kite, sits on another. The other pillars have holes for dowels, hence there may have been figures on these pillars as well. A figure of Anubis, the god of the necropolis, is attached to the lid, but is badly eaten by insects.

Four comparable model coffins were found in the family tomb G57 in cemetery G in Abydos dating to Dynasty 26 and this may be one of the four. They were placed close to the coffins of the four individuals, in each case together with a statue of Osiris. Their placement along with these statues suggests that the model coffins are related to the Ptah-Sokar-Osiris statues. Those figures or their bases were often hollow to include a funerary papyrus, animal parts, or a corn mummy. The base was often topped by a falcon or a sarcophagus representing the tomb of Osiris. (C.G.)

盤尼席塔木棺及木乃伊

於探勘早期，常有埃及官員對於貴賓冠以發現古埃及文物的榮譽。這顯然是埃及古文物部長奧古斯都・馬利耶特（Auguste Mariette）為了威爾斯王子愛德華在 1858-1859 年出訪埃及時而有的。愛德華，也就是日後即位的英王愛德華七世，發現了一處內有 30 具木乃伊的古墓。一般認為此具木乃伊與棺木即屬於此次發現所得。威爾斯王子將攜回英格蘭的文物分送各種學會；其中，此具木乃伊與棺木當時為杭亭頓文藝科學協會所保管，日後交予萊斯特博物館服務處。

經調查，此棺木係於第三中間期至晚期為盤尼席塔（Panesittawy）所雕製。其特色為巨大的寬板領型項鍊，於胸部飾有守護鳥；下方的圖像為盤尼席塔來生順利復活的畫面。但經 X 光檢查結果卻確認了棺木中的木乃伊為一具女性遺體。這很可能是因為當時在營造這處古墓的過程中，是以來源不同的棺木及木乃伊拼湊出了墓葬中的 30 具木乃伊，才會產生這種現象。（作者：C.R.）

Panesittawy Coffin and Wrapped Mummy

During the early days of exploration, it was usual for the officials in Egypt to honour high ranking guests with discovering ancient Egyptian antiquities. This was certainly what Auguste Mariette, the Director of Antiquities in Egypt, did for Edward, the Prince of Wales when he visited Egypt in 1858-1859. Edward, later Edward VII King of the United Kingdom, 'discovered a tomb' with 30 mummies in it. It is thought that this mummy and coffin were one of his finds. The items he brought back to England were given by the Prince of Wales to various societies and this mummy and coffin came to the Leicester Museums Service from the Huntingdon Literary and Scientific Society.

Upon examination, the coffin dates to the Third Intermediate to Late Periods and is inscribed for Panesittawy. It features a large broad collar with a protective bird over its chest. Below are scenes of the successful mummification and rebirth in the next life of Panesittawy. However, when X-rayed, the mummy that had been inside the coffin was that of a woman. It is probable in creating the tomb with the 30 mummies in it, that coffins and mummies were brought together to create a set for the prince to find. (C.R.)

187. 盤尼席塔木棺及木乃伊
來自底比斯西岸
第三中間期至後埃及時期，第 26 王朝（西元前 1069-332 年）
木，顏料
1900 x 500 x 350 mm
木乃伊 - 未知
人體組織，亞麻
1550 x 300 x 200 mm

Panesittawy Coffin and Wrapped Mummy
From Thebes, West Bank
Third Intermediate - Late Period, Dynasty 26 (1069-332 BC)
Wood, pigment, 1900 x 500 x 350 mm
Mummy – unknown
Human tissue, linen

女孩木乃伊

此具木乃伊為年約八歲的女孩。以她的年齡而言，身材算是十分瘦小衰弱。X 光檢驗結果顯示脊椎異常，說明她生前可能曾受結核病侵襲脊椎之苦。

此具木乃伊以繃帶悉心包裹，呈現精緻的重疊交叉圖案；而她的頭部則覆蓋著嵌有眼睛的鍍金面具。據捐贈者安妮巴洛（Annie Barlow）於致伯頓博物館館長威廉米德里（William Midgley）的信件中表示，木乃伊盒自埃及抵達時，其臉部已經脆弱受損。此木乃伊盒正面與頭部背面漆有明亮特殊的粉紅色，但棺木本身卻相當樸素，此為該處墓地當時普遍的設計形式。此棺木可能實際上是一個深度較深的蓋子，而木乃伊原安置於一低盤中。如此精心裝飾的墓葬在年幼兒童間相當罕見，說明了其雙親於當時必然具有顯赫家世。（作者：C.R.）

Mummy of a Young Girl in a Coffin

This mummy is of a young girl of about 8 years old. She was very small for her age and appeared to have been sickly. X-rays indicate abnormality in the spine and it has been suggested she may have suffered from tuberculosis of the spine.

The mummy is elaborately wrapped in bandages making an over-lapping crossing pattern. Her head is covered with a gilded mask with inlayed eyes. The cartonnage over the face was already brittle and damaged when it arrived from Egypt according to a letter from the donor, Annie Barlow, to the first curator at Bolton, William Midgley. The cartonnage in the front and around the back of the head was brightly coloured featuring a distinct pink colour. The coffin is quite plain, but typical of the cemetery and the time. It is possible that the coffin was actually a deep lid and originally the mummy sat on a low tray. Such an elaborate burial is rare for such a young child and suggests that she must have been the child of someone of importance. (C.R.)

188. 女孩木乃伊
來自古洛卜
托勒密時期後期至羅馬時期 (西元前 100 年 – 西元 100 年)
木，人體組織，亞麻，鑲金，木乃伊盒
910 x 750 x 360 mm

Mummy of a Young Girl in a Coffin
From Gurob
Late Ptolemaic Period – Roman Period (100 BC – AD 100)
Wood, human tissue, linen, gilding, cartonnage

納法森凱棺蓋板

納法森凱（Nefsekhet）為西索貝克（Sitsobek）女士之女，從她形式十分簡單的棺蓋判斷，家境並不富裕；母親也無任何頭銜。此棺蓋描繪了她的木乃伊形象：戴有面具和深領型項鍊；然代表腳部的木片現已遺失。遺失的木片下方為跪姿的有翼女神努特的圖像。自第十八王朝結束以後，努特圖像最常見於棺木的此部位。棺蓋下半部有五行象形文字，最中央一行是許諾合宜葬禮與死後世界的充分糧食。其他四行是將亡者與葬禮之神伊姆塞特（Imseti）、哈比（Hapy）、多姆泰夫（Duamutef）及凱布山納夫（Qebehsenuef）連結，此四者為荷魯斯的四個兒子，也是死者最重要的守護者。

關於此物件的詳細過程並無完整明確記錄。可以肯定的是此物件是來自佩托里（Petrie）於1888至1890年間在伊拉胡恩和古羅布的挖掘結果，此地為法尤姆地區的入口。此物件由伯頓博物館取得時，同批文物還包括來自伊拉胡恩的第二十二王朝棺木和木乃伊盒，以及在棺木中的羅馬孩童（本書編號188）。其中，最後一項首先於1890年贈予安妮巴洛（Annie Barlow，1863-1941），以為其贊助開挖資金的代價；並隨後出借給位於伯頓的前查德威克博物館，直到1892年4月由該博物館正式獲贈收藏。納法森凱棺蓋及伊拉胡恩物件可能也是循相同管道而來。

當時於伊拉胡恩開挖的墓群，即是後世所稱的堤脊（Dyke Ridge）墓地，年代屬於第二十二王朝。當地確實可能存在有更晚期的墓葬，或許納法森凱墓葬即包括在內。另一方面，古羅布有一處墓地顯然屬於「托勒密」時期，但由於該處棺木全部未加彩繪，推斷本物件應非來自於此。（作者：A.M.D）

Coffin-lid of Nefsekhet

Nefsekhet was the daughter of a lady named Sitsobek, and to judge from the rather summary form of her coffin-lid, a lady of modest means; she also bore no title. The lid depicts her as a mummy, wearing a mask and a deep collar; the piece of wood representing the feet is now missing. Below the latter is a winged, kneeling figure of the goddess Nut, who occupies this position on most coffins from the end of Dynasty 18 onwards. The lower half of the lid bears five columns of hieroglyphs, the middle one being a formula guaranteeing a proper burial and adequate sustenance in the next world. The other four columns associate the deceased with the funerary genii Imseti, Hapy, Duamutef and Qebehsenuef, known collectively as the Four Sons of Horus and amongst the most important protectors of the dead.

The details of the acquisition of this piece are not wholly clear. It certainly came from the excavations carried out by Flinders Petrie at the sites of Illahun and Gurob, situated around the entrance to the Fayum region, in 1888–90, and was associated in its acquisition by Bolton with a group of items including Dynasty 22 coffins and mummy-cases from Illahun and a Roman child in a coffin (Catalogue #188). Of these, the last had been first allocated in 1890 to Annie Barlow (1863-1941) in exchange for her subscription of funds towards the excavations, but then loaned to the former Chadwick Museum at Bolton until presented to it in April 1892. Nefersekhet's lid and the Illahun items may thus have come via the same route.

While the tombs excavated at Illahun at that time, in what was later known as the Dyke Ridge Cemetery, allegedly dated to Dynasty 22, it is certainly possible that later burials existed there, potentially including that of Nefsekhet. On the other hand, work at Gurob included an explicitly 'Ptolemaic' cemetery - but here coffins were apparently all unpainted and thus unlikely to have included the present piece. (A.M.D.)

189. 納法森凱棺蓋板
來自伊拉罕或古若卜
第30王朝或托勒密時期早期（西元前400 - 250年）
木，灰泥，顏料
1700 x 450 x 70 mm

Coffin-lid of Nefsekhet
From Illahun or Gurob
Dynasty 30 or early Ptolemaic Period (400 - 250 BC)
Wood, plaster and pigment

190. – 193. 卡諾皮克臟器罐組
來自阿比多斯，D48 號墓室
新王國時期至第三中間期，第 20-22 王朝
（西元前 1186-715 年）
石灰岩
260 x 118 x 113mm, 305 x 180 x 127mm,
290 x 140 x 121mm, 300 x 130 x 130 mm

Set of Four Canopic Jars
From Abydos, tomb D48
New Kingdom - Third Intermediate Period,
Dynasty 20-22 (1186-715 BC)
Limestone

卡諾皮克臟器罐組

古埃及晚期不再將經防腐處理的器官取出置於卡諾皮克臟器罐內，而是將之連同製成荷魯斯四子形象的蠟塑一同放回體腔中。此時期人們將卡諾皮克臟器罐及盒子視為完善墓葬的必備物品，因此開始以實心仿製罐取代新王國時期所製作的傳統卡諾皮克臟器罐。此罐組與另一組仿造的卡諾皮克臟器罐同時出土於阿比多斯某墓地。

一組四件的卡諾皮克臟器罐是用來盛裝在木乃伊製程中從亡者身上取出的內臟。自第十八王朝以後，卡諾皮克臟器罐的罐蓋開始加上了荷魯斯四子的頭像。

凱布山納夫（Qebehsenuef）的形象是隼，專司守護亡者的腸。他與西方有關，中王國時期以後的棺木將凱布山納夫繪於棺腳西側。此展件中的眼部為浮雕的烏加眼，其下有細部雕刻。

多姆泰夫（Duamutef）的代表形象為胡狼，守護著胃。他與東方連結，繪於棺腳東側。此展件中將他的臉部簡化，但眼、鼻和口部的細節則於石上精細雕琢。

哈比（Hapy）以猿為形象，守護亡者肺部。他與北方連結，自中王國時期起即繪於棺頭西側。此件以浮雕方式表現眼、鼻和嘴，口部則以雕刻方式呈現。

伊姆塞特（Imseti）守護亡者肝臟，其形象為人類。他與南方相關，自中王國時期起即繪於棺頭東側。此為本組四件罐體中唯一具有分離上蓋且內部略成中空狀者，但其內部並無任何內容物痕跡，因此很可能並非用於儲存。面部為製作精美的浮雕。
（作者：A.G.）

Set of Four Canopic Jars

During the Late Period, instead of being removed and placed in canopic jars the mummified organs were returned to the body cavity, together with small wax statuettes in the form of the four Sons of Horus. Because by this time canopic jars and boxes were viewed as an essential element of a good burial, solid dummy jars began to be made in place of the conventional jars produced during the New Kingdom. This group were found with a further set of dummy canopic jars in a reused Dynasty tomb 18 at Abydos.

From Dynasty 18 onwards the lids of the four canopic jars, made to hold the internal organs of the deceased removed during the mummification process, bore the heads of the four Sons of Horus.

Qebehsenuef was depicted as a hawk and protected the intestines of the deceased. He was associated with the west, and coffins from the Middle Kingdom onwards depict Qebehsenuef on the west side of the foot of the coffin. On this example the eyes are shown as udjat-eyes in relief, with incised detail beneath.

Duamutef took the form of a jackal, and protected the stomach. He was linked with the east, and was depicted on coffins on the east side of the foot. Here the face is simplified, and the details of the eyes, nose and mouth have been delicately incised into the stone.

Hapy took the form of an ape, and protected the lungs of the deceased. He was linked with the north, and was depicted upon the western side of the head of coffins from the Middle Kingdom. The eyes, nose and snout of this figure were shaped in relief, and the mouth was incised.

Imsety guarded the liver of the deceased and was depicted as a human. He was associated with the south, and occupied the eastern side of the head of coffins from the Middle Kingdom. This is the only jar of the group which has a separate lid and was slightly hollowed out, though as it does not preserve any traces of contents it was probably not used for storage. The face has been delicately carved in relief. (A.G.)

194. 薩布提人偶
來自阿比多斯
第三中間期，第 21-25 王朝（西元前 1069-664 年）
彩陶
149 x 45 x 40 mm

Shabti
From Abydos
Third Intermediate Period, Dynasty 21-25 (1069-664 BC)
Faience

薩布提人偶

此件藍色彩陶薩布提屬於標準木乃伊箱設計，雙臂交叉於胸前。此陶俑上具有各種以黑色墨水繪製的圖案：除了眼睛和眉毛，陶俑頭部周圍並繪有環帶，於背面有結。此陶俑手中握有兩把鋤頭，背後揹有籮筐，均是以黑色墨水描繪。薩布提身體上的文字為：「奧塞里斯，阿蒙祭司，Nes-ankh-ef-en-maat，所言屬實」。在薩布提上提到的「奧塞里斯」這個稱號是指薩布提的所有者，因為亡故之人即與來世之神奧塞里斯有關。而這件薩布提所有者所獲得的「阿蒙祭司」這個頭銜則是一種宗教角色。阿蒙祭司是古埃及最普遍也最具影響力的神職人員之一。「所言屬實」則是加諸亡者的典型敘述用語，在古埃及銘文中常附加於人名之後。（作者：H.M.）

Shabti

This blue faience shabti is of standard mummiform design, with arms crossed across its chest. The figure has various features drawn on in black ink: eyes and eyebrows are drawn on and a circlet is drawn around the figure's head, shown knotted at the back. The figure is holding two hoes and has a basket on its back, all drawn on in black ink. The text along the body of the shabti reads: 'The Osiris, Priest of Amun, Nes-ankh-ef-en-maat, True of Voice Forever'. On shabtis the designation 'The Osiris' refers to the owner of the shabti, as deceased individuals were associated with the god of the afterlife Osiris. The owner of the shabti is then given the title 'Priest of Amun', which is obviously a title indicative of a religious role. The Priests of Amun were one of the largest and most influential clergies of ancient Egypt. The phrase 'True of Voice' was a standard epithet for a deceased person and frequently appears after names in ancient Egyptian inscriptions. (H.M.)

195. 薩布提人偶
來自底比斯
第三中間期，第 21-25 王朝（西元前 1069-664 年）
彩陶
114 x 39 x 30 mm

Shabti
From Thebes, the Ramesseum
Third Intermediate Period Dynasty 21-25 (1069–664 BC)
Faience

薩布提人偶

此件藍色彩陶薩布提為標準木乃伊箱姿勢。兩把鋤頭是塑形於陶俑之上（不同於本書編號 194 之薩布提以墨水畫上的鋤頭），而陶俑頭部周圍的環帶和背後的籮筐則是以黑色墨水繪製。眼睛和眉毛也是畫上的，但磨損情況相當嚴重。陶俑腿部周圍有部分泛黑現象。沿著陶俑身體以黑色墨水寫上所有者的標準稱呼「奧塞里斯…」，但此具名稱無法翻譯：這可能是因為抄寫錯誤或異常，也可能表示對於埃及人而言，這並非典型的埃及名字，也就是其所有者或許是一名外國人。文字以典型敘述用語「所言屬實」結尾，但是以此片語的陰性形式書寫，因此說明此薩布提的所有者是一名女性。（作者：H.M.）

Shabti

This blue faience shabti is in the standard mummiform position. Two hoes have been shaped into the figure (as opposed to being drawn on as seen on Catalogue #194) while a circlet around the head and a basket on the back of the figure have been drawn on in black ink. Eyes and eyebrows have also been drawn on, but these features are rather worn. There is some black discolouration around the legs of the figure. The text written along the body in black begins with the standard identification of the owner as 'The Osiris...'. The name of the individual cannot be definitively interpreted: this may be due to a scribal error or abnormality, or may mean that the name is atypical for an Egyptian which perhaps indicates that the owner was a foreigner. The text ends with the epithet 'True of Voice', but written in the feminine form of the phrase, which therefore identifies the owner of the shabti as a woman. (H.M.)

薩布提人偶

此件綠色彩陶薩布提為木乃伊箱設計，以雕工十分精美的裝飾點綴。此薩布提手握兩把鋤頭，背後揹有籮筐，皆是雕刻於陶俑上，且此陶俑具有典型的晚期背部基座。此件薩布提上有一行橫向貫穿（從右至左）其中央部位的雕刻文字，其下另有一行沿陶俑身體方向垂直書寫的文字。可惜此件薩布提上的文字磨損情況相當嚴重，因此難以就文字內容整理出有條理的翻譯。不過，我們可以從橫向文字中讀出兩個頭銜：「精英分子」和「管轄者」。前者純屬名譽稱號，但後者說明了此件薩布提的所有者生前具有官吏身分。雖然上有部分構成文字符號可供辨識，但不足以明確譯出此件薩布提所有者的名字，不過銘文最後仍可以看出「所言屬實」這句典型敘述用語。（作者：H.M.）

Shabti

This green faience shabti is mummiform in design and bears rather finely inscribed detailing. The shabti is holding two hoes and has a basket on its back, all of which are incised into the figure. It also has a typical Late Period back plinth. The shabti has one line of text inscribed horizontally across its middle (read right to left) and another written vertically beneath it, along the length of the body. Unfortunately the text on this shabti is rather worn, which makes coherent interpretation difficult. It is possible, however, to make out two titles in the horizontal line of text: 'Member of the Elite' and 'Governor'. The former of these titles was a purely honorary title, whereas the latter indicates that the shabti owner held a bureaucratic role. The name of the owner of this shabti cannot be clearly interpreted, although some of the constituent signs can be recognised, but it is possible to read the epithet 'True of Voice' at the bottom of the inscription. (H.M.)

196. 薩布提人偶
來自哈瓦拉
後埃及時期，第26-30王朝（西元前664-332年）
彩陶
163 x 45 x 38 mm

Shabti
From Hawara
Late Period, Dynasty 26-30 (664-332 BC)
Faience

薩布提人偶

此件藍色彩陶薩布提屬於標準木乃伊箱設計，手握兩把雕刻於陶俑身上的鋤頭。此件薩布提臉部比例有些不尋常：頭部較小，但五官極大。它也設有背部基座，這是晚期薩布提典型特徵，除了有加強陶俑結構的作用，柱子上的太陽符號也說明此設計與太陽崇拜有關。此薩布提背面繪製的袋體部分存有黑漆痕跡，且沿陶俑身體可見一行文字。可惜此薩布提上的彩繪磨損嚴重，使得其上文字難以閱讀，但依據博物館記錄，此薩布提所有者名為哲爾霍爾（Djed-Hor）。（作者：H.M.）

Shabti

This blue faience shabti is of standard mummiform design and is holding two hoes, which are incised into the shabti. The facial features on this shabti are somewhat unusual, with a relatively small head but noticeably large features. This shabti also has a back plinth, a typical feature of Late Period shabtis, which served to strengthen the figure but also has connotations with sun-cults as the pillar was a solar symbol. There are traces of black paint on the back of the shabti, where a bag was drawn, and along the body where there was a line of text. Unfortunately the paint on this shabti is so worn that the text is largely unintelligible, but museum records indicate that the shabti owner was named Djed-Hor. (H.M.)

197. 薩布提人偶
來自阿比多斯
後埃及時期，第26-30王朝（西元前664-332年）
彩陶
116 x 45 x 21 mm

Shabti
From Abydos
Late Period, Dynasty 26-30 (664-332 BC)
Faience

薩布提人偶

此件彩繪陶製薩布提屬於標準木乃伊箱設計，陶俑身體漆成白色，繪有黑、紅、黃色裝飾。此件薩布提眼部及頭髮是以黑色繪成，眼白部分塗以白漆，鋤頭則是以紅色繪製。背部並無裝飾且完全未上漆。沿陶俑身上的黃底紅框部位書有一行黑色文字，文字內容為：「照亮奧塞里斯，瓦伯祭司，帕 - 漢 - 耐吉爾（Pa-Hem-Netjer）」，腳部可見「所言屬實」的文字痕跡。瓦伯祭司屬於較低階的神職人員，擔任神殿活動中多種次要任務。帕 - 漢 - 耐吉爾之名的文字意義為「神的僕人」。這類陶俑存放在與卡諾皮克臟器罐相同的陶製薩布提罐中。（作者：H.M.）

Shabti

This painted pottery shabti is of standard mummiform design and the body is painted white with detailing drawn on in black, red and yellow. The shabti's eyes and hair are painted on in black, with the whites of the eyes also painted, and it holds two hoes which are drawn in red. The back is undecorated and completely unpainted. There is a line of black text along the body of the shabti, which is written on a yellow background bordered by red lines. The text reads: 'Illumine the Osiris, Wab Priest, Pa-Hem-Netjer' with a trace of the epithet 'True of Voice' on the feet. Wab-Priests were relatively low ranking priests who attended to numerous minor duties within a temple context. Pa-Hem-Netjer's name literally means 'the servant of god'. Figures such as this one were found in ceramic shabti jars not unlike canopic jars. (H.M.)

198. 薩布提人偶
來自阿比多斯
新王國時期，第18-20王朝（西元前1550-1069年）
陶，顏料
137 x 50 x 40 mm

Shabti
From Abydos, cemetery v
New Kingdom, Dynasty 18-20 (1550-1069 BC)
Ceramic, pigment

薩布提人偶

此件木製彩繪薩布提屬木乃伊箱設計，製作略顯粗糙，其上的五官及文字繪製書寫均未加修飾。農具（兩把鋤頭及背部籮筐）和部分圍領是以紅色墨水繪製，而臉部五官、圍領剩餘部份以及文字則是黑色。俑身背面有一條相當大的裂痕，幾乎向縱向貫穿整個薩布提。沿著薩布提垂直方向書寫的文字內容為：「照亮奧塞里斯，工藝師，佩予特（Payuit），…之前」。文句看似未完即中斷。這種現象在此類文句並不罕見，由於制式用語廣為使用，文句的後續部分已經是不言可喻。文句未完的部分很可能是繼續敘述佩予特所要頌讀的神祇名稱。（作者：H.M.）

Shabti

This painted wooden shabti, which is mummiform in design, is slightly roughly executed, with both its painted features and its text somewhat crudely drawn. Its agricultural implements (two hoes and a basket on the back) and part of a collar are drawn on in red ink and its facial features, the rest of its collar and text are in black. There is a sizeable split in the back of the object, running vertically along almost the entire length of the shabti. The text, which goes along the length of the body of this shabti, reads: 'Illumine the Osiris, the Craftsman, Payuit, before...'. The text appears to break off mid-sentence. This is not unusual for texts such as this, where the formula was so established that the next part of the sentence was implicit. It is likely the implied sentence would have gone on to name a god or group of gods before whom Payuit was to be glorified. (H.M.)

199. 薩布提人偶
來自埃及
新王國時期，第18-20王朝（西元前1550-1069年）
木，顏料
225 x 50 x 32 mm

Shabti
From Egypt
New Kingdom, Dynasty 18-20 (1550-1069 BC)
Wood, pigment

薩布提人偶用農具

某些大型精美的成套薩布提製作時會配有縮小版的工具和農具模型，如這些銅合金袋、軛和鉤等等。當初的設計是將鉤掛於軛上，再將袋吊於鉤上（至今仍有一鉤處於原位）。其中兩只袋體在袋口略有剝落，第三件則保存完好，甚至留有將袋體掛於軛鉤的細緻吊帶。如此型態的袋和軛當時在農業中可能是用來裝載穀物等物質。古埃及人在薩布提身邊放置工具模型的目的是讓他們於來世執行相同任務。後期工具及器具通常改為繪製或雕刻在薩布提身上，而非另行製作。（作者：H.M.）

200. 薩布提人偶用農具
來自阿比多斯
新王國時期，第18-20王朝（西元前1550-1295年）
Copper-alloy
115 x 110 x 17 mm

Model Bags and Yoke
From Abydos, Hill R
New Kingdom, Dynasty 18 (1550-1295 BC)
Copper-alloy

Model Bags and Yoke

Some larger and more elaborate shabti collections were accompanied by miniature model tools and agricultural implements, such as these copper-alloy bags, yoke and hooks. The bags would originally have been suspended from the hooks, which in turn attached to the yoke (one hook is still in place). Two of the bags are somewhat fragmentary around the mouth, but the third is near perfect and retains the original fine loops used to suspend the bag from the yoke hooks. In agriculture, bags and yokes like these would have been used for carrying substances such as grain. The ancient Egyptians deposited models of such tools alongside their shabtis to enable them to undertake similar tasks in the afterlife. In later periods tools and implements were more commonly drawn or incised onto the shabti itself, as opposed to being modelled separately. (H.M.)

薩布提人偶－監督

此件陶製彩繪薩布提是「工頭」或「監工」薩布提的範例。此陶俑穿著的短裙說明了他的身分。標準薩布提不會穿著日常衣物，而是做成木乃伊箱形狀的陶俑。部分墓葬中包含監工薩布提，以監督標準薩布提在來世的工作。此件陶俑原本覆滿黃漆（現已有數處脫落），上以黑漆及紅漆畫出特定圖案。俑身上繪製的黑髮至今仍十分鮮明，但臉部所有彩繪皆已脫落，因此沒有顯著五官。此陶俑雙臂交叉，手中兩件以紅漆繪製的器具僅存痕跡，因此無法確定器具性質，不過監工薩布提通常是握有鞭或杖。此薩布提所有者的名字「魅蘇（Mersu）」是以黑色墨水書寫於短裙之下。（作者：H.M.）

Shabti

This painted pottery shabti is an example of a 'foreman' or 'overseer' shabti. This is denoted by the prominent kilt the figure is wearing. Standard shabtis would not be depicted wearing the clothes of the living, instead they were shaped as mummiform figures. Overseer shabtis were included in some tombs to supervise the work of the standard shabtis in the afterlife. This figure was originally covered in yellow paint (this is worn in several places now) with specific features drawn on in black and red paint. The painted black hair on the figure is still clear, but all the paint on the face has worn off and therefore no facial features are apparent. The figure is modelled with crossed arms and appears to be holding two implements, which are drawn on in red. Only traces of these implements remain, so their nature cannot be ascertained, but overseer shabtis were often drawn carrying whips or batons. The name of the owner of this shabti , 'Mersu', is written in black ink under the kilt. (H.M.)

201. 薩布提人偶－監督
來自阿比多斯
新王國時期，第18-20王朝（西元前1550-1069年）
陶，顏料
180 x 75 x 40 mm

Overseer Shabti
From Abydos
New Kingdom, Dynasty 18-20 (1550-1069 BC)
Ceramic, pigment

薩布提人偶盒

此件薩布提盒呈矩形，兩端高起，形似石棺，上蓋及底座已遺失。盒體漆為白色，以兩條紅色水平線上下框住圍繞盒體的藍色銘文；文字為頌讚來世與復活之神奧塞里斯的制式內容。

盒內原本裝有一批陪葬人俑，也就是所謂的薩布提。薩布提是墓葬裝備中的必要部分，放置於墳墓中以供亡者來世之需。據考證，薩布提最早是自古王國時期（西元前 2687-2190 年）和第一中間期（西元前 2220-2040 年）保存至中王國時期（西元前 2000-1659 年）的陪葬雕像和模型發展而來。薩布提通常呈木乃伊箱外形；新王國時期（西元前 1569-1076 年）的薩布提有時繪有衣著，並配備有鋤和籃模型。人俑的目的在於接替亡者進行勞動工作或做為亡者來世的僕役。因此，薩布提上通常刻有亡靈書第六咒語，以便雕像發揮作用。一開始墓中僅放置一件，但在新王國時期，數量大幅增加。通常會以代表一年 365 天的 365 具薩布提加上 36 具監工薩布提做為亡者陪葬。

隨著人俑數量增加，對於容器的需要也應運而生，因此產生所謂的薩布提盒。在第十八至十九王朝時期，是存放在模型棺木和石棺形或神龕形盒體中。到了新王國末期及第三中間期（西元前 1094 年至西元前 664 年），神龕形盒體擴大成為大型長方形的有蓋容器，如此才足以容納整組薩布提。上述的有蓋容器到了第三中間期後期及晚期（西元前 664 年至西元前 332 年）演變成兩端高起的石棺型式。蓋上通常繪有一或兩艘船隻的圖案，以代表前往奧塞里斯之城阿比多斯的朝聖，或代表薩布提在來世工作時的交通方式。盒體側面可能也繪有神祇、小型場景或亡靈書第六咒語縮寫等。

根據形狀判斷，這件伯頓薩布提盒應屬於第三中間期後期（第二十五王朝）或晚期（第二十六王朝）；遺失的蓋體可能繪有一或兩艘船隻的圖案。但其銘文包含頌讚來世與復活之神奧塞里斯的制式內容，這點與該時期盒體側面上通常會出現的敘述有所不同。這件薩布提容器應是出土自帝王谷。那維爾（Naville）在他的挖掘報告中提到第二十六至三十王朝的薩布提於晚期墓葬中已不復見。此件薩布提盒或許即與這項發現有關。（作者：C.G.）

Shabti Box

This shabti box has a rectangular shape with high carved ends, resembling a sarcophagus. The lid and the base are not preserved. The piece is painted white. Two red coloured horizontal lines frame a blue inscription that runs around the box; the text features an offering formula to Osiris, the god of the afterlife and resurrection.

The box originally contained a group of funerary figurines, so-called shabtis that were an integral part of the funerary equipment, placed in the tomb for the needs of the deceased in the afterlife. The first examples are attested from the Middle Kingdom (2000-1659 BC), originating from funerary statuettes and models, preserved from the Old Kingdom (2687-2190 BC) and First Intermediate Period (2220-2040 BC). Shabtis are usually modelled in mummiform shape; in the New Kingdom (1569-1076 BC) they are sometimes depicted with dresses and can be accompanied by model hoes and baskets. These figurines were supposed to take over the labour of the deceased or of his servants in the afterlife. Consequently, Book of the Dead spell 6 is usually inscribed on the shabtis enabling the figurines to work. At the beginning only one example was placed in the tomb, but during the New Kingdom the number increased immensely. Typically, 365 shabtis, for each day of the year one, as well as 36 overseers were buried with the deceased.

The high number of figurines caused the need for containers, the so-called shabti-boxes. During the Dynasty 18-19, the figurines were kept in model coffins and sarcophagi or shrine-shaped boxes. At the end of the New Kingdom and in the Third Intermediate Period (1094-664 BC) the shrine-shaped boxes became larger and resemble large rectangular chests in order to include the entire collection of shabtis. Typical for the late Third Intermediate Period and the Late Period (664-332 BC) are chests in the form of a sarcophagus with high-carved ends. The lid often shows one or two boats, either representing the pilgrimage to Abydos, the town of Osiris, or the transportation means for the work of the shabtis in the afterlife. Divinities, small scenes, or an abbreviated version of Book of the Dead spell 6 can be depicted on the sides of the chest.

Based on the shape, the Bolton shabti-box has to be dated to the late Third Intermediate Period (Dynasty 25) or the Late Period (Dynasty 26); possibly the lost lid showed the illustration of one or two boats. The inscription differs however from the typical depictions found on the sides of the chests dating to that period as it contains an offering formula to Osiris. Supposedly, the shabti-container was discovered in Deir el-Bahri. Naville mentions in his excavation report shabtis from the Dynasty 26-30 that had been thrown out from Late Period tombs. Maybe the box can be seen in connection with this find. (C.G.)

202. 薩布提人偶盒
來自巴哈里
第三中間期至後埃及時期，第 26 王朝（西元前
1069-332 年）
木，顏料
320 x 185 x 135 mm

Shabti Box
From Deir el-Bahri
Third Intermediate Period-Late Period, Dynasty
25-26 (750-526 BCE)
Wood, pigment

203. 薩布提人偶盒
可能來自法尤姆
新王國時期，第 18-20 王朝（西元前 1550-1069 年）
木，顏料
275 x 170 x 140 mm

Shabti Box
Probably from the Fayum
New Kingdom, Dynasty 18-20 (1550-1069 BC)
Wood, pigment

薩布提人偶盒

此木箱的功用為貯藏薩布提雕像，雕像為死者來世所需，代替死者從事農耕工作。薩布提箱由簡單的木製薩布提棺發展而來，可容納一具薩布提雕像，於中王國時期製造。

此薩布提箱有很厚一層亮色漆，四片木板原本以木釘接合固定。上頭的紅色及藍色分別由赭石與埃及藍製成，非常亮眼。雖然一些繪圖裝飾已經褪去，但其中兩邊還保存著荷魯斯四個兒子的圖樣，分別是：鷹頭的凱布山納夫（Qebehsenuef）、胡狼頭的多姆泰夫（Duamutef）、猿頭的哈比（Hapi）、人頭的伊姆塞特（Imsety）。他們負責保護死者的器官，因此這些神祇的圖樣比較常用於裝飾存放死者內臟器官的骨罈櫃。還有些片段圖畫，描繪哈托爾女神（Hathor）的正面，以及伊西斯（Isis）和奈芙蒂斯（Nephthys）哀悼奧塞里斯去世的樣子（一般認為死者是奧塞里斯），這在箱子的短側邊上也可以看見。

在箱子各邊所描繪的圖畫之下，是兩個水平部分，上頭保存著傑得柱（Djed-pillar）與伊西斯結（Tyet-knot）這兩個輪流變換的主題，分別象徵著對奧塞里斯與伊西斯的神聖儀式，並且具有保護箱中物的神奇力量。（作者：A.G.）

Shabti Box

Wooden boxes were made for the storage of shabti figures: the statuettes required by the deceased in the afterlife to undertake agricultural labour on their behalf. Shabti-boxes developed from simple wooden shabti-coffins, made to hold a single shabti, produced during the Middle Kingdom.

This box was plastered and brightly painted, and the four panels would originally have been joined together with wooden dowels. The red and blue colours, produced from ochre and Egyptian blue respectively, are particularly striking. Although some of the painted decoration has been lost, two of the sides clearly preserve the figures of the four Sons of Horus – the falcon-headed Qebehsenuef, the jackal-headed Duamutef, the ape-headed Hapi and the human-headed Imsety – who protected the internal organs of the deceased. These deities were more commonly used in the decoration of canopic chests made to store the internal organs of the deceased. Fragmentary scenes depicting the frontal-face of the goddess Hathor and the figures of Isis and Nephthys mourning the death of the god Osiris, who was identified with the deceased, can also be discerned on the short sides of the box.

Beneath the scenes on each side of the box are two horizontal registers preserving an alternating motif of djed-pillars and tyet-knots –emblems sacred to the cults of Osiris and Isis respectively - which magically protected the contents of the box. (A.G.)

黃金眼蓋片和玲片

身體部位（例如：眼睛、耳朵、腳、心臟）的護身符在古埃及文化中由來以久。活著的人佩戴護身符保護該符所描繪之身體部位；至於死者，由於真實器官會腐壞，所以護身符具有取代真實器官的神奇功用。或許最常被描繪於護身符上的主題是眼睛；然而應注意到護身符上的圖樣中，「烏加眼」（荷魯斯之眼）與一般人類雙眼是不同的，就像此處的展品。

考古發現為數眾多的舌部黃金玲片與羅馬時期埋葬的木乃伊有關。除了其本身具有奢侈品的價值外，黃金向來被視為是一種具有神奇保護能力的物質。在死者的舌頭上覆蓋黃金玲片，就能確保死者於來世仍保有講話的能力。此雙眼的黃金眼蓋片與舌部黃金玲片是在同個地點被發現。（作者：J.H.W.）

Gold Tongue and Eye Plates

Amulets of body parts such as eyes, ears, feet and hearts have a long history in ancient Egypt. Amulets were worn by the living to protect the body part depicted and the amulet could also serve as a magical replacement after death should the real member become damaged. Perhaps the most commonly depicted subject for amulets is the eye. However, a distinction should be made between the udjat ("Sound Eye of Horus") amulet and those depicting a regular human eye, like the example we see here.

Numerous examples of gold foil tongue amulets have been found associated with mummies from Roman Period burials. In addition to its inherent value as a luxury item, gold was esteemed for its magical and protective properties. By covering the tongue of the deceased with a gold amulet, the deceased's ability to speak in the afterlife was ensured. The gold foil eye amulet was found at the same site as the tongue amulet. (J.H.W.)

204. & 205. 黃金眼蓋片和玲片
來自壇尼斯
羅馬時期 (西元前 30 年 - 西元 395 年)
金
40 x 28 x 1 mm, 38 x 27 x 1 mm

Tongue and Eye
From Hawara
Roman Period (30 BC-AD395)
Gold

206. 黃金玲片
來自哈瓦拉
羅馬時期 (西元前 30 年 - 西元 395 年)
金
33x 28 x 1 mm

Tongue
From Hawara
Roman Period (30 BC-AD395)
Gold

207. 鑲金木乃伊盒
來自阿比多斯，G50 號墓室
後埃及時期，第 30 王朝（西元前 380-343 年）
金葉片，木乃伊盒
512 x 370 x 3 mm

Gilt Cartonnage
From Abydos, Tomb G50
Late Period, Dynasty 30 (380-343 BC)
Gold leaf, cartonnage

鑲金木乃伊盒

1901 至 1902 年，考古學家佩托里（Petrie）於阿比多斯的某墓地進行挖掘工作，發現一處保存完好的古埃及晚期家族墓室，其中共埋葬七位死者，包括：名為哲爾霍爾（Djed-Hor）的男子、其妻娜布黛海特（Nebtaihyt）夫人以及兩名兒子。

娜布黛海特夫人的屍體置於石棺內，石棺外另加上木棺。石棺內的木乃伊棺加上鍍金木乃伊盒套組：珠飾及花飾的寬版領型項鍊，以及神聖人像的胸前裝飾物。胸前裝飾物下為天空女神努特（Nut）展開雙翅的圖樣。努特的圖樣常出現在葬禮用品上，例如棺木與木乃伊裝飾物，因為在埃及神話中，每天讓太陽出現在天上是努特負責的工作。畫上努特的圖樣，希望在每個落日遲暮時太陽都能重生，死者在來世也能獲得重生。努特女神圖樣下，是木乃伊置於棺架上的畫面。正中央裝飾的二邊，荷魯斯的兩名兒子出現在長方形塊狀上。死者與其雙親姓名寫於鍍金木乃伊盒，位於腳部上方的姓名條上。（作者：J.H.W.）

Gilt Cartonnage

In his excavations of Cemetery G at Abydos in 1901-1902, the archaeologist Flinders Petrie discovered a largely undisturbed Late Period family tomb containing seven burials. The tomb (G50) contained the burial of a man named Djed-Hor and his wife, the Lady Nebtaihyt, together with at least two of their sons.

The body of Lady Nebtaihyt was contained within Sarcophagus D, which had an outer wooden coffin. Within this sarcophagus, her mummy was decorated with a set of gilded cartonnage elements consisting of a broad wesekh collar adorned with beaded and floral elements and a pectoral decorated with divine figures. Below the pectoral is a large image of the sky goddess Nut with outstretched wings. Nut is often shown decorating burial equipment such as coffins and cartonnage, for in Egyptian mythology, Nut was responsible for giving birth to the sun each day. It was hoped that just as the sun is reborn each dawn, the deceased would be reborn in the afterlife. Below the goddess is a scene of a mummy on a bier. On either side of the central elements, two of the four sons of Horus appear in rectangular fields. The names of the deceased and those of her parents are preserved on a strip of gilded cartonnage found above the legs of the mummy. (J.H.W.)

木乃伊盒碎片

法老的木乃伊盒通常只是個圍住屍體的單一外殼。到了托勒密早期，這樣的做法開始改變，我們看見木乃伊盒的分組套件直接黏在亞麻裹屍布上。分離部分包括：面具、衣領、胸飾以及腳蓋板。此梯形木乃伊盒元素推測為木乃伊盒組件的部分，木乃伊盒組件均置於包裹的屍體或木乃伊的胸膛上。裝飾品由一系列的元素組成，邊緣是多色長方形樣式。上面是展翅的太陽圖搭配懸吊的神蛇標誌裝飾。翅膀羽毛製作精細，並有多種色彩，包括：紅色、藍色、暗黃色以及綠色。

太陽圖下為水平的獻祭文，指出死者身份，是位名叫帕邱米斯（Pachoumis）的男人，銘文亦透露男子於52歲去世，這在托勒密時期並不常見。下方為明顯區分成五部份的名冊，中間為紅色底，上頭畫的是木乃伊和陵墓的守護神阿努比斯（Anubis），他在木乃伊上執行葬禮的儀式，兩側圖畫是伊西斯（左邊）和奈芙蒂斯（右邊），兩個女神都呈哀悼狀，背景為綠色。剩下的四個土黃色部份畫是荷魯斯的四個兒子：伊姆塞特（Imseti）、哈比（Hapy）、多姆泰夫（Duamutef）及凱布山納夫（Qebehsenuef）。剩下四分之三的木乃伊盒板由十六排的亮色珠飾和花飾組成。（作者：J.H.W.）

Fragment from mummy case

Pharaonic mummy cartonnage cases were typically a single shell that enclosed the body. In the early Ptolemaic period, this practice changed and we begin to see separate cartonnage components attached directly to the linen wrappings. These sections typically included the mask, collar, pectoral, and foot cover. This trapezoidal cartonnage element was probably part of a set of cartonnage pieces, which were placed on the chest of a mummified and wrapped body. The decoration consists of a series of elements bounded by a rectangular multicolor border. At the top is a winged sun disk with pendant uraei. The feathers of the wings are particularly detailed and executed in multiple colors: red, blue, yellow-buff and green.

Below the sun disk is a horizontal offering formula identifying the deceased, a man by the name of Pachoumis. The inscription also gives his age at death as 52 years, a feature not common prior to the Ptolemaic period. Below this is a register with five distinct sections. In the central section with a red background, the patron of embalmers, Anubis carries out funerary rituals on a mummy. Flanking this central scene are images of Isis (on the left) and Nephthys (on the right) both shown in the mourning pose with a greenish background. The remaining four, buff-coloured sections contain images of the fours sons of Horus: Duamutef, Imsety, Hapy and Qebehsenuef. A stylized collar with sixteen rows of brightly colored beaded and floral elements comprises the lower ¾ of the cartonnage panel. (J.H.W.)

208. 木乃伊盒碎片
來自阿特法
托勒密時期（西元前332-30年）
木乃伊盒
608 x 350 x 15 mm

Fragment from mummy case
From Atfih
Ptolemaic Period (332-30 BC)
Cartonnage

木乃伊盒

木乃伊盒板推測用來裝飾木乃伊胸前。此裝飾上方為一圖像，四周由多種顏色繪成的框圍住，下方為兩欄半神職用之銘文。上方圖像中的男性死者在兩名神祇面前，獻上小型容器。死者戴著剪短的假髮、寬版領型項鍊、手鐲、臂飾、踝飾、長版褶裙。他面對著木乃伊形式的奧塞里斯，奧塞里斯手上拿著傳統的皇室象徵物：曲柄杖和連枷。伊西斯女神站在奧塞里斯身後，她舉起左手，頭上戴著君王象形符號（其姓名的象徵符號）的裝飾物，每個人前面的欄位都是空白的，兩個欄位中的銘文非常難閱讀，開頭都是標準的用語：「由誰所說」接著下去似乎是「反邊的 Nemeh／Nehem…」。第二個欄位的版本較令人困惑，開頭是：「由誰所說」，緊接著的是死者的姓名（Nemeh／Nehem…），接著是「在奧塞里斯之前，…之神」其餘皆難以辨認。（作者：J.H.W.）

Cartonnage

This cartonnage panel probably adorned the chest of a mummy. The decoration consists of a scene bordered by multicolor rectangles above two columns of a semi-hieratic inscription. The scene shows the male deceased offering a small vessel before two deities. The deceased wears a cropped wig, broad collar, bracelets, an armlet, anklets and a long kilt. He faces the god Osiris, who is shown mummiform and holds his traditional royal attributes, the crook and the flail. The goddess Isis stands behind Osiris. She raises her left hand and wears the throne hieroglyph (which is the symbol used to write her name) on her head. The columns in front of each of the figures are blank. The two columns of inscription are difficult to read. It begins with the standard expression 'Words said by' and then seems to continue, 'The revered one Nemeh/Nehem…' The second column begins with a garbled version of 'Words said by' followed by the name of the deceased (Nemeh/Nehem…) then '(be)fore Osiris, Lord of… the rest is illegible. (J.H.W.)

209. 木乃伊盒
可能來自法尤姆
羅馬時期 (西元前 30 年 - 西元 395 年)
木乃伊盒
340 x 113 x 10 mm

Cartonnage
Probably from Fayum
Roman Period (30 BC-AD 395)
Cartonnage

210. 胸飾
可能來自法尤姆
托勒密時期 (西元前 332-30 年)
木乃伊盒
330 x 265 x 5 mm

Pectoral
Probably the Fayum
Ptolemaic Period (332-30 BC)
Cartonnage

胸飾

在古埃及文化中，寬版領型胸飾（又稱 wesekh）是種極受歡迎的首飾。以純金、珍貴玉石或彩陶所製成的本展品是很好的代表。寬版領型胸飾也可以真花製成，埃及便曾經挖出花飾的寬版領型胸飾。1907 年西爾鐸·戴維斯（Theodore Davis）在圖坦卡門墳墓中的防腐保存用品中發現了一些保存良好的例子[1]。埃及歷史上許多時期的棺木與面具上都可見寬版領型胸飾的裝飾。

此展品裝飾木乃伊胸前部分，為花樣領型胸飾，搭配橄欖葉、蓮花、蓮花蕾，並有玫瑰花飾與珠飾。領型胸飾的兩端為鷹頭形狀搭配展翅之太陽圖裝飾，代表的或許是赫拉克提這個神。在兩個鷹頭形狀的端點的正中央，有個聖物形狀裝飾，兩旁則為「烏加眼」。中央的裝飾為阿比底尼（Abydene）三人組坐下來的圖，分別是奧塞里斯、荷魯斯以及伊西斯。這些神的頭上都刻有象形的銘文，代表的是他們個別的名字。（作者：J.H.W.）

Pectoral

A popular form of Egyptian jewelry was the wesekh or broad collar. Examples created of gold, precious stones or faience are well represented. Broad collars could also be made of real floral elements. Examples of floral collars have been excavated in Egypt. Some of the best preserved come from the embalming cache of Tutankhamun discovered by Theodore Davis in 1907.[1] Broad collars were often featured on coffins and masks from many periods in Egyptian history.

This cartonnage example decorated the chest of a mummy and depicts a floral collar with olive leaves, lotus flower and buds together with rosettes and beads. The ends of the collar feature terminals in the shape of falcon heads with sun disk, perhaps representing the god Re-Horakhty. Between the falcon headed terminals are two udjat eyes flanking a shrine-shaped central decoration containing seated images of the Abydene triad, Osiris, Horus and Isis. A hieroglyphic inscription above the heads of these gods identifies each by name. (J.H.W.)

---

1. 圖坦卡門的花飾寬版領型胸飾的設計元素包括：橄欖葉、酪梨葉、矢車菊、藍色蓮花花瓣、匍枝毛連菜、水茄。

---

1. The floral elements of Tutankhamun's collar include olive leaves, persea leaves, cornflowers, blue lotus petals, picris flowers and nightshade berries.

供品盤

陶的供品盤是模仿石材祭壇與獻祭桌以陶土製成的物品，常置於葬禮的祭拜堂，流質的祭品常被倒在供品盤上。陶質的供品盤是種負擔得起，而且更容易取得的替代物品，它們通常製成不同食物的形狀，以及流質獻祭品的排水裝置。拖盤的形狀有T型祭壇（直接源自於石材的獻祭桌），也有馬蹄形、圓盤形搭配各種不同管道、隔板、水井的設計。之後常加上庇護所及房屋的設計，這些設計通常被稱作「靈魂之屋」，此設計原本的想法是為死者的靈魂提供住所，但是它們的重點顯然是在提供獻祭品。

供品盤原本的功用是代替祭壇，會放置在能讓活著的人為死者倒入奠酒的地方，常置於墓地的地面上方或是葬禮的廳堂。隨著時間過去，這種做法發展出一種概念：拖盤本身即含有營養物質，所以直接置於墳上即可。

拖盤有排水管設計，因此與石材祭壇相似，但其圓形四角與盤形及馬蹄形的拖盤相似。匯合於排水管的四條溝槽，是液體的排水道，這些溝渠僅僅以手指挖掘而成，讓奠酒能倒在獻祭品上。拖盤的遠端描繪的弓形物體，意圖象徵的是公牛的頭型，加上過大且彎曲的牛角，這是供品盤上常見的主題。在左邊的不是一堆蔬菜就是公牛的肋骨，在右邊的大概是麵包。

安琪拉・托利（Angela Tooley）已經證實供品盤的形態與其出處有很大的關連。尤其此供品盤的形態相當與眾不同，具有排水管設計，最類似祭壇形式的拖盤，但也有圓角設計，類似馬蹄形拖盤。托利僅記錄此種形式的幾種樣本，所有樣本均來自埃及中部的力斐（Rifeh）遺址。另一種祭壇形式有圓角設計的拖盤來自艾斯尤特（Asyut），但此種形式的特色又與圓角形槽形式極不相似。祭壇形式的拖盤主要於下埃及與埃及中部發現，馬蹄形式主要存在於上埃及，所以結合兩種特色的形式出現於兩地交會的埃及中部，看起來可能性很大。（作者：M.M.）

211. 供品盤
可能來自瑞法
第 11-12 王朝（西元前 2055-1773 年）
陶
365 x 270 x 61 mm

Offering tray
Possibly from Rifeh
Dynasty 11-12 (2055-1773 BC)
Ceramic

Offering tray

Ceramic offering trays are imitations in clay of the stone altars or offering tables placed in funerary chapels, onto which liquid offerings were poured for the deceased. Ceramic offering trays represented an affordable, more widely available alternative. They often feature models of various forms of food and drainage channels for the liquid offering. The trays range in form from T-shaped altars, derived directly from stone offering tables, to horseshoe- and plate-shaped forms with a variety of different channels, partitions, and wells. Later, model shelters or houses were sometimes added, and so these are often termed 'soul houses'. They were originally thought to provide a home for the soul of the deceased, but their emphasis was clearly the provision of offerings.

Offering trays originally served as substitute altars, and as such, were placed in a position where the living could pour libations for the dead, on the surface of burials or in funerary chapels. Over time, it seems that this practice developed into the concept that the trays themselves were self-contained providers of nourishment, which could be placed directly in the tomb.

With its spout, this tray is similar in form to a stone altar, but its rounded corners resemble plate- and horseshoe- trays. The four grooves converging in the spout were drainage channels for liquid, simply gouged out using the fingers, to allow for the pouring of water libations over the offerings. The bow-shaped object depicted at the far end of the tray was likely intended to represent the stylized head of an ox, with oversized, curved horns, a frequent motif on offering trays. On the left are either stacks of vegetables or the ribs of an ox, and on the right, possibly bread.

Angela Tooley has demonstrated that the morphology of offering trays is strongly correlated with provenance. This particular offering tray is unusual in form, most resembling an altar-style tray with its spout, but with rounded corners, like horseshoe-style trays. Tooley recorded only a few examples in this style, all of which come from the site of Rifeh in Middle Egypt. Another altar-style tray with rounded corners comes from Asyut, but features distinctly dissimilar corner tanks. Altar-style trays are found mainly in Lower and Middle Egypt, while horseshoe-trays are prevalent in Upper Egypt, so a combination of the two styles at the location of their intersection in Middle Egypt seems possible. (M.M.)

普塔－蘇卡－奧塞里斯雕像

此人形木乃伊雕像顯現的是復活重生之普塔－蘇卡－奧塞里斯。人形雕像的黃色是模仿金的質感，也代表著神明肌膚的顏色，黏在臉上的是神明鬍子。此雕像穿戴著藍色的三方假髮以及合攏的王冠，此王冠有兩隻公羊角，中間是日輪裝飾，上頭並有兩根羽毛。他的身體上畫了珠飾的網狀裹布，強調此雕像木乃伊形式的特色。雕像的頸子上細細描繪的是寬版領型項鍊，末端以鷹頭的裝飾作結，繪於肩膀上。獻給奧塞里斯的三欄祭文寫在腳的前方，在上頭的則是努特女神展開雙翅的插畫圖。精簡版銘文保留於雕像的背後，只有一欄。神的下方緊黏著長方形的底座，側邊有花卉主題的裝飾。上方再次出現獻給奧塞里斯的獻祭文，文本被複製於下方的三個欄位，其中可能包括雕像所有者的姓名，可能是：Iri-seset 或 Iri-set，但此姓名並未被證實。

普塔－蘇卡－奧塞里斯雕像是兩個神明的結合——阿比多斯的神明奧塞里斯與孟斐斯城的神明普塔－蘇卡，這兩個神明均與來世及重生有關。在木乃伊棺與繪有圖樣的裹布之下，奧塞里斯外觀的雕像顯而易見，而王冠和寬版領型胸飾代表的就是普塔－蘇卡。長方形的基座或是雕像本身通常會出現一個洞穴的設計，是用來放置葬禮用的紙莎草紙（亡者之書）。

這些中空的雕像源自皇室樣本，首先被證實出現在十八王朝阿蒙霍特二世（Amenhotep II）的墓室裡，第三中間期開始至托勒密時期（公元前1094-30年），成為私人墓地上典型的葬禮用品。有些樣本可追溯至新王國晚期之前。這些雕像能保護死者，具有與神祇相等的能力，也能保障死後的生活，因此被放置於靠近棺木的地方。依照插圖的元素，此雕像可分為四大類型：黑假漆雕像、多色彩的奧塞里斯雕像、綠面普塔－索卡－奧塞里斯雕像、金面普塔－索卡－奧塞里斯雕像。伯頓博物館的樣本屬於最後一類，被證實是二十六王朝以降至托勒密時期的產物，然而這類雕像並非中空形式，也沒有奧塞里斯的讚美詩歌。該類別之下的次分類雕像中的典型元素是：寬版領型胸飾、珠飾網狀裹屍布，以及雕像前方的銘文。銘文共有三欄，上頭的圖樣是努特女神。此雕像的黃色臉，以及對努特女神的描繪是分類的決定性指標。（作者：C.G.）

Ptah Sokar Osiris Figure

This human mummiform statue visualizes the resurrection god Ptah-Sokar-Osiris. The yellow colour of the figure imitates gold, and thus represents the skin colour of the gods. Attached to the face is the divine beard. The statue is wearing a blue tripartite wig as well as the Shuty crown, consisting of two ram horns with a sun-disk in the middle and two feathers on top. A bead netting shroud is painted on the body, stressing the mummyform character of the statue. A broad collar is traced around the neck, ending in a falcon's head on the shoulder of the figure. An offering formula to Osiris is written in three columns on the front of the legs, surmounted by an illustration of the goddess Nut with outstretched wings. An abbreviated version of the text is preserved on the back of the figure, written in only one column. A rectangular base is attached beneath the god, decorated with floral motives on its sides. The upper part shows again the offering formula to Osiris. The text is copied down in three columns, and might include the name of the statue owner, Iri-seset or Iri-set, at the end. The name is otherwise unattested however.

The god Ptah-Sokar-Osiris is a syncretism of two deities – the Abydenian god Osiris and the Memphite deity Ptah-Sokar; both are associated with the afterlife and resurrection. The Osiris aspect of the statue is visible in the mummiform shape and the painted shroud, whereas the crown and the collar represent Ptah-Sokar. The rectangular base or the figure itself often exhibit a cavity that originally contained a funerary papyrus (Book of the Dead or Amduat) or later on a corn mummy.

Originating from royal examples first attested in the tomb of Amenhotep II of the Dynasty 18, theses hollow statues became a typical funerary item in private tombs from the Third Intermediate Period until the Ptolemaic Period (1094-30 BC); some examples date to before the late New Kingdom. The statues guarantee the deceased, equated with the deity, a life after death and were thus placed close to the coffin. Based on the iconographic elements this statue type can be divided into four larger groups: the black-varnished statues, the polychrome Osiris statues, the Ptah-Sokar-Osiris statues with green face, and the Ptah-Sokar-Osiris statues with gilded face. The Bolton example definitely belongs to the last group, attested after Dynasty 26 until the Ptolemaic Period, although the figure does not exhibit a hollow or an Osiris hymn. Typical elements of the sub-category C of that group are the broad collar, the bead netting shroud, as well as the inscription on the front of the figure that is written in three columns and surmounted by the goddess Nut. The yellow face of the figure and the depiction of the goddess Nut are the decisive criteria for the classification. (C.G.)

212. 普塔－蘇卡－奧塞里斯雕像
來自埃及
後埃及時期，第27-30王朝（西元前525-332年）
木，顏料
750 x 450 x 200 mm

Ptah Sokar Osiris Figure
From Egypt
Late Period, Dynasty 27-30 (525-332 BC)
Wood, pigment

213. 盛有樹脂的碗
來自埃及
新王國時期，第18王朝（西元前1550-1069年）
陶，樹脂
164 x 158 x 70 mm

Bowl containing resins
From Egypt
New Kingdom, Dynasty 18 (1550-1069 BC)
Ceramic, resin

盛有樹脂的碗

這款造型簡單的淺碗有明確邊線，是陶拉坯成品。此種形式在新王國時期的陶藝中也有許多可對應的作品，其內部以與邊緣垂直的紅色的波浪紋路來裝飾。碗裡面裝著已經變硬的物質，很像是樹脂，樹脂可能是來自各種不同的樹木，大部分的樹脂是從國外進口至埃及，大概是由敘利亞或黎巴嫩進口的。在古埃及，樹脂最重要的用途是製作木乃伊；身體內的器官被移出後，可以樹脂填充，因為樹脂會散發香甜的氣息，並且具有抑制細菌滋生的功用。在中王國時期開始時，半液態的樹脂被倒在將製作成木乃伊的屍體上。

在這個漆成紅色的碗裡發現樹脂，這可能說明它是種防腐容器，其中還有製作木乃伊過程中會產生的碎屑，如：陶器、亞麻布料、泡鹼、樹脂或其他類似的東西；因為用在一具木乃伊上的材料無法重覆使用，必須埋起來，有時埋在墓地附近的坑洞，有時埋在墳墓裡面；因此這碗樹脂或許是在製造木乃伊的過程中留下的。在埃及曾經發現過幾個防腐容器，最剛開始是在中王國時期的遺址發現的，其中最知名的是圖坦卡門的陵墓中所貯藏的防腐用品。並非所有的防腐容器內容都相同；大型壺罐裡裝的是製作木乃伊過程中所留下來的碎屑，這是山谷中國王陵墓的特色；而在塞內姆特（Senenmut）位於底比斯的墳墓，木乃伊製作時的碎屑是放置於籃子裡的。在杜拉 阿布'1Naga（Dra Abu'1 Naga）所發現的防腐容器，裡面含有20至30件容器、幾包泡鹼、亞麻，以及一個大型的骨罈櫃。此處的淺碗正好可以放置於這寬闊的櫃裡。（作者：L.A.W.）

Bowl containing resins

This simple, shallow bowl has a direct rim and was made on the potter's wheel. The form has many parallels in the New Kingdom ceramic repertoire. Its interior is decorated with red painted wavy lines roughly perpendicular to the rim. The bowl is filled with hardened material which is most likely resin. Resin can come from many varieties of trees; most resin would have been imported into Egypt from abroad, perhaps from Syria and Lebanon. One of the most important applications of resin in ancient Egypt was in mummification. Resin could be used to fill the body cavity once the organs were removed, for resin is sweet-smelling and reduces bacterial growth. Beginning in the Middle Kingdom, semi-liquid resin was poured over the mummified body.

The presence of resin in this red-painted bowl would suggest that it possibly originated in from an embalmers' cache. Embalmers' caches included all the detritus from the mummification process – pottery, linen bandages, natron, resin, and the like – buried in a pit near the burial or sometimes deposited within the tomb. It seems that the materials used in one person's mummification could not be reused and were thus buried out of necessity. Therefore, perhaps this resin was left over from the mummification process of an unknown individual. Several embalming caches have been found in Egypt, beginning in the Middle Kingdom. Most famous is the embalming deposit of Tutankhamen. Not all embalming caches had the same contents. Large jars filled with the debris from mummification characterize the embalming caches in the Valley of the Kings; on the other hand, the mummification remnants from the Theban tomb of Senenmut were placed in a basket. An embalmers' cache found in Dra Abu'l Naga contained 20-30 pottery vessels, sacks of natron, linen, and a large canopic chest. Our bowl could fit comfortably within this broad corpus. (L.A.W.)

木乃伊腳裹布

古埃及人在葬禮用品上添加神祕圖畫，希望如此能確保死者在進入來世的路上一切順利。這塊繪有圖樣的布原本是蓋在木乃伊的腳上，裹屍布上對稱的裝飾看起來很簡單，但卻代表著複雜的宗教概念。在物體的上端是一雙穿著涼鞋的腳。裹屍布的這一端會被置於木乃伊腳上。正中央是展翅的日輪，配上垂墜的神蛇標記。置於木乃伊上時，可看見一個圓形太陽符號在腳上方，另一個就放在下方。裹屍布底部呈現的圖畫是：兩隻揮舞著刀子的獅子正面對著橋塔或是寺廟的入口。此設計元素會蓋過腳底[1]。

裹屍布的裝飾包含著太陽及守護的意象，例如：帶翼日輪、一對生命之符、一隻烏加眼（代表荷魯斯沉靜的雙眼）、蠍子以及一對玫瑰圖樣。整幅圖畫的邊邊是螺旋設計。面對橋塔、揮舞著武器的獅子扮演的角色為到達永恆國度入口的警衛，這是死者必經的通道[2]。把這些圖畫放在死者的腳底，這樣的作法被解讀為希望死者能夠「走」向通往來世的門。此外，腳部的外觀裝飾或許代表著死者對於來世的行動能力的希望。（作者：J.H.W.）

---

1. 此時期腳底的圖樣常繪於木乃伊的腳底盒上。常見的主題是被綑綁住的犯人，或是危險的生物，例如：蠍子（參考本書編號171）。
2. 成對的獅子為埃及藝術中常見的裝飾主題。成對的舒神與努特可以獅子的樣貌出現，還有雙獅（RWTY），是一種表現藝術的裝飾，表示昨天與明天的概念，這些雙獅也稱作 Aker，地平線之神，守衛著地下世界的入口，替太陽打開入口讓它通過。

Foot Cover

Through the use of magical imagery on funerary equipment, the Egyptians hoped to ensure the successful passage of the deceased into the afterlife. This painted shroud originally covered the feet of a mummy. The symmetrical decoration on the shroud is seemingly simple, yet represents complex religious concepts. A pair of feet wearing sandals appears at the top end of the object. This end of the shroud would have been placed atop the feet of the mummy. A pair of winged sun disks with pendant uraei occur in the center. When placed on the mummy, one sun disk would be visible on the top of the feet; the other would be positioned below. At the bottom of the shroud is a scene of two knife-wielding lions facing a pylon, or temple gateway. This element would have been positioned over the soles of the feet. [1]

The decoration of the shroud contains solar and protective imagery, such as the winged sun disks, a pair of ankhs (meaning "life"), an udjat eye (representing the sound eye of Horus), a scorpion and a pair of rosettes. The entire scene is bordered by a spiral design. The lions, which face the pylon and brandish weapons act as guardians of the entrance to eternity through which the deceased had to pass.[2] By placing this image on the soles of the feet of the deceased, perhaps it was to be understood as a wish that the deceased would be able to "walk" through the doors into the afterlife. In addition, he appearance of the feet may represent a wish for the deceased's mobility in the afterlife. (J.H.W.)

---

1. The soles of the feet are often depicted on cartonnage foot cases of this period. A common decorative motif is that of bound prisoners, or dangerous creatures such as scorpions. See, for example, Catalogue #171.
2. The motif of the paired lions is well-known in Egyptian art. The paired gods Shu and Nut can appear as lions. There are double lions (known as rwty), which are shown in artistic representations on either side of the horizon and represent yesterday and tomorrow. These double lions are also known as Aker, the god of the horizon, who guarded the entrance to the underworld and opened it for the sun to pass through.

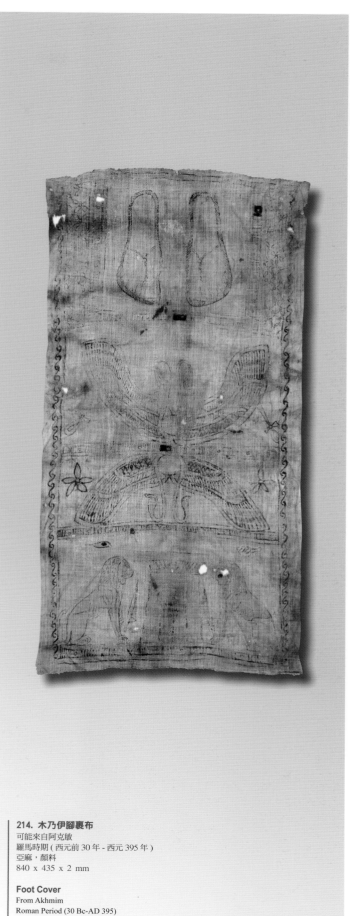

214. 木乃伊腳裹布
可能來自阿克敏
羅馬時期（西元前 30 年 - 西元 395 年）
亞麻，顏料
840 x 435 x 2 mm

Foot Cover
From Akhmim
Roman Period (30 Bc-AD 395)
Linen, pigment

215. 陶漢努棺木
來自底比斯西岸
新王國時期，第 21 王朝（西元前 1069-945 年）
木，灰泥，顏料
1845 x 508 x 285 mm

Coffin-Trough of Tayuhenet
From Thebes, West Bank
New Kingdom, Dynasty 21 (1069-945 BC)
Wood, plaster, pigment

陶漢努棺木

從十八王朝末期至二十二王朝早期，棺材通常以黃色為底色，彩色圖樣為裝飾，外層覆蓋的瀝青則因為時間的關係變黃，所以現在人會說那是「黃色」棺木。此棺木的棺蓋已經遺失，現在裝著的是一具男性木乃伊（本書編號 216），難以準確追溯其所屬年代，因為棺蓋的變化會比其他部分要來得明顯。然而，大概還是能推測此棺木的所屬年代應為二十一王朝的後半葉。棺木內部僅刷上紅色，並無特別裝飾。

外部裝飾由一連串神話的藤蔓花樣構成，旁邊有著亡者之書的內文，以及相關的文章，中楣為眼鏡蛇的造型，上方邊緣處有正義女神馬特（Maat）的羽毛。就細節來說它們有些不同，但仍屬這個較大的時間範圍內。

棺頭部分有奈芙蒂斯（Nephthys）站立的圖樣，棺頭的右手邊顯示的是死者將獻祭品獻給荷魯斯，以及在左邊的西方女神。棺木右手邊由肩膀至腰部的位置，繪著月神托特（Thoth）及一名眼鏡蛇頭的女神，站在眾神前面，整幅圖構成了荷魯斯在西方女神與眼鏡蛇頭女神的陪同下，對坐著的奧塞里斯的木乃伊表達敬意的圖樣，而她們全都在一條巨型蛇的保護之下。右手邊接下來的圖還有顯示死者崇拜著穿著普通服裝的奧塞里斯，身旁依舊伴著西方女神。緊接著下個圖：伊西斯女神、奈芙蒂斯以及「巴」（Ba，巴，古埃及文化中類似靈魂的概念。）正在哀悼木乃伊。右腳邊的最後一個圖，死者與西方女神站在西克莫無花果樹上的哈托爾（Hathor）的前方，這對她而言是至高的神聖。

回到棺木的左側，從肩膀到腰部的部分是舒神（Shu）與努特（Nut）分離的畫面，接下來有三幅圖畫。第一幅圖與棺木對面對應的圖很相似，不過是托特加入死者，站在奧塞里斯與西方女神前面的圖畫。第二幅圖上為荷魯斯的四個兒子支撐著祭壇的畫面。第三幅圖顯示為陶漢努（Tayuhenet）對著馬特女神與哈托爾獻上祭品的畫面，哈托爾的外表像隻牛出現在西方山的斜坡上。足部末端繪上的是關於奧塞里斯的迷信物節德柱。每幅圖畫中間皆以若干欄的文字做區隔。（作者：A.M.D.）

Coffin-Trough of Tayuhenet

From the end of Dynasty 18 to early Dynasty 22, coffins were generally decorated in polychrome on a yellow background, covered with a varnish that has yellowed with age - hence their modern description as 'Yellow' coffins. The tough of that of the Lady of the House and Singer of Amun, Tayuhenet, has now lost its lid and contains a male mummy (Catalogue #216). It has no lid, the loss of which makes the coffin more difficult to date with precision, as lid decoration changes more over time than that of the trough. However, it should certainly be dated to the second half of Dynasty 21, but probably not much beyond. The interior is undecorated, save a red wash of paint.

The exterior decoration comprises a series of mythological vignettes, accompanied by texts from the Book of the Dead and related compositions, with a frieze of cobras and the feather of Maat around the upper edge. In their details they are slightly unusual, but remain within the broader range of compositions of the time.

At the head of the coffin is a standing image of Nephthys, with the deceased shown offering to Horus on the right-hand side of the head, and to Horus and the Goddess of the West on the left. From the shoulders to the waist of the right-hand side of the coffin is a tableau of Thoth and a cobra-headed goddess in front of a group of gods, comprising Horus paying homage to a seated mummiform Osiris, who is accompanied by the Goddess of the West and a cobra-headed god, all under the protection of a great snake. Still on the right-hand side, the next tableau shows the deceased adoring a ordinarily-clad Osiris, who is accompanied again by the Goddess of the West, and is followed by a scene showing Isis, Nephthys and the ba-spirit mourning the mummy. The last one, on the right-hand side of the foot, has the deceased and the Goddess of the West before Hathor, who is shown in a sycamore tree, which was particularly sacred to her.

Moving back to the left-hand side of the coffin, the area from the shoulders to the waist has a scene of the separation of Shu and Nut, which is then followed by three further tableaux. The first is similar to the corresponding one on the opposite side of coffin, although Thoth now joins the deceased before Osiris and the Goddess of the West. The second comprises a shrine holding the Four Sons of Horus, while the third shows Tayuhenet making an offering to the goddesses Maat and Hathor, the latter in cow-form emerging from the slope of the Western Mountain. The foot-end of the coffin bears a depiction of the djed-pillar fetish of Osiris. Throughout, each tableau is separated from the adjacent ones by a number of columns of text. (A.M.D.)

拉美西斯二世之子木乃伊

在女唱吟者阿蒙陶漢努（Amun Tayuhenet）（本書編號215）的棺木內躺著的是一名年輕男子的屍體，此男子所屬年代應該比她早300年，屍體如何進入這具棺木至今仍不得而知。倫敦大學的埃及學者瑪格麗特‧莫瑞（Margret Murray）表示，古時候這口棺木可能用來重新埋葬木乃伊。1880年代剛開始在埃及發現木乃伊時，也曾發現過幾處此種埋葬方式的情形，最知名的是在巴哈里發現的皇室與僧侶的木乃伊埋葬處。另一種可能是，此具木乃伊是現代人放進去的，好讓歐洲人看起來覺得比較「有趣」，就像威爾斯親王造訪埃及時所「發現」的木乃伊（本書編號187）一樣。

駐約克大學的歷史頻道木乃伊鑑識系列的研究團隊負責研究此具木乃伊。他們表示此具木乃伊所屬年代為拉美西斯二世統治時期，根據他們分析臉部相似處，判定此木乃伊可能為拉美西斯二世之子，他們的研究也指出此男子死時年約25歲，但研究人員無法找出死因。此名男子有戽斗下巴、不對稱的眼窩以及鷹勾鼻，研究人員認為這是當時埃及皇室的臉部特徵。此具木乃伊呈現了高超的木乃伊製作技術，其中的屍體保存特別完好。研究團隊分析發現古埃及的防腐處理人員使用百里香和進口的開心果樹脂，右側身體以牛油處理，左側身體以綿羊或羔羊油處理。如此豐富的素材以及對細節的考究，可推測肯定是為古埃及精英階級所作的來世準備。（作者：C.R.）

216. 拉美西斯二世之子木乃伊
來自底比斯西岸
新王國時期，第19王朝（西元前1295-1186年）
人體組織，亞麻
1700 x 360 x 290 mm

Ramesside Mummy
From Thebes, West Bank
New Kingdom, Dynasty 19 (1295-1186 BC)
Human tissue, linen

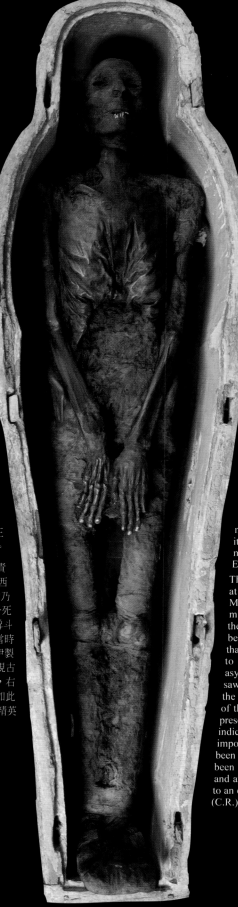

Ramesside Mummy

nside the coffin of the Chantress of Amun Tayuhenet (Catalogue 215) is the body of a young man who lived around 300 years before her. It is unclear how this body came to be in this coffin. Margaret Murray, an Egyptologist at University College London, suggested that the coffin may have been used to rebury the mummy in a cache of mummies in ancient times. There were several of these caches found around the time the mummy came from Egypt in the 1880s. The most famous were caches of royal and priestly mummies found at Deir el-Bahri. The other possibility is that the mummy was placed in the coffin in modern times to make it more interesting to Europeans in a similar manner to the mummy 'found' by the Prince of Wales when he visited Egypt (Catalogue #187).

The mummy was studied by a team of researches based at the University of York for the History Channel series, Mummy Forensics. Their suggestions were that this mummy dated to the reign of Rameses II and, based on their analysis of facial similarities, that the man may have been the son of Rameses II. Their findings also indicated that the man died around the age of 25, but they were unable to establish a clear cause of death. He had an overbite, asymmetrical eye orbits, and a 'hawk' nose, which the team saw as characteristic features of the Egyptian royal family of the time. The mummy itself shows an extremely high level of the mummification technique that resulted in exceptional preservation of the body. The team's analysis of the mummy indicated that the ancient Egyptian embalmers used thyme and imported pistachio resin and that the right side of the body had been treated with fat derived from cattle while the left side had been treated with fat from sheep or goat. Such rich materials and attention to detail would be typical of the treatment given to an elite ancient Egyptian man in preparation for the afterlife. (C.R.)

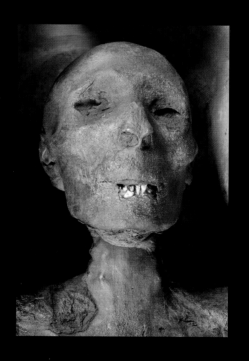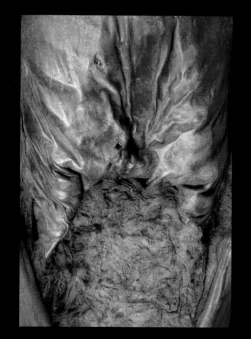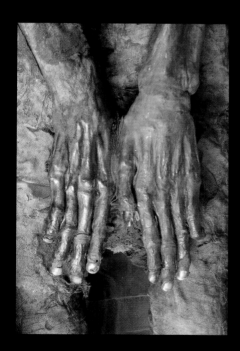

第一章

探索古埃及遺址

持續三千多年繁盛榮景的古埃及文明，直至今日仍令世人驚嘆不已。古埃及在歷史發展過程的多數時間中，皆為統治北非與中東大片領土的世界強國，古埃及除了令人著迷不已的歷史外，還有古埃及文明的知識為何消失的原因，也同樣引人關注，且自其消失後，探索埃及古文明的過程已持續了一千多年。

古埃及社會是完全由國王或法老操作所有功能，數千年來，這種統治方式僅出現過極短暫的中斷時期。埃及國王的統治權，在追隨亞歷山大大帝（Alexander the Great）的希臘人進入埃及後宣告終止，之後由希臘與羅馬統治者接收部分古埃及國王的標誌，但埃及統治者的社會角色則已逐漸削減。古埃及社會的功能，尤其是統治階級之間的社會功能，因希臘人與羅馬人在語言、宗教與政府結構方面引進的重大變化，加上失去自治的能力，而產生了極大的轉變，不過更大的變化，則是出現在基督教與伊斯蘭教等一神宗教進入之後。基督教與伊斯蘭教不同於能融入埃及宗教的希臘與羅馬宗教，其導致更多傳統埃及社會功能消失，以基督教而言，基督教認為傳統的聖書體象形文字（hieroglyphs）系統與宗教信仰有過多關聯，因此倡導以希臘文字書寫埃及語言，伊斯蘭教則是提倡以阿拉伯語替代埃及使用的語言。古老的埃及語與聖書體象形文字系統在伊斯蘭教成為埃及的主要宗教，阿拉伯語成為埃及的主要語言後便逐漸遭到遺忘。

僅管伊斯蘭教佔據中東地區，基督教佔據了歐洲，但對少數人而言，古埃及的異教徒歷史仍充滿神祕感且極具吸引力，可惜早期的探究者缺乏閱讀古代文字的能力，而無法瞭解古埃及的歷史，然而，至西元 1800 年時，因歐洲文化出現了一連串的變化，而創造出一個能深入調查古埃及的環境。在 18 世紀期間的啟蒙時代（the age of Enlightenment）中，知識份子可不受宗教束縛地以科學為依據，自由針對世界進行研究，此外，殖民主義（colonialism）與工業主義（industrialisation）的崛起，更使歐洲人有機會至遠處尋覓資源，以滿足其政治與經濟需求的野心。最後，這些力量皆匯集成拿破崙於 1798 年侵略埃及的行動，此時還有一大群學者與藝術家亦隨著拿破崙的軍隊到達埃及，開始探索埃及與其歷史的各個面向。

在探索埃及歷史方面，拿破崙的侵略戰役導致了兩個重大結果，即出版《埃及記述》（Description de l´Egypte）與發現羅塞塔石碑（Rosetta Stone）。《埃及記述》是一個多冊書籍（原書有 23 冊），書中對於當時拿破崙的學者造訪埃及的情形，以及他們發現的古老紀念碑皆有詳細的描述。

《埃及記述》引發了全歐洲學者與潛在探險家對埃及遙遠歷史的興趣，而由法國人發現，卻遭英國人奪走帶回到英國的羅塞塔石碑，則為解讀古埃及象形文字提供了重大線索。羅塞塔石碑銘刻了希臘文與兩種對照的古埃及文字：世俗體（demotic）與聖書體（hieroglyphs）象形文字，研究者耗費了數十年時間成功解碼聖書體，至 1800 年代末期時，學者已能理解古埃及文字並能重現其歷史。

19 世紀興起的工業主義使中產階級的財富與人口皆獲得增加，由於中產階級開始有能力收藏異國物品，因此 19 世紀初的發現與聖書體的破解，皆使日益茁壯的中產階級對埃及與其古老寶藏產生興趣，同時，中產階級的財富也創造出一批前往埃及觀光旅遊的群眾。此情形使古埃及文明的古老紀念碑及所有能帶得走的遺跡，皆陷入毀滅與消失的威脅中，因此有越來越多人開始認為古埃及的過往，正面臨再次消失的危機，而危機就是這種爭相掠取並將古老遺跡帶回歐洲的情形。

在英國國內，一個以小說家阿曼利亞·愛德華（Amelia Edwards）為首的團體，於 1880 年代初期設立了一個以至埃及挖掘古蹟，達到保存其古老歷史為目的之學會，此學會最初是命名為埃及古物挖掘基金會（Egypt Exploration Fund），之後則改為埃及探索學會（Egypt Exploration Society）。該學會係與埃及政府的埃及文物局局長馬斯佩洛（Gaston Maspero）共同合作，他們的構想是由英國人提供資金給學會，之後則可獲得部分出土文物作為回報，而埃及的國家博物館則是以這些出土文物，作為滿足需求與埃及政府利益的額外補貼。學會係聘用專業的埃及古物學家挖掘遺跡，並完成紀錄其工作情形的科學報告，讓埃及探索學會能據此回復古埃及的生活。

埃及探索學會的創辦者大多為大英帝國、美國的博物館以及私人收藏家，安妮巴洛（Annie Barlow）即是其中一位私人收藏家，她的父親詹姆斯巴洛（James Barlow）是伯頓市（Bolton）一位富有紗廠老闆。安妮巴洛為何會對古埃及產生興趣，如今已不得而知，可能是因為伯頓的紗廠從埃及進口大量棉花，而引起安妮對古老世界、聖經歷史與一般慈善事業的強烈興趣。安妮似乎於極早期即成為埃及探索學會的捐款人，至 1887 年時，已在伯頓地區運作一個當地的埃及探索學會分會，安妮巴洛與其兄長更曾於 1888 年一起造訪埃及，並完成大量記述其經歷的報導。

安妮巴洛亦與學會的主要考古學家威廉富林德斯派崔（William Flinders Petrie）發展出合作關係。派崔是首位開發以科學方式挖掘古蹟的考古學家，其開發的許多方式仍沿用至今，而埃及探索學會早期進行的許多文物開採工作亦皆由其負責，此次展覽展出的許多文物都是在他本人或經他訓練之學生的監督下挖掘出土。派崔是一位個性有趣的考古學者，生活十分簡樸，且工作非常努力，其最著名的事蹟係與阿比多斯（Abydos）遺址的工作有關：當他為探險隊購買了許多罐裝食品，並在當季工作結束時將未吃完的食品埋到地下，並於幾個月後他們再度回到遺址工作時，決定將扔向牆壁而的未爆罐頭食品分給大家吃掉。

安妮巴洛將自己獲得的文物，以及向當地民眾募集而得的文物一起交給伯頓博物館，即之後的查德威博物館（Chadwick Museum），且直至 1941 年辭世之前，安妮巴洛都一直持續為學會工作。安妮巴洛在與伯頓博物館合作初期，便已將獲得的文物以及與埃及探索學會聯絡的責任，轉移給伯頓博物館的首任館長威廉米德俐（William Midgley），而伯頓博物館也一直維持著與埃及探索學會的關係，並持續接收到文物，至 1970 年代埃及結束將部分出土文物授予挖掘者的做法。

由於伯頓博物館與埃及探索學會之間長久的關係，博物館中的大多數館藏文物都是屬於學會發表過的出土文物。至今日，我們也確實因為這些出版品而能瞭解多數文物的出處，事實上許多文物都是放置在古埃及人的墓地或房屋內，並在久遠之後再被挖掘出土。瞭解這些文物與其在古埃及文化中的作用，都是極為珍貴的資料，此外，埃及探索學會的檔案庫中還藏有與出土文物本身有關的無價資訊，包括一段阿瑪納（Amarna）挖掘古物現場，能窺看哈地亞（Hatiay）家門楣的舊影片。此挖掘現場係於 1931 年，由一個大型埃及工團進行開挖與搬移。

文物開挖地點的相關知識還可產生另一個有趣的結果，亦即再一次重新開挖埃及的同一個古老遺址時，往往都能找到更多與這些文物有關的額外資料，例如，波蘭代表在巴哈里（Deirel Bahri）進行的工作，讓部分文物在近期得見天日，本次展覽將展出的圖特摩斯三世（Thutmose III）墓室的原址，即是由他們發現出土。夢妮卡多林斯卡（Monika Dolinska）重建了此墓室的古老擺設，並提供下列描述內容：

英國許多博物館皆藏有從埃及探索學會分得的浮雕局部，這是埃及於 19 世紀末，20 世紀初授予作為學會提供文物開挖之經濟支持的回報。其中一部分屬於圖特摩斯三世位於巴哈里的神殿，則是在多年後由波蘭代表團於清理哈基蘇女王神殿（Temple of Hatshepsut）周圍區域時發現的，而伯頓博物館的 1906.144.1 墓室即屬其中之一。

經過多年的研究後，現在已能重建神殿的平面圖與神殿的場景設計。多數在文物開挖期發現且屬於此神殿的墓室與局部碎片，以及四散於全球各地

博物館的碎片，皆已完成辨識，並於虛擬空間中放回其原來的位置。

沙岩墓室 1906.144.1 是神殿西部，從多柱宮（Hypostyle Hall）通往最南端房間的入口，由於此入口的牆面，為此墓室的東牆，因此挖掘者命名為 G 室，此房間係與皇室祭祀有關的系列房間，且 G 室內更額外設置了皇室祖先的祭祀。本室北面牆上的第一個現場有圖特摩斯三世的父親與圖特摩斯二世（Thutmose II）的雕像，南面牆壁則有圖特摩斯三世的祖父與圖特摩斯一世（Thutmose I）的雕像，因此，能在右邊的圓柱及入口南邊側柱上找到圖特摩斯一世的名字，並在左邊的圓柱與北邊側柱上發現圖特摩斯二世一部分的名字開端。門楣上，還可看見雙重繪畫，包含國王圖特摩斯三世奉獻酒和清水以及成堆的各式貢品，給坐在神座上的太陽神阿蒙（Amun）。這座神殿的入口處還有一個最有趣的部分，是使用兩種不同類的石頭：沙岩與石灰岩，亦即門楣的下半部（包括伯頓博物館收藏的部分）與側柱的下半部分皆是以沙岩製成，而門楣的上半部與側柱的上半部則以石灰岩建造而成。

在埃及久遠歷史的探索中，仍持續揭露出令人興奮的發現與重要資訊，讓我們能更瞭解當時人們在此迷人文明中的生活情形。許多挖出將在本次展覽展出之文物的遺址，目前都仍在持續開挖中，如阿瑪納、阿比多斯和底比斯（Thebes），我們預期這些挖掘計畫將能發現更多與伯頓博物館館藏及全球各地博物館館藏文物有關的資料。本書呈現的最新研究，說明了由埃及考古學先鋒在許久之前發現的重要精選文物，這些獨一無二的文物將能協助我們瞭解這一段人類史中最壯麗輝煌的文化。

卡羅琳 ‧ 勞特利奇
伯頓博物館埃及古物學館長

Chapter 1
Exploration of Ancient Egyptian Sites

For over 3,000 years, ancient Egyptian civilisation flourished and today still astounds the world. For much of its history, ancient Egypt was a world power controlling significant amounts of territory in northern Africa and the Middle East. While we are fascinated with tracing this ancient history, what is as interesting is how knowledge of ancient Egyptian civilisation was lost to the world and is now in the process of being rediscovered over 1,000 years after that loss.

Ancient Egyptian society was very reliant on the role of the king or pharaoh to function fully. For several thousand years, there were only relatively short periods when there were breaks in this rulership. With the coming of the Greeks under Alexander the Great, the rule of indigenous kings came to an end. The Greek and Roman rulers took on some of the trappings of ancient Egyptian kings, but there was a slow erosion of the social role of the Egyptian ruler. The Greeks and Romans introduced significant changes in language, religion, and government structures. The combination of these changes with the loss of self rule caused significant shifts in social practice, particularly among the ruling classes.

Greater changes, however, came with the introduction of the monotheistic religions of Christianity and Islam. Unlike Greek and Roman religion, with which Egyptian religious practices could be integrated, Christianity and Islam promoted the ending of much of traditional Egyptian social practices. In the case of Christianity, it found the traditional writing system of hieroglyphs too connected to religious beliefs to be used and thus promoted the use of Greek letters to write the Egyptian language. Islam, however, promoted the use of Arabic as the language of choice. As Islam took over as the primary religion and Arabic as the primary language in Egypt, the ancient language and its hieroglyphic writing system were forgotten.

With the dominance of Islam in the Middle East and Christianity in Europe, interest in the pagan past of ancient Egypt remained an esoteric interest of a minority. However, without the ability to read the ancient writings, the history of ancient Egypt was not accessible to these early enquirers. However, around AD 1800 a series of changes in European culture created an environment that allowed for a stronger investigation of ancient Egypt. During the 18th Century, the age of Enlightenment gave intellectuals the freedom to approach the world from a scientific basis free from the limitation of religion. Additionally, the rise in colonialism and industrialisation meant that Europeans looked farther afield for resources to fuel both their political and economic ambitions. These forces came together in Napoleon's invasion of Egypt in 1798. Along with his army, Napoleon brought a large group of scholars and artists to Egypt to investigate all aspects of the country and its history.

The two most important outcomes of Napoleon's campaign, from the point of view of the exploration of Egypt's past, were the publication of the Description de l'Egypte and the discovery of the Rosetta Stone. The Description de l'Egypte was a multi-volume set of books (originally 23 volumes) that depicted and described Egypt at the time Napoleon's scholars visited and the ancient monuments they encountered. This work inspired scholars and potential adventurers across Europe to take an interest in Egypt's distant past. The Rosetta Stone, discovered by the French, but captured by the English and taken to England, provided an important clue to the decipherment of ancient Egyptian hieroglyphs. The stone had parallel inscriptions in Greek and two forms of ancient Egyptian script -- demotic and hieroglyphs. It took several decades of study before the hieroglyphs were deciphered, but by the late 1800s ancient Egyptian texts could be understood and history rediscovered.

The 19th Century saw the rise of industrialism and this resulted in an increase in the wealth and size of the middle classes. The discoveries in the early part of the century and the decipherment of hieroglyphs made Egypt and its ancient treasures of interest for an increasing segment of this middle class who had money to spend to collect exotic objects. This wealth also created a group of people who could travel to Egypt as tourists. This situation put the ancient monuments and the portable remains of ancient Egyptian civilisation under threat of destruction and removal. An increasing number of people recognised that the ancient Egyptian past was in risk of being lost again in the race to acquire ancient objects to take back to Europe.

Within Great Britain, one group headed by Amelia Edwards, a novelist, started up a society in the early 1880s in order to conduct excavations in Egypt with the aim of preserving the ancient past. This society was named the Egypt Exploration Fund, later the Egypt Exploration Society. This society co-operated with the Egyptian government's Director of Antiquities, Gaston Maspero. The idea was that individuals in England would give money to the society and in return would receive objects from the excavations that were deemed surplus to the needs and interests of the Egyptian government for their national museum. The society would employ professional Egyptologists to excavate the sites and write scientific reports describing their work. In this way, the Egypt Exploration Society would recover the life of ancient Egypt.

Many of the funders of the Egypt Exploration Society were museums from around the United Kingdom, the United States, and private individuals. One of those private individuals was Annie Barlow. She was the daughter of a wealthy cotton mill owner from Bolton named James Barlow. It is uncertain how Annie Barlow became interested in ancient Egypt, although it can be said that the Barlow mills were importing large quantities of cotton from Egypt and Annie had strong interests in the ancient world, the history of the Bible, and general philanthropy. Annie appears to have been a very early contributor to the Egypt Exploration Society. By 1887, she was running a local branch of the society for the region around Bolton. In 1888, Annie Barlow visited Egypt with her brother and produced a number of reports describing her experiences.

Annie Barlow developed a working relationship with the society's main archaeologist, William Flinders Petrie. Petrie was the first archaeologist to develop scientific methods of excavation, many of which are still used today. He was responsible for many of the excavations conducted by the Egypt Exploration Society in the early years and many of the objects in this exhibition were excavated under his supervision or that of the students he trained. Petrie was a colourful character. He lived simply and worked hard. One of the most famous stories concerning him relates to his work at the site of Abydos. He purchased tinned food for the expedition and at the end of a season of work he buried what they had not consumed. When they returned to resume work months later, he decided they could consume the tinned food if the tins did not explode when thrown against a wall.

Annie Barlow made arrangements for the divisions of finds from her contributions and the contributions she solicited from local people, to be presented to Bolton's Museum, then called the Chadwick Museum. Annie Barlow continued to work for the society until close to her death in 1941. Very early in her relationship with Bolton Museum, Annie Barlow turned over the responsibility for the division of objects and communicating with the Egypt Exploration Society to the first curator in charge of Bolton's Museum, William Midgley. Bolton Museum has retained this relationship with the Egypt Exploration Society and continued to receive divisions into the 1970s, after which time Egypt ended the practice of granting divisions of objects to excavators.

Bolton Museum's long relationship with the Egypt Exploration Society created the situation where the majority of objects in the museum's collection are from excavations that were published by the Society. Today these publications allow us to know exactly where a large number of the objects were discovered. Many objects can be located in the tombs and houses where they were left by the ancient Egyptians and much later discovered by the excavators. This information is invaluable in understanding the object and how it functioned in ancient Egyptian culture. Additionally, the archives of the Egypt Exploration Society contain invaluable information about the excavations themselves. Old film of the excavations at Amarna allow us to see lintel of the house of Hatiay, the cast of which is in this exhibition (catalogue #2), being excavated and moved across the site by a large team of Egyptian workmen in 1931.

Another interesting outcome of knowing where the objects were excavated is that when new excavations are conducted at the ancient sites in Egypt, additional information about these objects is often recovered. One exciting example that has come to light recently is due to the work of the Polish Mission at Deir el

Bahri. They have discovered the original location of the block of Thutmose III that is featured in this exhibition (catalogue # 162). Monika Dolinska, who has reconstructed the ancient setting of this block, contributed the following description:

In many museums in England there are fragments of reliefs distributed by the Egypt Exploration Society in return for the financial support of their excavations in Egypt at the end of the 19th and the beginning of the 20th century. Some of them have appeared to belong to the temple of Thutmose III at Deir el Bahri, discovered many years later by the Polish Mission during the clearance of the area around the Temple of Hatshepsut. The block 1906.144.1 in the Bolton Museum is one of them.

After many years of research it has become possible to reconstruct the plan of the temple and a layout of scenes adorning it. Most blocks and fragments found in the course of excavations of the temple as well as some fragments dispersed in museums around the world have been identified and located (virtually) in the places from which they originally came.

The sandstone block 1906.144.1 comes from the entrance leading from the Hypostyle Hall to the southernmost room in the western part of the temple. The entrance wall is thus the eastern wall of this room, called Room G by the excavators. This room belongs to the set of rooms connected to the royal cult; the Room G additionally houses the royal ancestors cult. The statue of Thutmose II, Thutmose III's father, is represented in the first scene on the north wall of this room and the statue of Thutmose I, Thutmose III's grandfather is represented on the south wall. Accordingly, we can find the name of Thutmose I in the third column of the right, southern jamb of the entrance and the beginning of the name of Thutmose II in the third column of the left, northern jamb. On the lintel we can see the double scene with King Thutmose III presenting wine and fresh water in addition to piles of various offerings to the god Amun seated on the throne. The interesting thing about this temple, also exemplified in this entrance, is that two varieties of stone are used: sandstone and limestone. The lower part of the lintel (including the block in Bolton) and the lower parts of the jambs are made of sandstone while the upper part of the lintel and the upper parts of the jambs are made of limestone.

Exploration of Egypt's distant past continues to reveal exciting discoveries and important information about what life was like for people living in this fascinating civilisation. Many sites where objects in this exhibition were found, such as Amarna, Abydos, and Thebes, are currently being excavated. We can expect that these projects will reveal even more about the objects in Bolton and in museums around the world. This catalogue reveals the latest research about a selection of significant objects discovered long ago by the pioneers of Egyptian archaeology. These unique objects tell us about one of the most spectacular cultures in human history.

Carolyn Routledge
Curator of Egyptology, Bolton Museum

第二章

古埃及歷史概述

緒論：從史前時代到歷史時代

尼羅河谷中最早被發現的人工製品是距今約 30 至 40 萬年的大型石造手斧。這是一段悠長的歷史旅程，從仔細琢磨而成的燧石工具起，歷經古王國時期（the Old Kingdom）以石灰岩、花崗岩及玄武岩所建造的偉大金字塔建築，然後，在好幾百年後，艾德夫（Edfu）、丹德拉（Dendera）等地出現以巨石建構的希臘羅馬式神廟（Graeco-Roman temples）。古埃及歷史是一部生動多樣的故事，帶領我們瀏覽從史前工匠到西元前兩三千年建築師、詩人及藝術家的事蹟，他們的作品預示了雅典和羅馬的古典文明成就，甚至經常使之相形失色。

古文明往往以文物和建築的形式存在，但它們基本上是由人類所建構成，而解剖學意義上的現代人（anatomically modern human）在埃及最早出土的遺骸（1994 年位於上埃及地區，丹德拉附近的塔拉姆薩丘（Taramsa Hill）所發現的某位孩童墓地），其年代距今約 55,000 年。首件人類化石的年代比舊石器時代手斧晚相當多的情況，純粹顯示在考古紀錄中，石頭比骨骸及其他有機物質來得較能完好保存。

埃及接下來的主要文化現象為新石器時代，此時代始於約西元前 5500 年之前，農業開始取代狩獵與採集，成為人類主要的生計。大約在西元前 4500 到 3000 年間被稱為前王國時期（Predynastic period），因為實際上這是最後的史前時期，此後埃及人共組成一個國家，遵循所謂「王朝」的繼承原則（世襲的帝王若非與前任有親屬關係，就是與其主要定居地有關）。

編年架構

在古埃及政治史上，約西元前 3000 年到西元 395 年的這段期間通常分成三個時期：法老時期（the pharaonic period）、托勒密時期（Ptolemaic period）和羅馬時期（Roman period）。其中法老時期（約西元前 3000-332 年）最長，是由連續三十王朝所構成，一般分為早王朝時期（Early Dynastic period）、古王國時期（the Old Kingdom）、第一中間期（the First Intermediate Period）、中王國時期（the Middle Kingdom）、第二中間期（the Second Intermediate Period）、新王國時期（the New Kingdom）、第三中間期（the Third Intermediate Period）及後埃及時期（the Late Period）。其中的三個「中間期」是相當奇怪的階段，部分原因是這些時期經常出現不只一位統治者或王朝同時在埃及不同地區進行統治。

法老時期的統治者及王朝的名字和年代出自於諸多文獻。包括《埃及通史》（Aegyptiaca），由一位名為馬內托（Manetho）的埃及祭司在西元前第三世紀初期所撰寫的，以及時代更早的「帝王世系表」，這些帝王列表大多記載於陵墓與神廟的牆上，但也記錄於莎草紙（papyri）製成的文獻中（例如第十九王朝的杜林國王名冊（Royal Turin Canon）），或是偏遠沙漠中的石刻上（例如刻在瓦地哈馬馬特（Wadi Hammamat）粉砂岩上的名冊）。一般推測馬內托是以這些世系表作為寫作依據。

「傳統的」完整埃及年表傾向仰賴錯綜複雜的文獻記載，將名字、日期和宗譜等資料整合成為一個全面性的歷史架構，這樣的年表在某些時期是較為可信的。有兩則天狼星的「偕日升」（heliacal rising）紀錄是非常重要的文獻，用來判定傳統埃及年表的確切日期。其中一次「偕日升」是發生在第十二王朝（記載於一封來自卡洪城（Kahun）的信，日期為辛努塞爾特三世（Senusret III）在位第七年的第二季，第四月的第十六天）；另一次發生在第十八王朝（記載於底比斯（Theban）的醫療文件〈艾伯斯紙草書〉（Papyrus Ebers），日期為阿蒙霍特普一世（Amenhotep I）在位第九年的第三季，第三月的第九天）。埃及古物學家藉由這兩份文獻所判定出的確切日期，並以中王國及新王國時期其他帝王的在位年限為基礎，推論出整個法老時期的確切日期。這種受到尊崇的傳統編年架構，讓埃及古物學成為最早受益於碳十四測年法的考古學科之一。

埃及史與碳十四測年法

在 1940 年代晚期有一批埃及古物被當作基準，用來評估新發明的碳十四測年法的準確度。由於這些早期測定的年代數據，標準差可達五百年，因此出現了各種讓考古樣本的碳十四測年法技術更為精進的研究，李比（W. F. Libby）率先研發的「固碳」法，首度被檢測技術更為精確的氣體正比計數法及液體閃爍計數法所取代，近年更出現了加速器質譜儀，以極小的樣本就能測定出更精確的結果。

自從專家發現大氣中碳十四濃度會隨磁場變化後，如何找出一條校準曲線（calibration curve）將碳十四測定的年代轉換成精確的日期成為關注的焦點。亞利桑那州的舒曼（E. Schulman）、佛格森（C. W. Ferguson）以及加州拉荷亞區的蘇斯（H. Suess）以紅衫及刺果松年輪的定期碳十四測定為研究基礎，在他們的樹木年輪的研究報告中提出第一條校準曲線。1983 年，一篇愛爾蘭橡樹年輪的碳十四測定報告公布了一條範圍達 6000 年的高精確率校準曲線，徹底改變了考古史。這項非凡的成就帶給北半球整個區域一條可應用的碳十四年代校準曲線。然而，有些問題仍舊存在，在埃及和努比亞（Nubia）測定的碳十四年代，有時明顯與傳統年表不符，而這個情形至今依舊無解。

國王與王朝

許多法老時期的社會及政治結構的主要特性，在早王朝時期（最早的兩個王朝）逐漸顯露出來。此一時期的考古文物及文獻資料大多來自於阿比多斯（Abydos）及薩卡拉（Saqqara）兩地的陵墓。埃及最早的文獻記載有一部分出自於這些帝王及大臣的墓室，大多記載於石碑、木頭製與象牙製標籤、附有雕刻的陶罐，以及陶製印鑑上。根據這些文獻以及碳十四測年的結果，考古學家已可建構出這段時期的粗略年表架構。目前一般大眾認可的第一王朝世系依序為：納美爾（Narmer）、哈（Aha）、哲爾（Djer）、傑特（Djet）、丹（Den）、埃德哲伯（Anedjib）、塞默克霍特（Semerkhet）及卡（Ka'a），而梅奈茨皇后（Queen Merneith）的攝政期可能出現在丹王朝之前或之後。第二王朝初期的帝王可能安葬於薩卡拉，他們的年表較不明確，推測的順序為：霍特普塞海姆威（Hetepsekhemwy）、拉內布（Raneb）、尼內特爾（Nynetjer）、溫內格（Weneg）與塞涅德（Sened）。第二王朝最後兩位統治者為伯里布森（Peribsen）及哈塞海姆（Khasekhemwy），兩人皆葬在阿比多斯。

古王國初期最重要的兩位人物為第三王朝統治者卓瑟（Djoser）以及他的首席建築師印何闐（Imhotep）。卓瑟建於薩卡拉的階梯金字塔是第一座石造埃及陵墓，鑿於金字塔下方的複雜通道包含了一部分最早的皇室浮雕，上面有卓瑟在皇家慶典塞德節（the sed-festival）中邁步前行的形象，並有隼神荷魯斯（Horus）在他上面盤旋保護他。古王國時期的繪畫與浮雕大多來自於陵墓建築，其中第三到第六王朝法老的金字塔坐落於古代首都孟斐斯（Memphis）的大墓場，地點就在現代首都開羅（Cairo）南邊，涵蓋範圍北起阿布拉瓦須（Abu Rawash），南至達休爾（Dahshur）。第四王朝以後，每座皇家陵墓建築通常包含了一座金字塔陵墓（由通道進入，通往一間或更多的墓室），外加一座位於金字塔東面的神殿，以及一條石造堤道往下通往河谷的神廟，推測是法老屍身進行防腐並製成木乃伊的場所。從第五王朝烏納斯（Unas）統治時期開始，金字塔內的通道和墓室以俗稱的「金字塔文」（Pyramid Texts）裝飾，金字塔文是一連串古老的符咒，與國王來世的命運有關。

在第六王朝末期，部分地方省長（nomarchs）資產日趨豐厚的情況，反映在他們裝飾繁華陵墓上，而當時法老的金字塔規模正逐漸縮減。不論古王

國的衰敗是因為環境因素，例如每年灌溉平原的洪水量不足或過多，或是因為社會、政治或經濟的管理不善（也可能是綜合以上所有因素），在後來的第一中間期（約西元前2181-2055年），藝術與建築水準出現明顯的頹勢，首要原因無疑是因為當時不再有任何統治者能強勢地領導優良工匠持續打造品質穩定的葬儀用品。這個時期，某些地方的藝術創作風格反映了國家政治分裂的情形，他們的作品有時因為展現出個人實驗特質，彌補了技術上的偶爾退步，從現代眼光來看，可令人眼睛為之一亮。

中王國時期始於底比斯第十一王朝統治者蒙圖荷泰普二世（Mentuhotep II）將上下埃及再度統一成為一個國家，在他繼任之前，雖然家族已經好幾代稱王，但事實上統治範圍僅限於上埃及的一小塊地區。蒙圖荷泰普在統治晚期，於自己的陵墓位址上建造了一座參拜神殿，坐落於底比斯峭壁西側的海灣，也就是今天的巴哈里（Deir el-Bahri）。就某種意義而言，這座建築具體呈現了他的政治成就，再現古王國時期孟斐斯大墓地的皇家陵墓建築，外加壯觀的階梯柱廊，令人聯想到他祖先在底比斯的神廟。他的繼位者蒙圖荷泰普三世（Mentuhotep III）在位時間相對較短，在巴哈里附近留下一座較小且未完成的墓室建築（雖然另一種推測也頗讓人信服：這座遺跡事實上可能是阿蒙涅姆赫特一世（Amenemhat I）在建造位於利斯特（Lisht）的金字塔之前所建）。第十一王朝的最後一位統治者蒙圖荷泰普四世（Mentuhotep IV）是一位在位更短且模糊的人物，主要是從記錄他採礦考察的銘文中得知他的存在。

第十二王朝的首位統治者為阿蒙涅姆赫特一世，他建立了新首都伊赤塔維（Itj-tawy），位在法雍（Fayum）地區北邊一處尚未發現的地點。第十二王朝的國王在利斯特、達休爾、哈瓦拉（Hawara）及拉罕（Lahun）等地建造金字塔（皆位於法雍及孟斐斯中間的區域），幾乎是回歸古王國時期的傳統，但這些金字塔本身稍小，石工品質較差，且室內通道已不再刻有金字塔文。

第十二王朝是埃及歷史中最穩定的統治家族，約兩百年的統治期間共歷經了八位帝王。杜林國王名冊記載了這些帝王的統治期，也在許多當時的銘文及莎草紙文獻裡獲得證實。在中王國時期（西元前2055-1650年），省長葬於其管轄地的大型石造陵墓，顯示非皇族的墓葬藝術發展到達了巔峰，這些陵墓坐落在中埃及的德爾柏夏（Deir el-Bersha）及班尼哈山（Beni Hasan）等省份，裡面的壁畫作品變得廣大，以便容納摔角及戰爭的壯闊場面（可能取自古王國時期金字塔神廟上的浮雕，至今僅存少許殘片），以及死者收到供品，或是在沼澤中打獵及釣魚等更為傳統的場景。

至西元前17世紀晚期為止，最後一位中王國統治者（第十三王朝晚期）的疆域已往南退至底比斯地區，而東尼羅河三角洲則被亞洲統治者所佔領，俗稱西克索王朝（Hyksos）。西克索王朝將尼羅河三角洲的首都設在亞華尼斯（Avaris）地區，在此地區的德爾達巴（Tell el-Dab'a）所進行的考古挖掘，顯示這些亞洲國王只篡奪並複製傳統埃及的雕塑與浮雕，而以尼羅河為據點的大多數居民，他們的物質文化比較近似銅器時代中期的巴勒斯坦（Palestine）。

埃及在驅逐了西克索統治者後，展開了超過400年的社經穩定期：新王國時期。這個時期，埃及與愛琴海及近東文明的貿易與外交快速成長，呈現勢不可擋的局面。新王國法老的神殿遺跡坐落於底比斯西岸，其中最早的一座是位於巴哈里的哈謝普蘇皇后（Queen Hatshepsut）陵墓。帝王谷（Valley of the Kings）及皇后谷（Valley of the Queens）則為新王國法老的最終安息處，其中第十八王朝初期圖特摩斯一世（Thutmose I，約西元前1500年）的陵墓走道稍為錯綜迂迴，而單一斜降的通道盡頭，則是第二十王朝的最後一位統治者拉美西斯十一世（Ramesses XI，約西元前1070年）的墓室。法老陵墓中的神話場景，相較於高級官員及皇家墓室工人的墓室裡所出現的家庭生活及葬禮安排等更為私人的細節，形成某種程度的對比。這些私人場景出現在位於科內穆萊（Qurnet Murai）、謝赫阿卜杜勒古爾奈（Sheikh Abd el-Qurna）及阿薩西夫（Asasif）等高級官員陵墓裡，以及位於麥地納（Deir el-Medina）的皇室墓室工人的墓室中。

雖然底比斯已成為埃及新王國時期的精神中心，第十八王朝的行政中心如同早期王朝的大部分情況，仍舊設在孟斐斯城的北邊，在今天的開羅附近，為王室的定居地。近來對新王國時期孟斐斯大墓地的調查，發現了部分第十八王朝高級官員的陵墓，包括軍方指揮官（後成為國王）哈瑞赫柏（Horemheb）、首相馬亞（Maya）以及大臣亞佩爾（Aper-el）。

新王國時期最不尋常的階段無疑是西元前十四世紀中期阿肯納頓（Akhenaten）的統治時期，又稱為阿瑪納時期（Amarna period）。他在開始統治的幾年後，王名尚為阿蒙霍特（Amenhotep）時，就已著迷於膜拜阿頓神（Aten，字面上的意義為「日輪」），這是比傳統埃及諸神更為抽象的神祇。最後他將自己的王名改成阿肯納頓（意指「他是阿頓神的權威代表」），並建立了阿肯納頓城（意指「阿頓神的地平線」）作為新首都，這座城市位於中埃及一處尚未開發的處女地，今日名為阿瑪納（el-Amarna）的地方。雖然阿瑪納時期「異教崇拜」背後的真正動機不明，但顯然這種對阿頓神的膜拜，在某種程度上是符合邏輯的結果，因為在先前的王朝時期，膜拜太陽的情況已經逐漸流行起來；但同樣很顯然地，阿瑪納時期發生的文化改變，絕大部份是阿肯納頓自己的構想。他的繼任者圖坦卡門（Tutankhamun）、埃（Aye），以及哈瑞赫柏明顯花了很多時間恢復傳統的藝術形式及信仰。

在歷經阿瑪納時期以及餘波盪漾的階段後，接著是第十九和第二十王朝，俗稱拉美西斯時期（Ramessid period），因為這個時期的十一位法老皆以拉美西斯（Ramesses）為名（意指「太陽神拉（Ra）所生」）。在拉美西斯時期，尼羅河三角洲東邊的皮拉美西斯（Piramesse）建立了新的皇居，緊鄰亞華尼斯（Avaris）古城的北方，但在第二十一到二十三王朝時，這個地區的大部分浮雕和雕像被移至附近的壇尼斯（Tanis）城裡的神廟中重覆使用，當時「利比亞時期」（Libyan period）的統治者企圖在該城創建一座北方版本的阿蒙（Amun）神廟。

在西元前一千年，埃及只有幾個時期是完全由土生土長的埃及人所統治，其他時期則受制於接連不斷的外族統治者，包括第三中間期利比亞人的穩定滲透，以及努比亞人、亞述人和波斯人的軍事佔領。自第二十一王朝起，帝王已不再埋葬於西底比斯，因此這些帝王陵墓或木乃伊經常無法遺留下來。第三中間期時，帝王谷中孤立的石窟墓穴被神殿周圍所鑿出的小型家族墓穴所取代，顯示皇室葬儀已有大幅變動，可能是帶有利比亞血統的法老所導致的。位於壇尼斯三角洲地區的阿蒙神廟內就有一群像這樣的家族墓穴，有些仍藏有皇族木乃伊以及數量頗豐的葬儀用品，在1939年由皮耶·蒙特（Pierre Montet）考古挖掘出來，

後埃及時期最精緻的非皇室藝術，部分出自於門特姆赫特（Mentuemhet）的陵墓，西元前七世紀正值第二十五王朝的庫什（Kushite）帝王首度被入侵的亞述人推翻，王位由位於尼羅河三角洲薩伊斯（Sais）的第二十六王朝統治者取而代之，在這段混沌不安的時期，門特姆赫特這位傑出人物掌控了底比斯地區。不過，門特姆赫特以及其他第二十五、二十六王朝的底比斯官員，例如帕巴薩（Pabasa）及伊比（Iby），他們的「仿古」陵墓所展現出創新性與一致性，將陵墓引用各種墓室裝飾的事實給掩蓋住。以其中一個最極端的仿古墓室為例，第二十六王朝晚期的大臣尼斯帕卡舒地（Nespakashuty）接手改建了一座第十一王朝的墳墓，他以舉貢品挑夫（offering bearers）的場景裝飾墓室內部牆壁，仿造遠溯至第四王朝的墓室藝術。

西元前525年春天，阿契美尼王朝（Achaemenid）的岡比西斯二世（Cambyses II，西元前525-522年）在佩魯修姆（Pelusium）打敗了埃及國王普薩美提克三世（Psamtek III，西元前526-525年）的軍隊，繼續拿下孟斐斯。接下來的第一波斯統治時期（First Persian Period，或第二十七王朝，西元前525-404年）所傳世的文獻中，最有趣的莫過於一篇銘刻在烏迦荷瑞斯尼（Udjahorresnet）雕像上的長篇文章（收藏於梵諦岡的葛利果埃及美術館（Museo Gregoriano Egizio），158）。烏迦荷瑞斯尼是一位埃及祭司兼醫師，資料顯示他與新的政權合作，但有些資料證明他也照應當地習俗，維持他的家鄉薩伊斯城（Sais）對女神奈斯（Neith）的膜拜。1990年代，捷克考古學家在阿布西爾（Abusir）發現烏迦荷瑞斯尼的井狀墓穴並挖掘出來。

埃及短暫回到埃及人統治後（第三十王朝），又陷入第二次的波斯統治期，從西元前343年到西元前332年亞歷山大大帝（Alexander the Great）

抵達埃及為止，歷經十年的統治期。政策上，亞歷山大大帝將自己塑造成埃及國王，將新的施政管理有效地轉移至埃及既有的政治宗教結構上，繼任的托勒密王朝帝王各懷著不同程度的野心延續這些政策，達到或多或少的成效。在希臘羅馬時期，神殿的建造與裝飾工程仍積極持續著，然而埃及文化中有許多傳統卻逐漸式微。托勒密法老的陵墓至今尚未發現，他們的墓地可能位於托勒密首都亞歷山大城的某處，顯示托勒密王朝由埃及往地中海地區進行疆域統整，而非朝非洲或西亞地區擴張。

托勒密一世（Ptolemy I）根據既有的奧塞里斯─阿匹斯神（Osiris-Apis）崇拜儀式，發展出塞拉皮斯神（Serapis）的新興宗教膜拜，希望能藉此達到政治統一，但結果卻出現女神伊西斯（Isis）信仰的風潮，並傳播至埃及境外。後埃及時期（西元前 712-332 年），埃及軍隊內向來包含了數量龐大的希臘傭兵，因此早在亞歷山大大帝抵達埃及前，埃及人就對馬其頓人及希臘人毫不陌生。然而，托勒密王朝不再受人民愛戴，西元前 208 年至西元前 186 年，以及西元前 88 年至西元前 86 年間，底比斯地區發生多起反叛事件。隨著王朝逐漸衰弱，托勒密皇室對羅馬的倚賴日趨漸深。克麗奧佩脫拉七世（Cleopatra VII，西元前 51-30 年）身為托勒密十二世（Ptolemy XII，西元前 55-51 年）女兒兼托勒密十三世（Ptolemy XIII，西元前 51-47 年）姐姐及妻子，她的所作所為給了羅馬皇帝奧古斯都（Augustus，西元前 30 年－西元 14 年）征服埃及的藉口。奧古斯都在西元前 30 年 8 月 30 日自立為法老，此後將埃及視為帝國的領土，而非羅馬的一省。後來繼任的羅馬皇帝仍讓埃及維持這種特殊的狀態。

表面上，羅馬的統治是托勒密時期的延續（希臘文仍為官方語言，而亞歷山大城仍為行政首都），只是不再有皇室定居埃及。這種情況造成重大的影響，讓埃及無意積極創造財富，而實際上埃及完全被羅馬當成遠方的糧食供應地。托勒密王朝引進的灌溉系統經改良後，獲得羅馬政府充分利用，埃及所產的糧食以賦稅形式被徵收，若出現短缺，則負責徵收的官員本人須負法律責任。

馬可·奧里略皇帝（Marcus Aurelius，西元 161-180 年）在位期間，埃及遭受一場嚴重的瘟疫肆虐，導致人口大幅下降。這個情形到了塞普蒂米烏斯·塞維魯（Septimius Severus，西元 193-211 年）在位時才稍微緩和。他重整地方政府，並進行各種建築工程，特別是修復底比斯的門農石像（Colossi of Memnon）。以希臘居民為主的法雍地區仍舊受到羅馬觀光客的青睞（他們需要特別許可才能入境），但根據西元四世紀的證據顯示，這個地區的人口同樣面臨逐漸減少的情況。西元 384 年，狄奧多西（Theodosius，西元 379-395 年）下令關閉所有異教神廟，並規定所有人民篤信基督教。在他統治末期，羅馬帝國最後分裂成東羅馬與西羅馬兩個自治區，傳統上，這個時期被視為「古埃及」歷史的結束，科普特（Coptic，拜占庭）時期的開始。

文化變遷

歷經近兩世紀的考古挖掘後，現在我們能夠描繪埃及在政治方面的歷史輪廓，還有物質文化方面的主要變化歷程。不同於前述的歷史概述，物質文化上的描述不著重於特定人物的職業或成就，而在於工藝品的形式變化，以及技術上的一連串發展與革新。

我們一般認知的埃及史前時期最初期（舊石器時代）的物質文化，重點大多在石製工具及武器的製造，以及最早發現的矽石礦場，例如位在納茲利卡特（Nazlet Khate）及薩卡拉的礦區（距今約 40,000 年）。不過，更多樣化的工藝技術自新石器時代遺留下來。除了人工培育的動植物以及陶器的出現（大部分的文化將這兩項因素視為新石器時代的特徵），也有跡象顯示工藝技術是採用有機素材進行製作，例如籃子編織、繩子編製，以及骨製用品打磨。

在進入前王國時期之前，埃及人的灌溉技術已有所進步，提升了尼羅河谷的農業生產力。他們在這個時期也製造了大量的石製容器，擁有無與倫比的陶器製作技術（西元前 3800-3500 年間，位於希拉康波利斯（Hierakonpolis））。最晚從內加達（Naqada）時期起，埃及人就懂得釀造啤酒和種植葡萄。他們也能夠建造籬笆、為建築上漆、煉銅（西元前 4000 年之前）、開採金礦，並將鉛、金與銀製成物品。籃子及繩子的部分編織技術開始運用於織品生產，採用的是亞麻紗。最早的地織機（或「水平式」織機）繪畫出現於巴達里時期（Badarian period）（約西元前 4500-3800 年）；這幅畫被描繪在一件陶器上，顯示紡織機是在兩根橫杆的兩端各打椿固定，經線在中間來回穿梭；紡織機中間的三條桿子可能分別是固定棒、綜絖棒及某種型式的打棒。同時大約在此時期第一件彩陶器製成，最初用來做成簡單的珠串，後來運用在小型動物雕像上。

然而，前王國時期的各項發展中，最能明顯預示法老時期的到來，莫過於越趨頻繁使用的圖像與符號，這些圖像符號據推測是象形文字的前身。在西元前四千年中期之前，埃及人所使用的圖像符號已進入複雜寫作系統的最初階段。目前現存最早的莎草紙（可惜未有書寫）是在第一王朝的赫瑪卡（Hemaka）位於薩卡拉的陵墓（約西元前 3000 年）裡發現的。早期王國時期出現了第一批為權貴打造的陵墓，這些墓穴包括了石造建築，位於亞斯文（Aswan）的花崗岩採石場開始啟用，而銅製專業工具也開始用於木工上。早期王國時期的其它發展包括引進染線與染布，以及出現最早的葡萄酒釀造證據。第二王朝（約西元前 2890-2686 年）之前，埃及已引進聞名的人造木乃伊製作方法，雖然更多證據顯示木乃伊製作最早可追溯至西元前五千年（完全端看「木乃伊化」或「屍體防腐」要如何定義）。嘉娜·瓊斯（Jana Jones）研究了位於巴達里（Badari）及莫斯塔傑達（Mostagedda）的新石器時代墓穴裡厚實乾燥的團狀繃帶，指出松香油浸泡過的繃帶，早在前王國時期初期就已運用在屍體處理上。然而就如瓊斯所言：「埃及最早時期包裹屍體的行為是否表現出人為保存屍體的企圖，或者這種行為是否為另一種墓葬儀式特色，皆尚未定論。」

自第三王朝（約西元前 2686-2613 年）起，埃及開始大規模開採石灰岩礦，主要用於金字塔的建造。在這個時期也出現了最早的層壓木板證據。第四王朝（約 2613-2494 年）之前，「埃及藍」（Egyptian blue）已開始作為雕塑材料及顏料，並出現了現存最早的彩陶工坊（位於阿比多斯）。約於此一時期，木乃伊製作的技術，至少對權貴遺體的處理而言，已開始包含內臟取出及脫水處理。製陶轉盤在第五王朝（西元前 2494-2345 年）之前就引進埃及，雖然一直到第一中間期（約西元前 2160-2055 年）才開始普及使用。

自第十一王朝（約西元前 2055-1985 年）起，埃及開始開採砂岩礦作為建築及雕塑材料。中王國時期（約西元前 2055-1650 年）以前，除腦術（excerebration，腦部移除）已成為木乃伊製作過程之一在此時，這種技術的應用對象已擴大至「中產階級」。將黃金顆粒細加工處理的技術也在這個時期引進。新王國時期初期出現了最早的埃及木材車削技術，並引進煉銅用的液態排渣爐。至少在圖特摩斯三世（西元前 1479-1425 年）在位之前，埃及人就能處理（甚至製造）玻璃，可能是採用了早期在近東國家米坦尼（Mitanni）所發展的技術。大約西元前 1500 年時，埃及出現了第一架直立式織機。這種直立式（或「雙橫杆」）織機，不像水平式織機佔著地面打椿，通常靠在牆邊，織布者則由底部往上進行作業，較低的橫杆不是置於地面淺坑處，就是放在有溝槽的磚塊上（在部分新王國時期的房子裡保有類似遺跡）。

後埃及時期（西元前 664-332 年）之前，埃及已發展專業的煉金術，而自西元前 600 年起，鍛鐵技術已經相當普遍。在托勒密時期初期（西元前第四世紀）的一座神殿裡，首度描繪了一塊木製品在車床上加工的畫面（雖然車床可能早在新王國時期就應用了）。托勒密時期引進了壓挑編籃法。在西元一世紀之前，棉花普遍用於紡織品，逐漸取代亞麻。

雖然古埃及往往被視為最保守又棘手的文明之一，但所有關於尼羅河谷地的物質文化研究都指出，埃及人能高度接納新的生產方式與創新技術，必要時將新素材發揮到極致。埃及的政治社會系統在本質上無疑是非常僵化而持久的，但不應讓我們無視他們在物質文化上所展現的活力與彈性。

依恩·蕭
利物浦大學資深講師

Chapter 2
Overview of Ancient Egyptian History

Introduction: From Prehistory to History

The earliest artefacts in the Nile Valley are finds of large stone hand-axes currently dated at about 400-300,000 BP. It is a long journey from the painstaking knapping of flint and chert tools to the stupendous limestone, granite and basalt pyramid complexes of the Old Kingdom, and, many centuries later, the vast stone Graeco-Roman temples at such sites as Edfu and Dendera. The history of ancient Egypt is a vivid and diverse narrative that takes us from prehistoric tool-makers to the architects, poets and artists of the third and second millennia BC, whose monuments prefigure, and frequently even overshadow, the achievements of Classical civilization in Athens and Rome.

Ancient civilizations may survive primarily in the form of objects and buildings, but they are ultimately composed of people, and the earliest known remains of an anatomically modern human in Egypt (the burial of a child discovered in 1994 at the Upper Egyptian site of Taramsa Hill, near Dendera) date to about 55,000 BP. The fact that the first fossilised remains of people are considerably later than the finds of Palaeolithic hand-axes is simply a reflection of the fact that stone has tended to survive much better than bone and other organic materials in the archaeological record.

The next major cultural phenomenon in Egypt was the Neolithic period, when agriculture began to replace hunting and gathering as the main subsistence strategy, from about 5500 BC onwards. The period between about 4500 and 3000 BC is known as the Predynastic period because it was essentially the last prehistoric epoch before the Egyptian people became united into one nation under the rule of a succession of so-called Dynasties (sets of kings linked either by kinship or by the location of their main place of residence).

The Chronological Framework

Ancient Egyptian political history from c.3000 BC to c.AD 395 is traditionally divided into three sections: the pharaonic, Ptolemaic and Roman periods. By far the longest of the three was the pharaonic period (c.3000-332 BC), which was made up of a sequence of thirty dynasties, conventionally grouped into the Early Dynastic period, the Old Kingdom, the First Intermediate Period, the Middle Kingdom, the Second Intermediate Period, the New Kingdom, the Third Intermediate Period and the Late Period. The three 'intermediate periods' have proved to be particularly awkward phases, partly because there was often more than one ruler or dynasty reigning simultaneously in different parts of the country.

The names and relative dates of the various rulers and Dynasties in the pharaonic period are derived from a number of textual sources. These range from the Aegyptiaca, a history compiled by an Egyptian priest called Manetho in the early 3rd century BC, to the much earlier 'king-lists', which were lists of the names of rulers mainly recorded on the walls of tombs and temples, but also occurring in the form of papyri (such as the Dynasty 19 document known as the Royal Turin Canon) or remote desert rock inscriptions (such as the list in the Wadi Hammamat siltstone quarries). It is usually presumed that Manetho himself used king-lists of these types as his sources.

The 'traditional' absolute chronology of Egypt tends to rely on complex webs of textual references, combining such elements as names, dates and genealogical information into an overall historical framework which is more reliable in some periods than in others. The two most important documents for assigning absolute dates to the traditional Egyptian chronological framework, are two records of the 'heliacal rising' of the dog-star Sirius, one dating to Dynasty 12 (a letter from Kahun, written on day 16, month 4 of the second season in year 7 of the reign of Senusret III) and the other dating to Dynasty 18 (Papyrus Ebers, a Theban medical document from day 9, month 3 of the 3rd season of year 9 in the reign of Amenhotep I). By assigning absolute dates to each of these documents, Egyptologists have been able to extrapolate a set of absolute dates for the whole of the pharaonic period, on the basis of records of the lengths of reign of the other kings of the Middle and New Kingdoms. Because of its well-respected traditional chronological framework, Egyptology was one of the first archaeological disciplines to benefit from radiocarbon dating.

Egyptian History and Radiocarbon Dating

In the late 1940s, a series of Egyptian artefacts were used as a bench-mark in order to assess the reliability of the newly invented radiocarbon dating technique. Since those early dates, with their wide standard deviations of up to five centuries, various technical refinements have been made in the measurement of C-14 in archaeological samples, and the 'solid carbon' method, pioneered by W.F. Libby, has given way firstly to the more precise gas-proportional and liquid-scintillation techniques of measurement, and, more recently, to accelerator mass spectrometry, providing even better results on the basis of extremely small samples.

Ever since the discovery of secular variations in the C-14 content of the atmosphere, the major preoccupation has been the need for a calibration curve to convert any given radiocarbon date into a precise and accurate calendar date. The first calibration curves were provided by the dendrochronological work of E. Schulman and C. W. Ferguson in Arizona and H. Suess in La Jolla, California, based on the routine radiocarbon dating of rings from the sequoia and bristlecone pine. In 1983 the publication of a 6000-year high-precision calibration curve based on the measurement of radiocarbon in tree rings from Irish oaks totally transformed the situation. This remarkable achievement had the effect of providing a radiocarbon curve of proven applicability to the whole northern hemisphere. Concerns, however, have still been expressed that the available radiocarbon dates for Egypt and Nubia sometimes appear to differ significantly from the conventional chronology, and this situation remains unresolved.

Kings and Dynasties

During the Early Dynastic period (the first two dynasties), many of the major aspects of the social and political structure of the pharaonic period emerged. Most of the archaeological and textual material pertaining to this period derives from the cemeteries of Abydos and Saqqara. The tombs of kings and high officials have yielded some of the earliest Egyptian textual evidence, primarily in the form of stone stelae, wooden and ivory labels, inscribed pottery jars and clay seal impressions. On the basis of these documents, together with the evidence of radiocarbon dating, archaeologists have been able to construct a rough chronological structure for the period. The sequence of Dynasty 1 kings is now widely accepted as Narmer, Aha, Djer, Djet, Den, Anedjib, Semerkhet and Ka'a, with Queen Merneith serving as a regent, probably either before or after the reign of Den. The chronology of the early Dynasty 2 kings, who were probably buried at Saqqara, is more nebulous, perhaps taking the form: Hetepsekhemwy, Raneb, Nynetjer, Weneg and Sened. The last two rulers of Dynasty 2 were Peribsen and Khasekhemwy, both buried at Abydos.

The early years of the Old Kingdom are dominated by two figures: the Dynasty 3 ruler Djoser and his chief architect Imhotep. Djoser's Step Pyramid at Saqqara was the first stone-built Egyptian tomb, and the labyrinth of corridors carved out below the pyramid complex contained some of the earliest royal reliefs, showing the striding figure of Djoser engaged in the celebration of the sed-festival (royal jubilee), with the falcon-god Horus hovering protectively above him. The majority of Old Kingdom paintings and reliefs derive from funerary monuments, including the pyramid complexes of the Dynasty 3-6 pharaohs in the necropolis of the ancient capital, Memphis, just to the south of modern Cairo, stretching from Abu Rawash in the north to Dahshur in the south. From Dynasty 4 onwards, each royal funerary complex consisted of a pyramidal tomb (entered through corridors leading to one or more burial chambers) with a mortuary temple on its east face, and a stone causeway leading down to the valley temple, where the embalming and mummification of the pharaoh may have taken place. Starting in the reign of the Dynasty 5 ruler Unas, the internal corridors and chambers were decorated with the so-called Pyramid Texts, a set of ancient spells concerned with the fate of the king in the afterlife.

At the end of Dynasty 6, the growing prosperity of some of the provincial governors (nomarchs) is reflected in the rich decoration of their tombs, at a time when the pyramid complexes of the pharaohs were diminishing in size. Whether the Old Kingdom state went into decline because of environmental reasons — such as an insufficiency or excess of annual flood-waters over the fields — or because of social, political or economic mismanagement (or perhaps a combination of all of these factors), there is a perceptible decline in the standards of art and architecture during the succeeding First Intermediate Period (c.2181-2055 BC), no doubt primarily because there was no longer a single ruler strong enough to maintain a central workforce of skilled craftsmen producing funerary equipment of a consistent quality. During this period the political fragmentation of the country is mirrored in the emergence of a number of provincial artistic styles, the occasional technical deficiencies of which are sometimes balanced by a sense of individual experimentation that can be refreshing to the modern eye.

The Middle Kingdom began with the reunification of Upper and Lower Egypt into a single state by the Theban Dynasty 11 ruler Mentuhotep II, whose family had claimed the kingship for several generations although they had, until his reign, only controlled a small area of Upper Egypt. In his later years Mentuhotep constructed a cult temple over the site of his tomb in a bay of the western Theban cliffs known today as Deir el-Bahri. This complex was in one sense an architectural crystallization of his political successes, combining a revival of the Old Kingdom royal funerary monuments of the Memphite necropolis with a spectacular sequence of columned terraces reminiscent of the mortuary chapels of his Theban ancestors. His immediate successor, Mentuhotep III, enjoyed a comparatively short reign and perhaps left behind a smaller, unfinished funerary complex in the vicinity of Deir el-Bahri (although it has been persuasively argued that this monument might actually have been built for Amenemhat I prior to the construction of his pyramid complex at Lisht). The last Dynasty 11 ruler, Mentuhotep IV, was an even more ephemeral and shadowy figure, known primarily from the inscriptions recording his quarrying expeditions.

The first Dynasty 12 ruler, Amenemhat I, established a new capital, Itj-tawy, at a still-undiscovered site somewhere to the north of the Fayum region. The pyramid complexes of the Dynasty 12 rulers, at Lisht, Dahshur, Hawara and Lahun (all situated in the region between the Fayum and Memphis), were very much a return to the traditions of the Old Kingdom, although the pyramids themselves were somewhat smaller, the masonry was of a poorer quality and the interior corridors were no longer inscribed with the Pyramid Texts.

Dynasty 12 was the most stable ruling family in the history of Egypt, consisting of the reigns of eight kings covering a period of about 200 years. The lengths of these reigns are listed in the Turin Royal Canon, and they have been broadly corroborated by many contemporary inscriptions and papyri. The funerary art of non-royal individuals during the Middle Kingdom (2055-1650 BC) reached its peak in the large rock-tombs of the governors buried at provincial sites such as Deir el-Bersha and Beni Hasan in Middle Egypt, where the repertoire of wall-paintings was enlarged to embrace large-scale depictions of wrestling and warfare (perhaps deriving from reliefs in Old Kingdom pyramid temples, only a few fragments of which have survived) alongside more traditional scenes, such as the deceased receiving offerings or hunting and fishing in the marshes.

By the late 17th century BC, the last Middle Kingdom rulers (the late 13 Dynasty) had retreated south to the Theban region, and the eastern Delta region was taken over by Asiatic rulers - the so-called 'Hyksos'. The excavations at Tell el-Dab'a, the site of Avaris, the Hyksos capital in the Delta, suggest that these Asiatic kings simply usurped and copied traditional Egyptian sculptures and reliefs, while the material culture of many of the people inhabiting their Delta strongholds was more typical of Middle Bronze Age Palestine.

After the expulsion of the Hyksos rulers, Egypt embarked on more than 400 years of economic and social stability: the New Kingdom. During this time there was an apparently inexorable growth in trade and diplomatic contacts with the Aegean and Near Eastern civilisations. On the west bank at Thebes are the remains of the temples dedicated to the funerary cults of the New Kingdom pharaohs, the earliest being that of Queen Hatshepsut at Deir el-Bahri. In the Valley of the Kings and the Valley of the Queens were the last resting places of the New Kingdom pharaohs, ranging from the gently curving passages of the early Dynasty 18 tomb of Thutmose I (c.1500 BC) to the single monumental descending corridor that led to the burial-chamber of Ramesses XI, the last ruler of Dynasty 20 (c.1070 BC). The mythological scenes in the pharaohs' tombs contrast to some extent with the more intimate details of family life and funerary arrangements in the tombs of high officials at Qurnet Murai, Sheikh Abd el-Qurna and Asasif and those of the royal tomb-workers at Deir el-Medina.

While Thebes appears to have been the spiritual focus of New Kingdom Egypt, the administrative centre of Dynasty 18 - as in many earlier periods - was the northern city of Memphis, near modern Cairo, where the royal Residence was situated. Recent investigations at the New Kingdom necropolis of Memphis have revealed the tombs of some Dynasty 18 high officials, including the military commander (and later king) Horemheb, the chancellor Maya and the vizier Aper-el.

The most unusual phase of the New Kingdom was undoubtedly the time of Akhenaten in the mid-14th century BC - the so-called Amarna period. After the first few years of his reign, when he was still known as Amenhotep, he appears to have developed an obsession with the cult of the Aten (literally the 'sun-disc'), a considerably more abstract deity than the traditional Egyptian pantheon, and eventually changed his name to Akhenaten ('he who is effective on the Aten's behalf') and established the city of Akhetaten ('horizon of the Aten') as a new capital, built on virgin ground at the site now known as el-Amarna, in Middle Egypt. Although the precise motivations behind the 'heresies' of the Amarna period are uncertain, it is nevertheless apparent that the cult of the Aten was to some extent a logical outcome of the gradual growth in the solar cult in the preceding reigns; it is equally apparent, however, that much of the cultural change which took place in the Amarna period was a product of the mind of Akhenaten himself. His successors, Tutankhamun, Aye and Horemheb, clearly wasted little time in restoring traditional forms of art and worship.

The Amarna period and its immediate aftermath were followed by Dynasties 19 and 20, now known as the Ramessid period, on the basis that eleven of the pharaohs during this period took the name of Ramesses ('Ra has engendered him'). During the Ramessid period, a new royal Residence was established at Piramesse in the eastern Delta, immediately to the north of ancient Avaris, but many of the reliefs and statues from this site were moved in Dynasties 21 - 23 to be reused in the temples of the nearby city of Tanis, where the rulers of the 'Libyan period' attempted to create a northern version of the precinct of Amun.

During the 1st millennium BC there were only a few periods of completely indigenous Egyptian rule, as the country fell victim to a succession of foreign rulers, from the steady infiltration of Libyans during the Third Intermediate Period to the military conquests of the Nubians, Assyrians and Persians. From Dynasty 21 onwards, kings were no longer buried in western Thebes; consequently, in most cases neither their tombs nor their mummies have survived. In the Third Intermediate Period, the isolated rock-cut tombs of the Valley of the Kings were replaced by small family vaults excavated within the precincts of temples, suggesting that a major change in royal funerary practices had taken place, probably as a result of the Libyan origins of the pharaohs concerned. A set of such vaults, some of which still contained royal mummies and substantial amounts of funerary equipment, were excavated by Pierre Montet in the temple of Amun at the Delta-site of Tanis in 1939.

Some of the finest non-royal art of the Late Period derives from the tomb of Mentuemhet, a remarkable individual who retained power over the Theban region throughout the tumultuous period in the 7th century BC when the Kushite kings of Dynasty 25 were first overthrown by an Assyrian invasion and then replaced by Dynasty 26 rulers at Sais in the Delta. The 'archaizing' tombs of Mentuemhet and other Dynasty 25 - 26 Theban officials, such as Pabasa and Iby, are, however, all characterized by a sense of freshness and internal consistency that belies the variety of their sources. In one of the most extreme cases of archaism, the late Dynasty 26 vizier Nespakashuty took over and remodelled a Dynasty 11 tomb, decorating its interior walls with scenes of offering bearers that harked back as far as Dynasty 4 funerary art.

In the spring of 525 BC, the Achaemenid ruler Cambyses II (525-522 BC) defeated the armies of the Egyptian king Psamtek III (526-525 BC) at Pelusium and went on to capture Memphis. The most interesting single document surviving from the ensuing First Persian Period (or Dynasty 27, 525-404 BC) is a long text inscribed on the statue of Udjahorresnet (Vatican, Museo Gregoriano Egizio, 158), an Egyptian priest and doctor who appears to have collaborated with the new regime, although there is some evidence that he looked after such local interests as the maintenance of the cult of the goddess Neith at his home-city of Sais. In the 1990s, Udjahorresnet's shaft-tomb was discovered and excavated by Czech archaeologists at Abusir.

After a brief period of renewed indigenous rule (Dynasty 30), Egypt was subject to a second period of Persian domination, covering the decade between 343 BC and the arrival of Alexander the Great in 332 BC. The policy pursued by Alexander the Great, in which he portrayed himself as an Egyptian ruler and effectively grafted the new administration onto the existing political and religious structure, appears to have been followed by his Ptolemaic successors with varying degrees of enthusiasm and success. The construction and decoration of temples continued unabated during the Graeco-Roman period, but there were many other traditional aspects of Egyptian culture that went into decline. None of the tombs of the Ptolemaic pharaohs has been discovered, although it is likely that their necropolis was located somewhere within the Ptolemaic capital at Alexandria, the very position of which indicated the Ptolemies' realignment of Egypt towards the Mediterranean region rather than Africa or Western Asia.

Ptolemy I devised the new religious cult of Serapis from the existing worship of Osiris-Apis, hoping perhaps to use it as a unifying political force, but in practice it was the cult of the goddess Isis that grew and spread from Egypt. The Macedonians and other Greeks were already familiar to the Egyptians long before the arrival of Alexander, since the Egyptian army in the Late Period (712-332 BC) had invariably included large numbers of Greeks as mercenaries. Ptolemaic rule, however, did not remain popular, and there were revolts in the Theban area in 208-186 BC and 88-86 BC. As Ptolemaic rule weakened, so the Ptolemies relied ever more heavily on Rome. Eventually the actions of Cleopatra VII (51-30 BC), the daughter of Ptolemy XII (55-51 BC) and sister-wife of Ptolemy XIII (51-47 BC), provided a pretext for the Roman conquest of Egypt under Augustus (30 BC-AD 14). The latter appointed himself pharaoh on August 30th, 30 BC thenceforth treating Egypt as an imperial estate, rather than a Roman province. This special status was retained under subsequent emperors.

Superficially, Roman rule was a continuation of the Ptolemaic period (Greek remained the official language, and Alexandria the dominant city), except that no ruling family was resident in Egypt. This had important consequences, in that it may have removed any incentive for Egypt to create wealth, given that it was effectively being exploited at a distance, as a source of food for Rome. Improvements in irrigation that had been introduced by the Ptolemies were exploited to the full by the Roman administration, and the produce was gathered up in tax by governors who could be held personally liable for any shortfalls.

During the reign of Marcus Aurelius (AD 161-180), Egypt was seriously affected by a plague, which seems to have resulted in a significant decrease in population. Conditions improved slightly under Septimius Severus (AD 193-211) who reorganized the local administration and carried out various building works, notably the repair of the Colossi of Memnon at Thebes. Although the Fayum region, heavily settled by Greeks, continued to be favoured by Roman visitors (who needed special permission to visit the country), it too gradually underwent depopulation, evident by the 4th century AD. In AD 384, Theodosius (A.D. 379-395) issued an edict commanding the closing of all pagan temples, and ordering the adherence of the entire populace to Christianity. The end of Theodosius' reign, when the Roman empire finally split up into autonomous western and eastern regions, is traditionally regarded as the end of the history of 'ancient' Egypt and the beginning of the Coptic (Byzantine) period.

Cultural Change

After almost two centuries of excavation, it is now possible to outline the history of Egypt not merely politically but also in terms of broad processes of change in material culture. Unlike the history outlined above, this kind of narrative is not concerned with the careers or achievements of specific individuals but with changing patterns of artefacts, and sequences of technological developments and innovations.

Most of our knowledge of Egyptian material culture during the earliest periods of Egyptian prehistory (the Palaeolithic period) centres on the production of stone tools and weapons, and the earliest known chert quarries, such as those at Nazlet Khater and Saqqara (c.40,000 BP). However, a much more varied range of crafts have survived from the Neolithic period. Apart from the domestication of plants and animals and the emergence of pottery (the two factors that tend to characterize this phase in most cultures), there also surviving indications of crafts using organic materials, such as basketry, rope making and bone working.

By the Predynastic period, the Egyptians' irrigation techniques had improved, thus expanding the agricultural capacity of the Nile Valley. By this time they were also producing large numbers of stone vessels and making pottery on an unparalleled scale (between 3800 and 3500 BC at Hierakonpolis). From at least the Naqada period onwards, they were brewing beer and cultivating grapes. They were also able to build wattle and daub buildings, smelt copper (by 4000 BC), mine gold, and work lead, gold and silver into artefacts. Some of the weaving techniques developed in basketry and rope making had begun to be applied to textile production, using linen. The earliest depiction of a ground (or 'horizontal') loom dates from the Badarian period (c.4500-3800 BC); the painting, executed on a pottery vessel, shows four corner pegs holding two beams, one at either end, with the warp running between them; three bars depicted in the middle of the loom may perhaps be the laze rod, heddle rod and some form of beater. It was also around this time that the first faience was being manufactured, initially for simple beads and later for small animal figurines.

However, the Predynastic development that most obviously foreshadowed the pharaonic period was the increasing use of images and symbols that are assumed to be the forerunners of hieroglyphics. By the mid-4th millennium BC, the Egyptians' use of pictorial symbols had evolved into the earliest stage of a sophisticated writing system. The oldest surviving sheet of papyrus (unfortunately uninscribed) was found in the Dynasty 1 tomb of Hemaka at Saqqara (c.3000 BC). In the Early Dynastic period the first élite tombs incorporating stone masonry were built, the granite quarries at Aswan began to be exploited, and specialized copper tools began to be used for wood working. Other Early Dynastic developments were the introduction of dyed threads and dyed cloth, and the earliest evidence for wine production. By the Dynasty 2 (c.2890-2686 BC), recognised forms of artificial mummification had been introduced, although evidence increasingly suggested that earlier stages of mummification can be identified as early as the 5th millennium BC (depending on precisely how 'mummification' or 'embalmment' are defined). Jana Jones's examination of thick, desiccated clumps of wrappings from the Neolithic cemeteries at Badari and Mostagedda has shown that resin-soaked bandages were already being applied to bodies in the early Predynastic period, although, as Jones points out, 'Whether the act of wrapping the body in the very earliest periods indicates an intention to preserve it artificially, or whether it was another aspect of the funerary ritual, is uncertain'.

From Dynasty 3 (c.2686-2613 BC) onwards, limestone quarries began to be exploited on a huge scale, primarily for the construction of pyramid complexes. From this date we also have the earliest evidence for the laminating of sheets of timber. By Dynasty 4 (c.2613-2494 BC), 'Egyptian blue' had begun to be used both as a sculpting material and as a pigment, and the earliest surviving faience workshop (at Abydos) had come into existence. At around this date, mummification techniques, for the élite at least, began to include evisceration and treatment with drying agents. By Dynasty 5 (c.2494-2345 BC) the potter's wheel had been introduced, although it was not until the First Intermediate Period (c.2160-2055 BC) that it began to be widely used.

From Dynasty 11 (c.2055-1985 BC) onwards, sandstone quarries began to be exploited for building and sculptural material. By the Middle Kingdom (c.2055-1650 BC), excerebration (removal of the brain) had become part of the mummification process, which had by now spread to the 'middle classes'. Techniques of gold granulation were also introduced at this date. From the early New Kingdom we have the earliest examples of Egyptian wood-turning, and the introduction of topped-slag furnaces for copper processing. By at least the reign of Thutmose III (1479-1425 BC), glass was being processed (and perhaps even manufactured) by Egyptians, probably adopting techniques developed at an earlier date in the Near Eastern polity of Mitanni. At around 1500 BC the first vertical loom is attested in Egypt. Unlike the horizontal loom, which was pegged out across the ground, the vertical (or 'two-beamed') loom was usually placed against a wall, with weavers working upwards from its base; the lower beam was either set into a shallow hollow in the ground or resting on grooved blocks (examples of which have survived in some New Kingdom houses).

By the Late Period (664-332 BC), specialized techniques of gold refinement had been developed, and, from about 600 BC onwards, iron working became fairly widespread. In a temple of the early Ptolemaic period (4th century BC) we have the first representation of a wooden object being turned on a lathe (although the lathe may have already been used as early as the New Kingdom). During the Ptolemaic period stake-and-strand basketry was introduced. By the 1st century AD, cotton was in general use for textiles, gradually beginning to replace linen.

Although ancient Egypt tends to be regarded as one of the most conservative and intractable of civilisations, even the briefest study of the material culture of the Nile Valley shows that the Egyptians had an enormous capacity both to absorb new modes of production and innovative techniques and to exploit new materials when necessary. The nature of the Egyptian political and social systems - which were undoubtedly remarkably rigid and enduring - should not blind us to the vitality and flexibility of much of their material culture.

Ian Shaw

Senior Lecturer, University of Liverpool

第三章

古埃及人民

古埃及人的自然環境

古希臘的歷史學家希羅多德（Herodotus）曾經形容埃及為「尼羅河的贈禮」，這句名言真是一點也不錯。坐落在非洲東北的埃及，降雨量非常少，沒有尼羅河，埃及就不可能發展出她那璀璨的文明。二十世紀亞斯文大壩還沒蓋起來以前，尼羅河每年的洪水氾濫為它所流經過的埃及帶來了泥沙淤積，在原本貧脊而不宜人居的沙漠上打造出一條狹長而且非常肥沃的農耕地。埃及人很明白他們有多麼依賴尼羅河，他們很清楚地區分出可以居住的「黑土」谷地跟未知而危險的沙漠「紅土」，並且把洪水氾濫所帶來的富足擬人化成生育之神「哈比」（Hapi）。儘管埃及人受益無窮，不過尼羅河也帶來不確定性，當洪水水位過低時，就會導致乾旱和飢荒。相反地，如果洪水水位過高不只會淹沒掉沿岸的村莊，毀掉灌溉渠道，傷害牲畜，還可能殃及未來好幾年的農業。

埃及的地理形勢決定了她國土四周的邊界以及國土內部的分野。傳統的南方邊界在今天的亞斯文（Aswan）以南，由連綿的湍流瀑布所組成，這一連串的急流與大瀑布使尼羅河道受阻。南埃及位於尼羅河上游，海拔也較高，因此稱為上埃及（Upper Egypt），而北埃及則稱為下埃及（Lower Egypt）。上埃及剛好位於尼羅河谷地，由洪水氾濫淤積的平原以及低平的沙漠所組成，長 660 英里（約 1062 公里），四周由峭壁所圍繞。埃及最南端的尼羅河谷地非常狹長，不過越往北，河谷地就明顯開展，這片寬闊的河谷地延伸了好幾英里，一直到中埃及的尼羅河兩岸，是埃及農業的中心地帶。下埃及從今天的開羅附近開始，剛好是尼羅河三角洲向地中海開展的地點。尼羅河三角洲延伸的範圍有 8500 多平方英里之大（13680 平方公里），是由低窪的沼澤、平坦遼闊的耕地以及龜背形的沙丘所組成，這些龜裂的沙丘即使在每年尼羅河氾濫的時期，也高於水平面，是史前時代人類最早的定居地之一，湖泊和瀉湖則分布在三角洲外圍的地中海岸一帶。上埃及與下埃及在某種程度上各自為政，當中央政府積弱不振時，便想要各自獨立。埃及歷史上大多時候的首都都坐落於上埃及與下埃及的交界處，就像今天的首都開羅一樣，有部分就是受這個原因的影響。

圍繞尼羅河谷地東西兩邊的沙漠則有野生動物供埃及人狩獵，也供給埃及人原料，像是建造和雕塑用的石材、各式各樣的礦物、金子以及其它不那麼貴重的寶石等。河谷以西的沙漠中有一連串的綠洲，將河谷中的聚落與通往非洲其它地區的貿易路線聯繫起來。法雍（Fayum）是其中最大的綠洲，就位於上埃及與下埃及交界處的南方，經由巴赫尤塞夫運河（Bahr Yusef canal）與尼羅河相連。法雍綠洲本來就是一塊豐饒之地，有大量的魚產和野生動物，後來中王國以及托勒密王朝的排水防洪計畫又為法雍綠洲增加了更多的農耕地，法雍綠洲因此變得更為豐饒，成為古埃及主要的人口中心區。而河谷以東的沙漠中，流經丘陵的河道或是已經乾涸的河床，則是將尼羅河谷地的村落與紅海的港口聯繫起來，透過這條連接路線，貿易團得以將奇珍異品，像是東南方的沒藥，引進埃及。

除了提供豐沃的農耕土壤，尼羅河也是埃及最主要的運輸、交通與貿易管道。當陸上交通困難時，旅客乘船就可以輕輕鬆鬆橫越整個尼羅河谷地，時間也更快。洪水氾濫的季節，甚至連沙漠的邊緣水路都可以到達，因此建築材料也可以被運送到法老的金字塔以及神廟的建造地點去。尼羅河在埃及人的心目中無所不在，因此搭船旅行的情節在埃及人的宗教信仰中也大量出現。埃及人相信太陽神，拉，在白天時乘船橫越天堂，而夜晚則行船經過冥界。死者也同樣是搭船到達來世。船的圖案出現在埃及最早有紋飾的墓穴中，還有早期的陶器上，並且在之後的幾百年也一直是陵墓裝飾的一部分。模型船在古埃及是普遍的陪葬品，而法老王的陵寢中有時候則會埋進真船大小的模型船，或甚至在墓碑旁邊擺上小型船隊。尼羅河的氾濫週期和太陽的日昇日落也深深影響著埃及人的世界觀、宗教信仰和創世神話。埃及的創世故事描述世界的開始是一座小山從渾沌的大水中浮出，就好像尼羅河谷地與三角洲裡的河堤與龜背形沙丘從每年的洪水氾濫中浮出來一樣。

埃及的植物與動物也在埃及人的宗教中佔有一席之地。古埃及常常以動物的形象來描寫神，同時，神也擁有與他們對應的動物的性格。因此，和天空跟太陽有關係的神就化身為隼鷹，而守墓的神就化身為狐狼，因為狐狼被認為是以荒廢墓穴中的腐肉為食。聖甲蟲，或稱為金龜子，滾著糞球越過沙漠，並在糞球上面產卵。看著小甲蟲似乎是自然而然從這些糞球中孵化出來，埃及人聯想到重生與回春。聖甲蟲也被視為是太陽神的化身，推著日盤越過天堂。聖甲蟲因此成為埃及人最常配戴的護身符之一。植物以及其它的自然圖騰也常常出現在埃及的藝術與建築當中。例如，埃及神廟的特色，就是將圓柱雕刻成沙草紙和蓮科植物的樣式，地面以濕地植物的紋樣來裝飾，而天花板則點上星星。夜晚闔上，旭日東昇時又重新盛開的蓮花，被埃及人視為重生的象徵。因此，死去的法老王被描繪成從盛開的蓮花中浮現，而埃及墓室中描繪的場景和雕刻也常常出現墓室的主人手持蓮花或是以蓮花供養。

埃及的曆法以尼羅河的氾濫週期為基礎。一年分為三個季節，每四個月合為一季，每一個月有三十天。每年的第一個季節—「阿克赫特」（akhet），或稱為氾濫季，從六月中旬持續到十月中旬。接著是「佩瑞特」（peret）—生長季，從十月中旬到二月中旬。最後是「施姆」（shemu）—收割季，從二月中旬到六月中旬。一年的最後會再加上額外的五天構成三百六十五天。除了這本民曆以外，埃及還有以月亮的盈虧為計算基礎的陰曆，埃及一些特定的宗教節慶日都是根據陰曆制定的。在埃及，節慶一到頭都在舉行，用來紀念或慶祝各式各樣的神祇、死去的祖先、季節的更迭、月亮的盈虧以及其它的重大事件。

古埃及的社會

古埃及以農業經濟為主，因此絕大多數的人口為農民。小麥與大麥是主要的穀物，用來製作麵包和啤酒，是埃及人的主食。亞麻則種植來製造亞麻布。埃及的農民也種植各式各樣的豆類，諸如豌豆、扁豆與蠶豆，還有萵苣、洋蔥、韭菜與香草等蔬菜。水果類則種有葡萄、香瓜、無花果、棗子和石榴。埃及人也飼養牛、綿羊與山羊等家畜，以供給他們日常所需的肉、奶與皮革。養豬也可以供給所需的肉類，鴨、鵝與鴿子提供埃及人蛋與肉類，而野鳥、野味和魚則豐富埃及人的飲食。牛與驢是埃及主要的駄獸，過去在埃及被用來駄重物還有拉犁與橇。輪車在古埃及的運輸中幾乎無用武之地，因為動物駄不動的重物往往交由船運。馬只有在大約西元前十六世紀的中王國時期被引進埃及，即便在當時，也只被養在皇家馬廄或精銳部隊中，用來拉馬車而已。而跟現今埃及分不開的駱駝，則一直要到羅馬時期才在埃及出現。

埃及是一個高度組織化且階級嚴明的社會，底層的人幾乎沒有甚麼機會可以往上爬。農民的生活艱苦而且常常吃力不討好。他們沒有自己的土地，卻被租約束縛在所耕種的田地上，這些田地則由富有的達官貴人、皇室或是神廟所擁有。農民的工資則以耕地上所收割的作物來支付，所得僅供餬口。他們在秋冬時節犁田播種，拿來挖土的手工具主要是一支簡單實用的 A 形鋤頭，將一片木製的平刃以特定的角度套進一支較長的木柄中，鋤頭就製成了。犁的形狀像是加大版的鋤頭，犁頭是木製或銅製的，用兩隻牛來拉。在生長季，作物主要以徒手灌溉，因此一定需要相當的勞力。熟成之後，以鐮刀收割穀物，送到篩穀場，然後儲存在地主、神廟或皇家機構的穀倉。

除了農民，埃及的平民階級還包括家僕、洗衣工、漁夫、磚匠、礦工、石匠以及其它的勞動人口。《行業之諷》（The Satire on the Trades）是一部古埃及的文學作品，在大力鼓吹從事書記官這個行業的好處時，這部作品也向讀者揭示了埃及這些勞動人口不僅過著艱苦的生活，而且還受到上層階級的鄙夷。談到磚匠，《行業之諷》說：「勞累和緊繃將他榨得一滴不剩，他的力氣已經耗費殆盡。」而談到洗衣工則說：「他的食物混著

髒汙，全身上下沒有一處是乾淨的。」有些情況是成批的工人受雇於皇家的建築工程，而在洪水氾濫的時節，如果耕地被淹了，政府就徵召農民去探勘礦業。新王國時期，當埃及將它的版圖擴展到了努比亞以及西非時，受俘的戰犯就被充當成奴隸。而罪犯所服的勞役則是一般平民老百姓最避之唯恐不及的，像是到努比亞沙漠掏金。

擁有專業技術的工人相對的社會地位也比較高，像是受雇於皇家或神廟工坊的陶工、寶石匠、雕刻師、裁縫師、傢俱木工，還有負責裝飾皇家陵墓的藝匠等等。從事這些行業的大部分是男人，不過有女人從事裁縫師的工作，有時候也有女人製陶。這些工作在埃及都傾向於世襲，下一代在當學徒的過程中承繼上一代的技術。在一個作坊內，技術較不純熟的工匠負責基本的準備工作，而師傅則負責最後的完工。從阿瑪納（Amarna）和麥地納（Deir el-Medina）等目前還遺留的工匠村遺址所發現的證據顯示，在工匠中，雕刻師和畫家所擁有的社會地位特別高，而到了中王國時期幾乎等同於「中產階級」。然而，對大多數的他們而言，生活還是一樣艱苦。《行業之諷》裡描寫銅匠時，說道：「他的手指看起來就像鱷魚的爪子，身上散發著比魚蛋還腥的臭味。」至於陶工，則說：「為了製作陶具，他在田地裡比豬還會挖土。」

真正有地位並且可能更上一層樓的只限於能讀能寫的書記官，只占埃及人口的極少數—在古埃及時期，大多數時候可能都沒有超過百分之五。埃及龐大的行政與祭祀體系都仰賴書記官，因此他們很受尊敬，收入也很可觀。有能力為自己的陵墓造像或題獻的權貴，常常選擇將自己塑造成書記官的形象一端坐著，莎草紙卷攤展在膝蓋上，肩頭掛著抄寫版與墨水瓶。雖然有些上層階級的女性也識字，不過專職的書記官都是由男性擔任。小男孩和青少年如果不是在家裡由父親訓練就是送到出了名嚴格的書記學校，養成訓練包括抄寫與背誦作業、表單和名著，當時學生的練習範例有許多也都還遺存至今。有些學生繼續鑽研外國語言、醫藥、數學、神學或行政管理，有些則成為一般的書記官。除了在政府機構任職外，他們也為村落中的一般民眾服務：紀錄書信、契約、合同、遺囑、結婚與離婚婚證書，還有訴訟等。

而處在埃及的社會金字塔頂端，僅次於法老王的，則是領導中央行政機構的權貴。他們由法老王直接欽點，並且在埃及早期的時候只有皇室成員可以雀屏中選。他們其中的最上位者在古埃及被稱為 tjaty，也就是今天埃及學者所說的「維西爾」（viziers），地位等同於總理，他們同時也兼任埃及的大祭司，擁有更多的權力。中央政府其它的領導權貴則掌管國庫守衛、皇家工匠、軍隊、糧倉、檔案卷宗以及祭司等。皇城以外，埃及劃分為四十二個行政區，今天希臘文稱之為「諾姆」（nomes），行政機關的編制比照中央單位，不過規模較小。「諾姆」的行政長官，或稱為「州長」，負責將中央的權力貫徹到地方。他由管轄底下的政務官員簇擁著，負責徵收賦稅，並代表法老王徵集軍隊。反過來，如果他管轄的地區發生飢荒，人民想必就寄望他開倉賑濟。名義上，地方長官由法老王直接任命，不過實際上這個職位通常都是世襲。

埃及的政治和宗教是密不可分的，神廟擁有自己的耕地和作坊，雇用人數成千上萬，以底比斯的阿蒙神廟為例，從上層的祭司到一般的農民和工匠就有好幾萬人，

因此神廟在埃及的經濟上扮演相當重要的角色。神職人員在埃及為數相當多而且階級嚴明，法老王是最至高無上的大祭司，而他底下位階較低的祭司則從一般老百姓當中挑選。在新王國以前，埃及沒有全職的祭司，相反的，都是由官員輪流擔任，而他們的妻子就擔任女祭司以及唱詩者。地方祭神典禮的大祭司則有該地的行政長官擔任。祭司的俸祿則由神廟的盈餘支付。只有最上位的祭司、先知、或是「神的侍者」—古埃及稱為 hem-netjer—才得以進到神廟的最內殿。他們底下則是由書記官擔任的讀經員（khery-hebet），負責朗誦經文，這些人身著寬幅腰帶，因而在陵墓的浮雕或壁畫場景中很容易辨認出來。地位較低的埃及男性則擔任為數眾多的純祭司，他們進入神廟的限制相對較多，也沒有獨特的配飾。殯葬祭司執行祭典以及特定的葬禮，剃光頭並且穿著醒目的豹皮衣袍。葬禮上的殯葬祭司通常由死者的子孫擔任。從新王國時期開始，特別是底比斯阿蒙神廟的祭典，世襲而全職的祭司變成了常態，權力也日益強大，最後，阿蒙神殿第一先知的影響力竟然足以跟南埃及的法老王相抗衡。女性通常不能擁有高階的神職，主要都擔任神廟的唱詩員。不過，底比斯的「阿蒙神的妻子」在第三中間期扮演的角色日益重要，而到了第二十五王朝還成為阿蒙祭典上最重要的人物。

在軍隊中，社會地位也有可能更上一層樓，因為出身微薄的士兵偶爾也可能因為戰功彪炳而大受賞賜。埃及史上大多數時期，除了最上階的司令官以外，軍人都不是全職的。常備軍主要都是從埃及境內各地區以及努比亞和西非等占領地徵召而來。努比亞人是有名的弓箭手，一直以來似乎都在埃及擔任士兵和警衛。由於埃及的士兵大多都是臨時徵召而非全職，因此幾乎年年都有的軍隊服役通常都選在洪水氾濫的時節進行，好讓士兵在洪水消退後趕得及回家種植來年的作物。軍隊中最多的是步兵，他們配備的武器為：矛、斧、弓、箭以及動物毛皮製作的盾。馬及馬車在第十八王朝引進埃及，不過當時只限於特別用途。一直到末王朝時期，埃及都沒有海軍，而是以徵召入伍的陸軍來駕船。就像政府其他機構一樣，埃及軍隊的特色是有一支書記官和政府官員組成的龐大官僚體系，受「部隊司令官」指揮，而全部則都服從於法老王的終極命令。

經濟與貿易

國家與神殿推動著古埃及的經濟，他們掌握著農產品的徵收與重分配。貯存的資源在面臨短缺的時候可以應急，多餘的則可以在機構之間交易流通。商人這個特殊的階級只有在新王國時期才出現，也就是西元前一千五百年左右。關於埃及有市集這一點，最佳的證據就是陵墓壁畫中出現食物交易的場景，像是麵包、啤酒、魚、肉以及其他的基本物品，大部分都是家庭自製的產品，也有神殿和國家機構多餘的物品。工匠交換工具、傢俱、拖鞋、拐杖與陶器。沙漠以及綠洲來的商人則出售畜養的或者捕捉到的獵物，或是用來製作木乃伊的泡鹼等礦產。當時沒有貨幣，所以完全是以物易物。至於價格則以赫卡特（hekat）這種標準容積單位而定。考古學上還沒有發現任何一個古代市集的證據。這些市集很可能是在港邊村落廣場裡臨時聚集的露天攤販。因為這些地方往往有大量來自四面八方的人聚集，自然就成了交換資訊與商品交易的中心。至於區域內的城鎮貿易則由神廟與地方政府的代表壟斷。這樣的貿易讓農產富饒的埃及中部地區得以用多餘的產品換取奢侈品與生產原料。地方官也會代表法老王，使用連通西部沙漠綠洲的商隊路線前往偏遠地區從事貿易。

埃及的房子、村落、城鎮與城市

相當不幸的，關於古埃及城鎮的證據非常少，因為不管是地方村落或者區域的主要城市，當時都坐落於尼羅河附近的沖積平原上，如今都已經被固定氾濫的洪水沉積物與現代建設所覆蓋。雖然埃及當時絕大地區是鄉村，但是很多小村落圍繞著較大的城市，這些城市就當成當時的區域首都，或者現在所謂的州首府，成為地方行政中心以及地方神廟的所在地。埃及最大的城市有北埃及的地方首府孟斐斯與南埃及的底比斯，所信仰的主神分別是普塔（Ptah）和阿蒙雷（Amun-Re），居民有三萬到四萬人。

埃及城鎮與鄉村生活的最佳證據是政府為安置建造與維護皇室陵墓與紀念碑的工人而開發的城鎮，比如中王國時期卡洪（Kahun）的城鎮、法雍附近以及南阿多比斯（South Abydos）的辛努塞爾特二世（Senusret II）金字塔區、還有位於上埃及的辛努塞爾特三世（Senusret III）墓葬區。位於底比斯西邊山區的麥地納，是建造帝王谷新王國皇家陵墓的工匠聚落，也是埃及保存最完好的古代村落。因為不僅僅有房舍遺跡，當時的文字記錄包括書信、清單、帳本還有法律文件都保存良好，所以麥地納詳盡生動的記錄著聚落的日常生活。阿肯納頓法老（King Akhenaten）時期的首都位於埃及中部的阿肯納頓（今天的阿瑪納），雖然為期不長，但是它的官府，皇宮，官員宅第、技工住所以及工匠的聚落讓我們得以一窺新王國首都的生活面貌。位於尼羅河三角洲的德爾達巴（Tell el-Dab'a），也就是古代的亞華尼斯（Avaris），從中王國時期一直使用到新王國初期，並且在第二中衰期的時候，被佔領北埃及的迦南人（又稱西克索人）設為首都。

當時的埃及人造屋用的是太陽烤乾的泥磚而不是火燒的窯磚，然後用茅草鋪蓋棕櫚木搭屋頂。地板則鋪上灰泥或磚。他們用木材做門，窗戶上有木欄或石欄。房屋的大小結構取決於每戶人家的財力，當然也依地點有所不同，但是多間且方正的格局是最常見的。城市裡的家庭格局比較狹長，甚

至有樓房。城市近郊或者鄉下的屋子占地較廣，多數是平房，有的還有游泳池和有圍牆的花園。

位於卡洪與南阿比多斯的城鎮有許多相似之處，它們都是建於沙漠邊緣與沖積平原附近的大城，周邊圍繞著城牆。不過它們都沒有完全被挖掘出來，部分遺跡要不是已經被破壞就是位於現代建築的下方。不過它們的城鎮規模已經被推估出來，卡洪大約是十三萬平方米，而南阿比多斯則是約四萬五千到六萬平方米。街道將城鎮劃分成矩形的里坊，當地仕紳佔地廣大的府邸只佔城鎮的一小部分，其他部分則是一般居民居住的區域，其中的房子規模小、數量多而且密度高，皆依照當時的標準興建。當地統治階級所住的仕紳府邸，特色是居住場所位於中央，由一個大廳（或客廳）與側翼的許多小廂房組成，面向一個開闊的庭院，邊緣圍繞著柱廊。供烹飪與貯藏的設施區安排在居住場所兩側的庭院，總管區則位於府邸後方，由各別獨立的入口進出。

麥地納是在埃及第十八王朝早期開闢的，然後一直使用到第二十王朝，歷經三期的興建工程，最後一期工程結束時麥地納的總占地面積約五千六百平方米，共有六十八戶，依中央道路兩旁排列，中央道路狹窄，另外還有更小的巷道供住戶進出。聚落外圍繞著一道石砌的城牆，北面與西面闢有城門。雖然聚落裡的房子都是依照相同的藍圖打造的，但是大小卻相當不一，面積從四十到一百二十平方米不等，而且大多都歷經改建以符合住戶需要。緊鄰麥地納村落西邊的山坡上有個家族墓園，墓上堆砌著小型的金字塔，有些還有精心彩繪的墓室。麥地納裡標準的房舍都是緊密相連，並呈狹長形排列。進屋時通常會經過一個方型的前廳，盡頭則是一間狹窄石砌的密閉空間，可能用來當臥房。過了前廳後就是主大廳，由一至多根的柱子支撐，特色是裡面有一個供祭拜祖先用的小型家庭神龕，以及一個可能是當成餐桌的泥磚平台。主大廳盡頭則是其他臥房，屋子後方則有一個作為廚房的小庭院，其中還有一間地窖與泥窯。有些房子的門牆漆成紅的，上面繪飾著家神。

阿肯大頓城（Akhetaten）建於尼羅河東岸的山壁上，在於中埃及的農業精華區。這座城只有一個世代的歷史，不過可以提供我們一窺第十八王朝的城市生活。城裡有條貫通南北的道路，約六公里長，得以連結城市與南北兩端的郊區。最北端是一座泥磚蓋的宮殿，可能是阿肯大頓的皇家寓所。往南走則會先經過一個住宅區跟行政區，然後抵達皇后與公主的宮殿，其四周圍繞著花園與池塘。再往南則會經過另一個住宅區然後到達城中心，主要的神殿與市政建築都坐落於此，像是行政中心、檔案辦公室、警察局、糧倉以及作坊等。城中心以南緊鄰的則是行政官員與雕刻師傅居住的城郊，最南端則還有另外一系列的神殿與宗教建築。城東部則另有一個獨立的村落，位於開鑿有國王與官員陵墓的岩壁附近，是讓墓地工人居住的，村落裡有自己專屬祭祀祖先的小型神龕。

在阿肯大頓的高級郊區內，富人居住的有圍牆的莊園，裡面不但有屋主的宅第，還有傭人區、作坊、糧倉、廚房、畜養區，以及馬廄。雖然房子的設計不一，還是可以看出典型的特徵。通常都是平房，起居空間包含柱式前廊、小前廳，以及作為主要起居室的大柱廳。個人的房間與寢室通常位於房子後方，還有另外分開的套房供女人、小孩與客人使用。有些階級較高的家庭在臥房邊有石砌的衛浴間，裡面有石椅或陶椅，下方放置一個裝滿沙土的盆子。

其它關於埃及房子的資料還可以從中王國時期陵墓裡的房屋模型與新王國時期的墓室壁畫中取得。新王國的墓室壁畫描繪的是底比斯貴族在市區裡的多層建築，地下室用來作為傭人織布與製造食品的家庭作坊，一樓的格局特色與中王國時期的仕紳宅第類似，有柱式前廊以及寬敞的柱式大廳。個人的房間在三樓，貯藏食物的籃子和爐子則位於頂樓。很多房子在屋頂甚至有露臺以便主人傍晚可以在此乘涼享受。

大多數埃及人家裡的傢俱樣子簡單而且數量也不多，但是有錢人則享受著用進口木料精雕細琢的工藝品。房間地板甚至走廊上鋪著蘆葦編織的蓆子。一般陳設簡樸的屋裡用的床是泥磚搭的平台，而佔埃及人口最多的窮人則只睡在地板鋪的墊子上。上流社會的人睡離地不高的木板床，床尾稍微比床頭低一點，床腳則通常刻成獸足的形狀，例如獅爪或牛蹄。床邊的木竿子上掛著遮棚以防蚊蟲，床單折成的墊子就當床墊，埃及人不用我們今天的枕頭，而是以木頭或石塊來當頭枕，這個風俗今天有些非洲文化還看得到。凳子是埃及最常見的椅子，有許多樣式一直存留下來，像是可攜帶的以及可折疊的板凳。埃及人也常常直接坐在地上，就在矮桌旁吃起東西。椅子是上流社會才有的奢侈品，就像床腳一樣，椅腳上常刻上獸足，最好的還鑲上黑檀、象牙以及其他的奇珍異品。衣服、首飾和其他私人物品則是收在箱子及櫃子裡而不是衣櫥或壁櫥裡。

由於每個家庭都會有各式各樣陶製的容器，所以陶器就成為古代遺留下來最常見的工藝品。有些陶器形制簡單，可能是在家裡自行捏就的，其他的就是由專門的作坊製作。陶罐的用途很廣，可以用來儲藏各類食物，陶缸或大碗用來盛放麵包的製作材料、啤酒或是供平常煮飯之用。像是穀物、肉、作物以及液體。做好的食物通常放在托盤上或者是碗裡，飲料則裝在杯子或者廣口杯裡。陶器也有其他用途，像是作為火盆、鍋底座，以及桌子等。埃及人吃東西的時候通常用手，用到的餐具很少，只有勺子或濾網。

古埃及的家庭

典型的古埃及家庭由丈夫、妻子以及他們未嫁娶的小孩所組成，可能還有他們老邁的父母。而貧窮家庭的小孩即便婚嫁了也可能還是帶著孩子跟父母親同住。父親為一家之長，通常被認為是家裡的經濟支柱；母親則操持家務、養育小孩並且看管傭人─在經濟負擔起的家庭。女性同時也耕種菜圃、製作麵粉、烘培麵包、烹煮肉食、將亞麻抽絲並織造成布。在古埃及，成婚需要經過父母同意，雖然古埃及的情詩與戀愛符咒顯示在擇偶時浪漫的元素也一定不可或缺，但是許多婚姻可能都由父母直接安排。目前還沒有發現婚禮相關的證據，不過在古埃及似乎是一旦婚姻被批准了，然後新人就住在一起而已。離婚應該還不普遍，不過的確有發生而且丈夫或妻子任一方都可以提出，必須要有離婚同意書才可以再婚。正常的情況下丈夫有資格分得婚後所得的三分之二，另外三分之一歸妻子所有，不過如果通姦的話，妻子可能會被迫放棄她所得的財產，至於婚前所得則歸原來擁有的一方。

古埃及人重視大家庭，而且男孩女孩一樣好。生產的時候，女眷以及其他家庭裡的女性成員都要助生，不過可能旁邊有產婆協助。大部分的女性都早婚，而且可能大半的人生都在懷孕生產或哺育小孩。小孩的出生在古埃及是憂喜參半的時刻，生產對於母親和嬰兒來說都是危險的，所以準父母都會向各式各樣的守護神祈求保佑，其中最重要的就是女神索埃里斯（Taweret）和侏儒神貝斯（Bes）。女神索埃里斯的身體被描繪成懷孕的河馬，還有鱷魚的尾巴；而貝斯則是一個長有獅鬃的侏儒，會吐蛇信，而且常常配戴匕首或其他武器。女神索埃里斯和侏儒神貝斯的外型都頗嚇人，不過他們也因為擁有守護母親與嬰兒的能力而確實受到古埃及人的喜愛。索埃里斯和貝斯的神像也常被拿來裝飾床枕。其他跟生產有關的神祇還有用輪轆造人的克嫩（Khnum），青蛙形象的生產女神希基特（Heqat），化為人身的分娩踏磚梅斯克內特（Meskhenet），以及眼鏡蛇女神瑞奈努泰特（Renenutet）。

古埃及的母親哺育小孩的時間長達三年。在古埃及，特別是四、五歲之前的小孩死亡率很高，不過從這些幼兒疾病中存活下來的孩童就很有可能長大成人大部分的小孩沒有受正式教育，不過很小的時候就要在家中、田裡或是工坊幫忙父母以便學習成人必備的技能。階級較高的男童則進入跟神殿相關的書記學校，學習閱讀、寫作、數學、天文學、地理以及其他科目。就像今天的小孩一樣，古埃及的小孩也喜歡玩玩具，像是洋娃娃、球、陀螺、箍環和動物玩偶。從墓室繪製的場景中發現他們還喜歡玩摔跤、跳高、戲法、跳舞和雜技，也和父母一起從事一些消遣活動，像是釣魚、狩獵和划船。

以今天的標準來看，古埃及的平均預期壽命很短，大部分人的壽命是三十歲，不過飲食較好而且生活比較沒有壓力的富人，平均壽命則較長。由於生產本身的危險，許多婦女早逝。因此當男性的墓室或墓碑提到一位以上的妻子，通常很難斷定他是享齊人之福還是續絃。不過皇室則另外，很少證據顯示古埃及是一夫多妻制。有幸活過平均壽命的人很有可能長壽，據我們所知，有些法老王活到九十幾歲。埃及的文學提到「完美的長壽年齡」是一百一十歲，不過這個數字無疑是一個理想而不是真實的情況。埃及人相當敬重老邁的親人，並且以照顧年長的雙親為榮。流傳下來的文學故事

也把老年和智慧、箴言聯想在一起。

古埃及有許多家庭也養寵物，特別是貓狗。狗特別受到埃及人的喜愛，從很早以前就常被畫進埃及的藝術裡。狗也是目前所知會被埃及人取名的動物，有些寵物狗甚至死後也會被製成木乃伊並放進屬於他們的棺木中。有些狗的品種近似於格雷伊獵犬，而貝吉生犬和薩路基犬可能主要是飼養來狩獵的。大約西元前兩千年，埃及人開始將豢養地方的野貓，不用說，這些豢養的家貓肯定是用來防範老鼠以保護穀倉的。墓室壁畫顯示貓也陪著埃及人去獵鳥，牠們會躡手躡腳地穿過蘆葦去捕捉沒有防備的小鳥。新王國時期的墓室場景顯示，貓被豢養在家裡的程度更深，牠們被畫成很舒適地坐在主人的椅子下。有錢的埃及人也飼養野生動物，像是猴子或是異國禽鳥。

古埃及人的飲食

埃及人的兩樣主食是麵包與啤酒，配菜有肉、魚、蔬菜、水果、植物油、蛋、奶油與蜂蜜。在前王朝時期，肉的來源是狩獵與捕魚。到了法老時代，牛隻成為最常見的肉類來源，人們在宰殺前會強迫進食牛隻讓增重。因為牛很珍貴，所以可能只有在慶典或者特殊場合才會吃牛肉。平常埃及人吃綿羊與山羊肉。雖然過去我們一直以為埃及人不吃豬肉，但是古城遺址挖到的豬骨似乎說明他們其實常吃豬肉。埃及人也吃小型動物，像是豪豬與老鼠。除了養的鴨與鵝，他們也吃各種野鳥，比如說鴿子、鵪鶉、鷗鴣、鷺以及鸛鳥。直到希臘羅馬時代人們才引進雞隻。

小麥與大麥是埃及主要的穀類作物，多數家庭都有石磨與土窯以便製作麵包。雕像與墓室繪製的場景中，都有出現婦女磨麵粉與烤麵包的工作情形。圓錐形的陶製麵包模子可以製作出長條型的麵包，至於要製作扁平或者圓狀的麵包，就直接把麵糰貼在爐壁上烤。由於磨麵粉的過程中，砂與小石頭會混到麵粉裡，麵包吃起來有砂礫，因此對牙齒造成嚴重的磨損。由於經年累月吃這種含砂的麵包，因此老年人製成的木乃伊上常常可以看到嚴重的牙齒問題。啤酒的製作原料與麵包相同，但是相同產區與原料所釀造出來的啤酒，古埃及和今天的味道卻不一樣，古埃及的啤酒味道濃郁且營養豐富。至於用葡萄、無花果與棗椰釀製的酒只有富人消費得起。

吃不起肉的人就必須靠豆類像是蠶豆、扁豆、豌豆，與鷹嘴豆以取得必須的蛋白質。其他埃及人能取得的蔬菜有萵苣、青蔥、大蒜、芥茉、大蔥、芹菜、香料與黃瓜。這其中有好幾種都還兼有療效，而萵苣則被埃及人認為具有催情作用。紙莎草最著名之處雖然在於它是古代紙稿的原料，不過本身也是很有營養的植物。椰棗是最常見的水果，其他常見的還有西克莫無花果，葡萄、杜姆棕櫚堅果，甜瓜與野莓。石榴在新王國時期首次出現。希臘羅馬時代，埃及水果的種類因為引進橄欖、桃子、梨與柑橘而大量增加。

醫療

就像工業化之前的所有社會一樣，古埃及人的生活充斥著疾病與受傷所帶來的危脅，包括毒蛇、蠍子，還有其他的危險生物。營養不良和寄生蟲是窮人常見的問題。當時在埃及沒有消毒藥品、抗生素，或者止痛劑，雖然有證據顯示古埃及進口鴉片，很可能是用來減緩疼痛。在田裡、軍隊、礦場與建地工作的人最容易因為受傷而惡化。因為感染機率高，現今很容易處理的外傷在古埃及卻時常致命。為了對付生活中無所不在的危險，埃及人依賴醫藥與赫卡（heka），也就是我們今天所謂的巫術。從許多古埃及保存下來的藥方看來，當時應該對病人的幫助不大，不過對於某些醫療議題，古埃及的醫生似乎已經擁有相當精確的知識。古埃及的醫學紙稿有相當數量被保存下來，提供我們關於當時的治療方法與許多疾病診斷的資訊，而對於木乃伊的研究則提供我們更多關於古埃及醫學的證據。這些類醫療類巫術的醫學紙稿描述了古埃及療程的三個階段：首先是診斷與預後，接下來是開處方，最後是配合處方進行的符咒與巫術，對古埃及人來說，最後的巫術療程和先前一樣重要。

在古埃及，醫生就是巫師，他們有藥草與手術器具，也配備有魔杖、附身符和咒語。不像今天我們所認為的巫術，赫卡在古埃及沒有任何既定的負面涵義，好壞完全取決於巫師。埃及人也從神靈求取醫療的幫助。托特（Thogh）為古埃及醫療，同時也是科學、數學與文字的守護神，以朱鷺或狒狒的造型出現。女神伊西斯（Isis）是古埃及的母性和巫術之神，被認為能保佑健康。而形象為獅頭的女神賽克麥特（Sekhmet）和伊西斯一樣，據信能抵禦所有傳染病。某些神祇具有更特殊的功能，像女神賽克麥特可以驅走蠍子。而第三王朝的先知印何闐（Imhotep），古埃及記載他建造了埃及最早的階梯金字塔，也就是位於薩卡拉（Saqqara）的卓瑟王（Djoser）金字塔，但是後來在埃及的歷史中他被神化成了有名的醫神。

個人信仰

古埃及的信仰與日常生活緊密相連，但是相較於今天大多數的宗教，當時的宗教活動相當沒有組織性。古埃及不認為神廟是供大眾膜拜的地方，而是諸神的住所。神廟在古埃及稱為 hut-netcher，字面的意思就是「神的家」；而位階最高的祭司則是 hem-netcher，意為「神的侍者」。神廟不對一般大眾開放，只有角色為「神的侍者」的祭司，才准許進入神廟最裡面的殿堂。每天都會有精心的儀式為神廟裡的神像沐浴、塗油、穿衣、祭酒和點香。即使是貴族與官員也只能進到全國性大神廟的外圍廣場，至於規模較小或地方性的神龕或神廟則會對更多的民眾開放。

對一般埃及人來說，想見到國內最重要的神只有通過慶典或遊行，在這些節慶活動舉行時，諸神的像會被放在船艙之外，象徵「遊」街或「航行」尼羅河。埃及曆法的特色就是常有慶典，其中有些是全國性的重要慶典，其中兩個被詳載的慶典在底比斯舉行，慶典中卡納克大神廟的阿蒙雷神像會出來遊行。「尼羅河谷的美麗慶典」在每年夏初的收割季舉辦。阿蒙（Amun）與祂的妻子穆特（Mut）還有兒子康斯（Khonsu）的雕像會被尼羅河東岸的神廟被抬到西岸的墳場。接著他們會被帶到皇家陵墓與其他聖地。在節慶的期間，家家戶戶會到他們死去的親人墓前祭拜，然後在廣場裡用餐。而在洪水氾濫的季節所舉辦的歐佩特（Opet）慶典中，阿蒙雷的神像會從卡納克神廟出發往南行到路克索（Luxor）附近的卡（ka）─保護法老生命力的神廟。歐佩特慶典是底比斯人最重要的假日，目標是為了重振阿蒙雷與法老王。遊神像不只在慶典遊行中可以看到，也會出現在其他地方，例如艾德夫（Edfu）的荷魯斯（Horus）神殿與丹德拉（Dendera）的哈托爾（Hathor）神殿。

阿比多斯（Abydos）是埃及最早的法老埋葬地，後來成為埃及主要的冥王奧塞里斯（Osiris）的神廟。每年一次的奧塞里斯慶典吸引了來自埃及各地的朝聖者，不管是到阿比多斯做生意的有錢人還是朝聖者，他們會在奧塞里斯遊行的路線上僱人建造小廟與紀念碑──遊行的路線從神廟到沙漠，據信是奧塞里斯冥界的範圍。關於古埃及慶典的記載，當時的文獻只有極少數留存下來，其中之一就是一塊中王國晚期的官員伊克諾弗特（Ikhernofre）所題獻的紀念碑。伊克諾弗特被法老王指派去翻修奧塞里斯的神像，因此有幸得以帶領遊行。根據他的描述，慶典當天的節目包括用戲劇重演當時奧塞里斯與塞特（Seth）的戰役，塞特是奧塞里斯的兄弟，同時也是他的敵人。

除了全國性的大型神廟與慶典，埃及的普羅大眾也可以透過地方與民間諸神來貼近神的世界。位於麥地納和阿瑪納的工匠村都有開放給民眾的小神殿。在麥地納最受歡迎的祭拜對象就是神格化的法老王阿蒙霍特一世（Amenhotep I），他是首先啟用帝王谷的法老也為陵墓工匠建造住所。一般人在家中也會進行地區性的膜拜儀式。工匠村有許多人的家裡都有神龕以便祭拜死去的親人或家神。這種神龕通常是嵌進牆內的壁龕加上一張小供桌就完成了，神龕裡面有時會供奉「祖先胸像」。在阿肯納頓（Akhenaten）法老短暫的宗教改革時期，阿瑪納地區禁止祭拜埃及傳統的諸神，因此，有些家庭就擺上神龕祭拜還在世的皇室家族，不過，城裡的居民還是繼續祭拜常見的家神。

法術在個人的宗教信仰上也占有一定的份量。從埃及有歷史以來，護身符和其他法器就被使用來召喚力量，以利狩獵、退敵、保護家畜、增強力量、生育力甚至是愛情。在古埃及常常聽聞在神廟裡擔任祭司的讀書人同時也身兼自己聚落的法師。這些施法術的人必須能夠根據不同的情況念出正確的咒語、祭文和頌詞；他們也要配備適當的器具，像是人偶、魔杖以及護身符。埃及的法器非常繁複，在孕婦、新手媽媽，還有小孩子的床邊用來畫圈圈的是用河馬牙製作的魔杖或刀子，上面刻繪有

侏儒神貝斯、女神塔沃里特（Taweret）和其他守護神的形象。放在床角落的眼鏡蛇石膏像可以保護熟睡的人。以外國俘虜的樣貌製作塑像並刻上敵

人的名字，然後在儀式中摧毀或破壞就可以確保敵人戰敗。埃及有個著名的故事描述一個亟欲報復妻子情人的丈夫在對方正在游泳的地方放了一隻蠟製的鱷魚，鱷魚被放進水中以後馬上活了過來然後咬死了妻子的情人。

埃及個人信仰與道德的根基是所謂的「馬特」（maat）觀，大致可以解釋成今天的「正義」。馬特基本上講的就是宇宙的自然之道，像是生活必須符合正確的社會準則，言行要能夠發揚埃及傳統的生活方式。貪婪、好吃與極端的自大是不被允許的，尤其在對待父母、長者或是有權勢的人更是如此。官員應該要照應屬下所需，滿足管轄地區的民眾，對窮苦的人慷慨解囊，取悅君王，滿足上蒼。

埃及人道德觀的證據來自於保存下來的各種文獻。最能提供相關資訊的文獻是那些從古王國時期以來就不斷流傳下來的教諭文學。這些「智慧文學」以父親對兒子或是老師對學生教導規矩的形式寫就，鼓勵讀者要利益眾生、尊敬父母長者、榮耀法老、照顧窮人、表現謙卑並慷慨大方。保存下來的中王國紙莎草稿「普塔霍特普箴言」（The Maxims of Ptahhotep）就給一位權貴如下的建言：

聽請願者訴願要有耐心；

在他還未說完之前不要急著打發他走；

受到不平對待的人渴望抒發他的苦惱；

超越他最終贏得正義的分享。

普塔霍特普建議丈夫要：

公平仁慈對待妻子；

讓她吃得好，給她穿得暖；

油膏可以讓她放鬆安歇。

生命裡的每天都要讓她喜悅；

因為她會予上帝豐滿的回報。

「棺木文」（Coffin Texts）和「亡者之書」（Book of the Dead）這些喪葬文學裡包含有「消極的告解」，其中死者會試圖為他們在世時的行為辯解以證明他們有資格進入來世，因此死者會證明他們沒有做出任何違反馬特的事情，不管是犯下今天看來是不道德或犯罪的行為還是做出埃及人認為有違常理的行為。天秤上的一端是死者的心，另一端則是代表馬特的羽毛，死者宣告：

我沒有帶給他人痛苦。

我沒有讓別人哭泣。

我沒有殺人也沒有因故被殺。

我沒有讓任何人受苦。

文學作品裡人物的行為提供我們更深的洞見。例如倡導夫妻忠誠和兄友弟恭的故事。而不管是墓室中美化的墓誌銘或是還願碑上的題記，官員往往自稱他們已經告慰諸神、取悅法老、並且謀求家人與聚落的福祉。墓誌銘則讚頌死者謹言、順從、知曉自己的責任，而且益發虔誠。例如，一個第六王朝的官員就在他的墓誌銘裡宣稱：

我對伴侶們品頭論足讓她們感到歡心，

強凌弱的時候我盡力拯救弱小幫他脫困，

我為挨餓的人添飯，給受凍的人添衣，

沒有船捕魚的人，我免費送他。

孤苦無子的死者我為他埋葬，

沒有錢坐渡船的人我替他出錢，

我尊敬我父親，

我取悅我的母親，

我幫他們帶大孩子。

古埃及的穿著與時尚

我們大部分關於古埃及穿著的資訊都來自於墓室中的藝術作品，但是保存下來的實體衣裳卻常常和藝術呈現的天差地遠。這表示，在使用墓室裝飾來解釋古埃及的服裝資訊這一點上，我們必須謹慎小心。就跟許多文化一樣，服裝是地位的象徵。特定的配件，尤其是頭飾，是只有法老王才可以穿戴的。一般來說，一個人的穿著越精緻華麗，他的社經地位就越高。古埃及的農夫和工匠常被描繪成穿著簡單的纏腰布，有時候甚至只圍一條腰帶。女侍者或舞者常出現裸體的形象，小孩也是，即便真實生活中小孩幾乎都一定是有穿衣服的。

亞麻是古埃及用來製衣最主要的纖維，有不同的厚度，而最好的亞麻布特別的柔順纖薄。墓室的繪製場景和模型出現的幾乎清一色是女性在忙著複雜的織造過程：

將亞麻纖維抽紡成亞麻線，然後織成亞麻布。古埃及最早使用的織布機是水平式織機，新王國時期以後也開始使用一種直立式的，用兩根柱子架起來的豎織機。古埃及大部分的衣服都是白色或米色的，而珠寶、腰帶和其他配飾則五彩繽紛。披肩和斗篷以綿羊或山羊毛製成，在寒涼的冬天，可以披在亞麻衣服上禦寒。

男性的主要裝束是圍一條裙布之後在腰上打一個結，裙布的長度從膝蓋到小腿肚不等。裙布外可能再穿上裙飾帶、斗篷或是流蘇無袖上衣。在中王國時期，很流行從胸到小腿圍上一條長而厚重的織品。古王國和中王國時期女性的典型形象則是穿著有肩帶的形緊窄連身裙。在流行過後很久一段時間，這種樣式又繼續出現在女神的形象上，因為埃及人推測女神會偏愛古典的服裝樣式。不過保存下來的連身裙通常都較寬鬆，有些還有袖子，這表示藝術上約定俗成的樣式不一定就是真實正確的。中王國時期男女都流行穿著長衣，上面有精巧的褶線跟流蘇。男女下半身基本的裝束是像尿布的三角形亞麻布，而且在田野裡工作的勞工只穿這樣。

除了皇家的頭飾以外，古埃及不流行帽子。藝術作品中有時候會出現的篩穀者或是碾穀的女性會在頭髮上綁著寬鬆的頭巾。女性在特殊的場合會戴上頭冠還有其他頭飾，或者緞帶和花環。鞋子的樣式簡單，大部分的埃及人大多數時候可能都打赤腳，就像今天鄉間的埃及人一樣。古埃及最常見的是用蘆葦或皮做的涼鞋，上面有 Y 字型的繫帶，有時候鞋子前面還會往上翻。皮製的包鞋最後才在羅馬時代引進埃及。

古埃及男女都會配戴精緻鮮豔的珠寶以便讓他們顏色相當單一的服裝顯得更出色。瑪瑙、天河石、長石和紫水晶等半寶石都在埃及開採，綠松石則由西奈半島進口，至於天青石的取得就必須仰賴遠至今天阿富汗的貿易路線了。珠子也用埃及當地的貝殼製造，有的則用河馬的牙齒和上釉的滑石。用彩釉來製造珠子和護身符在古埃及尤其受到歡迎。彩釉是以摻和礦物質的石英沙所製成的一種膠狀塗料，在高溫

燒造時會產生光彩奪目的釉色。藍色和綠色是燒造後最常見的顏色，不過從新王國時期開始工匠也製造出黃色、紫色、紅色和白色的彩釉。玻璃在新王國時期也開始出現，之後就常用來製造珠子或鑲嵌藝品。

古埃及最具特色的珠寶就是鑲有無數串的珠鍊和垂珠的大頸圈，可能是要仿造花環的樣式。要平衡這些頸圈的重量就得靠垂掛在背上的吊飾。除了頸圈，埃及人也會配戴項鍊、胸飾、手鐲、腕環、戒指、踝鍊、頭冠、鑲嵌珠子的腰帶和裙帶等。耳環和耳針引進埃及的時間相對較晚，大約西元前一千五百五十年才出現。新王國時期的埃及人常穿耳洞。而髮夾、髮篦和髮圈等髮飾的使用則是從最早的墓葬一直到整個古埃及時期都有發現。

除了裝飾，珠寶在古埃及也是一種象徵，有宗教或巫術的目的。不管是甚麼社會階級的男女都會配戴護身符，而且他們相信護身符的法力不只來自於外觀樣式而且來自於材質和顏色。獅子、鱷魚、河馬和眼鏡蛇等猛獸護身符不但可以守護配戴者，還可以將牠們的力量和本領轉化給配戴者。魚的護身符可以保護配戴者免於溺斃。神的護身符則可以召喚該神的法力。飾有索埃里斯女神、貝斯侏儒神和希基特女神的珠寶有助生產，此外，瑪瑙貝也有同樣的作用，因為埃及人認為瑪瑙貝形似於女性的生殖器。聖甲蟲則促使重生。最受古埃及歡迎的護身符可能是烏加眼（wedjat），象徵鷹頭神荷魯斯的眼睛。在和沙漠之神塞特的爭鬥中，荷魯斯失去了一隻眼睛，不過後來荷魯斯又把那隻眼睛奪回來。因而古埃及人認為荷魯斯的眼睛可以保佑健康。而配戴其他象形符號的護身符則會被賦予該象形文字的意義，例如「安卡」（ankh）表示生命，而「傑得柱」（djed-pillar）則表示穩定。

古埃及的髮型隨著時間呈現出不同的樣式，而不同的時間也有不同的偏愛款式。除了追隨當代的流行，頭髮的長度和樣式也反映出一個人的年齡、性別、職業或社會地位。例如，小孩一般都剃光頭，然後在一邊留著一條辮子。某些特定的祭司也剃頭象徵純潔。由於天氣炎熱，許多埃及人可能都留短髮或整頭剃掉，大部分農夫和工匠的形象就是平頭。要盛裝出席正式場合時，比較富裕的埃及人就會戴上真髮做成的假髮，也可能是用植物纖維做的。墓室場景和雕像都有出現精心編織而成的假髮，有時候會有幾撮真髮從假髮底下冒出來。古王國時期，埃及男女都流行厚重及肩的假髮，而直長的假髮則獲得中王國時期女性的青睞，至於厚重、長而捲的假髮則被新王國時期的男女視為時尚。為了防止頭髮乾枯，新王國時期的埃及人有時候會在頭上戴著混摻香料和牛油所製成的錐狀油膏。這塊圓錐狀的油膏會漸漸融化，就可以使頭髮潤滑並且飄出香味。指甲花則用來染灰白的頭髮。雖然鬍髭在古王國時期曾經短暫流行過──中王國初期有一些木乃伊面具也有鬍子──不過除了小山羊鬍，古埃及的男性不常蓄鬍。

衛生、美容與化妝品

清潔與個人衛生對埃及人來說是非常重要的，可以促進健康並端整儀容。有證據顯示古埃及人常常洗澡，祭司更被要求每日必行。因為沒有肥皂，所以他們製造清潔乳液與刷子。所有男女，不管甚麼社會階級，都會在皮膚上塗抹以植物與動物油製作，再摻以水百合、指甲花、香料、藥草與樹脂香味的油膏。如果有錢，也可以買到像是沒藥、乳香及其他異國原料。男女都描畫眼線以減低折射進入眼睛的陽光。綠色的眼影是孔雀石磨成的粉，黑色的則以方鉛礦──硫化鉛的一種──製成。醫學文獻指出，古埃及人認為眼圈敷上黑粉可以保護眼睛免於染疾。藝術作品中女性被描繪成塗抹著胭脂與口紅，不過這類化妝品的真實性目前還沒有被斷定出來。

埃及人製作的化妝用具種類繁多而且使用的材料相當廣泛。裝油膏的盒子有陶製、石製、玻璃、彩釉與木製，有時候還會做成禽鳥、動物或人的造型。黑色眼影粉裝在圓圓小小有平蓋的罐子或是柱狀的管子裡，附上用象牙、銅或者木製的塗抹棒。用來研磨顏料的硬石板在前王朝時期特別精緻，常被製成各種動物的造型，像是河馬、魚、龜和鳥，有時候是幾何圖形。至於用木頭、象牙或骨頭雕製成的「化妝匙」，確切的功能目前還不清楚，不過它的特色就是上面精雕細琢的裸女、禽鳥與動物圖案。鏡子則是高度拋光的金屬製成，嵌上銅製、木頭、象牙或彩釉的柄，它們不只是實用的化妝用具，也是喪禮的禮品，因為鏡子閃亮圓盤的形狀，使古埃及人聯想到太陽日盤與每天的重生。整套的美容用具還包括銅或青銅製的刀片還有用來捲髮的小夾子與工具。

休閒娛樂

許多證據顯示，在經濟狀況許可的條件下，埃及人很能享受娛樂活動。新王國時期繪製的墓室場景常出現晚宴與大餐。儘管這些場景描繪的可能是喪禮中用來向死者致敬的餐宴或慶典，但它們同時也透露些許埃及上流社會如何享樂慶祝的訊息。男人與女人穿著他們最好的服裝，在宴會中分開坐，旁邊跟著同性的侍者。食物與酒的份量都很大，舞者與樂師也在一邊娛樂大家。偶爾我們可以看到有人喝太多，醜態百出。

就像墓室壁畫、保存下來的歌詞與樂器所顯示的，歌與音樂是常見的娛樂活動。埃及人能彈奏多種樂器，包括類似響板的鈴舌，通常形狀很像人的手掌；搖鈴，或稱叉鈴，對女神哈托爾──音樂、舞蹈與愛的守護神──是種神聖的樂器；也有各式各樣的鼓；管樂器則包括長笛與蘆葦笛；弦樂器則有豎琴、七弦豎琴與詩琴。在慶典及宴席上的合樂團會包含歌者、打擊樂手、吹笛手還有豎琴家，以娛樂在場的貴賓。古埃及保存下來的歌曲中有讚頌法老與諸神的、有情歌，還有哈伯之歌（Harper's Songs）──鼓勵生者要「把握今朝」，因為人生短暫。

在家裡古埃及人似乎喜歡下棋。這從埃及的藝術作品與保存下來的棋具中可以證明。其中最有名的是賽尼特（senet）這種雙人遊戲，賽棋者爭奪的是幸福的來世。其他還有「耐力大挑戰」、「巨蛇」、「二十格」，和「獵狗與豺狼」等遊戲。體育活動可能源自於軍事訓練。埃及當時究竟有沒有舉辦體育競賽不得而知。但是從古王國時期開始，摔角手就出現在墓室所繪製的場景中，通常出現在繪有軍事活動的場景旁。陸上或是船上的棍鬥似乎也很受歡迎。狩獵不僅是運動也是取得食物的手段，尤其對於上等階級的人更是如此。家庭出遊去釣魚或獵鳥的畫面在整個法老時代所繪製的墓室場景中隨處可見。這樣的景象可能在喪禮中有儀式上的意義，但它們也一定反映了古埃及真實的生活習慣。

丹妮絲．多克西
波士頓美術館古埃及、努比亞及近東藝術策展人

Chapter 3
The People of Ancient Egypt

The Natural World of the Ancient Egyptians

The ancient Greek historian Herodotus famously called Egypt "the gift of the Nile," and in his description could hardly be more accurate. Located in northeastern Africa where rainfall is extremely rare, Egypt could never have developed its extraordinary civilization without the river. Prior to the construction of the twentieth century Aswan Dam, the Nile's annual flood deposited silt along its course through Egypt, creating a narrow band of exceptionally fertile agricultural land through what would otherwise have been uninhabitable desert. The ancient Egyptians were keenly aware of their dependence on the river, distinguishing between the habitable 'Black Land' of the valley and the chaotic and dangerous 'Red Land' of the desert. They personified the flood's abundance in the form of the fertility god Hapi. Yet, despite its obvious benefits the Nile also created uncertainty. A significantly low flood threatened drought and famine. Conversely, an overly high one could inundate villages along the banks, ruining irrigation canals, killing livestock and potentially damaging agriculture for years to come.

Egypt's geography determined both its external and internal boundaries. The traditional southern boundary, just south of modern day Aswan, was formed by a series of strong rapids, or cataracts, which prevented river travel. Southern Egypt, being upstream and at a higher altitude, was known as Upper Egypt, while the north was Lower Egypt. Upper Egypt corresponded to the Nile valley, a 660-mile long stretch of flood plain and low desert surrounded by steep cliffs. In southernmost Egypt the valley is very narrow but it widens considerably at certain points further to the north, extending to several miles on both sides of the river in central Egypt, the country's agricultural heartland. Lower Egypt begins near modern Cairo, where the Nile Delta opens toward the Mediterranean. The Delta extends over some 8,500 square miles (13680 km2) made up of low lying marshes, flat expanses of agricultural land and sandy 'turtle-backs' that were above water level even during the annual floods and were among the earliest settled areas in prehistoric times. Lakes and lagoons extend along the coast. Upper and Lower Egypt retained somewhat separate identities and, during periods of weakness in the central government, tended to break from one another. Partly for this reason the capital for much of Egypt's history was located near where the two regions join, just as it is today.

The Eastern and Western Deserts surrounding the Nile Valley provided wildlife for hunting, as well as raw materials such as stone for construction and sculpture, a variety of minerals, gold and semi-precious stones. A series of oases in the Western Desert linked the valley with trade routes leading to other parts of Africa. The largest of these oases, the Fayum, lies just south of the junction between Upper and Lower Egypt, and is connected to the Nile by the Bahr Yusef canal. A fertile area with abundant fish and wildlife, it was enhanced by drainage projects during the Middle Kingdom and Ptolemaic periods to create increased agricultural land, becoming a major population centre. Dry riverbeds, or wadis, running through the hills of the Eastern Desert connect the Nile Valley to the Red Sea ports, through which trading missions imported exotic products such as myrrh from regions to the Southeast.

In addition to providing fertile agricultural soil the Nile served as Egypt's principal means of transportation, communication and trade. While overland travel could be difficult, travelers by boat could easily access the entire length of the valley in a relatively short time. During the flood season even areas at the desert's edge were accessible, enabling building materials to be transported to the building sites of the royal pyramids and temples. So pervasive was the Nile in the Egyptians' minds, boat travel figured prominently in religious beliefs. The sun god, Ra, was believed to cross the heavens in a boat by day, and to travel through the world of the dead during the night. The dead likewise traveled by boat to the afterlife. Boats appear in the earliest decorated tombs and on early pottery, and remained a part of tomb decoration for centuries. Model boats were popular burial offerings and kings sometimes buried full-sized boats or even small fleets alongside their funerary monuments. The cyclical nature of the Nile's floods and the daily rising and setting of the sun also greatly influenced the ancient Egyptian worldview, religious beliefs, and creation myths. Stories of creation describe the world emerging from a watery abyss in the form of a mound, just as the levees and 'turtlebacks' of the Nile Valley and Delta emerged from the annual flood.

Egypt's flora and fauna played a role in their religion as well. Deities were often portrayed in the form of animals whose attributes they manifested. Gods associated with the sky and sun were therefore falcons, while the gods who protected cemeteries appear as jackals -- animals that could be seen scavenging in the desert cemeteries. The dung beetle, or scarab beetle, laid its eggs in balls of dung, which it pushed across the desert floor. Seeing the young beetles emerge seemingly spontaneously from these balls led the Egyptians to associate the scarab with rebirth and rejuvenation. It also came to be viewed as a manifestation of the sun god, pushing the solar disk across the heavens. Scarabs became one the most common amulets worn in Egypt. Plants and other natural motifs appear frequently in art and architecture. Temples, for example, featured columns in the form of papyrus and lotus plants, floors decorated with marsh plants and ceilings dotted with stars. Lotus blossoms, which close at night and reopen at sunrise, came to symbolize rebirth. Deceased kings were therefore shown emerging from lotus blossoms and tomb scenes and statues often show the tomb owners holding lotus blossoms or receiving them as offerings.

The Egyptian calendar was based on the schedule of the Nile's floods. The year was divided into three seasons, each containing four thirty-day months. The first season, akhet, or the inundation season, lasted from mid-June through mid-October. This was followed by peret, the growing season, from mid-October through mid-February and shemu, the harvest season, from mid-February through mid-June. Five additional days were added to the end of the year to bring the number of days to 365. In addition to this civil calendar, a lunar calendar based on the moon's phases determined the dates of certain religious festivals. Festivals occurred frequently though the year, honouring various deities, deceased ancestors, changes of season, moon phases and other significant events.

Ancient Egyptian Society

Ancient Egypt was primarily an agricultural economy, the vast majority of its population being farmers. Emmer and barley were the principal cereal crops, used to produce bread and beer, the staples of the Egyptian diet. Flax was grown for the manufacture of linen. Egyptian farmers raised a variety of legumes such as peas, lentils, and fava beans, along with other vegetables including lettuce, onions, leeks and herbs. Among the fruits grown were grapes, melons, figs, dates, and pomegranates. Domestic cattle, sheep, and goats were raised for their meat, milk and hides. Pigs also provided meat. Ducks, geese and pigeons furnished both eggs and meat. Wild birds, game and fish supplemented the diet. Cattle and donkeys were Egypt's primary beasts of burden, used to carry heavy loads and to pull plows and sledges. Wheeled carts played almost no role in ancient Egyptian transport; loads too heavy for a single animal were usually transported by boat. Horses were introduced only in the New Kingdom, around 1550 BC and even then served almost exclusively as chariot horses for the royal stables and elite military troops. Camels, now so closely associated with Egypt, did not appear until Roman times.

Egyptian society was highly structured and hierarchical, with little opportunity for upward mobility. The life of peasant farmers was harsh and usually thankless. They did not own their own land, but were indentured to the fields where they worked, which were owned by wealthy officials, the royal government or temples. They were paid in kind from the produce of these fields, wages that provided for little more than basic sustenance. During the fall and winter, they plowed the land and sowed seeds. The principal hand tool for breaking up soil was a simple, versatile, roughly A-shaped hoe composed of a flat wooden blade tied at an angle to a longer wooden handle. Plows, shaped like larger versions of the hoes, with wooden or copper plowshares, were pulled by pairs of oxen. During the growing season, irrigation was done primarily by hand and must have required substantial labour. After the harvest, cereal crops were cut with sickles, transported to winnowing facilities and stored in granaries owned by the landowners, temples or the royal administration.

In addition to farmers, the peasant class included household servants, launderers, fishermen, brick-makers, miners, stonecutters and other labourers. "The Satire on the Trades," a text extolling the virtues of becoming a scribe, demonstrates both the harsh lives of these labourers and the disdain with which they were regarded by at least some of the upper classes. About the brick-maker, it says, "his strength has vanished through fatigue and stiffness, kneading all his excrement," and about the launderer, "his food is mixed with filth and there is no part of him which is clean." In some cases, the gangs of workmen employed in royal building projects and mining expeditions were farmers conscripted by the government during the period when their fields were flooded. In the New Kingdom, as Egypt expanded its empire in Nubia and western Asia, prisoners of war entered the workforce as slaves. Convicted criminals laboured at some of the least desirable tasks of the peasantry, such as mining for gold in the Nubian deserts.

Somewhat higher on the social scale were relatively skilled workers employed in royal or temple workshops, such as the potters, jewellers, sculptors, weavers and furniture makers, as well as the artists responsible for decorating the royal tombs. Men held most of these positions, but women served as weavers and sometimes potters. These jobs tended to be passed down from parents to children, who learned their skills as apprentices. Within a workshop, the less experienced artisans carried out basic preparatory work while the master craftspeople performed the finishing work. Evidence from surviving town sites such as Amarna and Deir el-Medina demonstrates that master sculptors and painters enjoyed a particularly high status among these workers and by the New Kingdom formed something akin to a 'middle class'. For many such workers, however, life remained hard. The "Satire on the Trades" says regarding the coppersmith, "his fingers were like the claws of the crocodile and he stank more than fish eggs," and about the potter, "he burrows in the field more than swine to make his cooking pots."

Genuine status and the potential for upward mobility were restricted to the scribal class, the very small portion of the population – probably no more than five percent for most of ancient Egyptian history – who were able to read and write. Egypt's vast state and temple bureaucracy depended on scribes, and they were held in high regard and earned respectable incomes. Officials who could afford statues for their tombs or as temple dedications frequently chose to represent themselves in the characteristic pose of scribes, seated with papyrus rolls stretched across their laps and scribal palettes and inkwells hanging over their shoulders. Professional scribes were always men, although some upper class women were also literate. Preteen and teenage boys were trained either at home by their fathers or in scribal schools that were notoriously strict. They learned by copying and memorising exercises, lists and famous texts, and numerous examples have survived of scribal students' practice. Some students went on to specialize in foreign languages, medicine, mathematics, theology or administration, while others became more general practitioners. Along with working as government bureaucrats, they served the general population of their communities, recording correspondence, contracts, transactions, wills, marriage and divorce agreements, and lawsuits.

Near the top of Egypt's social pyramid, just below the king himself, were the elite officials who headed the various departments of the central administration. The king appointed these men directly, and early in Egypt's history only members of the royal family were selected. The highest of these officials, designated by the term tjaty in ancient Egyptian and called 'viziers' by Egyptologists today, were the equivalent of prime ministers, with additional powers as Egypt's highest judge. Among the other leading positions in the central government were the overseers of the treasury, royal works, the army, granaries, archives, and priests. Outside the capital, each of Egypt's forty-two administrative districts, known today by the Greek term 'nomes', was administered by a smaller-scale version of the central administration. The governor, or 'nomarch', who represented royal authority to his constituents, was served by his own council of ministers and was responsible for collecting taxes and conscripting troops on the king's behalf. In turn, he was expected to provide for the people of the district in times of shortage, presumably by drawing on accumulated reserves. Nominally, provincial governors were appointed directly by the king, but in reality the position was often hereditary.

Religion was inseparable from Egypt's government, and temples played a major economic role, owning farmlands and workshops and employing thousands or, in the case of temple of Amun at Thebes, tens of thousands of people, from high priests to farmers and craftspeople. The priesthood was vast and hierarchical, with the king serving as the ultimate high priest and ranks of priests below him drawn from a significant part of the population. There was not a full-time priesthood before the New Kingdom. Instead, officials rotated turns as priests and their wives as priestesses and temple singers. In provincial towns the governor was also the high priest in the cult of the local deity or deities. Priests were paid in the form of surplus produce from the temples. Only the highest ranked priests, the prophets, or 'god's servants' – hem-netjer in ancient Egyptian – had access to the innermost parts of the temple. Below them, members of the scribal class could serve as lector priests (khery-hebet) who read sacred texts and are identifiable in tomb scenes by their wide sashes. Lower status men formed a large class of wab-priests, or 'pure priests', with relatively limited access and no distinguishing accessories. Sem-priests, who performed offering rituals and certain funeral ceremonies, wore distinctive leopard-skin garments and shaved their heads. At funerals the heir of the deceased often filled the role of sem-priest. Beginning in the New Kingdom, particularly in the cult of Amun at Thebes, hereditary, full-time priests became the norm and gradually gained increasingly authority until eventually the influence of the First Prophet of Amun rivaled that of the king in southern Egypt. In general women did not hold high priestly offices, serving mainly as temple singers. However, during the Third Intermediate Period the 'God's Wife of Amun' played an increasingly important role at Thebes and by in the Dynasty 25 became the most important figure in Amun's cult.

The military was one field that offered some potential for upward social mobility, since soldiers from humble origins could occasionally be rewarded handsomely for their success in battle. For much of Egyptian history there was no full-time military staff with the exception of the highest-ranking commanders. Regular troops were primarily conscripted from districts within Egypt and its occupied territories in Nubia and western Asia. The Nubians were famed archers and seem to have served regularly as soldiers and policemen in Egypt. Military campaigns took place almost annually, usually during the flood season, with soldiers serving on a temporary basis, returning home in time to plant the next year's crop. Infantrymen, armed with spears, axes, bows and arrows and animal hide shields, made up the majority of the army. Horses and chariots were introduced during the Dynasty 18, but remained limited in use. Until the Late Period, Egypt had no navy, manning boats with the same conscripts who formed the army. Like most branches of the government, Egypt's military featured a large bureaucracy of scribes and officials, led by an 'Overseers of Troops', all under the ultimate command of the king.

Economy and Trade

The ancient Egyptian economy was driven by the state and by temples, which collected commodities and redistributed them to the population. Resources were stored for use in times of shortage and any surplus could be traded among institutions. A distinct class of merchants appeared only in the New Kingdom, about 1500 BC. The best evidence for marketplaces comes from tomb scenes that show the trade in food products such as bread, beer, meat and fish, and other basic, mainly home-produced goods, as well as surplus from temples and state institutions. Craftsmen exchanged tools, furniture, sandals, walking sticks and pottery, while traders from the deserts and oases offered domestic and captured animals, minerals such as the natron used in mummification, and other products. Coinage did not exist and trade was conducted entirely through a barter system. Prices for were measured in hekats, a standard grain measure. No ancient marketplaces have been identified archaeologically. They were probably open-air gatherings of temporary booths set up near harbours or in village squares. As places where large and diverse groups of people gathered, the markets must have served as centres for exchanging information as well as merchandise. Inter-regional trade among cities was conducted exclusively by representatives of temples and local governments. Such trade enabled areas such as central Egypt, which were rich in agricultural land, to exchange surplus grain for luxury goods and raw materials. Local governors also conducted trade missions on behalf of the king to distant areas via caravan routes linking the oases of the western desert.

Egyptian Houses, Villages, Towns and Cities

Evidence for ancient Egyptian towns and cities is unfortunately scarce because most settlements, from rural hamlets to regional capitals, were located on the flood plain close to the Nile and have now been covered by repeated flood deposits and modern construction. While most of Egypt was rural, its small villages were clustered around larger towns that served as the capitals of the districts known today as nomes. These centres housed the administrations of local governors and the temples of local gods. Egypt's largest cities were the regional capitals of Memphis in the north and Thebes in the south, the cult centers of Ptah and Amun-Re respectively, with populations that reached 30,000 to 40,000 people.

Some of our best evidence for Egyptian town and village life comes from government planned settlements built to accommodate the workers employed in building and maintaining the royal tombs and mortuary monuments. These include the Middle Kingdom towns at Kahun, the pyramid site of Senusret II near the Fayum, and at South Abydos, site of the mortuary complex of Senusret III in Upper Egypt. Deir el-Medina, located in the hills west of Thebes, was home to the workers who built the New Kingdom royal tombs in the Valley of the Kings and is Egypt's best-preserved ancient village. Because not only houses, but also written records such as correspondence, lists, accounts and legal documents survived, Deir el-Medina furnishes a lively account of everyday life in the village. King Akhenaten's short-lived capital at Akhetaten (present day Amarna) in central Egypt provides a unique glimpse of life in a New Kingdom capital city, including government buildings, royal palaces, residences for officials and skilled workers, and a workman's village. In the Delta, Tell el-Dab'a, ancient Avaris, was occupied from the Middle Kingdom through the early New Kingdom and served as the capital during the occupation of northern Egypt by the conquering Canaanites known as the Hyksos during the Second Intermediate Period.

The Egyptians built their houses with unfired, sun-dried mud brick, roofed with thatch laid over palm logs. The floors were covered with mud plaster or brick, while doors were made of wood and windows covered with wooden or stone grates. The size and configuration of homes depended on the family's wealth as well the house's location, but multi-roomed, rectangular floor plans were the norm. Urban homes tended to be long and narrow, and sometime had multiple stories. Suburban and rural homes had larger footprints and were usually single-storied, sometimes including walled gardens and pools.

The town sites at Kahun and South Abydos have much in common. Both are fairly large, walled settlements built at the edge of the desert, near the floodplain. Neither site has been completely excavated and portions of them are either destroyed or lie under modern construction, but their sizes have been estimated at approximately 130,000 square metres for Kahun and 45,000 to 60,000 square metres for South Abydos. Arranged in rectangular blocks divided by streets, the towns are made up of a relatively small number of very large mansions for the local elite and more numerous, smaller and more densely clustered houses for the rest of the population, all originally built to standard plans. The elite mansions of the local governing class featured a central residential unit with a large hall or 'living room' flanked by groups of smaller rooms and opening onto a broad courtyard with a columned portico. Courtyards to either side of the residential unit housed service areas for food preparation and storage, while an administrative area at the back was accessible through a separate entrance.

Deir el-Medina, built in the early part of Dynasty 18 and occupied through Dynasty 20, underwent three building phases, by the end of which it occupied about 5,600 square metres and contained some sixty-eight houses. The houses are arranged on either side of a narrow central lane, with smaller side streets providing additional access. A wall built of stone, with gates on the northern and western sides, surrounds the village. Although the houses adhere to the same basic plan, they vary considerably in size from forty to one hundred twenty square metres and most underwent modifications over time to accommodate the needs of their occupants. In the hills immediately west of the village was a cemetery of family tombs topped by small pyramids, some with elaborately painted burial chambers. Typical houses at Deir el-Medina were closely packed together and arranged in a long, relatively narrow plan. One entered the home through a square antechamber, off which was a narrow walled enclosure that probably served as a bedroom. Beyond the antechamber was the main living room, supported by one or more columns and featuring a small, private shrine for the worship of ancestors and a mud brick platform possibly for eating. Off the main room were additional bedrooms and at the back of the house was a small courtyard that served as the kitchen, with a storage cellar and clay oven. Some of the houses had red painted doors and walls decorated with images of household deities.

The city of Akhetaten, built in a bay of cliffs on the east bank of the Nile in central Egypt's agricultural heartland, was occupied for only a generation, providing a snapshot of urban life in the late Dynasty 18 capital city. A road running approximately 6 kilometres from north to south connected the central city with northern and southern suburbs. At the northernmost point was a mud-brick palace that may have been Akhenaten's royal residence. Proceeding south, a visitor would pass through a residential and administrative area before reaching the palaces of the queens and princesses, surrounded with gardens and pools, and then proceeding through another residential suburb to the central city. Here in the city's hub were the main temples and administrative buildings, such as the administrative palace, records offices, police headquarters, and government storage areas and workshops. Immediately south of the central city was a southern suburb that housed the families of administrative officials and master sculptors. Another series of temples and religious buildings marks the southern extent of Akhetaten. To the east of the city proper, nearer the cliffs into which were cut the tombs of the king and his officials, was a separate village for the necropolis workers, complete with its own small temples for ancestor worship.

The wealthy occupants of Akhetaten's upscale suburbs lived in walled estates that included not only the owner's house, but also servants' quarters, workspaces, granaries, kitchens, animal pens and stables. Although house designs varied, certain features are characteristic. They were generally built on a single story with a living area that included a columned porch, a small antechamber and a larger columned hall that served as the main living room. Private rooms and bedrooms were toward the back of the house, with separate suites for women, children and guests. Off the bedrooms, some upper class homes had stone-lined rooms for bathing and lavatories consisting of a stone or pottery seat over a pot filled with sand.

Additional information about Egyptian houses can be gleaned from house models placed in Middle Kingdom tombs and from New Kingdom tomb paintings showing houses. The latter depict the multi-level, urban dwellings of the Theban aristocracy. The basement level housed workshops for activities like weaving and food production, which were carried out by servants. The main floor had features reminiscent of the elite residences of the Middle Kingdom, including a columned entrance portico and a spacious main hall supported by a central column. Private rooms were located on the third floor, while food storage bins and ovens were built on the roof. Many homes also had roof terraces where the owners could enjoy cool evening breezes.

Furniture in most Egyptian homes was simple and spare, but the wealthy enjoyed finely crafted pieces made of imported wood. Woven reed matting covered the floors of houses and possibly interior doorways. In relatively modest houses the beds were built-in platforms of mud brick, while poorer Egyptians, the majority of the population, simply slept on mats on the floor. The upper classes slept in low wooden beds that slanted downward slightly toward the foot end, with legs often carved in the shape of animal feet, such as lions' paws or bulls' hooves. Canopies on frames of wooden poles protected them from insects. Pads of folded linen served as mattresses. Rather than pillows, the Egyptians used wood or stone headrests, as do some African cultures even today. Stools were the most common form of seating and a variety of types have survived including portable, folding stools. People often sat on the floor as well, eating on low tables. Chairs were luxuries limited primarily to the upper classes. Like beds, they often features legs carved to represent animal feet, and the best examples are inlaid with ebony, ivory and other exotic materials. Clothing, jewellry and other possessions were stored in boxes and chests rather than cupboards or closets.

Every home would have had a selection of pottery containers, as a result of which pottery is the most common type of artefact to survive from ancient times. Some basic shapes could be made at home while others were manufactured in specialized workshops. Jars served as versatile containers for storing all manner of foodstuffs, including grain, meat, and produce as well as liquids. Vats and large bowls were used in the preparation of bread and beer as well as for cooking. Prepared food was served on trays and in bowls, and beverages in cups and beakers. Pottery was also used for braziers, pot stands and tables. Most food was eaten with the hands and eating utensils are limited to such items as ladles and strainers.

The Family in Ancient Egypt

Ancient Egyptian families were typically composed of a husband and wife and their unmarried children, along with perhaps their elderly parents. The married children of poorer families may also have lived in their parents' homes, along with their children. The father, as head of the household, was expected to support the family financially, while the mother was responsible for maintaining the home, raising the children and, for families who could afford them, supervising servants. Women also harvested vegetable gardens, processed flour and baked bread, cooked meals, spun thread from flax and wove cloth. Egyptian marriages required parental approval and parents probably arranged many marriages outright, although love poems and charms suggest that romantic attachment certainly played a role in selecting a spouse. There is no evidence for wedding ceremonies and it seems that couples simply moved in together once the marriage was approved. Divorces were probably not common, but they did occur and could be initiated by either the husband or the wife. A divorce agreement was necessary for either party to remarry. Under normal conditions the husband was entitled to two-thirds of any property acquired during the marriage while one-third went to the wife, but adultery could force the wife to forfeit her share. Both spouses were allowed to keep any property owned prior to the marriage.

The Egyptians valued large families and held both male and female children in high regard. Female relatives and other women associated with the household assisted with the delivery of babies, perhaps accompanied by midwives. Most women married young and probably spent much of their lives either pregnant or nursing. The birth of children was a time for both celebration and concern. Childbirth was dangerous for both mothers and infants, leading expectant parents to invoke the aid of a variety of protective deities. Foremost among them were the goddess Taweret and the god Bes. Taweret is pictured with the body of a pregnant hippopotamus and the tail of a crocodile, while Bes appears as a dwarf with a lion's mane and serpentine tongue, and often armed with knives or other weapons. While both deities were fearsome in appearance they were clearly beloved for their perceived ability to safeguard mothers and babies, and their images often adorned beds and headrests. Other deities associated with childbirth included the god Khnum, who formed individuals on his potter's wheel, the frog goddess of fertility, Heqat, the personified birth brick, Meskhenet, and the serpent goddess Renenutet.

Egyptian mothers nursed their children for as long as three years. Childhood mortality rates were high, especially up to the age of four or five, but children who survived early childhood diseases stood a good chance of reaching adulthood. Most children received no formal education but from an early age they learned the skills necessary for adulthood by helping their parents in the home, fields or workshop. Higher status male children attended scribal schools associated with temples, being educated in reading, writing, mathematics, astronomy, geometry and other subjects. Like modern children, ancient Egyptian children enjoyed playing with toys, such as dolls, balls, tops, hoops and toy animals. Tomb scenes suggest that they also entertained themselves with wrestling, high jumping, juggling, dancing and acrobatics, and accompanied their parents in leisure activities like fishing, hunting and sailing.

The average life expectancy was low by today's standards, averaging about thirty years for most people, but higher for the wealthy who enjoyed better diets and less strenuous lifestyles. Due to the inherent dangers of childbirth, many women died young. As a result, when a man's tomb or stele mentions more than one wife it is often impossible to be certain whether he had multiple wives simultaneously or whether one succeeded the other. With the exception of the royal family, there is little evidence for polygamy. People who were lucky enough to survive past the average could potentially live to an old age, and some kings are known to have reached their nineties. Egyptian literature describes a "perfect old age" as one hundred and ten years, although this number is undoubtedly an ideal rather than reality. The Egyptians held elderly relatives in high esteem and took pride in caring for aged parents. Surviving literary tales also associate old age with wisdom and sage advice.

Many families kept pets, especially dogs and cats. Dogs were a particular favorite, and are pictured in Egyptian art from its earliest days. They are the only animals known to have been given names, and some pet dogs were mummified and provided with their own coffins. Some breeds similar to greyhounds, basenjis and salukis were probably bred mainly for hunting. Cats were domesticated from local wild cats, probably around 2000 BC, and undoubtedly served to help protect grain stores from rodents. Tomb paintings suggest that they also accompanied people on hunts for wildfowl, stalking through the reeds to catch unsuspecting birds. New Kingdom scenes show them in a more domestic context, seated comfortably beneath their owners' chairs. Wealthy Egyptians also kept wild animals such as monkeys and exotic birds.

The Ancient Egyptian Diet

The two staples of the Egyptian diet were bread and beer, supplemented by meat, fish, vegetables, fruit, eggs, oils, butter, and honey. In the Predynastic Period, the principal sources of meat were hunting and fishing. In pharaonic times oxen became the most popular meat source, being force fed to fatten them prior to slaughter. Because oxen were valuable, however their meat was probably reserved for festivals and other special occasions. Sheep and goats provided meat for everyday consumption. Although the Egyptians were long thought to have shunned pigs as a food source, pig bones excavated at town sites indicate that pigs were in fact frequently eaten. The Egyptians also ate small animals such as hedgehogs and mice. In addition to domesticated ducks and geese, they consumed a variety of wild birds including pigeons, doves, quail, partridges, herons and storks. Chickens were introduced only in the Graeco-Roman era.

Emmer and barley were Egypt's main cereal crops, and most houses would have had grindstones and clay ovens for preparing bread. Statuettes and tomb scenes show women at work grinding flour and baking bread. Conical pottery bread moulds produced long loaves of bread, and flat, circular loaves were baked by flattening dough directly on the sides of ovens. Because sand and grit from the querns found its way into the flour, bread was gritty and caused significant wear on teeth. The mummies of those who reached old age show the severe dental problems that resulted from a lifetime of bread consumption. Beer produced from the same ingredients as bread and in the same production areas was unlike modern beer, being thick and rich in nutrients. Wine, made from grapes, figs and date palms, was available primarily for the wealthy.

For those who could not regularly afford meat, legumes such as fava beans, peas, lentils, and chickpeas provided necessary protein. Among the other vegetables available to the Egyptians are lettuce, scallions, garlic, radishes, leeks, celery, herbs and cucumbers. Many of these items also had medicinal qualities and lettuce was thought to be an aphrodisiac. Papyrus, best known as a source of early "paper", also furnished a nutritious food plant. Dates were the most popular fruit, along with sycamore figs, grapes, doum palm nuts, melons and wild berries. Pomegranates first appeared in the New Kingdom. In Graeco-Roman times the variety of fruits expanded widely with the introduction of olives, peaches, pears and quince.

Medicine

As with all pre-industrial societies, life in ancient Egypt was fraught with danger from illness and injury, along with venomous serpents and scorpions and other dangerous creatures. Both malnutrition and parasites were commonplace among the poor. Disinfectants, antibiotics and pain relievers were unknown although there is evidence that the Egyptians imported opium, probably to relieve pain. Those who laboured in the fields, on military and mining expeditions or on building projects were especially prone to debilitating injuries. With the likelihood of infection, injuries that are easily treated today were frequently fatal. In an attempt to combat life's many dangers the Egyptians relied on both medicine and what they called heka, which would today be considered magic. Egyptian doctors seem to have had a surprisingly accurate knowledge of certain medical issues, although many preserved medical remedies would certainly have done very little to help the patient. A number of medical papyri have survived to provide information on treatment and diagnosis of a wide range of ailments, and further evidence comes from the study of human mummies. These medico-magical papyri describe three stages of care. The first included diagnosis and prognosis. Prescriptions and recipes for medications followed. Finally and of equal importance were the spells and incantations that accompanied treatment.

Magical and medical practitioners were one and the same, being equipped with wands, amulets and spells as well as medicinal plants and surgical tools. Unlike today's concept of magic, heka had no inherent negative connotations and could be used for both good and evil, depending upon the user. The Egyptians sought medical help from divine sources as well. Thoth, a god portrayed as an ibis or baboon, was the patron deity of medicine, as well as science, mathematics and writing. The goddess Isis, associated with both motherhood and magic, was thought to protect health, as was the lioness goddess Sekhmet, who defended against all forms of pestilence. Certain deities served more specialized functions. The goddess Sekhmet, for example, warded off scorpions. Imhotep, the Dynasty 3 sage remembered as the architect of the earliest pyramid, king Djoser's step pyramid at Saqqara, was deified later in Egyptian history and became a popular god of medicine.

Personal Religion

Religion was inextricably linked to everyday life in ancient Egypt, but it was practiced in a far less organized fashion than are most religions today. Temples were not considered places for public worship, but rather homes or estates for Egypt's gods and goddesses. The ancient Egyptian word for 'temple', hut-netcher, literally means 'house of the god' and the term for the highest class of priests, hem-netcher, translates as 'servant of the god'. Temples were off limits to the vast majority of the population; the king and certain priests, in their role as 'gods' servants', were the only people allowed to see the innermost sanctuaries. There, the cult statues underwent an elaborate daily ritual in which they were bathed, anointed, fed, clothed, and offered libations and incense. Even nobles and officials could enter only the outer courtyards of the great national sanctuaries. Smaller, local shrines and temples, however, offered access to a larger segment of the population.

For the average Egyptian, access to the state's most important deities took the form of festivals and processions, during which the cult images of gods and goddesses were carried outside in boats, symbolically 'sailing' through the streets or on the Nile. The Egyptian calendar featured frequent festivals, some of which had nationwide importance. Two of the best-documented festivals took place at Thebes and involved the procession of Amun-Ra's cult statue from the great temple at Karnak. The 'Beautiful Festival of the Valley' occurred at the beginning of the summer harvest season. Statues of Amun, his wife Mut, and their son Khonsu were carried from their temples on the east bank across the Nile to cemeteries on the west bank. There, they were taken to visit royal mortuary temples and other sacred sites. During the festival, families visited the tombs of their dead relatives and had meals in the courtyards. During the Opet festival, held during the inundation season, Amun-Ra's cult image traveled south from the Karnak temple to the temple of the royal life force, or ka, at nearby Luxor. The Opet feast was the most important Theban holiday, aimed at re-invigorating both Amun-Ra and the king. Festival processions in which sacred statues traveled from one temple to another are also attested at other sites including the sanctuaries of Horus at Edfu and Hathor at Dendera.

Abydos, the burial place of Egypt's earliest kings, became the sanctuary of Egypt's principal funerary god, Osiris. The annual festival of Osiris drew pilgrims from throughout Egypt, and wealthy visitors who came to Abydos on business or as pilgrims commissioned small shrines and stelae along the processional way from the temple to the desert location believed to be Osiris's burial place. A stela dedicated by the late Middle Kingdom official Ikhernofret contains one of the few preserved contemporary accounts of an ancient Egyptian festival. Sent by the king to refurbish Osiris's cult statue, Ikhernofret had the honour of leading the procession. According to his description, the day's activities included a dramatic reenactment of the battle between Osiris and his brother and adversary, Seth.

In addition to the great state temples and their festivals, local and private cults allowed ordinary Egyptians contact with the divine world. The workmen's villages at Deir el-Medina and Amarna both had small public chapels. A favourite subject of worship at Deir el-Medina was the deified king Amenhotep I, the first king to utilize the Valley of the Kings and the founder of the tomb-builders' settlement. Domestic cults were also practiced in individual homes. Many houses at these sites had shrines for the worship of deceased relatives or household deities. The shrines took the form of niches in the wall, sometimes occupied by an 'ancestor bust', and a small offering table. At Amarna, where the worship of Egypt's traditional state gods was prohibited by Akhenaten's new and short-lived religion, some households had shrines for the worship of the living royal family. Nevertheless, the city's inhabitants continued to worship popular household deities as well.

Magic played a part in personal religion as well. From the dawn of Egyptian history, amulets and other implements were called upon to facilitate prowess in hunting, ward off enemies, protect livestock and promote strength, fertility and even love. In many cases the same literate men who served as priests in the temple cults acted as the local magicians for their communities. Practitioners of magic were required to know the correct spells, prayers and hymns for a given situation, and to have the appropriate equipment, such as figurines, wands and amulets. The array of Egyptian magical devices is wide and varied. Wands or knives made from hippopotamus tusks decorated with images of Bes, Taweret and other protective creatures were used to draw circles around the beds of pregnant women, new mothers and young children. Clay serpent figurines were placed in the corners of bedrooms to defend sleepers. Figurines of foreign captives inscribed with the names of enemies were ritually damaged or destroyed to ensure the enemies' defeat. A famous tale tells the story of a man who seeks revenge against his wife's lover by placing a wax crocodile into the water where he is swimming. Once in the water, the crocodile comes to life and kills the victim.

Fundamental to Egyptian personal religion and morality was the concept of maat, loosely translated today as 'justice'. Maat essentially referred to the natural way of the world, including living in accordance with one's correct social standing and acting in a manner that promoted Egypt's traditional ways of living. Greed, gluttony, and flagrant self-promotion were frowned upon, especially when dealing with parents, elders or those in positions of authority. Officials were expected to look after the needs of their subordinates, provide for the people of their towns, show generosity toward the poor and afflicted and behave in a manner that pleased the king and satisfied the gods.

Evidence for Egyptian moral values derives from a range of surviving texts. Among the most informative of these are works of instructional literature, which began to be written down in the Old Kingdom and continued throughout Egyptian history. Phrased in the form of rules from fathers to sons or teachers to students, 'wisdom literature' encouraged readers to behave in the interest of public good, to respect parents and the elderly, honor the king, care for the poor and display modesty, humility and generosity. The "Maxims of Ptahhotep", preserved on a Middle Kingdom papyrus, offers the following practical advice for a man in a position of authority:

Be patient when you are listening to the words of a petitioner;

Do not dismiss him until he has completely unburdened himself…

A man who has been wronged desires to express his frustrations

Even more than the accomplishment of the (justice) for which he came.

Ptahhotep advises the husband:

Be gracious to your wife in accordance with what is fair.

Feed her well; put clothes on her back;

Ointment is the balm for her body.

Rejoice her heart all the days of your life,

For she is a profitable field for her lord.

Funerary texts such as the Coffin Texts and Book of the Dead included 'negative confessions' in which the deceased seek to defend their behaviour in life and justify their admission to the afterlife by proving that they have done nothing contrary to maat, including both committing what would today be considered sinful or criminal acts and engaging in actions that the Egyptians considered unnatural. As the heart of the deceased is weighed against a feather representing maat, he or she declares:

I have not caused pain.

I have not caused weeping.

I have not killed.

I have not caused to be killed.

I have not made suffering for anyone.

The behaviour of characters in literary works offers further insight. Stories, for example, promote fidelity between husbands and wives and loyalty among siblings. In idealized autobiographies in tombs and on votive stelae officials assert that they have appeased the gods, pleased the king and promoted the welfare of their families and communities. The biographies applaud careful speech, obedience, knowledge of one's responsibilities and, increasingly, personal piety. A Sixth Dynasty official, for example, claims in his tomb biography:

I judged two partners so as to content them,

I saved the weak from one stronger than he as best I could;

I gave bread to the hungry, clothes to the naked,

I landed one who was boatless.

I buried him who had no son,

I made a ferry for him who had none;

I respected my father,

I pleased my mother,

I brought up their children.

Dress and Fashion in Ancient Egypt

Much of our information about ancient Egyptian clothing comes from artistic representations in tombs. Actual surviving clothing, however, often differs dramatically from what appears in art, suggesting the need to exercise caution in interpreting tomb decoration as evidence. As with many cultures, clothing was an indication of status. Certain accoutrements, headdresses in particular, were reserved for the king. As a rule, the more elaborate a person's attire was, the higher his or her social and economic status. Farmers and labourers are depicted wearing simple loincloths or occasionally only a belt. Female servants and dancers are often shown nude, as are children, although children almost certainly wore clothing in reality.

Linen, the principal fabric used for clothing, came in varying degrees of thickness, with the finest being remarkably soft and sheer. Tomb scenes and models show almost exclusively women engaged in the complex process of spinning flax fibers into linen thread and weaving it into cloth. The earliest looms were horizontal ground looms, while from the New Kingdom onward an upright, two-beamed vertical loom also came into use. Most clothing was either white or off-white, while jewellry, belts and other accessories provided splashes of colour. Shawls and cloaks made of wool from sheep and goats supplemented linen clothing for cool winter weather.

The basic garment for men was a wrap-around kilt knotted at the waist and varying in length from the knee to the mid-calf. Aprons, cloaks and fringed tunics might be worn over the kilts. A longer, thicker, wrap-around garment that reached from the chest to the calves was popular during the Middle Kingdom. Women of the Old and Middle Kingdoms are typically shown wearing tight-fitting, sheath-like dresses with shoulder straps. Long after the style was popular it continued to appear in representations of goddesses, who were presumably believed to favour old-fashioned attire. Surviving dresses, however, are usually looser and some have sleeves, indicating that artistic conventions are not always reliable. During the New Kingdom long and elaborately pleated and fringed clothing became popular for both men and women. A triangular, diaper-like, linen loincloth was the basic undergarment for both sexes and was the only garment worn by field labourers.

Hats were never popular in ancient Egypt, with the exception of royal headdresses. Winnowers and women grinding grain sometimes appear in artistic representations wearing loose kerchiefs over their hair. For special occasions, women wore diadems and other hair ornaments, ribbons or garlands of flowers. Footwear was simple, and most people probably went barefoot for much of the time, as do rural Egyptians today. The most common shoes were sandals made of reeds or leather, with Y-shaped straps and sometimes upturned toes. Leather shoes that covered the entire foot were eventually introduced in Roman times.

Both men and women wore elaborate and brightly colored jewellry that enhanced their otherwise fairly monochromatic dress. Semi-precious stones such as carnelian, amazonite, feldspar and amethyst were mined in Egypt itself, while turquoise was imported from the Sinai Peninsula, and lapis lazuli was acquired via trade routes that reached as far as present-day Afghanistan. Beads were also produced from locally available shell and hippopotamus ivory, as well as glazed steatite. A particularly popular medium for beads and amulets was faience, a paste made of ground quartzite mixed with minerals that, when fired at a high temperature, produced a lustrous and colorful glaze. Blue and green were the most common colors but from the New Kingdom onward artisans could also produce faience in yellow, purple, red and white. Glass also became available in the New Kingdom, after which it became common for beads and inlays.

Among the most distinctive and characteristic items of ancient Egyptian jewellry were broad collars composed of numerous bead strands and pendant drop beads, probably modeled on floral garlands. Balancing the weight of these collars were counterpoises that hung down at the back. In addition to collars, the Egyptians wore necklaces, pectorals, bracelets, wristbands, rings, anklets, diadems and beaded belts and aprons. Earrings and ear studs were relatively late arrivals, appearing around 1550 BC. New Kingdom Egyptians often pierced their ears. Hair ornaments, including hairpins, combs and hair rings, are attested from the earliest burials throughout ancient Egyptian history.

In addition to being decorative, jewellry could serve a symbolic, religious or magical purpose. Both men and women of all social strata wore amulets, the power of which was believed to derive not only from their form but from their color and material as well. Amulets of ferocious animals such as lions, crocodiles, hippopotami and serpents afforded the wearer protection, while also transferring the animal's strength and prowess to the wearer. Fish amulets defended the wearer against drowning. Amulets of gods and goddesses invoked the special powers of the deities represented. Jewellry featuring Taweret, Bes and Heqat aided fertility, as did cowrie shells, which are thought to have reminded the Egyptians of female genitalia. Scarabs promoted rejuvenation. Perhaps the most popular amulet was the wedjat, representing the eye of the falcon god Horus, which was torn out during his conflict with the god of chaos, Seth, but later restored. The eye of Horus was thought to promote health. Other amulets take the form of hieroglyphs, bestowing the sign's meaning on the wearer, such as the ankh for 'life', and the djed-pillar for 'stability'.

Hairstyles in ancient Egypt changed over time, with different styles enjoying favour at different times. In addition to the current fashion, the length and style of hair could reflect a person's age, sex, profession or social status. Children, for example, are typically shown with their heads shaved, aside from a single, plaited sidelock. Certain priests also shaved their heads as a sign of purity. Because of the hot weather, many people probably wore their hair short or shaved their heads entirely, and most farmers and labourers are shown with closely cropped hair. When dressing for formal occasions well-to-do Egyptians wore wigs woven from human hair, possibly supplemented by vegetable fiber. Tombs scenes and statues show elaborately braided wigs, sometimes with a few curls of natural hair protruding from underneath. During the Old Kingdom, thick, shoulder-length wigs were fashionable for both sexes, while long, straight wigs gained popularity for Middle Kingdom women. Long, thick, curly wigs were in vogue for both men and women in the New Kingdom. To prevent the hair from drying out, New

Kingdom Egyptians sometimes wore cones of scented tallow, which would gradually melt to condition and perfume the hair. Henna was used to colour gray hair. Men usually did not sport facial hair aside from a short goatee, although moustaches enjoyed a brief period of popularity during the Old Kingdom and some early Middle Kingdom mummy masks feature beards.

Hygiene, Cosmetics and Toiletries

Cleanliness and personal hygiene were important to the Egyptians, promoting their health as well enhancing their appearance. There is evidence that they bathed frequently, and priests were required to do so daily. Lacking soap, they manufactured cleansing creams and scrubs, and both men and women of all social classes anointed their skin with unguents and oils made of vegetable or animal fat scented with water lily, henna flowers, spices, herbs and resins. For the wealthy, imported products like myrrh, frankincense and other exotic ingredients were also available. Both men and women wore eyeliner to reduce the sun's glare. Green eye makeup was ground from malachite, while black was made from galena, a sulfite of lead. Medical texts indicate that kohl was thought to protect the eyes from disease. Women are portrayed in art wearing rouge and lip colouring, although actual examples of these products have not been identified.

The Egyptians manufactured cosmetic equipment in a wide variety of types and materials. Containers for unguents were made of pottery, stone, glass, faience, and wood and sometimes took the form of birds, animals or human figures. Kohl was stored in small, squat jars with flat lids or in cylindrical tubes and was applied with sticklike applicators of ivory, bronze or wood. Hard stone palettes used for grinding pigment were particularly elaborate during the Predynastic era, when they were made in the shape of animals such as hippopotami, fish, turtles and birds, as well as in geometric shapes. 'Cosmetic spoons', the exact function of which remains unclear, were carved in wood, ivory and bone, sometimes featuring elaborate carvings of nude young girls, birds and animals. Mirrors of highly polished metal, with handles of copper, wood, ivory and faience, served not only as functional cosmetic tools but also as funerary gifts, since their shining discs reminded the Egyptians of the solar disc and its daily rejuvenation. The repertoire of cosmetic tools also included copper or bronze razors and tweezers and implements for coiling hair.

Entertainment and Recreation

There is ample evidence that the Egyptians, to the extent their economic ability allowed, enjoyed leisure activities. Banquets and feasts are frequently portrayed in New Kingdom tomb scenes. While these scenes probably represent funerary feasts or festivals honouring the dead, they provide a glimpse into the nature of other celebrations enjoyed by upper class Egyptians as well. Men and women, dressed in their finest attire, were seated separately and attended by servants of their own sex. Food and alcoholic beverages were served in large quantities, while dancers and musicians entertained the guests. Occasionally we see someone who has consumed too much alcohol and suffers the results.

Songs and music were popular forms of entertainment, as attested by tomb paintings, surviving song lyrics and actual musical instruments. A variety of instruments were enjoyed by the Egyptians, including castanet-like clappers, often shaped like human hands; rattles known as sistrums, which were sacred to the goddess Hathor, patron deity of music, dance and love; several types of drums; wind instruments including flutes and reed pipes; and stringed instruments like harps; lyres and lutes. Musical ensembles including singers, percussionists, flutists, and harpists entertained diners at festivals and feasts. Among the songs that have survived from ancient Egypt are hymns to the king and to various gods, Harper's Songs encouraging the living to "seize the day" since life is short, and love songs.

At home, the ancient Egyptians appear to have enjoyed playing board games. Several such games are attested both in art and by surviving boards and equipment. The best known is senet, a two-player game in which competitors vied for entrance to a happy afterlife. Others include 'endurance', 'serpent', 'twenty squares' and 'hounds and jackals'. Athletic events probably derived from what were originally military exercises. Relatively little is known about whether or not the Egyptians held organised competitions. Wrestlers appear in tomb scenes from the Old Kingdom onward, often near scenes of military activities. Stick fighting, both on land and in boats, also seems to have been popular. Hunting was a sport as well as a source of food, especially for the upper classes. Family excursions to fish or hunt wildfowl are ubiquitous among tomb scenes throughout pharaonic history. While such scenes may have ritual significance in the funerary context, they must also reflect actual practices.

Denise Doxey

Curator of Ancient Egyptian, Nubian and Near Eastern Art at Museum of Fine Arts, Boston

古埃及國王

遠從埃及王朝在西元前 3000 年成立之時，其中樞人物就是國王。他（或在少數的情況下為「她」）是神聖的存在，在皇家命名準則裡清楚地記載：國王的是隼頭人身的神祇荷魯斯（Horus）的化身、君主政體的守護神，以及太陽神「拉」（Re）之子。最完整的國王名稱發生於第五王朝。當時皇家命名單位給予國王五個名字：

- 「荷魯斯」名：將國王與荷魯斯做連結。通常寫於名為「賽瑞克」（serekh）的方框中，並加上荷魯斯的隼。
- 「奈布提」（Nebti）名：象徵國王為北方及南方女神的門徒。
- 「金色隼」名：含義不明。
- 「普力諾門（Prenomen）」：寫於於名為「卡達旭」（cartouche）的橢圓形框中，在「雙王」或後來的「兩地（南北埃及）主宰」頭銜之前。「雙王」通常翻譯為「上下埃及之王」，但或許實際上是意指他在物質及精神上的統治權。
- 「諾門（Nomen）」：同樣也是寫在「卡達旭」中、「拉神之子」或後來的「萬象之主」頭銜之前。

除了最後一個名字，所有上述稱號都在國王登基時授予；「諾門」則是國王出生時所給予的個人名字。

「法老」頭銜（埃及文為 per-aa）首度出現於新王國時期，字面上意義為「大房子」，也就是「皇宮」。它逐漸成為國王本人的代名詞，就像「白宮」意指美國總統，而「白金漢宮」意指英國女王。

國王的名字形式隨時間而改變，有時短如「格言」，有時長如政策說明。「普力諾門」總是與太陽神「拉」有關，而「諾門」在某些時期則是描述國王受到某些神「鍾愛」，或是統治了某些特定城市，特別是底比斯以及赫里歐波利斯（Heliopolis）兩處宗教重鎮。

在埃及大半的歷史中，「普力諾門」及「諾門」最為廣泛使用，當空間及內文只容許一個名字時，則使用「普力諾門」。這種情形在第三中間期及後埃及時期有所改變，「諾門」變成較常使用的名字。現代的史學家採用「諾門」來稱呼不同的國王，雖然有些人參照原始埃及文抄本，有些則採用古希臘文文章裡的譯名，例如「圖特摩斯」（Thutmose，譯自埃及文）之於「圖特摩西斯」（Tuthmosis，譯自希臘文），以及「尼斯班尼布傑德」（Nedibanebjedet）之於「斯門代斯」（Smendes）。值得注意的是，古代國王被賦予的序位（例如「圖特摩斯四世」）純粹只是現代慣例，在古代，擁有同樣出生名的國王則是以他們不同的登基名來區分。

在這些不同希臘文章來源裡看到的名字版本中，可以發現在西元前第三世紀時由馬內托（Manetho）所記述的、殘存的埃及歷史片段。他將第四世紀中以前的埃及國王區分為不同朝代，而這種分類方法仍為現代歷史學家所用。現代學者更進一步將數個政治及社會特徵相似的連續朝代歸納為不同的「王國」或「時期」。大體來說，「王國」一詞反映了國家在該時期的統一；而「時期」則暗指了國家的分裂或為他國所控制。

「朝代」、「王國」和「時期」的分類對歷史研究是很有幫助的。因為在西元前 690 年以前發生的歷史事件並無精確的日期，這樣的分類法使史實發生的相對年代得以排列出來，而不需要依賴西元前日期的記載。埃及人依當時國王的執政期間來記載史實，而非像今天所用的時代（例如：西元前、西元後）來記錄。有些事件的日期可以從太陽的活動現象大致計算出來，有些則可以參照其他國家較精確的大事表來推算出來。但這些方法仍有許多出錯的機會，而且學者們往往也因各自有不同詮釋而難以達成共識。

國王穿著特殊的服裝，擁有數頂王冠、帽子及權杖。最常見的兩頂王冠為紅色及白色，分別代表北埃及與南埃及的統治權；兩者結合的雙王冠則代表了統一的國家。然而這兩頂王冠似乎也象徵了之前所提到「雙王」頭銜的二元性。其他頭飾的含義就更難推測了，有些則僅出現於某些時期的文物中。

從不同史料所記載的國王列表看來，埃及國王原則上只有一位。然而，偶爾也有國王協同另一位統治者共同治理國家，通常是王位的繼承人。也有另一種情形是當國家分裂時，不同地區的人民各自擁戴自己的君主。他們可能早已在內戰時就是彼此的敵人，例如在第十九王朝後期，阿門邁蘇（Amenmessu）是塞堤二世（Sety II）的對手，或是當埃及陷入長期分裂時不同地區的君王，如第一、第二和第三中間期。

在埃及人的宇宙觀中，國王是人與神的媒介；他代表了神而管理並維持宇宙的平衡，在當時稱為「馬特」（Maat），通常譯為「真理」。因此，在廟宇中國王被描繪為唯一的主祭，雖然實際上主持例行儀式的是祭司。理論上，所有的政府官員皆由國王指派，所有土地也皆由國王處租借。國王推廣「馬特」的角色則是透過維持國家實質安全及抵制混亂的力量，特別是外侮。在第一王朝到羅馬時期文物裡常見的一種藝術雕像主題，便是國王使用鎚矛處死敵人的情境，而且往往裝飾於廟宇的入口處。

雖然現代歷史學家提出了多種的說法，我們對法老掌權的機制仍非全然了解。有論點指出埃及王權是由女性傳承，每一位男性國王候選人必須與「女繼承人」結婚，這種論點一直到二十世紀中期之前都還存在。雖然這個論點解釋了許多國王與其姊妹結婚的現象，因為這類通婚在古埃及社會裡並不常見，但例外實在太多，顯然這種繼承王位的方式應無法律根據。現在合理且實際的說法清楚地顯示：新國王須為前任國王的長子。最高的神化身為國王世間父親的神學解釋強化了對未來國王的概念。這個神話的完整版（阿蒙（Amun）在此為神聖父親）始於一些新王國時期的神廟。由長子繼承父業這個概念也深深根植於埃及人的思想與神學中。

在一場宣布繼承人的正式儀式中，繼承人會出席於一些重要人物面前。舉辦這場儀式的原因是為了確保在現任國王去世之時，真正的繼承人是毫無爭議的。當沒有皇子在世時，這個儀式也提供了一種提名繼承人的機制，這在孩童夭折率高的古代也是不無可能的。在歷史記載中，似乎至少有一次是女兒被提名為繼承人（妮菲如塔（Neferuptah）由阿蒙涅姆赫特三世（Amenemhat III）所提名，推測是由於沒有存活的兒子）。雖然在大部分的情形下會有男性親戚或非皇室成年男性被證明有資格而獲得提名（如拉美西斯一世（Rameses I）獲得哈瑞赫柏（Horemheb）的提名）。

在少數的例子裡，女人成了國王，但都是在特殊的例外情況下。蘇貝娜芙（Sobekneferu，第十二王朝末期）似乎是前述妮菲如塔的妹妹；哈謝普蘇（Hatshepsut）和娜芙妮佛拉頓（Neferneferuaten，第十八王朝）皆為國王的共治者，並無獨立的統治期；桃絲瑞特（Tausret，第十九王朝）在年輕王儲死後取得了王位，而之前她是攝政王的身分。在第六到第八王朝期間富傳奇性的尼托克裏斯（Nitocris），可能事實上是男性的名字被誤認為女性。在托勒密時期，雖然因為一些情況而有不少皇后成為唯一的統治者，如有名的克麗奧佩脫拉七世（Cleopatra VII），但她們從未獲得國王的全部頭銜，因此也不被列為女性法老。

在上述堪稱理想的繼位安排中，長子，也是將來當然的王位繼承人，必須是國王正妻的子嗣。從中王國時期末期開始，國王的正妻就擁有「大皇后」（King's Great Wife）的頭銜。許多例子顯示國王還擁有其他的配偶，通常也都擁有皇后的頭銜。如上面所說，有時候這些妻子中也包括了一位以上的親姊妹或同父異母妹妹。但大多數的妻子可能都是平民出身，而她們父母的資料也很少被清楚記載。又有些時候國王將大皇后的頭銜給予一個或以上的女兒，尤其在拉美西斯二世（Rameses II）在位後期。然而，對於他們彼此間是否有性關係，我們並不清楚，也或許只是這些女兒繼承了她們過世母親的義務及政治功能。

除了王位繼承人以及國王的妻子之外，皇室也包括了國王的母親（如果在世的話）及其他兒女。雖然在第四王朝期間，國王的兒子在政府體系中擁有很高的職位，但這很快就停止了，直到古王國時期結束前，只有少數幾位皇子為世人所知，到了中王國時期則更少了。雖然在第十八王朝期間，有些皇子曾擔任祭司的職務，不過一直要到第十九王朝之後，關於皇子比較重要的記載才被發現。這些記載也反映出當時皇室的擴張及公眾化。相關的行動包括了任命皇子擔任軍方要職和主要祭司職務。而這種情形一直延續到後埃及時期。

國王的女兒似乎並無特別的角色，雖然有些在神廟中擔任歌者，有些在第十八到二十六王朝期間擔任阿蒙神之妻（God's Wife of Amun），作為將對於大祭司的女性角色。這個職務一開始是次於大皇后的角色，但最後成為未婚公主的頭銜。除此以外，許多公主們嫁給官員、軍人及祭司階層為妻。

埃及的君主政體概念延續了超過三千年，甚至一直到她受外邦（波斯王朝、馬其頓王朝及羅馬帝國）統治之後。外邦的統治者通常採用埃及國王的頭銜及名稱，並被描繪為正規的埃及統治者，在神廟的場景中穿著一般的埃及服裝，雖然有些根本從未踏上埃及國土一步。

如上面所說，國王是埃及唯一的權力掌握者，並擁有無上權威，能夠任命國家所有官員與祭司。他個人的幕僚有時也承擔一些特別的任務，如為特定目的而召開委員會。除了在最早時期之外，最資深的事務官為「西維爾」（Vizier），地位大至與今天的首相相當；在當時，南北埃及有各自的大臣。他們在處理行政事務上是國王的代理人，也是首席法官。在大臣之下，政府機構分為不同的部門，其相對的角色與職責隨時代而有不同，但大致包括了公眾事務、經濟、糧食儲存與農業。在古王國時期，工程的監督者通常也是大臣，不過在新王國時期則設有特別的職司，並配有次要的負責人以涵蓋特定地區或機構。

除了中央政府以外，區域及地方管理機構也組成了龐大的網路系統。這些地方機構的組成、規模及概念隨著時間而有不同。在中間期的時候，這些地方權力中心有時形成軍閥，並抱著對王位的熱望。這在第三中間期晚期時特別常見。

進一步的管理機構在新王國時期於努比亞建立，被規劃成一個特別行政區，由國王的庫什之子（Son of Kush）所管轄。他並非國王真正的兒子，而是握有大權的總督。在他之下有官員組成的網絡，偕同當地的努比亞王子們共同組成有別於埃及政府本身的特別政府。

直到新王國時期，顯著的軍隊編制才出現。這是因為圖特摩斯一世及三世在巴勒斯坦及敘利亞攻佔了龐大的領土，並由他們的繼承人進行合併。在第十九王朝之前，這批軍隊被分為步兵團和戰車兵團，由皇子們擔任高級職位。埃及帝國在敘利亞及巴勒斯坦地區主要是以間接控制的方式統治，由留在當地的統治者、埃及督導及駐軍共同管理。這些當地統治者的孩子則被送往埃及接受教育，由此確保他們得到應有的教化，同時也作為可能的人質去牽制他們的父親，使之有良好的表現。

至於更廣泛的埃及對外政策，最佳資料來自新王國時期及其後的時代。由埃及的阿瑪納（Tell el-Amarna）及土耳其的波加斯卡列（Bo azkale）發現的西元前十三、十四世紀的外交檔案裡顯示，當時有一些統治者被視為「偉大的王」（Great Kings），以符合平等原則。他們稱彼此為「兄弟」（Brother），並與其他地位較低的領導人作出區分。在不同時代，埃及人把西臺、亞述、巴比倫、阿里沙（Alashia，今日的塞普勒斯）及米坦尼（Mitanni，今日的北敘利亞）的統治者歸類為「偉大的王」。

當領土的利益重疊時，這些掌權者之間的衝突就可能發生。尤其在新王國時期的西北敘利亞及其後的巴勒斯坦。然而，帝國的擴張也導致了主要強權間的國土侵略，如埃及在第二十五王朝末期被亞述人短暫占領，及之後依序被波斯、馬其頓及羅馬帝國所吞併。

當早期的羅馬皇帝代表法老的形象出現並資助傳統廟宇的建設時，埃及迅速淪為羅馬帝國的一省。殘存的古代君主體制符號逐漸式微。馬克西米努斯·代亞（Maximinus Daia，西元 305-313 年）似乎是最後一位擁有法老身分的羅馬皇帝。而隨著君士坦丁一世（Constantine I）改信基督教以後，很快地，法老的君主政體便徹底消失了。

古埃及的重要國王

丹
丹（Den）為第一王朝的國王，據推測他應為前任國王傑特（Djet）的兒子，其母為梅奈茨（Merneith），據說她在丹仍是個孩子時代為統治埃及。在丹至少長達 32 年的統治期間，有幾個重大事件在其中的六年間發生，並被記錄在第五王朝時編纂的皇家編年史裡。這些事件包括了三個在埃及東北方的軍事行動，以及神聖圖像的製造與宗教儀式的舉行。在國王墳墓裡發現的一系列標示暗示了該區域發生的軍事行動，其他標示則記錄了用魚叉刺河馬的儀式，以及即位週年慶典。

皇室的墳墓被建築在阿比多斯（Abydos）墓地的一區，稱為烏姆卡伯（Umm el-Qaab）。這裡是許多埃及最早期國王們的墓地。丹的墳墓設計在當時相當創新，是第一個擁有階梯入口的皇室墳墓，還有石塊鑿成的升降閘門及花崗岩鋪面。

古夫
古夫（Khufu，較完整的名字為「荷努姆古夫」（Khnumkhufu），希臘文為基奧普斯（Kheops））是第四王朝的第二位國王。他是前任國王斯尼夫（Sneferu）及其妻海特裴莉斯一世（Hetepheres I）的兒子，統治埃及可能有二十年之久，但幾乎沒資料記錄當時的歷史事件，除了在遠方礦場的一些活動。古夫的妻子是已被辨明身分的梅耶尤蒂一世（Meryetyotes I）及在後來資料中發現的第二位夫人荷努森（Henutsen）。他至少有六個兒子及三個女兒，其中兩個兒子雷吉德夫（Djedefra）及哈夫拉（Khafra）後來依序取得了王位。當時還有為數不少的皇室成員擔任包括大臣等的政府要職。

古夫最被世人所熟知的是他在吉薩（Giza）所建造的金字塔，被現代人稱為「大金字塔」（the Great Pyramid）。它除了是最大的金字塔外，也擁有許多革新的設計及結構。它是龐大墓地的一個部分，而這是第一次金字塔建築被納入整體的墓地規劃中。

古夫在後來的一些民間故事裡被描述為一位暴君，為了建造他的金字塔而奴役無數人民，還關閉了神廟。然而並沒有具體證據證明這些負面評價的真實性，而且人民對這位國王的膜拜一直延續到他過世兩千年以後。

哈夫拉
哈夫拉（Khafra）為古夫的兒子（希臘文：齊夫倫，Khephren）。他在其兄雷吉德夫及另一位可能的統治者塞斯卡（Seth-ka）之後得到王位。哈夫拉在位大約 25 年，並有至少四位妻子：梅莉珊卡三世（Meresankh III）、卡門羅內比蒂一世（Khamarernebty I）、荷肯努荷德潔（Hekenuhedjet）、波森妮（Persenet），還有至少十個孩子。

哈夫拉的主要紀念遺址是位於吉薩的第二金字塔，以及其附屬建築。這座埃及第二大的金字塔是埃及的金字塔複合建築邁向標準化的重要一步。它的複合建築體包括了比至今所見還要廣大的神殿，是世上保存最完整的神殿建築之一。神殿的裝飾品包括了數件特別精緻的國王雕像。

至今我們尚不清楚哈夫拉與吉薩大人面獅身像之間的關聯。雖然哈夫拉的金字塔和人面獅身像的相對關係很明顯，但沒有直接證據顯示是他修築了此像。它可能是由前任國王所建，或者早在幾世紀前就被修建完成亦不無可能。

蒙圖荷泰普二世
蒙圖荷泰普二世（Mentuhotep II）為第十一王朝上埃及國王因提夫三世（Intef III）與其妻伊雅哈（Iah）之子。在位 51 年間，他在前 20 年僅管理其祖先的領土，埃及北部則由定居赫拉克利奧波里（Herakleopolis，今天的 Ihnasiya el-Medina）的第十王朝所統治。然而，持續不斷的衝突導致蒙圖荷泰普最終統一了國家，並修改命名系統以紀念這個勝利。他首先採用了新的荷魯斯名以及登基名。之後，一些重要的事件又導致了荷魯斯名的更動及登基名拼法的調整。

證據顯示，再次統一後埃及的東方、西方及南方分別有若干軍事活動；與此同時，國內各地許多建設也正在進行。最主要的遺址包括來自象島（Elephantine）、艾卡伯（El-Kab）、格貝萊因（Gebelein）、托德（Tod）、代爾巴拉赫（Deir el-Ballas）、丹德拉（Dendera）、阿比多斯及卡納克（Karnak）。此外，設計新穎的神殿式墓穴也在底比斯西方的巴哈里（Deir el-Bahri）被修建，內部有階地的設計，據推測可能原本是金字塔，以及在石鑿廊道盡頭的棺室。這座墳墓在拉美西斯九世（Rameses IX）時曾被檢查過，仍然保存完好，不過隨後就被盜了。指向神廟的谷地內有國王主要官員的墓穴，而國王的許多家人則被葬在神廟裡面。這些家人包括蒙圖荷泰普二世六位已知的妻子，其中泰姆（Tem）及尼斐魯二世（Neferu II）顯然是最年長的。

哈謝普蘇

埃及歷史中，僅有寥寥可數的女性擁有國王的頭銜，其中最明確被證實的就是第十八王朝的哈謝普蘇（Hatshepsut）。她是圖特摩斯一世（Thutmose I）及其妻阿莫斯（Ahmes）的女兒，其後也成為她同父異母弟弟圖特摩斯二世的大皇后。在她姪子（也是繼子）圖特摩斯三世仍年幼的時候，由她先擔任攝政王，同時也還保留其皇后的頭銜。七年以後，她成為圖特摩斯三世的正式共治者，並享有法老的全部名號。她持續扮演這個角色有另外十四年之久。在這段時間哩，哈謝普蘇派遣了一商貿探險隊到東非的蓬特（Punt），並進行大量的建設，包括她在巴哈里的陵廟。歷史上對女王與她的高官塞奈穆特（Senenmut）之間的關係有許多爭論。身兼哈謝普蘇女兒教師的塞奈穆特，最後葬在女王陵廟外面不遠處，並塑像於陵廟內，而他的石棺也造得與女王相匹配。

哈謝普蘇在圖特摩斯三世 21 歲時失蹤，據推測是因為死亡。她的許多紀念遺跡在二十年後被毀壞，對此現象至今仍無清楚的解釋。在擔任攝政王期間，她在底比斯西邊的瓦底西卡達卡艾爾傑德（Wadi Sikkat Taqa el-Zeide）建造了一座陵墓，但最終還是在帝王谷裡面修建了 KV20 墓穴，作為其最後的安葬所。學者推測她的木乃伊可能在附近的 KV60 被重葬。

圖特摩斯三世

圖特摩斯三世（Thutmose III）是圖特摩斯二世（Thutmose II）與其次妃伊西特（Iset）之子。在他父親死亡時，他仍只是個小孩子。早期是由他的姑母哈謝普蘇攝政七年，大約在他成年時，哈謝普蘇成為他的共治者。他姑母失蹤以前，圖特摩斯三世的活動幾乎沒有記錄，但當他單獨掌權之後，便展開一系列的重要軍事行動，從第 22 年開始總共延續了有二十年之久。在這段期間，圖特摩斯越過了幼發拉底河，在敘利亞及巴勒斯坦地區將埃及帝國的版圖拓展到前所未有的大小，更對埃及在努比亞的控制進行擴張與合併。

圖特摩斯是偉大的建造者，卡納克神廟（Karnak）就是在其統治期間被大幅擴建的。他的建築遺跡遍布埃及與努比亞。他第一位妻子可能是他同父異母的姊姊涅弗魯利（Neferure），之後又先後娶了錫蒂亞（Sitiah）及梅耶契（Meryetre），後者比他還要長壽。這些妻子為他生了至少五個兒子，包括他的繼位者阿蒙霍特二世（Amenhotep II），還有至少兩個女兒。

圖特摩斯 53 歲過世之時被葬在帝王谷 KV34 墓穴中。他常被視為新王國時期最偉大的國王，被人民膜拜了一千五百年之久。他的木乃伊被發現與其他新王國時期的國王們一起藏在第二十一王朝大祭司皮努吉姆二世（Pinudjem II）的的墳墓（TT320）中，應是在第二十二王朝示撒一世（Sheshonq I）當政期間為了安全因素而存放於此的。

阿蒙霍特三世

當阿蒙霍特（希臘文：阿蒙諾菲斯，Amenophis）三世仍是王子的時候，他的形象就出現在其教師們的紀念碑上。那時他尚未繼承父親圖特摩斯四世（Thutmose IV）的王位。他是皇后穆諾梅特（Queen Mutnodjmet）的兒子，之後娶了提伊（Tiye）為妻，她是騎兵將軍尤亞（Yuya）與其妻提優（Tjuiu）的女兒。這段婚姻特別在一系列聖甲蟲寶石上被宣告，其他則是在慶祝統治早期的一些事件時被發布。

阿蒙霍特三世已知有兩個兒子：圖特摩斯及阿蒙霍特（後更名為阿肯納頓，Akhenaten），還有至少五位女兒。身為王儲的圖特摩斯後來在孟斐斯成為普塔（Ptah）的大祭司，但卻在大約第 30 年時英年早逝。最年長的女兒西塔蒙（Sitamun）則在阿蒙霍特三世在位的某個時間點得到了大皇后的頭銜。

阿蒙霍特三世的軍事活動相較於在中間期的前任國王們是比較少的。除了一些在努比亞的維安行動被證實之外，幾乎沒有什麼其他紀錄。相反地，這位國王的建設活動倒是分布得相當廣泛，且具有歷史意義。在底比斯西方的馬爾卡塔（Malqata），阿蒙霍特三世建造了一座複合宮殿建築，同時也在科梅爾哈坦（Kom el-Hatan）建造一座巨大且創新的神廟。在河對岸的卡納克，他也為阿蒙雷（Amun-Re）的神廟增建了一座新的塔門，並為鄰近的蒙圖（Mentu）及穆特（Mut）的神廟院落進行大量的建設。在稍微南邊的地方，一座新的神廟在樂蜀（Luxor）興建，和在努比亞索利卜（Soleb）地區的建築非常相似。在某些阿蒙霍特三世所建的聖殿裡面，他以神的形象出現，特別在他在位第 30 年時首次舉行即位慶典（jubilee）之後（他總共舉行三次即位慶典），他就被轉化為太陽神。這個神格化的過程也包含了提伊皇后，她在離索利卜不遠處的西迪因加（Sedeinga）以神的形態出現。

這種神格化的行為是以當時日益興盛的、對太陽神阿頓（Aten）的崇拜為背景。阿蒙霍特三世以「耀眼的太陽」作為暱稱，並將阿頓神的名字用在許多地方。對阿頓神的崇拜後來在下一任國王阿肯納頓統治期間變得更具獨占性。

阿蒙霍特三世在他在位四十年之後過世，被埋葬在帝王谷西支流的墓室（WV22）中。他的墳墓後來被盜，為了安全起見，他嚴重毀損的木乃伊便遷移至阿蒙霍特二世的墳墓（KV35）中，並在 1898 年被發現，後移至開羅。

阿肯納頓

阿肯納頓是阿蒙霍特三世與提伊的次子。他以阿蒙霍特四世（Amenhotep IV）之名即位，並在登基後很快地與娜芙蒂蒂（Nefertiti，可能是他母方的表姊妹）成婚。他們隨後就生了六女中的長女梅莉塔塔（Meryetaten）。這些女孩們被描繪在許多當時的紀念建築上，但卻只有一處提到他的兒子：圖坦庫阿頓（Tutankhuaten）。後來這個兒子成了國王圖坦卡頓（Tutankhaten，後來又改名為圖坦卡門（Tutankhamun））。

在剛即位的幾年間，阿肯納頓是以傳統方式被描繪；但他在位第四年以前，他和隨從們就被表現成扭曲而創新的造型，而且據他的主要雕塑師巴克（Bak）特別記述的文章裡，說是由國王所屬意。伴隨著國王造型的改變，太陽神阿頓的肖像畫法也從常見的擬人法變成抽象的日輪造型，光芒自太陽降下，每道光芒底端都有一隻手，後者舉著象徵「生命」的符號對著皇室成員的鼻孔。不久之後，國王便將他自己的名字改為阿肯納頓。

伴隨著這樣的轉變，尊阿頓為至高（如果尚非「唯一」的話）神的運動便展開了。據知這是世界上首次一神信仰的實驗。無論這是純粹神學上的轉變，或是因為政治因素欲降低傳統諸神祭司（特別是阿蒙）的權力，後來便僅成為學術上的爭論了。在某個時間點之後，許多在紀念碑上的神祇（特別是跟阿蒙相關）的名字和形象都被摧毀了。這場破壞偶像的行動在阿肯納頓整個在位期間都有許多記載。

最早出現新造型的紀念遺跡是一座位於卡納克的阿頓神大廟。它被建造在主要神廟建築體的東側。然而很快地，一座新的城市在阿瑪納（Tell el-Amarna）建立，大約位於舊首都孟斐斯及底比斯的中間。這座城市不但是阿頓虔誠的信仰中心，也是埃及的新首都。

有關阿肯納頓對外關係的資料是在一片刻有楔形文字的板子上發現的。這片板子是在阿瑪納所尋獲，因此被稱為阿瑪納書信（Amarna Letters）。這份資料代表了當時強權國與埃及的書信往來，也包括了埃及諸侯國與皇家法院間的通信。在阿肯納頓在位第 12 年時，埃及舉辦了一場大型的國際慶典，許多國家都派代表向國王致上賀禮。這場盛會的重要性目前無法確定，其中一個可能性是為了慶祝阿瑪納城的正式完工。沒想到不久之後，好幾位皇室成員死亡了，其中包括了提伊及多達三個女兒。據推測可能是在第 12 年時，外國代表將瘟疫帶入埃及而導致。

在第 12 年以後，阿肯納頓很快地指派了一位共治者斯蒙卡拉（Smenkhkare）。斯蒙卡拉與梅莉塔塔成婚，不過似乎很快就亡故了。之後，共治者的位置被一位女性娜芙妮佛拉頓所取代，這位女性的身分幾乎可以被確定就是娜芙蒂蒂。阿肯納頓在他在位第 17 年時過世，被埋葬於他在阿瑪納城的陵墓中。圖坦卡頓接替了他的位子，但很快地便反轉了阿肯納頓的宗教改革。在圖坦卡門去世以後，阿肯納頓在遺跡上的名字和形象盡被毀壞，他和他直接繼承人的名字也從正式的埃及國王名單中被刪除。

拉美西斯二世

拉美西斯二世（Rameses II）是第十九王朝的第三位國王，也是賽堤一世（Sety I）的長子及繼承人。他統治埃及長達 67 年。拉美西斯二世在位的第一個十年幾乎都在北敘利亞進行征戰，在該區域，埃及人長期以來和西臺人的一些當地領袖一直有霸權上的衝突。這些戰爭包含了第 5 年的卡疊石（Qadesh）戰役。雖然這場戰役充其量只是個隨機的戰略，卻在廟宇的牆上被大肆宣傳為一場埃及偉大的勝利。然而，因為這場戰役產生了一個根本的改變：在第 21 年時一項和平協議在埃及與西臺間被簽訂了。

拉美西斯二世在努比亞與西方的利比亞也有非常活躍的軍事行動。但他在位大部分時間是在埃及和努比亞進行大型的建築計畫。值得注意的是，國家的政治中心此時已轉移到尼羅河三角洲的東北方，在這裡拉美西斯建造了一座新的行宮 – 波拉美西斯（Per-Rameses），位置相當於現在的坎提

爾（Qantir）。

在即位第 30 年的時候，國王首次舉辦即位慶典，在他遜位前至少舉辦了十二次慶典。隨著國王年紀漸長，越來越多例行公事便由王儲代為執行。至少四位拉美西斯兒子相繼扮演這個角色，最後一位，也就是第十三個兒子麥倫普塔（Merenptah）繼承了他的王位。

拉美西斯二世的傑出成就使得皇室成員的形象也因而出現在公眾的紀念建築上。他有大約 50 位兒子及相似數量的女兒被排成一列，銘刻在神廟的牆上。在當政前期，他很不尋常地擁有兩位大皇后：妮菲塔莉（Nefertiry）及伊賽特娜芙瑞（Isetneferet）。在她們過世之後，幾位女兒們又承接了大皇后的頭銜；雖然我們並不清楚這只是因為公務上的目的，還是他們真有肉體關係。拉美西斯也將西臺阿圖西斯（Hattushilish）的一位女兒，以及他自己的妹妹荷努邁爾（Henutmire）封為大皇后。拉美西斯二世死後被葬於帝王谷的 KV7 墓穴裡，後來他和其他人的木乃伊一起被發現藏在皮努吉姆二世的墓室中。

麥倫普塔

麥倫普塔是拉美西斯二世的第十三個兒子，為妻子伊賽特娜芙瑞所生。麥倫普塔似乎在他父親在位的最後十年就已經擁有王儲的身分。他的大皇后和他的母親同名，都叫作伊賽特娜芙瑞。他有至少兩名兒子及一名女兒。在他當政第五年時，利比亞人與來自地中海東北方的海洋民族（Sea Peoples）組成聯盟入侵西北埃及，他們之後在尼羅河三角洲的西南邊被打敗。這些事件，包括在巴勒斯坦進一步的軍事活動，都被以文字和浮雕形式記錄在位於卡納克的阿蒙雷神廟中。

後來的這些事件也被記錄在一對勝利紀念碑上，分別被豎立在卡納克與底比斯西邊的麥倫普塔紀念神廟中。在上述被打敗的政體中，以色列也在記錄中被提及。這是唯一一在古埃及文字裡出現的紀錄。這段提及以色列名稱的記錄使得這紀念碑亦被稱為「以色列石碑」（Israel Stela），並使麥倫普塔成為「出埃及記的法老」（Pharaoh of the Exodus）的可能人選。在拉美西斯二世時期與西臺人建立的和平似乎仍維繫著，麥倫普塔甚至在西臺遭遇饑荒時運送穀物以「維持西臺土地的生命」。

麥倫普塔的建築工程分布很廣，他現存最大的作品於底比斯發現。他位於底比斯西邊的紀念神廟就建造在阿蒙霍特三世神廟的北邊，且運用了許多自該建築回收的石材在他自己的神廟上。在當政十年以後，麥倫普塔被埋葬在帝王谷的 KV8 墓室中，他的木乃伊在 KV35 貯藏室裡被發現，現保存於開羅博物館。

塞堤二世

賽堤二世（Sety II）是麥倫普塔的長子及繼承人。在阿門邁蘇（Amenmessu，可能是他的親生兒子）的侵略下，他在位第二年時似乎對努比亞及南埃及失去了控制。第五年的時候，賽堤奪回了整個國家的控制權，但卻在一年後即死去。有幾處重要的遺跡在後來被發現，除了位於卡納克的一座神龕和一對方尖碑以外，在別處還發現了一些次要的遺址。

由於賽堤二世在位期間發生的一些事件，位於帝王谷的賽堤之墓（KV15）修建時並不順利，最後草草結束，留下未完成的廊道及拼湊成的墓室。一具標上他名字的木乃伊在 KV35 貯藏室裡被發現，現保存於開羅博物館中。

拉美西斯三世

拉美西斯三世是塞斯那赫特（Sethnakht）的兒子及繼承人，也是第二十王朝的創建者。在第十九王朝的戰亂後，他在埃及的重建上貢獻良多。在這過程中，他時常有意地仿效拉美西斯二世。不僅在國王的名稱上以二世作模範，也將二世孩子們的名字直接用來命名自己的子女。拉美西斯三世也仿效拉美西斯二世，娶了至少兩位大皇后：伊賽（Iset）及蒂蒂（Tyti）。

在位早期，拉美西斯三世忙於處理利比亞及海洋民族再次與埃及的衝突，雖然他們之前曾遭麥倫普塔擊退。第五年的時候利比亞在西尼羅河三角洲處的戰況得到斬獲。但隨後的戰役中，拉美西斯的軍隊取得了勝利，也因此暫時安定了西部邊界。

然而，第二次更嚴重的危機在三年後發生，海洋民族顯然推翻了當時在黎凡特（Levant）的主要政權，這其中還包括了西臺人，逼近埃及東部的海陸邊界。再一次地，拉美西斯成功地打敗了敵人，並在他位在梅迪涅特哈布（Medinet Habu）的大神廟裡以許多裝飾品頌揚其勝利。第 11 年，利比亞再一次進攻，而他也再一次將之驅逐。超過 2000 名俘虜被殺，而被擄獲的首領也遭處死。

他在位最後的二十年以前，國家出現明顯的經濟問題；這個問題是因付不出薪水給西底比斯麥那（Deir el-Medina）村中修建皇陵的工人而揭露。這在第 29 年時導致了一場工人的靜坐罷工。在這樣的背景下，另一個危及國王生命的陰謀正醞釀著，動機是為了讓其中一位妻子的兒子取代現有王儲，也就是將來的拉美西斯四世。第 32 年時這個計畫執行了，拉美西斯三世也的確因此而死，但陰謀的目的卻沒有達成。國王最後埋葬在帝王谷中的 KV11 墓穴中，他的木乃伊最終則移到皮努吉姆二世墓穴的貯藏室裡。

奧索爾孔二世

奧索爾孔二世（Osorkon II）是第二十二王朝的代表人物，擁有利比亞人的血脈。他是前任國王塔克羅特一世（Takelot I）及其妻卡佩絲（Kapes）的兒子，統治埃及至少長達四分之一個世紀。自他在位早年，便於一座在首都塔尼斯（Tanis）的雕像上銘刻了他正式的計畫。計畫包括了將主要官職指派給他的孩子們，而這似乎違反了當時將主要封地分派給泛皇家成員的慣例。

奧索爾孔二世是相當大量的建設者。他為塔尼斯的阿蒙神廟增建了一個前庭及塔門，並於布巴斯提斯（Bubastis，今日的 Tell Basta）興建了不少建築物，包括一座在第 22 年時慶祝他即位週年的大廳堂。奧索爾孔二世其他的建築遺跡也存在於埃及境內許多地方。

這位國王有數位已知的妻子，最主要的一位是卡羅瑪瑪（Karomama），可能是他的姊妹。他的長子示撒在孟斐斯被指派為普塔的大祭司；而另一個兒子尼姆洛特（Nimlot）則成為中埃及的要塞赫拉克利奧坡里的大祭司，之後則被轉往底比斯擔任阿蒙的大祭司。還有另一位兒子赫納克特（Harnakht）亦成為阿蒙神在塔尼斯的大祭司，不過卻在還是個孩子時就死亡了。

在底比斯，控制權在某個時候轉讓給當地的國王海瑞西斯（Harisiese）。這成為啟動國家根本分裂狀態的第一個事件；國王在位末期，更因為塔克羅特二世（Takelot II）在底比斯的權力篡奪使分裂變得根深蒂固。這個分裂狀態持續了超過一個世紀。

奧索爾孔二世的王位在塔尼斯由示撒三世所繼承。他被埋葬在塔尼斯的 NRT-I 墓穴中。

夏巴卡

夏巴卡（Shabaqo）是努比亞國王卡斯塔（Kashta）的兒子。他接替了耗時三十年終於併吞埃及並建立第二十五王朝的皮耶（Piy），成為埃及與努比亞合併之後的王國統治者。然而，努比亞對埃及的控制在夏巴卡即位時退縮到僅剩南部地區，北部地區則落到薩伊斯（Sais）的國王巴肯瑞尼夫（Bakenrenef）手中。但這很快就被夏巴卡所扭轉。在夏巴卡的第二年間他推翻了巴肯瑞尼夫的政權，據傳並將他燒死。

政權安頓後，夏巴卡開始在埃及主要城市建造一些紀念建築，特別是孟斐斯和底比斯。另外也為位於卡納克的神廟增加不少附屬建築。許多夏巴卡的作品展現了仿古的風格，如收藏在大英博物館裡的夏巴卡石（Shabaqo Stone）文字就號稱是來自古王國時期宗教文章的抄本。政治上，位於阿敘得（Ashdod）的城邦黎凡特（Levantine），其國王以阿曼尼（Iamani）反叛亞述王叛統治，夏巴卡則提供以阿曼尼政治庇護。

夏巴卡有三位妻子為世人所知，並有好幾位兒女，包括後來的國王塔努塔蒙（Tanutamun）以及阿蒙神的大祭司哈瑞馬各（Haremakhet）。夏巴卡的王位由夏比特庫（Shabitqo）接任，這位繼任者應該也是他的兒子。他死後則被埋葬於位在蘇丹境內庫魯（El-Kurru）的金字塔 Ku15 中。

艾登·道森
布里斯托大學考古及人類學系資深研究員

Chapter 4

Kings of Ancient Egypt

From the moment the Egyptian state came into existence around 3000 BC, its pivotal figure was that of the king. He – or on a few occasions she – was a divine being, made explicit in the royal titulary, which named the king as the incarnation of the raptor-god Horus, the patron deity of the monarchy, additionally as the son of the sun-god, Re. In its fullest form, which came into being during Dynasty 5, that royal titulary gave the king five names:

- The Horus name, linking the king with Horus, and normally written in an enclosure known as a serekh, and incorporating the falcon of Horus.
- The Nebti name, signifying the king as protégé of the goddesses of the north and south.
- The Golden Falcon name, of uncertain significance.
- The Prenomen, written in an oval frame known as a cartouche, and preceded by the title 'Dual King' – often translated as 'King of Upper and Lower Egypt', but perhaps actually referring to his earthy and spiritual functions – or, later, 'Lord of the Two Lands' – i.e. northern and southern Egypt.
- The Nomen, also written in a cartouche, and preceded by the title 'Son of Re' or later, 'Lord of Appearances'.

All but the last of these names were conferred at the king's accession; the Nomen was the king's own personal name, bestowed at birth.

The title 'Pharaoh' (Egyptian: per-aa) first appeared during the New Kingdom, and means literally 'Great House', i.e. the royal palace. It only gradually came to be a way of referring to the king himself, much in the way that 'The White House' has come to mean the President of the United States of America, and 'Buckingham Palace' the Queen of the United Kingdom.

The styles of royal names vary with time, sometimes being very short 'mottos', at other times being long statements of policy. The Prenomen always included a reference to the sun-god Re, while the Nomen could during certain periods include statements that the king was 'beloved' of certain gods or had dominion over some particular city – in particular the key religious centres of Thebes and Heliopolis.

For much of Egyptian history, the Prenomen and the Nomen were the most widely used names, with the Prenomen being the name used where space or context could only allow one. This changed during the late Third Intermediate and Late Periods, when the Nomen became the name more usually employed. It is the Nomen that supplies the names used by modern historians to designate individual kings, although some employ a direct transcription of the original Egyptian, others use the forms of the names found in the writings of ancient Greek authors. Examples include 'Thutmose' (Egyptian)/'Tuthmosis' (Greek) and Nedibanebjedet/Smendes. It should also be noted that the ordinal numbers given to ancient kings (e.g. 'Thutmose IV') are purely a modern convention – in ancient times kings of the same Nomen were distinguished through their having different Prenomina.

Amongst the sources of these Greek versions of Egyptian royal names are the surviving fragments of an history of Egypt written by a priest named Manetho during the third century BC. In this, he divided the kings of Egypt prior to the mid-fourth century into a number of separate numbered dynasties, a classification that is still used by modern historians. The latter have, however, grouped the dynasties into a series of 'Kingdoms' and 'Periods' where common political and social themes applied. Broadly speaking, the kingdoms reflect eras of unity, the periods those of disunity and/or foreign control.

The use of dynasties, kingdoms and periods is useful because accurate dates for events prior to 690 BC do not exist, and allow a relative chronology to be developed that is largely independent of dates BC. The Egyptians dated by the regnal years of the contemporary king, rather than by an era such as is used today (e.g. BC/AD). Some broadly accurate dates can be calculated by reference to solar phenomena and events that can be linked to other nations with a more accurate chronology, but in all cases there are potentially significant margins of error or lack of consensus among historians as to their interpretation.

The king wore distinctive regalia, in particular a set of crowns, fabric head-coverings and a number of sceptres. The two most common crowns, the Red and the White, had associations with northern and southern Egypt, respectively, with the united country signified by their combination in the Double Crown. However, these two crowns also seem to have embodied the duality noted above in the Dual King title. The meanings of the range of other head-dresses are even more difficult to divine, with some only being found at certain periods.

In principle, there was only ever one king of Egypt, a view that was enshrined in the various lists of kings that have survived. However, there were occasions when a king took a co-regent to rule alongside him – in most cases the heir to the throne. Also, there were times when the country lost its unity and parts of Egypt acquired their own separate kings. These might have been rivals during a civil war – for example, Amenmessu as the opponent of Sety II during the latter part of Dynasty 19 – or represent a long-term division of Egypt, as was the case during the latter parts of the First, Second and Third Intermediate Periods.

At a cosmic level, the king was the intermediary between human beings and the gods on whose behalf he ruled and maintained the balance of the universe that was referred to as 'Maat' – often translated as 'Truth'. As a result, in temples he was depicted as the sole officiant, although in reality priests carried out the daily cult. All officials in the state were theoretically appointed by the king and all land was ultimately leased from him. Part of the king's role in promoting Maat was made concrete by maintaining the physical security of Egypt and holding back the forces of chaos - especially in the form of foreigners. A very common artistic icon was therefore the king executing enemies, usually with a mace, found from Dynasty 1 through to Roman times, and often adorning the outer gateway of a temple.

The mechanism by which a pharaoh came to power is not altogether certain, with various suggestions put forward by modern historians. For many years up to the middle of the twentieth century it was assumed that the right to the throne passed through the female line, with each male candidate for the crown having to marry the 'heiress'. While this theory helped explain the phenomenon of many kings marrying their sisters – something not otherwise generally found in ancient Egyptian society – it became apparent that there were far too many exceptions for this to have been the legal basis for succession to the throne. It now seems reasonably clear that in practical terms a new king should have been the senior son of his predecessor. This was theologically reinforced by the notion that on the occasion of the conception of the king-to-be, the chief god became incarnate in the king's earthly father. The full version of this myth (with Amun as the divine father) was set out in a number of New Kingdom temples. The concept of the eldest son succeeding to the offices of his father was also deeply embedded in Egyptian thought and theology.

There also seems to have been a formal ceremony of the proclamation of the heir by his presentation to an assembly of important persons. This ceremony may have been intended to ensure that there was no possibility of dispute as to who was the true heir at the death of a reigning king. It also provided a mechanism for nominating an heir where there was no surviving royal son - not impossible given the high level of child mortality in pre-modern times. There seems to have been at least one occasion when the opportunity may have been taken to nominate a daughter as heir (Neferuptah, by Amenemhat III, presumably in the absence of a surviving son), although in most cases it will have been a male relative or a non-royal adult male of proven worth (e.g. Rameses I by Horemheb) who received the nomination.

In a few cases a woman actually became king, but all these seem to have been in exceptional circumstances. Sobekneferu (end of Dynasty 12) seems to have been a sister of the aforementioned Neferuptah; Hatshepsut and Neferneferuaten (Dynasty 18) were co-rulers without independent reigns; and Tausret (Dynasty 19) took the throne on the death of the youth for whom she had previously been regent. A legendary 'Nitocris' during Dynasties 6/8 may actually been a misreading of a man's name. While a number of queens became sole rulers on occasion during the Ptolemaic Period - for example the famous Cleopatra VII - they never took full kingly titles and thus cannot be counted as female pharaohs.

In the above 'ideal' succession arrangements, the senior son, and thus prospective heir to the throne, would have been the offspring of the senior wife of the king. From the end of the Middle Kingdom this lady bore the title of King's Great Wife. In many cases the king also had a number of other spouses, generally with the title King's Wife. As noted above, on occasion these included one or more sisters and half-sisters of the king, but the majority of royal wives were commoners by birth, although the exact identity of their parents is only occasionally known. There are also instances where a king gave the title of King's Great Wife to one or more daughters, in particular during the latter part of the reign of Rameses II. However, it is unclear whether this included a sexual relationship, or whether the ladies in question were simply taking on the ritual and political functions of their deceased mothers.

Besides the heir to the throne and the king's wives, the royal family also included the king's mother (if alive), and the various other sons and daughters. Although sons of the king held high offices in the civil administration during Dynasty 4, this ceased shortly afterwards, with few king's sons known from the rest of the Old Kingdom - and still fewer during the Middle Kingdom. During Dynasty 18, some king's sons served in the priesthood, but it was not until Dynasty 19 that significant records of royal sons are found, reflecting a major expansion of the publicly-displayed royal family. This included the appointment of royal sons to senior army positions as well as those within the priesthood, a situation that endured into the Late Period.

Royal daughters seem to have had no particular roles, although some held office in temples as Singers, while during Dynasties 18 - 26 some served as God's Wife of Amun, a female counterpart to the high priest of the god. This office was at first a secondary role of a King's Great Wife, but ultimately came to be held by an unmarried royal daughter. Otherwise, many royal daughters married into the official, military and priestly classes.

The basic concept of the Egyptian monarchy endured for well over three thousand years, even when Egypt had been absorbed into foreign empires – those of the Persians, the Macedonians and the Romans. The foreign rulers usually adopted the titles and names of an Egyptian king and were depicted as normal Egyptian rulers, wearing the usual Egyptian regalia in temple scenes – even if they had never set foot in Egypt.

As noted above, the king was the sole font of power and authority in Egypt, as the person who nominally appointed all the officials and priests in the country. His own personal staff would also sometimes undertake specific duties, such as the running of commissions for specific purposes. Except in the very earliest times, the most senior civil official was the Vizier, roughly equating to a modern Prime Minister; at some periods there were separate Viziers for the north and south of the country. The vizier was effectively the king's deputy for administrative matters, as well as chief justice. Below the vizier, the administration split into specialized departments, whose relative roles and ramifications varied over time, but broadly covered public works, finance, grain storage and agriculture. During the Old Kingdom, the Overseer of Works was often also vizier, but during the New Kingdom it was a distinct post, with subordinate posts covering specific areas or institutions.

Beyond this central administration, there was an extensive network of regional and local authorities, whose configuration, size and conceptual basis varied with time. During the Intermediate Periods, these local power centres sometimes generated local warlords who aspired to kingly status, something seen in particular during the late Third Intermediate Period.

A further authority was found in Nubia during the New Kingdom, which was organised as a special region under the authority of the King's Son of Kush - not in fact a real royal son, but a viceroy with extensive powers. Below him was a network of officials who interfaced with some of the local Nubian princes to produce a distinctive administration separate from that in Egypt proper.

It was not until the New Kingdom that a significant military establishment came into being. This was a result of the extensive conquests carried out in Palestine and Syria by Thutmose I and III and consolidated by their successors. The army was divided into infantry and chariotry arms, with royal sons holding senior appointments from Dynasty 19 onwards. The Egyptian empire in Syria-Palestine was largely based on indirect control, with native local rulers left in place with Egyptian advisors and local garrisons. The children of these rulers were taken to Egypt for education, thus ensuring their indoctrination and also making them potential hostages for their fathers' good behaviour.

As regards broader Egyptian foreign policy, the best information comes from the New Kingdom and later. Diplomatic archives of the fourteenth/thirteenth century BC from Tell el-Amarna in Egypt and Boğazkale in Turkey indicate that a number of rulers were at that time regarded as 'Great Kings' who corresponded on terms of equality. They called each other 'Brother' and were distinguished from lesser rulers who were regarded as distinct inferiors. At various times the Egyptians included among the 'Great Kings' the rulers of the Hittites, Assyria, Babylon, Alashia (Cyprus) and Mitanni (northern Syria).

Conflict between these powers tended to occur where their territorial interests overlapped, in particular during the New Kingdom in north-western Syria and later in Palestine. However, imperial expansion led in some cases to the invasion of the home territories of the major powers, with Egypt temporarily occupied by the Assyrians at the end of Dynasty 25 and later absorbed successively into the Persian, Macedonian and Roman empires.

While the earliest Roman emperors had themselves represented as pharaohs and sponsored the construction of traditional temples, Egypt rapidly became simply a province of the Roman Empire. The residual symbols of the old monarchy were less and less seen, with Maximinus Daia (AD 305-313) the last emperor mentioned as though a pharaoh: with the conversion of Constantine I to Christianity shortly afterwards the pharaonic monarchy ceased to exist.

Significant Kings of Ancient Egypt
Den

A king of Dynasty 1, Den was presumably a son of his predecessor Djet, his mother being Merneith, who seems to have ruled Egypt for Den while he was a child. The events of six years from the middle of Den's long reign - at least 32 years - are recorded on one of the extant fragments of a set of royal annals compiled during Dynasty 5. These include three records of military activities to the north-east of Egypt, together with the manufacture of divine images and the carrying-out of religious ceremonies. The former tie in with a series of labels from the king's tomb that allude to military activities in this very area. Other labels record a ritual of 'spearing the hippopotamus' and a jubilee celebration.

The royal tomb was built in the portion of the Abydos cemetery known as Umm el-Qaab, which housed the tombs of Egypt's earliest kings. Den's tomb was of innovative design, being the first royal tomb with a stairway entrance, a stone portcullis-block and granite paving.

Khufu

The second king of Dynasty 4, Khufu (more fully Khnumkhufu: in Greek Kheops) was the son of his predecessor Sneferu and his wife Hetepheres I. He seems to have reigned for a little over two decades, but almost nothing is known of the events of that time, apart from some activities in remote quarrying locations.

Khufu's one certainly-identified wife was Meryetyotes I, with a second lady, Henutsen, known from later sources. The king had at least six sons – two of whom, Djedefra and Khafra, subsequently occupied the throne – and three daughters. A number of members of the royal family occupied senior governmental posts, including that of vizier.

Khufu is best known for the pyramid that he built at Giza, known in modern times as the Great Pyramid. It was the largest of its kind and incorporated a number of innovative features into its design and structure. It formed part of an extensive necropolis, laid out for the first time as part of an integrated plan.

The king features in later folk-tales, some of which depict Khufu as a tyrant who closed temples and resorted to mass slavery to build his pyramid. However, there is no contemporary evidence for negative memories of the reign, and the king's posthumous cult was maintained until some two thousand years after his death.

Khafra

A son of Khufu, Khafra (Greek: Khephren) came to the throne following the reigns of his brother Djedefra and (probably) the obscure king Seth-ka. Khafra appears to have reigned for around 25 years and had at least four wives - Meresankh III, Khamarernebty I, Hekenuhedjet, Persenet – and at least ten children.

Khafra's principal monument is the Second Pyramid at Giza and its subsidiary buildings. This is the second largest pyramid in Egypt and makes significant steps towards the standardization of the Egyptian pyramid complex. Its complex includes a significantly larger mortuary temple than hitherto known, and among the best preserved of all valley temples. The decoration of the latter included a number of particularly fine statues of the king.

It remains unclear how far, if at all, Khafra was responsible for the Great Sphinx at Giza. While his pyramid complex was clearly laid out with reference to it, there is no direct evidence as to whether it was actually carved by Khafra, or had been carved under a predecessor, possibly some centuries earlier.

Mentuhotep II

The son of Intef III, Dynasty 11 king of Upper Egypt, and his wife Iah, Mentuhotep II spent most of the first two decades of his 51-year reign as ruler of just his ancestral realm, the northern part of Egypt being ruled by Dynasty 10 at Herakleopolis (Ihnasiya el-Medina). However, ongoing conflict with the latter ultimately led to Mentuhotep reuniting the country, marking the occasion with a comprehensive change of his royal titulary, taking a new Horus-name and adopting a prenomen for the first time. Later, some important event lay behind a further change of Horus-name and an alteration in the spelling of the prenomen.

There is evidence for post-reunification military activities to the east, west and south of Egypt, while a considerable amount of building work was carried out throughout the country. The principal surviving remains derive from Upper Egypt, including material from Elephantine, El-Kab, Gebelein, Tod, Deir el-Ballas, Dendera, Abydos and Karnak. In addition, a temple-tomb of innovative design was constructed at Deir el-Bahri in Thebes-West, incorporating terracing, what was probably once a pyramid and the king's burial chamber at the end of a long rock-cut corridor. The tomb was inspected during the reign of Rameses IX and found to be intact, but was subsequently robbed. The valley leading up to the temple contained the tombs of the king's principal officials, many of his family being buried within the temple itself. These included Mentuhotep II's six known wives, of whom Tem and Neferu II were apparently the most senior.

Hatshepsut

Only a handful of women ever held the title of king, the best-attested being Hatshepsut of Dynasty 18. She was a daughter of Thutmose I and his wife Ahmes, and became the Great Wife of her half-brother Thutmose II. During the youth of her nephew and step-son Thutmose III, she first served as regent, retaining her queenly titles, but after seven years became his formal co-ruler with the full titulary of a pharaoh. She continued in this role for another 14 years. During this time, Hatshepsut sent a trading expedition to the territory of Punt in East Africa, and built extensively, including her mortuary temple at Deir el-Bahri. There has been much debate over the nature of her relationship with her high official Senenmut, who was tutor of her daughter, Neferure, possessed a tomb just outside the precincts of Hatshepsut's mortuary temple, was represented within it, and had a sarcophagus that was clearly made to match that of the female king.

Hatshepsut disappears from the records after Thutmose III's Year 21, when she presumably died. Her monuments were defaced some two decades later: the explanation of this phenomenon remains unclear. As regent, she built a tomb in the Wadi Sikkat Taqa el-Zeide at Thebes-West, but ultimately prepared tomb KV20 in the Valley of the Kings for her interment. It has been suggested that her mummy may have been later reburied in the nearby KV60.

Thutmose III

A son of Thutmose II and one of his junior wives, Iset, Thutmose III was only a child at the time of his father's death. He was at first under the regency of his aunt Hatshepsut but after seven years, probably at the time of his coming of age, Hatshepsut became his full co-ruler. Little is known of Thutmose III's activities until after his aunt's disappearance, but as soon as he embarked on his sole rule a major series of military operations were begun, stretching for two decades from Year 22. During these, Thutmose crossed the Euphrates and extended the Egyptian empire to its greatest extent in Syria-Palestine, while also expanding and consolidating Egyptian control in Nubia.

Thutmose was a great builder, the temple of Karnak being greatly extended during his reign, with traces of his work surviving at a wide range of sites throughout Egypt and Nubia. His first wife may have been his half-sister, Neferure, followed in turn by Sitiah and Meryetre, who survived him. By these ladies, he had at least five sons, including his successor, Amenhotep II, and at least two daughters.

On his death in Year 53, Thutmose was buried in tomb KV34 in the Valley of the Kings. He is often regarded as the greatest of all the New Kingdom kings, with a cult maintained for one and a half millennia; his mummy was found hidden along with a number of other New Kingdom kings in the Dynasty 21 tomb of the high priest Pinudjem II (TT320), where they had been placed for safety during the reign of the Dynasty 22 king Sheshonq I.

Amenhotep III

As a prince, Amenhotep (Greek: Amenophis) III appeared on the monuments of his tutors before succeeding his father Thutmose IV. A son of Queen Mutnodjmet, Amenhotep married Tiye, the daughter of cavalry General Yuya and his wife Tjuiu. The marriage was announced exceptionally on a series of scarabs, others being issued to celebrate a number of events of the earlier part of the reign.

The king had two known sons, Thutmose and Amenhotep (later Akhenaten), and at least five daughters. Thutmose, the crown prince, ultimately became High Priest of Ptah at Memphis, but died prematurely, possibly in Year 30. The eldest daughter, Sitamun took the title of King's Great Wife at some point during the reign.

Amenhotep III's military activities were limited as compared with those of his immediate predecessors, with little other than police actions in Nubia attested. In contrast, the king's building activities were widespread and monumental. At Thebes-West, Amenhotep III built a palace-complex at Malqata, together with a vast and innovative mortuary temple at Kom el-Hatan. Across the river, a new front pylon-gateway was added to the temple of Amun-Re at Karnak, with extensive work in the adjacent temple-precincts of the deities Mentu and Mut. A little further south, a new temple was built at Luxor, with a very similar structure erected at Soleb in Nubia. In a number of these sanctuaries, Amenhotep III appeared as a god, especially after the celebration in Year 30 of the first of his three jubilees, at which he was transformed into a solar deity. This deification also embraced Queen Tiye, who appears in a divinised form at Sedeinga, not far from Soleb.

This deification was against the backdrop of the growth of the cult of the sun-god the Aten, Amenhotep III taking the sobriquet of the 'Dazzling Sun' and including the god's name in a number of contexts. The Aten-cult would become predominant in Egypt during the reign of Amenhotep III's successor Akhenaten.

Amenhotep III's death came after four decades on the throne, the king being interred in a tomb (WV22) in the Western branch of the Valley of the Kings. After robbery, the king's badly-damaged mummy was moved for safety to the tomb of Amenhotep II (KV35), where it was found and moved to Cairo in 1898.

Akhenaten

The second son of Amenhotep III and Tiye succeeded to the throne under the name of Amenhotep IV and married Nefertiti, perhaps a maternal cousin shortly after his accession. They had Meryetaten, the first of six daughters, not long afterwards. These girls are depicted on many contemporary monuments, but there is only one mention of a son, Tutankhuaten, who ultimately became king as Tutankhaten (later Tutankhamun).

During his first years, the king was depicted in the traditional manner, but by his Year 4 he and his entourage were being shown in a distorted revolutionary style that is expressly stated in a text of his chief sculptor, Bak, to have been directed by the king. This was accompanied by a change of the iconography of the sun-god Aten from a conventional anthropomorphic representation to an abstract one comprising a sun-disk, from which descended rays terminating in hands, the latter holding the sign of "life" to the nostrils of the royal family. Soon afterwards, the king changed his own name to Akhenaten.

This transition was accompanied by a move to make the Aten supreme, if not yet sole, god – the first known experiment in monotheism in the world. Whether this was wholly a theological shift or had a political aspect of reducing the power of the priesthoods of the traditional pantheon – especially that of Amun – remains a matter for scholarly debate. At some point the names and images of a number of deities, especially those connected with Amun, were destroyed on a wide variety of monuments. This iconoclasm has been variously dated to the earlier part of the reign and to its very end.

The earliest monument of this new style was a large temple to the Aten that was built to the east of the main temple complex at Karnak. However, soon afterwards, a new city was founded at Tell el-Amarna, roughly half way between the old capitals of Memphis and Thebes, both as a dedicated cult-centre for the Aten and as a new capital for Egypt.

Information on Akhenaten's foreign relations is provided by an archive of cuneiform tablets found at Amarna and known as the Amarna Letters. These represent correspondence between the kings of the contemporary great powers and Egypt, as well between Egypt's Levantine vassals and the royal court. A major international festival was held in Year 12, with gifts to the king being brought by representatives from much of the known world. Its significance is uncertain, once possibility being that it could have marked the formal completion of the city of Amarna. Soon afterwards a number of deaths occurred within the royal family, including Tiye and up to three of the king's daughters. It has been suggested that a plague brought into Egypt by the Year 12 delegates may have been responsible.

Soon after Year 12, Akhenaten apparently appointed a co-ruler, Smenkhkare, who married Meryetaten but seems to have died soon afterwards. He was replaced as co-ruler by a woman, Neferneferuaten, who was almost certainly none other than Nefertiti. Akhenaten died in his Year 17 and was buried in his tomb at Amarna. He was succeeded by Tutankhaten, but steps were soon taken to reverse Akhenaten's religious revolution, and after the death of Tutankhamun, Akhenaten's names and images were mutilated on the monuments. He and his immediate successors were also omitted from official lists of the kings of Egypt.

Rameses II

The third king of Dynasty 19 and eldest son and successor of Sety I, Rameses II reigned for 67 years. The first decade of the reign was dominated by campaigns into northern Syria, where the Egyptians had for some time been in conflict with the Hittites for the overlordship of the various local rulers. These included the battle of Qadesh in Year 5 which, although at best a strategic draw, was widely publicised on temple walls as a great Egyptian victory. However, there was ultimately a fundamental change of approach, a peace treaty being agreed between Egypt and Hatti in Year 21.

Rameses II was also militarily active in Nubia and to the west in Libya, but much of his reign was taken up with a massive building program in Egypt and Nubia. Significantly, the political centre of gravity of the country shifted to the north east Delta, where he built a vast new residence city of Per-Rameses, around modern Qantir.

In Year 30, the king celebrated his first jubilee, at least twelve more being held prior to the end of the reign. As the king aged it is likely that more and more of his routine functions were carried out on his behalf by the current crown prince. At least four of Rameses' sons served successively as such, the last of them, Merenptah, the thirteenth son, following Rameses II on the throne.

Rameses II was exceptional in the degree to which his family was presented on public monuments, great processions of his approximately 50 sons and a similar number of daughters being carved on temple walls. For the first part of the reign the king, unusually, had two contemporaneous Great Wives, Nefertiry and Isetneferet; after their deaths, a number of their daughters received the title of King's Great Wife, although whether this was simply for official purposes or also reflected a physical relationship is unclear. Rameses also made a daughter of Hattushilish of Hatti and his sister Henutmire Great Wives. Rameses II was buried in tomb KV7 in the Valley of the Kings. His mummy was found hidden with others in the tomb of Pinudjem II.

Merenptah

The thirteenth son of Rameses II, by his wife Isetneferet, Merenptah seems to have been crown prince during the last decade of his father's reign. The King's Great Wife was named, like Merenptah's mother, Isetneferet; he had at least two sons and a daughter. In his Year 5, a coalition of Libyans and the so-called Sea Peoples from the north east Mediterranean made an incursion into north west Egypt before being defeated somewhere in the southern part of the western Delta. These events were recorded in texts and reliefs in the temple of Amun-Re at Karnak, as was further military activity in Palestine.

The latter events were also set down in a pair victory stelae, respectively erected at Karnak and in Merenptah's memorial temple at Thebes-West. Amongst the polities mentioned as defeated was Israel - its only mention in an ancient Egyptian text. This passing mention of Israel has caused the stela to be dubbed the 'Israel Stela', and once made Merenptah a candidate for being the 'Pharaoh of the Exodus'. The peace established with the Hittites by Rameses II seems to have been maintained, Merenptah even sending grain 'to keep alive the land of Hatti' at a time of famine.

The building works of Merenptah were widespread, but his largest surviving body of work is to be found at Thebes; his memorial temple at Thebes-West was built just north of that of Amenhotep III and employed many blocks salvaged from that building. After a decade on the throne, Merenptah was buried in KV8 in the Valley of the Kings; his mummy was found in the KV35 cache and is now in the Cairo Museum.

Sety II

The eldest son and successor of Merenptah, Sety II seems to have lost control of Nubia and the south of Egypt to the usurping king Amenmessu (probably his own son) during his Year 2. Sety regained control of the whole of the country during Year 5 but died only a year later. Few significant monuments are known, apart from a shrine and a pair of obelisks at Karnak, together with various minor elements elsewhere.

Sety's tomb in the Valley of the Kings (KV15) had a chequered building history owing to the events of the reign and was ultimately finished in a hurry, with a burial chamber improvised out of an unfinished corridor. A mummy anciently labelled as his was found in the cache in KV35 and is now in the Cairo Museum.

Rameses III

The son and successor of Sethnakht, founder of Dynasty 20, Rameses III, did much to restore the Egyptian state following the conflicts of late Dynasty 19. In doing so, he frequently consciously imitated Rameses II: not only were the king's names modelled on those of the earlier pharaoh, but also the names of Rameses III's children were directly taken from the brood of the earlier king. Rameses III also imitated the second Rameses by taking at least two Great Wives, Iset and Tyti.

The early years of the reign were dominated by renewed conflict with the Libyans and the Sea Peoples, previously repulsed by Merenptah. In Year 5 the Libyans made a new advance on the western Delta. In the battle that followed, Rameses' forces were victorious, thus temporarily securing the western frontier.

The second, far more serious, crisis came three years later when the Sea Peoples, having apparently brought about the downfall of the key regimes of the Levant – including even that of the Hittites – approached the eastern border of Egypt by land and sea. Once again, Rameses was successful in defeating the enemy, much of the decoration of his great mortuary temple at Medinet Habu being dedicated to his victory. Year 11 saw yet another invasion from Libya. Again, the enemy was driven back, over 2,000 men being killed, and the captured leaders executed.

By the late twenties of the reign, economic problems were becoming manifest, made most visible in failures to pay the workmen responsible for building the royal tomb, based at the West-Theban village of Deir el-Medina. This led to a sit-down strike by them in year 29. Against this background a plot was hatched against the king's life, carried out in Year 32 with the aim of placing one wife's offspring on the throne in place of the nominated heir, the future Rameses IV. Although successful in procuring Rameses III's death, the plot failed in its ultimate intent. The king was buried in tomb KV11 in the Valley Of The Kings; his mummy was eventually moved to the cache in the tomb of Pinudjem II.

Osorkon II

A representative of Dynasty 22, a line of Libyan origins, Osorkon II was the son of his predecessor Takelot I and his wife Kapes and had a long reign of at least a quarter-century. From early in his reign comes an inscription on a statue from the capital city, Tanis, setting out the king's formal program. This included the assignment of various key offices to his children, seemingly reversing the recent practice of parcelling key fiefs to wider members of the royal lineage.

Osorkon II was a considerable builder, in particular adding a forecourt and pylon to the Amun-temple at Tanis, and a number of structures at Bubastis (Tell Basta), including a hall to celebrate his jubilee in Year 22. Fragments of Osorkon II's buildings also exist at various other sites around Egypt.

The king had a number of known wives, the principal one being Karomama, probably his sister. A senior son, Sheshonq, was appointed High Priest of Ptah at Memphis, while another son, Nimlot, became High Priest at the important Middle-Egyptian stronghold of Herakleopolis, before being transferred to Thebes as High Priest of Amun. Yet another son, Harnakht, became High Priest of Amun at Tanis, but died while still a child.

At Thebes, control was ceded at some point during the reign to a local king, Harisiese. This marked the first episode of a fundamental split in the country that that would become entrenched with the assumption of power in Thebes by Takelot II around the end of Osorkon II's reign. This division would endure for over a century.

Osorkon II was succeeded at Tanis by Sheshonq III and was buried in tomb NRT-I at Tanis.

Shabaqo

A son of the Nubian king Kashta, Shabaqo became the ruler of the combined kingdom of Egypt and Nubia, succeeding Piy, who had progressively annexed Egypt over the previous three decades and founded Dynasty 25. However, Nubian control of Egypt seems to have shrunk back to merely the southern part of the country by Shabaqo's accession, with much of the north in the hands of King Bakenrenef of Sais. This was rapidly reversed by Shabaqo, with Bakenrenef overthrown in Shabaqo's Year 2 and allegedly burnt to death.

Once safely established in power, Shabaqo commissioned a number of monuments in the principal cities of Egypt, especially Memphis and Thebes, where a number of additions were made to the temple at Karnak. Much of Shabaqo's work displays archaising features, while a text known as the Shabaqo Stone in the British Museum purports to be copy of a religious text from an Old Kingdom papyrus. Politically, he gave asylum to Iamani, the king of the Levantine city-state of Ashdod, who had revolted against his overlord, the king of Assyria.

Three wives of Shabaqo are known, along with a number of children, including the later king Tanutamun and the High Priest of Amun Haremakhet. Shabaqo was succeeded by Shabitqo, who seems also to have been a son. Shabaqo himself was buried in pyramid Ku15 at El-Kurru in Sudan.

Aidan Dodson

Senior Research Fellow, Department of Archaeology & Anthropology, University of Bristol

第五章

完滿的墓葬

引言

初次探察古埃及文獻與遺址的現代觀察家，可能感到印象深刻的，是被多數人詮釋為埃及人迷戀死亡的現象。從多方面來看，這所謂的「迷戀」，與其說是在那遠古的年代真正存在的現實狀況，還不如說是一種現代觀點的演繹。大部分早期的考古勘查多在墓園裡進行，而非人類居住的區域。除此之外，埃及人的墳墓多建構在人類群居地邊緣乾旱不毛的西方沙漠——不折不扣的死亡之境——在這裡，為了長久保存墓地裡的陪葬品、殯葬銘文、人體遺骸等，所有天然與人工的保存方法都被發揮到極致。另一方面，埃及的村落與城鎮多分部在尼羅河沿岸，這些地區除了座落在地形偏高的河床上之外，人類的棲息地也持續開發拓展至今，因此，現代考古研究若要進入這些地區挖掘古文明，再再顯得困難重重。在上述因素的前提下，我們不難推演出，古埃及文明存留下的文物中，最令人驚豔、保存狀況最完善、最廣為人知者，都與墓葬有關。

然而，每一位埃及人在為亡者準備葬禮、墳墓的建造、殯葬銘文的匯集、贈予悼念祭品等方面，確實也會動用各種社會與經濟的關係，投入可觀的時間與資源。究竟，古埃及文明是否對死亡深深著迷呢？為了得到這個問題的答案，我們必須檢視埃及信仰中對生死命題提出的相對關係，以及木乃伊製作、墓葬、與墓群在冥世裡不斷變異的角色等議題背後所支撐的神學論點。

生與死

對古埃及人而言，肉體的死去意謂著存在狀態中兩種截然不同階段的轉移。第一階段是指在人世間的歲月，如古代文獻所述，古埃及人期盼享有的壽命是 110 歲，然而，從年代久遠的木乃伊上所作的科學鑑識報告指出，縱使有些埃及人確實活到 50 歲，甚至更久，但大部分人辭世時的年紀仍與期待的「榮光的高齡」（great old age）有很大的差距。一個人的壽限與死亡的方式，在出生時便受到掌管命運的七位女神—哈托爾（Hathors）—所設定。除了宿命的安排之外，一個人在有生之年依其自由意志所做的種種選擇，也佔有決定性的影響。《被詛咒的王子》（The Doomed Prince）這則寓言便是埃及人面對宿命與自由意志最佳例證，故事中，法老為了阻撓王子受到命運的注定而把他關在遠離塵囂的城堡中，男孩長大後，徵求國王的同意想要離開城堡去探索世界，他說：「我整天枯坐在此又有何用？這樣的我顯然已經受到宿命的束縛。何不讓我追隨內心的意志，自由來去，直到神明改變祂的決定。」故事的結局已失傳難尋，但其中的隱喻說明了即使一個人從生到死的期限已被安排，我們仍能依照自己的選擇，打造這條道路的風貌。今世的種種選擇，攸關著我們在未知世界存在時的狀態。

肉體死去之後，亡者的魂魄開始向靈界即埃及人所稱的「杜埃特」（Duat，意指「靈魂冥府」）—遊移。以法律術語來說，這個過渡時期是指亡靈來到陰間主神「奧塞里斯」（Osiris）所主持的聖庭之前的「最後審判」。審判中，真理女神「馬特」（Maat）以宇宙間的真理為準則，評量一個人在世間的所作所為。最廣泛用來作為神聖判決的例證起源於《亡者之書》（Egyptian Book of the Dead）（約西元前 1500 年）中的第 125 條咒語，這是一本可謂來世的「生存秘笈」。這項咒語附有的插圖描繪著一名亡者被帶領到埃及眾神之前，由胡狼頭神阿努比斯（Anubis，死神）掌管的磅秤或天平的一端放著亡者的心臟，代表他／她的道德特質的源頭，另一端則置有象徵真理女神「馬特」的一根羽毛。在天平的右側，一個「吃人魔」的妖獸等候著判決的結果，在往右邊一點，則是負責紀錄審判結果的鷺首之神托特（Thoth，智慧及書寫之神）。如果亡者心臟的成份良好，便會與另一端的羽毛等重，這個亡者也會因而被判擁有「真實之聲」的判決，即「亞庫」（akhu，可塑的靈體）之一，或受到祝福的亡靈，而獲准昇天，與其他眾神在聖界共同生存。若是亡者在生前未能遵從真理之神的準則，他的心臟便會重過羽毛，而被丟入吃人魔的口中，牠那張開的大嘴代表著二次死亡，足以將被送下地獄的靈魂徹底毀滅。

最後的審判這一事件具有某種必然性是值得我們進一步的審視。真理女神的天平最終會回到左右平衡的狀態，亡者在聖庭前的合理辯護乃預料中的必然結局，銘文和圖像總是以正義尊榮的形象刻劃墳墓的主人，《亡者之書》這類的作品就其實質的意義上，便是被用來作為確保有利判決的保證書。在最遠古的宗教文學—《金字塔文》（the Pyramid Texts）（約西元前 2375 年）中，便可見以墓葬銘文中展述的神奇力量來戰勝死亡的信心，其文本中不斷複述著：「你以生者而非亡者之軀離去。」埃及文中的「安卡」（ankh，生命之符）一字，現譯為「活著」，經常被用來形容人們「活」在世間的狀態。然而，放在眾神主宰的冥世裡來討論時，這一名詞的應用具有更為複雜的意義，超乎生物性的生與死之間的現代二分法可能帶有的寓意。用「安卡」形容神祇或亡者，則暗示著超越靈魂滅絕—亦即二次死亡，被詛咒的人的終極命運—的可能性而存在的狀態。另一方面，在聖界中，「安卡」所代表的意義不僅在於活著，更要成為「不朽」，照字面的意思則釋義為：不死的、超越死亡的。在此，我們面臨到從木乃伊的製作，到最後的安葬等等所有奠禮準備所隱藏目的：肉體死亡後個人身份的保存是為了讓他能與眾神共同「活」在聖界。

木乃伊製作與安葬

為生活於來世所作的準備必須從今世開始，包括安葬前為大體進行的儀式性處理，以及建造大體即將永駐的墳墓。安葬準備的重點在於，照料與維護埃及人信仰中個體肉身與精神的組成元素，其中某些元素，例如個體的名字及影子，同樣存在於陽世與陰間。其他元素，如能自由移動的「巴」（ba，意識、靈魂），和會發亮的「阿克」（akh，永生狀態的靈魂）則主要與來世的生活有關連。

前兩個組成元素是由陶神克努姆（Khnum）在創世之初塑造的，它們指的是一個人的肉身及其靈魂的複製品「卡」（ka）。「卡」是充滿生氣的「生命力量」，需要加以維護才能確保它的生存。一個人在世期間，「卡」從飲食中取得養分，死後，同樣的養分可從在世的親友，或執行殯葬儀式的祭司留在地表上的墓室裡的供品中取得。這些墓室通常離亡者安葬的地下墓寢相隔不遠。私人的陵墓與墓室，以及皇族殯葬廟宇與其他的遺址的結構中，通常設有「假門」，做為「卡」的出口。這些造型獨特的閘道口是陽世與冥府之間一道讓靈魂可以穿透滲入的過渡介面。在這些門上經常可見附有亡者姓名與稱謂的銘文，和象徵「卡」的圖像，在一些豪華至極的案例中，甚至將「卡」型塑成高度超高的浮雕，彷彿靈魂便可以鬼魅之姿從陵墓底處浮出地表，索取供奉給它的祭品。

相較於無形的「卡」，在埃及人的認知裡，有形的肉身為「ha'u」，即「四肢」的總和。人體重要的器官藉由「metu」的循環性載體系統串連起來，再由四肢保護其中。一個人的有生之年，這個有形的實體是「卡」以及其他精神性元素的屋宇，死後，人的「屍身」—埃及人稱為「khat」—幾乎就像靈魂的中途之家一般。雖然靈魂可以自由穿梭於聖界，最終還是期待能夠回到生前安穩棲居的身軀。埃及人具代表性的木乃伊製作的出發點，便是希望能妥善保存屍身，讓游移不定的靈魂得以重回主人的肉體。

在史前時期的埃及（約西元前 3400 年前），人類的遺體是安葬於低淺的土坑墓，而且沒有覆蓋任何衣物或加以包裹，由於大漠的風砂具有乾燥脫水效果，因此成為保存這些早期墳墓中的遺體最好的天然乾燥劑。在進入歷史時期前的過渡階段，隨著幾位初期執政者權力的擴張，在某種程度上為了有利於他們上綱的地位，而滋生加強後遺體保固的欲望，因而驅動了結構更為華麗的泥磚、木造，以及後期石造陵墓的發展。諷刺的是，這類進化的結構隔離了沙漠風塵與屍體的接觸，反而加速腐蝕的速度，接著便研發出一系列防腐與包裹屍體的技術，取代沙漠風塵的天然乾燥功能，並

於之後的數世紀間持續發展。儀式性防腐處理的全套過程，包括體內器官的取出及保存，首先出現在安葬第四王朝的帝后，即法老王古夫（Khufu）（約2513BC）之母—海特裴莉斯（Hetepheres）的吉薩金字塔（Giza）。

最高規的屍身包裹儀式總共需花費七十天的時間，執行地點為一座稱為「wabet」，即「純淨之屋」的淨房，第一階段是將一部份對來世生活無益的器官（包括腦）取出並丟棄，接下來取出肝臟、肺、胃、腸，以泡鹼鹽乾燥，放置於一式四組的「納卜卡諾皮克臟器罐」（canopic jars）中儲存保管。這些保存用的容器原本只以圓頂型的瓶塞蓋上，自古王國以降，漸漸演化成人頭造型的瓶蓋，可能是以此代表亡者的身份。到了新王國後期，則以神祇的頭取代人頭，包括伊姆塞提（Imsety，人頭造型，守護肝臟）；哈比（Hapy，狒狒造型，守護肺臟）；多姆泰夫（Duamutef，豺狼或狗頭造型，守護胃）；凱布山納夫（Qebehsenuef，老鷹造型，守護腸）。這些被稱為霍魯斯（Horus）之子的四個守護神，負責護衛亡者的重要器官，而其中最重要的心臟則原封不動的留在胸腔裡，成為道德倫理的保留所。

一旦內臟處理完畢後，屍身裡裡外外會被徹底的洗淨，再填入泡鹼和其他有乾燥作用的物質，讓屍身在接下來四十天的期間漸漸脫水。水分完全去除後，便以其他物質取代泡鹼混合物，重新填充乾癟的屍身，讓他恢復生前的樣貌，最後再以香料液與樹脂覆蓋屍身。屍身的外貌因塗上樹脂而變得像瀝青一般的漆黑，由於瀝青在阿拉伯文中為「mumia」，因此而演繹出現代人所稱的「mummies」（木乃伊）這個名詞。屍身表面完全被樹脂混合物塗滿後，便再以亞麻布將大體包裹，並附上具有神力的護身符來護衛靈魂，有利於靈魂過渡到聖界。木乃伊製作的儀式一旦完成，防腐師將屍身密封在木棺或石棺裡，最後由一組高度儀式性的葬禮隊伍將俗世的遺物從純淨之屋引迎送到陵墓，這支隊伍中包括了在世的親人、專業送葬者、表演者、和各種官方人員，另外還有一群稱為「讀經者」的特別祭司，他們負責朗誦聖歌和咒語，以確保亡者得以順利進入聖界。葬禮進行到最高點時，密封在棺木裡的木乃伊會被推移入地下的墓室，就此安葬。

人死後仍應享有與生前相同的物質條件是埃及自遠古以來的墓喪祭祀傳統裡不變的信條，地下陵寢的儲藏室裡極盡所能的置滿了裝著食物與飲料的瓶瓶罐罐，與在凡間被認為有用的工具和武器，以及價值不斐的珠寶和文物。一方面來說，在陵墓裡安置物件的用意在於希望亡者在聖界時得以運用，從另一方面而言，陪葬品的數量與品質可說明亡者生前的社為地位，希冀在冥界可以得到相同的位階。實際上，唯有社會上流份子才能負擔得起建構豪華正規的泥磚陵墓，大部分的埃及平民還是只能葬在簡陋的土坑墓。以第一與第二王朝的法老們為例，陪葬品中甚至包括僕人與牲口—這無疑是皇族成員在冥世享受特權的終極表現！雖然活體陪葬在第二王朝後便被廢除，然而，提供亡者未來永世的所需所用，一直是法老史上葬禮儀式的關鍵畫面向。

墓群與來世

古埃及陵墓在本質上是一種一分兩式（bi-partite）的結構。其一為地底下的墓室，以及在這一片亡靈世界中散佈的附屬房室和穿梭其間廊道，這些區域通常無法讓在世者進入。其二為地表上的祭品祀堂和其他相關結構，其功能在於延續殯葬的禮俗，讓在世的親人、祭司，和虔誠的路人能為亡者誦經，並獻上滋養「卡」的供品。以這個基本的二分法為前提，不論在地上或地下的殯墓葬結構群中，在任何特定的時間點所使用的祭文與圖像是否合宜，都受到既定禮儀的規範。從歷時性（不同的歷史時期）與共時性（同一時期內不同的資訊）的角度而視，都出現極大的多樣差異，新的元素不斷被加入，既有的元素則被擴張、簡略、廢除，或是在停用一段時間之後被重新啟用。除此之外，在早期只適用於皇族葬禮的一些治喪事宜到了後期「民主化」之後，也沿用到非皇族的私人陵墓。

在埃及早期王朝時期（第一與第二王朝），皇家與上流社會的私人陵墓主要是作為「來世的宮殿」，國王們來到這個世界可以繼續掌有統御之權，一般人也可照常實踐在世間的責任與義務。地下的墓室依格狀設計排列，由通道或門相互連結，與凡間的房舍相似。在一些泥磚陵墓中，甚至可見陸地上屋宇所具有的建築特徵，如木造屋頂的樑，或一綑綑捲起來的蘆葦草蓆。在地面上，長方形的上層結構，稱為「馬斯塔巴」（mastaba）（現代阿拉伯用語，意為「長凳」造型）則被用來標示出陵墓的位置。私人「馬斯塔巴」的室外通常模仿古代宮殿的外牆，以複雜的壁龕板片設計裝飾。反之，皇家墓群則多採用有平滑表面的「馬斯塔巴」，而將宮殿正面的設計主題留給另外的「喪葬闈場」（funerary enclosures），建造從陵墓出發幾公尺長，在國王的喪禮上可能是用來作為儀式進行的宮殿或廟宇。

在古王國期，皇家與私人的墓群在建築、設計、功能方面，產生了顯著的改變，在私人的範圍，藉由地層上祭品祀堂大張旗鼓的擴建，我們便可以很輕易的追查這些改變，以及官方高層日益擴充的權力及其重要性。自第三王朝起，祭品祀堂擴建的範圍更延伸到了「馬斯塔巴」，形成十字形的室內墓室。裝飾這個區域的元素包括假門、陵墓主人的畫像、生平介紹，以及稱為「祈禱祭品」的特殊祈禱文加以裝飾，希望透過神奇的力量將食物、衣服等必需品提供給靈魂。到了古王國後期（第五及第六王朝），許多上流社會成員的供品祀堂演化成規模龐大，房室眾多的結構，在財富與工匠技術方面足以與皇家抗衡，這些富麗堂皇的「馬斯塔巴」墓室中最常見的裝飾主題為所謂的「日常即景」。這些圖像代表著一大群工匠、技師、藝人，以及負責維護這些喪葬地產的祭司。俯視著這群次要角色的，正是墳墓主人與其家人的畫像，以「日常即景」為主題的銘文與圖像使人想到如人間天堂般的豐饒與太平，這樣的景象是以理想中的埃及為繪製的藍本。然而，縱使陵墓的主人彷彿在他的屬地上稱王，獲贈如此豐沛的獎賞，祭祀的咒語和生平的銘文上都還是清楚的陳述著，不論是在此世或來生，以眾神為名的國王才是提供社會地位與財富的最高來源，使亡者得以享用。

而在皇家的部份，認為陵墓是來世的宮殿的舊觀念已漸漸改變，取而代之的，是將陵墓視為一種具有神力的工藝表現，其設計的目的在於將亡者轉渡到發光的靈魂，或稱為「阿赫」（akh），如此便能進入神聖世界。這個過程差不多開始於位於埃及下墓地薩卡拉（Saqqara），卓瑟（Djoser）（第三王朝，西元前2668年）的階梯金字塔的建造。在首席建築師印何闐（Imhotep）的協助下，卓瑟是首位完全以石頭打造墓群的法老，捨棄了泥磚的作法。除此之外，過去在南方，另外建構一處「馬斯塔巴」和喪葬闈場的傳統作法，也被重新設計成為一個獨立存在於地表上的結構，代表著法老統御著上埃及與下埃及的權力，巨大的闈場外牆，以宮廷正面主題裝飾著，將一群仿造的建築物及其他儀式性的結構群圍繞著，在此，卓瑟的雙王權將可永世運行。在墓群的中央，一座巨大的石造馬斯塔巴藉由六度擴張，一層層往上堆疊，越往上層體積越小，所形成的階梯金字塔—埃及眾多金字塔中的先例—成為一座偉大的樓梯，好讓法老王可以登上，加入北方天空的星星。這座高聳的階梯同時代表著地球的原生土堆，在混沌的創世之初從水中升起。在地底下，建有兩座地下陵墓—在階梯金字塔底下一座具功能性的墓地，以及另一座建於墓群南端下方的儀式性墳地。一如地層上方的祠堂，這兩座地底下的墓地也將卓瑟延展到上埃及與下埃及的王權也轉移到冥世。這塊地下區域的外牆貼上了藍綠兩色的磁磚，代表混沌之水和宇宙的邊緣。天花板則裝飾著一片黃色星辰，下方襯托著深藍色的天空，指向亡者最終希望前往的天空的家，階梯金字塔的建築和裝飾讓我們看到陵墓首次產生了「cosmograph」的作用，以圖像的設計示意出世間，而金字塔在其中的意義便是作為冥界、塵世、天界之間的重要連結。

將陵墓視為將凡人神格化的工藝創作的發展在第四王朝初期，隨著史納夫（Sneferu）法老王所建造的完全平整金字塔，而來到了另一個重要的轉折點。史納夫 是史上建造最多金字塔的法老王，由他主持的三座金字塔分別是：在美杜姆（Meidum）一座改建的階梯金字塔，以及隨後在達舒（Dashur）的彎曲金字塔，及紅色金字塔。在這三座金字塔建構期間，史納夫 將滑面形式（smooth-sided）的金字塔推向了完美的境界。這些遺址的演進史或許反應了對金字塔基本的符號意含的重新分析，受到赫里歐波利斯（Heliopolis）這個地區盛行的太陽神「拉」（Ra）影響，金字塔原是通往天體的階梯，演化為一道固化的太陽光。與此同時，在金字塔東面，面對太陽升起的方向，建立一座作為祭品祀堂用的結構體，也被用來取代卓瑟階梯金字塔的代用宮殿建築，在尼羅河岸也開始蓋起一些以覆蓋住的堤道與主墓群相連結的獨立式山谷廟宇，除此之外，在史納夫 與其子嗣古夫（Khufu）在位期間，金字塔上層結構的規模顯著的擴張，由古夫建造的吉薩金字塔，位居全世界最高建物之首（146.5公尺）長達三千年。然而，在古夫次子卡夫拉（Khafre）執政之後，金字塔的規模開始大幅度的縮小，另外，在史納夫與卡夫所建的金字塔地上結構中廊道與上托墓室（corbelled chamber）的華麗設計也不復見，到了第四王朝末期，取而代之的是以一座單一的下降廊道、地下前廳與雕像室，以及葬禮室所組成

的簡化版排列次序。

到了第五王朝，金字塔的規模與內部結構多已規格化，進入第六王朝後，地層上廟宇似乎發展到某種經典的形式。然而，最關鍵性的發展則是喪葬咒語，或稱金字塔銘文的啟用，最早可見於第五王朝末代法老王烏那斯（Unas）的地下墓室。這些銘文是目前所知最古老的宗教文學的文獻，包含提供亡靈食物、衣物、藥膏、薰香的咒語，以及使法老復活的咒語，為他在前往神界的路上做好準備。烏那斯金字塔中的銘文被解讀為表現法老的亡靈，等同於太陽神的「巴」，從西方跟到東方，夜晚經過杜埃（Duat），在破曉時上升到天空的旅程。

古王國的崩解與接踵而至發生在第一中間時期（西元前 2200-2040 年，第七至第十王朝）的風暴，導致所有主要的皇族建設計劃的停擺，包括金字塔陵墓。第八王朝時期建於薩卡拉的伊比（Ibi）金字塔終結了金字塔建築的原始傳統，皇族陵墓牆上的金字塔銘文也從此不再出現，來自中王國時期的間接證據指出，甚至到了第九或第十王朝，法老都還繼續採用金字塔銘文一可能是撰寫在攜帶式的捲軸上，或刻在棺柩的四邊，但都已失傳。同一時期或不久之後，在私人棺柩與陵墓牆上開始出現金字塔銘文的節錄文本，以及一組專屬私人陵墓，稱為「棺木文」（Coffin Texts）的新式喪葬咒語。

中王國時期（第十一至第十三王朝，西元前 2040-1650 年）見證了皇族權力在全埃及境內的重建，大規模的遺址並在這個時期捲土重來。然而，中王國最初的幾位統治者出生於北方之城底比斯（Thrbes）（現為路克索（Luxor）），因為還帶著與北方舊王權的牽絆，並未立即重建金字塔的傳統。反而是底比斯第十一王朝才支持當地石窟陵墓的傳統，其具體表現可見於王朝創建者蒙圖荷泰普二世（Mentuhotep II）的喪葬遺址。然而，時代轉移到第十二王朝（西元前 1991 年）時，將首都從底比斯遷移到偏北的城市伊赤塔維（Itj-tawy），鄰近法雍（Fayum）綠洲。同一時期，在阿蒙尼赫特一世（Amenemhet I）的執政之下，重新恢復了以金字塔作為皇族喪葬遺址首選形式的傳統。

起初，中王國金字塔的地上廟宇及其他結構似乎是以古王國後期（第五及第六王朝）傳承下來的形式為藍本，然而，這份仿古與復刻的精神恰巧遇上了一段充滿實驗與創新的時代潮流。一開始時，中王國時期金字塔的子結構似乎完全未被記載下來，正當私人陵墓開始收錄金字塔銘文與棺柩銘文，皇族的陵墓靜肅低調的發展卻不禁令人起疑。埃及的神學家們極有可能在這段時間正在為法老的治喪儀式著手撰寫新的銘文，以供來世所需。這類文件的編纂並不會在大廷廣眾面前進行，而是在廟宇的繕寫室裡執行，由於存放在繕寫室的鉅著與手稿已不幸遺失，見證著風格演進的目擊者未能隨著時代存留下來，因此，形塑中王國時期金字塔建築發展的神學創意只能被間接地重新建構。

這些變化中最為顯著的為中王國時期金字塔的地上結構改由簡單的瓦礫組成，再以表面打磨得很平滑的石灰岩罩覆蓋住，如此一來，遺址施工的時間可大大縮短，但卻不能保證其耐久性。即使是從第十二王朝遺留至今保存最佳的金字塔，如今看來也不過是一堆錯落遍地的石塊與散沙。說明這個現象最常見的解釋為，建造金字塔的高額經費加速了古王國的崩解，中王國的統治者為了避免重蹈覆轍，開始尋求較為簡約的方式建造金字塔。要支持這種說法的先決條件是一套宏觀的經濟觀點，但就古埃及人的世界觀而言，這樣的說法不見得能夠成立。然而，即便經濟考量確實影響金字塔的結構發展，對於建構法老陵墓這樣如此重要的遺址而言，從神學考量出發的理論對任何改變也應有所貢獻。古王國初期由泥磚改為石塊的演進有著相當平鋪直述的理由：為永世打造的遺址需要使用能遠遠超越人類正常壽命的堅固材質，要解釋與這個趨勢背道而馳的反向操作便顯得有點困難。難道說，到了這個時期，金字塔的上層結構以被視為一種「一次性使用」的工藝作品，在將法老的靈魂成功轉渡到神聖世界後，便可卸除它的任務了？無論動機為何，改以瓦礫核心為地上結構的事實，恰巧與設置在地底下，即冥界的墓室在形式與功能上的轉變不謀而合。

在中王國金字塔地下墓室裡，我們意外發現完全缺乏標準化的設計，佈滿迷宮一般的曲折廊道與隱藏的門，這些發展肯定與杜埃地區　陵墓上層結構同樣受到尊重的現象有所關聯，然而，在更深的地層下那些下陷的墓室、沈瀆的廊道、令人暈眩的通風井等設計，都被解釋為與特定的神話場景有所關聯，如奧塞里斯的秘密陵墓，或是鷹頭造型的冥界神祇「蘇卡」（Sokar）的大洞穴。辛努塞爾特三世（Senusret III）（西元前 1843 年）位於中埃及阿比多斯（Abydos）的陵墓則是這類型的發展中最為顯著的一座金字塔。在此例中，建築師完全捨棄了金字塔的上層結構，反倒將陵墓的地下廊道蓋在西部大懸崖的陰影處，金字塔外型的天然山丘之下。地表上沒有任何標示進入陵墓的祠堂或遺址，連帶的山谷廟宇也不再以堤道的形式和陵墓連結。實際上，當時一般的埃及人對這位法老的喪禮完全一無所知。在上層結構中，可以清楚觀察到二分法的規劃：一座直線狀、下降的、表面處理為白色石灰岩廊道，通向彎曲的、表面處理為紅色石英岩的中心軸。在這兩個區域的交界處，有一座下陷的井道，通向一間隱藏嚴密的墓室，法老的遺體就安置其中。這座陵墓的現代挖掘者認為，阿比多斯的喪葬遺址索欲重建的神話場景，是奧塞里斯在入夜後的第六個小時與太陽神「拉」的重逢（見下述「太陽之旅」的討論），後者並隨即穿過蘇卡的大洞穴。即便繼承辛努塞爾特三世的法老並未沿用這些戲劇化的新意，當時代推進到新王國時期初期時，這些創意仍然對下一階段的皇族陵墓建設發揮了關鍵性的作用。

中王國時期終結後，埃及的政治與社會進入了一個動盪不安的新年代，今日稱為第二中間時期（第十三王朝末期至第十七王朝，西元前 1650-1569 年）。當這個時代來到尾聲時，一個來自底比斯這個南方城市的家庭再度重拾對上下埃及的統治權，正式進入新王國時期（第十八至二十五王朝，西元前 1569-1081 年），終止了一段長時間對大規模遺址建設的停滯期，正因如此，值得特別談談新王朝的創建者阿摩斯（Ahmose）：在阿比多斯，僅鄰辛努塞爾特三世的秘密陵墓數百公尺處，阿摩斯打造了埃及漫長的歷史上最後的一座皇族金字塔，在接下來的五百年裡，幾乎每一位新王國時期的統治者都被安葬在底比斯西岸一處石窟陵墓中，即今日所稱「帝王谷」的皇族墓地。

在帝王谷的陵墓理論上是被視為秘密的遺址，它們沒有連結到喪葬廟宇的堤道或其他的標誌記號，也沒有表示任何一座陵墓位置的金字塔上部結構。反而所有的遺址都是建置在一個巨大的金字塔型山丘的陰影處，成為望向西方山谷時最明顯的景色，其地底下的結構皆明顯分為兩部分，從一個深陷的井道開始，而十八王朝的其他案例卻都以明顯彎曲或凹折的軸線作為終點。整體說來，帝王谷的陵墓顯示了在意識形態上它們是阿比多斯辛努塞爾特三世偉大的喪葬遺址的傳承者，然而，從一個特定的層面來說，新王國的皇族陵墓卻有所不同。它們是六百餘年來首次出現刻有銘文的地下墓室，而這些銘文也是有史以來第一次與神祇形象的描繪、地理位置示意圖、神聖世界的居民融合彙整。剛開始，裝飾僅限於墓室與井道，但是到了新王國時期後期（第十九至第二十王朝）幾乎所有可用的牆面與天花板都成了描繪冥界與天界宇宙觀的畫布。

年代最久遠，最具影響力的宇宙觀的作品為《來世之書》（Amduat），這個古埃及的名詞意為「在冥界者」，實際上是一個可以應用在任何一本宇宙學書籍的統合性名詞，然而，在古埃及人的認知裡，我們現今所稱的《來世之書》中的文本指的是「密室的寫作」，其「寫作」可能意指石棺廳牆面上刻有的銘文與圖像，與四個地理方位有象徵性的連結。其「密室」指的就是石棺廳，奧塞里斯神聖墓室的皇族基礎。《來世之書》以圖像的方式紀錄太陽在夜晚十二小時的時間裡為達到冥界所需穿過的崎嶇路徑，及所見的居民。銘文理想上的排列，是以縱橫交錯的方式，將石造遺址轉化成一個具有神力及功能性的冥界模型，在太陽再生的輝煌時刻，法老的亡靈將從其深處浮現。

太陽之旅：以「拉」與「奧塞里斯」作為神聖再生的藍本

在最早期的宗教文學中一金字塔銘文一我們讀到亡靈加入神祇的行列，將祂們的屬性消化吸收，融入自身，甚至吃下祂們的肉身，以獲取神聖的力量與天性。在傳說中最古老的這些咒語中，亡者表達了希望成為北方天空極地之星的欲望，然而，在烏那斯時期，我們便遇到了在接下來的兩千年內，一直是埃及喪葬習俗的基石的神話方程式：法老王的屍身，加上奧塞里斯木乃伊後的遺體，長眠於杜埃，以及他行動自如的「巴」，加上太陽神「拉」，在破曉時從西方地平線升起。

似乎，從很久很久以前，每日上生下降的太陽對埃及人而言，代表了生一死一再生這恆常的輪迴。以傳統的進程來看，每一個在太陽神生命中重要的階段都有一個代表的神：破曉時稱為「凱普拉」（Kheprer），其形象為「聖甲蟲」（scarab），這個名字還有另外一種詮釋：「（永恆）來自他

的生靈」或「轉化者」。到了中午，成形的太陽「拉」（Re）以圓盤狀或鷹首人身的外型上升到天空的最高處。黃昏時，太陽化身為一位年邁駝背的老人，其形象是公羊頭的墓日神「阿圖姆」（Atum），這個名字的意義為「完成者」或「完美者」。就在這年老的神沉入西邊的地平線，日轉成夜，太陽也從凡間消失，直到十二小時之後，奇蹟似的又再以凱普拉之身從東方升起，新的一天於焉開始。

太陽的升起與落下是大自然贈予埃及人對冥世想像的一個完美模型，透過這個具體又令人信服的見證，生命的歷程不再只是一條從搖籃通往墳場的直線，它是一場生生不息的循環，死亡與誕生僅是這幅運轉之輪中的相對的兩端，然而，埃及人也很清楚地意識到這其中的一個主要的問題：從西方落下後，夜晚的太陽發生什麼事了？無疑地，介於傍晚與黎明間的十二小時中，發生了「某件事」，將老朽的墓日之神阿圖姆回春變身成活力四溢的太陽之子凱普拉。埃及最重要的冥王「奧塞里斯」的神話則為這個神學困境解套。

奧塞里斯法老在史前時代統治埃及，他的兄弟塞特（Seth）垂涎王位，因此將他殺害，並把屍體切成許多塊，分撒遍野。幸好，這位被殺害的法老的姊妹，同時也是他的妻子伊西斯（Isis），找回了這些屍體的碎塊。她用鬼斧神工般的技術，加上姊妹奈芙蒂斯（Nephthys）與狡頡的豺狼阿努比斯（Anubis）的幫忙，合力將奧塞里斯的遺體復原，為了安全起見，並用亞麻布加以包裹，成了第一個木乃伊。從此之後，重新復活的奧塞里斯便留在陰間，掌管冥界之事。

如前所述，在埃及前期的歷史中，木乃伊製作的發展似乎是針對喪葬習俗改變而衍生出的一種務實性回應，我們因此推斷，與奧塞里斯神話之間的關係可能只是附屬的發展。然而，我們可以肯定的是，到了第五王朝後期，死去的奧塞里斯的身份已經確認，如烏那斯金字塔銘文所陳：「塞特，這是你的兄弟，奧塞里斯，他的重生是為了懲罰你，只要他活著，烏那斯法老也會活著！他未死去，烏那斯法老也將不會死！…你的身體即烏那斯法老的身體，你的血肉及烏那斯法老的血肉，你的骨骸及烏那斯法老的骨骸。你走，烏那斯法老也走，烏那斯法老走，你也走。」

在冥界，奧塞里斯統治下行的陰間，埃及人看到了一個人世的翻版。在這個上下顛倒，處處充滿危險的陰暗領域，事物的運行仍遵循宇宙的原則及王權的統御，就像尼羅河流域與埃及這塊國土一樣。太陽無止境地在這兩個境域中推移渡過，它的到來驅散了黑暗，為人類與眾神祇帶來光明與生命，這是聖靈重生的最終解答：在某種情況下，奧塞里斯與被視為同一神祇的兩面，其神的屬性會反應在人類的肉體與靈魂上。每一位神祇各自為政時都，會施展各自對這個世界的重要功能，但是每一位神祇也有能力上的限制：出生與老去，死亡與腐敗。然而，每日入夜後，在冥界的最底部，「巴」將與屍身結合為一，「拉」會進入奧塞里斯的遺體，這兩個神祇短暫合體，懶洋洋的奧塞里斯受到這股催化作用的刺激，使太陽得以回到祂新生的狀態，而從東方的地平線再度升起。這個以太陽為中心的信仰裡隱藏的核心之謎，則可在第十九王朝拉美西斯二世（Rameses II）最寵幸的王后娜芙塔莉（Nefertari）的陵墓中獲得最清晰簡要的表述。改寫自偉大的太陽經連禱文《西方敬慕的太陽神拉之書》（Book of Adoring Re in the West），合體後的神與奧塞里斯的木乃伊之身，以及代表夜間的太陽的公羊頭共同出現，隨附的文本清楚的說道：祂是拉，祂安息於奧塞里斯之內，而奧塞里斯，則安息於拉之內。」

將亡者認定為太陽的信念或許可以遠溯至早期王國時期，我們發現許多最早期坑墓的方位多朝著太陽升起的東方，與奧塞里斯的聯想雖然可能是比較近期的發展，但仍可溯源至金字塔銘文最早出現的證據，然而，被稱為「太陽—奧塞里斯合體」（Solar-Osirian Unity）的原始概念─拉與奧塞里斯屬於同一神祇的不同面向，祂的「巴」和屍身在夜晚合為一體─則比較難作精確的展述。如此一來，舉例來說，在棺木銘文中，即埃及人所稱的《行Rosetjau之書》（Book of the Ways of Rosetjau），包含了現今已知最早的神聖世界的圖表式表現，其中或多或少提及了「太陽—奧塞里斯」神話，這些宇宙學的圖像出示了兩條可以通過「杜埃特」（Duat，陰間）的途徑，都與拉和奧塞里斯這兩個神祇有關，另外還有代表月亮神的「托特」（Thoth）。文本中對於這兩條路徑之間，或是與它們有關的兩位神祇之間的關係並未做出清楚的說明，然而，我們仍可以提出合理的推斷，太陽於白晝與黑夜兩段時間的運行存在著互惠的關係。

宇宙探索的傳統最早出現在中王國時期初期的《行Rosetjau之書》中，歷經了新王國時期，逐漸發展到前所未見的盛況。以《來世之書》為首，這些新的宇宙學書籍在太陽之旅的主題上大做文章─包括太陽神在夜間與奧塞里斯的神秘合體─對於像百科全書般細節的描述充滿了熱情無比的關注。新王國時期大部分正式的宇宙學文獻可約略分為以下兩類：《天空之書》（Books of the Sky），描述太陽通過天體之域上「杜埃特」的旅途，以及《冥界之書》（Underworld Books），著重在冥府之境的下「杜埃特」。

第十九王朝的《天空之書》以兩個部份描述太陽在日間的活動，《日之書》（The Book of the Day）與《諾特之書》（the Book of Nut），以及夜間的《夜之書》（Book of the Night）。《天空之書》全集以天空之后諾特（Nut）拱成半圓的身體描繪出天體之域，諾特是太陽之母，她以雙手落在西方地平線，雙腳踩在東方地平線之姿，將大地擁抱在懷中。描述白天的書以太陽神的在東方之境誕生為始，接下來循著諾特身體的外徑，描繪著太陽在日間十二個小時，經過並聚集了大批的神祇，朝向西方地平線前進，日落。埃及人以些許驚惶的態度看待這個行程中最後的項目，因為在這個時候，老化的太陽神從活人的世間消失，進入冥界。天空之書以神性的食人行為展示這個可佈的一章：天空之神活吞了祂的兒子─太陽神拉。在《夜之書》（Book of the Night）中所描述的接下來的夜晚十二個小時，便是太陽神在諾特的體內，從西方穿向東方的過程。這個過程同時也代表太陽神如何行經神聖世界的地景風光後，回到了母親的子宮，在黎明來臨祂將重新以幼兒之貌誕生之前，在母體內孕育成長的旅程。

另外一組重要的宇宙學文獻《冥界之書》則著重在通過下杜埃特的夜間之旅。《夜之書》將相同的區域視為一種存在諾特體內較下方的天空，《冥界之書》卻將下杜埃特描述為穿越地球的過道。除了「冥界者」之外，其他《冥界之書》包括所謂的《太陽—奧塞里斯合體之書》（Book of the Solar-Osirian Unity）、《通道之書》（Book of the Gates）、《洞穴之書》（Book of the Caverns）、《地之書》（Book of the Earth）。依據冥界的佈局與太陽神的圖像，這五冊書籍又可再分成部份稍微重疊的兩個類別。第一類為「冥界者」與《通道之書》，書中將夜晚的十二個小時刻畫為分別獨立的區域，太陽神駕著神聖的輕舟一一渡過。第二類則是《洞穴之書》、《太陽—奧塞里斯合體之書》、《地之書》，這三本書並不刻意將夜晚區分為十二小時，除了太陽神的輕舟之外，還將太陽神描繪成一個行走的人，或是一個在圓盤中旅行的人，甚至太陽神就是那片圓盤。縱使存在著這些形式上的差異，所有的《冥界之書》還是分享著一些共通點，尤其是它們都特別強調黑夜將結束前幾個小時的刻畫。

雖然各自呈現出相當多樣的變化，每一本《冥界之書》的最終章傳達出一個單一複雜的意象，「太陽穿越天堂、陰間與原生的海洋」。這些圖像通常帶有一些暗指東方地平線大圓弧的意含，分離陰間與天空的隱密境域。在這道弧形之下，太陽可能同時出現老化及回春後的樣貌，一個公羊頭形象的老人與太陽之子，或聖甲蟲「凱普拉」並肩站立。在其他的情況下，這些不同的造型會相互混雜配對─夜行公羊的頭從書行聖甲蟲的前肢冒出來─以強調不同類別的結合，來作為單一太陽神的佐證。通常，奧塞里斯的木乃伊會在周圍出現，影射神與拉的合體。在《來世之書》，這個木乃伊斜倚在冥界彎曲的邊界上；在《地之書》中，書行鷹頭造型的太陽將祂的光束射向奧塞里斯那被認為「載有拉之屍身」的木乃伊。稍早開始進行合體的兩位神祇，在夜間之旅的中途，在白晝降臨的那一刻，完成最終體現：神之合體，「雷—奧塞里斯」。祂有著能跨越宇宙的巨人身形，祂在黎明破曉時從東方地平線浮現，所射出的火熱光線會將創世的敵人殲滅。

冥世與墓葬的咒文

新王國時期皇族陵寢的牆面與天花板所裝飾的大量令人驚嘆的宇宙圖像與描繪咒文，與古王國初期金字塔裡簡樸的墓室成了強烈的對比，只不過，在這群遺址之間仍可觀察到理論發展的拋物線，其核心論點在歷經兩千年的時間淬鍊後，仍能產生顯著的效益。亡者被視與奧塞里斯與拉等同視之完滿了這個過程，使得死亡與再生有了務實性的神學理論支撐，對每一個埃及人而言，生死輪轉的例證近在眼前：每日的日昇日落；懷孕與生育的生理奇蹟；大自然現象的生生不息，行星的運轉，尼羅河的潮起潮落。藉由喪葬咒語、宇宙學文稿、宇宙圖像的銘刻，這些循環被轉移到陵墓的牆面，將代用的石造遺址變身成一個具有生命的小宇宙，亡者將從此處出現、重生，一如原始創世者，太陽神一般。

在埃及墓葬信仰與習俗的研究上，我們只能以逐步拼湊方式進行，所浮現的圖像也僅比最起碼的基礎輪廓多上幾筆，然而，在這個輪廓之內，我們已經看到了「完滿的墓葬」隨著時間的轉變：從只是為了幫助亡者打點在冥世宮殿中的生活，到在一座石造迷你宇宙的核心的一場偉大的神化行為。在這個漫長的過程中所滋生出的任何想法並未捨棄，而是受到。新一層的意義不斷被加附在既有的基層上，探索紀錄每一條可以推測想像到的打通冥界本質的手段與途徑，這樣的過程所推導出的結果經常難免是多重，甚至互相矛盾的詮釋，進而衍生出更多的提問，而非獲得確切的解答。夜幕低垂後，太陽究竟是進入了天空之神的身體，還是潛遊在地表之下？金字塔究竟是原生土墩的重建，還是一到固化的太陽光？拉、奧塞里斯、阿圖姆、凱普拉真的曾經一度是同一個神，還是祂們向來一直是不同的神祇？最終而言，這些提問反應了後代人追求雙重性與對立性的欲望，但這些卻是遠古時代的埃及人毫無猶豫會回答「是」的問題。這並不表示埃及人的思維是非理性、不務實、或無條理的一事實其實恰巧相反。對於生與死、神明，以及神所創造的世界，埃及人在這方面的觀點單純的建立在對符號的力量，對文字與圖像之間神奇的連結，以及它們所代表的現象為基礎的信仰上。然而，如果我們說，埃及人並沒有完全信服於他們的神話，或他們的宗教信仰「只是」由一套描述超越凡人能力所及的現象的寓言所構成，這對那些墓地是不公平的。《冥界之書》、《天空之書》等等的文獻「是」替代寓言，描述一種與相同的過程，但它們「同樣」也映照出埃及人認知中存在於神聖世界的真理。

因此，繞了一圈之後，我們回到了原始的提問：古代的埃及人很熱衷於死亡的命題嗎？從現代的觀點來看，答案無疑是肯定的。但這樣的回答完全無法說明死亡對古埃及人的意義。要認定一個人已「死亡」，是要將他貶謫到被詛咒的罪犯的等級，成為法治社會的敵人，將遭受聖靈界第二次死刑的懲罰，這無異是要將他送下地獄，然而，對大部分的埃及人來說，肉體的死亡，一如出生，是將存在狀態轉移到另一種明確的「活著」。「活在」世間，就是要渡過生老病死的正常程序，「活在」聖界，就是要受到「真實之聲」的神界審判，才能加入神的境域，祂們的存在超越肉體的死亡，也超越那些被詛咒者命中註定的終極毀滅。從這個角度我們得以歸證，所有投入於死亡與喪葬的準備上的時間與費用，反映出的絕對不只是對死亡的迷戀，或是某種拒絕接受死亡之實的幼稚企圖，對埃及人而言，一場完滿的墓葬是對在世生活的禮讚，是對生命以新的存在狀態，持續在聖界達到不朽與圓滿的保證。

喬許．羅伯森
賓州大學

Chapter 5
A Good Burial

Introduction

The modern observer, who considers the texts and monuments of ancient Egypt for the first time, may be impressed by what many have interpreted as the Egyptians' obsession with death. In many ways, this 'obsession' has more to do with modern perception than ancient reality. Most early archaeology was conducted in cemeteries, rather than settlements. In addition, Egyptian tombs were constructed in the arid, western desert at the very fringe of human society -- quite literally, the land of the dead -- where every natural and artificial means of preservation was exploited so that grave goods, mortuary texts, and human remains might be preserved for all time. Egyptian villages and towns, on the other hand, existed along the banks of the Nile River, where the high water table and continuous human habitation, up to the present day, have greatly complicated modern research into the ancient land of the living. Given these factors, it is hardly surprising that so many of the most beautiful, best preserved, and best known artefacts to survive from ancient Egypt derive from mortuary contexts.

However, it is a fact that the preparation for one's funeral, the construction of a tomb, the collection of mortuary texts, and the endowment of a memorial offering cult constituted some of the most significant investments of time and resources in the life of every Egyptian with the social and economic means to do so. Was ancient Egypt obsessed with death after all? In order to answer this question, we must examine Egyptian beliefs about the relationship between life and death, as well as the mythological rationales behind mummification, burial, and the changing role of the tomb complex in the afterlife.

Life and Death

For the ancient Egyptians, the death of the physical body marked a transition between two distinct phases of existence. The first phase consisted of the lifetime spent on earth. Ancient texts tell us that Egyptians hoped to enjoy an ideal lifetime of 110 years, although forensic examination of ancient mummies indicates that, while many Egyptians lived into their fifties and beyond, most died well before achieving the hoped-for 'great old age'. The actual number of years allotted to an individual and the manner of his or her eventual demise was ordained at birth by seven goddesses of fate, known as the Hathors. Alongside this element of pre-destination were the choices made during one's lifetime, which remained subject to the free will of the individual. A literary tale known as The Doomed Prince provides a wonderful illustration of Egyptian attitudes towards destiny and free will. In that story, the king hopes to prevent the fate ordained for his son by locking the boy away in a castle, far from civilization. After the boy matures, he demands that his father allow him to leave and explore the world, saying, "What is the point of my sitting around like this? Obviously, I am already commanded to this fate. Let me be released, so that I might follow my heart until God decides otherwise." The eventual end of the story is lost, but one lesson seems to be that, although the length of time from birth to death may be foretold, the path one takes to reach that fate was shaped by individual choices. Critically, it was these very choices, made during a lifetime spent on earth, which determined the outcome of the next phase of existence, in the world beyond.

After the death of the physical body, the spirit of the deceased began its transition into the divine world, which the Egyptians called the Duat. This transition was conceived in legal terms, as a final judgement before a divine tribunal, presided over by the great god of the dead, Osiris. At the judgement, an individual's prior actions on earth were measured against the standard of cosmic order and truth, known as Maat. The most widely attested representation of this divine judgement derives from 125th spell of the Egyptian Book of the Dead (c. 1500 BC), a sort of 'user's manual' for life in the next world. In the vignette to this spell, the deceased is led into the presence of the gods of Egypt. A large scale or balance, tended by the jackal-headed deity Anubis, holds on one side the heart of the deceased, the wellspring of his or her moral and ethical character, while on the other side rests a feather, representing Maat. To the right of the scale, a composite monster, 'She-who-devours', awaits the outcome of the judgement, which was also recorded by the ibis-headed scribe Thoth, on the far right. If the heart's character was good, it would balance evenly with the feather and the individual would be judged 'true of voice', as one of the akhu, or blessed dead permitted to dwell among the gods in the divine world. But if the deceased had failed to uphold the principles of Maat in life, then the heart would outweigh the feather and be cast into the mouth of She-who-devours, whose open jaws represent a second death, the total annihilation of the Damned.

There is a certain inevitability in the judgement scene that bears closer scrutiny. The scales of Maat always end in balance. The justification of the deceased before the divine tribunal is treated as a foregone conclusion. Texts and images invariably portray the tomb owner as righteous and honourable. In a very real sense, compositions like the Book of the Dead served as a sort of insurance to guarantee a favourable judgement. This confidence in the magical power of mortuary texts to overcome death appears already in the earliest religious literature, the Pyramid Texts (c. 2375 BC), where we find repeated the assurance that "You have not gone away dead, you have gone away alive!" The Egyptian word ankh, which we translate as 'alive', was often employed to describe people 'living' on earth. However, its use in the context of the afterlife—the world of the gods—was more complex than the modern dichotomy between biological life and death might suggest. To describe the gods or the deceased as ankh implied existence in a state that transcended the possibility of spiritual annihilation, or second death, which was the ultimate fate of the Damned. In the context of the divine world, ankh meant not merely alive, but 'immortal', in the literal sense: undying, beyond death. Here, we come to the purpose implicit in all mortuary preparations, from mummification to final interment: The preservation of individual identity in the wake of death, so that one might 'live' in the divine world, as the gods live.

Mummification and Burial

Preparations for life in the next world necessarily began in the land of the living, with the ritual treatment of the body for burial and the construction of a tomb to house it. These preparations focused upon the care and sustenance of various physical and spiritual components, which the Egyptians believed to constitute the individual. Some of these components, such as the individual's name and shadow, were common to both the living and the dead. Others, like the mobile ba-spirit and the luminous akh, were associated primarily with life in the next world.

The first two components, shaped by the potter god Khnum at the moment of conception, were the physical body and its spiritual double, the ka. The ka was the animating 'life force', which required sustenance for survival. During life, the ka drew its nourishment from the physical consumption of food and drink. After death, that same nourishment was extracted from offerings, which living relatives or mortuary priests might leave in above-ground chapels constructed near the subterranean tomb of the deceased. To facilitate the ka's egress, private tombs and tomb chapels, as well as royal mortuary temples and other monuments, often included structures known as 'false doors'. These stylized gateways served as a point of transition, a spiritually permeable interface between the land of the living and the abode of the dead. Such doors often included texts with the deceased's name and titles, as well as images representing the ka itself. In the most elaborate examples, the ka might be sculpted in ultra-high relief, such that the spirit appears to literally emerge, ghost-like, up from the depths of the tomb to claim the offerings left on its behalf.

In contrast to the immaterial ka, the Egyptians understood the corporeal body as a collection of ha'u, or 'limbs', enclosing the vital organs, which were connected by a system of circulatory vessels known as metu. This physical form housed the ka and the individual's other spiritual components during life. After death, the 'corpse', which the Egyptians called khat, functioned more or less as a way station for the spirit, which, while free to roam the divine world, hoped always to return to the familiar safety of the body that sheltered it during life. The desire to protect the body as a haven for the wandering spirit lies at the heart of the characteristically Egyptian practice of mummification.

Prior to the historic period in Egypt (before about 3400 BC), human bodies were buried in shallow pit graves, with no clothing or wrapping of any kind. The desiccating properties of the desert sands in these earliest, pre-historic graves served to preserve the bodies naturally. During the transition to the historic period, as the power of the early rulers grew, the desire to equip and protect their mortal remains in a manner befitting their elevated status led to the introduction of more elaborate tombs made of mud-brick, wood, and later, stone. Ironically, these developments actually served to accelerate the process of bodily decay, by isolating the corpse from the preservative properties of the arid desert sands. As a result, a series of techniques for the embalming and wrapping of the corpse was invented as an alternative to the natural preservation of the desert. These techniques were developed over many centuries, with evidence for the full process of ritual embalming, including the evisceration and preservation of internal organs, appearing first at Giza, in the Fourth Dynasty tomb of Hetepheres, the mother of Khufu (about 2513 BC).

In its most elaborate form, the embalming ritual took place over the course of seventy days, in a ritual building known as the wabet, or Place of Purification. In the first stage of this process, internal organs viewed as non-essential to the afterlife (including the brain) were removed and discarded. Next, the liver, lungs, stomach, and intestines were removed, dried with natron salt, and placed in a series of four so-called 'canopic jars' for storage and protection. After the Old Kingdom, the lids of these storage vessels -- originally, simple domed stoppers -- began to be sculpted in the form of human heads, perhaps representing the deceased. By the later New Kingdom, the human-headed jars came to be replaced by the heads of the deities Imsety (human-headed; liver), Hapy (baboon-headed; lungs), Duamutef (jackal-headed; stomach), and Qebehsenuef (falcon-headed; intestines). These protective deities, known as the four sons of the god Horus, were charged with protecting the vital organs of the deceased. The most important organ, the heart, was left intact in the chest, where it might continue to serve as the seat of moral and ethical character.

After evisceration, the body was washed inside and out, and then packed with natron and other substances, which served to desiccate the corpse over a period of forty days. After all moisture was removed, the natron mixture was replaced and the body re-stuffed to present a more life-like appearance, before being covered finally in perfumed oils and resin. This resin gave the bodies a blackened appearance, resembling bitumen pitch, which led to their modern designation as 'mummies', from the Arabic word for bitumen, mumia. Once the body was coated thoroughly with this resinous mixture, the corpse was wrapped in linen bandages and adorned with magical amulets in order to protect and facilitate the spirit's transition to the divine world. After the mummification ritual, the embalmer-priests sealed the corpse within a wooden coffin or stone sarcophagus. Finally, a highly ritualized funeral procession conducted the earthly remains from the Place of Purification to the tomb. This procession including living relatives, professional mourners and other performers, various officials, and a special class of priests known as Lectors, responsible for the recitation of hymns and spells to insure the deceased's successful transition into the divine world. At the culmination of the funeral ceremony, the mummified corpse, sealed and protected within its coffin, was deposited within the subterranean burial chamber of the tomb, which was to be its final resting place.

From the earliest periods, Egyptian burials reflected a belief in the necessity of provisioning the deceased with the same goods required in life. Storage chambers below ground were filled with as many jars for food and drink as they could possibly hold, together with tools, weapons, jewellery and other artefacts valued on earth. On the one hand, objects deposited within the tomb were intended to serve a practical function in the divine world. On the other hand, the amount and quality of burial goods also served as an indicator of the deceased's former social status, which they hoped to transmit to the afterlife. In fact, only the highest elite were afforded the luxury of a formally constructed mud-brick tomb, whereas the majority of private Egyptians continued to be buried in humble pit graves. In the case of kings from the first two Dynasties, human servants and beasts of burden were even sacrificed and buried alongside their rulers -- surely, the ultimate expression of royal privilege in the afterlife! This last practice was abandoned after Dynasty 2, but the importance of equipping the dead for eternity remained a vital aspect of burial for the rest of pharaonic history.

Tomb Complexes and the Afterlife

Ancient Egyptian tombs were conceived essentially as bi-partite complexes. Below ground, the burial chamber, plus any subsidiary rooms or corridors, lay within the land of the dead, which was generally inaccessible to living Egyptians. Above ground, offering chapels and other structures were erected for the perpetuation of the mortuary cult, so that living relatives, priests, and pious passers-by might recite prayers for the deceased and leave offerings of food and drink to nourish the ka. As a reflection of this basic, bi-partite division, specific rules of decorum governed which and what kinds of texts and images were appropriate for use in either the above- or below-ground areas of the mortuary complex, in any given period. This material shows tremendous variation both diachronically (from different historical periods) and synchronically (among different sources in a given period). New elements were added continuously, while others might be expanded, abbreviated, abandoned, or re-introduced after periods of disuse. In addition, what was appropriate only for royal tombs in an earlier period might become 'democratized' for use in non-royal, private tombs later.

In Egypt's Early Dynastic Period (Dynasties 1–2), both royal and elite private tombs appear to have functioned primarily as 'palaces for the afterlife', where kings might continue their rule in the Beyond and private persons might continue to perform their earthly offices and duties on his behalf. Subterranean chambers were arranged in grid-like plans, which might be connected with passageways or doors, similar to an actual house. Architectural elements from terrestrial dwellings, such as wooden roofing beams or rolled bundles of reed matting, were even occasionally imitated in mud brick. Above ground, the location of the tomb was marked with a rectangular superstructure known as a mastaba (a modern Arabic designation, meaning 'bench'-shaped). The exteriors of private mastabas were often decorated with a complex pattern of niched panels, in imitation of the walls of archaic palaces. Royal complexes, on the other hand, seem to have employed smooth-sided mastabas, reserving the palace façade motif for separate 'funerary enclosures', built several hundred meters from the tomb itself and serving perhaps as ritual palaces or temples during the king's funeral ceremony.

The Old Kingdom saw major changes in the architecture, design, and function of both royal and private tomb complexes. In the private sphere, we can trace these changes, as well as the increased importance and power of the highest officials, most easily through the dramatic expansion of the above-ground offering place. From Dynasty 3, the offering niche was extended deeper into the mastaba, forming a cross-shaped, interior chapel. This area might be decorated with false doors, images of the tomb owner, biographical texts, and special prayers known as 'invocation offerings', intended to magically equip the spirit with food, clothing, and the like. By the later Old Kingdom (Dynasties 5 and 6), the offering chapels of many of the highest elite had become enormous, multi-room structures, rivaling royal monuments in terms of their opulence and quality of workmanship. The dominant motifs in the decoration of the opulent mastaba chapels were the so-called 'Scenes of Daily Life'. These images represented veritable armies of workmen, artisans, entertainers, and priests responsible for the provisioning and maintenance of the mortuary estate. Towering over these minor figures was the image of the tomb owner, together with his family. The texts and images from the Scenes of Daily Life evoked a paradisiacal realm of abundance and order, whose imagery was modeled on an idealized vision of Egypt itself. But while the tomb owner appears as the overlord of his estate and the recipient of its considerable bounty, the offering spells and biographical texts make clear that it was the king, acting on behalf of the gods, who was the ultimate wellspring of any status or prosperity the deceased might enjoy, in this world or the next.

In the royal sphere, the old notion of the tomb as the palace for the afterlife gradually gave way to a more sophisticated idea of the tomb as a sort of magical artifact, designed to transform the deceased into a luminous spirit, or akh, capable of entering the divine world. For all intents and purposes, this process begins with the construction of the great Step Pyramid complex of Djoser (Dynasty 3, c. 2668 BC) at the Lower Egyptian necropolis of Saqqara. Djoser, through the agency of his chief architect Imhotep, was the first king to construct his mortuary complex entirely from stone, rather than mud brick. In addition, the older, southern tradition of a separate mastaba and funerary enclosure was re-envisioned as a single, above ground complex, symbolizing the king's rule over Upper and Lower Egypt. A massive enclosure wall, decorated with the palace façade motif, surrounded a series of dummy buildings and other ritual structures, from which Djoser's dual kingship might be exercised for eternity. At the center of the complex, a great stone mastaba was expanded through the addition of six tiers, each smaller than the last and stacked one atop the other. The resulting stepped structure -- the first of Egypt's many pyramids -- served as a monumental stairway, from which the king hoped to ascend, in order to join the stars in the northern sky. At the same time, the towering stairway also represented the primordial mound of earth, elevated from the waters of chaos at the moment of creation. Below ground, two subterranean tombs were constructed -- a functional burial, beneath the Step Pyramid itself, and a second, ritual tomb built beneath the south end of the complex. Like the cult buildings above ground, the two subterranean tombs stressed Djoser's kingship over Upper and Lower Egypt, transferred now to the land of the dead. The walls of this underground realm were lined with blue-green tiles, representing the waters of chaos and the very border of the created world. The ceiling was decorated with a field of yellow stars against a dark blue sky, pointing the way to the celestial abode that was the ultimate goal of the deceased. With the architecture and decoration of the step pyramid complex, we see the tomb functioning clearly for the first time as a cosmograph, a schematic representation of the created world, in which the pyramid itself served as the vital link between underworld, earth, and sky.

The next major watershed in the development of the tomb as an artifact for divine apotheosis came at the beginning of Dynasty 4, with the introduction of the true, smooth-sided pyramid under king Sneferu. The most prolific pyramid builder in history, Sneferu perfected the smooth-sided form over the course of three separate construction projects: a converted step pyramid at the site of Meidum, followed later by the Bent and Red pyramids at Dashur. The evolution of these monuments probably reflects a re-analysis of the pyramid's basic symbolism from a celestial stairway to a solidified bean of sunlight, under the influence of the cult of the sun god Re at Heliopolis. From this same time, the ersatz palace structures employed at the Step Pyramid of Djoser came to be replaced by a single structure for the offering cult on the east face of the pyramid, in the direction of the rising sun. Separate valley temples, connected to the main complex by means of a covered causeway, began to be constructed near the shore of the Nile. In addition, the size of the pyramid superstructures increased dramatically under Sneferu and his son, Khufu, whose Great Pyramid at Giza remained the tallest building in the world (146.5 meters) for more than three thousand years. However, after the reign of Khufu's second son Khafre, the size of the pyramids began to decline dramatically. In addition, the elaborate systems of corridors and corbelled chambers built inside the pyramid superstructures of Sneferu and Khufu gave way to a simplified sequence, consisting of a single descending corridor, subterranean antechamber plus statue room, and burial chamber by the end of Dynasty 4.

The size and internal structure of the pyramid was more or less standardized by Dynasty 5, while the above ground temple seems to have achieved its classic form by Dynasty 6. However, perhaps the most important development came with the introduction of mortuary spells known as Pyramid Texts, which appeared first in the subterranean chambers of Unas, the last king of Dynasty 5. These texts, the oldest known corpus of religious literature in the world, include spells to equip the deceased with food, clothing, ointment, and incense; spells of protection against chaotic desert animals, such as snakes and scorpions; and spells for the king's resurrection, intended to facilitate his journey to the world of the gods. The organization of these texts in the pyramid of Unas has been interpreted as a schematic representation of the course that the king's spirit, equated with the ba of the sun god, followed from west to east, passing through the Duat by night and ascending into the sky at dawn.

The collapse of the Old Kingdom and the ensuing turmoil of the First Intermediate Period (Dynasties 7–10, c. 2200–2040 BC) resulted in a hiatus on all major royal construction projects, including pyramid tombs. The pyramid of Ibi at Saqqara, dated to Dynasty 8, marks the end of the original tradition of pyramid building, as well as the last appearance of the Pyramid Texts on the walls of a royal tomb. Indirect evidence from the Middle Kingdom confirms that kings continued to employ Pyramid Texts—probably on portable scrolls or inscribed on the sides of coffins, which are no longer preserved—as late as Dynasties 9 or 10. Around that time or shortly after, excerpts from the Pyramid Texts began to appear on private coffins and tomb walls, together with a new group of mortuary spells attested exclusively in the private sphere, known as Coffin Texts.

The Middle Kingdom (Dynasties 11–13, c. 2040–1650 BC) saw the re-establishment of royal authority over all of Egypt and a resumption of large-scale monument construction. However, the earliest Middle Kingdom rulers, hailing from the southern city of Thebes (modern Luxor), did not immediately re-establish the tradition of pyramid building, with its ties to the old line of kingship in the north. Instead, the Theban Dynasty 11 upheld a local tradition of rock-cut tomb construction, exemplified above all by the great funerary monument of the Dynasty's founder, Mentuhotep II. However, with the transition to the Dynasty 12 (c. 1991 BC), the capital was moved from Thebes to the more northerly city of Itj-tawy, in the vicinity of the Fayum oasis. This movement also coincided with the re-introduction, under king Amenemhet I, of the pyramid as the preferred form of royal funerary monument.

Initially, the above-ground temples and other structures associated with the Middle Kingdom pyramids appear to have been modelled closely on their antecedents from the late Old Kingdom (Dynasties 5–6). However, this spirit of archaism and revival also coincided with a period of vigorous experimentation and innovation. From the first, the sub-structures of the Middle Kingdom pyramids appear to have been wholly uninscribed. Just as private tombs had begun to incorporate Pyramid Texts and Coffin Texts, the tombs of royalty now fell conspicuously silent. In all probability, Egyptian theologians had already begun composing new afterlife texts for use in the funeral and mortuary cult of the king. The composition and editing of such texts took place outside the public eye, in temple scriptoriums, where the master books and working drafts, which undoubtedly bore witness to the genre's evolution, have not survived. As a result, the theological innovations that shaped developments in pyramid architecture during the Middle Kingdom can be reconstructed only indirectly.

Certainly the most obvious of these changes was the fact that the superstructures of Middle Kingdom pyramids were now built from simple cores of rubble, overlaid with smooth casings of finished limestone. This allowed the monuments to be completed much more quickly, but at the expense of durability. Even the best preserved Twelfth Dynasty pyramids appear today as little more than heaps of loose stone and sand. The usual explanation for this change is that the Middle Kingdom rulers were seeking more economical solutions to tomb construction, the expense of which had supposedly accelerated the collapse of the Old Kingdom. Such an explanation presupposes a certain degree of macro-economic insight, whose relevance to the ancient Egyptians' worldview is questionable. However, even if economic considerations did play a role, it seems likely that a theological rationale would have accompanied any change to a monument of such importance as the king's tomb. The earlier shift from mud-brick to solid stone, at the dawn of the Old Kingdom, appears relatively straightforward: A monument for eternity required materials capable of enduring far beyond a normal human lifespan. It is more difficult to interpret the apparent reversal of this trend. Could the pyramidal superstructure have come to be viewed as a 'single use' artefact, whose function was served after transporting the king's spirit successfully into the divine world? Whatever its motive might have been, the adoption of a rubble-core superstructure also coincides with changes in the form and, presumably, function of the chambers located below ground, in the realm of the dead.

Within the subterranean chambers of the Middle Kingdom pyramids, we encounter a remarkable lack of standardization, an ever-changing labyrinth of twisting corridors and hidden rooms. These developments were surely connected with the venerable equation of the substructure of the tomb with the lower regions of the Duat. However, the sunken burial chambers, plunging corridors, and vertiginous shafts, excavated ever more deeply below ground, have also been linked with more specific mythological locales, such as the hidden tomb of Osiris or the cavern of the falcon-headed Underworld god, Sokar. The most significant development along these lines came with the construction of the tomb of Senusret III (c. 1843 BC), at the ancient site of Abydos in Middle Egypt. Here, the architects abandoned the pyramid superstructure altogether, instead constructing the tomb's subterranean corridors in the shadow of the great western cliffs, beneath a naturally pyramid-shaped hill. No cult buildings or other monuments marked the above-ground entrance to the tomb, while the associated valley temple was no longer linked to it by means of a causeway. The king's burial was, for all practical purposes, well and truly hidden from the sight of living Egyptians. Within the substructure, a clear bi-partite division may be observed: A linear descending corridor, faced in white limestone, gives way to a curved axis, faced in red quartzite. At the junction of these two areas, a sunken well shaft leads to a carefully concealed burial chamber, where the king's body was laid to rest. The tomb's modern excavator has suggested that the funerary monument at Abydos was intended to recreate the mythological location of Osiris's union with the sun god Re (see discussion of 'The Solar Journey' below), in the sixth hour of the night, following the latter god's passage through the cavern of Sokar. These dramatic innovations, although abandoned by Senusret's immediate successors, would yet play a pivotal role the next great phase of royal tomb construction, at the dawn of the New Kingdom.

The Middle Kingdom's end ushered in a new era of political and social unrest, which we refer to today as the Second Intermediate Period (late Dynasty 13–17,

c. 1650–1569 BC). At the end of this time, a family from the southern city of Thebes once again re-established control over Upper and Lower Egypt, ushering in the New Kingdom (Dynasties 18–20, c. 1569–1081 BC) and ending a protracted hiatus on large-scale monument construction. In this last regard, the founder of the new dynasty, Ahmose, deserves special mention: At the site of Abydos, only a few hundred meters from the hidden tomb of Senusret III, Ahmose constructed the last royal pyramid in Egypt's long history. For the next five centuries, nearly every ruler of the New Kingdom would be buried in a rock-cut tomb on the west bank of Thebes, in the royal necropolis known today as the Valley of the Kings.

The tombs in the Valley of the Kings were conceived, in principle, as hidden monuments. No causeways or other markers connected them to their mortuary temples and no pyramid superstructure marked the location of any one tomb. Instead, the monuments all lay in the shadow of a massive, pyramid-shaped hill, dominating the view of any westward approach to the Valley. The subterranean structures all exhibit a distinctive bipartition, commencing from a deeply sunk well shaft, while the Dynasty 18 exemplars all terminate in pronounced curved or bent axes. In all of these respects, the tombs of the Valley of the Kings reveal themselves as the ideological successors to the great funerary monument of Senusret III at Abydos. However, in one critical respect the New Kingdom royal tombs stand apart. For the first time in more than six hundred years, the subterranean chambers were inscribed with texts and for the first time ever these texts were integrated with figural representations of gods and schematic diagrams of the locations and inhabitants of the divine world. Initially, decoration was limited primarily to the burial chamber and well shaft but by the later New Kingdom (Dynasties 19-20) virtually every available wall and ceiling surface served as a canvas for cosmographic representations of the underworld and sky.

The earliest and most influential of these cosmographic works was the Amduat. This ancient Egyptian term, which literally means "that which is in the Duat," was actually a catch-all that could be applied to a virtually any cosmographic book. However, the specific text, which we now call the Amduat, was known to the ancient Egyptians as the "Writing of the Hidden Chamber." The 'writing' in question referred to the texts and images inscribed on the walls of the sarcophagus hall, which were linked symbolically to the four cardinal directions. The 'Hidden Chamber' was the sarcophagus hall itself, the royal hypostasis of the divine burial chamber of Osiris. The Amduat served as a pictorial record of the inhabitants and convoluted paths of the underworld, as traversed by the sun through the twelve hours of the night. The ideal layout of the text, criss-crossing the perimeter of the burial chamber in a convoluted spiral, transformed the stone monument into a magically functional model of Underworld itself, from depths of which the king's spirit emerged in a spectacular moment of solar rebirth.

The Solar Journey: Re and Osiris as a Model of Divine Rebirth

In the earliest religious literature -- the Pyramid Texts -- we read of the deceased joining the ranks of the gods, assimilating their attributes into his own being, and even consuming their bodies to acquire their magical power and divine nature. In what are thought to be the oldest of these spells, the deceased expresses his desire to join the circumpolar stars, in the northern sky. However, already by the time of Unas, we encounter aspects of the mythological equation that was to remain the cornerstone of Egyptian burial practices for the next two thousand years: The identification of the king's body with the mummified corpse of Osiris, who rests within the Duat, and of his mobile ba-spirit with the sun god Re, who emerges from the eastern horizon at dawn.

It seems that, from a very early period, the Egyptians interpreted the daily rising and setting of the sun as a cycle of perpetual birth, death, and re-birth. In its classic formulation, each major stage in the sun god's life was identified with a god: At dawn, the sun is (re-)born from the eastern horizon as Kheprer, the 'scarab', whose name also means "he who comes (perpetually) into being" and "he who transforms." By mid-day, the mature sun, Re, ascends to the height of the sky in the form of a disc or hawk-headed man. At dusk, the sun transforms into a bent and wizened old man, the ram-headed god Atum, whose name means both "the one who is complete" and "the one who is not." As the elderly god sinks into the western horizon, day yields to night and the sun disappears from the mortal world for twelve long hours until, miraculously, he re-emerges in the east as Kheprer, the following morning.

In the rising and setting of the sun, nature itself provided a nearly perfect model for the Egyptian afterlife. This model offered visible proof and daily assurance that life was not merely a straight line from the cradle to the grave but also a cycle, in which death and birth existed merely as antipodal points of transition on a larger journey. There was, however, one major problem, of which the Egyptians were acutely aware: What happened to the sun at night, after setting in the west? Clearly, something transpired in the twelve hours between dusk and dawn, which must account for the transformation from elderly Atum to Kheprer, the rejuvenated solar child. The solution to this theological dilemma was to be found in the mythology of Egypt's most important funerary deity, Osiris.

In the time before history, Osiris had ruled Egypt as king. His brother Seth, covetous of the throne, conspired to murder Osiris, whose body was cut to pieces and scattered throughout the land. Fortunately, Isis, the sister and wife of the slain king, was able to locate the scattered limbs. Through her unparalleled skill in magic, Isis, with the assistance of her sister Nephthys and the cunning jackal Anubis, was able to reunite the severed pieces into a whole, which they secured with linen wrappings, creating the first mummy. Thus reconstituted, Osiris took up residence in the Underworld as ruler over the land of the dead.

Since the development of mummification seems to have arisen as a practical response to changing burial practices at the dawn of the historic period, discussed above, we may infer that its association with the myth of Osiris was a secondary development. However, we may be certain that identification of the deceased with Osiris was firmly established by late Dynasty 5, when the Pyramid Texts of Unas assure us: "Seth, this one here is your brother, Osiris, who was caused to revive and to live, so that he might punish you. As he lives, so does this king Unas live! As he did not die, neither did this king Unas die! …Your body is the body of this king Unas. Your flesh is the flesh of this king Unas. Your bones are the bones of this king Unas. As you go, so does this king Unas go. As this king Unas goes, so do you go."

In the realm of the dead, the nocturnal Underworld where Osiris ruled as king, the Egyptians saw a mirror image of the living world. It was an inverted, shadowy realm fraught with peril, yet still a realm governed by the principle of cosmic order and divine kingship, as surely as the Nile valley and the land of Egypt itself. Passing forever from one realm to the next was the sun, whose arrival dispelled the darkness, bringing light and life to humans and gods alike. Here, at last, was the solution to the problem of divine rebirth: At some point, Osiris and Re came to be viewed as two aspects of a single deity, whose divided nature was reflected in the physical and spiritual components of humankind. Apart, each god exercised a vital function in the created world and yet each was subject to the limitations of their respective natures: Birth and aging, death and decay. However, every night, in the very depths of the Underworld, ba and corpse would unite, Re would come to rest in the body of Osiris, and for a time, the two gods would become one. This reunion acted as a catalyst, re-vivifying the inert god Osiris and enabling the sun to transform back into his nascent form, affecting his own rebirth from the eastern horizon. One of the clearest and most concise formulations of this, the central mystery of the solar cult, occurs in the Dynasty 19 tomb of Nefertari, the chief wife of Rameses II. Adapted from the great solar litany known as the "Book of Adoring Re in the West," the united god appears with the mummiform body of Osiris and the ram's head of the nocturnal sun. The accompanying text states unambiguously: "He is Re, who rests in Osiris, and Osiris, who rests in Re."

The identification of the deceased with the sun probably stretches back at least as far as the Pre-Dynastic Period, when we find many of the earliest pit graves oriented already eastward, in the direction of sunrise. The association with Osiris, although probably much more recent, must nevertheless date back at least to the earliest attestation of the Pyramid Texts. However, the original conception of what has been called the Solar-Osirian Unity -- Re and Osiris as aspects of a single god, whose ba and corpse united nightly -- is more difficult to pinpoint. Thus, for example, one group of spells from the Coffin Texts, known to the Egyptians as the "Book of the Ways of Rosetjau" included the earliest known schematic representations of the divine world, which might already allude to the Solar-Osirian myth. These cosmographic images show two paths through the Duat, identified with the gods Re and Osiris, but also with Thoth, in his capacity as the moon. The text is not yet explicit in the relationship between these two pathways or between the gods with whom they are identified. There is, however, every reason to suppose that a complimentary relationship between the day- and night-time courses of the sun was already present.

The tradition of cosmographic inquiry that appeared first in the Book of the Ways of Rosetjau, from the early Middle Kingdom, was developed to an unprecedented degree over the course of the New Kingdom. Beginning with the Amduat, these new cosmographic books elaborated upon the theme of the solar journey -- including the mysterious nightly union with Osiris -- with a zealous attention to detail that can only be described as encyclopaedic. Most of the formal cosmographic texts of the New Kingdom fall broadly into two categories: Books of the Sky, which depict the sun's journey through the celestial regions of the Upper Duat, and Underworld Books, whose focus lies upon the chthonic regions of lower Duat.

The Books of the Sky, attested from Dynasty 19 and later, include two compositions on the sun's diurnal travels, The Book of the Day and the Book of Nut, together with their nocturnal counterpart, the Book of the Night. All of the Books of the Sky depict the celestial regions in the form of the arched body of the sky goddess Nut, the mother of the sun, who stands braced with her hands upon the western horizon and her feet upon the eastern horizon. The diurnal books begin with the sun god's birth in the east and follow his course along the exterior of Nut's body, through the twelve hours of the day, past an assembled multitude of divine beings, toward the western horizon and sunset. The Egyptians viewed this last event with some trepidation, for here was the moment at which the aged sun god disappeared from the world of the living and entered the world of the dead. The Books of the Sky represent this fearsome passage as an act of divine cannibalism: The sky goddess literally swallows her child, the sun god Re, consuming him whole. The subsequent journey through the twelve nocturnal hours, as depicted in the Book of the Night, was envisioned as a trip back from west to east through the interior of Nut's body. This journey was simultaneously a passage through the landscape of the divine world and a return to the womb, allowing the sun to gestate inside his mother, prior to his rebirth as a child at dawn.

The other major group of cosmographic texts, the Underworld Books, deal exclusively with the nocturnal journey through the lower Duat. But whereas the Book of the Night had envisioned that same region as a sort of nether-sky inside the body of Nut, the Underworld Books represent the lower Duat as a passage through the earth itself. In addition to the Amduat, other Underworld Books include the so-called Books of the Solar-Osirian Unity, Gates, Caverns, and Earth. These five compositions may be further subdivided into two partially overlapping groups, based on the layout of the Underworld and the iconography of the sun god. The first group, which includes the Amduat and Book of Gates, depicts each of the twelve hours of the night as a discrete region, through which the sun-god sails in his divine barque. The second group, which includes the Book of Caverns, Book of the Solar-Osirian Unity, and Book of the Earth, does not emphasize the division of the night into twelve hours and might include, in addition to the solar barque, representations of the sun as a simple walking figure, as a figure travelling inside a disc, or even as the solar disc itself. Despite these formal differences, all of the Underworld Books exhibit certain commonalities in their content, above all in their shared emphasis on the concluding representation depicting the final hour of the night.

Although the individual components show considerable variation, each of the Underworld Books' concluding representations expressed in a single, complex image, "the entire daily course of the sun through Heaven, Underworld, and primordial ocean." Such images typically include some allusion to the great curving arc of the eastern horizon that separates the hidden realm of the Duat from the visible sky. Within this arc, the sun might appear simultaneously in his elderly and rejuvenated aspects, the ram-headed old man standing side by side with the solar child, or the scarab beetle Kheprer. In other cases, these forms might be blended—the nocturnal ram's head emerging from the forelimbs of the diurnal scarab—to emphasize the unity of the different forms as manifestations of a single, solar god. Usually, the mummiform figure of Osiris is present somewhere nearby, alluding also to that god's union with Re. In the Amduat, the mummy reclines along the curved border of the Underworld itself; in the Book of the Earth, the diurnal, falcon head of the sun sends its rays into the Osirian mummy, identified simply as "the corpse in which Re is." The union of the two gods, initiated earlier, at the midpoint of the nocturnal journey, achieves its ultimate expression at the moment of sunrise: The unified god, Re-Osiris, assumes the proportions of a giant, cosmos-spanning deity, whose fiery rays annihilate the enemies of creation with the first light of dawn, as he emerges from the eastern horizon.

Texts for the Afterlife and a Good Burial

The astonishing array of cosmographic images and descriptive texts that adorn the walls and ceilings of the royal tombs of the New Kingdom could not stand in more stark contrast to the austere burial chambers of the pyramids from the early Old Kingdom. And yet, between these groups of monuments, we observe a trajectory of theological development whose core principles remained vital and productive for more than two millennia. The crowning innovation in this process, the equation of the deceased with Osiris and Re, established a practical mythology of death and rebirth, whose proof was self-evident to every Egyptian with eyes to look: in the daily rising and nightly setting of the sun, in the biological mysteries of gestation and birth, and in all the cycles of nature itself, from the movement of the stars to the annual rise and fall of the Nile. Through the inscription of mortuary spells, cosmological texts, and cosmographic images, these same cycles were transposed onto the walls of the tomb, transforming the ersatz stone monument into a living microcosm from which the deceased emerged, reborn, in the same manner as the sun god, the primordial creator, himself.

Our survey of Egyptian mortuary beliefs and practices has been necessarily piecemeal and the picture that emerges is hardly more than the barest outline. And yet, within that outline, we have seen the 'good burial' transform over time from a mere equipping of the dead in a palace for the afterlife to a grand apotheosis at the heart of a miniature, stone cosmos. Throughout this long process, no idea was ever truly abandoned but only expanded and elaborated upon. New layers of meaning were overlaid atop the old, exploring and documenting every conceivable avenue of speculation into the nature of the afterlife. The very nature of this process often resulted in multiple, even contradictory, explanations that seem to raise more questions than definitive answers. Did the sun enter the body of the sky goddess at night, or did he travel beneath the earth? Was the pyramid a reconstruction of the primordial mound or a solidified beam of light? Were Re, Osiris, Atum, and Kheprer ever really aspects of a single god or were they always separate divinities? Ultimately, questions such as these reflect a modern desire to find dualities and oppositions where none were originally present: An ancient Egyptian might simply have replied, 'yes'. This does not mean the Egyptians were illogical, impractical, or unsystematic in their theological speculation—quite the opposite, in fact. The Egyptian view of life and death, the gods, and the divinely created world was simply informed by a fundamental belief in the power of symbols and signs, the magical connection between words, images, and the things they represented. However, we do a grave injustice if we suggest that the Egyptians didn't really believe their mythology or that their religion consisted 'merely' of metaphors describing phenomena that were otherwise beyond the powers of normal human observation. The Underworld Books, Books of the Sky, etc., were alternate metaphors describing one and the same process but they were also reflections of literal truths about the divine world, as the Egyptians saw it.

And so, having come full circle, we return to our original question: Were the Egyptians obsessed with death? From the modern perspective, the answer might very well be 'yes'. But such an answer fails utterly to convey what death meant in ancient Egypt. To qualify someone as 'dead' was to relegate them to the rank of a condemned criminal, an enemy of order subject to a second death in the divine world, which was tantamount to damnation. However, for most Egyptians, physical death, like birth, marked a transition to a stage of existence that they conceived explicitly as being 'alive'. To 'live' on earth, meant to pass through the normal stages of mortal existence. To 'live' in the divine world meant to be judged 'true of voice' by the divine tribunal and allowed to join the ranks of the gods, whose existence transcended both physical death and the ultimate destruction that was the fate of the damned. From this perspective, we see that all of the expense and time devoted to the preparation for death and burial never really reflected an obsession with death or some naïve attempt to deny its reality. For the Egyptians, a good burial was a celebration of the life led on earth and a guarantee of its perpetuation and perfection in a new state of existence, in the divine world.

Josh Roberson
University of Pennsylvania

阿蒙雷（Amun-Re）

阿蒙雷是阿蒙（Amun）和太陽神拉（Re）的結合。阿蒙原為法老的守護神，後來也成為代表國家的最重要的神。阿蒙雷參加了太陽神死亡和重生之旅。

阿努比斯（Anubis）

古埃及人認為胡狼與墓地有關。這也許可以解釋為什麼他們將胡狼與阿努比斯，防腐和墳場之神，聯想在一起，阿努比斯通常會引領亡靈前往審判，並協助秤量他們的心。

阿匹斯（Apis）

阿匹斯是公牛神，是最早將神性表現在動物上的神祇，他象徵豐饒及生產力，並戴有太陽和聖蛇。

貝斯塔（Bastet）

古埃及人飼養貓作為寵物並以貓來象徵許多神，在古埃及晚期，貓被用來代表貓神貝斯塔。埃及人製作了大量的青銅貓像用來祭祀女神或裝貓木乃伊。

貝斯神（Bes）

嬰兒、小孩、孕婦的守護神；埃及人會在家中放置貝斯神的塑像，以幫助分娩和養育年幼的子女。

哈托爾（Hathor）

荷魯斯的妻子，她是女性的保護者也是歡樂之神，她常以母牛的形體或一個女子頭戴著圓盤旁邊有兩個牛角的帽子。

荷魯斯（Horus）

荷魯斯為老鷹神、正義之神、復仇之神，父親是奧塞里斯、母親是伊西斯，妻子是哈托爾；另外，也有簡化成荷魯斯之眼的圖案。

印何闐（Imhotep）

印何闐在古埃及歷史中擁有近乎為神的神聖地位。他擔任埃及第一座金字塔 – 階梯金字塔的總設計師，也是古埃及一位重要的醫療專業人士。埃及人供奉印何闐的青銅雕像，頌揚他的技能和學習。

伊西斯（Isis）

伊西斯是奧塞里斯的妻子，奧塞里斯曾經統治埃及，然後被他的哥哥塞特謀殺。伊西斯不但讓丈夫復活，並幫助兒子荷魯斯成為埃及國王。埃及人為她製造了大量的雕像。

馬特（Maat）

馬特是真理女神。真理之羽就在她的頭上，這就是在前往來世的審判中用來秤量亡靈的心是否純潔的羽毛。馬特主張秩序，反對混亂。

奧塞里斯（Osiris）

奧塞里斯是冥界之王。埃及人崇敬奧塞里斯和不朽及永生的連結，他藉由妻子伊西斯的協助死後復活，就像給全埃及一個永生的承諾。

普塔（Ptah）

普塔是創造之神。普塔也和亡靈的復活有關，他被認為具有引領亡者通過陰間世界進入永生的力量。

普塔－蘇卡－奧塞里斯（Ptah-Sokar-Osiris）

普塔－蘇卡－奧塞里斯是一個複合的神，最早出現是和首都孟菲斯的信仰有關。這個神的權力結合創造、死亡和重生。古埃及人以普塔－蘇卡－奧塞里斯塑像陪葬，試圖經由建立自己冥神奧塞里斯的關聯，確保亡靈成功獲得奇蹟般地重生。

賽克麥特（Sakhmet）

賽克麥特是象徵激烈和強大的女神。她被認為和母獅有關。賽克麥特的暴力性格使她成為在陰間擊退邪惡的力量的優秀女神。

塞特（Seth）

塞特為奧塞里斯的弟弟，沙漠及黑暗之神，可以壓抑沙漠及外國的力量以保護埃及，也是奧塞里斯和荷魯斯最大的敵人。

托特（Thoth）

托特為寫作和知識之神。在前往來世的審判中，托特負責記錄審判的成果。托特本身被視為真實和誠實的，因此亡靈會想和托特神產生關聯。古埃及人認為朱鷺和托特神有關。

古　埃　及　年　表

王朝／年份		法老名稱	重要事件
前王國時期 (4500B.C.—3100B.C.)			◎ 來自中亞的移民進入尼羅河三角洲地區，與當地文化混合之後成為古埃及文明的前身。 ◎ 此時較接近部落族文化，國家的概念尚未完全成形，亦無法老制度。 ◎ 埃及進入定耕農業時期。 ◎ 原始的象形文字開始出現。
早王國時期 (3100B.C.—2700B.C)	第一王朝	從曼尼斯(Menes)到卡(Ka)共有8個法老，但這段歷史並不可信。	◎ 西元前3000年左右，法老王納美爾(Narmer)統一了南北兩個王國，定都孟菲斯(Memphis)，建立了埃及第一王朝，也促成了法老體制的誕生。 ◎ 早期泥磚方形大墓出現。 ◎ 大量的陶製與石製工具出現。 ◎ 太陽曆開始出現。
	第二王朝	從法老霍特普斯克摩伊(Hotepsekhemoui)到卡斯克摩伊(Khasekhemoui)共有6位法老，但這段歷史不可信。	
古王國時期 (2700B.C.—2160B.C.)	第三王朝	卓瑟(Djoser) 胡尼(Huni)	◎ 建都於孟菲斯，並以此為根據地往周邊地區發展。第四王朝開始遠征西奈半島及地中海沿岸區，埃及的國土開始擴大。 ◎ 古王國時期的埃及已經確立了君主專制的獨裁體系以及基本的官僚制度。 ◎ 農業、建築、手工業等得到當全面的發展。 ◎ 第三王朝法老王卓瑟(Djoser)於薩卡拉(Saqqura)建造了埃及第一座金字塔(階梯金字塔)，印何闐可能是督造人。 ◎ 第四王朝開始建築大金字塔(古夫、卡夫拉、門考拉三大金字塔)，以及附屬的享殿建築，陵墓建築完全成形；出現第一座人面獅身像。 ◎ 出現宗教都市赫利奧波利斯，太陽神信仰成形。採用天狼星曆作為宗教曆法。 ◎ 開始使用莎草紙 (5-8王朝)。 ◎ 第五王朝出現最早的喪葬文獻：金字塔文。 ◎ 第六王朝之後金字塔建築開始衰落，不再使用石頭，改用泥磚替代。
	第四王朝	史那夫魯(Snefru) 古夫(Khufu) 卡夫拉(Kafre) 門考拉(Menkaure)	
	第五王朝	烏瑟卡夫(Userkaf) 薩瓦雷(Sahure) 那夫易爾卡雷(Neferirkare) 易色西(Isesi) 烏那斯(Unas)	
	第六王朝	鐵提(Teti) 裴皮一世(Pepi I) 梅仁雷(Mernere) 裴皮二世(Pepi II)	
第一中間期 (2160B.C.—2010B.C.)	第七王朝 第八王朝 第九王朝 第十王朝	此時埃及南北分裂，王朝興替迭起，各地貴族自立為法老，戰爭頻繁，有些法老甚至不知姓名。	◎ 戰亂頻繁，孟菲斯及周邊地區破敗廢棄。 ◎ 此時僅有小型陵墓建築，大型公共工程完全停止。 ◎ 政權瓦解，由於地區貴族勢力興起，「諾姆」(nome，行省)行政制度因此成形，埃及再度進入分裂局面。
中王國時期 (2106B.C.—1786B.C.)	第十一王朝	英特夫(Intef) 蒙圖荷泰普一世(Montuhotep I) 蒙圖荷泰普二世(Montuhotep II) 蒙圖荷泰普三世(Montuhotep III) 蒙圖荷泰普四世(Montuhotep IV)	◎ 埃及再度統一，太平盛世為埃及帶來文學與藝術上所前未有的成就。 ◎ 中王國一開始，法老王積極發展海上與陸地上的對外貿易，讓埃及成為一個繁榮的國度。 ◎ 部分貴族往尼羅河上游的谷地區發展，底比斯興起。另一支系貴族往法尤姆綠洲發展。 ◎ 十一王朝，底比斯出現第一座神廟蒙圖荷泰普二世神廟。 ◎ 十二王朝，法尤姆綠洲水利計畫展開，大獲成功。 ◎ 十二王朝，開始開採西奈半島的銅礦，埃及的青銅製品大量出現。 ◎ 十二王朝以後，不再建築金字塔，改採地下陵墓替代。
	第十二王朝	阿蒙尼赫特一世(Amenemhet I) 申無施爾一世(Senwosert I) 阿蒙尼赫特二世(Amenemhet II) 申無施爾二世(Senwosert II) 申無施爾三世(Senwosert III) 阿蒙尼赫特三世(Amenemhet III) 索貝克那夫魯(Sobeknefru)	
第二中間期 (1786B.C.—1550B.C.)	第十三王朝 第十五王朝 第十六王朝 第十七王朝	西克索人(Syksos)入侵，建立政權，此時埃及法老充其量不過是西克索人的封臣，沒有實權。	◎ 埃及第一次面臨外族西克索(Hyksos)人入侵，西克索人並引進馬匹，埃及才開始出現戰車。埃及陷入爭戰局面。 ◎ 戰亂時期，貴族勢力完全崩解。
新王國時期 (1550B.C.—1069B.C.)	第十八王朝	阿摩斯(Ahmose) 阿蒙霍特一世(Amenhotep I) 圖特摩斯一世(Thutmosis I) 圖特摩斯二世(Thutmosis II) 哈謝普蘇(Hatshepsut) 圖特摩斯三世(Thutmosis III) 阿蒙霍特二世(Amenhotep II) 圖特摩斯四世(Thutmosis IV) 阿蒙霍特三世(Amenhotep III) 阿蒙霍特四世(Amenhotep IV) 史蒙卡雷(Smenkhkare) 圖坦卡門(Tutankhamun) 艾伊(Ay) 霍倫哈布(Horemhab)	◎ 新王國以底比斯為首都(Thebes)，法老們死後被葬於帝王谷。 ◎ 哈謝普蘇〔Hatshepsut〕自立為女性法老王，並利用宣傳手段合理化繼承的正統性。 ◎ 國力強盛不斷對外擴張勢力，圖特摩斯三世時代建立了埃及最大的版圖。 ◎ 拉美西斯二世成為埃及歷史上建神廟、方尖碑，生育子女最多的法老。 ◎ 新王國成為埃及最後一個強盛的年代。 ◎ 開始建築大規模的神殿，此時又稱為「大神殿時期」。 ◎ 十八王朝晚期法老阿蒙霍特四世改變宗教信仰，遷都阿瑪納，導致全國動盪不安。圖坦卡門時期重新恢復阿蒙信仰。 ◎ 十九王朝法老拉美西斯二世遠征努比亞，將國土範圍拓展到尼羅河上游。興建阿布辛貝神殿，此地為埃及最南方的疆域。
	第十九王朝	拉美西斯一世(Ramesses I) 塞堤一世(Seti I) 拉美西斯二世(Ramesses II) 梅仁普塔(Merneptah)	
	第二十王朝	拉美西斯三世(Ramesses III) ↓ 拉美西斯十一世(Ramesses XI)	
第三中間期 (1069B.C.—656B.C.)	第二十一王朝		◎ 底比斯的最高祭司有著至高無上得地位，但是北方出現了一股勢力與底比斯政權平起平坐，國家分裂為兩大中心。 ◎ 利比亞等政權相繼崛起，埃及成為各地強權覬覦的對象。 ◎ 亞述人占領了孟菲斯。 ◎ 公共建築幾乎完全停止，此時以小型貴族陵墓為代表。
	第二十二王朝	示薩(Shoshenq I)	
	第二十三王朝		
	第二十四王朝	特夫那克特(Tefnakht)	
	第二十五王朝	皮安赫(Piankhy) 夏巴卡(Shabaka) 謝比特古(Shebitku) 塔哈卡(Taharqa)	
後埃及時期 (656B.C.—332B.C.)	第二十六王朝	涅可一世(Necho I) 薩美提克一世(Psammetichus I) 涅可二世(Necho II) 薩美提克二世(Psammetichus II) 阿普利(Apries) 阿瑪西斯(Amasis) 薩美提克三世(Psammetichus III)	◎ 波斯帝國兩次入侵，波斯總督統治埃及，埃及傳統貴族勢力幾乎完全瓦解。 ◎ 三十王朝是埃及人建立的最後一個王朝。 ◎ 西元前332年亞歷山大征服埃及。
	第二十七王朝	波斯人第一次統治期	
	第二十八王朝	阿米爾泰(Amyrtee)	
	第二十九王朝	納菲里蒂斯一世(Nepheritis I) 納菲里蒂斯二世(Nepheritis II) 普薩摩蒂斯一世(Psammouthis I) 普薩摩斯二世(Psammouthis II) 阿科里斯(Achoris)	
	第三十王朝	納克塔內波一世(Nectanebo I) 納克塔內波二世(Nectanebo II) 提奧斯(Teos)	
	第三十一王朝	波斯人第二次統治期	
托勒密王朝 (332B.C.—30B.C.)		托勒密一世(Ptolemaios I) ↓ 托勒密十五世(Ptolemaios VX) 克麗歐佩托拉(Kleopatra)	◎ 埃及被亞歷山大的將軍托勒密所統治，建立了托勒密王朝，進入了希臘時期。 ◎ 埃及完全喪失尼羅河流域以外地區的控制權。 ◎ 羅馬凱撒大帝協助埃及豔后(Clepopatra VII)成為女王。 ◎ 奧古斯都率軍攻打埃及，埃及豔后(Clepopatra VII)自盡，成為埃及王國最後的統治者，埃及從此進入羅馬時代。
羅馬統治期 (30B.C.—395A.D.)			◎ 屋大維入侵埃及，廢除法老制度，埃及成為羅馬的行省。也改為基督教的國家，西元前640年埃及又被阿拉伯統治，變成回教國家。

英文撰稿人 Contributors

專文 Essays

Aidan Dodson
Senior Research Fellow, Department of Archaeology & Anthropology, University of Bristol
Denise Doxey
Curator of Ancient Egyptian, Nubian and Near Eastern Art, Museum of Fine Arts Boston
Nicholas Reeves
Sylvan C. Coleman and Pamela Coleman Memorial Fellow, Department of Egyptian Art, The Metropolitan Museum of Art
Josh Roberson
Lecturer in Egyptology, University of Pennsylvania
Carolyn Routledge
Curator of Egyptology and Archaeology, Bolton Museum
Ian Shaw
Senior Lecturer in Egyptian Archaeology, University of Liverpool

展件說明 Object Entries

A.D.	Aidan Dodson, Bristol University
A.H.	Amber Hutchinson, University of Toronto
A.G.	Anna Garnett, University of Liverpool
A.M.	Antonio Morales, University of Pennsylvania
A.C.	Ashley Cook, National Museums Liverpool
B.R.	Bruce Routledge, University of Liverpool
C.G.	Christine Geisen, University of Toronto
C.P.	Campbell Price, University of Liverpool
C.R.	Carolyn Routledge, Bolton Museum
C.W.	Cordula Wierschkun, University of Liverpool
D.N.	Daniel Nikolov, University of Liverpool
D.D.	Denise Doxey, Boston Museum of Fine Arts
E.L.	Emma Libonati, Oxford University
H.M.	Hayley Meloy, University of Liverpool
J.A.H.	Jane A Hill, University of Liverpool
J.C.	Jennifer Cromwell, Macquarie University
J.H.W.	Jennifer Houser Wegner, University of Pennsylvania Museum
L.A.W.	Leslie Anne Warden, West Virginia University Institute of Technology
L.F.	Liz Frood, Oxford University
M.M.	Margaret Maitland, Oxford University
N.H.	Nicola Harrington, Oxford University
R.G.	Rachel Grocke, Durham University Museums
R.L.	Ronald Leprohon, University of Toronto
T.H.	Tom Hardwick, Grand Egyptian Museum Cairo

書　　名：木乃伊傳奇—埃及古文明特展
主辦單位：國立中正紀念堂、國立自然科學博物館、旺旺中時媒體集團時藝多媒體

發 行 人：蔡衍明
總 策 畫：林宜標
策展顧問：邱建一、吳駿聲、謝哲青
展覽企劃團隊：張慧菁、譚傳穎、陳彥如、何煥文、張心瑜、周宜靜、吳雅嫻
　　　　　　　張耀尹、謝博丞、張一山
主　　編：林秋芳
執行編輯：雅凱藝術事業有限公司
文字編譯：譚傳穎、陳彥如、張心瑜、傅惠慧、莊雅珊、王舒津、徐佳琳、沈怡寧
美術設計：吳俊輝

出 版 者：時藝多媒體傳播股份有限公司
　　　　　台北市萬華區艋舺大道 303 號
　　　　　TEL：02-6630-3888
製版印刷：日動藝術印刷有限公司
出版日期：2011 年 6 月

I S B N：978-986-85469-5-0（平裝）
定　　價：新台幣 1200 元

The exhibition is organised by UEG ADM., Denmark